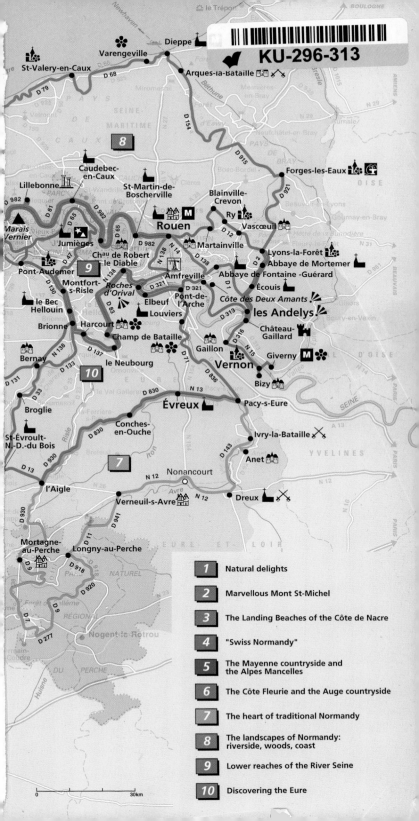

KU-296-313

1	Natural delights
2	Marvellous Mont St-Michel
3	The Landing Beaches of the Côte de Nacre
4	"Swiss Normandy"
5	The Mayenne countryside and the Alpes Mancelles
6	The Côte Fleurie and the Auge countryside
7	The heart of traditional Normandy
8	The landscapes of Normandy: riverside, woods, coast
9	Lower reaches of the River Seine
10	Discovering the Eure

NORMANDY

A. de Valroger/MICHELIN

Chief Editor   Cynthia Clayton Ochterbeck

THE GREEN GUIDE NORMANDY

Editor   Jonathan P. Gilbert
Principal Writer   Margaret LeMay
Production Coordinator   Natasha G. George
Cartography   Alain Baldet, Michèle Cana, Peter Wrenn
Photo Editor   Lydia Strong
Proofreader   Gaven R. Watkins
Layout & Design   Franz Pinga, Tim Schulz
Cover Design   Laurent Muller and Ute Weber

Contact Us: The Green Guide
                                     Michelin Maps and Guides
                                     One Parkway South
                                     Greenville, SC 29615
                                     USA
                                     www.michelintravel.com
                                     michelin.guides@us.michelin.com

                                     Michelin Maps and Guides
                                     Hannay House
                                     39 Clarendon Road
                                     Watford, Herts WD17 1JA
                                     UK
                                     ☎01923 205240
                                     www.ViaMichelin.com
                                     travelpubsales@uk.michelin.com

Special Sales: For information regarding bulk sales,
                                     customized editions and premium sales,
                                     please contact our Customer Service
                                     Departments:
                                     USA   1-800-432-6277
                                     UK   01923 205240
                                     Canada 1-800-361-8236

Note to the reader
While every effort is made to ensure that all information printed in this guide is
correct and up-to-date, Michelin Apa Publications Ltd. accepts no liability for
any direct, indirect or consequential losses howsoever caused so far as such
can be excluded by law.

One Team ...
A Commitment to Quality

There's just one reason our team is dedicated to producing quality travel publications—you, our reader.

Throughout our guides we offer **practical information**, **touring tips** and **suggestions** for finding the best places for a break.

Michelin driving tours help you hit the highlights and quickly absorb the best of the region. Our descriptive **walking tours** make you your own guide, armed with directions, maps and expert information.

We scout out the attractions, classify them with **star ratings**, and describe in detail what you will find when you visit them.

Michelin maps featured throughout the guide offer vibrant, detailed and easy-to-follow outlines of everything from close-up museum plans to international maps.

Places to stay and eat are always a big part of travel, so we research **hotels and restaurants** that we think convey the essence of the destination, and arrange them by geographic area and price. We walk you through the best shopping districts and point you towards the host of entertainment and recreation possibilities on offer.

We **test, retest, check and recheck** to make sure that our guidebooks are truly just that: a personalized guide to help you make the most of your visit. And if you still want a speaking guide, we list local tour guides who will lead you on all the boat, bus, guided, historical, culinary, and other tours you shouldn't miss.

In short, we remove the guesswork involved with travel. After all, we want you to enjoy traveling with Michelin as much as we do.

The Michelin Green Guide Team

PLANNING YOUR TRIP

INTRODUCTION TO NORMANDY

MICHELIN DRIVING TOURS   12

WHEN AND WHERE TO GO   14
Seasons.......................... 14
Themed Tours.................... 14

KNOW BEFORE YOU GO   18
Useful Web Sites 18
Tourist Offices.................... 18
International Visitors 18
Accessibility..................... 21
The Channel Islands 21

GETTING THERE   22
By Air........................... 22
By Sea 22
By Rail 22
By Bus 23
Driving in France 23

WHERE TO STAY AND EAT   25
Where to Stay 25
Where to Eat 28

WHAT TO DO AND SEE   29
Outdoor Fun 29
Activities for Children 35
Calendar of Events............... 35
Shopping 40
Sightseeing 40
Books 41
Films 41

USEFUL WORDS AND PHRASES   43

BASIC INFORMATION   44

© François Pinon

Dielette Harbour, Normandy

NATURE   50
Regions of Normandy............ 50
Horses: the Pride of Normandy ... 52

HISTORY   54
Timeline 54
Normans Throughout History 57
Monasticism in Normandy 58
The Battle of Normandy 60
Reconstruction.................. 62

ART AND CULTURE   64
Architecture 64
Norman Dovecotes 75
Decorative Arts.................. 77
Painting 77
Literature 79
Music........................... 81

THE REGION TODAY   81
Food and Drink.................. 81

SYMBOLS

🛈	**Tourist Information**
🕐	**Hours of Operation**
🕐	**Periods of Closure**
👁	**A Bit of Advice**
👁	**Details to Consider**
💰	**Entry Fees**
Kids	**Especially for Children**
🚶	**Tours**
♿	**Wheelchair Accessible**

CONTENTS

DISCOVERING NORMANDY

L'Aigle 86
Alençon 88
Les Andelys 93
Argentan 95
Arques-la-Bataille 100
Arromanches-les-Bains 101
Pays d'Auge 103
Avranches 107
Bagnoles-de-l'Orne 110
Barfleur................................114
Barneville-Carteret 115
Bayeux 117
Le Bec-Hellouin 125
Bellême................................127
Bernay.................................129
Blainville-Crevon 132
Brionne................................133
Forêt de Brotonne....................134
Cabourg 136
Caen...................................138
Château de Carrouges 154
Caudebec-en-Caux...................156
Pays de Caux 160
Ancienne abbaye de
    Cerisy-la-Forêt 165
Château du Champ de Bataille 165
Îles Chausey..........................167
Cherbourg-Octeville 168
Clécy 172
Clères..................................174
Conches-en-Ouche...................175
Presqu'île du Cotentin 176
Coutances 186
Crèvecœur-en-Auge..................192
Deauville 193
Plages du Débarquement........... 198
Dieppe 207
Dives-sur-Mer.........................212
Domfront..............................213
Dreux..................................216
Écouis 220
Elbeuf 222
Étretat 224
Eu 227
Évreux 229
Évron 233
Falaise 235
Fécamp................................238
Flers...................................241
Château de Fontaine-Henry.........243
Forges-les-Eaux 244
Fresnay-sur-Sarthe 246
Gisors..................................247
Giverny 248
Granville..............................250

Le Havre 254
Honfleur.............................. 262
Ville Romaine de Jublains........... 271
Abbaye de Jumièges 272
Lassay-les-Châteaux.................274
Laval 275
Lessay 281
Lillebonne 282
Lisieux 283
Louviers.............................. 287
Abbaye de Lucerne................. 289
Lyons-la-Forêt 290
Mayenne............................. 293
Mont-St-Michel 294
Mortagne-au-Perche 304
Mortain............................... 307
Neufchâtel-en-Bray 310
Nogent-le-Rotrou 311
Omaha Beach 313
Orbec..................................316
Ouistreham-Rive-Bella 316
Haras National du Pin................318
Château de Pirou 319
Pont-Audemer 320
Pontmain 321
Pontorson 322
Quillebeuf 323
Rouen 324
St-Évroult-Notre-Dame-du-Bois..... 342
St-Lô...................................343
St-Martin-de-Boscherville 347
St-Pierre-sur-Dives 348
St-Sauveur-le-Vicomte.............. 349
St-Vaast-la-Hougue...................351
Abbaye de St-Wandrille............. 352
Ste-Mère-Église 353
Ste-Suzanne 355
Sées 356
Sillé-le-Guillaume 359
La Suisse Normande.................. 360
Thury-Harcourt 362
Le Tréport............................. 363
Trouville-sur-Mer..................... 364
Valognes.............................. 366
Varengeville-sur-Mer 368
Château du Vendeuvre 369
Verneuil-sur-Avre 370
Vernon 372
Villedieu-les-Poêles..................376
Vimoutiers............................ 378
Vire................................... 378
The Bailiwicks........................ 382
Alderney.............................. 383
Guernsey 388
Herm 397
Jersey 399
Sark 413

Index 416
Maps and Plans 429
Legend............................. 430

HOW TO USE THIS GUIDE

Orientation

To help you grasp the "lay of the land" quickly and easily, so you'll feel confident and comfortable finding your way around the region, we offer the following tools in this guide:

- Detailed table of contents for an overview of what you'll find in the guide, and how it is organized.
- Map of Normandy at back of the guide, with the principal sights highlighted for easy reference.
- Detailed maps for major cities and villages, including driving tour maps and larger-scale maps for walking tours.
- Map of Normandy Regional Driving Tours at the front of the guide, each one numbered and color coded.

Practicalities

At the front of the guide, you'll see a section called "Planning Your Trip" that contains information about planning your trip, the best time to go, different ways of getting to the region and getting around, basic facts and tips for making the most of your visit. You'll find driving and themed tours, and suggestions for outdoor fun. There's also a calendar of popular annual events in Normandy. Information on shopping, sightseeing, kids' activities and sports and recreational opportunities is also included.

WHERE TO STAY

We've made a selection of hotels and arranged them within the cities, categorized by price category to fit all budgets (see the Legend at the back of the guide for an explanation of the price categories). For the most part, we selected accommodations based on their unique regional quality, their Normandy feel, as it were. So, unless the individual hotel or bed & breakfast embodies local ambience, it's rare that we include chain properties, which typically have their own imprint. If you want a more comprehensive selection of Normandy accommodations, see the red-cover Michelin Guide France.

WHERE TO EAT

We thought you'd like to know the popular eating spots in Normandy. So we iselected restaurants that capture the Normandy experience—those that have a unique regional flavor and local atmosphere. We're not rating the quality of the food per se. As we did with the hotels, we selected restaurants for many towns and villages, categorized by price to appeal to all wallets. If you want a more comprehensive selection of dining recommendations in the region, see the red-cover Michelin Guide France.

Attractions

Principal Sights are arranged alphabetically within the Discovering section. Within each Principal Sight, attractions for each city or town, or geographical area are divided into local Sights or Walking Tours, nearby Excursions to sights outside the town, or detailed Driving Tours—suggested itineraries for seeing several attractions around a major town. Contact information, admission charges and hours of operation are given for the majority of attractions. Unless otherwise noted, admission prices shown are for a single adult only. Discounts for seniors, students, teachers, etc. may be available; be sure to ask. If no admission charge is shown, entrance to the attraction is free.

If you're pressed for time, we recommend you visit the three- and two-star sights first: the stars are your guide.

STAR RATINGS

Michelin has used stars as a rating tool for more than 100 years:

★★★	Highly recommended
★★	Recommended
★	Interesting

SYMBOLS IN THE TEXT

Besides the stars, other symbols in the text indicate sights that are closed to the public ⊶; on-site eating facilities ✕; also see 👁; breakfast included in the nightly rate ⌷; on-site parking 🅿; spa facilities 𝐒𝐩𝐚; camping facilities △; swimming pool ⛵; and beaches ⌂.

See the box appearing on the Contents page for other symbols used in the text. See the Maps explanation below for symbols appearing on the maps.

Throughout the guide you will find peach-coloured text boxes or sidebars containing anecdotal or background information. Green-coloured boxes contain information to help you save time or money.

Maps

All maps in this guide are oriented north, unless otherwise indicated by a directional arrow. The term "Local Map" refers to a map within the chapter or Tourism Region. See the map Legend at the back of the guide for an explanation of other map symbols. A complete list of the maps found in the guide appears at the back of this book. Addresses, phone numbers, opening hours and prices published in this guide are accurate at press time. We welcome corrections and suggestions that may assist us in preparing the next edition. Please send your comments to:

Michelin Maps and Guides
Hannay House
39 Clarendon Road
Watford, Herts WD17 1JA
UK
travelpubsales@uk.michelin.com
www.michelin.co.uk

Michelin Maps and Guides
Editorial Department
P.O. Box 19001
Greenville, SC 29602-9001
USA
michelin.guides@us.michelin.com
www.michelintravel.com

Trouville

G. Guittot/POTONONSTOP

MICHELIN DRIVING TOURS

1 Natural delights
290km/180mi from Saint-Lô and back
At the western edge of the continent of Europe, off the main tourist routes, the Cotentin Peninsula (also known as the Cherbourg Peninsula) faces the sea on three sides. Where the countryside is lush and green, cows graze placidly. In the regional nature park, canals, rivers and ponds provide a cool resting place for tourists and migratory birds alike. Sandy beaches are protected by cliffs and promontories. The towns and villages are picturesque, and the cities have been built (or rebuilt, after the war) in local granite. To get the most out of your tour, pack good walking shoes and a bathing suit.

2 Marvellous Mont-St-Michel
210km/130mi from Granville and back
The tour starts in Granville, a town proud of its maritime heritage. The route takes you through quiet hamlets and lively small towns, mostly rebuilt after the Second World War, using the typical regional granite blocks. The most unforgettable spot is of course Mont-St-Michel, a pinnacle of art, architecture, spirituality and European culture. If you decide to walk across the bay from Genêts or Courtils, check the tide tables first.

3 The landing beaches on the Côte de Nacre
180km/112mi from Caen and back
This tour takes you along the lovely coast known as the mother-of-pearl, and also inland through a landscape steeped in memories of the momentous D-Day landings. Caen is well worth a visit, for its art collections, abbeys, lively town centre, and the moving Museum for Peace just outside the town, which was at the centre of the Battle of Normandy. Bayeux is known for its precious tapestry and also as the only town in the region to have survived the war relatively unscathed. Arromanches-sur-Mer was the site chosen for the famous artificial or mulberry ports towed across from Great Britain to assist the allied landing. The coast is also a fine place for sunbathing and swimming in the many family-style resorts.

4 Swiss Normandy
210km/130mi from Alençon and back
Perhaps you have to live in Normandy to appreciate why this area is likened to Switzerland. The hills here rise no higher than 360m/1181ft but that is enough for them to form a landscape of steep cliffs, deep valleys with rivers winding through them, and hair-pin bends; meadows and woods alternate on the slopes.

5 The Mayenne countryside and the Alpes Mancelles
210km/130mi from Laval and back
The Mayenne Valley is quite different from the popular tourist areas of the coast. The charm of this hidden corner of Normandy lies in its many ponds, lakes and streams, and the hills of the Sarthe Valley. The granite houses with slate roofs echo the neighbouring region of Brittany, and the mild climate and gracious lifestyle are reminiscent of the Loire. An especially enjoyable section of this drive is through the Nomandie-Maine Regional Nature Park, where traditional agriculture and crafts are still practised, and you can engage in outdoor sports, including cycling, climbing, or rambling on one of the many way-marked paths.

6 The Côte Fleurie and the Auge countryside
200km/124mi from the Pont de Normandie and back
After admiring the graceful span of the Normandy bridge, take this drive to the charming town of Honfleur, on the Seine estuary, and continue to the popular beach resorts of Trouville, Deauville, Houlgate and Cabourg. When you leave the coast, you enter the Auge country, a land of green

pastures and half-timbered houses, famous for its fine aged calvados and savoury cheeses. The route goes through Lisieux, birthplace of St Theresa, then on to Camembert, Vimoutiers and the Vie Valley. The Valley de la Risle leads back to the Seine estuary by way of the Bec-Hellouin Abbey, Pont-Audemer and the Vernier wetlands.

7 The heart of traditional Normandy
300km/180mi

This tour carries you through the heartland of historic, rural and culinary Normandy. Visit the site of the Battle of Ivry, the Château d'Anet, the Perch Nature Park; keep an eye out for sturdy Percheron horses grazing in the fields; enjoy blood sausage in Mortagne or rillettes in Mamers. The gentle hills are wooded and serene.

8 The landscapes of Normandy: riverside, woods, coast
400km/249mi from Les Andelys and back

This drive follows the north bank of the River Seine, winding along past many spectacular sights: Les Andelys and Château-Gaillard, the Fontaine-Guérard Abbey, the old town of Rouen, Duclair, the monasteries of St-Martin-de-Boscherville, Jumièges and St-Wandrille, Caudebec-en-Caux, Villequier, Ételan Castle, the Roman amphitheatre at Lillebonne. Across the Pont de Normandie lies the major port of Le Havre, which is well worth a visit for its many museums and modern architecture (the city was almost obliterated during the war). The suggested tour next follows the shore known as the Alabaster Coast, with its striking chalk cliffs and shingle beaches. The arch and needle, two unique rock formations off the coast of Étretat, are emblematic of this area; Fécamp and Dieppe are typical fishing ports with many interesting things to see and do. The route turns inland, crossing the Eawy Forest, and passing through the picturesque town of Forges-les-Eaux, continues along the Andelle Valley and into the lovely Lyons Forest. The tour finishes in the delightful village of Lyons-la-Forêt.

9 Lower reaches of the River Seine
300km/186mi from Vernon and back

Vernon is the starting point for a trip to Bizy Castle and Monet's famous house and garden in Giverny. Follow the north bank of the Seine through the gentle meanders of the Gaillon Valley to Les Andelys; the remains of the formidable Château-Gaillard rise above the river. On the road to Rouen, you can stop and admire the statues at Notre-Dame d'Écouis, the regional art centre in Vascoeuil, and the château-museum in Martainville. After touring the historic city of Rouen and its famous cathedral, carry on as far as the estuary and the Pont de Normandie. Here you can cross the estuary to enjoy the beaches at Trouville and Deauville before discovering the delights of the south bank. The first stop is Pont-l'Évêque, home of the eponymous cheese. After the pretty village of Pont-Audemer, the road leads into the Brotonne Regional Nature Park, with its traditional crafts museums and recreational facilities. The château of Champ de Bataille illustrates a more refined way of life with its elegant rooms and formal French gardens. From here, the route offers splendid views from the castle of Robert le Diable, the rocks at Orival and the Amfreville canal locks.

10 Discovering the Eure
200km/124mi

After a tour of the city of Rouen, take a trip into the département of the Eure. You can see the châteaux of Robert le Diable and Champ de Bataille along the way. Drive along the Charentonne Valley as far as St-Évroult, then head north-east towards Évreux. The tour meets up with the River Eure at Pacy-sur-Eure, and follows the valley back north. Between Elbeuf and Rouen, the Roches d'Orival rise up on the horizon in silhouette.

WHEN AND WHERE TO GO

Seasons

The most pleasant season is July to September, although the mildness of the coastal climate makes it possible to visit Normandy at any time of the year. In spring the blossoming of the apple trees transforms the Normandy countryside. Apples flower last, after the Gaillon cherries and the Domfront pears. Apple blossom time is really without equal, and this would therefore be the ideal time to explore the countryside by driving through the Pays d'Auge and along the Seine Valley.

In summer the hot weather comes earlier inland than on the coast. The beach season does not begin before June, when the last storms have died away. From Le Tréport to Mont-St-Michel, the coast is taken over by the people in search of sea air, relaxation and amusement. The sky remains hazy, the sunshine has a special quality. The inevitable changes in the weather are felt most inland.

The autumn months are the wettest of the year but as soon as November approaches there are many magnificent days. It is the time of year to enjoy the wonderful changing colours of the forest trees. The light is incomparably soft, making the stone buildings appear all the more substantial. It is never very cold.

Themed Tours

HERITAGE TRAILS

To help tourists discover France's national heritage in its historical context, municipalities have set up a number of routes focusing on a given theme. Each itinerary is clearly signposted by panels laid out along the roads and is described in leaflets available from regional tourist offices. Information on literally dozens of specialized itineraries is available at **www.normandy-tourism.org**. Information, which can be accessed in English, includes daily programs, tourist office addresses, mileage, maps and links to commercial sites such as lodging. Here is a sample of the itineraries:

Highways and Byways for Americans in Normandy

For visitors from the US, 13 itineraries have been mapped out, including the area around the town of Vernon, from which Mount Vernon takes its name; Arromanches, with its D-Day history; Giverny, the home of Claude Monet, restored with funds from American donors; Rouen, including the Romanesque School of the Jews, a remarkable archeological discovery.

Following in William the Conqueror's Footsteps

A suggested 7-day itinerary, with supporting information and links, follows the career of the Conqueror from Fécamp through 20 towns and sites. You can also write for information to Mme Morel, President of the Route, 5 pl du Chauchix-St-Léonard, 22510 Moncontour-de-Bretagne. ☏ 02 96 69 39 74.

Chateaux, Parks and Gardens

This week-long itinerary takes you through some of the loveliest sites in Normandy, including Giverny, Mont-St-Michel, Rouen and lesser-known gardens of châteaux such as the 18C "chartreuses" of Mézidon-Canon and the "surprise gardens" of Vendeuvres.

Ivory and Spice Road

This itinerary takes you back to the Middle Ages, when the commerce of ivory and spices thrived, concentrating on the harbours of Eu and Le Havre, with a few glimpses inland (Dieppe, Cany-Barville, Varengeville, Étretat, etc.). You can also write for information on this route to Route de l'Ivoire et des Épices, 110 rue

Alexandre-le-Grand, 76400 Fécamp, ☎ 02 35 10 26 00. www.routes-historiques.com

Route Historique des Abbayes Normandes

This route takes you to some 30 abbeys and priories (of 60 surviving in Normandy) as well as châteaux along the valley of the Seine, around Caen and in Basse-Normandie. Route historique des Abbayes normandes, 6 rue Couronné, BP 60, 76420 Bihorel. ☎02 35 12 41 60. **www.abbayes-normandes.com**, or **www.routes-historiques.com**. Or contact Mme Robic, Présidente de la Route, 6 r. Couronné, BP 60, 76420 Bihorel. ☎ 02 35 12 41 60.

Routes Historiques

The Féderation Nationale des Routes Historiques distributes booklets outlining specialized historical itineraries. The Norman tours are the **Abbayes Normandes**, **Maisons des Écrivains**, **Ivoire et des Épices** and **Normandie-Vexin**. The website, www.routes-historiques.com offers useful information, in French only. You can request brochures in tourist offices, or write to the Féderation at Hôtel de Nesmond, 57 quai de la Tourelle, 75005 Paris.

Route historique du Patrimoine Cultural Québécois

Three circuits have been developed especially for French Canadians seeking to learn about the land of their ancestors.
Comité Chomedey de Maisonneuve, Centre Culturel Maisonneuve, 10190 Neuville-sur-Vanne, Aube, France. **http://perso.orange.fr/comite.maisonneuve**

THEMATIC ITINERARIES

A wide choice of routes devoted to traditional aspects of Norman life is also available to tourists visiting the area. Subjects include food and drink, notably cheese,Calvados, and cider; dovecots; gardens; copper-working, trains etc. Tourist offices have maps and itineraries, and the www.Normandy-tourism.org website lists many local tours. The following is a sample.

Visiting Mont-St-Michel Bay

The bay surrounding Mont-St-Michel, which features on UNESCO's list of World Nature and Culture Heritage Sites, is also an exceptional place on account of its tidal range – the greatest in continental Europe. During spring tides, the sea level can rise up to 15m/49ft between low and high tide. The water recedes 15km/9.5mi from the coast, then rushes back, accelerating its pace towards the end.

Throughout the year, the **Maisons de la Baie** welcome tourists, organize tours of the Bay, provide information and stage exhibits aimed at promoting the heritage of the bay. The Maisons are located at Genêts, Vains-St-Léonard, Courtils and Le Vivier-sur-Mer (on the Breton side). The Maisons and local tour guides organize visits, crossings (5–6hr), walks, hikes (2hr30min–4hr) and even horseback and bicycle (25–30km/15–20mi; you can rent bicycles) tours. Most tour agencies are open daily April through October, weekdays only November through March.

To obtain further information, or to make reservations (essential), apply to:

Maison de la Baie du Mont-St-Michel, Relais de Courtils, 21 Route de la Roche Torin, 50220 Courtils. ☎02 33 89 66 00. **www.baie-mont-saint-michel.fr**

Maison de la Baie (Brittany) Pont Le Vivier, Cherrueix, 35960 Le Vivier-sur-Mer. ☎02 99 48 84 38. **www.maison-baie.com**

Chemins de la Baie, 34 rue de l'Ortillon, 50530 Genêts. ☎02 33 89 80 88. **www.cheminsdelabaie.fr**.

Découverte de la Baie, La Maison du Guide, 1 rue Montroise, 50530 Genêts, ☎02 33 70 83 49. **www.decouvertebaie.com**

Route des Colombiers Cauchois

Visit Normandy's famous dovecots nestling along the valleys of the Durdent, Valmont or Gonzeville. A website gives a detailed itinerary, in English, as well as photos and links:
www.francerama.com/escapade/colombiers cauchois.

Route de la Pomme et du Cidre

The countryside stretching from the Pays de Caux and the Pays de Bray is dotted with cour-masures planted with venerable apple trees. Leaflets about apples and cider making are available from local tourist offices.
http://routeducidre.free.fr
There is also a **Route du Poiré**, a sparkling drink made from pears, around the town of Domfront: Maison du Parc, BP05, 61320 Carrouges. ☎02 33 81 75 75. **www.parc-naturel-normandie-maine.fr**

TRADITIONAL MARKETS

All cities and nearly all towns have weekly markets, usually held in the morning. The following are only examples – there literally hundreds. Check with tourist offices.

Calvados

Bayeux (rue St-Jean Wed, Place St-Patrice Sat);**Dives-sur-Mer** (Sat year-round, July-Aug Tue); **Honfleur** (Sat; organic produce Wed; antiques 2nd Sun of month; flowers Sat); **St-Pierre-sur-Dives** (Mon) **Trouville** (Wed and Sun).

Eure

Les Andelys (Sat); **Bernay** (Sat); **Évreux** (town centre Wed and Sat, la Madeleine Sun); **Lyons-la-Forêt** (Thu and weekends); **Le Neubourg** (Wed); **Pont-Audemer** (Mon and Fri); **Verneuil-sur-Avre** (Sat).

Manche

Coutances (Sun); **St-Hilaire-du-Harcoët** (Wed in summer, market of artisanal objects); **St-Vaast-la-Hogue** (Sat); **Valognes** (Fri)

Orne

L'Aigle (animal market at 7.30am Tue, followed by traditional market); **Bagnoles-sur-l'Orne** (Tue and Sat)

Seine-Maritime

Caudebec-en-Caux (Saturdays); **Dieppe** (Saturdays); **Étretat** (Thursdays); **Eu** (Fridays); **Fécamp** (Saturdays); **Forges-les-Eaux** (Thursdays and Saturdays); **Harfleur** (Sundays); **Le Havre** (Les Halles centrales daily except Sunday and holidays; antiques, cours de la République, Fri); **Vieux Rouen** place St-Marc (Sundays); **Yvetot** (Wednesdays).

GARDENS OF NORMANDY

The mild climate has long inspired inhabitants of both Basse- and Haute-Normandie to cultivate lovely gardens which are the perfect setting for a leisurely stroll.
The **Comité Régional de Tourisme de Normandie** (www.normandy-tourism.org) offers a free brochure, available at local tourist offices, listing some 60 gardens open to the public.
The **Comité des Parc and Jardins de France** has regional associations in Normandy. The excellent website, www.parcsetjardins.fr, (in French only) lets you locate gardens by type, region, name or on interactive maps.

- ◆ **Union des Parcs et Jardins de Basse-Normandie**: Maison des Quatrans, 25 rue de Geôle,14000 Caen. ☎02 31 15 57 35.
- ◆ **Union des Parcs et Jardins de Haute-Normandie**: 7 rue de Trianon, 76100 Rouen. ☎02 32 18 76 18.

Here is a selection of gardens and parks described in this guide:

- ◆ Jardin des Plantes in **Caen**.
- ◆ Gardens of the **Château de Brécy**.
- ◆ Park and gardens of **Thury-Harcourt**.
- ◆ Botanical gardens in **Vauville**.
- ◆ Parc Emmanuel-Liais and its greenhouses in **Cherbourg**.
- ◆ Jardin des Plantes Quesnel-Morinière in **Coutances**.
- ◆ Jardin Christian-Dior in **Granville**.

- Park of the **Château de Nacqueville**.
- Floral park of the **Bois des Moustiers** at Varengeville-sur-Mer.
- Jardin des Plantes at **Rouen**.
- Park of the **Château de Miromesnil**.
- Gardens and terraces of the **Château de Sassy**.
- Park of the **Château d'Acquigny**.
- Park of the **Château de Beaumesnil**.
- Parc zoologique Jean-Delacour at **Clères.**
- Claude Monet's garden at **Giverny**.
- Park of the **Château de Launay**.

BATTLE OF NORMANDY ITINERARIES

Eight themed itineraries take in the sites, museums and memorials relating to the events of June 1944. The symbol is a sea gull: Association Normandie-Mémoire, 88 rue Saint-Martin, 14000 Caen. ☎02 31 94 80 26.
www.normandiememoire.com

- **Overlord-L'Assaut** *(70km/43.5mi)* from Pegasus Bridge to Bayeux via Sword, Juno and Gold beaches.
- **D-Day-Le Choc** *(130km/81mi)* from Bayeux to Carentan taking in Omaha Beach and St-Lô.
- **Objectif-Un Port** *(95km/59mi)* from Carentan to Cherbourg via Ste-Mère-Église and Valognes.

Road Numbering

In France, some national roads are being transferred to *départements*, and their numbering is being changed. This process will take years, so is not yet captured on maps. As a rule, the number of the national road is found in the last numbers of the new departmental road. Thus, in Calvados, N 13 becomes D 613.

- **L'Affrontement** *(207km/129mi)* this itinerary completes the Overlord-L'Assault one and carries on from Bénouville to Vire coming back by Caen.
- **Cobra-La Percée** *(155km/96mi)* from Cherbourg to Avranches via Coutances.
- **La Contre-Attaque** *(162km/100mi)* from Avranches to Alençon via Mortain.
- **L'Encerclement** *(145km/90mi)* from Alençon to L'Aigle via Chambois and Montormel.
- **Le Dénouement** *(122km/76mi)* from Caen to L'Aigle via Montormel and Vimoutiers.

An entry ticket purchased full price at any of the museums of the Espace historique de la bataille de Normandie entitles the holder to a pass (costing 1€) giving reduced fares at all other museums on the tour. For links to some 30 tours of the battlefields, go to **www.normandy-tourism.com**

Mean Temperatures						
	Jan	Feb	Mar	Apr	May	Jun
min/max°F	33°/44°	35°/46°	37°/51°	41°/55°	46°/62°	50°/68°
min/max°C	1°/7°	1°/8°	3°/11°	5°/13°	8°/17°	10°/20°
	Jul	Aug	Sep	Oct	Nov	Dec
min/max°F	53°/71°	53°/71°	51°/68°	40°/59°	40°/51°	35°/46°
min/max°C	12°/22°	12°/22°	11°/20°	7°/15°	4°/11°	2°/8°
Precipitation						
Average monthly fall	Jan	Feb	Mar	Apr	May	Jun
	68mm	55mm	44mm	47mm	54mm	43mm
Average monthly fall	Jul	Aug	Sep	Oct	Nov	Dec
	50mm	57mm	65mm	72mm	75mm	60mm

KNOW BEFORE YOU GO

Useful Web Sites

The following selected websites offer information in English and provide links to other useful sites.

www.normandy-tourism.org

This official site of the Normandy Tourist Board provides information in about places to visit, maps, suggested itineraries as well as tips for those interested in sports, gastronomy, the travel industry, etc. There are also links to tourist offices, for booking hotels and lodging, transport and other services.

www.francetourism.com

This commercial site offers information about France generally, with a section on each region, including Normandy. Maps, information on tours, places of interest, hotel and transport bookings and lots of links.

www.franceguide.com

The site of the French Government Tourist Office offers information aimed at foreign visitors to France, with sites adapted for each country. It has a particularly good practical information section, and a list of facilities accessible to handicapped people.

www.normandie.visite.org

This site is updated daily and provides weather news, schedules for festivals and other events, and tourist information as well as links to websites covering news, education, business, shopping, chat sites, electronic post cards etc.

www.abmc.gov

The site of the American Battle Monuments Commission offers information on events at the Normandy American Cemetery and Memorial. There is a link to the World War II database giving the location of individual casualties buried in ABMC cemeteries.

www.info-france-usa.org

The French Embassy's web site provides practical information (visa requirements, driving, transport, tipping), a link to the US embassy website in Paris (www.amb-usa.fr), recent news stories, and links (consulates in the US, regions, cities, ministries, commercial sites).

www.ambafrance-ca.org

The Cultural Service of the French Embassy in Ottawa has a bright and varied site information about travel in France, France-Canada relations, links to consulates, and much more.

www.visiteurope.com

The European Travel Commission provides useful information on travelling in 30 European countries, and includes links to commercial booking services (such as vehicle hire), rail schedules, weather reports and more.

Tourist Offices

For information, brochures, maps and assistance in planning a trip to France, you should apply to the French Tourist Office in your own country.

AUSTRALIA – NEW ZEALAND

Sydney – Level 22, 25 Bligh St, NSW 2000 Sydney. ☎(02) 9231 5244. http://au.franceguide.com.

CANADA

Montreal – 1981 McGill College Avenue, Suite 490, Montreal PQ H3A 2W9. ☎(514) 288-2026. http://ca-uk.franceguide.com.

EIRE

Dublin – No office. ☎15 60 235 235 (Irish information line). http://ie.franceguide.com

SOUTH AFRICA

Craighall – PO Box 41022,2024
Craighall. ☎00 27 11 523 82 92.
http://za.franceguide.com

UNITED KINGDOM

London – 178 Piccadilly, London WIJ
9AL ☎09068 244 123.
http://uk.franceguide.com.

UNITED STATES

Website: http://us.franceguide.com

East Coast: New York – 444 Madison
Avenue, 16th floor, NY 10022-
6903. ☎(514) 288-1904 (Montreal
office).

Midwest: Chicago – Consulate General of France, 205 North Michigan
Avenue, Suite 3770, Chicago, IL
60601-2819. ☎(514)288-1904
(Montreal office).

West Coast: Los Angeles – 9454
Wilshire Boulevard, Suite 715, Los
Angeles CA 90212-2967. ☎(514)
288-1904 (Montreal office).

REGIONAL TOURIST OFFICES

To telephone directly to a local tourist
office or *syndicat d'initiative* from
within France, even if you don't know
the number, dial 3265 (costs 0.34
€/min), then pronounce clearly the
name of the town that interests you.
You will be connected directly.

◆ **Comité Régional de Tourisme
de Normandie,** 14 rue Charles-
Corbeau, 27000 Evreux. ☎02 32
33 79 00. www.normandy-
tourism.org

Departmental Tourist Offices

◆ **Calvados**: 8 rue Renoir, 14054
Caen Cedex 4. ☎02 31 27 90 30.
www.calvados-tourisme.com.
◆ **Eure**: 3 rue du Cdt-Letellier, BP
367, 27003 Evreux Cedex. ☎02 32
62 04 27. www.cdt-eure.fr.

◆ **Manche**: Maison du Département,
Route de Villedieu, 50008 Saint-Lô
Cedex. ☎02 33 05b98 70.
www.manchetourisme.com.
◆ **Mayenne:** 84 av Robert Buron, BP
0325, 53003 Laval. ☎02 43 53 18
18. www.tourisme-mayenne.com
◆ **Orne**: 86 rue St-Blaise, BP 50,
61002 Alençon Cedex. ☎02 33 28
88 71. www.ornetourism.com
◆ **Seine-Maritime**: 6 rue Couronné,
BP 60, 76420 Bihorel. ☎02 35 12
10 10. www.seine-maritime-
tourisme.com

TOURIST INFORMATION CENTRES

♿In the Sights section *(Exploring
Normandy)*, the address, telephone
number and web address of the local
tourist office *(Syndicats d'Initiative)*
appear after the introduction to
the Principal Sight, flagged by the
symbol.

International Visitors

EMBASSIES AND CONSULATES

Australia   **Embassy**
4 rue Jean-Rey, 75015 Paris
☎01 40 59 33 00.
www.france.embassy.gov.au

Canada   **Embassy**
35 avenue Montaigne, 75008 Paris
☎01 44 43 29 00. www.amb-canada.fr

Eire   **Embassy**
4 rue Rude, 75016 Paris.
☎01 44 17 67 00.
www.embassyofireland.paris.com

New Zealand   **Embassy**
7 ter rue Léonard-de-Vinci, 75116 .
☎01 45 01 43 43.
www.nzembassy.com

South Africa   **Embassy**
59 quai d'Orsay, 75343 Paris. ☎01 53
59 23 23. www.afriquesud.net

UK   **Embassy**
35 rue du Faubourg-St-Honoré,
75008 Paris
☎01 44 51 31 00.
www.britishembassy.gov.uk/france

UK   **Consulate**
16 rue d'Anjou, 75008 Paris;
☎01 44 51 31 00 (visas)

USA   **Embassy**
2 avenue Gabriel, 75008 Paris.
☎01 43 12 22 22. www.amb-usa

USA   **Consulate**
2 rue St-Florentin, 75382 Paris
☎01 43 02 22 22.
http://france.usembassy.gov.

DOCUMENTS

Passport
Nationals of countries within the European Union entering France need only a national identity card or, in the case of the British, a passport. Nationals of other countries must be in possession of a valid national **passport**. In case of loss or theft report to the embassy or consulate and the local police. **You must carry your documents with you at all times**; they can be checked anywhere.

Visa
No **entry visa** is required for Australian, Canadian, New Zealand and US citizens traveling as tourists and staying less than 90 days, except for students planning to study in France. If in doubt, apply to your local French Consulate..
US citizens should obtain the booklet *Safe Trip Abroad* ($2.75) from the Government Printing Office. ☎(202)512-1800. or order at http://bookstore.gpo.gov, or consult on-line and download at www.pueblo.gsa.gov (click on travel publications). General passport information is available by phone toll-free from the Federal Information Center (item 5 on the automated menu), ☎800-688-9889. US passport forms can be downloaded from http://travel.state.gov.

Duty-Free Allowances	
Spirits (whisky, gin, vodka etc)	10 litres
Fortified wines (vermouth, port etc)	20 litres
Wine (not more than 60 sparkling)	90 litres
Beer	110 litres
Cigarettes	800
Cigarillos	400
Cigars	200
Smoking tobacco	1 kg

CUSTOMS

In Britain, go to the Customs Office (UK) website at http://customs.hmrc.gov.uk for information on allowances, travel safety tips and to consult and download documents and guides. For questions contact the National Advice Service at 0845 010 9000.

The US Customs Service offers a publication, *Know Before You Go* to consult and download at www.customs.ustreas.gov (click on travel).

Canadians can consult and download *I Declare* at www.canadaonline.about.com. For **Australians**, *Know Before You Go* is available at www.customs.gov.au. For **New Zealanders**, *Advice for Travellers* is at www.customs.govt.nz.. **Americans** can bring home, tax free, US$800 worth of goods; **Canadians** CDN$750; **Australians** AUS$900 and **New Zealanders** NZ$700.
People living in a Member State of the European Union are not restricted in regard to good for private use, but the recommended allowances for alcohol and tobacco are shown in the table. There are no customs formalities for holidaymakers bringing their cars or caravans into France for a stay of less than six months. No customs document is necessary for pleasure boats and outboard motors for a stay of less than six months but the registration certificate should be kept on board.

HEALTH

First aid and medical advice are available from chemists/drugstores (*pharmacie*) identified by the green cross sign. In every town, a *pharmacie* remains on duty at night, based on a revolving schedule. All prescription drugs must be clearly labeled; it is essential you carry the prescriptions You should take out comprehensive insurance coverage as the recipient of medical treatment in French hospitals or clinics must pay. Nationals of non-EU countries should check with their insurance companies about policy limitations. **Americans and Canadians** can contact the International Association for Medical Assistance to Travelers: for the US ☎ (716)754-4883 or for Canada ☎ (416) 652 0137 or ☎ (519) 836-0102. www.iamat.org. **British and Irish citizens** (and all EU citizens) should apply for a European Health Insurance Card (EHIC), which has replaced the E111. Everyone in the family must have one, even children. **UK subjects** can apply online to www.dh.gov.uk/travellers, or telephone ☎0845 606 2030, or pick up an application at the Post Office. **Irish citizens** may contact info@health.gov.ie or www.ehic.ie.

Accessibility

The sights described in this guide which are easily accessible to people of reduced mobility are indicated for the Sights in the *Admission times and charges* by the symbol ♿.
For a list of accessible sites, carrying the Tourisme et Handicap designation, go to **www.franceguide.com**.
The principal French source for information on facilities is the **Association de Paralysés de France**, 17 bd Auguste-Blanqui, 75013 Paris, www.apf.asso.fr. The APF publishes a *Guide vacances* available on the website, or by mail (5.30 € plus postage).
The **Michelin Guide France** and the **Michelin Camping Caravaning France**: Revised every year, these guides indicate where to facilities accessible to the disabled.

The French railways (SNCF) gives information on travel at www.voyages-sncf.com, as does **Air France** at www.airfrance.fr.

The Channel Islands

ENTRY REGULATIONS

Passports are not required for British subjects. The same requirements apply for other tourists as in France.

TRAVEL

By Air
There are flights to **Jersey**, **Guernsey** and **Alderney**:
- Jersey, Guernsey and Alderney airports are served by regular flights operated by British Airways, (ba.com);British Midland (flybmi.com); Thompsonfly.com and Flybe.com, as well as Swiss (www.swiss.com) from Zurich and Blue Islands (www.blueislands.com) and Twin-Jet (www.twinjet.com) from Paris.
- Aurigny Air Services offers flights between Guernsey, Jersey and Alderney and several British airports as well as Dinard in France. Tickets are electronic only: www.aurigny.com.

By Sea
Fast catamaran ferries run to the Channel Islands from England (Poole, Weymouth and Portsmouth) and France (Granville, Diélette, Carteret, St-Malo). Contact www.condorferries.co.uk; www.hdferries.org; www.manche-iles-express.com. Scheduled ferries run among the islands. Note that, for all ferry services, where they land and at what time depends on tides.

CURRENCY

Legal tender is the British pound. The local currency issued by the banks of Jersey and Guernsey is not legal tender outside the islands. All the British clearing banks have branches in the Channel Islands.

GETTING THERE

By Air

The principal cities of Normandy are served out of St-Exupéry airport in Lyons. **Brit'Air** (Air France) has flights to and from Caen, Rouen and Le Havre daily. Information and reservations: ☎0 820 820 820. www.airfrance.com. or www.britair.com. **Twin Jet** has flights connecting Paris/Orly and Cherbourg-Jersey. ☎0 892 707 737. www. twinjet.net

The regional airports are:
Aeroport de Caen-Carpiquet – ☎02 31 71 20 10
Aéroport de Cherbourg-Maupertus – ☎02 33 88 57 60.
Aéroport Le Havre-Octeville – 02 35 54 65 00
Aéroport Rouen Vallée de Seine – ☎02 35 79 41 00

By Sea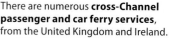

There are numerous **cross-Channel passenger and car ferry services**, from the United Kingdom and Ireland.

- ♦ **P & O Ferries**, Channel House, Channel View Road, Dover CT17 9JT, ☎08705 980 333 (in the UK) or ☎0825 120 156 (in France) **www.poferries.com**. Service between Dover and Calais
- ♦ **Norfolk Line**, Norfolk House, Eastern Docks, Dover CT16 1JA Kent. ☎870 870 10 20 (in the UK) or ☎03 28 59 01 01 (in France). **www.norfolkline-ferries.co.uk**. Service between Dover and Dunkerque.
- ♦ **Brittany Ferries**, Millbay Docks; Plymouth, Devon, PL1 3EW, ☎0870 9 076 103 (in the UK) ☎0825 828 828 (in France). **www.brittany-ferries.co.uk.** Service between Portsmouth, Poole and Plymouth and ports in France and Spain.
- ♦ **Irish Ferries**, Ferryport, Alexandra Road, Dublin 1. ☎8705 17 17 17 (in the UK); ☎00 353 818 300 400 (Northern Ireland); ☎0818 300 400 (Republic of Ireland); ☎(01) 44 88 54 50 (France). **www.irish-ferries.com.** Service between Dublin, Rosslane and Roscoff and Cherbourg.
- ♦ **Seafrance Ferries Ltd.** Whitfield Court, Honeywood Close, Whitfield, Kent CT16 3PX. ☎0871 663 2546 (In the UK). **www.seafrance. fr.** Service between Dover and Calais.

By Rail

Eurostar runs via the Channel Tunnel between **London** (Waterloo) **Paris** (Gare du Nord) in 3hr; in late 2007, service will move to **St Pancras** station and the trip will take 2hr20min. The trip from **London** to **Lille** takes 2hrs. At present, the only high speed train serving Normandy connects **Marseilles** and **Le Havre** in 6hrs 30mins. Bookings and information ☎0345 303 030 in the UK; ☎1-888-EUROSTAR in the US or **www.eurostar.com**. Or contact the French national railways **www.voyages-sncf.com**. SNCF operates a **telephone information, reservation and prepayment service in English** from 8am to 7pm (French time). In France call ☎0892 33 35 39 (When calling from outside France, drop the initial 0 and add 33). Dial 42 as soon as the connection is made.

The **Corail Intercités** network connects Paris with Norman cities: Rouen, Le Havre, Dieppe, Trouville, Dreux, L'Aigle, Beauvais and LeTréport. Trains run several times daily. **Trains express régionaux** (**TER**) form an efficient local network which also makes use of buses.

Eurailpass, Flexipass, Eurailpass Youth, EurailDrive Pass and **Saverpass** may be purchased by residents of countries outside the EU. In the Western Hemisphere go to **www.raileurope.com**. Alternatively, in the **US**, contact Rail Europe

☏1-877-257-2887. In **Canada**, contact ☏1-800-361-RAIL. **Australians** go to www.railplus.com.au. ☏1300 555 003, and for **New Zealanders**, go to www.railplus.com.nz. ☏649 377 5415.
European residents can buy an individual country pass if not a resident of the country where they plan to use it. In the **UK or Ireland**, contact Rail Europe ltd at www.raileurope.co.uk or ☏0870 848 848.
Tickets bought in France must be validated (*composter*) by using the orange automatic date-stamping machines at the platform entrance. Failure to do so may result in a fine.

By Bus

Each *départment* in Normandy operates local and intercity bus services. You can travel anywhere within a *département*, no matter how far, for 2€ one-way adult fare, 1€for children. Information is available, in French, from the website of each *département*. The website of **Calvados** is www.cg14.fr; **Eure** is www.cg27.fr; **Manche** is www.cg50.fr (the direct bus site is www.stenligne.fr); **Orne** is www.cg61.fr; **Seine-Maritime** is www.cg76.fr (or www.seine-maritime.net).
You can also consult local tourist offices once you arrive in Normandy.

Driving in France

PLANNING YOUR ROUTE

Michelin **Local** maps give a close, detailed look at two or three *départements*, with maps of major towns. For Normandy, you will need **Local 310** (covering the *départements* of Mayenne, Orne, Sarthe), **303** (Calvados, Manche) and **304** (Eure, Seine-Maritime), and may also want the **Regional 513** (Normandy, including maps of Caen and Rouen) and **517** (Pays-de-la-Loire) maps, which list towns, show secondary roads and offer information for tourists. **The map of France 721** offers a view of all

Normandy, with major arteries leading from your point of arrival.
The latest Michelin route-planning service is available on the Internet, **www.ViaMichelin.com**. Travellers can calculate a precise route using such options as shortest route, route avoiding toll roads, GPS navigation, Michelin-recommended route and gain access to tourist information (hotels, restaurants, attractions).
The roads are very busy during the holiday period (particularly weekends in July and August), and you should consider recommended secondary routes (signposted as *Bison Futé – itinéraires bis*). For information on traffic conditions, consult **www.autoroutes.fr** or ☏0 892 681 077.

DOCUMENTS

Travellers from other EU contries or North America can drive in France with a valid national, home-state or provincial **driving licence** for up to a year; you should have a French translation attached. An **international driving licence** is recommended, however. To procure one in **the US**, contact the National Automobile Club, 1-800-622-2136, www.nationalautoclub.com, or contact your local branch of the American Automobile Association or go online to www.aaa.com. **In Canada**, contact www.caa.ca.
The Australian Automobile Association is at www.aaa.asn.au and the **New Zealand Automobile Association** is at www.aa.co.nz.
For the vehicle, you must have the registration (*carte grise*) and the insurance certificate (*carte verte*).

INSURANCE

Certain motoring organisations (AAA, CAA, AA, RAC) offer accident insurance and breakdown service schemes for members. Check with your current insurance company in regard to coverage while abroad. If you plan to hire a car using your credit card, your may have liability insurance automatically (and thus save paying for optimum coverage).

ROAD REGULATIONS

The minimum driving age in France is 18. Traffic drives on the right. It is compulsory for all passengers, in front and back seats, to wear **seat belts**. Children under the age of 10 must travel on the back seat of the vehicle. In the case of a **breakdown** a red warning triangle or hazard warning lights are obligatory. In the absence of stop signs at intersections, as in roundabouts, cars must **yield to the right**. Vehicles must stop when the lights turn red at road junctions and may filter to the right only when indicated by an amber arrow. The regulations on **drinking and driving** (limited to .05% or 0.50g/l) and **speeding** are strictly enforced – usually by an on-the-spot fine and/or confiscation of the vehicle.

Rental Cars – Central Reservation in France		
Avis:	☏ 08 20 05 05 05	www.avis.fr
Europcar:	☏ 08 25 35 23 52	www.europcar.fr
Budget France:	☏ 08 00 10 00 01	www.budget.fr
Hertz France:	☏ 01 39 38 38 38	www.hertz.fr
SIXT- Eurorent	☏ 01 40 65 01 00	www.sixt.fr
National-CITER	☏ 01 45 22 88 40	www.citer.fr
Barron's Limousines:	☏ 01 45 30 21 21	www.barrons-limousines.com

Speed Limits

Speed limits, generally speaking, are 50kph (31mph) in towns and built-up areas; 90kph/56mph on ordinary roads; 110kph/68mph on dual car-riageways and motorways without tolls; and 130kph/80mph on toll motorways (*autoroutes*). Limits are posted along the road.

Parking

In town there are zones where parking is either restricted or subject to a fee; tickets should be obtained from the ticket machines (*horodateurs* – small change necessary) and displayed inside the windscreen on the driver's side; failure to display may result in a fine, or towing and impoundment. In some towns where you find blue parking zones (*zone bleue*) marked by a blue line on the pavement or road and a 🅿 sign, a cardboard disc gives you 1hr 30min (2hr 30min over lunch time) free. Discs are sold in supermarkets or gasoline stations (ask for a *disque de stationnement*) and are sometimes given away free.

Tolls

In France, most motorway sections are subject to a toll *(péage)*. You can pay in cash or with a credit card (Visa, Mastercard).

Fuel

French service stations dispense *sans plomb 98* (super unleaded 98), *sans plomb 95*, *diesel/gazole* (diesel) and GPL (LPG) Gas in France is far more expensive than in North America. It is usually cheaper off the motorway; check the hypermarkets.

CAR RENTAL

There are car rental agencies at air-ports, railway stations and in all large towns throughout France: consult the websites. Most European cars have manual transmission; automatic cars are available only if an advance reser-vation is made. Drivers must be over 21; between ages 21 and 25, drivers are required to pay an extra daily fee. It is expensive to hire a car in France: take advantage of fly-drive offers, or seek advice from a travel agent.

MOTORHOME RENTAL

Several companies offer motorhome rental in France. Note that caravans are not allowed into the Channel Islands. Websites include:
www.motorhomesworldwide.com.
www.ukandeuropetravel.com
www.car-rental-hire.co.uk
www.ideamerge.com

WHERE TO STAY AND EAT

The *Michelin Green Guide* is pleased to offer a selection of accommodations and restaurants for Normandy. Turn to the green Address Books within the individual Sights for descriptions and prices of typical places to stay (**Where to Stay**) and to eat (**Where to Eat**). The Legend on the cover flap explains the symbols and abbreviations used in these sections.

Where to Stay

FINDING A HOTEL

Use the **Places to stay** map in the following pages to identify recommended places for overnight stops. It can be used in conjunction with the **Michelin Guide France**—with its well known star-rating system—which lists an even greater selection of hotels and restaurants.
For further assistance, **La Fédération Loisirs Accueil** is a booking service that has offices in most French *départements*: 280 boulevard St-Germain, 75007 Paris, ☎01 44 11 10 44 , http://www.loisirsaccueilfrance.com.
Relais et châteaux provides information on booking in luxury hotels with character: 15 rue Galvani, 75017 Paris, ☎01 45 72 90 00, www.relaischateaux.com.

ECONOMY CHAIN HOTELS

If you need a place to stop en route, these can be useful, as they are inexpensive (35-45€ for a double room) and generally located near the main road. There may not be a restaurant; rooms are small, with a television and private bathroom. Rather than sort through hotels yourself, you can go to websites that cover several chains, where you can select your hotel and book online:
www.accorhotels.com covers some 1 400 hotels in france, including the Formule 1 chain, at about 35€, as well as Novotel, Mercure, Sofitel, etc.
www.activehotels.com covers a wide range of hotels, with cutomer reviews.
www.day-tripper.net covers reasonably priced hotels, by location, throughout France.
www.envergure.fr covers more expensive hotels (more than 60€) Campanile, Kyriad, Bleu Marine, Première Class and Louvre.
Here are some modestly-priced chains:
- **Akena** ☎01 69 84 85 17. www.hotels-akena.com
- **B&B** ☎02 98 33 75 00. www.hotel-bb.com
- **Etap Hôtel** ☎08 92 68 89 00. www.etaphotel.com
- **Best Hôtel** ☎03 28 27 46 69. www.besthotel.fr

RURAL ACCOMMODATION

The **Maison des Gîtes de France et du Tourisme vert** is an information service on self-catering accommodation in the regions of France. *Gîtes* usually take the form of a cottage or apartment decorated in the local style where visitors can make themselves at home. The organization also covers specialized *gîtes*, for fishing, camping, hiking, etc.
Contact Gîtes de France: 59 rue St-Lazare, 75439 Paris Cedex 09. ☎01 49 70 75 75. **www.gites-de-france.com**, where you can purchase a booklet, *Normandie* (17€) updated yearly. In total, the association lists some 2000 rural gîtes and more than 1000 bed-and-breakfasts in Normandy.
The publication **Bienvenue à la Ferme** lists some 300 Norman farmers who offer accomodation of varying degrees of comfort on their farms, including meals: Service Agriculture et Tourisme, 9 av George V, 75008 Paris, ☎01 53 57 11 44. You can find the book in stores, or at **www.bienvenue-a-la-ferme.com**

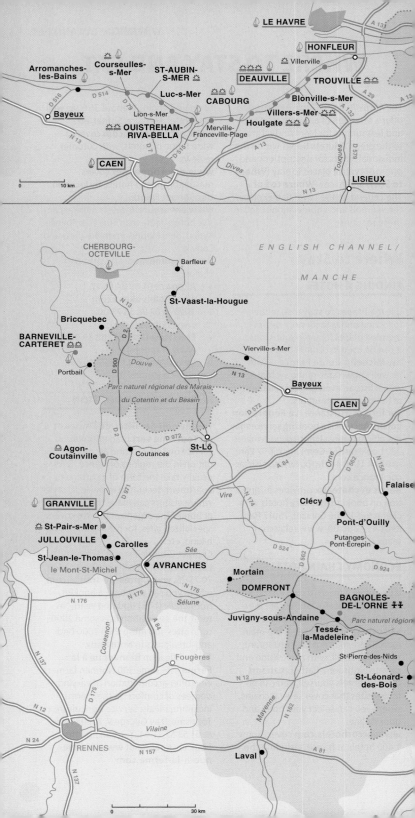

Places to stay

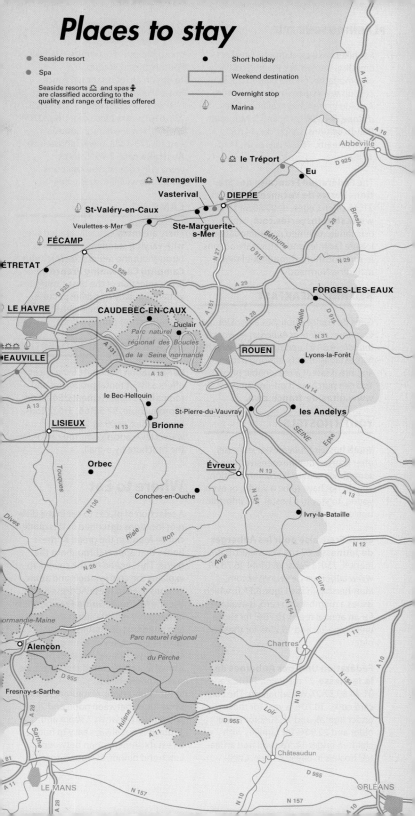

Legend:

- ● Seaside resort
- ● Spa
- ⚓⚓ Seaside resorts and spas ⚓ are classified according to the quality and range of facilities offered
- ● Short holiday
- ▭ Weekend destination
- — Overnight stop
- ⛵ Marina

Abbeville

⚓ ⚓ le Tréport
● Eu

⚓ Varengeville
Vasterival
⚓ DIEPPE
⛵ St-Valéry-en-Caux
Veulettes-s-Mer
Ste-Marguerite-s-Mer

⚓ FÉCAMP

ÉTRETAT

LE HAVRE

FORGES-LES-EAUX

CAUDEBEC-EN-CAUX
Duclair

Parc naturel régional des Boucles de la Seine normande

ROUEN
Lyons-la-Forêt

⚓⚓⚓⛵
EAUVILLE

le Bec-Hellouin
St-Pierre-du-Vauvray
les Andelys

LISIEUX
Brionne

Orbec
Évreux
Conches-en-Ouche
Ivry-la-Bataille

Chartres

Alençon

Parc naturel régional du Perche

Fresnay-s-Sarthe

Châteaudun

LE MANS
ORLÉANS

For hikers, skiers, climbers, kayakers, bicyclists and others seeking rustic accomodation off the beaten track, consult **www.gites-refuges.com**. A guide in French is available: *Gîtes d'étape, Refuges* by A. and S. Mouraret, Rando Éditions, La Cadole, 74 rue A.-Perdreaux, 781 Vézily. ☎01 34 65 11 89.

The **Fédération Française des Stations Vertes de Vacances**, BP 71698, 21016 Dijon Cedex. ☎03 80 54 10 50, **www.stationsvertes.com**, which lists family-oriented accommodation, leisure facilities and natural attractions in rural locations throughout France, including Normandy.

BED AND BREAKFAST

Gîtes de France publishes a booklet *Chambres d'Hôte et Auberges en Normandie* (4.50€) updated yearly, which lists establishments offering a room and breakfast at a reasonable price. You can purchase it on-line at **www.gites-de-france.com**.

YOUTH HOSTELS

Youth hostels (*auberges de jeunesse*) offer spartan but inexpensive and sometimes convivial accommodation. You do not have to be a youth, or even young, to stay in a hostel. For information contact:

Ligue Française pour les Auberges de Jeunesse, 67 rue Vergniaud, Bâtiment K, 75013 Paris. ☎01 44 16 78 78, www.auberges-de-jeunesse.com. Membership in the Ligue (LFAJ), which issues a membership card, is available for an annual fee of 10.70€ for those under age 26, and 15.25€ for those older.

Fédération Unie des Auberges de la Jeunesse, 27 rue Pajol, 75018 Paris. 01 44 89 87 27. wwwfuaj.org. The Fuaj card costs 10.70€ a year for those under age 26, and 15.30€ for those older and 22.90€ for families with children under 14. You will find affiliated hostels in Bayeux, Caen, Cher-

bourg, Dieppe, Eu, Genêts, Granville, Pontorson and Vernon.

To obtain an International Youth Hostel Federation card, contact the IYHF in your own country: **US** ☎(202) 783-6161, www.hiusa.org; **UK** ☎1707 324 170, www.iyhf.org; **Canada** ☎(613) 273-7884, www.hihostels.ca; **Australia** ☎61-2-9565-1669. www.yhg.com.au. You can book through www.hihostels.com.

CAMPING

There are many officially graded sites with varying standards of facilities throughout the region; the **Michelin Camping Caravaning France** guide lists a selection of the best camp sites, visited regularly by our inspectors. Tourist offices and their websites also provide lists of campgrounds.

VACATION RENTAL PROPERTIES

La Fédération National Clévacances offers a list of rental properties and rooms in 79 départements: 54 bd de l'Embouchure, BP 52166, 31022 Toulouse Cedex. ☎05 61 13 55 66. www.clevacances.com. You can order the brochure by e-mail

Where to Eat

A selection of places to eat in the different locations described in this guide can be found in the green Address Books that appear throughout the guide. The Legend on the cover flap explains the coin symbols and abbreviations used in these Address Books. Use the **Michelin Guide France**, with its famously reliable star-rating system and hundreds of establishments all over France, for an even greater choice. If you would like to experience a meal in a highly rated restaurant, be sure to book ahead.

In the countryside, restaurants usually serve lunch between noon and 2pm and dinner between 7.30pm and 10pm. It is not always easy to find an establishment open between lunch and dinner, as "round-the-clock" restaurants are still scarce in the provinces. However, a hungry traveller can usually get a sandwich in a cafe, and ordinary hot dishes may be available in a brasserie.

For information on local specialities, 🖝 see *The Region Today* in the Introduction. Many restaurants participate in the **Assiette de pays** programme, which promotes local specialities at 6–18€ for a single dish and drink; participants post the logo in their windows, and you can get a list at **www.norman-diepays.com**, under *Assiette de pays*.

In French restaurants and cafes, a service charge is included. Tipping is not necessary, but French people often leave the small change from their bill on their table.

Menu reader

La Carte	The Menu
Entrées	**Starters**
Crudités	Raw vegetable salad
Terrine de lapin	Rabbit terrine (pâté)
Frisée aux lardons	Curly lettuce with lardons
Escargots	Snails
Cuisses de grenouille	Frog's legs
Salade au crottin	Goat's cheese salad
Plats (Viandes)	**Main Courses (Meat)**
Bavette à l'échalote	Sirloin with shallots
Faux filet au poivre	Sirloin with pepper sauce
Côtes d'agneau	Lamb chops
Filet mignon de porc	Pork filet
Blanquette de veau	Veal in cream sauce
Plats	**Main Courses**
Filets de sole	Sole fillets
Dorade aux herbes	Sea bream with herbs
Saumon grillé	Grilled salmon
Coq au vin	Chicken in red wine sauce
Poulet de Bresse rôti	Roast Bresse chicken
Fromage	**Cheese**
Desserts	**Desserts**
Tarte aux pommes	Apple pie
Boissons	**Beverages**
Bière	Beer
Eau minérale (gazeuse)	(Sparkling) mineral water
Une carafe d'eau	Tap water
Vin rouge, vin blanc, rosé	Red wine, white wine, rosé
Jus de fruit	Fruit juice
Menu Enfant	**Children's Menu**
Jambon	Ham
Steak haché	Ground beef

WHAT TO DO AND SEE

Outdoor Fun

CRUISES ON THE RIVER SEINE

A number of boats able to accommodate between 80 and 350 passengers visit the main harbours (Le Havre, Honfleur, Rouen). Trips can take half a day or a whole day, including meals on board, or you can opt for luxury cruises between Paris and Honfleur lasting up to a week, with stops along the way.

The following list features the most popular boats offering this type of excursion:

♦ **CroisiEurope** – 12 rue de la Division-Leclerc , 67000Strasbourg. ☎03 88 76 44 44. www.croisieurope.com. Cruises between Paris and Honfleur, or the reverse, in 5–7 days.

♦ **Viking Croisières Fluviales** – Enquire at Athenaeum, 39 rue de Marbeuf, 75008 Paris. ☎01 58 36 08 36. On a luxury boat-hotel, from late March through October, 7-day cruises between Paris and Le Havre, with bus excursions.

◆ **Le Guillaume-le-Conquérant**
– Contact Rives de Seine Croisières,
72 rue Scheurer-Kestner, 76320
Caudebec-lès-Elbeuf. ☎02 35 78
31 70. www.rives-seine-croisieres.
fr. Shorter cruises, about 4 hrs
there and back, between Poses
and Muids.

◆ **Fécamp Boat Tours**. ☎02 35
28 99 53, tim76@wanadoo.fr. In
July–August, leaving from Fécamp,
boat trips along the cliffs of Étretat
and fishing excursions; from September–June, tours of the port of
Le Havre and fishing excursions.

PARKS AND GARDENS

*Information on parks and gardens
in Normandy is provided on page 16 of
this guide.*

SWIMMING

The first thing to do is become
acquainted with the rhythm of the
tides, which alternate from high tide
to low tide every 6hrs. It is usually safer
and warmer to bathe on an incoming
tide. On steeply sloping shingle
(stoney) beaches high tide can be
dangerous as children are rapidly out
of their depth. Low tide on the other
hand is often impatiently awaited by a
happy group with nets for shrimping
or forks and spades to dig for bait or
pails for gathering mussels and crabs.
The Norman beaches are of two
types: **sandy** along the Côte Fleurie
(Cabourg, Houlgate, Deauville,
Trouville, Honfleur etc.) and **shingle**
(stoney) along the Alabaster Coast
(Étretat, Yport, Fécamp, St-Valéry-en-
Caux, Varengeville, Dieppe etc.)
Guarded beaches have a system of
flags to warn bathers of possible
risks: **green** – safe bathing; **orange**
– dangerous, be careful; **red** – bathing
prohibited; **violet** – polluted water.
If you want to know the water quality
of any beach (tested each June), go
to **www.infosplage.com**. The rating
goes from A (good) to D (questiona-
ble).

SAILING

The Channel coast is a favourite venue
for boaters and sailors. Many sailing
clubs offer lessons at all levels of
skill, and in the bigger coastal towns,
annual regattas are a glorious sight.
The main moorings and marinas for
visiting yachtsmen are indicated on
the **Places to Stay Map**. They usually
provide fuelling facilities, convenient
water stands for drinking water and
electricity points, WCs, showers and
sometimes laundry facilities, handling
equipment and repair facilities and a
24-hour guard.

France Stations Nautiques is an
association of coastal villages, tourist
sites and marinas offering first-rate
facilities for nautical sports.
France Stations Nautiques: 17, rue
Henri-Bocquillon, 75015 Paris. ☎01 44
05 96 55. **www.france-nautisme.com**
For further information on sailing,
contact the **Fédération Française de
Voile:** 17, rue Henri-Bocquillon, 75015
Paris. ☎01 40 60 37 00. **www.ffvoile.
org.**

Foreigners who own or want to rent
a boat (with an engine of more than
6hp) in France must take a compulsory
test in sailing skills (carte mer).

SPAS

Normandy has several centres for
thalassotherapy and water cures
aimed at preventing or treating certain
ailments. In addition to the bracing climate and vivifying sea air, they rely on
the curative virtues of the local waters,
mud and algae. The Normandy coast
offers five establishments of this type:

Granville

Le Normandy: Centre de rééeducation
et de réadaptation fonctionnelles en
milieu marin – 1 rue J.-Michelet, BP
619, 50406 Granvile Cedexb02 33 90 33
33. www.lenormandy.com.

Prévithal Institut de thalassothérapie
–3 r. J.-Michelet, BP 618, 5-406 Granville Cedex. ☎02 33 90 31 10.
www.previthal.com

Luc-sur-Mer
Institut de Cure Marine – rue Guyne-mer, 14530 Luc-sur-Mer. ☎02 31 97 32 22. www.thalasso-normandie.com.

Deauville
Thalsasso-Deauville – 3 rue de Sem, 14800 Deauville. ☎02 31 87 72 00. www.thalasso-normandie.com.

Ouistreham
Thalazur Ouistreham-Normandie – Av. du Cmdt-Keiffer, 14150 Ouistreham. ☎02 31 96 40 40. **www.thalazur.fr.**

Bagnoles-de-l'Orne
The Grande Source, **a hot spring** with slightly radioactive mineralized water, is said to provide relief for circulatory problems, especially in the legs, and for arthritis and rheumatism as well as problems of the endocrine glands. The season lasts from mid-March to early November.

T**hermes de Bagnoles-de-l'Orne** rue du Prof.-Louvel, BP 33, 61140 Bag-nole-de-l'Orne. ☎0811 902 233. www.thermes-bagnoles.com. You can take a tour Tue–Fri at 5pm.

Centre d'animation de Bagnoles-de-l'Orne – 1 rue du Prof.-Louvel, BP 27, 61140 Bagnoles-de-l'Orne. ☎02 33 30 72 70. www.bagnoles-de-lorne.com

WINDSURFING

This sport, which is permitted on lakes and in sports and leisure centres, is subject to certain rules. Apply to local sailing clubs. Boards may be hired on all major beaches. **www.ffvoile.org**.

LAND SAILING

The great stretches of sandy beach on the Calvados and Cotentin coasts are ideal for land sailing (*char-à-voile*), an exhilarating sport performed on a three-wheeled cart equipped with a sail; speeds can reach 100kph/63mph. A new, similar sport has recently seen the light of day: **speed sailing**, a form of windsurfing on wheels. Further information may be obtained from

R. Corbel/MICHELIN

Bisquine La Granvillaise drawing

the **Fédération française de Char à voile**, 17 rue Henri-Bocquillon, 75015 Paris. ☎01 45 58 75 75. **www.ffcv.org** The federation offers a list of clubs, guidebooks and calendars.

SKIN DIVING

The right conditions for deep-sea diving are to be found between Dieppe and Le Havre and between Barfleur and Avranches on the Cotentin coast. Further information can be obtained from the **Fédération française d'étude et de sports sous-marins**, 24 quai de Rive-Neuve, 13284 Marseille Cedex 07. ☎04 91 33 99 31. **www.ffessm.fr**

FISHING

For those interested in freshwater fishing, it is necessary to know the dates of the *saison de la pêche*: all over France, the second Saturday in March heralds the start of the fishing season for rivers belonging to the first cate-gory *(première catégorie)*, ending on the third Sunday in September. In the case of second category rivers *(deux-ième catégorie)*, fishing is permitted all year round, except for pike, which can usually be caught between July and January, depending on the area.

Normandy is dotted with a great many lakes, rivers and ponds of astounding variety. This particular type of topography makes it one of France's most treasured regions for fishing. The fast-flowing rivers abound in fario trout, a local variety, and rainbow trout, brought over from America, whereas the various lakes and ponds are the favourite haunt of carnivorous species such as pike, pikeperch and salmon. The most popular rivers among anglers are the **Risle** (fario trout, carnivores), the **Iton** (pike, rainbow trout), the **Charentonne** (fario trout), the **Huisne** (grayling, fario trout), the **Touques** (fario trout), the **Yères** (fario trout), the **Bresle** (sea trout), the **Arques** (salmon and sea trout) and the **Durdent** (fario trout and sea trout).

Wherever you choose to go fishing, make sure you obey the laws on angling and apply for details from the relevant federations and associations. You have to become a member (for the year in progress) of an affiliated angling association in the *département* of your choice, pay the annual angling tax or buy a day card, and obtain permission from the landowner if you wish to fish on private land.

- **Fédération de Calvados pour la pêche,** 18 rue de la Girafe, 14000 Caen. ☎02 31 44 63 00.
- **Fédération de la Manche pour la pêche**, 16 rue du Pont-l'Abbé, 50190 Périers. ☎02 33 46 96 50.
- **Fédération de l'Orne pour la pêche,** 59 rue Julien, BP 91, 61014 Alençon Cedex ☎02 33 26 10 66. **www.unpf.fr**.
- **Fédération de l'Eure pour la pêche et la protection du milieu aquatique**, Av. de l'Europe, Immeuble Leipzig, BP 412, 27504 Pont-Audemer Cedex. ☎02 32 57 10 73.
- **Fédération de Seine-Maritime pour la pêche**, 11 cours Clemenceau, 76100 Rouen. ☎02 35 62 01 55.

A leaflet with a map and information called La Pêche en France (Fishing in France) is available from the **Conseil Supérieur de la Pêche**, immeuble Le Péricentre,16 av. Louison-Bobet, 94132 Fontenay-sous-Bois Cedex. ☎01 45 14 36 00.

Anglers are expected to comply with legislation on fishing, in particular concerning the size of their catch. They are expected to throw back certain fish into rivers if their length does not meet the required standards (40cm/16in in the case of pike; 23cm/9.2in in the case of trout).

It is possible to take up sea fishing, both along the coast or on board one of the boats leaving from Trouville, Honfleur, Fécamp, Dieppe, Le Tréport or St-Valery-en-Caux. The waters near Dieppe are said to be teeming with fish and anglers who settle near the piers often see their patience rewarded by landing mackerel, pollock, sole or bass. Details are available from regional tourist offices.

CANOEING/KAYAKING

Normandy's many rivers, lakes and reservoirs are ideal for this sport. The fast-flowing rivers in the Suisse Normande are particularly good for canoes and kayaks. Notable sites in Normandy are Pont-d'Ouilly, Clécy, Sillé-le-Guillaume and St-Léonard-des-Bois. The rivers **Eure** (around Dreux-Louviers) and **Risle** (around L'Aigle-Seine estuary) have excellent sites; contact clubs in **Rouen** or **Belbeuf**. You can also practice sea-kayaking out of major nautical centres such as Le Havre and Fécamp.

- **Comité Départemental de Canoë-Kayak Calvados**, 4 quai Caffarelli, 14000 Caen. ☎02 31 53 92 23.
- **Fédération Française de Canoë-Kayak**, 87 quai de la Marne, 94344 Joinville-le-Pont. ☎01 45 11 08 50. **www.ffcanoe.asso.fr**

The Fédération publishes a map, *Les Rivières de France,* showing all the good canoeing and kayaking watercourses in France.

- **Comité régional de Normandie de canoë-kayak** – 40 rue des Mouettes, 76960 Notre-Dame-de-Bondeville. ☎02 35 75 16 10. **www.crck.org/normandie**

HIKING

Walking is one of the best ways of discovering the countryside – the superb beech forests and the occasional manor houses on well-kept farms. Throughout the region there are long-distance footpaths (*sentiers de grande randonnée*, or GR – one- or two-day hikes) marked with red and white lined posts and shorter, local paths (*petite randonnée* or PR) marked on posts with a single yellow line. Detailed topographical guides are available showing the routes and giving good advice to walkers. The Topo-guides are published by the **Fédération Française de la Randonnée Pédestre** (Comité National des Sentiers de Grande Randonnée) and are on sale at 14 rue Riquet, 75019 Paris. ☎01 44 89 93 90. **www.ffrandonnee.fr**

Several of these well-marked footpaths cross Normandy.

◆ The **GR 2** follows the north bank of the Seine and crosses the Londe and Roumare forests.
◆ The **GR 21** runs up the Lézarde Valley to meet the coast at Étretat.
◆ The **GR 22** from Paris to Mont-St-Michel crosses the southwest of Normandy up to Mamers.
◆ The **GR 23** follows the left bank of the Seine and crosses the Forest of Brotonne.
◆ The **GR 211** leaves from the Seine and reaches the coast passing through the forest of Mauléverier.
◆ The **GR 221** crosses parts of the Suisse Normande and the Cotentin Penninsula.
◆ The **GR 222** starts in the Yvelines *département* and then winds its way across the Eure and Calvados *départements* to reach the Côte de Nacre at Deauville.
◆ The **GR 223** (444km/278mi) runs along the north coast and the Cotentin Penninsula, often following old customs agents' trails with superb views, notably at Cap de La Hague.
◆ The **GR 225** passes from the Vexin to the Lyons Forest and then the

Hikers on Cap de la Hague

D. Hée/MICHELIN

Pays de Bray before reaching the sea near Dieppe.

◆ The **GR «Sur les traces du chasse-marée»** (on the trail of the fish-mongers) follows the ancient medieval cart-track that, until the arrival of the railroad in 1848, brought fish from Dieppe to Rouen and Paris. Information and a topographic map are available from the tourism offices in Dieppe and Rouen and from the tourist office of the *département* of Seine-Maritime.

◆ The **Chemins de Saint-Michel** follow routes taken by pilgrims in the years when Mont St-Michel drew penitants from all over France. These trails, long forgotten, have been progressively traced and marked with bright blue posts. Two 200km/125m trails in the North Cotentin are collectively named the *Chemins aux Anglais,* while the *Chemin de l'Intérieur* leaves from Barfleur and crosses Sainte-Mère-l'Église, Carentan, Saint-Lô, Coutances, La Haye-Pesnel, to arrive in Genêts. The *Chemin Côtier* links Cherbourg with Genêts following the seacoast. Other trails lead to St-Michel from Caen, Rouen Chartres and Paris. For information, contact **Les Chemins du Mont-Saint-Michel**, rue de Picardie, 14500 Vire. ☎02 31 66 10 02. **www.lescheminsdu-montsaintmichel.com**

◆ **Voies vertes, sentiers de découverte and sorties natures** are shorter, less ambitious trails organized locally or in regional parks. Contact tourist offices for information.

Regional parks are a popular destination for hikers and nature lovers alike since they provide countless opportunities for a wide range of open-air activities. In these highly protected areas, extensive facilities have been set up to introduce visitors to local flora and fauna and to increase their awareness of environmental concerns. There are a great many sports in which to indulge, depending on the time of year. *For more details, read about the regional nature parks described in this guide: the parks of Boucles de la Seine Normande (see Forêt de BROTONNE) Brotonne, Perche (see MORTAGNE), Normandie-Maine (see CARROUGES) and Marais du Cotentin et du Bessin (see COTENTIN).*

CYCLING

Good cycling country is found in the Brotonne Forest, Lyons Forest, Eure Valley, Seine Valley and along the Caux coast; there are steeper gradients in the Alpes Mancelles, the Suisse Normande and the Cotentin peninsula. Voies vertes (ecolo-paths for all-terrain bikes) are being developed throughout the region. Consult tourist offices. You can take the train for part of your circuit; your bike travels for free. Certain train stations even rent bikes, which you can turn in at another station.

For up-to-date information, consult the **Fédération Française de Cyclotourisme**, 12 rue Louis-Bertrand, 94207 Ivry-sur-Seine Cedex. ☎01 56 20 88 88. **www.ffct.org**. The Fédération supplies itineraries covering most of France, giving mileage, difficult routes and sights to see.

Fédération francaise de cyclisme, 5 rue de Rome, 93561 Rosny-sous-Bois Cedex. ☎01 49 35 69 24. **www.ffc.fr**. This group produces an annual repertry covering 46 000km/28,750mi of marked trails for all-terrain bicycling.

◆ **Comité Départemental de Cyclotourisme de l'Eure**, Mme

Monique Loride, Le Clos Tiger, 27170 Beaumonte. ☎02 32 45 35 06.
◆ **Comité départemental de Cyclotourisme de Seine-Maritime**, 86, rue Léon-Gambetta, 76320 Caudebed-lès-Elbeuf. ☎02 35 77 03 37. **www.ffct-codep76.fr**.
◆ **Comité Départemental de Cyclotourisme de la Manche**, Maison Tollemer, 50190 Périers, ☎02 33 47 93 51.**www.velo-manche.org.**

CLIMBING

Climbers are attracted to the steep rocky slopes of the Alpes Mancelles and Suisse Normande, particularly the vertical walls of the Rochers des Parcs near Clécy or the Fosse-Arthour northwest of Domfront. For information apply to Tourist Information Centres or to the **Club Alpin Français**, 92 rue de Geôle, 14000 Caen ☎02 31 86 29 55 or to the **Comité Départemental de la montagne et de l'Escalade**, M. Lebègue, 25 rue André-Letard, 61600 St-Georges-des-Groseilliers. ☎02 33 96 13 19.

HORSEBACK RIDING

In such a well-known horse-breeding region many riding clubs and centres organise rides on the many miles of bridle paths through the woodlands or exhilarating canters along the shore as well as pony-trekking holidays. There are many local gymkhanas and equestrian events and racegoers are spoilt for choice for a day at the races. From September to Easter, experienced riders can hunt in the forests of Écouves or Andaines to the sound of the horn. Some *gîtes* will even put up both you and your horse!

Information is available from:
◆ **Comité National de Tourisme Équestre**, 9 boulevard Macdonald, 75019 Paris, ☎01 53 26 15 50, **cnte@ffe.com**. The committee publishes an annual brochures listing equestrian events,horseback rides and acco-

modation welcoming horse
and rider.

◆ **Comité Régional d'Équitation de Normandie, www.chevalnormandie.com.**

◆ **Comité Départemental de Tourisme Equestre du Calvados**. Jean-Louis Faucher, Le Haut de la Vallée, 14480 Lantheuil, ☎/fax 02 31 08 23 95, **www.cheval-calvados.fr.st.**

◆ **Comité Départemental de Tourisme Equestre de la Manche**, rue Corbeauville, 50500 Meutis

◆ **Comité Départemental d'Equitation de l'Orne,** Centre équestre Sagien, BP 4, route d'Essay, 61500 Sées, ☎02 23 27 55 11, **www.equitorne.org.**

Horse-drawn caravans
In the Orne and Calvados départements you can hire a horse-drawn caravan (*roulotte*). Information on holidays in a horse-drawn caravan is available from Tourist Information Centres.

HUNTING

For all enquiries apply to the various Fédérations départementales de Chasse: **Calvados**, rue des Compagnons, 14000 Caen. ☎02 31 44 24 87; **Eure**, rue de Melleville, 27930 Angerville-la-Campagne, ☎02 32 23 03 15; **Seine-Maritime**, Maison de la Chasse et de la Nature, rue de l'Étang, 76890, Belleville-en-Caux. ☎02 35 60 35 97 **www.fdc76.com**
Union Nationale des Fédérations Départementales des Chasseurs, 48 rue d'Alésia, 75014 Paris. ☎01 43 27 85 76, **www.chasseurdefrance.com**

GOLF

Normandy has some 35 golf courses; all the major resorts have clubs, many very beautiful. For information about golf in Calvados, la Manche or Orne départements, contact the **Ligue de Golf de Basse-Normandie**, Mairie de Varaville, 2 av. du Grand-Hôtel, 143 Le Home Varaville ☎02 31 28 31 00. **www.liguedegolfdebassenormandie.com**.

For information about courses in the Sarthe and La Mayenne départements, contact **www.planet.golf.**
For the Eure and Seine-Maritime, contact the **Ligue de Golf de Haute-Normandie**, 94 rue St-Jacques, 76600 Le Havre. ☎ 02 35 42 71 19, fax 02 35 42 71 19.
The **Fédération Française de Golf**, 68 rue Anatole-France, 92309 Levallois-Perret Cedex, ☎01 41 49 77 00, **www.ffgolf.org.**

Activities for Children 🄺🄸🄳🄸

In this guide, sights of particular interest to children are indicated with a KIDS symbol (🄺🄸🄳🄸). Some attractions may offer discount fees for children.

Calendar of Events

MARCH
Caen – Aspects of Contemporary Music
Deauville – Festival of Asian Film and Festival of Scientific Film
Rouen – International Festival of Nordic Film. ☎02 32 08 32 40. www.festival-cinema-nordique.asso.fr

30 APRIL TO 1 MAY
Rouen – 24-hour motorboat races. ☎02 32 08 32 40

APRIL TO OCTOBER
Le Havre – International Regattas

SUNDAY PRECEDING ASH WEDNESDAY
Granville – Carnival. ☎02 33 91 30 03

1 MAY
Le Marais Vernier – Branding of cows. ☎02 32 57 61 62

MAY TO DECEMBER
Montivilliers – Les Concerts de l'Abbaye: Music Festival. ☎02 35 30 96 58

IN MAY

Coutances – Jazz Festival Under the Apple Trees (Ascension week). ☎02 33 76 78 50. www.jazzsous-lespommiers.com

Conches-en-Ouche – Meetings of area farmers (Les Comices Agricoles). ☎02 32 30 20 41.

Deauville – Easter Festival, two weeks of classical music (Easter-time)

Le Tréport– ⚓Nautical Sports Festival

Mont-Saint-Michel - 🚶Rando-Baie du Mont-Saint-Michel (hike around the bay, 2nd weekend of month). ☎02 33 89 64 00

Mont de Cerisi – Rhododendron Fair (end of month)

Pacy-sur-Eure – Stock fair (Les Foulées pacéennes). ☎02 32 36 29 38

Rouen – Joan of Arc Festival, performances in medieval dress. ☎02 32 08 32 40. www.rouentourisme.com (last weekend of May)

Ste-Adresse – Dixie Days Jazz Festival

WHIT SUNDAY AND WHIT MONDAY (PENTECOST)

Bernay – Pilgrimage to Notre-Dame-de-Couture

Honfleur – Seamen's Festival – Sunday: Blessing of the sea; Monday morning: Seamen's Pilgrimage

La Perrière – Art Market. ☎02 33 73 35 49

JUNE

Pays d'Auge – Heritage Days. ☎02 31 48 52 16

Cabourg – Cabourg Film Festival. ☎02 31 91 20 00 (mid-June)

Deauville – ⚓International Sailing Week

Deauville – 🏇International Jumping Competitions (Equestrian)

Évreux – Rock Music Festival

Fécamp – Festival of the Sea and Music (Estivales – last weekend before 21 June)

Haucourt – Festival of St-Jean (midsummer – last weekend of month)

Le Havre – Biannual Show of Contemporary Art (every 2 years)

Ste-Mère-Église – Commemoration of the D-Day Airborne Landings (6 June). ☎02 33 41 41 35

Utah Beach – Commemoration of the landings of 6 June 1944. ☎02 33 71 58 00

JUNE-JULY

Blainville-Crevon - Archéo-Jazz, festival of jazz and contemporary music in a medieval setting. www.archeojazz.com

Mortagne-au-Perche - Les Musicales de Mortagne, festival of chamber music (last weekend in June and first 2 weekends of July)

Pont-Audemer – Les Mascarets street festival. 02 32 36 29 38

JULY

Barneville-Carteret – ⚓Jersey-Carteret Sea Race. ☎02 33 04 90 58

Bayeux – Medieval Festival (first weekend in July) ☎02 31 51 28 28

Le Bourg-Dun– Festival of Linen Products

Deauville – Swing'in Deauville

Dives-sur-Mer – Festival de la Marionnette: Puppet Festival (around July 15). ☎02 31 28 12 53

Domfront – Orne Music Festival, lyrical and classical music. ☎02 33 38 56 66

Haras National du Pin – 🏇Festival Équestre la Équit'Orne: international equestrian competitions (mid-July). ☎02 33 36 68 68

Le Haye-de-Routot – Saint-Clair bonfire night (16 July)

Le Tréport – ⚓Festival of the Sea

Mont-St-Michel - 🚶Pilgrimage from Genêts across the sands at low tide. ☎02 33 60 14 05

Pontmain – 🚗Blessing of cars and motorcycles (2nd Sun of July), ☎02 43 05 07 26

St-Christophe-le-Jajolet – 🚗Motorists' Pilgrimage (last Sunday of July). ☎02 33 35 34 24

St-Vaast-la-Hougue – Festival of books about sea adventures (2nd or 3rd weekend of July). ☎02 33 23 19 32.

Rouen - Les Terraces du Jeudi, concerts in front of bars and cafés on Thursdays.

Rouen – ⚓Armada of Tall Ships (every 4 years, scheduled for 20008)

LAST SUNDAY IN JULY OR FIRST SUNDAY OF AUGUST

Granville - Pardon of the Corporations of the Sea: Procession of guilds with their banners; open-air mass and torchlight procession. ☎02 33 91 30 03

JULY–AUGUST

Bellême – Perche Terre des Légendes: night-time show (3 last weekends in July and first 2 of August). ☎02 33 25 23 23

Dreux – L'Été sous les charmes, festival of world music, free concerts. ☎02 37 38 87 00. www.dreux.com

La Mayenne region – Les Nuits de la Mayenne: entertainment organized in some 15 sites around the region (Ste-Suzanne, Jublains, Laval) from mid-July to mid-August. ☎02 43 53 34 84. www.nuitsdelamayenne.com

Montgothier – Les Féeriques de Montgothier (Saturdays in July and August): Sound and light show illustrating the history of the Norman *bocages*. ☎02 33 60 60 70

EARLY AUGUST

Barfleur – Regattas (2nd weekend of August). ☎02 33 54 02 48

Carrouges - Festival of hunting and fishing. (1st weekend of August). ☎02 33 37 15 88.

Crèvecoeur-en-Auges - Les Medié-vales: Medieval festival (first 2 weeks of August). ☎02 31 63 02 45. www.chateau-de-crevecoeur.com

Jobourg – Foire aux moutons: sheep fair (1st Saturday of August). ☎02 33 10 00 40

St-Lô – Normandy Horse Show (2nd week of August). ☎02 33 06 09 72. www.normandie-horse-show.com

Ste-Marguerite-sur-Mer – Fishing Competition. ☎02 35 04 03 74

FESTIVALS OF THE VIRGIN, ON OR ABOUT 15 AUGUST

Douvres-la-Délivrande – Feast Day of the Coronation of the Virgin: Procession of the Black Virgin (1st or 2nd Saturday after 15 August)

Lisieux – Procession to the Smiling Virgin. ☎02 31 48 55 08. www.therese-de-lisieux.com

Pontmain – Pilgrimage to the Virgin. www.sanctuaire-pontmain.com

Pont d'Ouilly – The Pardon of St-Roche (Sunday after 15 August). ☎02 31 69 80 46

St-Cyr-la-Rosière – Festival of the Percheron Horse at the Priory of Ste-Gauburge. ☎02 33 73 48 06

AUGUST

Barfleur – Antiques Show (3rd or 4th weekend of August). ☎02 33 43 22 09

Blangy-sur-Bresle – Glass Festival

Deauville – Sale of yearlings (3rd or 4th week of August). ☎02 31 14 40 00

Deauville - Grand Prix: Horse racing events and Polo Championship Cup (last Sunday of month). ☎02 31 14 40 00

Deauville – Musical August, a week of classical music

Houlgate – Festijazz 3rd weekend of August.

Laval – The Uburlesques, humour festival (last weekend of August)

Île de Tatihou - Les Traversées de Tatihou: Music festival on the island, near St. Vaast-la-Hougue (2nd or 3rd week of August, depending on tides). www.tatihou.com

AUGUST–SEPTEMBER

L'Aigle, Alençon, Argentan, Bagnoles-de-l'Orne, Mortagne, Domfront, Croutes, Carrouges, Ceton, Prieuré de Vivoin, Flers, Mortrée, Sées, Laval - Musical September on the Orne: concert series (end of August, beginning of September). ☎02 33 26 99 99

IN SEPTEMBER

Deauville – American Film Festival (1st week of September). ☎02 31 14 14 14

Dieppe – International Kite Festival (from 2nd to 3rd weekend of August, even-numbered years). ☎02 32 90 04 95. www.dieppe-cerf-volant.org

Haras National du Pin – 🐴Competition for Percheron horses (last Friday and Saturday of September). ☎02 33 36 68 68

Lessay – Foire de la Sainte-Croix: Holy Cross Fair, the largest and most typical fair in Normandy (2nd weekend of September). ☎02 33 76 58 80

Lisieux – Feast of Ste-Thérèse (last weekend of September). ☎02 31 48 55 08

OCTOBER–SEPTEMBER

Bellême – International Mushroom Festival. ☎02 33 73 34 16. www.mycologiades.com

Fécamp– 🚣Multicup 60' Catamaran sailing races, boat salon (4 or 5 days)

OCTOBER

Caen - International Organ Festival ☎02 31 30 46 86

Deauville – Paris–Deauville Rally, with classic cars

Deauville – Equi'Days, Festival of Calvados horses and races.

Dieppe-Le Havre-Rouen - Octobre en Normandie: Music and Dance Festival ☎ 02 32 10 87 00

Haras national du Pin - 🐴Horse racing events; prestigious cross-country race and procession of carriages and stallions.☎02 33 36 68 68

Mont-St-Michel – Feast of the Archangel Michael: Mass in the abbey church in the presence of the bishops of Bayeux and Coutances (1st Sunday of October). ☎02 33 60 14 05

Pacy-sur-Eure – Pedestrian relay races. ☎02 32 36 29 38

OCTOBER – NOVEMBER

Calvados – 🐴Equi' Days: Horse riding events throughout the region. ☎02 31 27 90 30

Caen – Puces Caennaises: Flea-market (last weekend of November) ☎02 31 29 99 99.

Seine-Maritime and Eure départements – Several cities participate in Autumn in Normandy, music, theatre and dance. ☎02 32 20 87 00

DECEMBER

Sées - Turkey Fair. ☎02 33 28 74 79

Dreux - Les Flambarts Carnival: festivities celebrating light ☎ 02 37 46 01 73

St-Hilaire-du Harcouët - Nativity Play (2nd fortnight of December). ☎02 33 79 38 88. www.creche-vivante.org

GASTRONOMIC FAIRS

Every year a number of fairs and events are held throughout Normandy in connection with local specialities. The following list offers a sample:

MARCH

International *Boudin* (white or blood sausages) Festival in **Mortagne-au-Perche** (3rd weekend of March)

MAY AND JUNE

Saturday-morning foie gras market in **Bernay** in June.

Gastronomic fair and competition in **Cherbourg**, early May

Festival of local products in **Crèveco-eur-en-Auge**, mid-May

Mussels Fair in **Le Tréport (**1st weekend in May or June). ☎02 35 86 05 69

Cherry Fair in **Vernon** (4 days over Whit' weekend/Pentecost).

JULY AND AUGUST

Cheese fair in **Pays d'Auge** (1st weekend of August) ☎02 31 63 47 39

Camembert festival in **Camembert** (last Sunday of July)

Carrot Festival in **Créances** (2nd Sat in August)

Fair of cheese and regional products at **Livarot**, 1st weekend of August

SEPTEMBER

Norman pastries competition in **Caudebec-en-Caux** (3rd Sunday of September)

Cheese Fair in **Neufchâtel-en-Bray (mid-September.)** ☎02 32 97 53 01

IN OCTOBER

Cider festival in **Beuvron-en-Auge**, end of October-early November.

Prawn Festival in **Honfleur** (1st week-end of October)

Foie gras market in **Le Neubourg** October through December

Apple Fair in **Vimoutiers** (mid-October)

IN NOVEMBER

Herring Fairs in **Dieppe, Fécamp, Le Tréport** and **St-Valery-en-Caux**

Feast of St-Martin autumn festival at **Neufchâtel-en-Bray** (mid-November)

THE CHANNEL ISLANDS

IN APRIL

Guernsey – Floral Guernsey Spring Festival Week (3rd week of April) Throughout April, there are springtime gastronomic events as well.

Herm – Garden tours on Tuesdays

9 MAY

Guernsey and Jersey – Liberation Day, commemorating the liberation of Guernsey during WWII, holiday with a parade and a carnival

MAY–JUNE

Sark – Wildflower Event (last week of April, first week of May,

IN JUNE

Guernsey – Carnival at St Peter Port

Guernsey – Floral Guernsey Summer Festival Week with Battle of Flowers in Saumarez park (early June). www.visitguernsey.com

Jersey - Floral Festival (end of June)

Sark – Sark's Midsummer Show

IN JULY

Jersey – Wet and Wild Festival (early July) celebration of water sports. Starts with out of the Blue Festival in St Helier Harbour.

Jersey – Artisan Showcase displaying work of artists and crafts workers from Jersey and the UK. www.mnig.com/art

IN AUGUST

Alderney - Carnival (early August)

Jersey – Battle of Flowers Carnival (mid-August).www.battleofflowers.com

Jersey – Samarès Manor Autumn Fair (end of August) www.samaresmanor.com

Sark – Carnival (mid-August)

AUGUST–SEPTEMBER

Jersey and Guernsey –Sea Guernsey regattas (end of August–early September)

SEPTEMBER

Guernsey and Jersey - Commemoration of the Battle of England and Battle of Britain Air Display (mid-September) www.jerseyairdispay.org.uk

Guernsey and Jersey – Channel Islands Festival of Arts and Crafts (last 2 weeks of September) www.cifestivalofartsand crafts.com

OCTOBER

Guernsey – Jazz Festival (late September)

Guernsey – Floral Guernsey Autumn Festival (2nd week of October)

Jersey – Standard Chartered Jersey Marathon. A run through S. Helier and across the island. www.jersey-marathon.com

Jersey – Autumn, Fruit, Flower and Vegetable Show (mid-October). This also includes a poultry show and the Autumn Cattle Show.

OCTOBER–NOVEMBER

Guernsey–Jersey – Tennerfest, gastronomic festival with meals at reduced prices, throughout October and early November. www.tennerfest.com

IN DECEMBER

Jersey – La Fête de Noué fair from 1 December up to Christmas: moonlight island walks, lighting displays, traditional markets, parades, street theatre...

Shopping

In France, the big stores and larger shops are open Mondays to Saturdays from 9am to 6.30 or 7.30pm. Smaller, individual shops may close during the lunch hour, almost universally so in smaller towns. Food shops – grocers, wine merchants and bakeries – are generally open from 7am to 6.30 or 7.30pm; some open on Sunday mornings. Many food shops close between noon and 2pm and on Mondays. Hypermarkets usually remain open non-stop until 9pm or later.

People travelling to the USA cannot import plant products or fresh food, including fruit, cheeses and nuts. It is all right to carry tinned products or preserves.

Channel Islands

In Jersey, shops are open from 9am to 5pm, 5.30pm or 6pm, and are closed on Sunday and Thursday afternoon. On Guernsey, shops are open Monday through Saturday from 9am until 5.30pm.

VALUE ADDED TAX

There is a **Value Added Tax** (VAT) in France of 19.6% on almost every purchase (books and some foods are subject to a lower rate). VAT **refunds** are available to visitors from outside the EU only if purchases exceed 175€ on one day in one store; the VAT cannot be refunded for items shipped. The system works in large stores which cater to tourists, in luxury stores and other shops advertising Duty Free. Show your passport, and the store will complete a form which is to be stamped by a customs agent at the airport or at whatever point you are leaving the EU (if you are visiting several EU countries, this would be done at your final exit point); at Paris airports, enquire where this procedure is done as it is not always evident. You may have to show the agent the items purchased, so don't pack them in checked luggage. For more information go to the French Customs website www.douane.gouv.fr and scroll down to the English-language on-line booklet about VAT refunds.

Channel Islands

There is no VAT on the Channel Islands, which accounts for the profusion of very busy shops. The most popular purchases are alcohol, tobacco, perfume, cream caramels and the famous Jersey and Guernsey wool sweaters.

Sightseeing

GUIDED TOURS

Many sights, such as châteaux, can be visited only on a guided tour. The departure time of the last tour of the morning or afternoon may be up to 1hr before the actual closing time. Most tours are conducted by French-speaking guides; some of the larger and more popular sights may offer guided tours in other languages. Enquire at the ticket office or book-stall. Other aids commonly available are notes, pamphlets or audio-guides.

LECTURE TOURS

These are organised during the tourist season in towns of special interest. In towns labelled Villes d'Art et d'Histoire and Villes d'Art, tours are conducted by lecturers/guides approved by the Caisse Nationale des Monuments Historiques et des Sites, and tours may be offered in English. Enquire at the local tourist office.

CHURCHES

Admission times are indicated if the interior is of special interest. Churches are usually closed from noon to 2pm. Visitors should refrain from walking about during services. Visitors to chapels are accompanied by the person who keeps the keys. A donation is welcome.

TOURIST INFORMATION CENTRES

In the Sights section (*Exploring Normandy*) the addresses, telephone numbers and, if available, websites are given for the local Tourist Information Centres, which can provide information on local market days, early closing days etc.

Books

Norman Conquest

1066: The Hidden History in the Bayeux Tapestry
Andrew Bridgeford (*Walker 2005*)

The Normans and the Norman Conquest
R Allen Brown
(Boydell , 2nd edition 2000))

Mont St-Michel

Mont-Saint-Michel from A to Z
Henri Decaens, Adrien Goetz, Gerard Guiller (Flammarion 1997)

Tides of Mont St-Michel
Roger Vercel (1938, reissued by Kessinger Publishing, 2005))

Gardens

Gardens in Normandy
Marie-Françoise Valéry (Flammarion 2000)

Claude Monet

Monet in Normandy
Richard Bretteil (*Rizzoli, 2006*)

Claude Monet
Christoph Heinrich (Taschen, revised 2000)

Cuisine

Cuisine Grandmere: Brittany, Normandy, Picardy and Flanders
Jenny Baker (*Faber and Faber, 1995*)

The Cuisine of Normandy
Princess Marie-Blanche de Broglie (Houghton-Mifflin 1984)

Battle of Normandy

D-Day: the First 24 Hours
Will Fowler (*Barnes and Noble, 2006*)

The Germans in Normandy
Richard Hargreaves, Pen & Sword, 2006)

The Americans at Normandy, The Americans at D-Day
Two volumes by John C. McManus (Tom Doherty, 2004-5)

British Armour in the Normandy Campaign 1944
John Buckley (Frank Cass 2004)

The D-day Landings
Philip Warner (Pen & Sword, 2004)

Overlord-D-Day and the Battle of Normandy, 1944
Max Hastings (Pan MacMillan, reissued 2004)

Codebreakers: The Inside Story of Bletchley Park
Edited by FH Hinsley and Alan Stripp (Oxford, reissued 2001)

The D-Day Landing Beaches: The Guide
Georges Bernage (Heindal 2001)

A Traveller's Guide to D-Day
Carl Shilleto, Mike Tolhurst (Interlink 2000)

Films

The Umbrellas of Cherbourg (1964)
Starring Catherine Deneuve: Jacques Demy's charming musical about love and loss in Normandy.

Tess (1979)
Roman Polanski's gorgeous version of Thomas Hardy's novel was shot in the lush Norman countryside.

The Longest Day Fox Video (1962)
Re-creation of the Normandy landings.

Saving Private Ryan (1998)
Steven Spielberg drama about the Battle of Normandy

Band of Brothers (2001)
TV drama (HBO) based on the Stephen Ambrose book

Dunkirk MGM/UA, (1958)
Sombre portrait of the Dunkirk evacuation.

USEFUL WORDS & PHRASES

SIGHTS

abbaye	abbey
arc-boutant	flying buttress
beffroi	belfry
chapelle	chapel
cimetière	cemetery
cloître	cloisters
cour	courtyard
couvent	convent
écluse	lock (canal)
église	church
gothique	Gothic
halle	covered market
jardin	garden
mairie	town hall
maison	house
marché	market
monastère	monastery
moulin	windmill
musée	museum
place	square
pont	bridge
port	port/harbour
quai	quay
remparts	ramparts
romain	Roman
roman	Romanesque
tour	tower

NATURAL SITES

barrage	dam
belvédère	viewpoint
cascade	waterfall
corniche	ledge
côte	coast, hillside
étang	pond
falaise	cliff
forêt	forest
grotte	cave
lac	lake
marais	marsh
plage	beach
rivière	river
ruisseau	stream
signal	beacon
source	spring
vallée	valley

ON THE ROAD

car park	parking
diesel	diesel/gazole
driving licence	permis de conduire
east	Est
garage (for repairs)	garage
left	gauche
LPG	GPL
motorway/highway	autoroute
north	Nord
parking meter	horodateur
petrol/gas	essence
petrol/gas station	station essence
right	droite
roundabout	rond-point
south	Sud
toll	péage
traffic lights	feu tricolore
tyre	pneu
unleaded	sans plomb
west	Ouest
wheel clamp	sabot
zebra crossing	passage clouté

TIME

today	aujourd'hui
tomorrow	demain
yesterday	hier
winter	hiver
spring	printemps
summer	été
autumn/fall	automne
week	semaine
Monday	lundi

Tuesday	mardi
Wednesday	mercredi
Thursday	jeudi
Friday	vendredi
Saturday	samedi
Sunday	dimanche

NUMBERS

0	zéro
1	un
2	deux
3	trois
4	quatre
5	cinq
6	six
7	sept
8	huit
9	neuf
10	dix
11	onze
12	douze
13	treize
14	quatorze
15	quinze
16	seize
17	dix-sept
18	dix-huit
19	dix-neuf
20	vingt
30	trente
40	quarante
50	cinquante
60	soixante
70	soixante-dix
80	quatre-vingts
90	quatre-vingt-dix
100	cent
1000	mille

SHOPPING

antiseptic	antiseptique
bank	banque
bakery	boulangerie
big	grand
butcher shop	boucherie
chemist's/drugstore	pharmacie
closed	fermé
cough mixture	sirop pour la toux
entrance	entrée
exit	sortie
fishmonger's	poissonnerie
grocer's	épicerie
newsagent, bookshop	librairie
open	ouvert

painkiller	analgésique
plaster (adhesive)	pansement adhésif
post office	bureau de poste
pound (half kilo)	livre
push	pousser
pull	tirer
shop	magasin
small	petit
stamps	timbres

FOOD AND DRINK

beef	bœuf
beer	bière
butter	beurre
bread	pain
breakfast	petit-déjeuner
cheese	fromage
chicken	poulet
dessert	dessert
dinner	dîner
duck	canard
eel	anguille
fish	poisson
fork	fourchette
fruit	fruits
glass	verre
ham	jambon
ice cream	glace
ice cubes	glaçons
jug of water	carafe d'eau
jug of wine	pichet de vin
knife	couteau
lamb	agneau
lunch	déjeuner
lettuce salad	salade
meat	viande
mineral water	eau minérale
mixed salad	salade composée
mussels	moules
orange juice	jus d'orange
oysters	huîtres
plate	assiette
pork	porc
red wine	vin rouge
salt	sel
sparkling water	eau gazeuse
spoon	cuillère
still water	eau plate
sugar	sucre
tap water	eau du robinet
turkey	dinde
vegetables	légumes
white wine	vin blanc
yoghurt	yaourt

PERSONAL DOCUMENTS AND TRAVEL

airport	aéroport
credit card	carte de crédit
customs	douane
passport	passeport
platform	voie
railway station	gare
shuttle	navette
The Shuttle	Le Shuttle
suitcase	valise
train/plane ticket	billet de train/d'avion
wallet	portefeuille

CLOTHING

coat	manteau
jumper	pull
raincoat	imperméable
shirt	chemise
shoes	chaussures
socks	chaussettes
stockings	bas
suit	costume/tailleur
tights	collant
trousers	pantalon

COMMONLY USEFUL WORDS

goodbye	au revoir
hello/good morning	bonjour
excuse me	excusez-moi, pardon
thank you	merci
yes/no	oui/non
please	s'il vous plaît

USEFUL PHRASES

Do you speak English?
Parlez-vous anglais?
I don't understand
Je ne comprends pas
Talk slowly Parlez lentement
Where's...? Où est...?
When does the ... leave?
A quelle heure part...?
When does the ... arrive?
A quelle heure arrive...?
When does the museum open?
A quelle heure ouvre le musée?
When is breakfast served?
A quelle heure
sert-on le petit-déjeuner?
What does it cost?
Combien cela coûte?
Where is the nearest petrol/ gas station?
Où se trouve la station
essence la plus proche?
Where can I change traveller's cheques?
Où puis-je échanger
des traveller's cheques?
Where are the toilets?
Où sont les toilettes?
Do you accept credit cards?
Acceptez-vous les cartes de crédit?
I need a receipt. Je voudrais un reçu.

BASIC INFORMATION

Electricity

The electric current is 220 volts (in North America it is 110). Circular two-pin plugs are the rule – an electrical adaptor may be necessary. Adapters are sold in electronics stores and also at international airports. if you have a rechargeable device (camera, portable computer, battery recharger) you may need only a plug adapter, but you may need a voltage converter as well.

Public Holidays

Public services, museums and other monuments may be closed on public holidays: National museums and art galleries are closed on Tuesdays; municipal museums are generally closed on Mondays. In addition to the usual school holidays at Christmas and in the spring and summer, there are long mid-term breaks in February and early November.

1 January	New Year's Day (*Jour de l'An*)
	Easter Day and Easter Monday (*Pâques*)
1 May	May Day (*Fête du Travail*)
8 May	VE Day (*Fête de la Libération*)
Thurs 40 days after Easter	Ascension Day (*Ascension*)
7th Sun-Mon after Easter	Whit Sunday and Monday (*Pentecôte*)
14 July	France's National Day (*Fête de la Bastille*)
15 August	Assumption (*Assomption*)
1 November	All Saint's Day (*Toussaint*)
11 November	Armistice Day (*Fête de la Victoire*)
25 December	Christmas Day (*Noël*)

Post (Mail)

Post offices are open Monday to Friday 9am to 6.30pm and Saturdays, 9am to noon. Smaller branch post offices often close at lunchtime between noon and 2pm and may close early in the afternoon. Stamps are also available from newsagents and tobacconists.

Money

CURRENCY

There are no restrictions on the amount of currency visitors can take into France; however, the amount of cash you may take out of France is subject to a limit, so visitors carrying a lot of cash should complete a currency declaration form on arrival.

PRICES AND TIPPING

Since a service charge is automatically included in the prices of meals and accommodation in France, an addi-tional tip is up to you, generally not more than 5%. Taxi-drivers and hair-dressers are usually tipped 10–15%.
Restaurants usually offer a fixed-price *menu* with 2 or 3 courses for a stated price, or you can order *à la carte*, the more expensive way, with each course ordered separately.
At **cafes** the price of a drink or a coffee is cheaper if you stand at the counter (*comptoir*) than if you sit down (*salle*) and sometimes it is even more expensive if you sit outdoors (*terrasse*).

BANKS

Bank opening hours vary widely. Generally, they are open from 9am to noon, and 2pm to a variety of afternoon closing times; branches are closed either on Monday or Saturday, or open only in the morning if open at all. Banks close early the day before a bank holiday. A passport is needed when cashing travellers' cheques; hotels usually charge more than banks for this service.
The most economical way to access your money in France is to use **ATM machines** to get cash. Code pads are numeric; use a telephone pad to trans-late a letter code into numbers. PIN codes in France have four numbers; enquire with your issuing company or bank if yours is longer.

CREDIT CARDS

Credit cards are widely accepted in shops, hypermarkets, hotels and restaurants, at tollbooths and petrol stations. Visa and Mastercard networks have merged in France, so merchants take both interchangeably. However, cash advance functions have not merged, and Visa is more widely accepted for this than MasterCard. Other credit and debit cards are accepted in some cash machines and businesses. Most places post signs indicating the cards they accept. Your bank's hotline is printed on the back of your card: make a note of it. If your card is stolen, you can call a 24-hour hotline to make a report: ☎08

American Express ☎ 01 47 77 72 00	
Visa ☎ 08 36 69 08 80	
MasterCard/Eurocard ☎ 01 45 67 84 84	
Diners Club ☎ 01 49 06 17 50	

36 69 08 80. You must report any loss or theft of credit cards or travellers' cheques to the local police, who will issue you a certificate (useful proof to show the issuing company).

Telephones

Most public phones in France use pre-paid phone cards *(télécartes)*, rather than coins. Some telephone booths accept credit cards (Visa, Mastercard/Eurocard). *Télécartes* (50 or 120 units), used for local or international calls, can be bought in post offices, branches of France Télécom, *bureaux de tabac* (cafés that sell cigarettes) and newsagents; some places sell cards for overseas calls that can be used for public or private phones. Calls can be received at phone boxes where the blue bell sign is shown; the phone will not ring, so keep your eye on the little message screen.

NATIONAL CALLS

French telephone numbers have ten digits. Paris and Paris region numbers begin with 01; 02 in north-west France; 03 in north-east France; 04 in south-east France and Corsica; 05 in south-west France.

INTERNATIONAL CALLS

When calling abroad from France dial 00, then dial the country code followed by the area code and number of your correspondent.

- **International Information, US/Canada:** 00 33 12 11
- **International operator:** 00 33 12 + country code
- **Local directory assistance:** 12
- Toll-free numbers in France begin with 0 800.

MINITEL

France Télécom operates a system offering directory enquiries (free of charge up to 3min), travel and entertainment reservations, and other services (cost per minute varies). 3614 PAGES E is the code for **directory assistance in English** (turn on the unit, dial 3614, hit the *connexion* button when you get the tone, type in PAGES E, and follow the instructions on the screen).

CELLULAR PHONES

Cellular phones across Europe operate on the GSM standard. Those who have GSM phones can arrange with their service providers to use a SIM card, so they can keep their number and be billed by their provider. However, it is cheaper to buy or rent in France.

To use your personal calling card	
AT&T	☎ 0-800 99 00 11
Sprint	☎ 0-800 99 00 87
MCI	☎ 0-800 99 00 19
Canada Direct	☎ 0-800 99 00 16
Emergency numbers	
Police:	17
SAMU (Paramedics):	15
Fire (Pompiers):	18

Time Difference

When it is **noon in France**, it is	
3am	in Los Angeles
6am	in New York
11am	in Dublin
11am	in London
7pm	in Perth
9pm	in Sydney
11pm	in Auckland

In France "am" and "pm" are not used but the 24-hour clock is widely applied.

CONVERSION TABLES

Weights and Measures

EU	US	UK	
1 kilogram (kg) 6.35 kilograms 0.45 kilograms	**2.2 pounds (lb)** 14 pounds 16 ounces (oz)	**2.2 pounds** 1 stone (st) 16 ounces	*To convert kilograms to pounds, multiply by 2.2*
1 metric ton (tn)	**1.1 tons**	**1.1 tons**	
1 litre (l) 3.79 litres 4.55 litres	**2.11 pints (pt)** 1 gallon (gal) 1.20 gallon	**1.76 pints** 0.83 gallon 1 gallon	*To convert litres to gallons, multiply by 0.26 (US) or 0.22 (UK)*
1 hectare (ha) **1 sq. kilometre (km²)**	**2.47 acres** 0.38 sq. miles (sq.mi.)	**2.47 acres** 0.38 sq. miles	*To convert hectares to acres, multiply by 2.4*
1 centimetre (cm) **1 metre (m)**	**0.39 inches (in)** 3.28 feet (ft) or 39.37 inches or 1.09 yards (yd)	**0.39 inches**	*To convert metres to feet, multiply by 3.28; for kilometres to miles, multiply by 0.6*
1 kilometre (km)	**0.62 miles (mi)**	**0.62 miles**	

Clothing

Women	EU	US	UK
	35	4	2½
	36	5	3½
	37	6	4½
Shoes	38	7	5½
	39	8	6½
	40	9	7½
	41	10	8½
	36	6	8
	38	8	10
Dresses & suits	40	10	12
	42	12	14
	44	14	16
	46	16	18
	36	06	30
	38	08	32
Blouses & sweaters	40	10	34
	42	12	36
	44	14	38
	46	16	40

Men	EU	US	UK
	40	7½	7
	41	8½	8
	42	9½	9
Shoes	43	10½	10
	44	11½	11
	45	12½	12
	46	13½	13
	46	36	36
	48	38	38
Suits	50	40	40
	52	42	42
	54	44	44
	56	46	48
	37	14½	14½
	38	15	15
Shirts	39	15½	15½
	40	15¾	15¾
	41	16	16
	42	16½	16½

Sizes often vary depending on the designer. These equivalents are given for guidance only.

Speed

KPH	10	30	50	70	80	90	100	110	120	130
MPH	6	19	31	43	50	56	62	68	75	81

Temperature

Celsius (°C)	0°	5°	10°	15°	20°	25°	30°	40°	60°	80°	100°
Fahrenheit (°F)	32°	41°	50°	59°	68°	77°	86°	104°	140°	176°	212°

To convert Celsius into Fahrenheit, multiply °C by 9, divide by 5, and add 32.
To convert Fahrenheit into Celsius, subtract 32 from °F, multiply by 5, and divide by 9.
NB: Conversion factors on this page are approximate.

Dielette Harbour, Normandy

© François Pinon

NATURE

Normandy is not a homogeneous geographical unit but an old province, formerly a dukedom, embracing two large areas with different geological structures, which become progressively younger from west to east. The sandstone, granite and primary schists of the Armorican Massif in the west give way to the Secondary and Tertiary Era strata of clay, limestone and chalk which belong to the geological formation of the Paris basin. Normandy can therefore be conveniently divided into two quite distinct regions, Haute-Normandie, which lies north-west of the Paris basin, and Basse-Normandie, which resembles its neighbour Brittany and consists of an eroded foundation of ancient rocks.

The administrative region of Haute-Normandie is made up of the départements of Eure (27) and Seine-Maritime (76); Basse-Normandie includes the départements of Calvados (14), Manche (50) and Orne (61).

Regions of Normandy

The inland areas can be divided into two types of regions, **open country** and **woodland**. In the strictest sense, the open country (*campagne*) consists of dry, windswept plains and cultivated fields. The woodland (*bocage*) is typical of the Armorican Massif, although to the east it spills over into the Maine, the Perche and the Auge regions. Typical of the countryside, and sometimes confusing for casual ramblers, a network of dense hedges grows on earthen banks, enclosing fields and meadows and forming a sort of labyrinth. The people living on the farms and hamlets scattered along the sunken roads have for a long time lived in relative isolation. Lastly, the different parts of the **coast** of Normandy also have distinctive characteristics.

OPEN COUNTRY

The **Pays de Caux** is a vast limestone plateau covered with fertile silt, ending along the coast in cliffs famous for their hanging valleys *(valleuses)* and bordered to the south by the Seine Valley. The area produces wheat and industrial crops such as flax, sugar beet and rape. Most of the cattle grazing here are raised for meat rather than milk.

The Secrets of the Tide

This curious phenomenon, which manifests itself quite spectacularly in the English Channel, is due to the influence of the moon and, to a lesser extent, to that of the sun. When the moon passes over the sea, it attracts the water and the water level rises as a result, creating a **high tide**. Six hours later, after the earth has accomplished a quarter of a turn, the moon is no longer above the sea and its influence wanes: the water level drops, causing a **low tide**.

Every fortnight, when the tide-generating force of the sun acts in the same direction as that of the moon, it causes the greatest difference in tidal level – the **spring tide** – which occurs either at new moon or full moon. When the tide-generating forces of the sun and the moon oppose each other, they produce the smallest difference in tidal level – the **neap tide** – which occurs at the first or last quarter of the moon. In France, the highest spring tides, known as **equinoctial springs**, occur at the equinoxes, in March and September.

The difference in the water level between the high and low tide is called the **tidal range**. In France, this phenomenon is at its most striking in Granville, where the water is known to rise 16m/53ft during spring tides!

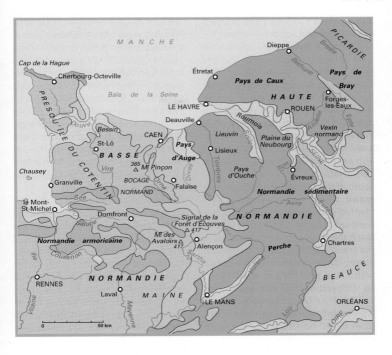

Quaternary Era		Alluvial deposits
Tertiary Era		Sedimentary deposits
Secondary Era	{	Cretaceous limestone
		Jurassic limestone
Primary Era	{	Granite
		Metamorphic rocks

Bordered by the valleys of the Epte and the Andelle, the **Vexin normand** is covered by a particularly thick layer of alluvial soil which favours the intensive cultivation of wheat and sugar beet.

The **Plaine du Neubourg** and the **Évreux-St-André** district present a flat landscape of open fields, similar to the area known as **Caen-Falaise**. The fertility of the soil favours large-scale arable farming coupled with cattle-breeding for the production of meat. Vegetables are grown in the region of Caen.

The **Argentan-Sées-Alençon** country, north of the Sarthe Valley and the Alpes Mancelles, are composed of small chalk regions where horses and cattle graze in the open orchards.

TRANSITIONAL REGIONS

The **Roumois** and **Lieuvin** plains are separated by the Risle Valley; hedges and apple orchards create the texture of the landscape. The **Pays d'Ouche** is more densely forested, whereas the rolling hills of the **Perche normand**, a famous horse-breeding district, form a transition between the Paris basin and the Armorican Massif.

WOODLANDS

The Norman part of the **Pays de Bray** is a vast clay depression, known as the buttonhole, bordered by two limestone heights. It is stock-raising country and has increased its production of meat; it also specialises in fresh dairy produce such as yoghurts and *petits-suisses*.

The **Pays d'Auge**, which contains the river valleys of the Touques and the Dives, is different from the other regions in that the chalk strata have been deeply fissured by a network of streams. High local humidity promotes the growth of grassland and hedges. Apples are turned into cider and Calvados. Milk is used to make Camembert. Horse breeding is also a tradition near the coast and the Perche region.

South of the Bessin is the **Bocage normand**, where meadows, sometimes planted with apple or pear trees, are enclosed by hedges. Raising dairy cattle is still the main activity. In addition to the traditional Normandy cream and butter, farmers produce sterilised milk with a long shelf life and which needs no refrigeration *(UHT milk)* and a great variety of low-fat dairy products.

The **Bessin** lies on the edge of the Armorican Massif north-west of the open country. The famed local dairy produce is represented by the name Isigny. Bayeux is the capital of this region, where the breeding of saddle-horses and trotters has been a long-standing tradition.

The remote peninsula of **Cotentin**, which lies between the Vire estuary and Mont-St-Michel Bay, is part of the Armorican Massif. The peninsula itself is divided from the Bocage Normand by a sedimentary depression, which is flooded at certain times of the year; there are three distinct areas within the peninsula: the Cotentin Pass, the Val de Saire and Cap de la Hague. The region is still largely devoted to stock raising except along the coast where vegetables are grown, as they are in nearby Brittany.

THE COAST

The coast of Normandy from the River Bresle west to the River Couesnon is as varied as its hinterland. Erosion by the sea has transferred material from rocky projections and deposited it in sheltered coves. The sea has brought shingle to the bays and ports of the Pays de Caux, mud to the Seine estuary and to more than one port (Lillebonne was a sea port in Gallo-Roman times).

The Pays de Caux meets the sea in what is known as the **Côte d'Albâtre** (Alabaster Coast), a line of high limestone cliffs, like the White Cliffs of Dover, penetrated by shingle-bottomed inlets. The sea beating at the foot of the cliffs has eroded the cliff face, forming hanging valleys.

The **Côte Fleurie** offers miles of fine sand beaches where the sea may withdraw more than a mile at low tide; it also enjoys a high level of sunshine. The Calvados coast is composed of the low Bessin cliffs, interspersed with sand dunes and salt marshes (Caen area).

To the west are the sand or sand and shingle beaches of the bracing **Côte de Nacre** (Mother-of-Pearl Coast). The Cotentin peninsula resembles Cornwall and Brittany with its rocky inlets, although sand dunes and beaches stretch along the coast where the continental rock base does not reach the shore. Mont-St-Michel Bay is known for its vast sands and mud flats from which the sea seems to withdraw completely at times.

The **lighthouses** along the Normandy coast, which guide navigators in the Channel, also make good vantage points. The Norman engineer **Augustin Fresnel** (1788-1827) replaced the conventional parabolic reflector with compound lenses, which led to great progress in the length of beam projected out to sea. The nature of light sources has changed and their candlepower has considerably increased but the Fresnel system is still in use. At night, in the more difficult sectors, several lighthouses can be seen at once, each with its own peculiarities: fixed, revolving or intermittent beam.

Horses: the Pride of Normandy

More than 70 per cent of all French thoroughbreds and trotters are bred in Basse-Normandie as well as the most powerful draught horses (Percherons) and some of the best carriage-horses (Cobs).

Thoroughbreds are the fastest and the most refined horses, but their racing career does not exceed three years. The sale of yearlings at the end of August in Deauville attracts international racing stable owners. The sale of brood mares and foals is held in late November.

French trotters were developed from Normandy mares and Norfolk-roadster trotters. Their racing career lasts longer than that of thoroughbreds.

The term "**French saddle-horse**", which first appeared in 1958, encompasses almost all French competition horses. Excellent jumpers as well as trotters, these horses are ideal all-rounders for show-jumping competitions.

Whether chestnut or bay, the **Norman cob** is strong, compact, likeable, full of energy and has a pleasant way of trotting. Cobs can work in the fields or be harnessed to a carriage.

Percherons are the most sought-after heavy draught horses in the world; the race was developed from cobs and Arabs, some say as far back as the Crusades. Dappled grey or black, Percherons were used for work in the fields, deliveries and army duties.

Finally, one can't ignore the **Cotentin donkey**, recognized by the national stud in 1997, which has a soft gray coat, with a cross of St. Andrew on its back. Some 1 200 of these gentle beasts now carry tourists on treks across the Cotentin.

NATIONAL STUD FARMS

They form one of the oldest French institutions since one was founded by Colbert in 1665. They still have the same mission: to supervise all matters concerning horse breeding and equestrian activities. In France there are 23 national studs which work in close collaboration with the Institut National de la Recherche Agronomique to improve breeding techniques; they also supervise horse racing and betting.

Normandy breeds of horses

English thoroughbred

Pony

Thoroughbred mare and foal

French trotter

Percheron

Illustrations: M. Dewynter

Barfleur

HISTORY

Time Line

ROMAN PERIOD

58-51 BC — Roman conquest. New towns appear: Rotomagus (Rouen), Caracotinum (Harfleur), Noviomagus (Lisieux), Juliobona (Lillebonne), Mediolanum (Évreux).

56BC — The Unelli crushed by Sabinius in the Mont Castre area.

1C — Growth of main settlements (Coutances, Rouen, Évreux etc).

2C — Nordic (Saxon and Germanic) invasions of the Bessin region. Conversion to Christianity.

260 — Bishopric of Rouen founded by St Nicaise.

284 and 364 — Nordic invasions.

FRANKISH DOMINATION

497 — Rouen and Évreux occupied by Clovis.

511 — Neustria or the Western Kingdom inherited by Clothaire, Clovis' son.

6C — The first monasteries founded (Castles of God).

7C — Monasteries flourish: St-Wandrille, Jumièges.

709 — Mont Tombe consecrated to the cult of St Michael by Aubert, Bishop of Avranches.

VIKING INVASIONS

The Vikings or Norsemen who sailed from Scandinavia harassed Western Europe, parts of Africa and even headed into the Mediterranean.

800 — Channel coast invaded by Vikings.

820 — Seine Valley laid waste by Vikings.

836 — Christians persecuted in the Cotentin region.

858 — Bayeux devastated by Vikings.

875 — Further persecution in the West.

885 — Paris besieged by Vikings.

911 — Treaty of St-Clair-sur-Epte: Rollo becomes the first Duke of Normandy.

THE INDEPENDENT DUKEDOM

Under William Longsword the dukedom takes on its final form with the unification of the Avranchin and the Cotentin.

10-11C — Consolidation of ducal powers. Restoration of the abbeys.

1027 — Birth of William, the future conqueror of England, at Falaise.

1066 — Invasion of England by William. King of France threatened by his vassal, the Duke of Normandy, now also King of England.

1087 — Death of William the Conqueror in Rouen.

1087-1135 — William's heirs in dispute; ducal authority restored by Henry Beauclerc who becomes King of England as Henry I (1100-35) after his brother William Rufus.

1120 — The wreck of the White Ship off Barfleur Point with the loss of Henry I's heir, William Atheling and 300 members of the Anglo-Norman nobility.

1152 — Marriage of Henry II Plantagenet, to Eleanor of Aquitaine, whose dowry included all south-west France.

1154-89 — Henry II of England.

1195 — Château-Gaillard built by Richard Lionheart.

1202 — Loss of Norman possessions by John Lackland, King of England.

1204 — Normandy united to the French crown

FRENCH DUKEDOM TO THE PROVINCE OF NORMANDY

1315 — Granting of the Norman Charter, symbol of provincial status, which remained in being until the French Revolution.

1346 — Normandy invaded by Edward III of England.

1364-84 — The Battle of Cocherel marks the start of Du Guesclin's campaigns.

1417 — Normandy invaded by Henry V of England.

1424 — English repulsed by Louis d'Estouteville, defender of Mont-St-Michel.

1431 — Trial and torture of Joan of Arc at Rouen.

1437 — Founding of Caen University.

1450 — Normandy recovered by the French crown after the victory at Formigny and the recapture of Cherbourg.

1469 — Charles of France, last Duke of Normandy, is dispossessed of his dukedom.

1514 — The Rouen Exchequer becomes the Parliament of Normandy.

1517 — Founding of Le Havre.

1542 — Rouen created as a self-governing city for treasury purposes.

1589 — Henri of Navarre victorious at Arques and the following year at Ivry-la-Bataille.

1625 — Alençon also created as a treasury district.

1639-40 — Revolt of the Barefoot Peasants provoked by the introduction of the salt tax (gabelle).

1692 — Naval battle of La Hougue.

1771-75 — Suppression of the Parliament at Rouen.

CONTEMPORARY NORMANDY

1789 — The Caen Revolt.

1793 — The Girondins' attempted uprising; siege of Granville.

1795-1800 — Insurrection of the Norman royalists, the Chouans.

1843 — Inauguration of the Paris-Caen railway.

1870-71 — Franco-Prussian War; occupation of Haute-Normandie and Le Mans.

June 1940 — Bresle Front breached.

August 1942 — Dieppe Commando raid by Canadian and British troops.

June 1944 — Allied landing on the Calvados coast. Battle of Normandy.

1954 — René Coty, born in Le Havre, is elected President of the Republic.

1959 — Inauguration of the Tancarville Bridge.

1967 — Commissioning of the Atomic Centre at La Hague.

1971 — Launch of the Redoutable, the first French nuclear submarine, at Cherbourg.

1974 — Creation of the Brotonne Regional Nature Park.

1975 — Creation of the Normandie-Maine Regional Nature Park.

1977 — Completion of the Normandy motorway (A 3).

1983-84 — Start-up of Paluel Nuclear Power Station.
Start-up of Flamanville Nuclear Power Station

1987 — Commemoration of the 900th anniversary of William the Conqueror's death.

1991 — Inauguration of France's 27th regional nature park in the Cotentin and Bessin area.

6 June 1994 — 50th anniversary of the Battle of Normandy.

January 1995 — Inauguration of the Pont de Normandie.

1997 — A violent controversy breaks out between Greenpeace environmentalists and COGEMA over nuclear waste dumped near La Hague.

1999 — Tall Ships Armada of the Century on the Seine, from Rouen to Le Havre.

1999 — Violent windstorms in December uproot innumerable trees and damage buildings.

2000 — Wreck of the Evoli Sun, an Italian ship loaded with chemicals, off Cap de la Hague.

2004 — Sixtieth anniversary of the Normandy landings attended, for the first time, by leaders of Germany and Russia.

2005 — The centre of Le Havre, rebuilt by Auguste Perret, is named UNESCO a world heritage site.

2006 — Port 2000 at Le Havre opened.

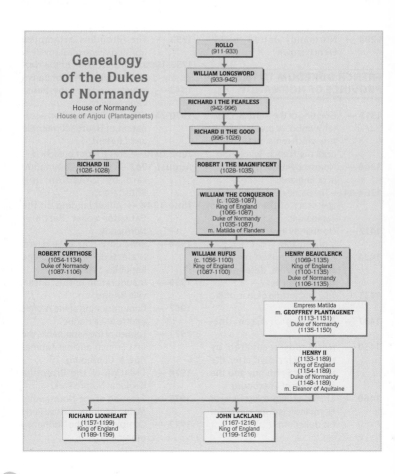

Normans Throughout History

The story of the Norsemen, or Vikings, who settled in the Frankish kingdom and from there set out on expeditions of conquest to southern Italy and Sicily as well as to England, Wales, Scotland and Ireland has inspired many tall tales and cinematic extravaganzas.

In the 8C, pagan barbarians from Denmark, Norway and Iceland began their plunder of coastal settlements in Europe and by the 9C they had established a permanent foothold in the region that is now Normandy. In the year 911, **Charles III (The Simple)** signed the treaty of **St-Clair-sur-Epte** with the Viking chief **Rollo**. According to Dudon de St-Quentin, the first historian of Normandy, the Viking simply placed his hands between those of the French king to ratify the agreement creating the dukedom of Normandy: no written treaty was ever drafted. The Norsemen continued to expand their holdings until well into the 11C, ruling through a succession of ruthless dukes and counts.

Eventually, the Norse converted to Christianity and adopted the French language, but retained a reputation for recklessness, love of combat, cunning, and outrageous treachery. At the same time, wherever they went, they showed a remarkable capacity for adapting to local customs. William, Duke of Normandy, became king of England in a coup known as the **Norman Conquest** (1066), while the Norman kingdom of Sicily was founded by the descendants of Tancrède de Hauteville. Norman rulers were among the most powerful and successful of their time, and established enduring political institutions.

In Normandy, the Normans quickly adopted the precepts of feudalism, became masters of cavalry warfare and fostered the cult of knighthood. Eventually, their reputation for fierceness and brutality was softened by religion, marked by pilgrimages to Rome and the Holy Land. In England, their rule made the kingdom safer from foreign invasion and brought discipline to church organisations.

Later still, explorers continued to embark from Normandy in search of new lands:

1402 — Jean de Béthencourt, of the Caux region, became king of the Canary Islands, but ceded his realm to the King of Castile.

1503 — Paulmier de Gonneville, gentleman of Honfleur, reached Brazil in the Espoir.

1506 — Jean Denis, a sailor from Honfleur, explored the mouth of the St Lawrence, preparing the way for Jacques Cartier.

1524 — Leaving Dieppe in the caravel La Dauphine, Giovanni da Verrazano, a native of Florence and navigator to François I, discovered the site of New York City, which he named Land of Angoulême.

1555 — Admiral Nicolas Durand de Villegaignon set up a colony of Huguenots from Le Havre on an island in the bay of Rio de Janeiro, but they were driven away by the Portuguese.

1563 — Led by René de la Laudonnière, colonies of Protestants from Le Havre and Dieppe founded Fort Caroline in Florida but were massacred by the Spaniards.

1608 — Samuel de Champlain, Dieppe shipbuilder, left Honfleur to found Quebec.

1635 — Pierre Belain of Esnambuc claimed Martinique in the name of the King of France; the colonisation of Guadeloupe followed soon after.

1682 — Cavalier de La Salle of Rouen, after reconnoitring the site of Chicago, sailed down the Mississippi river and took possession of Louisiana.

WILLIAM THE CONQUEROR

The story of William has roots in Viking mythology and culminates with the seizing of the crown of England.

William was the son of Robert the Magnificent and his concubine Herleva, from the town of Falaise. A descendent of the great chief Rollo, he was first known as William the Bastard. In 1035, when his father died on his way back from a trip to the Holy Land, William, then eight years old, became the seventh duke of Normandy. His tutors instructed him in the rudiments of Latin and the fine points of military strategy, and also instilled in him a deep religious faith. Later, three of his guardians and his tutor were assassinated by parties who objected to the Bastard's succession. In 1046, barely 20 years old, he confounded yet another plot to undo him, and wisely sought out the support of the king of France, Henri I.

For the Love of Matilda

With the king's soldiers at hand to support his own faithful warriors, William firmly established his authority. He built castles (Falaise – his birthplace – and Cherbourg) and towns (Saint-James), expanded Saint-Lô and Carentan, created the city of Caen as a second capital for his dukedom, and negotiated a peace treaty with his enemies.

Between 1054 and 1060, William held fast against the allied forces of the king of France, Guillaume d'Arques and the Geoffrey Martell of Anjou. He consolidated his power by marrying Matilda, daughter of Baldwin V, count of Flanders. Mindful of all he had suffered as an illegitimate son, William was a faithful and trusting husband. When called away from Normandy, he left the realm in his wife's able hands. Tradition assigned the Bayeux tapestry to Matilda (it is also referred to as Queen Matilda's tapestry), but it is unlikely that she busied herself with embroidery when William was abroad.

The Conquest

Edward the Confessor, king of England, had recognised William as his heir, but in January 1066 news arrived that **Harold** had claimed the English throne. The duke appealed to the Pope and Harold was subsequently excommunicated.

Within seven months, William, henceforth the Conqueror, was master of England. On 12 September 1066, protected by the Pope's ensign, about 12 000 knights and soldiers embarked upon

696 ships followed by smaller boats and skiffs bringing the total number of vessels to 3 000. On 28 September, at low tide, the Normans landed at Pevensey, Sussex. William, the last to disembark, stumbled and fell full length. The superstitious Normans were alarmed, but William laughed and, according to the records, retorted: "My Lords, by the glory of God have I seized this land with my own two hands. As long as it exists it is ours alone."

The Normans occupied Hastings. Harold, who had been busy fighting other attackers, rushed to the scene and pitched camp on a hill. On 14 October William launched an assault, and after a terrible struggle the Normans were victorious; Harold died in combat. The history of the invasion is recounted in the Bayeux Tapestry, which shows fascinating details of combat dress and equipment and the gory consequences of the momentous Battle of Hastings.

While remaining Duke of Normandy, William was crowned King of England on Christmas Day, 1066, at Westminster Abbey. For the century that followed, England was politically united with continental Europe. William suppressed revolts, brought to heel the corrupt aristocracy, encouraged noble Norman families to settle in England, and overcame the Pope's opposition to his control over church affairs. Norman art flourished, as the cathedrals at Canterbury, Winchester and Durham show.

Ruling 52 years in Normandy and 21 years in England, William the Conqueror maintained a large measure of peace and justice in his realm. He died on 9 September 1087 near Rouen and was was buried at St-Étienne Church in Caen, as he had requested.

Monasticism in Normandy

Normandy, like Champagne and Burgundy, was a centre of monasticism during the religious revival that swept the 11C. Today a great many Norman abbeys still testify to the strong fervour that characterised the period. The greatest legislator of Latin monasticism was undoubtedly St Benedict of Nursia (c 480-547), who laid down a series of precepts for his monks at Monte Cassino in Italy. Under the Benedictine Rule, which gradually supplanted other religious rules, nuns and monks made three vows on entering the monastery: obedience, poverty and chastity. They were placed under the absolute authority of the abbots, who were elected for life, and practiced fasting, silence and abstinence.

The monks' working day was taken up by divine office, holy reading and, to a greater extent, manual labour.

Divine office consisted of prayers and hymns scheduled throughout the day (matins, lauds and vespers) and night. The monks also studied the Bible and other sacred texts, and practiced solitary meditation in their cells.

Manual labour consisted of daily chores such as baking bread, weaving cloth for the monks' tunics, carrying firewood, sweeping floors, serving meals, preparing the sacristy, growing vegetables, helping in the fields etc.

Throughout the Middle Ages monasticism played a vital role in society, securing the propagation of Christianity, promoting the authority of the Pope and contributing to the conservation and transmission of learning. In its most prosperous years, monasticism was also a powerful economic and cultural force.

MEDIEVAL MONASTERIES

The monastic buildings were arranged around the cloisters as in the plan below.

Cloisters

Generally, four galleries surrounded a central courtyard, often laid out as a garden; some monasteries made this their herb garden. The east gallery opened onto the sacristy, the chapter-house and the calefactory. The south gallery featured a lavabo, a large stone basin with water flowing from a fountain where the monks washed their hands before eating or praying. The west gallery bordered the lay brothers' quarters and the cellars. The north gallery adjoined the church, providing access through the monks' doorway, at the east end, and the lay brothers' doorway, at the west end.

Abbey Church

The monks spent a large part of the day and sometimes the night in church for Mass and other religious offices. The abbey church was characterised by an extremely long nave. In Cistercian churches, a rood screen placed near the high altar separated the monks' choir from that of the lay brothers.

Sacristy

The room in which ecclesiastical garments and altar vessels were stored and in which the priest would don his robes before leading the service.

Chapter-house

Used for daily monastic activities, including prayers before the day's work and the reading of a chapter taken from the monastic rule. It was here that the abbot imposed penance on those who had transgressed the rule.

Calefactory

The only heated room in the monastery. It was accessible to all monks under carefully regulated conditions.

Scriptorium

A room set aside for the copying out of manuscripts, often adjoining the calefactory.

Refectory

A large bare room where the monks took their meals, endowed with surprisingly good acoustics. During meals, the reader would recite passages from the Bible in the elevated pulpit.

Dormitories

There were generally two; one for the monks above the chapter-house and one for the lay brothers above the cellars. In the Cistercian order seven hours were allowed for rest. The monks slept fully dressed in a communal dormitory.

Outbuildings

Other conventual buildings included the barns and the porter's lodge or gatehouse, often a grand building with a huge gateway to allow the passage of both carriages and people on foot. The porter's lodge had living quarters on the first floor, where alms were distributed and justice was dispensed to the population.

The Battle of Normandy

On 6 June, 1944, the coast of Normandy was the setting for yet another crucial invasion which would, in its own turn, change the course of history.

From the autumn of 1941 the British authorities had envisaged a landing on the continent of Europe, but it was only after the entry of the United States that offensive action on such a scale could be seriously considered. The COSSAC plan, approved at the Churchill-Roosevelt meetings in Washington and Quebec in May and August 1943, foresaw the landing of invasion troops along the Calvados coast, which was defended by the German 7th Army. This sector was preferred to the Pas-de-Calais because it meant that the Germans' lines of communication would be more vulnerable: lower Normandy would be isolated if the bridges over the Seine and Loire were destroyed. It was also known that the enemy was preoccupied by the defence of the Pas-de-Calais (15th German Army).

PREPARATION

The building of artificial ports – a lesson learned as a result of the costly Dieppe commando raid of 1942 – and the construction of landing craft was carried out with other training in the winter of 1943-44. On 24 December 1943 General Eisenhower was named Chief of the Allied Expeditionary Force and General Montgomery made responsible for tactical coordination of all land forces (21st Army Group) for Operation Overlord.

Air raids to paralyse the French railway system began on 6 March 1944. During the spring of 1944 Marshal Rommel had the beaches and their approaches covered with obstacles. It became urgent to find a means of destroying these obstacles by using tanks as bulldozers or sending frogmen to dispose of them.

FIRST WEEK OF THE LANDING

Circled numbers refer to the map.
①Originally D-Day had been planned for the 5 June but it was postponed for 24 hours owing to bad weather.

At dawn on D-Day, 6 June 1944, British and Commonwealth ground forces established beachheads at **Sword**, **Juno** and **Gold** and rapidly linked up with the airborne troops dropped to their east. The Americans, landing on **Omaha** beach, joined up with their airborne flank only after the capture of Carentan on 12 June.

LAYOUT OF THE BRIDGEHEAD

Advances were substantial but of unequal depth: the Americans threatened Caumont on 13 June; the British and Canadians were held up by very fierce fighting 6km/4mi north of Caen in the Tilly-sur-Seulles sector on 7 June and broke through only on the 20th – the village changed hands some 20 times. The Caen sector, as Montgomery had foreseen, became the principal hinge of the whole front.

Isolation of the Cotentin Peninsula and the Capture of Cherbourg

②The Americans attacked across the Cotentin Peninsula on 13 June and secured it, capturing Barneville on 18 June. Turning north they attacked Cherbourg which fell on 26 June – a victory in the battle to ensure supply lines.

Battle of the Odon and Capture of Caen

③On 26 June a hard battle, which was to last a month, began for a crossing over the Odon upstream from Caen and the taking of Hill 112. Montgomery decided to outflank Caen to the south-west. The city of Caen on the left bank was attacked in force from the west and north-east and fell on 9 July.

BREAKTHROUGH PREPARATION

In early July General Montgomery laid out his breakthrough strategy: "Keep the greatest possible number of the enemy divisions on our eastern flank, between Caen and Villers-Bocage, and pivot the western flank of the Army Group towards the south-east in a vast sweeping movement in order to threaten the line of retreat of the German division."

WAR OF THE HEDGEROWS

For the American soldiers of 1944 the Cotentin campaign – the advance to Cherbourg and the Battle of St-Lô – was simply "the war of the hedgerows."

Leafy hedges and sunken lanes such as those that divide the Normandy countryside came as an unpleasant surprise for the attackers, but for defensive warfare or guerrilla tactics the terrain offered unending opportunities.

Modern arms were not much help: four-inch shells scarcely shook the tree-covered embankments which constituted natural anti-tank barriers; only the foot soldier could fight successfully in this hell of hedges.

The effort of fighting against an invisible enemy was exhausting; every field and orchard crossed was a victory in itself; progress was slow and was often estimated by the number of hedges passed. So that the tanks could operate with a maximum of efficiency, an American sergeant devised a system whereby a sharp steel device, not unlike a ploughshare, was attached to the front of each tank.

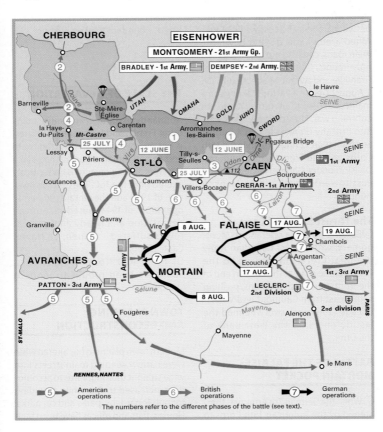

The Battle for St-Lô

④On 3 July the American 8th Corps launched its offensive, in the face of fierce German resistance, towards the road centre of St-Lô, thus assuring more favourable positions for the large-scale operations to come. Fighting was fierce for La Haye-du-Puits and Mount Castre. St-Lô fell on 19 July and the Americans entrenched their position behind the Lessay-Périers-St-Lô stretch of road. Progress at this time was slow in the Caen sector. A breakthrough was attempted towards the south-west of the town but was halted in the Bourguébus sector on 19 July. For one interminable week, from 19 to 25 July, bad weather suspended operations on all fronts.

THE BREAKTHROUGH (OPERATION COBRA)

⑤At midday on 25 July, following intense aerial bombardment, the 7th corps attacked west of St-Lô, the 8th between Périers and Lessay. By 28 July, Allied armour was driving down the main roads, carrying out vast encircling movements. Coutances fell on 28 July, Granville and Avranches on 31 July. On 1 August General Patton, taking command of the 3rd Army, hurled it into the lightning war. The 8th Corps burst west into Brittany (Rennes fell on 4 August and Nantes on 12 August), while the 15th Corps and the French 2nd Armoured Division under General Leclerc moved east towards Laval and Le Mans (9 August).

The Thrust South of Caen

⑥Backing up these operations, Montgomery, with the 1st Canadian Army (General Crerar) moved up to the Caen-Falaise road at the eastern end of the front; the British divisions, pushing south-east from Caumont and Villers-Bocage (5 August), overwhelmed the last defences on the west bank of the Orne.

BATTLE OF THE FALAISE-MORTAIN POCKET

⑦When the German 7th Army was threatened by the American 15th Corps to their rear and the British to the north, Hitler himself organised a counter-offensive to cut off the 3rd Army from its supply bases by taking control of the Avranches bottle-neck. The German 7th Army began its westerly counter attack on 6-7 August in the Mortain region. The Allied air forces crushed the move at daybreak. After a week of bitter fighting the Germans retreated east (12 August).

During this time the French 2nd Division moved northwards from Le Mans, took Alençon on 12 August and on 13 August breached the Paris-Granville road at Écouché.

The Canadians, halted between the 9 and 14 August at the River Laison, entered Falaise on 17 August, thus forming the northern arm of the pincer movement. Meeting with the Americans at Chambois (19 August), they cornered the German 7th Army and forced its surrender at Tournai-sur-Dive. By the night of 21 August the Battle of Normandy was over – it had cost the Germans 640 000 men, killed, wounded or taken prisoner.

Reconstruction

THE SCALE OF DEVASTATION

Normandy, like Britain and unlike many other French and European territories, is not on any European invasion route and so had remained unscathed since the Wars of Religion; towns had scarcely altered since the 16C. The German invasion of 1940 and the air raids and army operations of 1944 caused widespread devastation and nearly all the great towns suffered – Rouen, Le Havre, Caen, Lisieux.

Of the 3 400 Norman *communes*, 586 have been rebuilt to modern standards.

TOWN PLANNING AND RECONSTRUCTION

Modern town planning has altered what were narrow winding main streets into wide straight thoroughfares to accomodate increased traffic, while providing for public gardens, parks and car parks. Houses, flats and offices have been built and an effort has been made to restore individual character to towns and villages; limestone is used for buildings on the Norman sedimentary plain and plateaux, while sandstone, granite and brick are used in the woodland regions. Many historic monuments were damaged but most have been restored and are enhanced by improved settings.

Commanders in the Battle of Normandy

General Dwight Eisenhower (1890-1969) was the Supreme Allied Commander for Overlord. He was present when the German capitulation was signed in Berlin on 8 May 1945. Eisenhower was then to become US president from 1953 to 1961.

General George Patton (1885-1945) commanded the 3rd American Army. After the Avranches breakthrough his units swept across Brittany, the Paris basin, participated in the defence of Bastogne in the Battle of the Bulge then went as far as Bohemia.

General Omar Bradley (1893-1981) commanded the American assault forces during the landing operation. He then led his troops from Brittany across Europe in the Advance to the Elbe.

General Bernard Montgomery (1887-1976) commanded the land forces for the Allied landing operation. Montgomery then led the northern wing of the 21 Army Group through the Netherlands and Denmark in the Drive to the Baltic.

General Philippe de Hauteclocque (1902-47) known as **Leclerc**, commanded the 2nd Armoured Division of Free French Forces. He landed at Utah Beach on 1 August and took the 2nd Armoured Division from Cotentin to Colmar, liberating Paris on the way.

Field Marshal Erwin Rommel (1891-1944) was overall commander of German forces along the North Sea and Atlantic coasts and chief of the armies of the B group. Wounded on 17 June, suspected of having taken part in a plot against Hitler, he committed suicide on 14 October 1944.

Eisenhower *Patton* *Montgomery*

Leclerc *Rommel*

ART AND CULTURE

The Norse, a people long considered barbaric, were in fact masters of wood-carving and metal-working, as their sophisticated domestic implements and fine jewelry testify. Over the centuries, their descendents produced the great Norman and Gothic religious architecture of the 11C through 13C, and later proved great innovators in the decorative arts, music (Saint-Saëns, Honegger, Satie), literature (Corneille, de Toqueville, de Maupassant, Flaubert, Maurois), painting (the 19C Impressionists) and, most recently, the cinema.

Architecture

See the illustrations of Religious, Rural, Military and Seaside Architecture beginning on page xx.

NORMAN BUILDING MATERIALS

Rouen and the towns of the Seine are built with chalky limestone from the valley sides. A similar affinity exists between the local materials and the buildings in the Caux region, where pebbles are set in flowing mortar. Clay, in cheap and plentiful local supply, was used for the cob of the timber-framed thatched cottages and for making bricks, which were often ingeniously set to make decorative patterns.

ROMANESQUE (11C-EARLY 12C)

The Benedictines and Romanesque Design

In the 11C, immediately after the period of Viking invasions, the Benedictines returned to their task of clearing the land and constructing churches and other monastic buildings. These architect monks retained the robust building methods employed by the Carolingians and then embellished their constructions with the Oriental dome or the barrel vault used by the Romans for bridges and commemorative arches. This new architectural style, created by the Benedictines, was named Romanesque by Arcisse de Caumont, an archaeologist from Normandy, who in 1840 outlined the theory of regional schools of architecture. Despite its apparent simplicity Romanesque architecture is wonderfully diverse. In England the style is known as Norman.

Norman School and its Abbey Churches

The Benedictines, supported by the dukes of Normandy, played an immensely important part in the whole life of the province; only their work as architects and creators of the Norman School is described below.

The first religious buildings of importance in Normandy were the churches of the rich abbeys. Early monastic buildings may have disappeared or been altered, particularly after the Reform of St Maur, but examples of the Benedictine flowering have survived – the ruins of Jumièges Abbey and the churches on Mont-St-Michel, in Cerisy-la-Forêt, St-Martin-de-Boscherville as well as Église St-Étienne and Église de la Trinité in Caen.

The Norman School is characterised by pure lines, bold proportions, sober decoration and beautiful ashlared stonework. The style spread to England after the Norman conquest. Durham Cathedral provides the first official example of quadripartite vaulting, erected at the beginning of the 12C. The Norman style is to be seen in Westminster Abbey, which was rebuilt by Edward the Confessor, in the two west towers and the square crossing tower of Canterbury Cathedral and in the cathedrals of Southwell, Winchester and Ely.

Norman architecture also appeared in Sicily in the 11C in the wake of noble Norman adventurers; in France it paved the way for the Gothic style.

The abbey churches are characterised by two towers on either side of the west

ABC of architecture

Religious Architecture

ROUEN – Ground plan of the Cathédrale Notre-Dame (12-15C)

Lady chapel: in churches that are not dedicated to the Virgin, this chapel is often consecrated to Our Lady.

Ambulatory: semicircular or polygonal aisle enclosing the apse, originally used for processional purposes in pilgrimage churches

Arms of the transept: sometimes projecting

Bay: transverse section of the nave between two pairs of pillars

East end

Radiating chapel

High altar

Chancel

Apsidal chapel

Transept crossing

Nave

Side aisles, sometimes double

Narthex: enclosed vestibule stretching across the entrance to the church

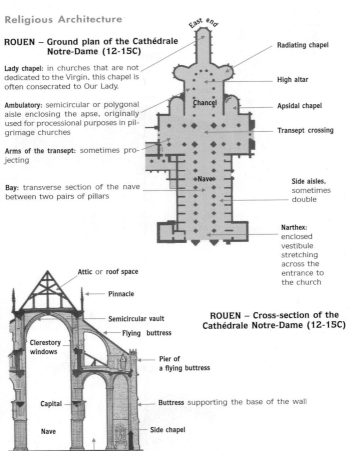

Attic or roof space

Pinnacle

Semicircular vault

Flying buttress

Clerestory windows

Pier of a flying buttress

Capital

Buttress supporting the base of the wall

Nave

Side chapel

Side aisle

ROUEN – Cross-section of the Cathédrale Notre-Dame (12-15C)

**CAUDEBEC-EN-CAUX
Vaulting in the Lady Chapel of the
Église Notre-Dame (14C)**

Keystone

Quarter or cell

Lierne: subordinate rib connecting two main ribs in Gothic vaulting

Tierceron: intermediate rib inserted between the transverse and diagonal ribs

Pendant: characteristic of Late Gothic

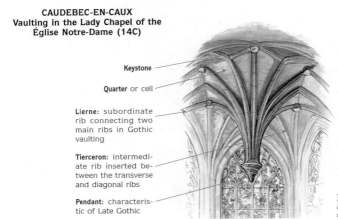

R. Corbel

CAUDEBEC-en-CAUX – Église Notre-Dame (14C)

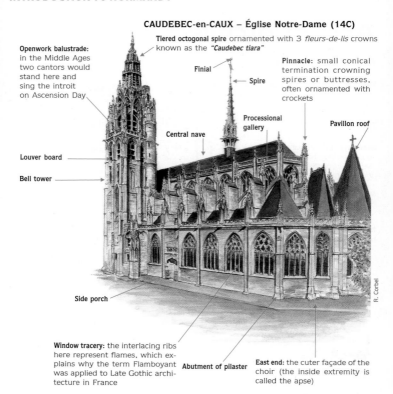

Tiered octogonal spire ornamented with 3 *fleurs-de-lis* crowns known as the *"Caudebec tiara"*

Finial

Spire

Pinnacle: small conical termination crowning spires or buttresses, often ornamented with crockets

Openwork balustrade: in the Middle Ages two cantors would stand here and sing the introit on Ascension Day

Processional gallery

Pavillon roof

Central nave

Louver board

Bell tower

Side porch

Window tracery: the interlacing ribs here represent flames, which explains why the term Flamboyant was applied to Late Gothic architecture in France

Abutment of pilaster

East end: the outer façade of the choir (the inside extremity is called the apse)

R. Corbel

ROUEN – Portail des Librairies, Cathédrale Notre-Dame (1482)

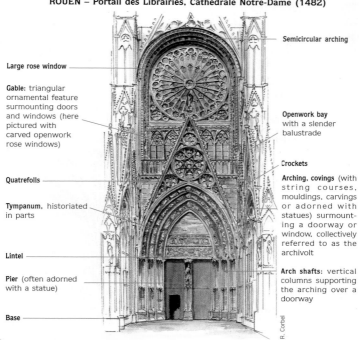

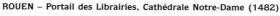

Semicircular arching

Large rose window

Gable: triangular ornamental feature surmounting doors and windows (here pictured with carved openwork rose windows)

Openwork bay with a slender balustrade

Crockets

Quatrefoils

Arching, covings (with string courses, mouldings, carvings or adorned with statues) surmounting a doorway or window, collectively referred to as the archivolt

Tympanum, historiated in parts

Lintel

Pier (often adorned with a statue)

Arch shafts: vertical columns supporting the arching over a doorway

Base

R. Corbel

ROUEN – Chancel and Transept Crossing in the Abbatiale St-Ouen (14C)

Main arcade

Clerestory windows

Arcature with mouldings

Tracery: ornamental stone ribwork in the upper part of a window

Sculpted spandrel: triangular area comprised between an arch and its framing

Equilateral arch

Mullion: vertical shaft dividing a window into two or several lights

Triforium

Diagonal rib

Compound pier

CAUDEBEC-EN-CAUX – Grand Organ in the Église Notre-Dame (1541-1542)

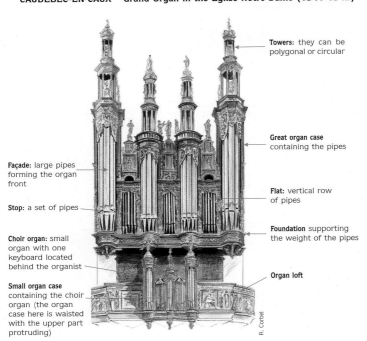

Towers: they can be polygonal or circular

Great organ case containing the pipes

Façade: large pipes forming the organ front

Flat: vertical row of pipes

Stop: a set of pipes

Foundation supporting the weight of the pipes

Choir organ: small organ with one keyboard located behind the organist

Organ loft

Small organ case containing the choir organ (the organ case here is waisted with the upper part protruding)

R. Corbel

ÉVREUX – Stained glass (early 14C) in the Cathédrale Notre-Dame

The main function of stained glass is to provide a translucent framing for church windows and to regulate the intensity of the light inside the building. "The stained-glass windows in the chancel of Évreux Cathedral are the finest examples of 14C work. They are pure in the extreme, artfully combining light yellows and limpid blues with transparent reds and silvery whites... They are in perfect harmony with the radiant chancel, suffused with dazzling day light", remarked Emile Mâle

Glass edging surrounding the finished panes

French T-bar armature: iron band used between panels to fix them onto the saddle-bar

Ferramenta: iron framework that provides a fixing for the panels within the window

Internal lead: strip of lead used to fit together the pieces of glass in the panel

Silver stain: pigment made of silver nitrate mixed with ochre that produces a lovely yellow after firing in the kiln

Grisaille: pigment made with iron oxide producing a variety of greys and blacks after firing in the kiln

Saddle-bars: iron shafts embedded in the masonry of windows to support the panels

R. Corbel

ÉCOUIS – Stalls in the chancel of the Collégiale Notre-Dame (14C)

High back

Elbow rest

Cheek: narrow upright face forming the end of a row of stalls

Separation between two stalls

Misericord: ledge projecting from the underside of a hinged seat which, when the seat is raised, provides support to worshippers or choir singers out of mercy (per misericordiam). 15C and 16C stalls were often sculpted with amusing grotesques or bizarre creatures called "**drolleries**"

R. Corbel/MICHELIN

Rural Architecture

Thatched Cottage at LYONS-LA-FORÊT

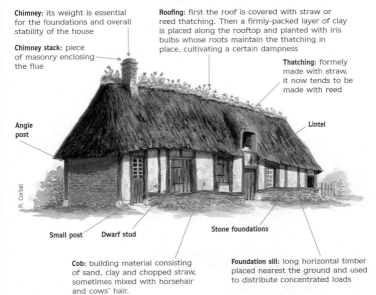

Chimney: its weight is essential for the foundations and overall stability of the house

Chimney stack: piece of masonry enclosing the flue

Roofing: first the roof is covered with straw or reed thatching. Then a firmly-packed layer of clay is placed along the rooftop and planted with iris bulbs whose roots maintain the thatching in place, cultivating a certain dampness

Thatching: formely made with straw, it now tends to be made with reed

Angle post

Lintel

Small post   **Dwarf stud**

Stone foundations

Cob: building material consisting of sand, clay and chopped straw, sometimes mixed with horsehair and cows' hair.

Foundation sill: long horizontal timber placed nearest the ground and used to distribute concentrated loads

Military Architecture

Château d'HARCOURT (13C)

Although it has suffered from the ravages of time and history, the **Château d'Harcourt** remains a perfect example of medieval defensive architecture.

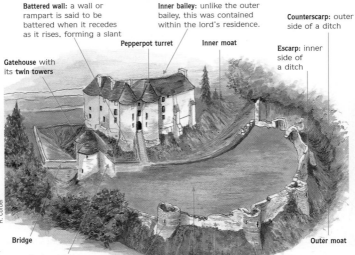

Battered wall: a wall or rampart is said to be battered when it recedes as it rises, forming a slant

Inner bailey: unlike the outer bailey, this was contained within the lord's residence.

Counterscarp: outer side of a ditch

Pepperpot turret   **Inner moat**

Escarp: inner side of a ditch

Gatehouse with its **twin towers**

Bridge

Outer moat

Garrison quarters

Arrow silt: loophole through which archers shot their arrows, converted here to receive artillery cannons in the 14C

Flanking Towers: they facilitated the firing of weapons along the outer face of the walls

Curtain wall: enclosing rampart connecting two bastions or towers

Outer bailey: courtyard lying outside the castle perimeter but protected by its ramparts: it was used to accommodate the quartermasters' lodgings and to receive the population in the event of a siege

69

Seaside Architecture

DEAUVILLE – Villa Strassburger (early 20C)

This villa is a pastiche of the half-timbered mansions typical of the area. Its genuine Norman characteristics are combined with those from Alsace and some other French regions, complemented by a few eccentric touches prompted by the imagination of architect **G. Pichereau**: asymmetrical rooftops, profusion of skylights and dormer windows, projecting eaves.

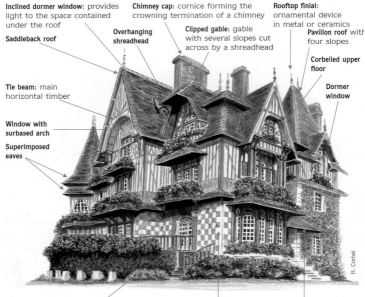

Inclined dormer window: provides light to the space contained under the roof

Saddleback roof

Overhanging shreadhead

Chimney cap: cornice forming the crowning termination of a chimney

Clipped gable: gable with several slopes cut across by a shreadhead

Rooftop finial: ornamental device in metal or ceramics

Pavillon roof with four slopes

Corbelled upper floor

Dormer window

Tie beam: main horizontal timber

Window with surbased arch

Superimposed eaves

R. Corbel

Balustrade: parapet formed by a row of balusters

Stacked bond: a bond in masonry in which the bricks form a chequered pattern

Wind-brace

Civil Engineering

The Pont de NORMANDIE (1988-1994)

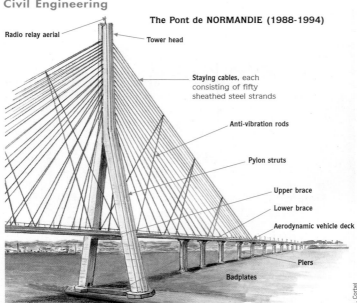

Radio relay aerial

Tower head

Staying cables, each consisting of fifty sheathed steel strands

Anti-vibration rods

Pylon struts

Upper brace

Lower brace

Aerodynamic vehicle deck

Piers

Badplates

R. Corbel

Entrance providing access inside the pylon

front, giving the west face an H-like appearance, and a square lantern tower above the transept crossing, which also served to increase the light inside.

The towers, bare or decorated only with blind arcades below, get lighter with multiple pierced bays the higher they rise (in the 13C many were crowned by spires quartered by pinnacles). Charming country churches are often surmounted by Romanesque belfries, which are crowned with a saddleback roof or a four-sided squat wood or stone pyramid, the forerunner of the Gothic spire.

The interior light and size of Norman abbeys is very striking. The naves are wide with an elevation consisting of two series of openings above great semicircular arches – an amazingly bold concept for a Romanesque construction. The Norman monks eschewed the heavy barrel vault in favour of a beamed roof spanning the nave and galleries, reserving groined stone vaulting (the crossing of two semicircular arches) for the aisles. The vast galleries on the first level open onto the wide bays of the nave and repeat the design of the aisles. At clerestory level a gallery or passage in the thickness of the wall circles the church. A dome over the transept crossing supports a magnificent lantern tower which lets in the daylight through tall windows.

Norman Decoration

The abbey churches, like all others of Romanesque design, were illuminated on a considerable scale with gilding and bright colours as were the manuscripts of the time. The main themes were those of Byzantine iconography.

Norman sculptural decoration is essentially geometric; different motifs stand out, of which the most common is the key or fret pattern (straight lines meeting at right angles to form crenellated or rectangular designs). The decorative motifs are sometimes accompanied by mouldings, human heads or animal masks emphasising recessed arches, archivolts, cornices and mouldings. Sometimes the monks executed low-relief motifs copied from cloth, ivories or metalwork brought back from the Ori-

G. Targat/MICHELIN

ent; this is the origin of the cornerstones in the great arcade in Bayeux.

Capitals are rare and, where they exist, they are carved with gadroons or stylised foliage.

GOTHIC (12C–15C)

The style, conceived in Île-de-France, apart from quadripartite or rib vaulting which originated in Norman England, was known as French work or French style until the 16C when the Italians of the Renaissance, who were resistant to the Parisian trend, scornfully dubbed it Gothic. The name survived. The French copied the H-shaped façades and great galleries of the Norman abbeys (the west front of Notre-Dame in Paris is based on that of the Église de la Trinité in Caen and its galleries on those of the Église St-Étienne).

The Cathedrals

Gothic is an ideal artistic style for cathedrals, as it symbolises the religious fervour of the people and the growing prosperity of the towns. In an all-embracing enthusiasm, a whole city would participate in the construction of the house of God. Under the enlightened guidance of bishops and master builders, all the guilds contributed to the cathedral's embellishment: stained-glass makers, painters, wood and stone carvers went to work. The doors became the illustrated pages of history.

Gothic Architecture in Normandy

Gradually the national Gothic style percolated into Normandy before the province was seized by Philippe Auguste in 1204.

In the 13C the Gothic and traditional Norman styles merged. The best example of this fusion is Coutances Cathedral, where the pure proportions and the lofty austerity of the Norman style combine with Gothic sophistication as in the lantern tower.

This was also the period of the superb belfries of the Caen and Bessin plains, typified by their tall stone spires, often pierced to offer less resistance to the wind, and quartered with pinnacles.

The magnificent Merveille buildings of Mont-St-Michel give an idea of total Norman Gothic ornamentation. Sobriety provides the foundation over which foliated sculpture reigns supreme; plants of every variety decorate the round capitals, cover the cornerstones and garland the friezes. The three- and four-leafed clover in relief or hollowed out is a frequent motif but statuary is rare. Lisieux Cathedral and the Tour St-Romain of Rouen Cathedral show the degree of French Gothic influence in Normandy by the end of the 12C.

The Flamboyant Style

By the 14C, the period of great cathedral building had come to an end. The Hundred Years War (1337-1453) killed architectural inspiration; bits were added, buildings were touched up, but little created. When the war was over a taste for virtuosity alone remained – and the Flamboyant style was born. Rouen is the true capital of the Flamboyant, which was particularly widespread in Haute-Normandie.

In this new style, the tracery of bays and rose windows resembles wavering flames – the derivation of the term Flamboyant. The Flamboyant style produced such single masterpieces as the Église St-Maclou in Rouen, the Tour de Beurre of Rouen Cathedral, the belfries of Notre-Dame in Caudebec and La Madeleine in Verneuil-sur-Avre. Civil architecture developed in importance and passed from Flamboyant to Renaissance – a change symbolised in the gables, pinnacles and balustrades of the Palais de Justice in Rouen.

Feudal Architecture

In medieval Normandy permission to build a castle was granted to the barons by the ruling duke, who, prudent as well as powerful, reserved the right to billet his own garrison inside and forbade all private wars. Over the years the building of castles along the duchy's frontiers was encouraged – Richard Lionheart secured the Seine with the most formidable fortress of the period, Château-Gaillard.

Originally only the austere keeps were inhabited, but from the 14C a courtyard and more pleasing quarters were constructed within the fortifications. This evolution can be seen in the castles at Alençon, and Dieppe and some of the Perche manor houses.

A taste for comfort and adornment appeared in civil architecture; wealthy merchants and burgesses built tall houses where wide eaves protected half-timbered upper storeys that overhung stone walled ground floors. The results were as capricious as they were picturesque: corner posts, corbels and beams were decorated with lively and fantastic carvings.

THE RENAISSANCE (16C)

Georges I d'Amboise, Archbishop of Rouen and patron of the arts, introduced Italian taste and usage to Normandy. The new motifs – arabesques, foliated scrollwork, medallions, shells, urns etc – were combined with Flamboyant art. Among the outstanding works of this period is the chevet of the Église St-Pierre in Caen, a masterpiece of exuberance.

Castles, Manor Houses and Old Mansions

The Renaissance style reached its fullest grace in domestic architecture. At first, older buildings were ornamented in the current taste or a new and delicately decorated wing was added (Château d'O and the château at Fontaine-Henry); fortifications were replaced by parks and gardens.

The Classicism rediscovered by humanists took hold so that architects aimed for correct proportion and the imposition of the three Classical Orders of Antiquity.

Imperceptibly the search for symmetry and correctness produced aridity; fantasy was stifled by pomposity.

In Normandy, the Gothic spirit survived, appearing most successfully in small manor houses and innumerable country houses with sham feudal moats, turrets and battlements incorporated in either half-timbering or stone and brick.

Norman towns contain many large stone Renaissance mansions. The outer façade is always plain and one must enter the courtyard to see the architectural design and the rich decoration (Hôtel d'Escoville, Caen; Hôtel de Bourgtheroulde, Rouen).

In the 16C decoration became richer and less impulsive but the half-timbered construction technique remained the same. Many of these old houses have been carefully restored and there are good examples in Alençon, Bayeux, Bernay, Caen, Domfront, Honfleur, Pont-Audemer, Verneuil-sur-Avre and Rouen.

CLASSICAL (17C–18C)

In this period, French architectural style, now a single concept and no longer an amalgam of individual techniques, imposed its rationalism on many countries beyond its borders.

Louis XIII and the "Jesuit Style"

The reign of Henri IV marked an artistic rebirth. An economical method of construction was adopted in which bricks played an important part: it was a time of beautiful châteaux with plain rose and white façades and steep grey-blue slate roofs.

The first decades of the 17C coincided with the Counter-Reformation. The Jesuits built many colleges and chapels – cold and formal edifices, their façades characterised by superimposed columns, a pediment and upturned consoles or small pavilions joining the front of the main building to the sides.

The Grand Siècle in Normandy

The symmetrical façades of the Classical style demanded space for their appreciation as in the châteaux at Cany, Beaumesnil, Balleroy and elsewhere. The Benedictine abbeys, which had adopted the **Maurist Reform** (the Benedictine Congregation of St Maur was founded in 1621), rediscovered their former inspiration. At the beginning of the 18C, the monastery buildings of the Abbaye-aux-Hommes in Caen and at Le Bec-Hellouin were remodelled by a brother architect and sculptor, **Guillaume de la Tremblaye**. The original plan was conserved but the design and decoration were given an austere nobility.

The urban scene was transformed by the construction of magnificent bishops' palaces, town halls with wide façades and large private houses.

CONTEMPORARY (19C–20C)

Following the extensive destruction caused by the Second World War many towns and villages in Normandy were rebuilt in the mid-20C in accordance with the precepts of modern town planning. A good example of successful reconstruction is Aunay-sur-Odon, with its large and imposing church.

Auguste Perret (1874-1954), the architect who pioneered the use of reinforced concrete construction, was appointed Chief Architect for the reconstruction of Le Havre; his works include the modern district of Le Havre and the Église St-Joseph. His work makes use of textured concrete and is designed to take the best advantage of natural light.

Normandy is a region of innovation as well; in Le Havre, note the **Espace Oscar-Niemeyer**, named after the Brazilian architect as an example. Two surprising white structures evoke a volcano, and stand out in contrast to the buildings designed by Perret. The Musée des Beaux-Arts André-Malraux, also in Le Havre, ressembles a glass ship at anchor. In Rouen, the renovation of place du Vieux-Marché in the 1970s included the construction of the Église Ste-Jeanne-d'Arc, based on a design by Louis Arretche. The roof of the church is in the shape of a boat hull (upside down).

Three of Normandy's bridges are also noteworthy examples of modern architecture: the **Tancarville bridge** was inaugurated in 1959, the **Brotonne**

bridge in 1977, and the colossal **Pont de Normandie**, spanning the Seine estuary, opened in 1995. The most recent bridge is not only a boon to travellers, it is also a work of art and a technological feat, a milestone of civil engineering. It is a cable-stayed bridge, more elegant and cheaper to build than a suspension bridge, made of steel and concrete, able to withstand winds of 440kph/274mph.

POPULAR ARCHITECTURE

Normandy is often associated with **half-timbered** houses. The basic box frame is essentially composed of horizontal and vertical beams, but there are very often different local methods of construction. Footings or a base of some solid material is laid to prevent damp from rising. A wooden sill or horizontal beam is laid along this base to ensure the correct spacing of the upright posts or studs. It is divided into as many sections as there are intervals between the vertical posts. The upper horizontal beam, sometimes known as a summer or bressumer, consists of a single beam. Along the gable ends it is known as a tie-beam. Bricks are often ingeniously used to make attractive patterns between the timbers.

Roofing materials such as thatch, which is so vulnerable to fire, and shingles of sweet chestnut, are becoming increasingly rare. The schist slabs of the Cotentin are a typical part of the landscape. The slate which has been used since the 18C for houses and outbuildings alike has a silver tinge. A watertight roof depends on the correct hanging of the slates. The appearance of the villages is conditioned by the local materials used and the trades of the various villagers. One well-known building material, **Caen stone**, is quarried from the Jurassic deposits. It can be either friable or durable and varies in colour through grey and off-white to its more characteristic light creamy colour. The ashlar blocks are divided into two groups, one with the grain running vertically for façades, corner stones and gables and the second with a horizontal grain for courses and cornices.

Farms

In the open landscape of the **Caen plain** the typical courtyard farms are surrounded by high walls. A gateway gives access to the courtyard with the one or two storeyed farmhouse at the far end. The smaller crofts usually consist of two buildings, one long house for the living quarters and cowshed or barn and another for the stable or byre.

The farm buildings of the **Bessin** stand round a large courtyard that has two entrances, side by side, one for wheeled vehicles and a second for people. The house stands at the far end with the service and outbuildings to the right and left. There is usually a well in the middle. Built of limestone or Jurassic marls, the house has a pristine appearance. The windows are tall and wide; the roofing is either tiles or slates.

The small flat-tiled houses in the **Argentan** area have symmetrical façades. The buildings are usually a harmonious mixture of schist, brick (chimneys and window surrounds) and limestone (the walls). Some are surrounded by walls or a screen of vegetation. Large barns are frequently adjoined by sheds.

Brick and small laminated schist tiles predominate in the **Sées** countryside. Sometimes the buildings fit snugly one against the other, creating a jumble of roofs of varying pitch.

The farms in the region of **Alençon** are built around an open courtyard. The infinitely varied architecture reflects the wide range of rocks: granite, schist, flint, clay and kaolin.

The most common house type in the **Falaise** countryside is akin to those found in the Caen region. The walled courtyard predominates. The brick chimney replaces the rubblework one and tiles are used for roofs in the area bordering the Auge region.

The houses in the **Suisse Normande** are built of schist known as Pont-de-la-Mousse slate quarried near Thury-Harcourt and the settlements often have the rugged appearance of mountain villages. In the Orne Valley the houses huddle closely together on the floor whereas those on the slopes are scattered, even isolated.

The farm courtyard in the **Vire** *bocage* is often planted with apple and pear trees. On either side of the farmhouse are the barns, cattle sheds and outbuildings for the cider press. Brown or red schist is the main building stone.

Seaside Architecture

In the 19C, the coast became a popular destination and bathing in the sea a novel pastime. Wealthy patrons ordered quirky houses for their holiday pleasures. Sometimes they were built in or near existing fishing villages, and in other places whole resort communities sprang up. Many of these villas are still standing along the coast at Cabourg, Houlgate, Villers, Deauville, Trouville, Villerville, Ste-Adresse, Étretat, Dieppe, Le Tréport, Mers-les-Bains etc. Generally, they are remarkable for their multicoloured façades, busy with balconies, bow windows, railings, gables and other decorative elements. A profusion of skylights, projecting eaves and rooftop finials adds to the exuberance. Other models are more reserved and even stately, recalling the Renaissance style. Some are more modestly termed chalets, and are said to be in the Swiss, Spanish or Persian style, depending on their features.

Norman Dovecotes

The practice of keeping pigeons, formerly known as doves, dates back to the earliest civilisations. Although domestication is believed to have originated around 4500 BC, the practice became widespread some 2 000 years later, in ancient Egypt, where pigeon was appreciated for its succulent flesh, a fact evidenced by the many frescoes of feasts and banquets.

THE CARRIER PIGEON

The carrier pigeon is mostly known for its military role in times of war. News of the conquest of Gaul by Julius Caesar was relayed to the capital by means of pigeons, as was Napoleon's defeat at Waterloo. During the Siege of Paris in 1870, 400 birds helped defend the city by carrying tiny strips of film attached to their claws.

More recently, during the First World War, English troops entrusted some 10 000 messages to their feathered friends. Several warrior birds became legendary figures and some were even awarded a military decoration: *The Mocker, Lord Adelaide, Burma Queen* etc. The cities of Brussels and Lille have erected memorials to these worthy messengers.

THE HOMING PIGEON

In the early 19C, a new sport appeared in Belgium – pigeon racing, in which birds are trained to return to their home loft after being released in the wild. The first long-distance race (160km/100mi) was held in 1818 and the sport gradually gained prominence in Great Britain, France and the United States. Today, many French villages have their own Pigeon-Fanciers Club (*Société Colombophile*) and organise races regularly.

FOR THE BIRDS

A familiar sight in Normandy, especially in the Pays de Caux, is the dovecote (*colombier*). Norman dovecotes are square, polygonal or round; the last type is the most common. The door is at ground level, usually rectangular but sometimes rounded at the top and often surmounted by the arms of the owner. The projecting ledge half way up (*larmier*) is designed to prevent the entry of rodents. There are openings for the pigeons all round. The roofs, conical on circular dovecotes and faceted on square or polygonal dovecotes, are often covered with slates. The lead finial may be in the shape of a pigeon or a weathervane.

The interior is lined with pigeon-holes (*boulins*) – one hole for each pair of pigeons – and the number varies according to the wealth of the owner. They are reached by a ladder fixed to an arm attached to a central post which pivots on a hard stone. In some dovecotes only the upper part is intended for pigeons; the lower part may be used as a hen house or a sheep pen. When the two parts are separated by a wooden floor, the door to the upper part is above the stone rat ledge and reached by an external detachable ladder.

There are two kinds of dovecote. The standard or classic type is built of ashlar stone (not common), in an attractive contrast to black flint and white stone (north and north-east of Le Havre), in brick, black flint and ashlar stone (brick tended to replace black flint after the 17C), or in brick and stone (fairly common). The type of dovecote called

Dovecotes of Normandy

Manoir de Caudemonde

Château de Crèvecoeur-en-Auge

Manoir d'Auffray, Oherville

Dovecote in the hamlet of Petit Veauville, Héricourt-en-Caux

Château de Betteville

M. Dewynter/MICHELIN

secondary includes buildings in light coloured flint (a similar shade to ashlar stone), in flint and stone, or in flint, brick and stone.

The first known laws on pigeon breeding were instituted in the Middle Ages. In Normandy, the owners of fiefs were the only ones entitled to build dovecotes. This right, known as the *droit de colombier*, was abolished on 4 August 1789 and very few new dovecotes were built after the French Revolution. A total of 535 were officially registered in the Seine-Maritime in the early 20C. However, many have been abandoned and are now in a state of neglect. The French government and local authorities have recently taken measures to finance the restoration of these charming buildings, which are an essential part of Normandy's rural heritage.

Decorative Arts

CERAMICS AND POTTERY

The glazed pavement in the chapterhouse of St Pierre-sur-Dives (13C) demonstrates the long tradition of ceramic art in Normandy. In the mid-16C Masséot Abaquesne was making decorated tiles, which were greatly prized in Rouen, whereas potteries in Le Pré-d'Auge and Manerbe (near Lisieux) were producing "earthenware more beautiful than is made elsewhere." In 1644 **Rouen faience** made its name with blue decoration on a white ground and white on blue. By the end of the century production had increased so that when the royal plate was melted down to replenish the Treasury, "the Court changed to chinaware in a week" (Saint-Simon). The so-called radiant style is reminiscent of the wrought-iron work and embroidery for which the town was well known. The desire for novelty brought in the vogue for chinoiserie. In the middle of the 18C came the Rococo style with its quiver decoration and the famous Rouen cornucopia, a horn of plenty overflowing with flowers, birds and insects. This industry was ruined by the 1786 trade treaty, which allowed the import of English chinaware into France.

Rouen faience

NORMAN FURNITURE

Sideboards, longcase clocks and wardrobes – the three most characteristic and traditional pieces of furniture in Normandy – are valued for their elegance, solidity and generous proportions.

The wardrobe, which gradually replaced the medieval chest, first appeared in the 13C; by the beginning of the 17C the sideboard was already in existence and in the 18C longcase clocks became widespread. The golden age of furniture making in Normandy produced wellproportioned and delicately carved sideboards or kitchen dressers; coffin clocks (broader at the top than at the bottom); longcase clocks characterised by carved baskets of fruit and flowers round the clockface; tall pendulum clocks, with delicately chased dials in gilt bronze, copper, pewter or enamel; majestic oak wardrobes, ornamented with finely worked fittings, in brass or other metals, or with medallions, surmounted with carved cornices of doves, birds' nests, ears of corn, flowers and fruit or Cupid's quiver etc. The wardrobe was often part of a young woman's dowry and contained her trousseau; its transfer from her parents' house to her new home was the occasion for traditional celebrations.

Painting

Painting took first place among the arts in 19C France. Landscape totally eclipsed historical and stylised paint-

Furniture from Basse-Normandie

Box bed (Pays d'Auge – 18C)

Longcase clock (St-Lô – 19C)

Marriage wardrobe (Bayeux – 18C)

Dairy cupboard (Avranchin – 18C)

Kitchen dresser (Crotentin – 19C)

Sideboard (Vire – 19C)

ing and Normandy was to become the cradle of Impressionism.

THE OPEN AIR

While the Romantics were discovering inland Normandy, Eugène Isabey, a lover of seascapes, began to work on the still deserted coast. **Richard Bonington** (1801-28), an English painter who went to France as a boy, trained there, and, in his watercolours, captured the wetness of sea beaches.

In the second half of the 19C artistic activity was concentrated on **Eugène Boudin** (1824-98) round the Côte de Grâce. This painter from Honfleur, named King of the Skies by Corot, encouraged a young fifteen-year-old from Le Havre, **Claude Monet**, to drop caricature for the joys of real painting and urged his Parisian friends to come and stay in his St-Siméon farmstead.

IMPRESSIONISM

The younger painters, nevertheless, were to outstrip their elders in their search for pictorial light. They wanted to portray the vibration of light, hazes, the trembling of reflections and shadows, the depth and tenderness of the sky, the fading of colours in full sunlight. They – Monet, Sisley, Bazille and their Paris friends, Renoir, Pissarro, Cézanne and Guillaumin especially – were about to form the Impressionist School, which gave France a front rank in the history of painting.

From 1862 to 1869 the Impressionists remained faithful to the Normandy coast and the Seine estuary. After the Franco-Prussian War they returned only occasionally – although it was in Normandy, at Giverny, that Claude Monet set up house in 1881 and remained until he died in 1926.

Impressionism, in its turn, gave birth to a new school, **Pointillism**, which divided the tints with little touches of colour, applying the principle of the division of white light into seven basic colours, to get ever closer to a luminous effect. Seurat and Signac, the pioneers of this method, also came to Normandy to study its landscapes.

In the early 20C **Fauvism** was born as a reaction against Impressionism and neo-Impressionism. These brightly coloured linear compositions exploded on the canvas.

For half a century, therefore, the Côte de Grâce, the Pays de Caux, Deauville, Trouville and Rouen were the sources of inspiration of a multitude of paintings.

A PLEIAD OF PAINTERS

Numerous artists still came to Normandy in the first half of the 20C, notably Valloton and Gernez (the latter died in Honfleur); Marquet, who had worked in Gustave Moreau's studio in Paris; Othon Friesz, who particularly enjoyed Honfleur which he portrayed in its many aspects; and Van Dongen, painter of the worldly and the elegant and a frequent guest at Deauville.

Marquet, Friesz and Van Dongen were strongly influenced by Fauvism, whereas **Raoul Dufy**, a native of Le Havre, soon overthrew accepted convention to associate line drawing and richness of colour in compositions which were full of movement.

Literature

Literature and architecture both sprang from the monasteries. It is therefore hardly surprising that Normandy and its abbeys became rich in literary activity from the 13C. Monks and clergymen with a sound knowledge of history and legend, together with travellers and pilgrims, provided the poets with the inspiration needed to create the Christian epics known as the *chansons de geste*. Such verse appeared chronologically after the early hagiographic literature (lives of saints) but remains one of the first examples of the use of French as a literary mode of expression. In the 12C the Anglo-Norman **Robert Wace**, who was born in Jersey but brought up in Caen, wrote two notable verse chronicles. *Le Roman du Rou* (1160-74) was commissioned by Henry II of England and is a history of the dukes of Normandy.

17C

Pierre Corneille (1606-84) is often called the father of French classical tragedy. His main works are known together as the classical tetralogy: (1637), *Horace* (1640), *Cinna* (1641) and *Polyeucte* (1643). The dramatist enjoyed a happy life with his extended family in Rouen (He married and had seven children; his brother married his wife's sister and their households were very close), and despite occasional brushes with the authorities, his plays were generally well received. Balzac praised him, Molière acknowledged him as his master and the foremost of dramatists, Racine lauded his talent for versification. From the 20C viewpoint, it is clear that Corneille also had a great impact on the rise of comedy, and in the development of drama in general, in particular in regard to his ability to depict personal and moral forces in conflict.

18C

Born in Le Havre, **Bernardin de St-Pierre** (1737-1814) travelled the world to fulfil his dreams, and spent part of his life on the Indian Ocean island of Mauritius. In Paris, he became the disciple of the Romantic philosopher Jean-Jacques Rousseau. His best-known works are *Paul and Virginie* (1787) and *Studies of Nature* (1784).

19C

The founder of Norman regionalism is **Barbey d'Aurevilly** (1808-99), a nobleman from Cotentin, who was born in St-Sauveur-le-Vicomte. In a warm and bright style, illuminated with brilliant imagery and original phrases, he sought, like the Impressionists, to convey the atmosphere, the quality, the uniqueness of his region. Valognes, the town where he spent most of his adolescence, is mentioned in several of his works *(Ce qui ne meurt pas; Chevalier des Touches* and *Les Diaboliques)*.

Although born in Paris, **Charles Alexis de Tocqueville** (1805-59) was from an old Norman family. It was during stays at the ancestral home, the Château de Tocqueville, not far from Cherbourg, that he wrote many of the works which were to bring him fame. This political scientist, politician and historian is best-known for his timeless classic *Democracy in America*.

Gustave Flaubert (1821-80), a prime mover of the Realist School of French literature, considered art as a means to knowledge. His masterful *Madame Bovary* (1857), a portrait of bourgeois life in the provinces, took him five years to complete. The French government sought to block its publication and have the author condemned for immorality – he narrowly escaped conviction.

Flaubert greatly influenced **Guy de Maupassant** (1850-93), a family friend born in Dieppe who regarded himself as the older author's apprentice. Maupassant's work is thoroughly realistic, the language lucidly pure and the imagery sharp and precise. The author wrote best-selling novels *(Une Vie, Bel-Ami, Pierre et Jean)*, but his greatest achievement lies in his short stories; he perfected the form and many of these works are considered among the finest in French literature. Today, he is one of the most widely read French authors in English-speaking countries.

Octave Mirbeau, (1848-1917) from Trévières near Bayeux, was an active participant in the literary and political quarrels of his time, speaking out in defence of anarchist ideas. As a novelist, he was fiercely critical of the social conditions of the time, and his work *Journal of a Lady's Maid (Le Journal d'une femme de chambre*, 1900) is typical of this attitude.

20C

Alain (1868-1951), made a name for himself by his columns in a Rouen newspaper. A professor of philosophy and author of many essays, he revolted against all forms of tyranny. His works *Remarks on Happiness* (1928) and *Remarks on Education* (1932) are noteworthy.

André Maurois (1865-1967) is known for his war memories, novels, biographies (*The Life of Disraeli*, 1927) and historical works (*History of England*, 1937).

Jean de la Varende (1887-1959), from the Ouche region, evokes in his novels the Normandy of yesteryear. His work *Par Monts et Merveilles de Normandie* is a description of all he saw and admired in the region.

Armand Salacrou (1899-1989), born in Rouen, called his dramatic works a "meditation on the human condition." He experimented with different dramatic styles. Two of his popular successes were *Un homme comme les autres* (1926) and *Boulevard Durand* (1961).

Raymond Queneau (1903-76) was born in Le Havre and achieved distinction as the director of the prestigious Encyclopédie de la Pléiade, a scholarly edition of past and present authors. As the author of many poems, novels and plays, Queneau stands out for his quirky style and verbal juggling, revealing the absurdity that underlies our everyday world. One of his best-loved works, *Zazie dans le métro* (1959), was made into a charming film. He created a surprising book called *100 000 Billion Poems* on the following principle: he took a sonnet (14 lines) and printed each line on 10 strips of paper, then arranged them in a spiral binding so that by flipping the strips one way and another, a reader can construct 10^{14} (10 to the 14th power) poems. Although the book is small, if you were to read a different poem every 10 seconds, it would take you millions of years to read them all!

Music

Composer operas and comic operas, **François-Adrien Boieldieu** (1775-1834) was born in Rouen. His work *The Caliph of Baghdad* (1800) earned him a glowing reputation throughout Europe. From 1803 to 1810 he was Director of Music at the Imperial Opera of St Petersburg at the request of Czar Alexander I. His talent was universally recognised with his masterpiece *La Dame Blanche* in 1825. **Camille Saint-Saëns** (1835-1921) was born in Paris, but his father was from Normandy. A brilliant pianist, he composed symphonies, operas, concertos and religious works. His most famous works include the *Danse Macabre* (1875) and *Samson et Dalila* (1877).

Arthur Honegger (1892-1955) was born in Le Havre, of Swiss origin. At first he composed melodies to poems by Cocteau, Apollinaire and Paul Fort, then *Pacific 231* (1923) and *King David* (1924). *Joan at the Stake* (1935) and *The Dance of the Dead* (1938) have texts by Paul Claudel. Born in Honfleur, **Erik Satie** (1866-1925) began as a pianist in the cabarets of Montmartre (The Black Cat), where he met Debussy. Sarcasm and irony permeate his works, his greatest being the symphonic drama *Socrates* (1918) for voice and orchestra based on texts by Plato. Satie exerted an undeniable influence both on his time and on musicians such as Ravel, Debussy and Stravinsky.

THE REGION TODAY

Normandy today takes pride in its agricultural and fishing traditions as one of the most rural regions of France, while adapting to the wider European economy as a major centre for maritime trade; technology-based industries are also coming to the fore. The old rural pursuits have been maintained, although in modern facilities, and Normandy markets its milk, cider and Camembert cheese around the world.

Food and Drink

The people of Normandy have a reputation for being hearty eaters who appreciate good cooking. Most family celebrations and reunions are marked by leisurely meals for which the French are so famous. Normandy is known for its traditional recipes and specialities based on the wonderful flavour of local produce.

LOCAL SPECIALITIES

According to Normandy tradition one should eat duck in Rouen, tripe in Caen and La Ferté-Macé, leg of lamb from the salt meadows of Mont-St-Michel Bay and an omelette in Mont-St-Michel; one should also taste Dieppe sole, Duclair duckling, Auge Valley chicken garnished with tiny onions, Vire chitterlings (*andouillette*), black pudding from Mortagne-au-Perche and white pudding from Avranches. Among the tasty meat dishes, try the *côtes de veau vallée d'Auge*, which are veal cutlets fried in butter and flambéed in Calvados then braised in cider and fresh cream.

The range of seafood is impressive: shrimps and cockles from Honfleur, mussels from Villerville and Isigny, lobsters from La Hague and Barfleur and oysters, Atlantic crabs, spider crabs, winkles and whelks from Courseulles and St-Vaast. Any selection of seafood may be accompanied by rye bread, slightly salted butter and a glass of dry cider.

The many different varieties of fish – sole, turbot and mackerel to mention only a few – are often served with a delicious sauce.

Local pastries, which are all made with butter, include apple turnovers (*chaussons aux pommes*), flat cakes baked in the oven (*falues or fouaces*), biscuits (*galettes*), shortbread (*sablés*) and buns (*brioches*). Those who have a sweet tooth will enjoy the Calvados-flavoured cream chocolates from Caen and Putanges, the caramels (*chiques and balivernes*) from Isigny and the boiled sweets (*berlingots*) from Bayeux, Caen and Falaise, not to mention the scrumptious Rouen sugar apples. *Douillons* are pears hollowed out and filled with butter, wrapped in pastry and baked.

CREAM AND NORMANDY SAUCE

Cream is the mainstay of the Normandy kitchen: ivory in colour, velvety in texture and mellow in taste, it goes as well with eggs and fish as with chicken, white meat, vegetables and even game. This delicious cream is at its best in the so-called Normandy Sauce (*sauce normande*), which elsewhere is nothing but a plain white sauce, but in Normandy both looks and tastes quite different.

CHEESE

If cream is the queen of Normandy cooking, cheese is the king of all fare. Pont-l'évêque has reigned since the 13C; Livarot is quoted in texts of the same period; the world renowned Camembert first appeared early in the 19C.

To be really creamy and soft, a **Pont-l'évêque** should be made on a farm in the Pays d'Auge when the milk is still warm from the cow. **Livarot**, whose strong odour may alarm the uninitiated, is made from milk which has been left to stand. Although cheeses claiming to be **Camembert** are now made in factories all over France, only Normandy Camembert is authentic.

The Normandy cheeseboard also includes fresh cheeses from the Pays de Bray – the **bondons**, demi-sel or double cream – whose repute is more recent but nonetheless firmly established.

Originally a local product, like the **Neufchâtel** in its various forms, the **petit-suisse** was also a much appreciated farmhouse cheese. Neufchâtel cheese can be eaten within only 12 days of being made, although a mature Neufchâtel takes up to three months.

Le Trou Normand

In the middle of a generous repast, the people of Normandy are prone to take a small break, often accompanied by a glass of Calvados: this is the famous *trou normand* (Norman hole) that revives the appetite of the most satiated guests. Nowadays, in restaurants, an apple sorbet doused with Calvados has replaced the traditional *trou normand*. This said, at the end of the meal, coffee can still be liberally spiked with the brandy!

CIDER

Apple orchards have always been a characteristic feature of the Normandy landscape and cider has been made locally since the Middle Ages when it took second place to barley beer. Although most of the cider now made in Normandy is manufactured in huge factories, it is still possible to find a farmhouse brew distilled in the traditional way.

The apples are gathered in huge baskets then stored for a short while before being emptied into a circular granite trough, where they are crushed by a round wooden mill-stone pulled by a horse. The crushed apples (*marc*) are transferred to the press, where they are laid between layers of rye straw and then pressed; the juice runs out at the bottom onto a flat surface from which it is drained into the surrounding gutter and is then drawn off through a spout. After pressing, the rye straw is extracted and the apple pulp is put to soak in a vat before being pressed a second time. The first pressing produces pure cider juice; subsequent pressings produce a weaker brew which is kept for use on the farm. Whether it is *brut* (dry, strongly flavoured with apple with an alcohol content of 4-5%), *demi-sec* or *doux* (made artificially sweet by stalling the fermentation process when the alcohol content reaches 2.5-3%), cider is the perfect accompaniment for both gastronomic dinners and lighter meals such as pancakes or desserts made with apples. It should always be served chilled.

When it matures, cider loses its sweetness and takes on a distinctive, earthy flavour. The fruity quality of cider is best preserved when it is stored in a cool cellar, where the temperature does not exceed 15°C/59°F, and it should be drunk in the months following its purchase. Bottles that have travelled or remained lying horizontally should be left to rest for a while before being opened. The most famous *appellation* is the Cidre de la Vallée d'Auge, which is subject to strict controls and tastings. It covers five different *crus*: Blangy-le-Château-Pont-l'Évêque, Cambremer, Lisieux-Orbec, Livarot and Vimoutiers.

CALVADOS

Calvados, or *calva* as it is better known, is a cider brandy made from a mash of apples fermented with yeast; it is distilled twice and matured in oak for six to ten years. The use of the name Calvados, from one of the regions which produces this brandy, probably dates from the early 19C, although cider brandy was first mentioned in the 16C; it was made by Gilles de Gouverville in a little village in the Cotentin. The tradition of the *trou normand* (Norman hole – *see above*) is still observed; during a heavy meal a small glass of Calvados is swallowed at one go to help the digestion. Restaurants often serve an apple and calvados sorbet instead. Calvados is usually drunk after coffee, one or two glasses; for just a taste, eat a sugar lump dipped in Calvados. The AOC label for Calvados dates from 1942 and applies to two *appellations*: Calvados and Calvados du Pays d'Auge. A great many distilleries and storehouses are open to the public.

PERRY

Perry (*poiré*), is similar to cider but is made from pears and usually comes from the areas around Mortain and Domfront.

POMMEAU

This alcoholic beverage is made by mixing two thirds of apple juice with one third of Calvados and features an alcohol content of 16-18%. The ageing process is carried out in oak casks for a period of 18 months. In 1991 it was officially awarded an AOC label *(appellation d'origine contrôlée)* on account of its excellent taste and outstanding qualities. It can be drunk chilled as an apéritif (without ice) and served with dried apples. It can also be drunk at room temperature to accompany oysters (warm oysters with Normandy Pommeau), foie gras, melon or dessert (especially apple pie). When it is used in cooking, its full flavour matures and delicately enhances the flavour of the dish.

Mont-St-Michel

© Dieter Basse

DISCOVERING NORMANDY

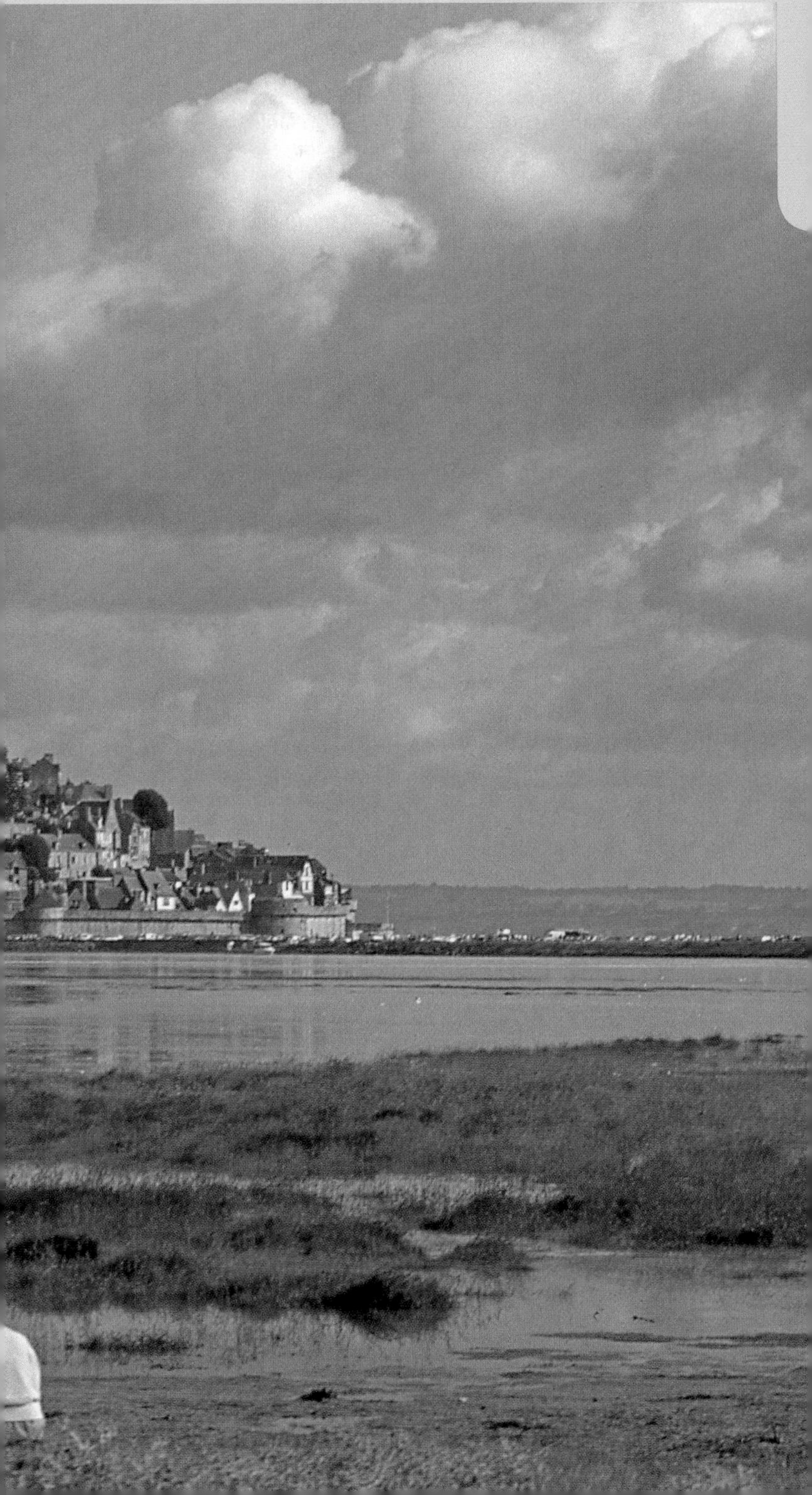

L'AIGLE

ORNE, POPULATION: 8 972 – MICHELIN MAP 310: M-2

L'Aigle is at its best on Tuesday, when it holds the third largest market in France. One of the main towns in the Upper Risle Valley, l'Aigle is a centre for traditional metalwork industries: steel drawing mills produce pins, needles, staples and more. The historic centre is place St-Martin, with its attractive church.

- **Information:** Place Fulbert-de-Benna, 61300 L'Aigle, ☎02 33 24 12 40. www. paysdelaigle.com. The tourist office has a practical brochure available, which describes a walking tour through town (allow 1hr 30min) and a longer walk around the 15 neighbouring cantons. ⊜1€.
- ▶ **Orient Yourself:** L'Aigle lies between the Pays d'Ouche and the Perche, on the road linking Dreux, 59km/39mi to the east, to Argentan. Lisieux is only 56km/35mi northwest on D 519.
- 🅿 **Parking:** You will find parking on the public squares: de la Halle, de l'Europe, de Verdun and de Bois-Landry.
- ⊛ **Don't Miss:** The Tuesday market; the museum of La Grosse Forge at Aube.
- 🕓 **Organizing Your Time:** Give yourself a half-day at l'Aigle before visiting the museums at Aube.
- 🅺🅸🅳🆂 **Especially for Kids:** The museum of the Comtesse de Ségur (1799–1874), France's most famous children's author, and the machinery at the Grosse Forge museum at Aube.
- ♿ **Also See:** The Perche nature park and the villages of Mortagne-au-Perche, Verneuil-sur-Avre, Conches-en-Ouche, Bernay and Vimoutiers.

Sights

Église St-Martin

An elaborate late-15C square tower contrasts with a small 12C one built of red iron agglomerate (*grison*) and sur-mounted by a more recent spire. Beautiful modern statues stand in niches between the windows of the south nave, added in the 16C.

Above the high altar (1656) is a beautiful carved wooden altarpiece, consisting of four twisted columns capped by Corinthian capitals and decorated with vine leaves, bunches of grapes and cherubs. The central composition, attributed to

---

Address Book

♿*For coin ranges see the Legend on the cover flap.*

WHERE TO EAT

⊜ **Le Manoir de Villers** – *61550 Villers-en-Ouche, 9km/5.6mi N of St-Évroult via D 230 dir Bocquencé. ☎02 33 43 98 00. http://perso.wanadoo.fr/ le.manoir.Closed Jan, Tue, Wed and Thu, except for hotel guests. Reservations suggested.* This 17C farm includes an equestrian centre and small hotel, as well as the restaurant. The proprietors offer their native Italian cuisine, with delicious home-made pasta, served in friendly, rustic surroundings.

WHERE TO STAY

⊜⊜**Hôtel du Dauphin** – *Place de la Halle. ☎02 33 84 18 00. regis.ligot@ free.fr* 🅿*30 rooms.* ⊡*10€. Restaurant* ⊜⊜. The oldest of these two buildings was already a hotel in 1618. The rooms are comfortable, with a mixture of old and modern furniture. A shops sells local products, while the restaurant offers a daily menu in the pleasant dining room. A nice, old-fashioned Renaissance sort of place.

Lebrun, a celebrated artist under Louis XIV, shows the Descent from the Cross.

Château

The château, which houses the town hall and two museums, was built in 1690 on the site of an 11C fortress, by Fulbert de Beina, Lord of L'Aigle and vassal of the dukes of Normandy. He is said to have discovered an eagle's nest on the site, hence the name of the town. The plans were the work of Mansart (Jules Hardouin 1646-1708), who designed the Château of Versailles for Louis XIV.

Musée des Instruments de Musique

🕐Open Mon-Fri 8.30-noon, 1.30-5pm (Fri 4pm). 🕐Closed public holidays. ➾No charge. ☎02 33 84 16 16.

A double spiral staircase leads to the first floor of the museum. A collection of musical instruments, the gift of a former bandmaster, includes an archaic bass wind instrument known as a serpent used in military music.

Musée Juin 44 : bataille de Normandie

♿🕐 Open May–Sept Tue, Wed, weekends and holidays 2-6pm .🕐Closed Aug 15. ➾3.60€ (under 15 years old, 1.80€). ☎02 33 24 99 44.

Located beside the castle, the Battle of Normandy Museum contains wax figures of De Gaulle, Churchill, Leclerc, Roosevelt, Stalin etc. and their recorded voices. The Battle of Normandy is represented on a relief map and events are traced on dioramas. A small archeological museum houses some interesting objects.

Excursion

St-Sulpice-sur-Risle

3km/2mi NE by D 930. 🕐Open Mon–Fri 3-5pm, telephone beforehand. ☎02 33 24 15 76 The **church** adjoins the 13C priory, which was partially rebuilt in the 16C.

Among its artworks are a 16C tapestry, a 17C painting of St Cecilia, a statue of St Anne and two stained-glass windows from the 13C and 14C.

Aube

Musée de la Comtesse de Ségur

Kids 7km/4mi SW of L'Aigle by N 26. 3 rue de l'Abbé-Derry 🕐Open mid-June–Sept daily except Tue, 2–6pm. Wed in June and Sept 4–6pm (last entry 5pm) 🕐Closed public holidays. ➾4€ (6-12 years old 1.50€). Ticket combined with Grosse Forge 6€(children 2€). ☎02 33 24 60 09. www.musee-comtessedesegur.com.

Musée de la Grosse Forge d'Aube

Kids rue de la Vieille-Forge. 🕐Open mid-June to end of Sept daily except Tue, 2–6pm. Wed in June and Sept 2-4pm (last entry 1hr before closing) ➾guided audio tours (45min) every hr. ➾4€(6-12 years old 1.50€). ☎02 33 24 60 09.

The **Château des Nouettes**, now a medico-pedagogical institute, was once the residence of Countess Eugène de Ségur.

In the former presbytery at the foot of the church stands the **Musée de la Comtesse de Ségur** which contains exhibits evoking the life and literary career of the countess. Characters from the writer's novels are represented by a collection of dolls and exhibits (toys, games, books, furniture etc).

On the River Risle, as you leave Aube towards L'Aigle, stands the **Musée de la Grosse Forge d'Aube**, which retraces five centuries of metallurgy. This museum has changed very little since the 17C. Note the furnace for refining metals, the massive camshaft hammer and the wooden bellows (a 1995 replica) operated by a paddle wheel.

ALENÇON ★

ORNE, POPULATION: 28 935

MICHELIN MAP 310: J-4 – LOCAL MAP ALPES MANCELLES

A royal lace manufactory under Louis XIV, Alençon has a rich architectural heritage, a Fine Arts Museum with a collection of lace work and paintings from the 15C-19C, and pleasant waterways and gardens surrounding the pedestrian town centre. Alençon was liberated on 12 August 1944 due to the decisive role of the French 2nd armoured division in the battle of the Falaise-Mortain Pocket.

- **Information:** Maison d'Ozé, place de la Magdelaine, 61000 Alençon. ☎02 33 80 66 33. www.paysdalencontourisme.com.
- ▶ **Orient Yourself:** From Alençon, roads lead to Paris (195km/122mi east via N 12), and to Brittany, Belgium and Spain. The A 28 leads to LeMans (58km/36mi to the south) and to Rouen (160km/100mi to the north).
- **Don't Miss:** The little villages of the Alpes Mancelles, especially St-Léonard-des-Bois and St-Cénéri-le-Gérei.
- **Organizing Your Time:** Take a half-day in the town, then enjoy the lovely countryside in the forest of Perseigne or in the Alpes Mancelles.
- **Especially for Kids:** At St-Léonard-des-Bois, the domaine of Gasseau offers nature hikes under the trees.
- **Also See:** Argentan, the national stud at Pin, the château of Carrouges, Sées, Fresnay-sur-Sarthe, Sillé-le-Guillaume and Bagnoles-de-l'Orne.

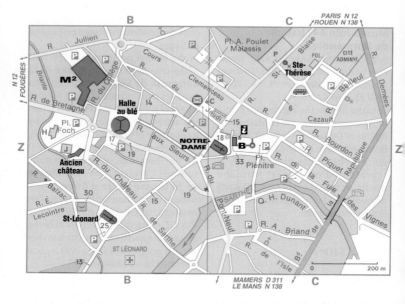

ALENÇON			Fresnay R. de	BZ	13	La Magdelaine Pl.	CZ	18
			Grande-Rue	BZ	15	Marguerite-de-Lorraine Pl.	BZ	25
Bercail R. du	BZ	4	Grandes-Poteries R. des	BZ	14	Porte-de-la-Barre R.	BZ	30
Capucins R. des	CZ	6	Halle-au-Blé Pl. de la	BZ	17	Poterne R. de la	CZ	33
Clemenceau Cours	BCZ		Lattre-de-Tassigny R. du Mar.-de	BCZ	19	Sieurs R. aux	BZ	

Maison d'Ozé	CZ	BMusée des Beaux-Arts et de la Dentelle	BZ M²

From the Venice Point to the Alençon Point

Around 1650, Madame de la Perrière perfected the Venice Point, very fashionable at the time in all the European courts, and taught her skill to the young women of Alençon. As a result, lacemaking developed and soon 8 000 people were involved in the manufacture of point lace. In order to keep up with fashion, men and women were tempted to spend large sums of money and to buy lace abroad, which prompted Colbert in 1665 to ban imported lace and to establish a royal factory in Alençon to produce French point lace. The needlewomen of Alençon subsequently developed their own style based on a specific technique and a new pattern consisting of delicate motifs arranged in close symmetry on a plain background. This was the origin of Alençon lace which, by the end of the 17C, was the only one in fashion. The Atelier National du Point d'Alençon (National Workshop of Alençon Lace, not open to the public) has preserved this ancient tradition of needlepoint lace, acknowledged in the 19C as the best lace.

Sights

Musée des Beaux-Arts et de la Dentelle★

Open July–mid-Sept daily 10am–noon, 2–6pm. Sept–June daily except Mon 10am–noon, 2–6pm. Closed 1 Jan, 1 May, 25 Dec. 3.05€ (no charge under 18 and on 1st Sun of the month). ☎02 33 32 40 07.

Located in the former Jesuit college (17C), the Museum of Fine Arts and Lace houses paintings from the 15C to the 19C as well as collections of lace. The French and Nordic Schools of the 17C are well represented with canvases by Philippe de Champaigne, Jean Jouvenet, Allegrain, Voet, Ryckaert, Wyck. There is also a fine selection of 19C French painting with works by Boudin, Courbet, Fantin-Latour, Lacombe, Laurens, Legros, Veyrassat etc.

The presentation of the **lace collection**★ offers a broad review of the principal lacemaking centres in Italy and France. Its display of Alençon lace, which uses a needlepoint technique unique in France, includes the elegant creations of the Alençon lacemakers from the 17C to the present day.

There is also a collection of Cambodian objects brought back by **Adhémar Leclère** (1853-1917), a native of Alençon and 19C governor of Cambodia.

Église Notre-Dame★

Allow at least 15min. Open daily 9:30am–noon, 2–6pm. In June–Aug, guided tours available, ask at the tourist office.

The beautiful 14C-15C Flamboyant Gothic Church of Our Lady was begun during the Hundred Years War. The tower, transept and chancel were rebuilt in the 18C. The elegant three-sided **porch**★, built by Jean Lemoine from 1490 to 1506, is an example of the purest Flamboyant style. All the decoration is concentrated on the upper parts of the church. The Transfiguration in the central gable shows Christ with the Prophets Moses and Elijah; below are the Apostles Peter, James and John, with their backs to the street.

Inside, the sweeping lines of the nave rise to the lierne and tierceron **vaulting** which is highly decorated. The lines of the triforium merge with those of the

Descent from the cross, Église Notre-Dame

E. Lambere/MICHELIN

Address Book

For coin ranges see the Legend on the cover flap.

WHERE TO EAT

Le Saint-Léo – *Pl. de l'Église, 72130 St-Léonard-des-Bois. ☎02 43 33 81 34. lesrleo@aol.com. Closed Wed off-season and Tue .* A simple, convivial halt in this picturesque village in the Alpes Mancelles. The dining room faces the Sarthe and offers local fare with an accent on fresh ingredients, galettes and crepes.

Auberge Normande – *Le Pont-du-Londeau, 61250 Valframbert. ☎02 33 29 43 29. www.chateau-des-requetes.com. Closed 1 May, 24-25 Dec, Sun evening and Mon. Reservations suggested.* This restaurant is often fully booked for lunch; the locals appreciate the updated regional cuisine and reasonable prices.

Le Chapeau Rouge – *117 r. de Bretagne. ☎02 33 26 57 53. Closed Fri evening, Sat noon and Sun .* A luminous range of yellow tones on the walls, flamboyant tablecloths and straw-bottomed chairs compose the emphatically cheerful decor of this restaurant hidden behind a stone façade. Well-prepared traditional cuisine and a few dishes blending sweet and savoury flavours.

Au Petit Vatel – *72 place Cdt-Desmeules. ☎02 33 26 23 78. Closed 27 July–10 Aug, Sun evening and Wed.* There is nothing "petit" about the cuisine of this restaurant with its pleasantly rustic decor, where the chef offers traditional fare enlivened by regional touches.
One menu is devoted entirely to Norman specialities.

WHERE TO STAY

Hôtel Marmotte – *Les Grouas– 61250 Valframbert, 1km/.6mi N of Alençon centre, dir. Dreux. ☎02 33 27 42 64 . 46 rooms. 5.40€. Restaurant .* Since the town centre offers limited accomodation, head towards the outskirts where you will find this traditional family hotel. Its rooms offer contemporary furnishings and modern plumbing. A good base from which to explore the area.

La Garencière Bed and Breakfast– *72610 Champfleur 6.5km/4mi SE of Alençon dir Mamers and Champfleur via D 19, then towards Bourg-le-Roi. ☎02 33 31 75 84. denis.langlais@ wanadoo.fr. Closed Jan. 5 rooms. Restaurant .* At the time of the Crusades, this hamlet was the fief of the knights of Garencière and a stop on the pilgramage route to Compostelle in Spain. Today, you will enjoy the prettily decorated rooms and the covered swimming pool facing the countryside. Billiards room and second-hand crockery on sale to guests.

Le Moulin de Linthe Bed and Breakfast – *Rte de Sougé-le-Ganelon, 72130 St-Léonard-des-Bois. ☎02 43 33 79 22. Closed Jan–Feb. 5 rooms. 8.50€.* The bedrooms have character in this old mill which looks quite picturesque even if its paddle wheel no longer turns. Amateur anglers can fish for trout or pike in the River Sarthe.

Château de Sarceaux – *61250 Valframbert. ☎02 33 28 85 11. sarceaux@wanadoo.fr. Closed Jan. . 5 rooms. .* A large park with a pond surrounds this château built in the 17C and 19C. The south-facing rooms are elegantly decorated with antique furniture and family portraits. Candlelight dinners in the guest dining room, with classic cuisine.

SHOWTIME

La Luciole – *171 rte de Bretagne. ☎02 33 32 83 33. www.laluciole.org. Opening times follow the calendar of performances - Closed Aug, Sun and Mon.* This music hall is no doubt the locals' favourite haunt, with more than 70 concerts each year. Pop-rock is the main genre, but both established and aspiring young groups of all horizons perform here.

clerestory to form a unified whole. Note the admirable **stained glass**★ by the master-glaziers of Alençon and the Maine region. The glass in the clerestory windows dates from 1530.

The first chapel off the north aisle is where Marie-Françoise-Thérèse Martin (1873-1897) was baptised. She is better known as St Therese of Lisieux.

In place de La Magdelaine, to the left of the church, is the attractive 15C **Maison d'Ozé** (Ozé House), now the Tourist Information Centre, where the future king Henri IV is said to have stayed in 1576.

Additional Sights

Ancien Château

From place Foch, you can see the 14C and 15C towers of the old castle, built by Jean II le Beau, first Duke of Alençon and ally of Joan of Arc. The central tower, known as the crowned tower, has an unexpected outline: the main tower with machicolations is itself crowned by a slimmer, round tower. The other two towers, which defend the main gate, can be seen from rue du Château. The fortress is used as a prison.

Halle au Blé

Built at the beginning of the 19C, this circular grain market was covered towards the end of the century with a glass dome which the ladies of the town nicknamed the hoopskirt of Alençon. It is today a cultural centre.

Église St-Léonard

Apply to the presbytery to visit. ☎02 33 26 20 89.

The rebuilding of the present church was begun in 1489 by René, second Duke of Alençon, and was completed in 1505 by his widow, Marguerite de Lorraine.

Nearby (*no 10 rue Porte-de-la-Barre*) is a 15C house (Maison à l'Étal) with a slate-hung façade.

Chapelle Ste-Thérèse

⏱*Open year-round.* •Visit by guided tour (30–45min) June–Sept daily 9am–noon, 2–6pm. Oct–May open daily except Tue 9.30am–noon, 2.30–7pm. ⏱*Closed Jan.* ✉*No charge.* ☎02 33 26 09 87.

Opposite the Préfecture, a fine 17C building and former military headquarters, a double staircase leads to the chapel which adjoins the house where St Therese of Lisieux was born on 2 January 1873.

⏱*The itinerary known as L'Encerclement (The Encircling Movement), one of several in the Historical Area of the Battle of Normandy, runs from Alençon to L'Aigle, tracing the progress of the 2nd Armoured Division under General Leclerc.*

Driving Tour

Forêt de Perseigne★

Round trip – 53km/33mi – allow about about 3hr.

▶ *From Alençon take D 311 SE in the direction of Chartres. Beyond Le Buisson turn left onto D 236. After 4km/2mi turn sharp right onto a forest road towards Aillières-Beauvoir and right again towards Ancinnes; at the Rond de Croix-Pergeline turn left by a milestone to Gros Houx.*

La Belle Échappée

8 rue de la Forêt de Perseigne, La Fresnaye-sur-Chédouet. 🎫♿⏱*Open April–Sept daily except Mon and Tue 10am–noon, 2–7pm. Rest of the year daily except Mon and Tue (last entrance 1hr before closing).* ⏱*Closed 25 Dec–1 Jan.* ✉*5€ (children: 3€).* ☎02 43 34 39 11.

⚲ Exhibitions retrace the history of cycling and of its great champions.

▶ *At the Carrefour des Trois-Ponts turn left uphill.*

The road enters the picturesque **Vallée d'Enfer** (Hell Valley). The tower-belvedere (30m/90ft high) is the highest point (349m/1 145ft) in the Sarthe district.

⚑*There are 8km/5mi of waymarked paths round the belvedere and in Hell Valley.*

▶ *Take D 234 SE to the twin villages Aillières-Beauvoir and take D 116 S via Villaines-la-Carelle. At the crossroads with D 311 continue SW on D 310.*

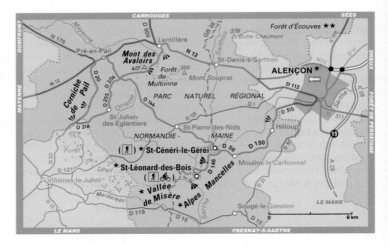

Chapelle Notre-Dame-de-Toutes-Aides

The doorway of this graceful pilgrimage chapel is surmounted by a Virgin and Child. Above the 17C altarpiece is an Assumption; below is a painting of the Annunciation.

▶ *In St-Rémy-du-Val turn right in front of the church onto the road to Neuf-châtel-en-Saosnois (D 117). Turn left onto D 165. From Ancinnes take D 19 to Alençon.*

The Alpes Mancelles★

82km/51mi – about 3hr round-trip from Alençon (excluding the Misère Valley). The Alpes Mancelles is part of the Normandie-Maine Regional Park.

▶ *On leaving Alençon take N 12 W via St-Denis-sur-Sarthe; in Lentillère turn left towards Champfrémont; then bear right to Mont des Avaloirs.*

Mont des Avaloirs

A belvedere marks the summit (417m/1 368ft), one of the highest points in western France.

▶ *At the second crossroads turn left onto D 204 and then fork right onto D 255. In St-Julien-des-Églantiers turn right onto D 245, then right onto D 218 and right again onto D 20.*

Corniche du Pail

The road, which climbs slowly, provides a view over the Mayenne basin.

▶ *In Pré-en-Pail take N 12 E and D 144 S via St-Pierre-des-Nids.*

St-Céneri-le-Gérei★

This village has a charming setting: hilltop Romanesque church, bridge spanning the Sarthe and stone houses.

▶ *From St-Céneri-le-Gérei take D 56 S; turn right onto D 146.*

St-Léonard-des-Bois★

This village is an ideal excursion centre for the Alpes Mancelles.

Vallée de Misère★

Round trip - 1hr 30min on foot.
On the church square take the path from the corner by the Hôtel Bon Laboureur. At the crossroads marked by a stone cross take a path uphill. Beyond Le Champ-des-Pasfore turn left. At the next crossroads turn left onto a path marked in red and white. From a bench there is an attractive **view**★ of the wild Misère Valley, St-Léonard and the Manoir de Linthe farther downstream.

▶ *From St-Léonard-des-Bois take D 146 N. Turn right onto D 56; in Moulins-le-Carbonnel turn left onto D 150 which becomes D 315, which will take you back to Alençon.*

LES ANDELYS ★★

EURE, POPULATION: 9 049

MICHELIN MAP 304: I-6 – LOCAL MAP SEE VALLÉE DE LA SEINE

Les Andelys, dominated by the impressive ruins of Château-Gaillard, lies in a lovely setting along the Seine. It once consisted of two distinct areas, Le Petit-Andely to the west and Le Grand-Andely to the east. The latter was the site of a 6C monastery founded by Clotilde, who converted her husband, King Clovis, to Christianity. At a fountain at 29 rue Ste-Clotilde, she is said to have turned water into wine for the workmen building the monastery chapel.

- **Information:** 24 rue Philippe-Auguste, 2770 Les Andelys. ☎02 32 54 41 93. www.ville-andelys.fr
- ▶ **Orient Yourself:** The two Andelys are linked by avenue de la République and the rue du Maréchal-Leclerc. Paris is 100km/63mi away, and Rouen 40km/25mi.
- **Don't Miss:** The view of the Seine valley from the heights of the château.
- **Organizing Your Time:** Visit the château in the morning, then enjoy Les Andelys and its surroundings.
- **Especially for Kids:** Children will be thrilled by the massive fortress.
- **Also See:** Lyons-la-Forêt, Gisors, Vernon, Giverny and Louviers.

A Bit of History

In 1196 **Richard Lionheart**, King of England and Duke of Normandy, decided to bar the King of France's way to Rouen along the Seine Valley by building a massive fortress on the cliff commanding the river at Andely. Work progressed so rapidly that within the year Château-Gaillard was erected and Richard was able to cry aloud "See my fine yearling!"

Despite his boldness, **Philippe Auguste**, king of France, did not at first dare attack so formidable a redoubt. But when Richard I was succeeded in 1199 by the vacillating King John, the French went into action. When a seige of the castle stalled, the French filled in the moat, mined the walls and took the castle by storm on 6 March 1203.

Three months later Rouen, too, had fallen to the French king.

Château-Gaillard ★★

Allow 1hr. To reach the château by car: from Grand-Andely, follow the signs from rue Louis-Pasteur. On foot (allow 30min ascent): from Petit-Andely, follow the rue Richard-Coeur-de-Lion, near the

Office de Tourisme. Open mid-Mar to mid-Nov daily except Tue 10am–1pm, 2–6pm (last entry 1hr before closing). Closed 1 May. 3€(under 10 years no charge). ☎02 32 54 41 93 (Office de Tourisme).

From the car park there is a **view**★★ of the castle, the Seine and Les Andelys.

Barbican

The redoubt, separated from the main castle by a deep moat, possessed five towers of which only one, the barbican, remains, encircled by a narrow path.

Castle

The outer ward, the esplanade, is situated between the redoubt and the castle. Around the wall to the left are the foundations of the keep which rises from the natural rock. At the far end of the wall there is a fine viewpoint.

By returning along the bottom of the moat, one passes in front of casemates (*right*) hollowed out of the rock to store the garrison's food supplies. The keep is round (8m/26ft in internal diameter) and has thick walls (5m/16ft). Formerly it had three floors linked by mobile wooden ladders. Adjoining (*right*) are the ruins of the Governor's residence.

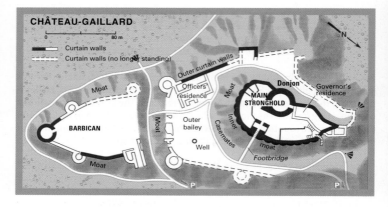

CHÂTEAU-GAILLARD

Inside a path leads to the edge of the rocky escarpment which provides an extended view of the Seine Valley.

▶ *Take the one-way descent to rue Richard-Cœur-de-Lion to return to the town.*

Additional Sights

Église Notre-Dame★

A well-balanced façade of twin towers flanked by a square staircase tower fronts Notre-Dame Church. The 16C south side is a good example of the Flamboyant style and the 16C and 17C north side is Renaissance in style with round arches, Ionic pilasters, balustraded roofs, caryatids and Antique-style statues.

Inside, the well-proportioned nave is 13C; the delicately ornamented triforium was remodelled in the 16C and the windows enlarged; the **organ★** and loft are Renaissance. In the north transept and a nearby chapel are two lovely paintings by Quentin Varin, teacher of Nicholas Poussin. The Entombment in the south aisle beneath the tower is 16C, the Christ in the Tomb is 14C.

Église St-Sauveur

St Saviour's is Greek cross in ground plan and Gothic in style; the chancel is late 12C, the nave early 13C. The wooden porch stands on an early-15C stone foundation. Inside there is an organ dating from 1674.

Address Book

WHERE TO EAT

🍽🍽 **De Paris** – *10 av. de la République.* ☎*02 32 54 00 31. www.giverny.org.* Attractive residence from the early 20C, with a restaurant in a style part bourgeois, part rustic. A few simple rooms are also available.

🍽🍽🍽 **La Chaîne d'Or** – *27 r. Grande.* ☎*02 32 54 00 31. www.planete-b.fr/la-chaine-d-or. Closed 1 Jan–4 Feb, Sun evening, Tue lunch, Mon and Tue in Nov–Mar.* This pleasant house on the banks of the Seine offers lovely views of the river. Try for a window seat, but wherever your table, you will enjoy the renowned cuisine. Rooms are available.

WHERE TO STAY

🛏 **Mme Vard Bed and Breakfast** – *29 r. de l'Huis, village of Surcy, 27510 Mézières-en-Vexin, 13km/8mi SE of Les Andelys via D 1.* ☎*02 32 52 30 04. Closed Nov–Mar. 4 rooms.* 🍴. Fresh air, peace and quiet, plus the charm of a bustling farm. Although the house's façade is rather glum, the old furniture, fine half-timbered stairway and rustic bedrooms make for an authentic sojourn. Farm products for sale.

Musée Normandie-Niémen

🕐*Open June to mid-Sept daily except Tue 10am–noon, 2–6pm. Rest of the year daily except Tue 2–6pm.* 🕐*Closed 1 Jan, 1 May, 24, 25 and 31 Dec.* 👁3.50€ *(children 1€).* ☎*02 32 54 49 76.*

"The 'Normandy Regiment', my companion in arms, upholds, confirms and increases the glory of France on Russian soil as on French soil for they have both suffered at the hand of a common enemy!" General de Gaulle wrote these words in Moscow on 9 December 1944 to pay homage to the **Normandie-Niémen squadron**. Two galleries are devoted to Marcel Lefèvre.

ARGENTAN

ORNE, POPULATION: 16 596 – MICHELIN MAP 310: I-2

From its hillside site, the small town of Argentan overlooks the confluence of the River Orne and the River Ure. The marked itinerary known as L'Encerclement (The Encircling Movement), one of several in the Historical Area of the Battle of Normandy, goes through this town.

- **Information:** Chapelle St-Nicholas, 6 place du Marché, 61200 Argentan.☎02 33 67 12 48. www.argentan.fr
- ▶ **Orient Yourself:** Argentan lies on the River Orne, surrounded by forests, between Flers and Alençon, each 45km/28mi away.
- **Don't Miss:** Examples of local lacemaking at the Maison des dentelles and at the Benedictine abbey. Also, visit the château of Bourg-St-Léonard.
- 🕐 **Organizing Your Time:** Spend a morning in town, then visit one of the châteaux.
- **Also See:** The town of Falais, the national stud at Pin, Sées, the château at Carrouges, Bagnoles-de-l'Orne and the Suisse Normande.

A Bit of History

From Kingly Disputes to Lacemaking – It was in Argentan in the 12C that the papal legates assembled to settle the disagreement between the English king, Henry II Plantagenet, and his chancellor, Thomas Becket, Archbishop of Canterbury. The assassins of the sainted archbishop set out from here to accomplish their dire deed.

Although Colbert set up a lace factory in Alençon, he did not neglect the lacemakers of Argentan. The rediscovery of 18C lace patterns for the Point d'Argentan in 1874 enabled the characteristic Argentan pattern to regain its popularity.

Battle of Normandy – In 1944 the closing stages of the Battle of Normandy were fought around Argentan. Following the success of the American breakthrough at Avranches and the failure of the German counter-attack of 7 August, the enemy rear-guard was vulnerable. On 13 August the French 2nd Armoured Division at Écouché together with the American 5th Armoured Division in the Argentan sector formed the southern arm of the pincer action. When the Canadians took Falaise on 17 August, the German 7th Army retreated via Dives Valley. A chaotic rush ensued. On 19 August the allied troops met at Chambois and by nightfall (6.30pm) on 21 August the fall of Tournai-sur-Dive marked the final stage in the Battle of Normandy.

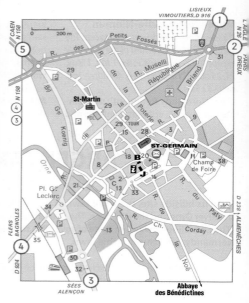

ARGENTAN	
104e-Régiment- d'Infanterie R. du	38
2e-Division-Blindée Av. de la	35
Beigle R. du	2
Boschet R. P.	3
Carnot Bd	7
Chaussée R. de la	8
Collège R. du	9
Forêt-Normande Av. de la	13
Gaulle Bd Général-de	14
Griffon R. du	15
Henri-IV Pl.	18
Marché Pl. du	20
Panthou R. E.	21
St-Germain R.	28
St-Martin R.	29
Semard Pl. Pierre	30
Trois-Croix Pl. des	31
Victor-Hugo Bd	32
Vimal-du-Bouchet Pl.	33
Wolf R. J.	34

Ancienne chapelle St-Nicolas	B
Château (Palais de Justice)	J

Visit

Église St-Germain★

Open June–Aug Mon, Wed, Thu, Fri 10.30am–noon, 2.30–6pm, Tue and Sun 2–6pm. Closed Sat. ☎02 33 67 12 48 (Office du Tourisme).

The church, badly damaged by shelling in 1944, was built in the Flamboyant style from the 15C to the 17C.

Walk round the church clockwise to view the unusual pentagonal east end (16C) and the unusual circular chapels terminating the transepts. At the base of the belfry a fine Flamboyant **porch** opens on to rue St-Germain.

Additional Sights

Château

Not open to visitors. The castle now serves as the Law Courts. This imposing rectangular castle, flanked by two square towers, was built in 1370 by Pierre II, Count of Alençon.

Ancienne Chapelle St-Nicolas

The chapel, which was built in 1773, belonged to the castle. Marguerite de

Lorraine, founder of the monastery of Ste-Claire, took her vows here.

The Tourist Information Centre occupies the ground floor, and the first floor houses a lovely carved 17C altarpiece (displayed on request).

Église St-Martin

Guided tours by appointment with the Tourist Office. ☎02 33 67 12 48.

The church, which was damaged in 1944, is dominated by an octagonal tower surmounted by a decapitated spire. The overall style is Flamboyant Gothic but presents several Renaissance innovations.

The Point d'Argentan (Argentan Lace Stitch)

Take boulevard du Général-de-Gaulle and rue de la Noë SE, following signs to Abbaye des Bénédictines.

Benedictine Abbey

Open daily except Sun and public holidays 2.30-4pm. 2€(children no charge). Closed one week in Aug. ☎02 33 67 12 01. The enclosed order of nuns has exclusive rights to the Argentan stitch, a needlepoint lace comprising a variety of motifs on a honeycomb-like background.

There are no workshops, but one can ask to see specimens illustrating steps in the working of Argentan lace and samples of old and modern needlepoint lace.

Maison des Dentelles

Open Apr to mid-Oct Tue–Sat 9am–noon, 2–6pm, Sun 2–6pm. Closed Mon and public holidays except 14 July and 15 Aug. 3€ (10-18 years 2.30€). Guided tours available. ☎02 33 67 50 78.

This museum presents a charming incursion into the history of lacemaking right up to the present day. A number of dresses and other outfits are on show, many the work of famous designers.

Pays d'Argentan

The region around Argentan is a plain circled by woods: Écouves to the south, Gouffern to the north. The Orne Valley, separating this region from the Pays d'Auge, entered into military history in August 1944.

Meanders of the River Orne 1

32km/19.2mi – 1hr from Argentan and back.

▶ *Leave Argentan travelling SW on D 924.*

Écouché

Church – Open July-Aug daily 2.30-5pm. If it is closed, apply to the Syndicat d'Initiative. ☎02 33 36 88 82.

The 15C-16C **church** was never completed and the ruined 13C nave never rebuilt. The Renaissance triforium in the transepts and the chancel are worthy of note.

▶ *Take D 29 N towards Falaise; turn left.*

Ménil-Glaise★

The **view**★ from the bridge takes in the rock escarpment crowned by a castle on the south bank of the Orne; there is another good view from a terrace.

Address Book

For coin ranges see the Legend on the cover flap.

WHERE TO EAT

Restaurant de Fleuré – *61200 Fleuré, 6.5km/4mi SW if Argentan via D 924 and D 2, rte de Carrouges. ☎02 33 36 10 85. Closed Sun evening, Thu evening and Mon.* In a little village outside Argentan, this family restaurant is a favourite of locals who appreciate the carefully prepared cuisine and cordial ambiance. The menu has both traditional and more elaborate fare, with efficient and welcoming service.

WHERE TO STAY

Le Refuge du P'tit Fischer – *1 place des Trois-Croix. ☎2 33 67 05 43. 17 rooms. ☐ 5.60€. Restaurant.* Just at the entrance to Argentan, on a busy street, this hotel offers modern, fuctional rooms on three storeys, well soundproofed. The restaurant is in the

Alsacien brasserie style, offering coffee and croissants as well.

Pavillon de Gouffern – *61310 Silly-en-Gouffern, 11km/6.8mi E of Argentan via N 26 and D 729. ☎02 33 36 64 26. pavillondegouffern@wanadoo. fr. 20 rooms ☐ 11€. Restaurant.* At this former 19C hunting lodge, you can wake up to birds singing sweetly in the century-old trees. If the hotel exterior is rustic, with typical Norman half-timbering, the renovated interior is chic and contemporary.

LEISURE

Hippodrome d'Argentan – *Rte de Crennes (D 113) 61200 Urou-et-Crennes-☎ 02 33 67 08 02 www.hippodrome-argenton.com. Open for training on Tue, Thu and Fri 8am–1pm.* Vast racecourse where some 20 meetings take place every year. The timetable is available at the tourist office.

▶ *Turn round; continue straight ahead passing (left) the path from the bridge and (right) the Batilly road; turn left onto D 924 to Argentan. 9km/4.4mi S.* ▶*Take N 158 from Argentan.*

St-Christophe-le-Jajolet 2

The village church is a place of pilgrimage to St Christopher, the patron saint of travellers. On the day of pilgrimage *(last Sunday in July and first Sunday of October)* a procession of cars files past.

Château de Sassy

◔*Open Easter to Sept.* ◂◂*guided tour (45min) daily mid-June to mid-Sept 10.30am–12.30pm, 2–6pm; Easter to mid-June and last half Sept, weekends and public holidays 3–6pm.* ◎*6€ (under 12 no charge).* ◎*02 33 35 32 66.*

Building began in 1760, was interrupted by the Revolution and continued in 1817 by the Marquis d'Ommy. In 1850 the château became the property of Étienne-Denis Pasquier (1767-1862), an important political figure. The main salon presents several 17C tapestries and mementoes of Pasquier. The **chapel**, partly hidden by trees, contains a 15C Flemish oak altarpiece carved with scenes from the Passion, formerly in St Bavon Abbey in Ghent.

3 Le Vaudobin

⤒*12km/7mi – plus 15min walk round trip* ◎*on slippery paths.*

▶ *From Argentan take D 916 NE; after 7km/4mi (beyond Gouffern Forest) turn left and cross La Londe. Park near the quarry; take the path left of the quarry entrance.*

The path crosses the Meillon stream, bears left round a large rock and climbs uphill past a rock bearing fossil imprints. From the top of the grassy mound there is a view of the Meillon Gorge and the Dives Valley.

4 Gouffern Forest

About 3hr 30min.

▶ *Leave Argentan to the NE via N 26, then take D 113 to the right.*

As you leave Argentan, the road crosses Gouffern Forest, then winds back down into the Dives Valley.

Chambois

A stele near a central crossroads recalls the joining up of Polish (1st Canadian Army) and American 3rd Army troops

Château de Bourg-St-Léonard

S. Targat/MICHELIN

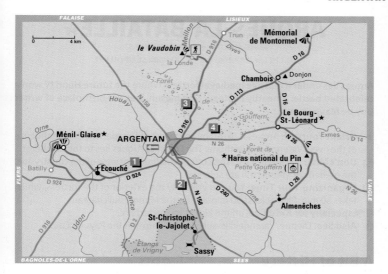

on 19 August 1944 to cut off the retreat of the German 7th Army.

The huge rectangular **keep** (*donjon*) buttressed by four towers is a good example of 12C military architecture. The church has an 11C stone spire and a fine Descent from the Cross.

▸ *Take D 16 uphill to Montormel.*

Mémorial de Montormel

♿ 🚶*Visit by guided tour (1hr) only, May to Sept 9am–6pm. The rest of the year Wed and Sat-Sun 10am–5pm.* 🕐*Closed mid-Dec–mid-Jan.*⊜*4.50€ (children 2€).* ☎*02 33 67 38 61.*

The **Battle of the Chambois Pocket**, raged from 18 to 22 August 1944, causing 10 000 to 12 000 deaths. Marshall Montgomery declared that it marked the "beginning of the end of the war." A monument commemorates the fierce fighting in this sector. From the American tank there is a wide **view**★ over the plain. Two galleries are particularly interesting: in one of them, a large relief map shows the stages of the battle; the other gallery is devoted to the soldiers of the Polish 1st Armoured Division.

Le Bourg-St-Léonard★

11km/8mi E by N 26. Château– ♿🕐*Telephone for opening hours and admission charges.* ☎*02 33 67 10 40.*

The 18C **château** was built by Jules David Cromot while chief of the Treasury under Louis XV. The elegance of its lines and the harmony of its design make it a most attractive building. The interior is embellished with panelling, tapestries and 18C furniture.

Haras national du Pin★

🐎🐴*See Haras national du PIN.* From the stud farm, to the south, you can see the outline of the Écouves Forest.

Almenêches

The Renaissance church used to belong to a Benedictine **abbey**. The altars are decorated with sculptures representing, on the left, the canonisation of St Opportune, a well-known local abbess.

Médavy

Château 🐴*Visit by guided tour (30min) only, July– Aug daily 10am–noon, 2–7pm. May–June and Sept Sun and public hilidays 3–7pm. Park and outbuildings open without tour.* ⊜*6€ (under 14 years 3€).* ☎*02 33 35 05 09.*

A 11C fortified house built to defend the Orne crossing was replaced in the 16C by a stronghold with four corner towers. The site is now occupied by a sombre 18C **château**.

ARQUES-LA-BATAILLE★

SEINE-MARITIME, POPULATION: 2 535
MICHELIN MAP 304: G-2 – 8.5KM/5MI SE OF DIEPPE

Arques lies under a massive medieval fortress where the future Henri IV won a celebrated battle. A nearby château, Miromesnil, was the birthplace of writer Guy de Maupassant.

▶ **Orient Yourself:** Arques is 8km/5mi southeast of Dieppe, near the confluence of the rivers Varenne and Béthune. The Forest of Arques lies to the northeast.

🕉 **Don't Miss:** The medieval fortress offers a magnificent view of the countryside; the gardens of Miromesnil are splendid.

🕐 **Organizing Your Time:** You can visit only the exterior of the fortress, which takes 30 min. Plan at least 90 minutes for the Miromesnil château.

Especially for Kids: Cool off the kids at the waterpark.

🕯 **Also See:** Dieppe, Varengeville-sur-Mer, Fécamp and the Pays de Caux.

A Bit of History

When **Henri IV** was still a king without a kingdom, he possessed the fortress of Arques, said to be "capable of withstanding cannon". He gathered within the ramparts every piece of artillery he could find and dug in, with 7 000 men, to await 30 000 soldiers under the Duke of Mayenne.

The battle took place on 21 September 1589. A fog delayed the artillery action but finally lifted and Henri's cannon thundered into the besiegers. Mayenne, who had promised to bring back his enemy "tied and bound," beat a hasty retreat. In the vicinity of Arques, on the edge of a lake, the recreational centre **Varenne Plein Air** offers facilities for water sports 🚤 and other nautical activities. *Varenne Plein Air, 76510 St-Aubin-le-Cauf. ☎02 35 85 69 05.*

Château d'Arques ruins

Sights

Château★ *Allow 30min.*
From place Desceliers, where the town hall (Mairie) is located, take the second road to the right, uphill to the castle entrance, about 45 min; the road is very narrow, steep and winding. ⚠ *Closed for safety reasons. Admission to the château grounds, no charge.*

The 12C keep occupies the highest point. The earliest part was built between 1038 and 1043. In 1053 it was attacked by William the Conqueror, then reconstructed by Henri I in 1123. Two new towers were added in the 14C. It played a vital role in the wars of religion that raged in the late 16C, as Protestant forces under the future Henri IV repelled the Catholic League in 1589. A triple door leads into the castle. On the back of the last one a carved low relief depicts Henri IV at the Battle of Arques. Follow the old sentry path along the moat to enjoy a view of the Arques Valley.

Église Notre-Dame-de-l'Assomption

Rebuilt around 1515, the Church of Our Lady of the Assumption was given a belfry in the 17C. Inside, the nave was roofed in the 16C with wood cradle vaulting on pendentives. The apse windows are 16C (restored). A chapel to the right of the chancel contains a small bust of Henri IV and an inscription commemo-

G. Targat/MICHELIN

rating the battle. Note a 15C Pietà in the south chapel.

Excursions

Château de Miromesnil★

4km/2.5mi SW of Arques. ♿📷🚗*Visit of château by guided tour (1hr15min) only, Apr – Oct daily 2-6pm.* ☞*6€ (children 4€),* ☞*garden and park 5€ (children 4€).* ☎*02 35 85 02 80. www.chateaumiromesnil.com*

The château was built after the Battle of Arques (1589). Facing the main courtyard is the monumental Louis XIII central façade, capped by a great slate roof.

In the hall there is a display of documents connected with the birth of the great writer Guy de Maupassant in the château on 5 August in 1850.

The **south front**, in the Henri IV style, is flanked by two cylindrical pepper-pot towers; brick predominates with stone trim round the windows and corners.

Beyond a magnificent stand of beech trees is a 16C **chapel**, part of an earlier château. The sober flint and limestone walls contrast with the rich interior decoration dating from 1780.

Jardins et potager fleuri★

Flowers border the well-ordered vegetable plots. Brick walls enclose the garden and serve as a support for espaliered fruit trees.

Forêt d'Arques

From Arques-la-Bataille take D 56 . ☺ *The forest roads are sometimes narrow; drive carefully.*

This forest of beech trees crowns a spur surrounded by the River Eaulne and the River Béthune; the two join forces to become the Arques. D 56 crosses the river, then the southern part of the forest, alongside traces of an ancient Roman road. Several pretty villages in the area are worth visiting: **St-Nicholas-D'Allermont**, a "street-village" which grew up in medieval fashion along either side of the road. **Envermeu** has an unfinished Gothic church with Renaissance touches; its remarkable chancel★ has hanging keystones. On D 1 between Enverneu and Arques is an **obelisk** commemorating the battle of Arques. From the site (*15min walk from the carpark*) is a view of the château of Arques-la-Bataille across the river.

ARROMANCHES-LES-BAINS

CALVADOS, POPULATION: 552
MICHELIN MAP 303: I-3 – LOCAL MAP SEE PLAGES DU DÉBARQUEMENT

Arromanches is a modest seaside resort, which owes its fame to the gigantic landing operation of June 1944. In the little port are the remains of a Mulberry harbour, the most extraordinary industrial and maritime achievement of the war.

- ▪ **Information:** 2 rue Mar.-Joffre, 14117 Arromanches-les-Bains. ☎02 31 22 36 45. www.arromanches.com.
- ▸ **Orient Yourself:** Arromanches is on the coast, 10km/6mi northeast of Bayeux via D 516 and 38km/24mi northest of Caen via D 516 and N 13.
- ▸ **Don't Miss:** The remains of the allied artificial "Mulberry" port.
- ▸ **Organizing Your Time:** In three hours you can see the beach, the museum and the film.
- ▸ **Also See:** The landing beaches at Fontaine-Henry, Ouistreham-Riva-Bella, Caen, Bayeux and Omaha Beach.

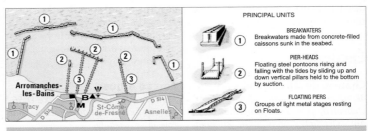

Arromanches 360	B	Musée de Débarquement M

A Bit of History

Artificial Port – "If we want to land, we must take our harbours with us." The failed Dieppe raid of 1942 confirmed that fighting during a landing would make Channel ports unusable by the Allies. The Calvados coast offered no natural protection: bad weather could have catastrophic effects on the landing operations. The creation of a prefabricated port was given the code name "Mulberry," perhaps after a restaurant where War Office staff often ate.

Mulberries – Arromanches harbour was the landing point for Mulberry B for British troops, while the Americans' Mulberry A went to Omaha Beach. In all, 146 Phoenix caissons were laid, representing 500 000t of concrete (each one was 70m/230ft long, 20m/66ft high and 15m/49ft wide). Along with 33 jetties and 16km/10mi of floating roads, they were towed across the Channel at just over 6.5kph/4mph.

Mulberry B at Arromanches ★, later known as Port Winston, enabled 9 000t of material to be landed each day, equivalent to the tonnage handled by the port of Le Havre prior to the war. More than 500 000t had been landed by the end of August.

The best place from which to spot the remaining caissons (preferably at low tide) is the belvedere situated on D 514 leading to Asnelles (see *Plages du DÉBARQUEMENT*).

Visit

Musée du Débarquement

Musée du Débarquement – ♿ ⏱Open Apr–Sept 9am–7pm. Mar and Oct 9.30 am–12.30pm, 1.30-6pm. Feb and Nov– Dec 10am-12.30pm, 1.30-5pm. ⏱Closed 20 Dec–31 Jan. ≈6.50€ (children 4.50 €). ☎02 31 22 34 31. www.normandy 1994.com.
The D-Day Landing Museum contains a collection of models, photographs, dioramas, arms and equipment of the Allied forces. A large model of the pre-fabricated port shows how it functioned regardless of the tides. Royal Navy films of the landing are shown.

Arromanches 360

♿ ⏱Open June– Aug 9.40am–6.40pm. Apr–May and Sept–Oct 10.10am–5.40pm. Mar and Nov 10.10am–5.10pm. Feb and Dec 10.10am–4.40pm. ⏱Closed in Jan. ≈4€ (children 3.50€). ☎02 31 22 30 30. www.arromanches360.com
The Price of Freedom mixes archive footage with scenes re-enacted on the landing sites. The 360-degree viewing gives an intense dramatic effect.

PAYS D'AUGE★

CALVADOS, MICHELIN MAP 303: M-4 TO N-6

With its pastures, thatched cottages, manor houses, apple orchards and winding hedgerows, the Pays d'Auge provides a picturesque transition to the beaches of the Côte Fleurie. The heart of traditional rural Normandy, the Auge Region is partially covered in original woodland, with a chalk escarpment (30m/98ft high), known as the Côte d'Auge, overlooking the Dives Valley and the Caen area.

- **Information:** R. Pasteur, 14340 Cambremer. ☎02 31 63 08 87. www.pays-auge-culture.org, www.pays-auge.fr
- ▶ **Orient Yourself:** The Pays d'Auge, between the River Dives on the west and the River Touques on the east, surrounds Lisieux, 36km/22.5mi south of Honfleur.
- ⊚ **Don't Miss:** The beautiful château of Crèvecoeur-en-Auge, with its half-timbering typical of the region.
- ⊙ **Organizing Your Time:** Give yourself a few hours to visit the Manoir des Évêques de Lisieux, the château de Crèvecoeur and to visit gardens.
- ⓒ **Also See:** Lisieux, Crèvecoeur-en-Auge and Pont-l'Évêque.

Driving Tour

1 Côte d'Auge: Sieux to Cabourg

26km/16mi – allow 1hr.

Lisieux★★ ⓒ *See LISIEUX.*

▶ *From Lisieux take N 13 W. In La Boissière turn right onto D 59.*

Ancienne Abbaye du Val Richer

(o― *not open to the public*) Following the destruction of the Cistercian abbey during the Revolution, only the 17C hospice remained. François Guizot (1787-1874), a historian and leading politician during the reign of Louis-Philippe (1830-1848), retired here after the 1848 revolution until his death in 1874. The Schlumberger brothers, early 20C petroleum engineers, worked here on inventions that would transform the industry. (ⓒ *See CRÈVECOEUR-EN-AUGE*).

▶ *At the crossroads turn left onto D 101 and bear right onto D 117. At the next crossroads turn left onto D 16 and right onto D 85.*

Clermont-en-Auge★

Chapel – ⊙ *Open Easter through Oct 10am-7pm*

▶ *Follow the signs Chapelle de Clermont – Panorama.*

Leave the car at the start of the avenue leading to the **chapel** *(15min round-trip).* From the east end there is an extensive **panorama**★ of the Dives and Vie valleys; in the distance stretches the Caen countryside, bounded by the dark line of the Bocage hills. The church contains statues of St Marcouf and St Thibeault in polychrome stone in the chancel and on either side of the altar St John the Baptist and St Michael.

Beuvron-en-Auge★

This charming village has kept around 40 lovely old timber-framed houses set around the central square. The former covered market is now a shopping centre. There is a very pretty manor at the south exit from the village, decorated with wood carvings.

▶ *Take D 49 N through Putot-en-Auge; cross N 175 and pass under the motorway. Fork right to Cricqueville.*

Criqueville-en-Auge

The **château** (o― *not open to the public*), completed in 1584, and its three main buildings with vast roofs are typically medieval whereas its chequered stone and brick decoration are Norman.

▶ *From Sarlabot to Dives there is a beautiful panorama over the Calvados coast.*

Dives-sur-Mer★
See DIVES-SUR-MER.

▶ *Continue to Cabourg via D 45.*

2 Traditional Normandy: From Villers-sur-Mer to Lisieux
36km/22mi – about 1hr.

▶ *From Villers take D 118 SE.*

Beaumont-en-Auge
This small town, remarkably situated on a spur commanding the Touques Valley, was the birthplace of the mathematician and physicist **Pierre Simon, Marquis de Laplace** (1749-1827). His house and statue are on place de Verdun.

▶ *D 58 S; left on N 175; right on D 280 and pass under the motorway.*

St-Hymer
Pleasantly set in a valley, the village has a 14C **church** with traces of Romanesque in its style. Its belfry is a replica of that of Port-Royal-des-Champs, the famous Jansenist abbey south-west of Paris.

Pierrefitte-en-Auge
Church – ⏱*Contact the Auberge des 2 tonneaux.* ☎*02 31 64 09 31.*
In the 13C **church** the nave arches are decorated with cameo paintings of landscapes. There is a fine 16C rood beam.

Coquainvilliers
Distillerie Boulard – ♿*Visit by guided tour only July–Aug hourly 10.30–11.30am, 2.30–5.30pm; Apr–June and Sept–Oct 11.30am, 2.30–4.30pm.* ⊜*2.50€(under 12 no charge).* ☎*02 31 48 24 01. www. lebistronormand.fr*
A guided tour describes the making of apple brandy (Calvados) and traditional distillation techniques.

Ouilly-le-Vicomte
Church – Apply to the town hall to visit. ☎*02 31 61 12 64 or to M. Aillaume* ☎*02*

31 62 29 02. The **church** standing beside the road which spans the Touques is one of the oldest in Normandy, dating from the 10C and 11C.

▶ *Continue E; at the crossroads turn right onto D 579 to Lisieux.*

3 Vallée de la Touques: From Lisieux to Trouville
28km/17mi – about 1hr.

▶ *Leave Lisieux via boulevard Herbert-Fournet, D 579 N; right onto D 263.*

Rocques
The village **church** in the centre of its old burial ground has two wooden porches. The chancel and the tower date from the 13C. Inside note the torches and painting of the Brothers of Charity and several polychrome wooden statues.

▶ *Take D 262 NW back to D 579.*

Pont-l'Évêque
Since the 13C Pont-l'Évêque has been famous for its cheese. Only a few old houses remain, mostly in rue St-Michel and rue de Vaucelles. The Aigle d'Or Inn (*68 rue de Vaucelles*) was a post house in the 16C and has retained the Norman courtyard of the period.
The **Église St-Michel** is a fine church in Flamboyant style flanked by a square tower. The modern stained-glass windows (1963-64) are by François Chapuis. An interesting wooden balcony decorates the old **Dominican Convent**, a 16C half-timbered building beside the Law Courts (Tribunal). The **Hôtel Montpensier**, a building in the Louis XIII style has two corner pavilions. The 18C Hôtel Brilly (restored) now houses the town hall and the Tourist Information Centre.

La Belle Époque de l'Automobile★
South of the town along D 48, follow the marked itinerary. ♿ 🚸 ⏱*Open July–Aug 10am–7pm. Apr–June and Sept 10am–12.30pm, 1.30–6pm. Oct–mid-Nov 2–6pm* ⏱*Closed 11 Nov – mid-March.*

Address Book

For coin ranges see the Legend on the cover flap.

WHERE TO EAT

Auberge de la Boule d'Or – Pl. Michel-Vermughen, 14430 Beuvron-en-Auge. ☎02 31 79 78 78. Closed Jan, Tue evening and Wed except July–Aug. The half-timbered façade is magnificent, and inside are rafters, tile floors, rustic furniture and an open hearth. The Norman menu offers lashings of rich cream, cider and calvados.

WHERE TO STAY

Les Marronniers Bed and Breakfast –Les Marronniers, 14340 Cambremer. ☎02 31 63 08 28. chantal. darondel@wanadoo.fr. 5 rooms. This charming 17C residence, surrounded by a flower garden, has a superb view over the Dives valley. The guestrooms are spacious, and breakfast is served on a pleasant terrace.

Le Manoir de Cantepie Bed and Breakfast –Le Cadran, 14340 Cambremer, 11km/7mi W of Lisieux via N 13, then D 50. ☎02 31 62 87 27. Closed 15 Nov–1 Mar. 3 rooms. Reservations required. This splendid 17C manor offers a delightful stay in elegant surroundings at a reasonable price .

6€ (children 4.50€). ☎02 31 65 05 02. On the grounds of the Château de Bette-ville, this collection features around 600 vehicles. Among the most remarkable are a Marne Renault AG taxi cab (1911), a Clément-Bayard fruit and vegetable van (1910), a 1910 Vinot et Deguingand, a 22 horse-power Delaunay-Belleville (1911) which once belonged to Marshall Joffre, a model 30 Cadillac (1912) and a Ford T.

Canapville

Manoir des Évêques de Lisieux – Visit by guided tour (30min) only July–Aug daily except Tue 2-7pm. 6€(children no charge). ☎02 31 65 24 75.www.man-oirdeseveques.fr

The 13C-15C **Manoir des Évêques de Lisieux** is one of the most charming country houses in the Pays d'Auge. It consists of the large manor, with three monumental stone chimneys, and the small manor with a bishop's head carved on the entrance post. The 18C ground-floor rooms display Chinese porcelain.

Bonneville-sur-Touques

William the Conqueror's 11C castle, of which only the moat and fortified enclo-sure remain, offers a fine panorama of the sea and Deauville to the north, the Touques Valley to the south. Between 1203 and 1449 the castle belonged in turn to the English and the French. Only in 1451 did it become French for good.

Touques

Église St-Pierre – Information on exhib-its at Tourist Office. 2€. www.ville-

In apple-blossom time

G. Targat/MICHELIN

Touques.com William the Conqueror's port stands at the mouth of the river. Old houses line the Ouies stream. The Église St-Thomas (12C) owes its name to a visit by Thomas Becket; the **Église St-Pierre** (11C), now deconsecrated, is used for exhibitions.

▶ *Take N 177 to Deauville, then Trouville.*

Deauville☆☆☆
See DEAUVILLE.

Trouville☆☆
See TROUVILLE.

Haute Vallée de la Touques 4

75km/47mi – about 3hr round-trip from Lisieux – see LISIEUX.

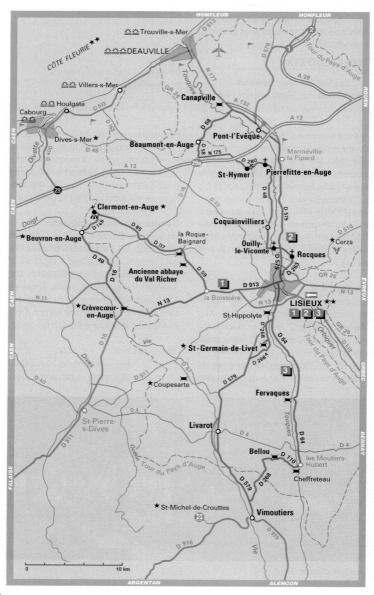

AVRANCHES★

MANCHE – POPULATION 8 500
MICHELIN MAP 303: D-7
LOCAL MAP SEE BAIE DU MONT-ST-MICHEL

The pretty and lively city of Avranches is one of the oldest towns in Normandy; its origins date back to early antiquity. St Aubert, Bishop of Avranches in the 8C, instigated the foundation of Mont-St-Michel and the two centres are therefore closely linked not only geographically but also historically.

▌ **Information:** 2 rue Général-deGaule, 50300 Avranches.
☎02 33 58 00 22. www.ot-avranches.com
▶ **Orient Yourself:** The town, on a granite spur, has a commanding view of Mont-St-Michel, 25km/15.6mi to the west. It can be reached by A 84, linking Ville-dieu-les-Poêles (23km/14mi) to the northeast and Rennes, 87km/54mi to the southwest.
🅿 **Parking:** At the town centre, near the Museum, Plate-forme and gardens.
☻ **Don't Miss:** The superb view of Mont-St-Michel from the Jardin des Plantes.
🕐 **Organizing Your Time:** One can easily spend a half-day at Avranches, between the museums and the Jardin des Plantes.
🧒 **Especially for Kids:** At the Scriptorial, children are welcomed with a special tour led by the elf Titivillus.
👣 **Also See:** The marked itineraries La Contre-attaque (the Counter-Attack) and Cobra-La Percée (the Breakthrough), described in the Historical Area of the Battle of Normandy, both go through Avranches; the former starts from here, whereas the latter ends here.

A Bit of History

The Vision of Bishop Aubert (8C) – Legend has it that St Michael appeared twice before **Aubert** and commanded him to raise a chapel in his honour on the rock then called Mount Tombe, but the sceptical Bishop of Avranches vacillated. St Michael reappeared and dug an imperious finger into the doubting man's skull. Aubert could delay no longer. A skull with a hole in it in the St Gervase Basilica recalls this legend.

Henry II Repents (12C) – Relations between the King of England, **Henry Plantagenet**, who was also Duke of Normandy, and his Archbishop of Canterbury, **Thomas Becket**, became very bitter. One day the King cried out, "Will no one rid me of this insolent priest?" Four knights took the words as a command and, on 29 December 1170, Thomas Becket was murdered in Canterbury Cathedral. The Pope excommunicated Henry II, who begged absolution. Robert of Torigni, Abbot of Mont-St-Michel, held a council attended by the King at Avranches, and so it was that at the door of the cathedral (collapsed in 1794) Henry II, barefoot and dressed only in a shirt, made public penance on his knees on 22 May 1172.

The Avranches Breakthrough – It was from Avranches on 31 July 1944 that General Patton began the swift advance which smashed the German Panzer counter-offensive launched from Mortain, beginning the attack which was to take the American 3rd Army through to Bastogne in Belgium.

Sights

The Museum, the Plate-forme and the town hall (Mont St-Michel manuscripts) are located around the site of the former episcopal palace while the botanical gardens are slightly down the hill. The Basilica of SS Gervais and Protais is a short walk from the town hall. Entry to the Basilica Treasury is included in the

Mont-St-Michel Abbey

© Dieter Basse/Normandy Tourism

museum and manuscript ticket. The Patton Monument is a 20-minute walk down rue de la Constitution.

Jardin des plantes

The botanical gardens were once the property of a Capuchin monastery that was destroyed during the Revolution. From the terrace at the far end of the garden is a **panorama**★ of the bay.

La Plate-forme

From place Daniel-Huet, walk along the garden of the Sous-Préfecture to reach the site of the old cathedral. This little square contains the paving stone on

which Henry II made public penance in 1172. From the terrace there is a wide **view**★ embracing Mont-St-Michel.

Monument Patton

This memorial commemorates the deployment of General Patton's troops towards Brittany and the Basse-Normandie (in July 1944 with the American 3rd Army). The square on which it stands is now American territory.

Museum

◷*Open June-Sept, 10am–noon, 2-6pm.* ➣*1.50€.* ☎*02 33 89 29 49.*
Housed in the outbuildings of the former episcopal palace restored in the late 15C the museum contains rich and varied collections illustrating the history of the town.

Manuscrits du Mont-St-Michel

♿ ◷ *Open July–Aug 10am–7pm; May–June and Sept, daily except Monday 10am–6pm. Oct–Dec and Feb–Apr Tue–Fri 10am–12.30pm, 2–5pm, weekends 10am–12.30pm, 2–6pm.*◷*Closed 1 May, 1 Nov, 25 Dec and Jan.* ➣*7€ (10-18 years 3€, family ticket 15€).* ☎*02 33 89 29 49. www.ville-avranches.fr*
Inside the town hall, an old library houses a collection of 8C-15C **manuscripts**★★, largely from Mont-St-Michel Abbey: famous texts from ancient Greece and Rome and from the Middle Ages.

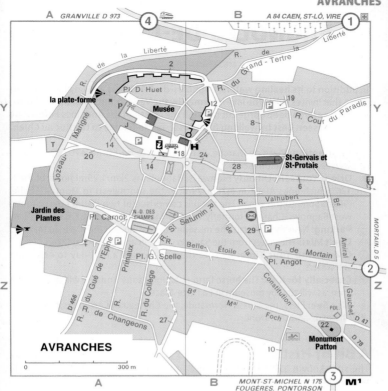

AVRANCHES

Abrincates Bd des	AY 2	Estouteville Pl. d' Gaulle	BY 12	Patton Pl. Gén	BZ 22
Bindel R. du Cdt	BZ 4	R. Gén.-de	AY 14	Pot-d'Étain R. du	BY 24
Bremesnil R. de	BY 6	Littré Pl.	AY 18	Puits-Hamel R. du	AZ 27
Chapeliers R. des	BY 8	Marché Pl. du	BY 19	St-Gaudens R.	BY 28
Constitution R. de la	BZ	Millet R. L.	AY 20	St-Gervais R.	BZ 29
Écoles R. des	BZ 10				

Manuscrits du Mont-St-Michel (Hôtel de Ville)	AB H	Musée de la Seconde Guerre mondiale	BZ M¹

Basilique St-Gervais-et-St-Protais Treasury

🕙*Open June–Sept 10am-noon, 2-6pm, Sunday 2-6pm,* 🚫*no charge.* This vast basilica dating from the late 19C is interesting for its treasury of St Gervase. ☏*02 33 58 00 22.*

Musée de la Seconde Guerre mondiale

5km/3mi S on N 175. 🕙*Open July–Aug: 9am–7pm; Apr–June and Sept–mid-Nov 9.15am–12.15pm, 2-6.30pm; mid-Nov – March Sun and school holidays 10am-noon, 2-5pm.* 🕙*Closed 1 Jan, 25 Dec.* 🎟*7€ (under 10 years 4€).* ☏*02 33 68 35 83.* This museum is devoted to the Avranches breakthrough during the Second World War. The German exhibits are on the ground floor (note the bell that sounded the alarm on the morning of 6 June 1944 on Pointe du Hoc) whereas the Allied exhibits are upstairs.

BAGNOLES-DE-L'ORNE⚜⚜

ORNE, POPULATION: 893
MICHELIN MAP 310: G-3

In addition to its healing waters, Bagnoles-de-l'Orne has a lovely lakeside set-ting★ that invites calm. The lake is formed by the Vée, a tributary of the Mayenne, before it enters a deep gorge cut through the massif of the Andaines Forest. The site can be seen best by walking from Tessé-la-Madeleine to the Roc au Chien.

- **Information:** Place du Marché, 61140 Bagnoles-de-l'Orne, ☎02 33 37 85 66 www.bagnolesdelorne.com.
- **Orient Yourself:** Off busy highways, Bagnoles is 2km/1.25mi north of the N 176, which links Alençon (47km/29mi to the southwest) to Mont-St-Michel (90km/56mi to the west). The town is comprised of two distinct parts: to the west Bagnoles-Château, formerly Tessé-la-Madeleine, and east, Bagnoles-Lac.
- **Parking:** Near the château, the museum, the casino and the Place du Marché.
- **Don't Miss:** The views from the Saut du Capucin and the roc au Chien.
- **Organizing Your Time:** Be sure to give yourself a half-day to enjoy the spa waters.
- **Especially for Kids:** The horse farm at Juvigny-sous-Andaine will delight chil-dren, as will the toy museum at La Ferté-Macé.
- **Also See:** Flers, the Suisse Normande, the Château of Carrouges, Lassay-les-Châteaux and Domfront.

A Bit of History

The spot known as Capuchin's Leap received its name when a Capuchin monk, cured of his ills by a magical spring, fulfilled a vow by making a gigantic leap (4m/13ft) between the rock spikes high above the water.

Sights

Parc de l'établissement thermal★

The park surrounding the spa building is planted with pines, oaks and chest-nut trees. The Allée du Dante on the east bank of the Vée, which is often crowded with bathers, leads from the lake to the spa building. Other alleys in the park wind towards Capuchin's Leap and to the site known as the Abri Janolin. Shops line the lake front rue des Casions.

Le Roc au Chien★

🕐 *Tours by tourist train (30min) June–Sept 3.15 and 4.30pm. Apr–May and Oct weekends and public holidays 3.15 and 4.30pm.* 🎫*5.60€.* ☎*02 33 30 72 70. www. bagnolesdelorne.com*

🚶*45min round-trip on foot.* Start from the church and walk up the avenue du Château; the main gateway opens on to the avenue and the public park of Tessé *(arboretum containing 150 different tree species, bird-watching trail, children's playground and other amusements).*

The château, built in the 19C in the neo-medieval style. now houses the town hall. Take the avenue on the right which overlooks the Bagnoles Gorge and leads to the rocky promontory, the Roc au Chien, where there is a lovely **view**★ of Bagnoles beside the lake (*left*) and the spa building and its park (*right*).

Musée départemental des Sapeurs-Pompiers de l'Orne

♿ 🕐 *Open Apr–Oct 2–6pm.* 🎫*3.80€(children 2.30€)* ☎*02 33 38 10 34.*

A deconsecrated church houses the Fire Brigade Museum with its collection of horse-drawn hand pumps, the oldest being La Distinguée, which is pre-1790. The collection includes badges, medals, helmets, uniforms, fire-fighting appli-ances, breathing apparatus and radios.

Address Book

🖐For coin ranges see the Legend on the cover flap.

WHERE TO EAT

⊖ **Chez Marraine** – 6 r. du Square. ☎02 33 37 82 91. chezmarraine@wanadoo.fr. Closed 15 Feb–15 Mar. "To be happy, be discreet!" This motto surely applies to this restaurant hidden in a narrow street between town and lake. Meals are served on the pleasant covered terrace, a good opportunity for you to try calf's head, a speciality of the house.

⊖ **Maison Chatel EURL Le Goff** – 31 r. St-Denis, 61600 La Ferté-Macé. ☎02 33 3711 85. Daily except Sun afternoon and Mon 7am–7.30pm. If you like rural treats such as calf's head or tripe cooked in beer or with vegetables, you can purchase them in the renowned shop, or enjoy them in the small restaurant.

⊖ **La Terrasse** – R. des Casinos. ☎02 33 37 81 44. Closed 26 Nov–4 Jan, Sun evening and Mon. With an unexceptional exterior, this restaurant may escape your notice. But you'll be glad you walked in when you taste the good regional cuisine and the fish specialities. Inviting rustic interior and sheltered terrace.

⊖⊖ **Auberge de Clouet** – Le Clouet, 61600 La Ferté-Macé, 7km/4.3mi NE of Bagnoles via D 916. ☎02 33 37 18 22. Closed 1-15 Nov, Sun evening and Mon Nov– Easter.
In spring, the terrace of this peaceful inn overlooks a small vale covered in flowers. Regional cuisine from local produce, chickens from the farm and vegetables from the garden in season. A few rooms decorated in 1970s style are available.

WHERE TO STAY

⊖ **Auberge de la Source**– La Peras, 61600 La Ferté-Macé, 5km/3mi NW of Bagnoles via D 908, towards Mount-St-Michel. ☎02 33 37 2823. http://perso.wanadoo.fr/auberge.lasource. 5 rooms ⊐⊇. This new building follows the old Norman style with bricks and half-timbering. Upstairs, the rooms, one of them for families, have excellent beds and parquet floors. The restaurant has an open hearth and regional fare.

⊖⊖ **Hôtel Ermitage**– 24 bd Paul-Chalvet. ☎02 33 37 96 22. www.hotel-de-l-ermitage.com. Closed Nov– Mar. 🅿. 37 rooms ⊇8€. An old building surrounded by smaller century-old cottages and shaded gardens. Guestrooms are simply decorated and have tiny balconies.

Excursions

Château de Couterne

1.5km/1mi S of Bagnoles by D 335. 🅿 Park the car by the bridge. ⚹ The interior is not open to the public. The massive brick and granite château (16C and 18C) is reflected in the waters of the Vée.

La Ferté-Macé

6km/3.6mi N via D 916. This small town has retained a number of 18C and 19C buildings and houses that recall its past role in the textile industry. Today, it is a centre for light industryr. Its gastronomic renown is due to tripes en brochettes, skewered onto hazel wood sticks.

A large tourist complex includes a leisure park (pedalos, windsurfing, fishing, climbing, swimming, golf etc) and a dozen holiday houses. A big, lively market is held on Thursday mornings. An 11C Romanesque tower is all that remains of the old church demolished in 1861.

The **hôtel de ville** (town hall) houses works by the local artist **Charles Léandre**, as well as facinating 19C paintings celebrating the postal service and local manufacturing.

Musée du Jouet

🔲 🕐Open July–Aug daily 3–6pm. Apr–June and Sept weekends and public holidays 3-6pm. ⚹3.20€ (under 6 years no charge). ☎02 33 37 47 00 or 02 33 37 04 08. Set up in the former municipal baths, this museum shows 19C and 20C games and toys.

Healing Waters

The establishment in the Vée Gorge is supplied exclusively by the Great Spring (Grande Source) where water gushes forth at the rate of 50 000L/11 000gal an hour at a temperature of 25°C/77°F. It is the only hot spring in western France and its acidic, mildly radioactive waters have a low mineral content. Bathing, the essential part of any treatment, can be accompanied by showers or localised treatment with water jets, and pulverisations.

Rânes

13km/8mi from La Ferté-Macé via D 916.
Rebuilt in the 18C, the castle, which now houses the local gendarmerie, has retained its 15C two-storeyed keep, fortified with crenels and machicolations. (*panoramic view from the top*).

Vallée de la Cour

5km/3mi SE.
A forest road leads to a pool, a popular beauty spot known for its good fishing🪝.

Forêt des Andaines

🅺 *La Ferme du Cheval de Trait –* ♿🕐 *Horse shows mid-July–Aug Wed, Thu,* *weekends and public holidays at 3.30pm. Rest of the year, check the website.* 🎫*9€ (5-12 years 4€).* 🐴🅿 *Book for lunch on the farm.* ☎ *02 33 38 27 78. www.chevaldetrait.com.*

This forest, part of the Normandie-Maine Regional Nature Park, offers pleasant walks and glimpse of stags, does and the smaller roedeer. Of particular interest are: **Tour de Bonvouloir**, a slender observation tower; **Chapelle Ste-Geneviève**, a picnic site; and **Juvigny-sous-Andaine** , a picturesque village where the **Ferme du Cheval de Trai-** which offers a 1hr horse show sure to please youngsters.

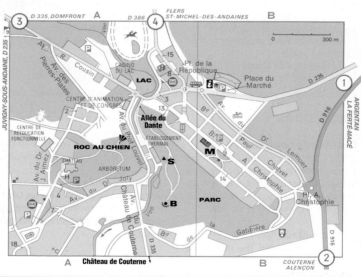

BAGNOLES-DE-L'ORNE			Château Av. du	A	4	Lemeunier-de-la-Raillère Bd	B	14
			Dr-Pierre-Noal Av. du	A	7	Rozier Av. Ph.-du	A	15
			Dr-Poulain Av. du	A	8	Sergenterie-		
Bois-Motté Bd du	A	2	Gaulle Pl. Général-de	B	9	de-Javains R.	A	18
Casinos R. des	A	3	Hartog Bd G.	A	13			

Abri Janolin	A B	Musée départemental des Sapeurs-Pompiers de l'Orne	B M	Saut du Capucin	A S

CHÂTEAU DE BALLEROY★

CALVADOS, MICHELIN MAP 303: G-4 – LOCAL MAP SEE BAYEUX

The Château of Balleroy, built between 1626 and 1636, was designed by François Mansart (1598-1666). It was owned by successive Marquis de Balleroy for three centuries. It was purchased in 1970 by Malcolm Forbes (1919-1990), the American publisher and aeronaut, whose family still owns it. The plain but majestic brick and stone building dominates the village's main street. Symmetrical outbuildings lie behind formal flower beds designed by Le Nôtre.

- **Information:** ☎ 02 31 21 60 61. www.chateau-balleroy.com.
- ▶ **Orient Yourself:** Take D 572 from Bayeux (19km/12mi to the southwest) then D 13. Balleroy is at the exit for the Forest of Cerisy.
- **Don't Miss:** The salon d'honneur, reached by one of the earliest cantilevered stairways built in France.
- **Organizing Your Time:** Give yourself a good two hours to see everything.
- **Also See:** Saint-Lô, the abbey of Cerisy-la-Forêt, Bayeux, Aunay-sur-Odon and the Cotentin penninsula.

Tour

Interior

Open mid-March–mid-Oct 10am–6pm. Visit of château by guided tour (45min) only, daily 10am–6pm. Museum and park out of season 10am–noon, 2–5pm. 6.86€ (Museum 4.27€, Château 5.35€, Park 3€). ☎ 02 31 21 60 61. www.chateau-balleroy.com.

The château's sober exterior gives no hint of its rich interior decoration. On the ground floor the salons display portraits of past counts. The dining room is painted with scenes from the Fables of La Fontaine.

On the first floor, the bedrooms are decorated lavishly in period styles. The drawing room ceiling portrays the Four Seasons and the signs of the zodiac.

Musée des Ballons

Kids – *For times and prices see the Château, above.*

A museum of hot-air balloons is housed in the stables. Dioramas tell the story of major flights in the history of ballooning.

Salon d'Honneur, château de Balleroy

B. Kauffman/MICHELIN

BARFLEUR★

MANCHE, POPULATION: 642

MICHELIN MAP 303: E-1 – LOCAL MAP SEE PRESQU'ÎLE DU COTENTIN

This charming fishing port, with its granite houses and its quays, is one of the most beautiful villages of France. Tradition has it that the boat that carried William, Duke of Normandy, to England was built here. A bronze plaque placed in 1966 at the foot of the jetty marks his departure (1066). In 1194 Richard Lionheart also embarked from Barfleur on his way to be crowned King of England.

- **Information:** 2 rond-point Guillaume-le-Conquerant, 50760 Barfleur. ☎02 33 54 02 48. www.ville-barfleur.fr
- ▶ **Orient Yourself:** Barfleur is reached from Cherbourg (29km/18mi to the west) via D 116, which follows the coast, or by D 901, which is more direct.
- **Don't Miss:** The view from the top of the Gatteville lighthouse, and the arrival of the day's catch from fishing boats in the port.
- **Organizing Your Time:** The area requires at least a half day of your time.
- **Also See:** The Cotentin penninsula, the regional nature park, St-Vaast-la-Hougue, Valognes and Cherbourg-Octeville.

Sights

Église St-Nicholas

This squat 17C church has the appearance of a fort. In the south transept is a remarkable 16C Pietà while in the north transept above the font is a stained-glass window of St Mary Magdalene Postel.

Maison de Julie Postel

&🕐Open *9am-7pm.* 🚫*No charge.* ☎02 33 54 02 17. *La Bretonne hamlet.* Julie Postel was born in Barfleur in 1756. As Sister Mary Magdalene she founded the Sisters of the Christian Schools of Mercy (La Congrégation des Sœurs de la Miséricorde). She lived in this house, which was also a school of domestic science, for 30 years. Scenes from her life are depicted in the stained-glass windows of the adjoining chapel.

Port de Barfleur

Pointe de Barfleur★★

4km/2mi N by D 116 and D 10.

Gatteville-le-Phare

The church, rebuilt in the 18C, still has its original 12C belfry. The Mariners' Chapel (Chapelle des Marins), in the square, is built over a Merovingian necropolis. Beyond Gatteville the scenery is wilder and rough seas pound the rocky coast.

Phare★★

🕐*Open May–Aug 10am–noon, 2–7pm. Sept and Apr 10am–noon, 2–6pm. Oct and Mar 10am–noon, 2–5pm. Feb, 1st half Nov, last half Dec 10am–noon, 2–4pm.* 🕐*Closed Jan, 1 May, 25 Dec, and if winds are too high.* 🚫*2€(children under 17 free).* ☎02 33 23 17 97.

The lighthouse, on the north-eastern extremity of the Cotentin peninsula, is one of the tallest in France (71m/233ft). The light, with a range of 56km/35mi, and the radio beacon, installed in a small 18C tower, guide ships into Le Havre. From the top (365 steps) there is a **panorama**★★ stretching over the east coast of the Cotentin peninsula, St-Marcouf Islands, Veys Bay and, in clear weather, the cliffs at Grandcamp. The shallow waters and swift currents have caused many shipwrecks, including the *White Ship* in 1120, with Henry I's heir, Wil-

G. Guégan/MICHELIN

liam Atheling, and 300 members of the Anglo-Norman nobility on board.

Montfarville
2km/1mi S by D 155.
This 18C granite church has a chapel and belfry dating from the 13C and a highly colourful **interior**★. The paintings on the vaulting are by a local artist, Guillaume Fouace. Note the 18C rood beam and a 14C polychrome Virgin.

BARNEVILLE-CARTERET ☖ ☖

MANCHE, POPULATION: 2 429
MICHELIN MAP 303: B-3 – LOCAL MAP SEE PRESQU'ÎLE DU COTENTIN

This popular seaside resort, the closest port to the Channel Islands, is lively, the dunes windswept, and the long beach is of fine sand.

- 🛈 **Information:** 10 rue des Écoles, 50270 Barneville-Carteret. ☎02 33 04 90 58. www.barneville-carteret.net
- ▶ **Orient Yourself:** Valovnes is 28km/17.5mi northeast via D 902, Cherbourg 37km/23mi northeast via D 650 and Caen 120km/75mi to the east.
- ☻ **Don't Miss:** You may want to tour Carteret on the tourist train, before trying some of the hikes and walks giving views over the sea.
- ◴ **Organizing Your Time:** The Saturday morning market is worth your time.
- **Kids** **Especially for Kids:** Children will enjoy the tourist train.
- ⚫ **Also See:** The Cotentin penninsula, the marshes of Cotentin and Bessin, Valognes, Cherbourg-Octeville, St-Sauveur-le-Vicomte, and Lessay.

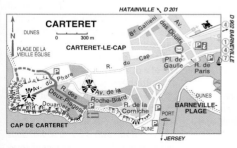

SE LOGER		
Chambre d'hôte	Hôtel des Îsles...................⑦	
La Roque de Gouey..........①	SE RESTAURER	
Chambre d'hôte	L'Hermitage......................①	
La Tourelle.....................④	Le Berlingot.....................④	

Carteret★

Tourist train operates late June–mid-Sept. ⌘7€ (children 4€). Le Clos St-Jean, 50270 Barneville-Carteret, ☎02 33 04 70 08.
A headland to the north protects the Gerfleur estuary and the delightful small beach (☻beware of coastal currents).

Walking Tour

Cap de Carteret★★
Allow a total of 2hr for these two walks.
🚶Follow the signs La Corniche, le Phare; park near the roundabout by Carteret beach. Take Sentier des Douaniers (left) which is very narrow, to the Plage de la Vieille-Église.
🚶Take the road leading down to this beach to return inland. At the crossroads either turn right up to the **lighthouse** (*phare*) or turn left (avenue de la Roche-Biard) to a viewing table: **views**★ of the coast, the Channel Islands and inland.

▶ *Alternatively, continue straight ahead at the crossroads to return to the car.*

Address Book

&For coin ranges see the Legend on the cover flap.

WHERE TO EAT

⊜**Le Berlingot** – Rte de Bricquebec (D 902), 50270 Sortosville-en-Beaumont, 7km/4.4mi NE of Barneville-Carteret via D 902. ☎02 33 53 87 16. Closed mid-Nov–Mar and Wed out of season. Reservations suggested on weekends. This restaurant specializing in crepes is popular with locals, who appreciate the friendly atmosphere and regional food, including meat grilled over the open hearth.

WHERE TO STAY

⊜⊜ **La Tourelle Bed and Breakfast** – 5 r. du Pic-Maillet, in Barneville-Bourg. ☎02 33 04 90 22. 3 rooms. ⌇ ☐
A real Grandma's house, with its old-fashioned air, old furniture, polished parquet floors and, every morning, the delicious odors of a good breakfast. The 16C century house faces the village church.

Barneville

Église

The 11C church was given a fortified tower in the 15C. The the arches and capitals of the Romanesque nave have delightful **decoration**★. On one of these capitals, note the figure portraying the Prophet Daniel confronting a fierce lion. The monument on the way out of Barneville commemorates the cutting-off of the Cotentin peninsula on 18 June 1944 during the Battle of Normandy.

Excursion

Fierville-les-Mines

9km/5.6mi E. Leave Barneville S on D 903 until La Picauderie, then turn left onto D 50 to Fierville-les-Mines and follow signs to Le Moulin à vent du Cotentin.

Moulin à vent du Cotentin

○Open Jul-Aug. ☛Guided tours (30min) 10am-noon, 2-7pm. May–June and Sept daily except Mon 2-7pm (in Sept. until 6pm). Mar–Apr and Oct–Nov Wed, weekends, and public holidays 2-6pm. School holidayss except Christmas daily except Mon 2-6pm. ○Closed Dec–Jan. ☛3.50€(children 1–12 years 1€).
This 18C mill was restored in 1997 and continues to produce flour. The tour (30min) explains the mechanism and the this traditional profession.

Mont Castre Driving Tour

29km/18mi. About 2hr 15min.

▶ From Barneville-Carteret take the Coutances road. At La Picauderie, bear right onto D 50.

Portbail

This popular resort has two beaches of fine sand, a sailing school and a marina. A 13-arch bridge links the town to the harbour and the beaches. The 11C **Église Notre-Dame**, was built on the site of a 6C abbey founded in the reign of Childebert. (Église Notre-Dame – ○open Apr-Sept: 10.30am-noon, 3-7pm; ☛ guided tours available in July-Aug every hour Tue–Sat 10.30am–12.30pm, 3.30–6.30pm, Sun 3.30-6.30pm. Sept and June visits by appointment at Tourist Office. ☛2€(children no charge) ☎02 33 04 03 07.)

▶ Take D 15 and D 903 inland via La Haye-du-Puits towards Carentan. 1.5km/0.9mi from the first level crossing E of La Haye-du-Puits turn right onto a narrow uphill road.

Mont Castre★

Beyond the houses, take the path to the church ruins, then go round a field to reach the ruins of a Roman watch post – still a strategic point in July 1944 during the Battle of Normandy. The **view** extends from Carteret to St-Côme-du-Mont.

BAYEUX★★

CALVADOS, POPULATION 14 961

Today the Bayeux Tapestry still presents its unique record of the events of 1066 and the Battle of Hastings. Its home, the former capital of the Bessin, was the first French town to be liberated (7 June 1944) in WWII. The town escaped damage during the war, leaving a cathedral and old houses—many tastefully restored—as well as a pedestrian precinct, for explorers in the 21st Century.

- **Information:** Pont St-jean, 14400 Bayeux. ☎02 31 51 28 28. www.bayeux-tourism.com.
- **Orient Yourself:** A short distance away from the D-Day beaches of Omaha and Arromanches, Bayeux is midway between Caen (30km/19mi southwest) and Carentan (47km/29mi northwest).
- **Don't Miss:** The Bayeux Tapestry, Notre-Dame cathedral, the Battle of Normandy museum and the gardens of the château of Brécy and the Priory of St-Gabriel
- **Organizing Your Time:** Give yourself at least an hour to view the Bayeux Tapestry.
- **Especially for Kids:** The special children's audio guide will make the tapestry more interesting for them.
- **Also See:** The marked itineraries D-Day–Le Choc (D-Day–The Impact) and Overlord–L'Assaut (Overlord–the Onslaught) described in the Historical Area of the Battle of Normandy pass by Bayeux.

A Bit of History

Cradle of the Dukes of Normandy – Bayeux, a Gaulish town, became a Roman centre, then was successively captured by the Bretons, the Saxons and the Vikings.

Rollo, the famous Viking, married Popa, the daughter of Count Béranger, Governor of the town. In 905, their son, the future William Longsword, ancestor of William the Conquerer, was born here.

Oath of Bayeux – In the 11C Edward the Confessor ruled over England. He had previously found refuge in Normandy for many years, and Norman accounts claim that he thus chose his cousin, William of Normandy, as his successor. He allegedly sent **Harold**, a powerful favourite of the Saxon nobles, to officially inform the Duke.

Harold was shipwrecked on the coast of Picardy and captured by Count Guy of Ponthieu. Freed by **William**, he was received at the Norman court where the Duke's daughter, Edwige, was presented as his wife to be.

Harold swore on saintly relics to recognize the Duke's right to the English throne. However, when Edward died on 5 January 1066, Harold accepted the English crown.

The Conquest of England – Harold's accession provoked William to set sail with the Norman fleet on 27 September 1066 from Dives-sur-Mer, to fight for his claim to the throne. On 28 September the Normans set foot on English soil at Pevensey in Sussex and occupied Hastings. Harold dug in on a hill. On 14 October William advanced and emerged victorious by that evening. The Bayeux Tapestry, a propaganda created after the invasion, claims that Harold fell in the fighting with an arrow in his eye.

Visit

Bayeux Tapestry★★★

Centre Guillaume-le-Conquérant: &⊙Open May–Aug 9am–7pm. Mid-Mar–Apr and Sept–Oct 9am–6.30pm. Rest of the year 9.30am–12.30pm, 2–6pm (last

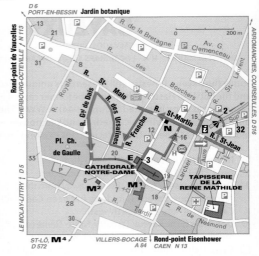

BAYEUX

Aure Q. de l'	2
Bienvenu R. du	3
Bois Pl. au	4
Bourbesneur R.	6
Chanoines R. des	7
Chartier R. A	8
Cuisiniers R. des	12
Dr-Michel R.	13
Foch R. Mar.	15
Laitière R.	16
Leforestier R. Lambert	18
Liberté Pl. de la	19
Maîtrise R. de la	20
Marché R. du	21
Poterie R. de la	28
St-Jean R.	
St-Loup R.	30
St-Malo R.	
St-Martin R.	
St-Patrice R. et Pl.	31
Teinturiers R. des	32
Terres R. des	33

Conservatoire de la Dentelle	E	Musée-mémorial de la		Mémorial Charles-de-Gaulle	M²
Hôtel du Doyen	M¹	Bataille de Normandie	M⁴	Maison à colombages	N

entry 45min before closing). 🕐*Closed 2nd week of Jan, 1 jan and 25 Dec.* 👁*7.50€ (children 3€). Audio guide included in ticket price.* ☎*02 31 51 25 50.*

The **Bayeux Tapestry** *(Tapisserie dite de la Reine Mathilde)* is displayed in the **Centre Guillaume le Conquérant** in an impressive 18C building which was a seminary until 1970.

Visitors are introduced to this jewel of Romanesque art as they pass through a series of rooms, with films and dioramas explaining the history and content of the tapestry, which is itself displayed under glass round the walls of the specially designed Harold Room.

Wrongly attributed in the 18C to Queen Mathilde, the tapestry was probably commissioned in England soon after the conquest from a group of Saxon embroiderers by Odo of Conteville, Count of Kent and Bishop of Bayeux. The embroidery is in coloured wool on a piece of linen, 50cm/19in high by 70m/203ft long.

The work is the most accurate and lively document to survive from the Middle Ages and provides detailed information on the clothes, ships, arms and general lifestyle of the period.

In 58 detailed scenes, the illustrations give a very realistic account of the events of 1066. The English are distinguished by their moustaches and long hair, the Normans by their short hairstyles, the clergy by their tonsures and the women (three in all) by their flowing garments and veiled heads. Latin captions run above the pictures.

The outstanding sections are Harold's embarkation and crossing (4-6), his audience with William (14), crossing the River Couesnon near Mont-St-Michel (17), Harold's Oath (23), the death and burial of Edward the Confessor (26-28), the appearance of Halley's comet, an ill omen for Harold (32), the building of the fleet (36), the Channel crossing and the march to Hastings (38-40), cooking and eating meals (41-43), the battle and Harold's death (51-58).

Cathédrale Notre-Dame★★

Only the towers and crypt remain from the original church, which was completed in 1077 by Odo of Conteville, William's turbulent companion in arms.

Exterior

The east end is a graceful composition; flying buttresses support the chancel which is flanked by two bell turrets. The central tower dates from the 15C but was unfortunately recapped in the

Address Book

For coin ranges, see the Legend on the cover flap.

WHERE TO STAY

La Ferme des Châtaigniers Bed and Breakfast – *14400 Vienne-en-Bessin, 7.5km/4.6mi E of Bayeux via D 126.* ☎02 31 92 54 70. *3 rooms.* Set apart from the farmhouse, this converted stable contains simple yet pleasant, comfortable rooms. Guests have the use of a well-equiped kitchen. Peace and quiet is guaranteed by the tranquil surrounding fields.

Le Grand Fumichon Bed and Breakfast – *14400 Vaux-sur-Aure, 3km/1.9mi N of Bayeux via D 104.* ☎02 31 21 78 51. duyckja@wanadoo.fr. *4 rooms.* Once part of Longues-sur-Mer Abbey, this fortified 17C farm, with its square courtyard and characteristic porch, is today a dairy and cider-making farm. The attic rooms are plain but pleasant.

Hôtel Reine Mathilde – *23 r. Larcher.* ☎02 31 92 08 13. www.hotel-reinemathilde.com . *Closed 15 Nov–15 Feb. 16 rooms.* If you wish to stay in the old town, this small family hotel is conveniently situated a stone's throw from the cathedral and the famous tapestry. Exposed beams and light-wood furniture. Plain rooms, some of them with sloping ceilings. Bar, tea room and ice-cream shop.

Le Manoir de Crépon Bed and Breakfast – *Rte d'Arromanches, 14480 Crépon.* ☎02 31 22 21 27. www.manoirdecrepon.com. *Closed 10 Jan–10 Feb. 5 rooms.* This house built in the 17C and 18C is typical of the area, with its oxblood-coloured exterior. You will like the stone floors and fireplaces, the vast, tastefully furnished bedrooms and the authentic atmosphere of the former kitchen converted into a breakfast room.

WHERE TO EAT

L'Amaryllis – *32 r. St-Patrice.* ☎02 31 22 47 94. *Closed 15 Dec–31 Jan, Sun evening and Mon.* The modest facade just off the narrow streets of old Bayeux hides a dining room full of greenery and furnished in bistrot style. The menu is traditional local fare: sausage in pastry, steamed fish and deserts featuring apples and Calvados.

Le Pommier – *40 r. des Cuisiniers.* ☎02 31 21 52 10. www.restaurantlepommier.com. *Closed 7– 28 Feb, 21 Nov–2 Dec, Tue evening and Wed, except during July–Aug.* This restaurant near the Cathedral has an apple-green façade and offers a celebrated daily menu of Norman specialities, many featuring apple products. The vaulted dining-room with stone walls adds charming authenticity.

Le Bistrot de Paris – *Pl. St-Patrick.* ☎02 31 92 00 82. The daily menu of this bistrot-style restaurant is written on a slate, based on what the chef finds at the market: oysters, foie gras, rabbit stewed with prunes, fish and cheese are offered in a relaxed ambiance and at reasonable prices.

Hostellerie St-Martin – *Pl. Edmond-Paillaud, 14480 Creully.* ☎02 31 80 10 11. www.hostelleriesaintmartin.com. The large vaulted rooms dating from the 16C used to house the village market. Exposed stone, a fireplace, sculptures and a view of the wine cellar make up the curious decor. Classic cuisine. A few bedrooms.

SHOPPING

Markets – *R. St-Jean, Wed 8.30am–1.30pm.* The St-Jean pedestrian street Wednesday market features some 25 stalls including greengrocers, butchers, fishmongers, cheesemakers and honey-sellers. On the Place St-Patrice, every Saturday, some 120 merchants offer their wares, about half of them foodstuffs.

Naphtaline – *14–16 parvis de la Cathédrale.* ☎02 31 21 50 03. www.naphtaline-bayeux.com. *Open Apr–Oct daily except Sun 10am–7pm. Nov 2–6.60pm. Mar & Dec 11am–12.30pm, 2–6.30pm. Closed Jan and Feb, Sun and holidays off-season.* Two boutiques housed in a fine 18C building offer antique and modern lace, Bayeux porcelain and reproductions of traditional tapestries woven on Jaquard looms. Next door is a boutique called Autre Temps that specializes in medieval objects.

19C. The south transept is pure in style; the tympanum over the door shows the story of Thomas Becket, Archbishop of Canterbury, assassinated in his cathedral on the orders of Henry II.

The small porch further west on the south side is late 12C.

The two Romanesque towers on the west front must have been redesigned in the 13C with massive buttresses to take the weight of the Gothic spires. The only points of interest are on the tympana over the two side doors: the Passion and the Last Judgement.

Interior

The well-lit nave is a harmonious blend of Romanesque and Gothic. The clerestory and the vaulting date from the 13C but the wide arches are in the best 12C style. Their justly famous decoration is typical of Norman Romanesque sculpture. Against an interlaced or knotted ground the spandrels are decorated with low-relief sculptures which show oriental influence transmitted by the illuminators of manuscripts.

The transept crossing is supported by four huge pillars. The south transept contains two interesting pictures low on the right: the Life of St Nicholas and the Crucifixion (15C).

The three-storey chancel, with its ambulatory and radiating chapels, is a magnificent example of Norman Gothic architecture. The great arches are separated by pierced rose windows.

The high altar is a majestic 18C piece; the six candelabras in chased bronze, the tabernacle and the cross are by Caffieri the Elder.

The paintings (restored) on the chancel vault represent the first bishops of Bayeux. The ambulatory, like the transepts, is lower than the chancel and separated from it by handsome wrought-iron screens. The third and fourth chapels on the south side contain 15C frescoes.

Crypt

Beneath the chancel is the crypt (11C). Above the decorative foliage of the capitals are 15C frescoes (restored) of angel musicians. A recess (*left*) contains the recumbent figure of a canon (15C).

Chapter-house

This is a beautiful late-12C Gothic construction. The vaulting, which was renewed in the 14C, is supported by consoles decorated with monsters or grotesque figures. A graceful blind arcade adorns the lower walls. The floor of 15C glazed bricks includes a labyrinthine design in the centre. The tiles on the risers at the back of the room depict hunting scenes. The beatification of St Thérèse of Lisieux was signed at the desk.

Old Bayeux

The old stone or timber-framed houses have been splendidly restored.

Rue St-Martin

No 6 is a 17C house known as the Maison du Cadran because of the sundial on the façade. On the corner of rue des Cuisiniers stands a very elegant **half-timbered house**★ with two overhanging upper storeys and a slate roof. Just after the rue Franche, on the right, is the Hôtel d'Argouges, a 15C-16C timber-framed house.

Conan capitulates and surrenders the keys of the city on the end of his lance to Duke William. The Siege of Dinan Duke William gives arms to Harold

Rue Franche

Several private houses: no 5, Hôtel de Rubercy, is a 15C-16C turreted manor house; no 7, Hôtel de la Crespellière, is set back behind a courtyard and dates from the mid-18C; no 13, Hôtel St-Manvieu, is from the 16C.

Rue du Général-de-Dais

No 10, Hôtel de Castilly (18C), is in the Louis XV style. No 14, Hôtel de la Tour du Pin (18C), has an imposing façade in the Louis XVI style.

Rue du Bienvenu

No 6 is decorated with wooden carvings inspired by religion or legend. It houses the Conservatoire de la dentelle de Bayeux (*See Additional Sights*).

Rue St-Jean

East of rue St-Martin, part of this street is within the pedestrian precinct which has been attractively restored. The Tourist Information Centre is housed in the old fish market. No 53 is the Hôtel du Croissant (15C-16C).

Rue des Teinturiers

Two handsome half-timbered houses face a row of stone houses.

Quai de l'Aure

On turning into this street from rue des Teinturiers, one has a fine view of the river, the water mill in what was once the tanning district, the arched bridge, the old fish market and the towers of the cathedral in the background.

Additional Sights

Hôtel du Doyen

Open July–Aug 10am–12.30pm, 2–7pm. Rest of the year 10am–12.30pm, 2–6pm. 3€ (under 10 years or with a ticket from the Tapestry museum no charge). 02 31 92 14 21.

A huge 17C porch leads into the 18C mansion which houses the collection of the Baron-Gèrard Museum, which is closed for repairs (*see below*).

Conservatoire de la dentelle de Bayeux

6 rue du Bienvenu. Open daily except Sunday and public holidays 10am–12.30pm, 2–6pm. 02 31 92 73 80.

Bayeux lace is characterised by floral motifs. The workshop, where the lacemakers are reviving the Bayeux pattern, has displays of lace specimens.

Musée Baron-Gérard

The collection of this museum is temporarily housed in the Hôtel du Doyen, rue Lambert-Leforestier. 02 31 92 14 21. The museum building, the former Palais des Évêques, is temporarily closed.

Bayeux was once an important manufacturing centre for porcelain. Founded in 1812 by J Langlois, the workshop's famous glazing (red, gold and blue) made the reputation of the town. Production ended in 1951. The museum displays several of these abundantly decorated porcelain pieces, some quite rare.

The upstairs rooms contain furniture and painting, mainly 15C and 16C Italian and Flemish Primitive works and 17C-19C French works including those of Philippe de Champaigne, David, Baron François Gérard, Boudin and Caillebotte.

Tapestries of Bayeux 16C, Courtesy Ville de Bayeux

Harold swears allegiance to William on two reliquaries
They set out together for Bayeux Harold sets sail again for England

Bayeux porcelain

Musée-Mémorial de la Bataille de Normandie★

&🕒*Open May–mid-Sept 9.30am–6.30pm. Rest of the year 10am–12.30pm, 2–6pm (last entry 1hr before closing).* 🕒*Closed 25–26 Dec, 1 Jan and last 2 weeks of Jan.* ✍6.50€ *(children 3€).* ☎02 31 51 46 90.

Situated on the line separating the British and American sectors in 1944, the Memorial Museum recalls the dramatic events of summer 1944. Two large galleries, named Overlord and Eisenhower, explain the chronology of the Battle of Normandy and give a detailed account of the equipment and uniforms of the various nations involved in the conflict.

The closing of the Falaise Pocket is illustrated by a diorama recreating the village of Chambois where, on 19 August, part of the 90th US Infantry Division joined forces with the 1st Polish Armoured Division.

A great variety of heavy equipment is exhibited. Note in particular the Churchill MK VII tank (GB) – the anti-tank armoured vehicle called Destroyer M 10 (US), the anti-tank Jagdpanzer (Germany) – a quadruple 20mm German Flak gun as well as a Caterpillar D 7 Bulldozer.

Mémorial Charles-de-Gaulle

🕒*Open June–Aug 9.30am–12.30pm, 2–6.30pm (last entry 1hr before closing). Sept–Nov and Mar–May 10am–12.30pm, 2–6pm.* 🕒*Closed Dec–Feb.* ✍3.50€ *(children 2€).* ☎02 31 92 45 55.

The Governor's mansion (15C-17C) houses a museum which retraces the life and career of the General through events associated with Bayeux (liberation of the town and speech of 1946). Personal belongings, newspaper articles and manuscripts are also on display.

Jardin botanique

🕒*Open April–Sept 9am–8pm. Rest of the year 9am–5pm.*The pleasant sloping botanical gardens include a huge weeping willow.

Excursion

Abbaye de Mondaye

11km/7mi – about 45min. From Bayeux take D 6 S. After 8km/5mi turn right onto D 33; follow the signs. &🕒*Open July–Aug.* 💬*Guided tours (45min) daily at 3pm and 4.30pm. Sept–May Sun and public holidays 3pm and 4pm.* ✍4€ *(under 12 no charge).* ☎02 31 92 58 11. www.mondaye.com.

St Martin's Abbey was founded in 1215 but rebuilt in the 18C and 19C. The abbey church, which also serves the parish, is in the Classical style (early 18C). Its uniformity of design is due to its architect and decorator, **Eustache Restout**, a canon in the Premonstratensian Order. The interior contains some fine pieces: high altar, woodwork in the chancel including a beautiful Crucifixion, the Assumption (a terracotta group in the Lady Chapel) and the Parizot organ (restored).

The 18C **conventual buildings** – refectory, sacristy (18C woodwork) and library – are open to the public.

Driving Tours

1 South-West of Bayeux

Round-trip of 46km/29mi – about 3hr 30min.

▶ *From Bayeux take D 572.*

St-Loup-Hors
The 12C-13C church has retained its Romanesque tower and many old tombs.

Noron-la-Poterie
This is a well-known centre producing salt glaze ware; some of the workshops are open to the public.

▶ *In La Tuilerie turn left onto D 73 which leads to Balleroy via Castillon.*

Château de Balleroy★
See Château de BALLEROY.

▶ *On leaving turn left onto D 13. At the Embranchement crossroads take D 13 and D 8 W through Cerisy Forest.*

Cerisy-la-Forêt
See CERISY-LA-FORÊT.

▶ *From Cerisy take D 34, D 160 and D 15 NE to Le Molay-Littry.*

Le Molay-Littry
The village was once a busy coal mining centre. The mine was opened in 1743 and flourished until the late 19C. During the Second World War it was reopened and produced coal until 1950.

The **Musée de la Mine**★ (Kids &. ⊙*Open Apr–Sept daily except Mon (open holidays) 10am–noon, 2–6pm. ∞5.40€ (children 3€). ☎02 31 22 89 10. www.ville-molay-littry.fr)* presents the history of mining and the life of the miners through an audio-visual presentation, a reconstruction of a mining gallery, a scale model of a pithead, and a range of tools.

▶ *Take D 5 E to return to Bayeux.*

2 East of Bayeux

Round-trip of 34km/20mi. Allow 2hr.

▶ *From Bayeux take D 12 and D 112 towards Ver-sur-Mer.*

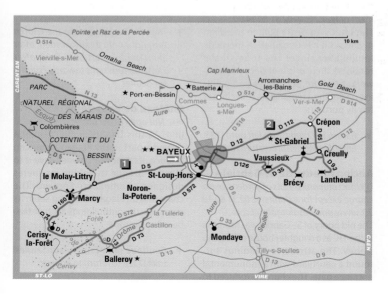

Crépon

The Romanesque church with its 15C tower and the smart farms attract attention.

▶ *Turn right onto D 65.*

Creully

Guided tours (45min) July–Aug Tue–Fri 10.30am–12.30pm, 2.30–5.30pm.1st half Sept Tue– Fri 2.30–5.30pm by appointment only. 3€(children 1.50€) ☎02 31 80 67 08.

The **château** is built on the foundations of an 11C castle. The main 12C building is flanked by a 16C round tower adjoining a square keep. During the Second World War, the BBC used it to relay news of the Battle of Normandy.

From the terrace there is a view of **Château de Creullet** standing in a loop of the Arromanches road. On 12 June 1944 King George VI and Sir Winston Churchill met here with General Montgomery.

Grange aux Dîmes

On the Bayeux road, level with no 82.

The Tithe Barn is a powerfully buttressed building where wheat was stored and where the taxes were collected.

▶ *Take D 93 S to Lantheuil.*

Château de Lantheuil

Guided tours for groups by appointment only. 7€ ☎02 31 80 14 00.

This imposing castle built in the reign of Louis XIII has remained in the same family ever since. The rooms have retained their original decor: woodwork, furniture, sculptures and paintings including a remarkable collection of family portraits.

▶ *Return to Creully; turn left onto D 35. Enter St-Gabriel-Brécy; turn right.*

Ancien Prieuré de St-Gabriel★

Unaccompanied visits of gardens. No charge except for exhibits. ☎02 31 80 10 20. www.prieuresaintgabriel.com.

The old priory of St-Gabriel was founded in the 11C as a daughter house of Fécamp Abbey. The attractive buildings surround a courtyard with a monumental entrance gate. The church is reduced to

The Old Priory of St-Gabriel

A. de Valroger/MICHELIN

the magnificently designed and decorated east end and chancel (11C-12C). Beyond the church is a garden, planted with fruit trees and banks of flowers. The 15C Justice Tower, buttressed at the corners, contained a prison on the lower floor and a look-out place at the top.

▶ *Return to D 35; continue W towards Bayeux; then follow the signs S.*

Gardens of the Château de Brécy ★

Open June Tue, Thu, Sat–Sun and public holidays 2.30–6.30pm. Easter–May and July–Oct Tue, Thu, Sun and public holidays 2.30–6.30pm. 6€ (under 12 no charge). ☎02 31 80 11 48.

The castle is approached through a magnificent great **gateway**★ (17C). The terraced **gardens**★ offer a beautiful perspective which terminates in a high wrought-iron grill ornately decorated.

▶ *Take D 158; just before the church turn right onto a narrow road; after 2km/1mi turn left onto D 35; after 2km/1mi turn right towards Esquay-sur-Seulles.*

Château de Vaussieux

Not open to the public.

In 1778 this beautiful 18C mansion played a part in the Franco-American alliance. Its American owner gave it to Marshal Broglie to hold manoeuvres designed to intimidate England. The château is an elegant building set in its own park; the outbuildings are half-timbered or of stone.

▶ *Continue onto Esquay-sur-Seulles; take D 126 to return to Bayeux.*

LE BEC-HELLOUIN★★

EURE, POPULATION 434
MICHELIN MAP 304: E-6

Le Bec-Hellouin Abbey, a medieval religious and cultural centre, produced two great Archbishops of Canterbury for England.

- **Information:** Place du Mal-Leclerc, 27110 Le Neubourg.
  ☎02 32 35 40 47. www.le-neubourg.fr/tourisme
- **Orient Yourself:** The abbey is 35km/22mi southwest of Rouen, and within 40km/25mi of Honfleur (northwest), Lisieux (west) and Évreux (southeast). Paris is only 150km/94mi, and Caen 80km/50 miles, away.
- **Don't Miss:** The abbey of Le Bec-Hellouin, the château and gardens at Champ-de-Bataille, and the Harcourt fortress with its arboretum.
- **Organizing Your Time:** Spend your morning at the abbey, then go to Champ-de-Bataille or Harcourt in the afternoon.
- **Also See:** Brionne, Bernay, Pont-Audemer, the Boucles de Seine Regional Nature Park, Elbeuf, Louviers and Évreux.

A Bit of History

In 1034 the knight **Herluin** found God and founded the Bec abbey; its pious reputation attracted an Italian scholar, **Lanfranc**, who later became young **Duke William's** trusted advisor.
Pope Alexander II, a former student of Lanfranc at Bec, appointed him Archbishop of Canterbury, which made him virtual Regent of England whenever William returned to Normandy. On Lanfranc's death in 1093, **Anselm**, the theologian who was now Abbot of Bec, was transferred to Canterbury.
In the 17C Bec rose to new eminence under **Guillaume de la Tremblaye** (1644-1715), one of the greatest sculptors and architects of his period.
The monks were driven out during the Revolution and the church, one of the largest in Christendom, was demolished under the Empire. In 1948 the site was restored to the Benedictine Order.

Visit

Abbaye de Bec-Helouin★★

○ *Open for unaccompanied visit daily 7am–9pm.* *Guided tours (45 min) available daily except Tue 10.30am, 3pm and 4pm.* ○ *5€ for tour.* ☎02 32 43 72 60. www.abbayedubec.com

---

Address Book

WHERE TO STAY

○○ **Château de Boscherville Bed and Breakfast** – 27520 Bourgther-oulde, 10km/6mi NE of Bec-Helouin via N 138, D 80 then D 38. ☎02 35 87 62 12. ○ ○ 5 rooms. The rooms of this small 18C family château are comfortable and bright, the small drawing room is elegant and the welcome is pleasant indeed. A must, if only to enjoy following in the footsteps of Jean de La Fontaine while strolling among the centuries-old oaks in the park.

WHERE TO EAT

○○ **Le Canterbury** – R. de Canterbury. ☎02 32 44 14 59. Closed Sun and Tue evenings and Wed. The aim here is not to impress, but to satisfy. The result: scrupulously well-prepared cuisine served in a fine half-timbered 18C house. Over 60 kinds of Calvados to sample. Small terrace open in fine weather.

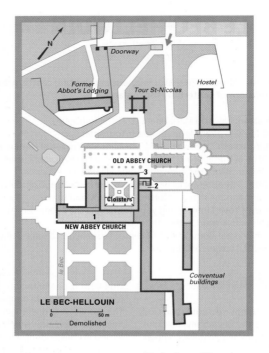

LE BEC-HELLOUIN

0   50 m

Demolished

New Abbey Church

The new abbey stands in what was the former refectory. At the entrance is a 14C statue of the Virgin, the Fathers of the Church are 15C; before the high altar lies the 11C sarcophagus of Herluin, founder of Bec (1). Turn left on leaving to reach the other sights.

Old Abbey Church

Only the column, foundations and fragments of the south transept of the old abbey church remain.

Cloisters

A monumental 18C grand staircase (2) leads to the cloisters. Built between 1640 and 1660, the cloisters were modelled after those of Monte Cassino (Italy).

Tour St-Nicolas

Closed for reasons of security. The 15C tower is the most important remainder of the old abbey church.

Driving Tour

Neubourg and Roumois

Allow about 2hr30min

▷ *Leave LeBec on the D 38 to the Château de Tilly, then E on the D 124 to the crossroads with the D 576, where you turn N to Ecaquelon, then N to Routot and S on the D 144 to Bouquetot, then the D 313 to Bourgtheroulde, then back to LeBec via the N 138, turning right on the D 39.*

Château de Tilly (1500)

Guided tours of interior (30min) mid-July–mid-Aug 2–6pm. 4€. Tours of exterior 10am–6pm. 2.50€ (children no charge).

Lozenge-patterned stone and glazed-brick front, perimeter wall quartered by pointed turrets. The winding staircase★in brickwork in the courtyard recalls that of the Rihour Palace in Lille.Villages churches that merit a stop include Bouquetot (11C-12C), Bourg-Achard (15C-16C), Bourgtheroulde (Renaissance), Cesseville, Écaquelon.

BELLÊME

ORNE, POPULATION 1 774

MICHELIN MAP 310: M-4 – LOCAL MAP SEE MORTAGNE-AU-PERCHE

Bellême, a very typical village of the region, overlooks the forest and the beautiful Perche countryside. The town had a particularly turbulent history in the Middle Ages, when Blanche of Castile and the future St Louis (Louis IX,1214-1270) took the fortress by storm in 1229.

- **Information:** Blvd Bansart-des-Bois, 61130 Bellême.
  ☎ 02 33 73 09 69. www.lepaysbellemois.com
- ▶ **Orient Yourself:** Bellême is 22km/14mi northwest of Nogent-le-Rotrou and 17km/10.6mi south of Mortagne-au-Perche, its long-time rival.
- **Don't Miss:** The old houses of the Ville-Close, and the forest walks.
- **Organizing Your Time:** Give yourself an hour to see the town, and 3h to visit the Écomusée at Ste-Gauburge.
- **Also See:** Nogent-le-Rotrou and Mortagne-au-Perche.

Sights

Ville close

The **gate**, flanked by two reconstructed towers, together with towers now incorporated into domestic buildings, are the only remains of the 15C ramparts which once enclosed the town and were built upon 11C fortress foundations. Rue Ville-Close, on the site of the former citadel, is lined with fine 17C and 18C houses. Outstanding are No 24, the Governor's house, and especially No 26, the **Hôtel de Bansard des Bois**.

Église St-Sauveur

The late-17C St Saviour's Church has a richly decorated interior. Note in particular the imposing high altar and canopy (1712) made of stone and marble, the chancel woodwork from the old abbey of Valdieu, and the windows, each composed of six scenes from the life of Jesus. The font, decorated with garlands, stands against a three-panelled altarpiece.

Driving Tour

Forêt de Bellême★

27km/17mi – about 1hr 30min.
This forest (2 400ha/5 930 acres) is one of the most beautiful in the Perche region with its majestic oaks and its beautiful and varied site.

▶ *From Bellême take D 938 NW.*

From the road there is a very pretty **view** of the town. It then crosses woodland before reaching the Herse Pool.

Étang et Fontaine de la Herse

A path circles the pool – 15min on foot.
The calm waters of the pool reflect the surrounding greenery and offer freshness much appreciated by tourists. Opposite the forester's lodge is a Roman fountain and two blocks of stone bearing Latin inscriptions.

▶ *Turn round and continue straight ahead; turn right at the Colbert crossroads.*

The forest road (surfaced) affords lovely **views**.

▶ *At the Creux Valley crossroads, turn left. Follow the road along to the edge of the forest. Turn first right and enter the forest once again. Before reaching the Montimer crossroads the road crosses a thicket. Descend on the left for 400m/0.3mi.*

Chêne de l'École

This oak tree stands 40m/130ft tall and has a circumference of 22m/66ft. Even after 300 years it is still perfectly straight.

▶ *Return to the Montimer crossroads and continue to La Perrière.*

La Perrière

The name comes from the Latin *petraria*, meaning stone quarry. Many of the houses have been built with dark-red ferruginous sandstone (*grison*).

The village offers one of the best **panoramas**★ of the Perche countryside, including Perseigne Forest (*west*) and Écouves Forest (*northwest*) which can be seen from the cemetery path near the church.

👣 To admire the old dwellings (15C-17C) and streets of the town, follow the discovery path *(sentier de la découverte: plan available locally).* 🚲 To organize cycle tours and country walks, contact Les Marcheurs du Perche Ornais, La Grange Rouge, 61130, St-Germain-de-la-Coudre. ☎02 33 83 22 90. marchers-du-perche-mb@wanadoo.fr

▶ *Return to the forest road that crosses Bellême Forest from W to E and passes through the delightful Creux Valley. At the Rendez-vous crossroads turn right onto D 310.*

St-Martin-du-Vieux-Bellême

The houses of this picturesque village are clustered round the 14C-15C church. *Continue on the road which joins D 955 and turn left to Bellême.*

Perche Tours

Owing to its rich meadows the Perche is devoted to stock raising, particularly

Percheron

H. Dewynter/MICHELIN

to the breeding of the draught horses known as **Percherons**. The region is subdivided into two areas, the Norman Perche, and the southern sector, the Perche-Gouet or Lower Perche.

Whereas manors in the Pays d'Auge appear as country houses, those in the Norman Perche resemble small castles, built of stone and fortified. Although most of these late-15C or early-16C lordly houses are now farmhouses, they have retained features such as towers, elegant turrets and the delicately carved ornaments decorating many façades.

①From Bellême to Logny-au-Perche

68km/43mi – Allow about 2hr.

▶ *From Bellême take D 7 S.*

Château des Feugerets

👁 *Not open to the public.* A cluster of buildings – two square pavilions with a fine balustrade and moat and an elegant 16C central block – form a harmonious, well-balanced ensemble.

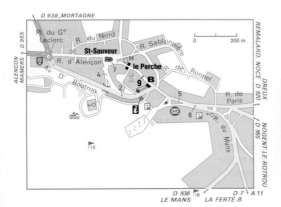

> *In La Chapelle-Souëf turn left onto D 277.*

St-Cyr-la-Rosière
The church has a beautiful Romanesque doorway, a remarkable 17C polychrome terracotta **Entombment**★ and a 17C painting of St Sebastian.

> *Take the road S towards Theil.*

Manoir de l'Angenardière
⚭ *Not open to the public.* This manor house, built in the 15C and 16C, is circled by well-preserved ramparts. Note the massive towers with machicolations.

> *Continue to the S.*

La Pierre Procureuse
According to legend, this stone serving as a roof to a late Neolithic (2500BC) dolmen brings luck if you touch it.

> *At the T-junction turn right; go through Gémages.*

St-Germain-de-la-Coudre
The church has an 11C crypt containing a beautiful Virgin and Child in stone.

> *Return to Gémages and take the road to Ste-Gauburge.*

Priory of Ste-Gauburge
At St-Cyr-la-Rosière. ◷*Open Apr–Sept daily except Tue 10.30am–6.30pm. Rest of the year daily except Tue 10.30am–6pm.* ◷*Closed 1 Jan, 24–25 and 31 Dec.* ⊕*3.90€ (children 3€) with guided tour of the priory during school holidays, public holidays and weekends 2–5.30pm 5€.* ☎*02 33 73 48 06. www.ecomuseedu-perche.free.fr*

The church has been transformed to house the **Écomusée du Perche**. Crafts of the past – blacksmith, saddler, cartwright, woodcutter, cooper – are brought to life again.

Adjoining the church is an imposing monastic ensemble (13C-18C) laid out around the courtyard.

> *Continue along D 277. Turn left at the crossroads onto D 9. In Colonard-Corubert turn right onto D 920.*

East of Rémalard the country is greener and hillier; the road is picturesque.

> *In Moutiers turn left onto D 918 to Longny-au-Perche.*

2 From Mortagne-au-Perche-to Logny

25km/16mi –Allow about 30min. ⦿*see MORTAGNE-AU-PERCHE.*

3 From Mortagne-au-Perche to Bellême

35km/22mi – Allow about 1hr. ⦿*see MORTAGNE-AU-PERCHE.*

> *D95 from Mortagne-au-Perche.*

BERNAY

EURE, POPULATION 11 024
MICHELIN MAP 304: D-7

Bernay developed rapidly around an abbey founded early in the 11C by Judith of Brittany, wife of Duke Richard II. The town, which nestles in the Charentonne Valley, has a number of interesting, renovated, half-timbered houses.

🛈 **Information:** 29 rue Thiers, 27300 Bernay. ☎02 32 43 32 08. www.ville-bernay27.fr

▶ **Orient Yourself:** Bernay lies at the junction of the Carentonne and the Cosnier rivers. Take N 138 from Rouen (65km/40.6mi northeast) or Alençon (92km/57.5mi southwest), or the N 13 from Lisieux (34km/21mi northwest) or Évreux (52km/32.5mi southeast).

☺ **Don't Miss:** The view from the boulevard des Monts, the municipal museum, and the lovely château de Beaumesnil.

🕐 **Organizing Your Time:** Spend a morning in town, then drive the Risle river.

Kids Especially for Kids: The museum has activities for children.

👢 **Also See:** Conches-en-Ouche, L'Aigle, Vimoutiers, Lisieux, Brionne, Le Bec-Hellouin and the Pays d'Auge.

Sights

The principal streets are rue Thiers and du Générale-de-Gaulle, along which the abbey, the museum and the Ste-Croix Church are clustered. The information office is also here.

Boulevard des Monts★

This lovely hillside road north of the centre commands good views of the town and the Charentonne Valley.

Hôtel de ville★

The 17C town hall buildings, which were formerly Bernay Abbey, are in the style of the Maurists, a Benedictine order.

Ancienne église abbatiale

Same as for the municipal museum.
The abbey church was begun in 1013 by **Guglielmo da Volpiano**, summoned from Fécamp by Judith of Brittany. In the 15C the semicircular apse was replaced by a polygonal one. Note the carved capitals above the nave and the twin bays in the galleries. The north aisle, rebuilt in the 15C, has diagonal vaulting.

Musée municipal

Place Guillaume-de-Volpiano 🕐*Open mid-June–mid-Sept daily except Mon 10am–noon, 2–7pm. Rest of the year daily except Mon 2–5.30pm.* 🕐*Closed 1 Jan, 1 May, 25 Dec.* ⊚*3.50€ ticket combined with the abbey church, (no charge Wed and for children).* ☎*02 32 46 63 23.*
The museum is housed in the 16C abbot's lodge. Exhibits include a fine collection of Rouen, Nevers and Moustiers faience and old Norman furniture.

Église Ste-Croix

Started in the 14C, the church is heavily restored and contains fine works of art from Le Bec-Helleloun. The remarkable **tombstone** of Guillaume d'Auvillars, Abbot of Bec (1418), stands at the entrance to the sacristy. Sixteen great statues of Apostles and Evangelists from the end of the 14C are in the nave.

Basilique Notre-Dame-de-la-Couture

Access by rue Kléber-Mercier, about 1km/.6mi S of town centre. Ask for information at the presbytery, 12 r. Alexandre 🕐*unaccompanied visit Sat 2–6pm.* ☎*02 32 43 06 82.*
The interior of this 15C church, established as a basilica in 1950, has wooden vaulting; the statue Notre-Dame-de-la-Couture (16C), highly venerated by pilgrims is placed on a modern altar in the north transept.

Address Book

👢*For coin ranges, see the Legend on the cover flap.*

WHERE TO EAT

⊖ **Le Bistrot de Bernais** – *21-23 r. Gaston-Follope.* ☎*02 32 46 06 06. Closed 2 weeks in Aug, Sun and Mon.* A narrow passage leads to a delightful courtyard, where there is a terrace in fine weather. Behind a creaking door is a medieval room (the house dates from the 15C) with an enormous fireplace. Traditional cuisine and cheese specialties.

⊖⊖ **Auberge de la Truite** – *127390 Montreuil-l'Argillé, 12km/7.5mi SW of Bernay via N 138.* ☎*02 32 44 50 47. aubergelatruite@aol.com. Closed 15 Jan–15 Feb, 25 June–5 July, Tue evening and Wed.* A pleasant village inn that has on display in the rustic dining room a collection of disparate objects: monkey organs, copper pots, coffee grinders, lanterns, etc. The cuisine, however, is familiar Norman fare.

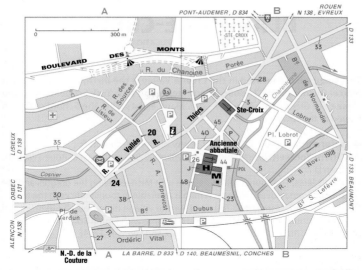

BERNAY			Gaulle R. Gén.-de	A	24	Parissot R. A.	B	40
			Héon Pl. G.	B	26	Le-Prévost-de-		
Alexandre R.	B	3	Kléber-Mercier R.	A	27	Beaumont R.	B	33
Charentonne			Leclerc R. Gén.	B	28	République		
R. de la	B	5	Lemoing R. M.	A	30	Pl. de la	B	44
Delamotte R.	B	8	Liberge-de-			Thiers R.	AB	
Folloppe R. G.	A	20	Granchain Av.	A	35	Union R. de	B	45
Gambetta R.	B	23	Morsan R. de	A	38	Victoire R. de la	B	48
Hôtel de ville	B	H	Musée municipal	B	M			

Excursion

Château de Beaumesnil★

13km/8mi SE by D 140. ⏱*Open July–Aug daily 11am–6pm. Easter–June Fri–Mon and public holidays 2-6pm. Sept daily except Tue 2-6pm.* ⏱*Closed Oct to mid-April.*

✎*7€ (under 12 no charge).* ☎*02 32 44 40 09. www.chateaubeaumesnil.com.*
The château, a masterpiece of the Louis XIII style, is built of brick and stone. The formal gardens and the 60ha/149-acre **park** echo the sumptuous lines of the château.

Château de Beaumesnil

L. Baret/MICHELIN

BLAINVILLE-CREVON

SEINE-MARITIME, POPULATION 1 113

MICHELIN MAP 304: H-4 – 20KM/12MI NE OF ROUEN

This small village located in the Crevon Valley is the birthplace of the artist Marcel Duchamp (1887-1968), forerunner of the New York School of painting (see *The Green Guide New York City*). Many artists from the School of Rouen stayed in the town.

- **Information:** 02 35 23 19 90. www.blainville-crevon.fr
- **Orient Yourself:** Blainville-Crevon is 20km/12.5mi northeast of Rouen via N 31, then D 7
- **Don't Miss:** The church, with its statue of St Michael killing the dragon, and the tour of Emma Bovary country. A map is available in tourist offices in the area.
- **Organizing Your Time:** You can tour the village in an hour; a 60km/37.5mi marked itinerary around Ry lets you pass time with Emma Bovary.
- **Also See:** Rouen, Clères, Forges-les-Eaux and Lyons-la-Forêt.

Sights

Église

Guided tours June–Sept weekends 2–6.30pm. Rest of the year, contact the town hall. 02 35 34 01 60.
The church, which was founded in 1488 has a chequered sandstone and silex facing. The interior is in the Flamboyant style. In the left transept there is a monumental late-15C statue in painted wood of St Michael slaying the dragon.

Château

Visits by appointment only. 01 42 88 95 29.
Excavations begun in 1968 on the ruins of a medieval castle have exposed a number of interesting features: a staircase buried by an 11C motte, a stretch of curtain wall, ditches and two towers.

Château de Martainville

Driving Tour

South of Blainville

Tour of 10km/6mi by D 12.

Ry

The village of half-timbered and brick houses is said to be the model for Yonville-l'Abbaye, where **Gustave Flaubert** (1821-80) set his novel *Madame Bovary*. The 12C **church** is surmounted by a lantern tower entered through a charming Renaissance wooden **porch**★.

- *Take D 13 SW.*

Château de Martainville★

Open Apr–Sept daily except Tue 10am–12.30pm, 2–6pm, Sun 2–6.30pm . Rest of the year daily except Tues 10am–12.30pm, 2–5pm, Sun 2–5.30pm. Closed 1 Jan, 1 May, 1 and 11 Nov, 25 Dec. 3€, (children no charge). 02 35 23 44 70.
The elegant brick and stone château, little changed since its contruction in 1485-1510, has a massive dovecot (16C) and a half-timbered cart shed (18C).
The château houses the **Musée Départemental des Traditions et Arts Normands** ★, with displays of furniture from Rouen and the Pays de Caux, chests, 17C buffets, 18C cupboards, earthenware and pottery, glass, pewter and copper, regional ceramics and costumes.

BRIONNE

EURE, POPULATION 4 449

MICHELIN MAP 304: E-6

In medieval times Brionne was a stronghold commanding the Risle Valley. While William of Normandy was besieging Brionne from 1047 to 1050, he encountered the monks of Bec-Helluoin Abbey, an event which had a profound impact on religious life in England.

Information: 1 rue Générale-de-Gaulle, 27800 Brionne. ☎02 32 45 70 51.

▶ **Orient Yourself:** Brionne is 40km/25mi northwest of Évreux via N 13 and D 130, and nearly the same distance east of Lisieux.

Don't Miss: The square Norman keep and the banks of the Risle.

Organizing Your Time: After an hour or two in the village, visit Le Bec-Helluoin and the châteaux of Harcourt and Champ de Bataille nearby.

Also See: Pont-Audemer, le Bec-Helluoin, Elbeuf and Bernay.

Sights

Donjon

Park in place du Chevalier-Herluin or by the church.

▶ *Take rue des Canadiens and 45m/50yd farther on turn right onto sente du Vieux-Château. 15min on foot there and back.*

The steep path leads to the ruins of one of the best examples of a square Norman keep (11C), once supported by solid buttresses. From the base of the keep (*viewing table*) there is a pleasant view over the town and the Risle Valley.

Église St-Martin

The nave is 15C and the Gothic wood vaulting in the chancel 14C. The marble altar and altarpiece (17C) come from Bec-Helluoin Abbey. The modern windows are by Gabriel Loire.

Driving Tour

28km/17mi – Allow about 1hr.

The Lieuven is a region of pastures and cereal crops. Together with the Roumois, from which it is separated by the Risle Valley, it forms the transition between the Caux and the Auge regions.

▶ *From Brionne take D 46 N. In Authon turn left onto D 38.*

BRIONNE

Chevalier-Herluin Pl. du	3
Croix-Béranger Pl. de la	5
Gaulle R. du Gén.-de	8
Lemarois R.	12
Martyrs R. des	13
République Bd de la	15
Vieux-Château Sente du	18

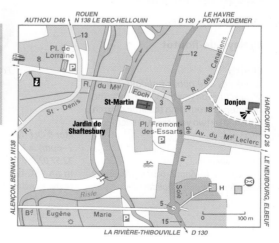

Livet-sur-Authon

A picturesque village with half-timbered houses, a castle and a church.

St-Benoît-des-Ombres

The chapel's 15C wooden porch is crowned by a wooden statue of St Benedict. Inside, a fine vault and 16C font.

▸ *Bear right towards St-Georges-du-Vièvre.*

Château de Launay

Guided tours (45min) mid-Aug – Sept. 5€.

From the main gate, approached on foot, there is a good view of this attractive early 18C building. There are also a remarkable **dovecot**★ with beams carved to depict monsters and generally grotesque characters, and attractive formal gardens. *Return to Brionne by D 137 and D 130.*

FORÊT DE BROTONNE

EURE AND SEINE-MARITIME, MICHELIN MAP 304: D-5 TO E-5

The creation of the Parc naturel régional des boucles de la Seine in 1974 and the construction of the Brotonne Bridge in 1977 have made the forest readily accessible. A village on the southern edge of Brotonne Forest, La Haye-de-Routot is part of the Écomusée de la Basse-Seine (regional open-air museum), which preserves ancient crafts.

🄸 **Information:** Maison du Parc, 76940 Notre-Dame-de-Bliquetuit. ☎02 35 37 23 16. www.pnr-seine-normande.com

▸ **Orient Yourself:** The Park extends on either side of the Seine below Rouen. Bridges at Tancarville and Brotonne as well as ferries pass from one bank to the other.

☺ **Don't Miss:** The many marked paths in the forest, as well as Vieux-Port and its surroundings.

🕓 **Organizing Your Time:** This is an opportunity to bring along a picnic lunch.

🖑 **Also See:** Pont-Audemer, Honfleur, Caudebec-en-Caux and Jumièges.

Driving Tour

From Routot to Caudebec-en-Caux

33km/20mi. Allow 1hr.

La Haye-de-Routot

Church

Weekends and public holidays 2-7pm. Lectures on yew trees Sat 2-7pm. The cemetery surrounding the little **church** is shaded by two **yew trees**★, over 1 000 years old.

Bread oven

🖑🕓*Open July–Aug: 2–6.30pm. Apr–June & Sept Sun and public holidays 2–6.30pm.*

Parc Naturel Régional de Brotonne

Mar & Oct–Nov Sun and public holidays 2–6pm. 1.80€ (children 1.50€) ☎02 32 57 07 99.

In an 18C building the **bread oven** revives ancient baking methods.

Musée du Sabot

&♿ ⏰*Same hours as bread oven.* ☞*2€ (Children 1.80€)* ☎*02 32 57 59 67.*
The **Musée du Sabot** set up in a 17C house presents tools and techniques used by makers of wooden shoes.

▶ *Take D 40 for 4.5km/3mi; turn left onto the narrow forest road which crosses D 131.*

This pleasant road passes through beautiful woods as descends into the Seine Valley. Near the river *(3km/2mi from D 131)* is a beautiful **view** *(left)* of the Seine Valley west as far as Tancarville Bridge.

▶ *Turn right onto D 65; at Le Quesney bear right onto the road to La Mailleraye and right again onto the forest road to St-Maur Chapel.*

The road passes through one of the thickest parts of the forest.

▶ *Turn left onto D 131; continue N via Rond-Victor to St-Nicolas-de-Bliquetuit. Turn left onto D 65.*

From St-Nicolas-de-Bliquetuit (site of the **Maison du Parc**), pretty gardens and half-timbered houses are strung along the silver waters of the River Seine.

Pont de Brotonne★

☞*Toll bridge.* The bridge, which spans the Seine above Caudebec-en-Caux, was opened in 1977. *Return to Caudebec via D 982.*

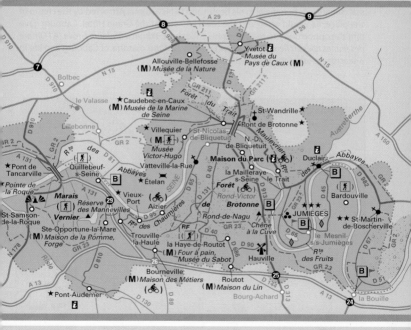

PARC NATUREL RÉGIONAL DES BOUCLES DE LA SEINE NORMANDE

0   6 km

Park boundary	**M** Museum or exhibit	🚶 Discovery trail	🛈 Information centre
GR Main footpaths	♦ Recreation area, park	🚲 Bike trail	B

CABOURG ⚏ ⚏

CALVADOS, POPULATION 3 520
MICHELIN MAP 303: L-4 – LOCAL MAP SEE PAYS D'AUGE

The large seaside resort of Cabourg, created at the time of the Second Empire (1852-70), centres on the Casino and Grand Hôtel on the seafront, from which streets radiate inland, intersecting with two semicircular avenues. Many avenues and streets are lined by attractive houses set in shaded gardens.

- 🛈 **Info:** Jardins du Casino, 14390 Cabourg. ☎02 31 91 20 00. www.cabourg.net.
- ▶ **Orient Yourself:** Take D 513 from Caen (33km/20.6mi to the southwest), Deauville (19km/12mi) and Honfleur (51km/32mi) to the east; take D 45 from Lisieux (30km/19mi to the southeast).
- 👁 **Don't Miss:** The lovely residences of Cabourg, the magnificent view from Promenade Marcel-Proust and the pretty port of Dives-sur-Mer.
- 🕓 **Organizing Your Time:** Explore in the morning to avoid crowds.
- 🏃 **Also See:** Houlgate, Deauville, Trouville, Honfleur, Lisieux, Pays d'Auge.

Famous Guest

Marcel Proust went to Cabourg for the first time in 1881, when he was 10. The coastal climate was beneficial to his health and to his asthma. Attracted by the charm of the place, he would often visit the town and stay at the Grand Hôtel. Cabourg gave him the opportunity to rediscover his childhood. *Within a Budding Grove (À l'Ombre des jeunes filles en fleurs),* was a vivid portrayal of the customs of Cabourg and life in a seaside resort at the turn of the 20C.

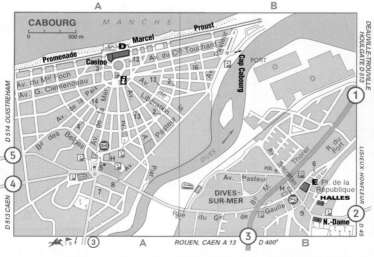

CABOURG					
		Hastings R. d'	B 6	Mermoz Av. Jean	A 12
		Hippodrome Av. de l'	A 7	Prempain Av. A.	A 3
Bertaux-Levillain Av. du Cdt	A 2	Leclerc Av. du Gén.	A 8	Prés. R.-Poincaré Av. du	A 13
Castelnau Av. Gén.-de	A 4	Manneville R. Gaston	B 9	République Av. de la	A 14
Coquatrix Pl. B.	A 5	Mer Av. de la	A	Roi-Albert-1er Av. du	B 16

Grand Hôtel	A D	Village Guillaume-le-Conquérant	B E

Excursions

Merville-Franceville-Plage
6km/4mi W of Cabourg by D 514.
When the Allies landed in June 1944 the strongest point in the defences was the Merville Battery. It was captured by the 6th British Airborne Division. One of the casemates has been converted into a museum, the **Musée de la Batterie** ♿🕐*Open Apr –Sept daily 10am–6pm. Last half of Mar & all Oct Mon, Wed, week-* ends 10am–5pm. 🚌*4.50€ (schoolchildren 2.50€)* ☎*02 31 91 47 53.*

Ranville
8km/5mi S of Merville-Franceville-Plage on D 223.
Ranville was captured at 2.30am on 6 June 1944 by the 13th Battalion of the Lancashire Fuseliers of the 6th British Airborne Division; it was the first village to be liberated on French territory. A War Cemetery to commemorates these events.

Address Book

♿*For coin ranges see the Legend on the cover flap.*

WHERE TO STAY
🛏 **Le Moulin du Pré** – *Lieu-dit le Moulin du Pré, 14860 Bavent, 7km/5mi SW of Cabourg via D 513, rte de Caen.* ☎*02 31 78 83 68. Closed 1–15 Mar, Oct, Sun evening, Mon, Tue except 15 July-15 Aug and public holidays. Reserv. advisable. 10 rooms.* 🅿️🖥. *Restaurant* 🍽🍽🍽.
A spacious garden full of trees and flowers surrounds this charming half-timbered farm from the 19C. Meals are served in an inviting, rustic dining room featuring a fireplace where meat is grilled. Pleasant rooms.

🛏🛏**Ferme de l'Oraille Bed and Breakfast** *–Chemin de Deraine, 14430 Douville-en-Auge, 7km SE of Dives-sur-Mer via D 45, D 27 between la Maison-Blanche and La Croix d'Heuland, chemin de Deraine.* ☎*02 31 79 25 49. 2 rooms.* 🖥. At this 18C Norman farm, which still produces dairy products, you can enjoy simple country comfort and sample farm milk and home-made jam at breakfast.

WHERE TO EAT
🍽**Dupont avec un Thé** – *6 av de la Mer.* ☎*02 31 24 60 32. sasdupont.dives@wanadoo.fr. Closed Tue and Wed out of season, noon on Mon, Thurs and Fri out of season except school holidays.* A tea salon offering a range of delicious cakes and sweets, notably chocolate and caramel. Branches are located in Dives, Deauville and Trouville.

🍽🍽 **Le Champagne** – *11 pl. du Marché.* ☎*02 31 24 23 39. www.hr-lechampagne-cabourg.com. Closed Mon out of season.* 🖥🖥. Opposite the market, this modest hotel-restaurant is both convenient and well managed. An elegant dining room with a menu specializing in seafood. Upstairs, comfortable guestrooms.

ON THE TOWN
Grand Casino – *Prom. Marcel-Proust.* ☎*02 31 28 19 19. Call for opening times. Discotheque Fri–Sat 11pm–5am.* In addition to its gambling facilities, the casino houses a disco (500 people), a performance hall (500 seats), an Italian-style theatre (up to 500 seats) and a panoramic restaurant facing the ocean. Terrace by the sea.
Bar du Grand Hôtel – *Prom. Marcel-Proust.* ☎*02 31 91 01 79. www.grandhotel-cabourg.com. Open daily 11.30am–1am.* The Grand Hôtel, with its Belle Epoque style, huge chandeliers and full draperies, is a monument to nostalgia. You needn't be a guest to have tea here, or better yet, enjoy a snifter of 40-year-old Calvados, while gazing out to sea.

SPORT AND LEISURE
Les écuries de la Sablonnière – *Av. Guillaume-le-Conquérant, rte de Caen, opposite the Vert Pré campsite.* ☎*02 31 91 61 70. http://sablonniere.neuf.fr. Open daily except Thur (open daily during school holidays) 9am–12.30pm, 2-6pm. Lesson 22€/hour. Tours 32€/hour.* This club organizes horseback rides on the beach and in the hinterland for all levels of experience.

CAEN★★★

CALVADOS, POPULATION 111 200
MICHELIN MAP 303: J-4 – LOCAL MAP SEE PLAGES DU DÉBARQUEMENT

Caen is the cultural capital of the Basse-Normandie, a lively city with a distinctive identity. The bombs that fell here in 1944 could have left Caen lifeless for all their violence, but the city proved resilient and drew on the strength of its history to rebuild and recreate. Today Caen is a charming place to visit. It has a modern spirit and a strong university; founded in the 15C, it now has more than 30 000 students.

- **Information:** 12 Place St-Pierre, 14000 Caen.
  ☎02 31 27 14 14. www.caen.fr/tourisme.
- ▶ **Orient Yourself:** At the junction of the rivers Orne and Odon, Caen can be reached by the A 13, some two and a half hours, or 235km/147mi from Paris.
- **Don't Miss:** The Mémorial, the Abbaye-aux-Hommes and the Fine Arts Museum (Musée des Beaux-Arts) housed in the château.
- **Organizing Your Time:** You need at least two hours to visit the Mémorial.
- **Especially for Kids:** There is an amusement park called Festyland nearby.
- **Also See:** The marked itinerary L'Affrontement (The Attack), one of several described in the Historical Area of the Battle of Normandy, starts from here.

A Bit of History

William and Matilda

The city achieved importance in the 11C when it became Duke William's favourite place of residence.

After establishing himself as Duke of Normandy, William asked for the hand of Matilda of Flanders, a distant cousin. She replied that she would rather take the veil than be given in marriage to the bastard son of the Beautiful Arlette. One fine day, mad with love and anger, the Duke rode headlong to Lille and burst into the palace of the Count of Flanders. According to the Chronicler of Tours, he seized Matilda by her plaits and dragged her round the room kicking her. Then he left her gasping for breath and galloped off. Proud Matilda was vanquished and consented to the marriage. The Pope, however objected to the cousins' distant kinship. In 1059, through the efforts of **Lanfranc,** the Pope relented. As an act of penitence the Duke and his wife founded two abbeys – the Abbey for

Abbaye-aux-Hommes

Address Book

For coin ranges see the Legend on the cover flap.

WHERE TO STAY

Hôtel St-Étienne – *2 r. de l'Académie.* ☎*02 31 86 35 82. www. hotel-saint-etienne.com. 11 rooms.* . This house, going back to the 1789 Revolution, is located in a quiet district close to the Abbaye-aux-Hommes. Note the fine wooden staircase with its beautiful patined woodwork and the smart bedrooms, some of them with fireplaces. Breakfast served in the dining room.

Hôtel Bernières– *50 r. de Bernières.* ☎*02 31 86 01 26 www.hotelbernieres. 17 rooms.* . Don't walk past the discrete entry of this hotel, or you'll regret it. The welcome is friendly, the breakfast room and lounge are charming and the rooms nicely decorated. All is touched up with bouquets of dried flowers.

Hôtel du Havre – *11 r. du Havre.* ☎*02 31 86 19 80. www.hotelduhavre. com. 19 rooms.* . Located near La Prairie and its racecourse, this post-war hotel offers modern, colourful and well-soundproofed rooms at very attractive prices.

Le Bristol – *31 r. du 11-Novembre.* ☎*02 31 84 59 76. hotelbristol@wanadoo. fr. 24 rooms.* . Those who would rather distance themselves from the bustle of the centre city will appreciate this hotel close to the Orne and the racetrack. The bedrooms, recently updated, are all identical: yellow tones, modern furnishings, sound beds and efficient double-glazed windows.

Hôtel du Château – *5 av du 6-Juin.* ☎*02 31 86 25 37. www.hotel-chateau-caen.com. 24 rooms.* . Well located in the town centre, between the marina and the chateau. Rooms are small but pleasant, painted in pastel tones.

WHERE TO EAT

Maître Corbeau – *8 r. Buquet.* ☎*02 31 93 93 00. www.maitre-corbeau.com. Closed 3 weeks in Aug, 25 Dec and 1 Jan.* This place is entirely dedicated to cheese: boxes, adverts, implements etc. Of course, your task is to choose between this cheese and that cheese, hot cheese, cold cheese and warm cheese! The establishment's generous helpings draw local connoisseurs.

Le Bouchon du Vaugueux – *12 r. Graindorge.* ☎*02 31 44 26 26. Closed 3 weeks in Aug, Sun, Mon & Wed. Reservations required.* This popular tavern (*bouchon*) is situated near the château and old Caen. Two fixed-price menus are listed on the carte du jour.

Saint-Andrew's – *9 quai de Juillet.* ☎*02 31 86 26 80. http://restaurant. st.andrew.free.fr. Reserv. advisable.* This is a good place to relax after a stroll along the Orne. In a decor reminiscent of an English pub, you will find a traditional menu, carefully prepared from local products.

L'Insolite – *16 r. du Vaugueux at the foot of the château.* ☎*02 31 43 83 87. Closed Sun–Mon except Jul–Aug. Reservations advisable.* Take the time to discover this half-timbered 16C house with its unconventional interior, mixing the rustic and the rétro: frescos, mirrors, dried flowers. On your plate, seafood. Heated terrace in winter, and a basement cigar room.

L'Embroche – *17 r. Porte-au-Berger.* ☎*02 31 93 71 31. Closed Sat lunch, Monday lunch and Sun. Reservations advisable.* This spot in the Vaugueux district has three specialties: a camembert cheese on lettuce dressed with Calvados, steak with a caramelized balsamic sauce, and *tripes Père Michel*. Good selection of cheese and wine.

A PLEASANT INTERLUDE

Café Mancel – *Le Château.* ☎*02 31 86 63.64 www.cafemancel.com. Daily 10am–midnight, closed Feb holidays, Sun evening, 1 May and Easter Mon.*This café and shop, whose name celebrates the great patron of the museum, offers high-quality local produce, as well as products from Italy, Flanders, Holland and England, partners in the museum.

Stiffler – *72 r. St-Jean.* ☎*02 31 86 08 94. www.stifflertraiteur.com. Open Wed–Sat 9am–1pm, 2.30–7.30pm, Sun 8am–6pm. Closed winter school holidays and 10 Jul–16 Aug.* This magnificent pastry shop offers specialties such as the celebrated *charlotte aux fruits de saison,* the *bavaroise au chocolat,* or the *méringue aux amandes.* Pause to enjoy the bounty. The delicatessan counter offers delicious lunch dishes and salads.

ON THE TOWN

Caen is a highly convivial and lively town. Don't hesitate to take a stroll in the pedestrian district; you will be pleasantly greeted by all the shopkeepers. In the evening tour the small Vaugueux district: several pubs and restaurants have opened in fine houses spared by the war.

Centre dramatique national de Normandie (Comédie de Caen) – *32 r. des Cordes.* ☎*02 31 46 27 27. www.cdn-normandie.com. Opening times follow the calendar of performances. Box office open Mon– Fri noon–6.30pm. Closed Jul–Aug.* The programming explores the full range of theatrical performance. Classical plays alternate with contemporary ones. Two halls, one of 300 seats and one of 700 seats.

Théâtre de Caen – *135 blvd du Mar.-Leclerc.* ☎*02 31 30 48 00. www.theatre.caen.fr. Opening times follow the calendar of performances. Closed Jul–Aug. Box office open Tue–Sat 1-6.30pm.* Inaugurated in 1963, this vast theatre with over 1 000 seats was entirely renovated in 1991. Operas, ballets and contemporary dance alternate with theatre, classical concerts, jazz sessions and traditional music programmes. Concerts are free on Saturday at 5pm Oct–May, and some evenings in the Café Cour.

SHOPPING

Librairie Guillaume – *98 r. St-Pierre.* ☎*02 31 85 43 13. librairie.gen.calv. guillaume@wanadoo.fr. Daily except Sun 9am–1pm, 2.30–7.30pm.* The carved-wood façade of this splendid bookshop dates from 1902. There is a choice of books about the region and, on the upper floor, a first-rate selection of antique books.

Poupinet – *8 r. St-Jean.* ☎*02 31 86 07 25. Tue–Thu 8am–1pm, 3–8pm, Fri–Sat 8am–8pm, Sun 8am–1pm. Closed July.* To taste authentic *tripes à la mode de Caen,* you must visit Poupinet, where you can buy this specialty put up in jars. You can also find a range of regional specialties including pâtés, terrines, country-style blood puddings, pork ears in jelly, and prepared dishes of highest quality.

MARKETS

Marché St-Pierre (Sun), rue de Bayeux (Tue), boulevard Leroy (Wed and Sat), boulevard de la Guérinière (Thu), Marché St-Sauveur (Fri), Christmas Market (Dec).

LEISURE

Hippodrome de Caen – *La Prairie.* ☎*02 333 42 41 07. Open Mar–June, Sept–Nov. Closed July–Aug.* This racecourse, nearly 2km/1.2mi long, in located in the heart of Caen. On the second floor, the panoramic restaurant offers a lovely view of the city. Visits are organised on mornings when races are held (30 times a year). Absolutely worth a visit.

Festyland – *Rte de Caumont, Boulevard Péripherique N, exit for Carpiquet, 14760 Bretteville-sur-Odon.* ☎*02 31 75 04 04. www.festyland.com. Open Jul–Aug daily 10am–7pm. June & Sept Wed 11am–6.30pm, weekends and public holidays 11am–6.30pm, school holidays 10.30am–7pm. April–May consult website for times. Closed Oct–Mar. 13€ (under 12, 11€).* This leisure park offers some 30 attractions along a Norman theme, including: giant loop the loop, bumper boats, nautical trail, old bangers, babyland, clockwork horses, 1900-style merry-go-round, water toboggans and, the latest attraction, The 1066, a super roller coaster. Food service available.

PARKS AND GARDENS

Caen is a "green city" with hundreds of acres of parks and gardens, open every morning at 8am during the week and 10am on weekends; closing times vary with the season. Tours and exhibits throughout the summer months.

The **Prairie**, a 90hectare/36 acre green space in the centre of the city, dates from the middle ages. The small lake is frequented by acquatic birds.

Parc floral de la Colline-aux-oiseaux, *av. Amiral-Montbatten, 14000 Caen.*

Jardin Botanique – *5 Pl Blot. Open daily 2–5pm.* This 300-year-old garden is the oldest in Caen and contains remarkable greenhouses with exotic plants.

Le parc Michel-d'Ornano, part of the Abbaye-aux-Dames, is a superb garden "à la française."

Men and the Abbey for Women. Bayeux remained the episcopal see.

When William departed to conquer England, faithful Matilda became regent of the duchy; in 1068 she was crowned Queen of England. She was buried in the Abbey for Women in 1083. William died in 1087 and was buried in the church of the Abbey for Men.

Battle of Caen

Two Agonizing Months – The battle lasted for over two months. On 6 June 1944 there was a heavy bombing raid; fire raged for 11 days and the central area was burnt out. On 9 July the Canadians, who had taken Carpiquet Airfield, entered Caen from the west but the Germans, who had fallen back to the east bank of the Orne in Vaucelles, began to shell the town. The liberation ceremony took place in Vaucelles on 20 July but German shelling lasted another month.

Under the Conqueror's Protection – On 6 June many people sought shelter in St-Étienne Church. During the battle over 1 500 refugees camped out in the abbey church. An operating theatre was contrived in the refectory of the Lycée Malherbe, which was housed in the monastery buildings of the Abbey for Men. The dead were buried in the courtyard. Some 4 000 people found accommodation in the Hospice of the Good Saviour (Bon Sauveur) nearby. The Allies were warned by the Préfet and the Resistance and these buildings were spared.

The quarries at Fleury, 2km/1mi south of Caen, provided the largest refuge. Despite the cold and the damp, whole families lived like troglodytes until the end of July.

Port of Caen – Although the River Orne has always enabled Caen to serve as a port, no major development took place until the middle of the 19C, when Baron Cachin dug a canal parallel to the river. The canal (12km/7mi long) was regulated by several locks and served by an outer basin at Ouistreham. Since then the increased output of the Caen steelworks has required the deepening and widening of the canal and the creation of five more docks: St-Pierre for pleasure boats, the New Dock, the Calix Dock, the Hérouville Dock and the Blainville Dock, which came into use in 1974.

Today the transportation of cereals is the chief function of Caen harbour, the largest one in the Basse-Normandie, which can receive ships of up to 19 000t fully laden and up to 30 000t partially laden. Because of its broad range of activities, this port is ranked 11th in France.

The opening of a cross-Channel car ferry service on 6 June 1986 has established daily links between Caen-Ouistreham and Portsmouth, catering to an estimated one million passengers every year.

Walking Tour

Hôtel d'Escoville★

This mansion, which now houses the tourist office and the Artothèque, was built between 1533 and 1538 by Nicolas Le Valois d'Escoville, a wealthy merchant. The bomb damage incurred in 1944 has been repaired.

Behind the plain street façade there is a **courtyard** flanked by two wings at right angles; the harmonious proportions, the arrangement of the various elements and the majestic sculptures make an elegant composition. The main block facing the entrance is surmounted by an unusual ornament, a large two-storey dormer window supported by flying buttresses projecting from a steep pavilion roof. Climb up to the loggia for a view of the whole courtyard.

Église St-Pierre★

🕐Open daily except some Sun afternoons. Restoration work is underway.

Although only a parish church, St Peter's is richly decorated. Construction started in the 13C, was continued during the 14C and 15C and completed in the 16C in the Renaissance style. The impressive tower (78m/256ft), which dated from 1308, was destroyed during the Battle of Caen in 1944. "The king of Norman belfries" has, however, been rebuilt as well as the nave into which it fell (all the vaulting

Académie R. de l'	CY	2	Bir-Hakeim Pont de	EZ	9	Caumont R. A. de	CY	15
Alliés Bd des	DY	3	Bosnières R.	CX		Chanoine X. de		
Arquette R. de l'	DEZ		Briand Bd A.	DZ		St-Paul R	CDX	16
Auge R. d'	EZ		Brunet R. H.	EYZ	10	Chanoines R. des	EX	
Bagatelle Av. de	CX	4	Caffarelli Q.	EY		Chaussée-Ferrée R. de la	EZ	18
Barbey-d'Aurevilly R.	CX	7	Calix R. de	EX		Churchill Pont	EZ	21
Basse R.	EXY		Canada Av. du	CXY		Clemenceau Av. G.	EX	
Bayeux R. de	CX	8	Canada Pl	CX		Cordeliers R. des	DXY	
Berrières R. de	DEY		Caponière R.	CY	12	Cordes R. des	EX	
Berthelot Av. P.	EY		Carel R. du	CZ		Courtonne Pl.	EY	26
Bertrand Bd	CDYZ		Carmes R. des	EYZ		Creully R. de	CX	27
Bicoquet R.	CY		Carrières-St-Julien R. des	CDX	13	Croisiers R. des	DY	

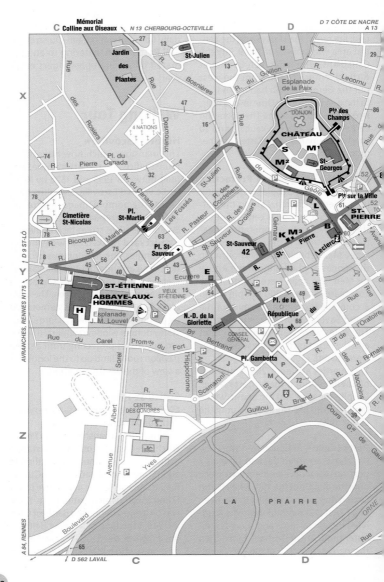

Croix-Guérin Av.	EX	
Decaen R. Gén.	EZ	28
Délivrande R. de la	DX	29
Desmoueux R.	CX	
Docteur-Rayer R.	CX	32
Doumer R. Paul	DY	33
Écuyère R.	CY	
Édimbourg Av. d'	DX	35
Engannerie R. de l'	DEY	
Falaise R. de	EZ	38
Foch Pl. Mar.	DZ	39
Fontette Pl.	CY	40
Fort Prom. du	CZ	
Fossés-St-Julien Les	CXY	
Froide R.	DY	42
Fromages R. aux	CY	43
Gaillon R. du	DX	
Gambetta Pl.	DZ	
Gare R. de la	EZ	
Gaulle Cours Gén.-de	DEZ	
Gémare R.	DXY	
Géôle R. de	DXY	
Guillaume-le-Conquérant R	CY	45
Guillou Bd Yves	CDZ	
Guillouard Pl. L.	CY	46
Hamelin Q. Amiral	EZ	
Haute R.	EX	
Havre R. du	EZ	
Jacobins R. des	DYZ	
Juifs R. aux	CX	47
Juillet Q. de	EZ	
Lair R. P.-A.	DY	49
Laplace R.	EZ	
Lebisey R. de	EX	50
Lebret R. G.	DYZ	51
Leclerc Bd Mar.	DYZ	
Lecornu R. L.	DX	
Lenoir R. R.	EY	
Libération Av. de la	DXY	52
Londe Q. de la	EY	
Louvel Espl. J.-M.	CY	
Malherbe Pl.	CDY	54
Manissier R.	EX	55
Marot R. J.	CY	56
Meslin Q. E.	EZ	57
Miséricorde R. de la	EYZ	58
Montalivet Cours	EZ	59
Montoir-Poissonnerie R.	DY	61
Oratoire R. de l'	DYZ	
Orne Rd-Pt de l'	EZ	
Paix Espl. de la	DX	
Pasteur R.	CY	
Pémagnie R.	CX	63
Petit-Valleren Bd du	CZ	65
Pierre R. I.	CX	
Pigacière R. de la	DEX	
Pont-St-Jacques R. du	DY	68
Reine-Mathilde Pl.	EX	69
République Pl. de la	DY	
Résistance Pl. de la	EYZ	
Romain R. J.	DEZ	
Rosiers R. des	CX	
Sadi-Carnot R.	DZ	72
St-Gabriel R.	CX	74
St-Jean R.	DEYZ	
St-Manvieu R.	CY	75
St-Martin Pl.	CY	
St-Martin R.	CY	
St-Michel R.	EZ	77
St-Nicolas R.	CY	78
St-Pierre Pl.	DY	80
St-Pierre R.	DY	
St-Sauveur Pl.	CY	
St-Sauveur R.	CDY	
Scamaroni R. F.	CDZ	
Sévigné Prom. de	EZ	81
Sore Av. Albert	CZ	
Strasbourg R. de	DY	83
Tourville Av. de	EY	
Vaucelles Pont de	EZ	
Vaucelles R. de	EZ	85
Vaugueux R. du	DX	86
Vendeuvre Pont	EZ	
Vendeuvre Q.	EYZ	
Verdun R. de	DEZ	
Victor-Hugo Av.	EY	
11-Novembre R. du	DEZ	90
6-Juin Av. du	DEYZ	

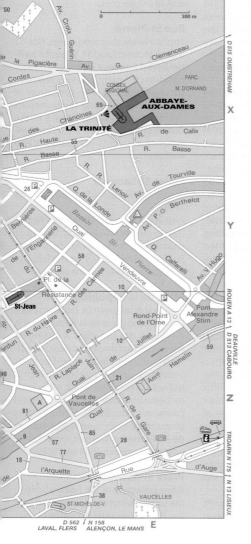

D 515 OUISTREHAM

ROUEN A 13

DEAUVILLE
D 513 CABOURG

TROARN N 175 / N 13 LISIEUX

D 562 / N 158
LAVAL, FLERS   ALENÇON, LE MANS

Abbaye-aux-Dames	EX		Église St-Julien	CX	Maison des Quatrans	DY	L
Abbaye-aux-Hommes	CY		Église St-Pierre	DY	Maisons à pans de bois	DY	K
Batiments conventuels			Église St-Sauveur	DY	Musée de Normandie	DX	M²
(Hôtel de ville)	CY	H	Église St-Étienne	CY	Musée de la Posteet des		
Cimetière St-Nicolas	CY		Église de la Trinité	EX	Techniques de		
Colline aux Oiseaux	CX		Hôtel d'Escoville	DY	B	Communication	DY	M³
Église N.-D.-de-la-			Jardin des Plantes	CX	Musée des Beaux-Arts	DX	M¹
Gloriette	CDYZ		Le Mémorial	CX	Porte des Champs	DX	
Église St-Georges	DX		Le château	DX	Porte sur la Ville	DY	
Église St-Jean	EZ		Maison de Malherbe	CY	E	Salle de l'Échiquier	DX	S

has been redone). The west front has been restored to its 14C appearance; the Flamboyant porch is surmounted by a rose window.

The **east end**★★, built between 1518 and 1545, is remarkable for the richness of its Renaissance decor, in which the shapely and graceful furnishings (ornate pinnacles, urns, richly scrolled balustrades, carved pilasters), have replaced the Gothic motifs.

Some of the **capitals**★ (*second and third pillars on the left*) are interesting for their carvings which are taken from the bestiaries of the period and chivalrous exploits. The third pillar shows (*from left to right*) Aristotle on horseback threatened with a whip by Campaspe, Alexander's mistress; the Phoenix rising from the flames (Resurrection); Samson breaking the lion's jaw (Redemption); the Pelican in her Piety (Divine Love); Lancelot crossing the Sword Bridge to rescue his Queen; Virgil suspended in his basket by the daughter of the Roman emperor; the unicorn (Incarnation), pursued by hunters; Gawain on his deathbed with an arrow wound (*image is damaged*).

The Renaissance vaulting in the second part of the nave, near the chancel, contrasts with the vaulting in the first part: each arch is embellished with a hanging keystone, finely carved. The most remarkable keystone, in the fifth arch over the high altar, is 3m/10ft high and weighs 3t; it is a life-size figure of St Peter.

The chancel is enclosed by four arches (late 15C-early 16C) surmounted by a **frieze**★★ in the Flamboyant Gothic style with a delicate decoration of flowers and foliage.

The Gothic style prevails up to 2.75m/9ft from the ground but above that level the Renaissance influence increases to predominate in the **vaulting**★★ by Hector Sohier. The vaulting in each chapel is highly ornate; the pendants look like stalactites.

Rue St-Pierre

This is a lively shopping street. Nos 52 (Postal Museum) and 54, beautiful **half-timbered houses**★ with steep gables, date from the early 16C; very few have survived in Caen. The profusion of carved decoration and the numerous small statues of saints belong to the Gothic style but there are a few Renaissance elements (balustrades and medallions).

Église St-Sauveur

🕐*Open daily 9am–5pm.* ☎*02 31 86 13 11.*

Also known by its old name of Notre-Dame-de-Froide-Rue, St Saviour's church has twin chevets facing rue St-Pierre: Gothic (15C) on the left and Renaissance (1546) on the right.

Place de la République

The pedestrian precinct, between place St-Pierre and place de la République, is lively both day and night. A turning off the west side of boulevard du Maréchal-Leclerc and rue Pierre-Aimé-Lair leads onto place de la République, which is laid out as a public garden; it is bordered by beautiful Louis XIII houses (Hôtel Daumesnil at nos 23-25) and the modern offices of the Préfecture. **Notre-Dame-de-la-Gloriette**, a former Jesuit church, was built between 1684 and 1689.

Place St-Sauveur

A fine collection of 18C houses borders the square, where the pillory stood until the 19C. At the centre is a statue of Louis

XIV as a Roman emperor. The north-east side of the square is the site of the old St Saviour's which was destroyed in 1944.

▶ *Continue along rue Guillaume-le-Conquérant.*

On your way, note the row of attractive houses in rue Jean-Marot; they date from the early 20C.

▶ *Turn right on rue St-Martin, which will take you to the Abbaye-aux-Hommes and the Église St-Étienne (described below).*

Place St-Martin

Note the statue of Constable Bertrand du Guesclin. Interesting view of the two towers of St-Étienne.

▶ *Continue NE along the Fossés St-Julien and turn right onto rue de Géôle.*

The 15C half-timbered house (no 31) is called **Maison des Quatrans**.

Rue du Vaugueux

Rue Montoir-Poissonnerie leads to this lovely pedestrian street which has kept its quaint charm: cobblestones, stone and timber houses, old-fashioned street lights.

▶ *Return to place St-Pierre.*

Visit

The Abbeys★★

Allow 2hr total.

Abbaye-aux-Hommes★★

Despite their different styles, St-Étienne Church and the monastery buildings of the Abbey for Men constitute a historical and architectural unit.

Église St-Étienne★★

This is the church of the abbey founded by William the Conqueror; Lanfranc was the first abbot before being appointed Archbishop of Canterbury and it was probably he who drew up the plans.

The church was started in 1066 in the Romanesque style, and was completed in the 13C in the Gothic style (east end, chancel, spires). The building was damaged during the Wars of Religion in the 16C and painstakingly restored in the early 17C by Dom Jehan de Baillehache, the Prior.

Following the Maurist reforms of the Benedictine order (1663) the abbey enjoyed a period of prosperity until the French Revolution: the church was richly furnished and the monastery was rebuilt. In the 19C St-Étienne became a parish church and the monastery was converted for use as a school. Fortunately the buildings survived the Battle of Caen unscathed.

Romanesque art has produced few more striking compositions than this plain **west front**; there are no ornate porches, no rose windows, only a gable end resting on four sturdy buttresses and pierced by two rows of round-headed windows and three Romanesque doors. Lanfranc seems to have exercised the artistic severity of Ravenna and Lombardy in his native country. The austerity of the west front is, however, tempered by the magnificent soaring towers (11C). The first storey is decorated with fluting, the second with single pierced bays and the third with paired bays. The octagonal spires with their turrets and lancets in the Norman Gothic style were added to the two towers in the 13C; the north tower is finer and more delicate in style.

The vast nave is almost bare of ornament except for the great round-headed arches. The construction of the sexpartite vaulting in the 12C altered the arrangement of the clerestory which is decorated with fretwork typical of the Norman style. At the west end of the church is the organ (1747) flanked by two telamones.

The lantern tower above the transept crossing was constructed in the 11C but rebuilt early in the 17C. The gallery in the north transept houses a large 18C clock in a carved wooden surround. In the 13C the Romanesque chancel was replaced by a Gothic construction, including an ambulatory and radiating chapels; it was the first of the Norman Gothic chancels and subsequently served as a model. With the Gothic style new decorative motifs were introduced: chevrons on the archivolts, rose windows in the spandrels of the lateral arches, trefoils piercing the tympana of the bays in the galleries, capitals ornamented with crochets and foliage. Note the spacious galleries above the ambulatory and the elegant central arches. The handsome stalls and pulpit are 17C.

In front of the altar is a stone inscribed with an epitaph. The sarcophagus containing the body of William the Conqueror was originally placed beneath the lantern but when the church was sacked by the Huguenots in the 16C ,the Conqueror's remains were scattered; all that remains is a femur which is interred beneath the stone. A monumental 18C paschal candlestick stands on the north side of the altar. The chancel is enclosed by a beautiful 19C wrought-iron screen; the cartouches bear the names and arms of the former abbots, priors and other dignitaries of the abbey.

In the sacristy there hangs an unusual portrait of William the Conqueror, painted in 1708, in which he is made to resemble Henry VIII.

▶ *Leave the church by the chancel door and skirt the handsome east end★★ of St-Étienne (13C-14C) to reach the gardens in Esplanade Louvel which have been restored according to the 18C plans.*

Monastery Buildings★

Monastery buildings of the Abbaye-aux-Hommes – ♿ 🔊*Guided tours (1h 30min), circuit A (buildings, cloister and chapter-hall) at 9.30 am, 2.30 and 4pm. Circuit B (buildings, cloister, press, guardroom) at 11 am. Additional visits (45min) offered Jul–Aug 10.15am, 3.15 and 5.15pm.* 🕐*Closed 1 Jan, 1 May, 25 Dec.* 💶*2€ (under 18 years and Sun, no charge).* ☎*02 31 30 42 81.*

Entrance through the town hall. These fine buildings were designed early in the 18C by Brother Guillaume de la Tremblaye, the great master builder of the Congregation of St Maur; the **woodwork**★★ is particularly beautiful.

The east wing comprises the monks' **warming room**, now a municipal exhibition hall; the **chapter-house**, formerly a collegiate chapel and now a registry office, is panelled in light oak and hung with 17C paintings; the chapel **sacristy**, panelled in oak, contains a painting by Charles Lebrun (1619–1690) (*Moses Confronting an Egyptian Shepherd*) and a collection of Norman headdresses. The hall, which features 18C stairs with a wrought-iron banister, leads to the **cloisters** (18C), where the groined vaulting centres on octagonal coffers. From the south-east corner of the cloisters there is a very fine **view**★★ of the towers of St-Étienne and the south side of the church. Fixed to the door into the church is a dark oak timetable of the offices said by the monks (1744). A doorway leads into the **parlour**, a large oval room with an unusual elliptical vault and beautiful Louis XV wooden doors. The **refectory**, now used for meetings, is sumptuously decorated with late-18C oak panelling and broken barrel vaulting. Some of the paintings above the door and the blind apertures are by Lépicié, Restout and Ruysdael. The wrought-iron banister of the **grand staircase** is decorated with floral motifs. The bold design has no central support. The remarkable Gothic hall in the courtyard, known as the **guard-room**★, was built on the remains of a Gallo-Roman structure and is now used for meetings. The panelled ceiling is shaped like an upturned hull. Originally there were two rooms as the two chimneys suggest.

View of the Abbey★★

Walk through the gardens in Esplanade Louvel to reach the east side of place Louis-Guillouard near Old St-Étienne Church (Vieux St-Étienne), a charming ruin, with the Jesuit church of Notre-Dame-de-la-Gloriette in the background. This is the best view of the 18C monastery buildings flanking the impressive east end of St-Étienne with its bristling bell turrets, flying buttresses, clustering chapels and steep roofs, topped by the lantern tower and the two soaring spires.

Abbaye-aux-Dames★

Founded in 1062 by **Queen Matilda**, the Abbey for Women is the sister house to the Abbey for Men; the towers of St-Étienne Church can be seen at the end of rue des Chanoines from place de la Reine-Mathilde.

Église de la Trinité★★

🚹 ◔ *Open 9am–6.30pm.* ☎*02 31 86 13 11.*

The old abbey church, which dates from the 11C, is a building in the Romanesque style. Its original plan was inspired by that of Benedictine abbeys, characterised by sturdy tiered apsidioles. The spires were replaced early in the 18C by heavy balustrades.

The vast nave of nine bays is a fine example of Romanesque art. Broken barrel vaulting marks the transition from the nave into the spacious transept. Adjoining the south transept is an attractive chapel, which is now used as the chapter-house. It was built in the 13C replacing two Romanesque chapels similar to the two in the north transept. The late-11C groined vaulting in the chancel covers a magnificent span. In the centre of the chancel is Queen Matilda's tomb, a simple monument consisting of a single slab of black marble, which has survived unscathed despite the Wars of Religion and the Revolution.

The crypt *(access by steps in the chapel in the south transept)* is well preserved. The groined vaulting rests on 16 columns, standing close together, which define five bays. An attempt at historiated decoration can be seen on one of the capitals, illustrating the Last Judgement, in which St Michael is portrayed gathering up the dead as they rise from their graves.

Conventual Buildings

🚹 ▰*Guided tours (1hr15 min) 2.30 and 4pm.* ◔*Closed 1 Jan, 1 May, 25 Dec.* ⊜*no charge.* ☎*02 31 06 98 98.*

From the French-style garden in the main **courtyard** one can admire the luminous golden façades. The cloisters (only three sides were completed) are a replica of the one in the Abbey for Men. Leading off them is a small oval room, the washroom *(lavabo)*, decorated with stone pilasters and a carved frieze like those in Greek temples; it is furnished with four black-marble basins set in recesses ornamented with a shell. In the **refectory** (used as a reception room or as a gallery for temporary exhibitions), pilasters with Ionic capitals and two columns which flanked the abbess' chair have survived whereas the oak panelling which covered the lower walls has been removed.

The **Great Hall**, which is the focal point of the whole abbey and leads into the church, is graced by **two flights** of stairs decorated at first-floor level with a cartouche bearing a plant motif; the walls are adorned with portraits of the two last abbesses, Anne de Montmorency and Marie-Aimée de Pontécoulant.

Château★

Allow 3hrs including museums.

The imposing citadel dominating the mount was begun by William the Conqueror in 1060 and fortified in 1123 by his son, Henry Beauclerk who added a mighty keep (demolished in 1793). During the 13C, 14C and 15C it was repeatedly enlarged and reinforced.

Throughout the 19C it was used as soldiers' barracks and was severely damaged in the bombardment of Caen in 1944. Since then its massive walls have been restored to their early grandeur.

The line of the ramparts has changed little since the days of William the Conqueror. In some places the walls date from the 12C, but most of them were built in the 15C. The two main gateways are protected by barbicans.

▶ *Enter the castle by the ramp which approaches the south gate opposite St Peter's Church.*

After passing a round tower, a defensive outwork, one enters the citadel by the town gate *(porte sur la ville)*.

From the terrace (east) and the rampart sentry walk there are fine **views**★ of St Peter's Church and western Caen as far as the Abbey for Men. On the west side of the gate, behind the Normandy Museum, a platform provides an interesting **view**★ over the south-west sector of the town and the belfries of the many churches.

The north rampart, the first to be restored under the current program, can be visited for a remarkable view★ of Caen (♿ 📷 *Guided tour (35min). Times posted at the entry to the Musée de Normandie. 🚫No charge.*)

The castle precinct encloses the modern **Musée des Beaux-Arts** (*east*) near the **Porte des Champs** (Field Gate), an interesting example of 14C military architecture; the **Chapelle St-George**, a 12C chapel which was altered in the 15C; the **Musée de Normandie** (*west*) in a building which was the residence of the Bailiff in the 14C and of the Governor of Caen in the 17C and 18C; a rectangular building, incorrectly called the **Salle de l'Échiquier** (Exchequer Hall), which is a rare example of Norman civil architecture in the reign of Henry Beauclerk and was the great hall of the adjoining ducal palace (foundations only visible); adjoining it was the Normandy Exchequer (the Ducal Law Court). Farther north lie the foundations of the keep which was built by Henry Beauclerk and altered in the 13C and 14C; it was a huge square structure, a round tower at each corner, surrounded by a moat which was joined to the castle moat. 📷 *You can stroll in the castle moat; descend from the porte des Champs.*

Musée des Beaux-Arts★★

♿🕐*Open daily except Tue 9.30am–6pm. 🕐Closed 1 Jan, Easter Sunday, 1 May, Ascension, 1 Nov, 25 Dec. 🎟Temporary exhibits 3–5€. Permanent collection no charge. ☎02 31 30 47 70.*

😊 *The Café Mancel offers a pleasant pause inside the museum where you can enjoy a meal or a drink.*

Situated within the precinct of William the Conqueror's castle, the Fine Arts Museum offers its collections from a chronological, thematic and geographical point of view. Large religious paintings and imposing historical and allegorical scenes hang in vast halls, bathed in light, whereas works of religious fervour and smaller paintings are essentially displayed in the small cabinets. The large galleries display landscapes, battle scenes and portraits.

The first three rooms on the ground floor are devoted to 15C, 16C and 17C Italian painting: the *Marriage of the Virgin* by Perugino, with a remarkable new frame, a triptych representing the *Virgin and Child between St George and St James* by Cima da Conegliano; in a room entirely devoted to Veronese, two paintings are of particular interest: the Temptation of St Anthony and Judith and Holofernes; also worth noting are *Coriolanus Implored by His Mother* by Il Guercino and *Glaucus and Scylla* by Rosa Salvatore.

The next room deals with 17C French painting with outstanding works by Philippe de Champaigne (*Louis XIII's Vow*) and also religious or mythological paintings by Vouet, Vignon, La Hyre and Le Brun.

Three intimate rooms are devoted to Dutch and Flemish 17C painting with works such as *A Seascape* by Solomon van Ruysdael, *Virgin and Child* by Roger van der Weyden and *Abraham and Melchizedek* by Rubens.

In the gallery devoted to the 18C are displayed works by French and Italian portrait and landscape painters: Hyacinthe Rigaud (*Portrait of Marie Cadenne*), François Boucher (*Young Shepherd in a Landscape*), Locatelli, Lalemand, Tournières.

On the lower level, the various aspects and the evolution of painting during the 19C and the early 20C are depicted through works by Romantic painters (Géricault, Delacroix, Isabey), Realists (Courbet: *The Lady with the Jewels*, Ribot), landscape painters (Corot, Dupré), Impressionists (Vuillard: *Portrait of Suzanne Desprez*, Bonnard, Dufy, Van Dongen: *Portrait of Madame T Raulet*), and Cubist painters (Gleizes, Villon, Meitzinger). Local artists are also represented: Cals, Fouace, Gernez, Lemaître, Lépine, Lebourg, Rame.

Innovations by contemporary painters such as Tobey (*Appearances*), Mitchell (*Fields*, 1990), Soulages, Dubuffet (*Migration*), Vieira da Silva, Szenez, Asse and Deschamps illustrate the different postwar trends: Conceptual art, Abstract landscape, Abstract art, Environmental art. From one end to the other, the museum thus presents an impressive chronology of the history of painting.

Musée de Normandie★

🕐 *Open daily except Tue 9.30am–6pm.* 🕐 *Closed 1 Jan, Easter, 1 May, Ascension, 1 Nov, 25 Dec.* 🎫 *No charge.* ☎ *02 31 30 47 60.*

The history and traditions of Normandy are illustrated by the presentation of the many archaeological and ethnographical exhibits.

The first section is devoted to the prehistoric period up to the arrival of the Vikings in 911 and concentrates on the culture and technology of the era: excavated artefacts, miniature replica of the burial mound at Fontenay-le-Marmion, statue of a mother goddess found at St-Aubin-sur-Mer, weapons and jewellery found in medieval cemeteries (tomb of a metalworker buried with his tools).

The second section follows the evolution of agriculture: land use (models comparing different types of cultivation and farms), agricultural techniques (display of ploughs, scythes and millstones).

The third section is devoted to crafts and industrial activities: stock breeding, ceramics (jugs, funerary ornaments and decorative ridge tiles), wood (beautifully carved marriage chests), metallurgy (iron and copper work: craftsman's tools, copperware from Villedieu-les-Poêles), textiles (costumes, headdresses and bridal ware in silk lace); the last room concentrates on the work of the candlemaker (interesting collection of candles for Easter, funerals and as votive offerings) as well as ceremonial articles belonging to the different brotherhoods (gold thread embroidery and tintenelles, the tiny hand-bells used in processions by the Brothers of Charity).

Musée de la Poste et des Techniques de Communication

🕐 *Open mid-June to mid-Sept daily except Sun and Mon 10am–noon, 2–6pm, Sat 2–6pm. Mid-Sept to mid-June daily except Sun and Mon 1.30–5.30pm.* 🕐 *Closed public holidays. 2.50€ (children 1€)* ☎ *02 31 50 12 20.*

This Postal and Telecommunications Museum, in a lovely half-timbered 16C house, illustrates the history of the

The Marriage of the Virgin by Perugino

M. Segve/Musées des Beaux-Arts, Caen

postal service through documents and equipment.

Le Mémorial★★

Allow 3hrs. ♿🕐 *Open mid-Feb–Oct 9am–7pm (last entry 1hr15min before closing). Nov–Dec and last week Jan–mid-Feb daily except Mon 9.30am–6pm.* 🕐 *Closed 1st 3 weeks of Jan and 25 Dec.* 🎫 *17.50€ (under 10 years no charge).* ☎ *02 31 06 06 44. www.memorial-caen.fr.*

ℹ *Directions to the memorial are signposted from the centre-city and from the Péripherique Nord.*

The memorial erected by the city, which in 1944 was at the centre of the Battle of Normandy, takes the form of a Museum for Peace; it is primarily a place of commemoration and of permanent meditation on the links between human rights and the maintenance of peace.

The façade of the sober building of Caen stone, facing Dwight-Eisenhower Esplanade, is marked by a fissure which evokes the destruction of the city and the breakthrough of the Allies in the Liberation of France and Europe from the Nazi yoke. It stands on the site of the bunker of W Richter, the German general, who on 6 June faced the British-Canadian forces.

The main events of the Second World War, the causes and the issues at stake, are presented in the light of the latest historical analysis. A particularly imaginative display, centred on a spiral ramp, on such themes as the inter-war years and the advance of Fascism; the use of extensive archive material, including

Recent Recipients of the Nobel Peace Prize

2006– Mohammad Yunnus, Grameen Bank (Bangladesh)

2005 – International Atomic Energy Agency, Mohamed ElBaradei

2004– Wangari Maathai (Kenya)

2003 – Shirin Ebadi (Iran)

2002 – Former American President Jimmy Carter

2001 – The UNO and its Secretary-General Kofi Annan

2000 – Kim Daejung (South Korea)

1999 – Doctors Without Borders

1998 – David Trimble (Protestant) and John Hume (Catholic) in Northern Ireland

1997 – International Campaign to Ban Landmines (ICBL, founded in 1992)

1996 – His Eminence Carlos Belo and José Ramos-Horta (East Timor)

1995 – Joseph Rotblat and the Anti-Nuclear Pugwash Campaign (Great Britain)

1994 – Yasser Arafat (Palestine), Yitzhak Rabin and Shimon Peres (Israel)

1993 – Nelson Mandela and Frederik De Klerk (South Africa)

1992 – Rigoberta Menchu (Guatemala)

1991 – Aung San Suu Kyi (Burma)

1990 – Mikhaïl Gorbatchev (Soviet Union)

1989 – The Dalai Lama (Tibet)

1988 – The United Nations' Peacekeeping Forces

a gripping panoramic projection of D-Day, seen simultaneously from the Allied and the German standpoint, as well as moving testimonies by witnesses of and participants in the drama, confers on this presentation of our recent past the authenticity of living experience.

The film *Hope* uses strong images and original music by Jacques Loussier to trace the alternating outbreaks of war and peace which have followed.

A walk to the Vallée du Mémorial will enable visitors to see the Parc de la Colline aux Oiseaux, in which the Floralies de la Paix has been created. The **Mur de la Liberté** (Wall of Freedom) pays tribute to the hundreds of thousands of American soldiers who fought for freedom in Europe.

▶ *Return to place St-Pierre.*

Additional Sights

St-Nicolas Cemetery★

🕓*Open Mar–Oct 8am–6pm. Nov–Feb 8am–5pm.* ✆*No charge.* 🅿*Park in the lot to the right of the church.*

St Nicholas' Church (deconsecrated) was built late in the 11C by the monks of the Abbey for Men and has not been altered

since. The west door is protected by a beautiful triple-arched Romanesque porch, an exceptional feature in Normandy.

The church is surrounded by an old graveyard (entrance left of the west front); one may stroll among the mossy tombstones under the shade of the trees and admire the magnificent apse at the east end beneath its steep stone roof.

Église St-Jean

The fine Flamboyant Gothic building was begun in the 14C, and repaired in the 15C. The bell-tower, of which the base and first storey are 14C, was inspired by the tower of St Peter's but, owing to the instability of the marshy ground, the spire and the belfry were never built, nor was the central tower; the lower courses of its second storey were capped with a dome.

The vast nave has a remarkable Flamboyant triforium and a highly ornate cylindrical **lantern tower**★ over the transept crossing. The highly venerated statue of Our Lady of Protection dates from the 17C. In the south transept there is an old retable (17C) from the Carmes Convent depicting the Annunciation and bearing statues of St Joseph and St

Le Mémorial

Teresa of Avila. In 1964 a statue of Joan of Arc was transferred from Oran to a site near the east end of the church in place de la Résistance.

Église St-Julien

🕐*Open daily except Sat afternoon and Sun 9.30am–noon, 2–5pm.* ☎*02 31 85 44 53.*

The old church, which was destroyed in 1944, was replaced in 1958 by this modern building. The sanctuary wall, elliptical in shape, forms a huge piece of latticework like that of a stained-glass window.

Excursions

Cintheaux

15km/9mi. From Caen take N 158 S. about 30min.

The village, renowned for its late-12C church, stands on the southern edge of the Caen countryside, in an old mining area marked by solitary slag heaps.

The road from Caen to Falaise passes through country laboriously recaptured during the Battle of Normandy between 8 and 17 August 1944 by the Canadian 1st Army (Gaumesnil cemetery) and its Polish units (Langannerie cemetery).

Troarn

14km/8mi about 30min. Leave Caen going E and then take N 175. In Troarn

take rue de l'Abbaye (second turn on the right after the church).

This little town, which was founded in 1048 by Roger de Montgomery, contains the remains of a 13C abbey.

Driving Tours

1 North of Caen

Round-trip of 31km/19mi – allow half a day.

▶ *From Caen take D 7 and at the top of the hill, turn right on D 401, then D 60 to the left.*

The road bends to the right and there is a panoramic view of Caen.

Biéville-sur-Orne

The blind arcades and oculi which decorate the west front of the church recall the architecture of Tuscany.

▶ *Take the road W to Épron.*

Épron

This small locality, which was razed in 1944, has been called the Village of the Radio since 1948. The origin of the nickname was a radio programme which sought to determine which of France's départements had been most severely damaged. Calvados was named, and a lottery draw among 10 communes fell

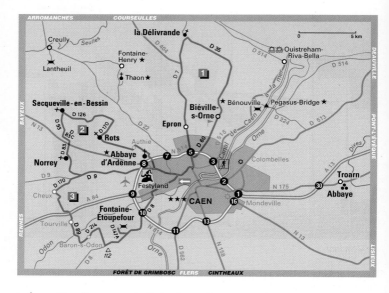

to Épron. The village was rebuilt thanks to a collection of small change taken up on its behalf.

②Churches and Abbeys

35km/21mi – about 2hr

▶ *From Caen take D 9 W towards Bayeux on rue de Bayeux and then rue du Général-Moulin. Half way up a hill on the outskirts of the town turn right onto the road to the abbey.*

Abbaye d'Ardenne★

🕐 *Open daily except Mon 2–6pm.* 🚶*Guided tour on weekends of convent every 30 min.* 🚫*No charge. Leave the car at the main gate (12C).* ☎02 31 29 37 37. www.imec-archives.com.

The abbey, which was founded in the 12C by the Premonstratensians, fell into ruins during the 19C but has recently benefited from a major restoration project. An exhibit describing its history can be seen at its sister abbey of Mondaye. In the first courtyard stands a huge 13C tithe barn (*back left*) with aisles which is covered by a single asymmetrical wooden roof (*restored – open during temporary exhibitions*). The 13C **abbey church**★ has been damaged on the outside but the nave is a very pure example of the Norman Gothic style.

Since 1998, the abbey has housed a major archive of French publications. The abbey church is now a research library.

▶ *Drive W to Rots via Authie.*

Rots

The **church** has an attractive Romanesque west front; the nave dates from the same period; the chancel is 15C.

▶ *Take D 170 N; in Rosel turn left onto D 126.*

Secqueville-en-Bessin

The 11C **church** has a fine three-storey tower and a 13C spire. The nave and transept are decorated with blind arcading.

▶ *Take D 93 and D 83 S.*

Norrey-en-Bessin

Church. 🚶*Guided tour available on written request to M. Roland Audes, Mairie, pl. Charles-de-Gaulle, 14740 St-Manvieu-Norrey.*

The little Gothic **church** boasts a great square lantern tower but no spire; the interior is richly carved; the chancel was built in the 13C.

▶ *Return to Caen by D 9.*

③ The Battle of Odon

37km/23mi – Allow about 2hr.
The name of this river recalls the hard-fought battles which took place between 26 June and 4 August 1944 south-west of Caen.

▶ *Leave Caen by the r. de Bayeax, then take D 9.*

The road skirts the airfield which the 12th SS Panzers held for three days, from 4 to 7 July, against the Canadian 3rd Division.

▶ *After another 3km/2mi bear left on D 170; in Cheux turn left behind the church onto D 89; after crossing N 175, at the top of a slight rise, follow D 89 round to the right and straight through Tourville.*

This is the line of the British advance, which began on 26 June in pouring rain at Tilly-sur-Seulles (*northwest*); the objective was the River Orne to the south-east. A memorial has been erected (*right*) to pay tribute to the men of the 15th Scottish Division who fell here.
Just when it seems that the road has reached the floor of the Odon Valley it drops into a rocky ravine, hitherto hidden by thickets; the river has created a second valley within the main valley. It is easy to see what a valuable line of defence this natural obstacle would have been and to appreciate the difficulties of the British troops exposed to heavy fire from the Germans on the far side of the valley. In fact the British lost more men crossing the Odon than crossing the Rhine.
The road climbs the opposite slope to a crossroads. The road on the left (D 214) passes straight through Baron-sur-Odon and continues to a T-junction marked by a stone monument surmounted by an iron cross (*right*). The raised roadway to the right, an old Roman road also known as Duke William's Way, leads to another T-junction where a stele has been set up to commemorate the battles fought by the 43rd Wessex Division. To the south stands **Hill 112** later known as Cornwall Hill.

▶ *Take D 8 to the left towards Caen.*

A monument at the junction with D 36 recalls the operations which took place in July and were marked by some fierce duels between armoured vehicles. A night attack on 15 June took place by the light of an artificial moon created by the reflection of searchlights on low cloud.

▶ *Turn left onto D 147A.*

Near a farm on the right the Château de Fontaine-Étoupefour comes into view.

Château de Fontaine-Étoupefour
Access by a track on the right beyond the farm. 🚶 *Guided tours (1hr) July–Sept Sun–Tue 2–6.30pm.* 🕐*Closed 26–28 Aug.* 💶*5€ (under 13 years no charge).* ☎*02 31 26 73 20.*
Nicolas d'Escoville, who built the Hôtel d'Escoville in Caen, owned this castle. It is surrounded by a moat spanned by a drawbridge which leads to an elegant 15C gatehouse bristling with turrets and pinnacles. The dining room is hung with three interesting paintings of hunting scenes. On the far side of the paved courtyard stand the ruins of one of the two main blocks (late 16C), currently undergoing restoration.
The refectory houses an exhibit about the battle of Hill 112 in 1944, of which the château was the centre.

▶ *Return to D 8 to reach Caen.*

CHÂTEAU DE CARROUGES★★

ORNE, POPULATION 743

MICHELIN MAP 310: I-3

For almost five centuries this immense château and park (10ha/25 acres), belonged to a famous Norman family, Le Veneur de Tillières; in 1936 it was bought by the nation. The town of Carrouges is part of the Parc naturel régional Normandie-Maine.

- **Information:** Rue du Crochet, 61320 Carrouges. ☎02 33 26 78 43.
- ▶ **Orient Yourself:** Set on a high point northwest of the Écouves forest, Carrouges is 26km/16mi east of Bagnoles-de-l'Orne and 30km/18 mi northeast of Alençon.
- **Don't Miss:** The majestic grand staircase at the château.
- **Organizing Your Time:** Count on at least 90 minutes to see the château.
- **Especially for Kids:** The apple orchard at the entrance to the château may revive their interest in this familiar fruit.
- **Also See:** Argentan, Sées, Alençon, Lassay-les-Châteaux and Bagnoles-de-l'Orne.

The Château

Guided tours (45min, last tour 45 min before closing). Mid-June–Aug 9.30am–noon, 2-6.30pm. Apr–mid-June 10am–noon, 2–6pm. Rest of the year 10am–noon, 2–5pm. Closed 1 Jan, 1 May, 1 and 11 Nov, 25 Dec. 6.50€ (under 18 years no charge). ☎02 33 27 20 32.

Park

From the park with its fine trees and elegant flower beds there are good views of the château.
The **Conservatoire botanique des pommiers de Bretagne et de Normandie**, at the entrance to the property, includes 152 varieties of apple trees.

Exterior

The 16C **gatehouse**★ is an elegant brick building with decorative geometric patterns. It was almost certainly built by Jean Le Veneur, bishop of Lisieux and abbot of Bec, who helped fund Jacques Cartier's 1534 expedition to Canada.
The château itself is austere but imposing. Surrounded by a moat, the buildings are arranged around an inner courtyard. The stables and domestic quarters occupy the ground floor; the apartments and state rooms are on the first floor.

Interior

The **kitchen** presents an imposing array of copper pans. The **Louis XI Bedroom** was named after the King's visit on 11 August 1473. The panelling is adorned with delicate panels of foliage highlighted in a different colour.
In the principal **antechamber** the chimney breast is decorated with a hunting scene. The remarkable fireplace in the **dining room** is flanked by two polished granite piers with Corinthian capitals. The sideboards are Louis XIV; note the Restoration chairs. The **portrait gallery** with its Louis XIII chairs assembles past lords and owners. The **drawing room** occupies part of one of the corner tow-

© CRT Normandie

Château de Carrouges

Address Book

⚬For coin ranges see the Legend on the cover flap.

WHERE TO EAT

⚬⚬ **Le Jean-Anne** – *2 r. de la Fée-d'Argouges. 61150 Rânes,11km/6.6mi NW of Carrouges via D 908 and D 909. ☎02 33 39 75 16. Closed last 2 weeks of Feb, Tue evening and Wed except public holidays.* Enjoy the view of the small Romanesque church and the châteauwhile dining in this simple, spick-and-span restaurant. The wife presides over the stoves while the husband takes your order. Traditional bourgeois cuisine.

SHOPPING

La Maison des métiers – Maison du Parc, *61320 Carrouges. ☎02 33 81 75 75 - www.parc-naturel-normandie-maine. fr. Open July-Aug & Dec.* Located in the restored buildings of the l5C chapter house at the château, the House of Crafts of the Parc Naturel Régional Normandie-Maine offers arts and crafts exhibitions and has objects for sale.

---

ers. The straw-coloured panelling dates from the late 17C or early 18C. The visit ends with the monumental great **staircase**★ and its brickwork vaulting and round headed arches as they wind up and round the square stair well.

The Village

La Maison du Parc – BP 05, 61320 Carrouges. ◷Open daily except weekends and public holidays 9am–noon, 2-8pm. *☎ 02 33 81 75 75. www.parc-naturel-normandie.fr.*

Carrouges stands within the boundary of the **Parc Naturel Régional Normandie-Maine**. The **Maison du Parc** (park's visitor centre) occupies the restored buildings of a 15C chapter of canons, an outbuilding of the château.

Normandie-Maine Regional Nature Park

Created in 1975 and spread over two regions (Basse-Normandie and the Pays de Loire), the **Parc Naturel**

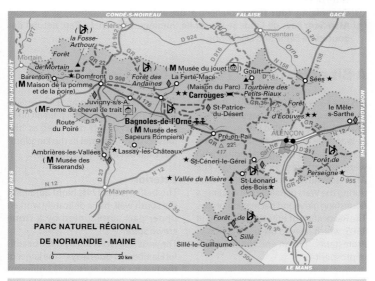

PARC NATUREL RÉGIONAL DE NORMANDIE - MAINE

0   20 km

◆ Recreation area, park   M Museum   🧗 Climbing   ⊙ Of special interest to children

Régional Normandie-Maine covers 235 000ha/907sq mi and includes 150 communes from the Orne, Manche, Mayenne and Sarthe départements.

Lying on the boundaries of both Normandy and Maine, the park can be divided into an upper stretch *(haut pays)*, featuring crests and wooded escarpments in the Alpes Mancelles, and a lower stretch *(bas pays)*, characterised by a bocage landscape, the rolling hills of Saosnois and open fields around Sées and Alençon.

The park can be explored by car or on a bicycle via four itineraries: the **Route des Trois Forêts** (three forests); the **Route Historique des Haras et Châteaux de l'Orne** (historic châteaux and stud farms); the **Circuit au Pays de Lancelot du Lac**; the **Route du Poiré,** (techniques of making cider, Calvados and perry).

There are 2 500km/1 553mi of signposted paths, including 250km/155mi associated with different themes.

CAUDEBEC-EN-CAUX ★

SEINE-MARITIME, POPULATION 2 342 MICHELIN MAP 304: E-4

Caudebec settles around the Seine where the Ste-Gertrude Valley runs into the river. The Brotonne Bridge leads directly to the forest of the same name. A fire in 1940 destroyed most of the old buildings, but the fine Church of Our Lady was virtually undamaged and three old houses to the left of the church give some idea of what Caudebec must once have looked like.

- **Information:** Place du Général-de-Gaulle, 76490 Caudebec-en-Caux. ☎02 32 70 46 32. www.caudebec-en-caux.com.
- **Orient Yourself:** At midway between Rouen (48km/30mi east) and Le Havre (52km/32.5mi west), Caudebec is on the banks of the Seine.
- **Parking:** Public lots are located on Place du Marché (except Saturday mornings), Place Henri-IV and Place d'Armes.
- **Don't Miss:** The Flamboyant architecture of Notre-Dame church, and the pretty town of Villequier.
- **Organizing Your Time:** You need a day at Caudebec.
- **Also See:** Pays de Caux, St-Wandrille, Jumièges, Rouen, Le Parc naturel des Boucles de Seine and Lillebonne.

A Bit of History

A Short-Lived Prestigious Past –
The name Caudebec first appears in the 11C on a charter granted to the monks of St-Wandrille Abbey. In the 12C the town was fortified to resist the English who were nevertheless victorious in 1419. After submitting to Henri IV in 1592, during the Wars of Religion, it became a flourishing glove and hat making centre. The Revocation of the Edict of Nantes in 1685, which revived the persecution of Protestants, put an end to this period of prosperity.

Église Notre-Dame ★
30min
This fine Flamboyant edifice (☞*see illustration in Introduction: Religious architecture)* which Henri IV described as "the most beautiful chapel in the kingdom" was built between 1425 and 1539.

Exterior
The belfry (53m/174ft high) adjoining the south wall, has a delicately worked upper part surmounted by a stone crown spire.

The west face is pierced by three beautiful Flamboyant **doorways** – the larger of the two is said to portray 333 different characters – and by a remarkable rose window surrounded by small statues.

CAUDEBEC-EN-CAUX		Cordonnerie R. de la	5	Poissonnerie R. de la	10
		Gaulle Pl. Gén.-de	6	Rive R. de la	12
Baillage R. du	2	Havre R. du	7	St-Clair R.	13
Basin R.	3	Letellier R.	8		
Churchill Av. W.	4	Marché Pl. du	9		

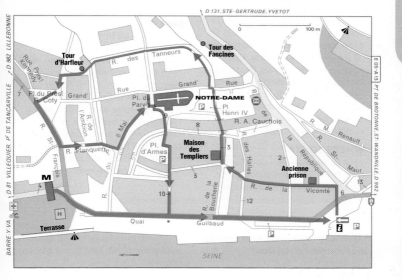

Interior

There is no transept. The triforium and tracery are the most characteristically Flamboyant features.

The 17C **font** (*left*) is decorated with intricately carved panels. The **great organ** ★ (early 16C – &*see illustration in Introduction: Religious architecture*) was restored in 1972; it has 3 345 pipes of repoussé pewter.

Chapelle du Saint-Sépulcre

The Chapel inspired Fragonard, who made a sketch of it. Beneath the 16C baldaquin a recumbent Christ, carved in incredible detail, faces some very large stone statues – all from Jumièges Abbey. The Pietà between the windows is 15C.

Chapelle de la Vierge

The Lady Chapel is famous for its **keystone**★, a 7t monolith supported only by the dependent arching and forming a 4.30m/13ft pendentive. The architect of this feat, Guillaume Le Tellier, lies buried in the chapel and is commemorated in a plaque beneath the right window.

Walking Tour

2km/1.25mi. About 1hr starting from the tourist office. From place du Général-de-Gaulle, take rue de la Vicomté. The Sentier de la Gribane (signposted and dotted with explanatory panels) provides an interesting itinerary for visiting the city. The promenades of La Vignette and Mont-Calidu offer lovely vistas of the town. On the right , the old prison is set in the 14C ramparts.

▶ *Continue along rue Thomas-Basin.*

Maison des Templiers

🕐 *Open Mar–Oct Wed–Thur 2.30–6.30pm, Fri–Sat 10am–noon, 2.30–8pm. Sun and public holidays 10am–noon, 2.30–6.30. ∞4€ (under 16 years no charge)☎02 35 96 95 91.*

The Templars' House is a precious specimen of 13C civil architecture which has retained its two original gable walls.

▶ *Follow cours de la Sainte-Gertrude.*

Address Book

For coin ranges see the Legend on the cover flap.

WHERE TO EAT

⊜⊜ **Auberge du Val au Cesne** – *Le Val au Cesne, 76190 Yvetot.* ☎*02 35 56 63 06. valaucesne@hotmail.com. Closed 10 Jan–1 Feb, 23 Aug–7 Sept, Mon– Tue.* ⊑ Lying in a remote vale, this Norman inn, with timber-framed walls, an exuberant garden and an aviary, is delightful. The cuisine is in harmony with the decor: it tastes of the authentic. A few comfortable guestrooms.

WHERE TO STAY

⊜⊜ **La Normandie** – *Quai Guilbaud.* ☎*02 35 96 25 11. www.le-normandie. fr. 16 rooms.* 🅿⊑. *Restaurant* ⊜⊜.

Located along the road that skirts the Seine, this small, unpretentious hotel offers simple, very tidy, functional rooms with a view of the river in the front. View of the river in the restaurant; traditional Norman cuisine.

⊜⊜ **Les Poules Vertes Bed and Breakfast** – *68 r. de la République.* ☎*02 35 96 10 15.http://villamaux.ifrance. com . 4 rooms.* 🍴⊑. This former barn, nestled in a lush English-style garden, is the ideal home base for discovering the region. The bedrooms, where family souvenirs abound, are cosy and comforting. The exceptionally kind welcome will have you planning your next visit before you leave.

You walk by two towers: **tour des Fascines** and **tour d'Harfleur**.

▶ *Take rue du Havre, on the left, and then left again on rue Planquette.*

Église Notre-Dame
See description above.

Musée de la Marine de Seine
🕐*Open daily Apr–Sept 2–6.30pm. Rest of the year 2–5:30pm.* 🕐*Closed 1 Jan and 25 Dec.* ⊕*3.25€(under 8 years no charge).* ☎*02 35 95 90 13.*
The museum is devoted to the history of navigation along the River Seine: ports, commercial exchanges, shipbuilding, crossings. Visitors can learn about a bygone phenomenon, the **tidal bore,** which used to rip down the Seine.

▶ *Return to Place du Gén.-de-Gaulle along the quai Guilbaud.*

Driving Tours

Around St-Wandrille

▶ *Round-trip of 8km/5mi. Leave Caudebec by rue St-Clair and follow chemin de Rétival keeping to the right.*

The road runs along the top of a small escarpment with tantalising glimpses of the bend in the river.

▶ *At the bottom of a steep descent take D 37 on the left.*

The road goes up a delightful little **valley**★ with thatched farmhouses scattered here and there.

▶ *Before Rançon, turn right on D 33 to St-Wandrille.*

Abbaye de St-Wandrille★
See Abbaye de ST-WANDRILLE.

▶ *Take D 22 and D 982 back to Caudebec.*

Latham-47 Monument
This commemorates the polar explorer **Roald Amundsen** and his companions, who disappeared in the Arctic in 1928.

▶ *Take D 22, than D 982 to return to Caudebec.*

Around Barre-y-Va

▶ *Round-trip of 21km/13mi. Leave Caudebec to the N on the Yvetot road and turn left onto D 40.*

Ste-Gertrude

The small **church** stands in attractive surroundings. It was consecrated in 1519 and is Flamboyant in style.

▶ *Head W on D 40, then D 30. Turn S on D 440 towards Anquetierville. At the junction with D 982 turn left, then at St-Arnoult right onto D 440. Turn right onto D 281 and almost immediately left down a steep hill to Villequier.*

Villequier★

Musée Victor-Hugo – Access through the rue Ernst-Binet. ○*Open Apr–Sept daily except Tue 10am–12.30pm, 2–6pm, Sun 2–6pm. Rest of the year daily except Tue 10am–12.30pm, 2–5pm, Sun 2–5.30pm.* ○*Closed 1 May, 1 and 1 and 11 Nov.* ◉*3€ (children no charge).* ☎*02 35 56 78 31.*

Villequier occupies a beautiful **site**★ on the banks of the Seine at the foot of a wooded height crowned by a castle. In 1843, six months after their marriage, Charles Vacquerie and his wife, Léopoldine Hugo, the daughter of the novelist and poet Victor Hugo, were drowned in the Seine at Villequier.

A house once owned by the Vacquerie family, rich boat-builders from Le Havre, has been converted into the **Musée Victor-Hugo**★.

▶ *Take D 81 back to Caudebec.*

Barre-y-Va

Chapel – ○*Daily 2-6.30pm.*

This tiny hamlet is named after the tidal wave or bore (*barre*) which used to swell upstream along the Seine.

▶ *Return to Caudebec via D 81.*

Around Yvetot

▶ *22km/14mi – 1hr 30min. Leave Caudebec and go N on D 131. After 4km/2mi, turn right on D 33 then left on D 37 towards Yvetot.*

Yvetot

Église St-Pierre – ○*Open daily 9am–noon, 2–6pm, Sun 9am–noon. Audioguides available at tourist office.*

The town, made famous in a song as the capital of an imaginary kingdom, is in fact a large market town on the Caux plateau. The **Église St-Pierre** (1956) contains remarkably large **stained-glass windows**★★ by Max Ingrand, which produce a dazzling effect; other windows show founders of religious orders, saints of the Rouen diocese and the saints of France. The Lady Chapel (*behind the altar*) windows depict episodes in the life of the Virgin.

▶ *Take D 131 S; turn right on the by-pass; turn left on D 34.*

Allouville-Bellefosse

The village is known for the **oak tree** (*chêne*) which grows in front of the church; it is believed to be more than 1 300 years old, one of the oldest in France and the most famous tree in Normandy.

▶ *Follow the signs to the Musée de la Nature (1.5km/1mi).*

Musée de la Nature

♿○*Open July–Aug daily 10am–noon, 2–7pm. Apr–June & Sept Mon–Sat 2–6pm, Sun and public holidays 10am–noon, 2–6pm. Rest of the year Wed, Sat and school holidays 4–6pm, Sun 10am–noon, 2–6pm.* ○*Closed 1 Jan, 25 Dec.* ◉*3.50€.* ☎*02 35 96 06 54.*

The Nature Museum is located in an old Caux farmhouse. Two diorama displays show local bird families and a reconstitution of the Normandy countryside (coastline, marsh, plain, forest and farmyard). The coastline is shown before and after the effects of pollution.

▶ *Return to Allouville, take D 34 then turn left on D 40; take D 131 back to Caudebec.*

PAYS DE CAUX★

SEINE-MARITIME, MICHELIN MAP 512 FOLDS 7-10, 19-22

The Caux is mainly known for its impressive coastline. Visitors delight in the natural beauty of the area, returning each year to the vast beaches below the splendid chalk cliffs. The surrounding countryside offers a swathe of remarkable churches, castles and manor houses.

- **Information:** Several villages have their own tourist offices. Those of Dieppe, Étretat, Le Havre and Caudebec-en-Caux also serve the Caux region.
- ▶ **Orient Yourself:** The Pays de Caux is bounded on the south by the Seine valley, on the west and north by the Alabaster Coast and on the east along a line extending between Dieppe and Rouen.
- **Don't Miss:** The resorts and little villages of the Alabaster Coast, as well as the charming villages of the interior and the Parc des Boucles de la Seine.
- **Organizing Your Time:** You will need several days to tour this region.
- **Especially for Kids:** The outdoor centre on Lac de Caniel offers sports and games. (*See address book*).
- **Also See:** Dieppe, Varengeville-sur-Mer, Fécamp, Étretat, Le Havre, Honfleur, Lillebonne, Caudebec-en-Caux, St-Wandrille, Clères and Neufchâtel-en-Bray.

Geological Notes

Côte d'Albâtre – Along the Alabaster Coast the chalk cliffs, with alternate strata of flint and yellow marl, are worn away ceaselessly by the action of the tides and the weather. The Étretat needle rocks and underwater shelves 1.6km/1mi from the shore indicate the former coastline. At the particularly exposed point of **Cap de la Hève** erosion is 2m/6ft a year; the water is milky with chalk, and flints are pounded endlessly upon the beaches. The hollows (valleuses) cut into every cliff top as far as the eye can see are dry valleys, truncated by the retreating coastline.

Caux Farmsteads – The farms appear as green oases surrounded by 2m/6ft-high windbreaks topped by a double row of oaks, beeches or elms. The **farmstead** comprises a meadow planted with apple trees in which stand the half-timbered farm buildings. The entrance is often through a monumental gateway. In spring cattle and horses pasture tethered to a post (**tière**) and each animal marks out his territory in the form of a perfect circle. Milk is the chief source of income.

Driving Tours

1 Côte d'Albâtre★

From Dieppe to Étretat – 104km/65mi – about 5hr
Glimpses of the sea and cliffs and pleasant views of resorts are the main features of the drive, which is at its best in the morning.

Dieppe★★
See DIEPPE.

▶ *Leave Dieppe by D 75.*

G. Targat/MICHELIN

Port of St-Valery-en-Caux

Address Book

For coin ranges, see the Legend on the cover flap.

WHERE TO STAY

Le Château de Grosfy Bed and Breakfast – *61 r. du Calvaire , 76570 Hugleville-en-Caux.* 02 35 92 63 60.*www.chateaudegrosfy.com. 4 rooms.* . A lovely alley of lime trees leads to this 18C-19C family home, formerly a hunting lodge. Both rustic and reproduction antique furniture in the large, peaceful guestrooms. Billiards, library, board games and kitchen available. Large park with a little woods.

Mme Genty Bed and Breakfast – *Hameau de Ramouville, 76740 St-Aubin-sur-Mer, 4km/2.4mi N of Bourg-Dun, then dir. Quiberville.* 02 35 83 47 05.*www.gisele.genty.free.fr. 5 rooms.* . Skilful restoration work has revived the ancient appeal of this typical late-18C farm. Bedrooms are decorated in the country spirit. Mornings, the delicious scent of warm bread will draw you towards the breakfast room.

Château de Mesnil Geoffroy Bed and Breakfast – *76740 Ermenouville, 12 kim/7.5mi S of St-Valery-en-Caux via D 20 and D 108.* 02 35 57 2 77. *www.chateau-mesnil-geoffroy.com. 5 rooms.* . A 17C-18C château, ranked as an historic monument, surrounded by a park with a superb rose garden. Guestrooms are refined and furnished with antique family furniture and art objects. Pleasant welcome by true princes, fortunate proprietors of this remarkable site.

WHERE TO EAT

La Boussole – *76460 St-Valery-en-Caux. Closed Jan–Feb, Mon and Tue.* Prettily set in a navy blue half-timbered house, this restaurant opposite the port is entirely devoted to seafood. Two cosy rooms with bistrot chairs and wooden tables. Shellfish platters in summer and many fish specialties. Piano music in the evening.

Le Belvédère – *76280 St-Jouin-Bruneval, 10km/6mi S of Étretat via D 940 then D 111.* 02 35 20 13 76. *Closed 10 Jan–9 Feb, Wed evening, Sun evening and Thu.* A curious blue building perched upon the cliffs of the Pays de Caux. The comfortable dining room, nicely renovated, offers an exceptional view of the sea. Enjoy fish, mussels and other shellfish while gazing over the deep blue sea.

LEISURE

Parc de Loisirs Eau et Nature – *Société du Lac de Caniel, 76450 Cany-Barville, between St-Valery-en-Caux and Fécamp.* 02 35 97 40 55. *www. lacdecaniel.fr. Open daily except Sun evening 11am–7pm. Longer hours for bowling.* This outdoors centre offers nautical activities: water skiing, rowing, canoeing, kayaking, windsurfing etc. Supervised beach (July–Aug).

Pourville-sur-Mer

This seaside resort, pleasantly situated near jagged cliffs, has risen from the ruins of the Dieppe commando raid of 19 August 1942; the Cameron Highlanders and a Canadian Regiment, the South Saskatchewan, landed to the sound of bagpipes, inflicted severe damage on the enemy and, under cover of the Navy and by sacrificing their rearguard, re-embarked early in the afternoon. A commemorative stele of pink marble stands on the seafront.

▶ *Continue W on D 75.*

Varengeville-sur-Mer
See VARENGEVILLE-SUR-MER.

Ste-Marguerite-sur-Mer

The 12C church, which has no transept, was considerably remodelled in the 16C. Inside, four of the original **arches**★ remain on the north side; those on the south date from 1528. The high altar dates from 1160 and is one of the very few of this date still extant.

▶ *At St-Aubin bear left onto D 237.*

Le Bourg-Dun

Notre-Dame-du-Salut is a vast composite church, remarkable for its **tower**★ built on a massive square 13C base. The hatchet-shaped roof is 17C. A Renaissance door opens into the south aisle. Beneath Flamboyant vaulting in the south transept are a Renaissance bay and piscina; the beautiful south aisle was added in the 14C. The font in the north aisle is Renaissance.

▶ *Return to St-Aubin.*

Veules-les-Roses★

The seaside resort, sheltered in a small valley, has pretty surroundings, notably windmills and picturesque villas. **St-Martin**, in the town itself, is a 16C-17C church with a 13C lantern. A timber-framed roof covers the nave and aisles. Inside are five 16C twisted, limestone columns and ancient statues.

▶ *Turn left onto D 37.*

Église de Blosseville

The church, surmounted by a 12C belfry, possesses beautiful Renaissance stained-glass windows and some old statues.

▶ *Continue towards Ermenouville on D 37.*

Château du Mesnil-Geoffroy

Ermenouville. ◐ *Open May–Sept.* ☞*Guided tours (45min) Fri–Sun and public holidays 2.30-6pm.*◉*5.30€ (under 15 years no charge). Park: May–Sept daily except Mon and Tue 2.30–6pm.*◉*4.30€ (under 15 years no charge).*☎*02 35 57 12 77.www.chateau-mesnil-geoffroy.com*

A. de Valroger/MICHELIN

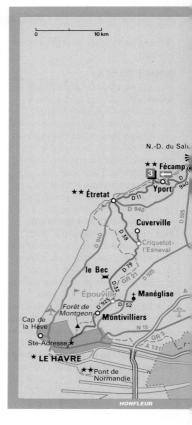

Surrounded by a 9ha/22.3-acre formal French park with a famous rose garden containing 2 500 species, this 17C and 18C château is a interesting testimony to the gentle art of living under Louis XV.

▶ *After leaving the château, turn onto D 70.*

Le Mesnil-Durden

Do not fail to visit this charming village and its wild garden, an irregular plot of land with many paths and embankments, planted with all manner of herbs carrying quaint, old-fashioned names.

St-Valery-en-Caux★

St-Valery is both a popular seaside resort, with a promenade overlooking the long shingle beach, and a fishing and coastal trading port.
The **Falaise d'Aval**★ (West Headland) *(access on foot via sentier des Douaniers*

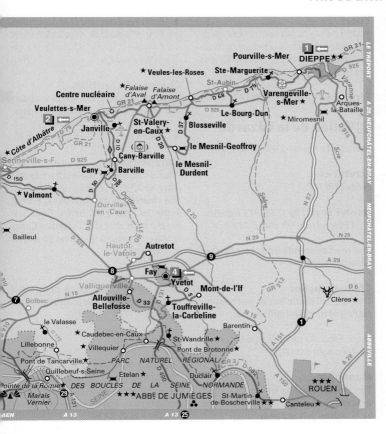

and steps) is crowned by a monument commemorating the battles of June 1940 (51st Highland Division and the French 2nd Cavalry Division). The view embraces the Ailly lighthouse and, on a clear day, Dieppe. The **Maison d'Henri IV** (quai du Havre) is a beautiful Renaissance house with carved beams. On the **Falaise d'Amont** (East Headland) (access by steps) stands the 51st Highland Division Monument overlooking the town, harbour and beach. The more modern monument nearby was erected in memory of Coste and Bellonte who in 1930 made the first flight from Paris to New York.

Centre nucléaire de production d'électricité de Paluel.

Tours are suspended for security reasons. For information: ☎02 35 57 69 99.
The nuclear power station consists of 45 autonomous units each with a capacity of 1 300 MW. It is fueled by enriched uranium and cooled by sea water pumped from the ocean. The thermal energy generated is transformed into mechanical, then electrical energy. A **visitor centre** has an exhibition on energy sources.

Veulettes-sur-Mer

The 11C and 13C church stands half way up a hill overlooking the seaside resort in the wide green valley below.
The finest **panorama**★★ is between Senneville (narrow road) and Fécamp, near the **Chapelle Notre-Dame-du-Salut** (sailors' pilgrimage), from the belvedere with a viewing table.
The cliffs to the west of Fécamp stretch as far as Étretat. Fécamp and its harbour appear after a sharp bend to the left.

Fécamp★★
⌂See FÉCAMP.

Yport

Yport is a seaside resort tucked away in a valley. Despite the lack of harbour facilities, there was a sizeable fishing fleet until 1970.

Étretat★★ – *See ÉTRETAT.*

②Vallée de la Lézarde

Étretat to Le Havre –33km/21mi – 1hr

Étretat★★
See ÉTRETAT.

▶ *Leave Étretat by D 39. At Criquetot-l'Esneval turn left onto D 239.*

The road descends into the pleasant Lézarde Valley.

Château du Bec

The 12C-16C castle has an enchanting setting of trees and still waters.

▶ *In Épouville turn left onto D 925 and then right onto D 52.*

Manéglise

The small church is one of the most graceful examples of Romanesque architecture in Normandy.

▶ *Return to Épouville; continue S.*

Montivilliers
See Le HAVRE.

▶ *The road leaves the Vallée de la Lézarde via Rouelles, just outside Le Havre.*

The road goes along the edge of Montgeon Forest, and leads to the Jenner tunnel, which leads to the town centre.

Le Havre★★
See Le HAVRE.

③Vallée de la Durdent

From Veulettes-sur-Mer to Fécamp – 36km/23mi – about 3hr

Veulettes-sur-Mer
See above.

▶ *From Veulettes take D 10 S. In Paluel turn left onto D 68. After a sharp right hand bend, turn left at the top of a rise to the chapel.*

Chapelle de Janville

The old pilgrimage church has an attractive wrought-iron grille in the chancel.

▶ *Return to Paluel. Turn left onto D 10.*

Cany-Barville

Guided tour on request from tourist office. ☎02 35 57 17 70.
The **church** on the west bank, rebuilt in the 16C, has a 13C belfry. Dominating the high altar (18C) stands a Christ in Majesty consisting of over 80 angels in relief work.

Barville

The small church has a delightful **setting**★ between two arms of the River Durdent.

▶ *Take D 131.*

Château de Cany

Guided tours (45min) July–Aug daily except Fri 10am–noon, 3–6pm. Closed 4th Sun in July. 6€ (children 7–18 years 3€). ☎02 35 97 87 36.
Surrounded by moats fed by the River Durdent stands an imposing stone and brick château built at the end of the Louis XIII era. The apartments have retained fine 17C and 18C furnishings. In the basement, a kitchen contains utensils, crockery and costumed figures.

▶ *Take D 50 to Ourville, then turn right onto D 150 which descends into the Valmont Valley.*

Valmont
See VALMONT.

▶ *Return to D 150 towards Fécamp.*

Fécamp★★ *See FÉCAMP.*

④Plateau de Caux★

Round-trip starting from Yvetot – See CAUDEBEC-EN-CAUX.

ANCIENNE ABBAYE DE CERISY-LA-FORÊT

MANCHE, POPULATION 839

MICHELIN MAP 303: G-4 – 8.5KM/5MI W OF BALLEROY – LOCAL MAP SEE BAYEUX

The abbey at Cerisy is a remarkable example of Norman Romanesque architecture. The first monastery dates from around 510. In 1032 Robert I of Normandy, the father of William the Conqueror, founded a new monastery here dedicated to Vigor, former bishop of Bayeux.

▶ **Orient Yourself:** Between Bayeux (22km/13.75mi northwest) and St-Lô (18km/11.25 mi southwest), at the exit from the forest of Cerisy near D 572.
- **Don't Miss:** The remarkably light and clear vaulting of the apse.
- **Organizing Your Time:** You will need 2hrs to see the abbey.
- **Also See:** The D-Day beaches, Bayeux, the château of Balleroy, Aunay-sur-Odon, Saint-Lô and the Parc naturel régional des marais.

Visit

Église Abbatiale★

15min ⏱Open Apr–mid-Nov daily except Mon 11am–6pm. 3€ (Children no charge) Guided tour (45min) 4€. ☎02 33 57 34 63.

The nave is remarkable for its height. The choir and especially the apse are a striking example of Romanesque architecture characterised by their delicacy and abundance of light, when most 11C buildings were massive and sombre.

Walk round the church to the east end to admire the **chevet**★ with its tiered effect formed by the apse, the choir and the belfry.

Conventuel Buildings

30min ⏱Same as the Eglise.

Following the Revolution, these 13C buildings were used as a stone quarry.

Musée lapidaire

A low chamber with pointed vaulting houses the Archaeological Museum. At the far end of the chamber, on the left, is a dungeon with 15C and 16C graffiti.

Chapelle de l'Abbé

The Abbot's Chapel, built in the 13C with a gift from St Louis, is a good example of Norman Gothic architecture.

CHÂTEAU DU CHAMP DE BATAILLE★

EURE, MICHELIN MAP 307: F-7 – 4KM/2.5MI NW OF LE NEUBOURG

The name, which means "Castle of the Battlefield", may recall a battle in 935 between forces of the count of Cotentin and of William Longsword, ancestor of the Conquerer: Or it may be that a peasant named Bataille owned the field ("champ"). The 17C château was built by Alexandre de Créqui and occupied by the Harcourt family before it was looted in 1795. In the 20C it was used as a hospice, a camp for war prisoners and a jail for women. The Duke of Harcourt bought it in 1947 and began restoration, continued by the present owner, Jacques Garcia.

🅱 Gardens open June–Aug 10am–6pm. Mid-Apr–May, Sept–Oct weekends and public holidays 2–6pm. 10 € (children 8€).

Interior of château: ✎Audio-guided tour July–Aug 3.30–5.30pm. Mid-Apr–June, Sept–Oct weekends 3.30–5.30pm. ✏20 € (children 15€).
☎02 32 34 84 34. www.chateauduchampdebataille.com.

▶ **Orient Yourself:** The château is just outside Le Neubourg, some 23km/14.4mi southwest of Rouen, by N 138, then D 83 south.

⊛ **Don't Miss:** The park, recently restored according to designs by Le Nôtre.

◷ **Organizing Your Time:** It takes at least an hour to explore the chateau and surrounding gardens.

⚶ **Also See:** Harcourt, Le Neubourg, Le Bec-Hellouin, Rouen

Visit

Main Courtyard

This quadrangle is entered through a gate pierced in a wall adorned with pilasters; it is closed off by a monumental gate.

Interior

Entrance through the main courtyard on the left.

The entrance (inspired by the 16C Italian architect Andrea Palladio) gives access to the grand staircase embellished with wrought-iron banisters. On the first floor, north wing, is a Louis XVI dining hall and a billiards room decorated with 16C **tapestries** from Brussels.

The south wing has an outstanding collection of antiques and sumptuous neo-Egyptian furniture. A small gallery features Chinese and Japanese porcelain (17C-18C). The visit ends with the chapel (17C-18C), which has recently been restored.

Château du Champ de Bataille

Excursions

Harcourt★

7km/4mi SE of Brionne by D 26 and D 137.

This small town near Le Neubourg is at the intersection of roads leading to the banks of the River Risle and River Charentonne and Beaumont Forest.

Not far from the 13C **church** (◷Mon–Fri except Wed 9am–noon, 1.30–4.30, Sat 9am–11.30. The key may be picked up at the town hall. ☎02 32 45 02 40), the old wooden market place stands intact.

Château d'Harcourt★

◷ Open mid-Jun–mid-Sept daily 10.30am–6.30pm. Mar–mid-June and mid-Sept–mid-Nov daily except Tue 2–6pm. ✏4€ (children 1.5€) ☎02 32 46 29 70.

Since 1827 the château (⚶see illustration in Introduction: Military architecture) and its park have belonged to the French Agricultural College.

The castle was built in the late 12C by Robert II of Harcourt, companion to Richard Lionheart. It was modernised in the 14C by John IV of Harcourt and, in the 17C, was converted into a comfortable residence.

At the end of the drive stands the imposing mass of the castle, sheltered by its curtain wall, 20m/66ft-wide moat, and ramparts flanked by dilapidated towers. The medieval entrance and its bridge have been restored.

Arboretum★

⚶*Same as for the château.*

Adjoining the main courtyard, a 10ha/25-acre arboretum presents over 400 tree species coming from the five continents.

ÎLES CHAUSEY★

MANCHE, MICHELIN MAP 303: B-6
ACCESS: SEE THE MICHELIN GUIDE FRANCE

According to legend the Chausey Islands were part of the ancient Scissy Forest submerged by the sea in 709. The islands are a popular day excursion *(1hr by boat)* **and are uninhabited except for Grande Île, which has a population of 100 in summer and just six in winter.**

▶ **Orient Yourself:** The islands are 17km/10.6mi from Granville.
🐾 **Don't Miss:** The remarkable spectacle of the high tide.
🕐 **Organizing Your Time:** The excursion takes a day; you can spend the night.
🐾 **Also See:** Granville, Coutances, the abbey of Lucerne, Carolles, the Parc naturel régional des marais du Cotentin et du Bessin and the Cotentin penninsula.

Visit

La Grande Île★

The Island (2km/1.25mi long by 700m/ 2 300ft at its widest point) is the largest and the only one accessible to visitors. The **lighthouse** stands 37m/121ft above the sea. The beam carries 45km/38mi.

Fort

The fort was built between 1860 and 1866 against a British attack that never came. It now serves as a shelter for local fishermen.

▶ *Go round the fort counter-clockwise. The path goes past an old cemetery with four tombs.*

Vieux fort

The Old Fort was rebuilt in 1923 on the remains of one built in 1558. It dominates all the coastline. Below it, on the beach at Plage de Port Homard, the enormous tidal range is 14m/46ft.

The Moines and the Éléphant

These granite rocks, which can be reached at low tide, are thought to resemble monks and an elephant.
More than 200 rocks, known locally as *grunes*, are revealed when the tide is out. Sailors should get some advice and double-check charts before setting out on an adventure.

WHERE TO STAY AND EAT

😊😊 **Hôtel Fort et des Îles** –*50400 Iles Chausey.* ☎*02 33 50 25 02. Closed 27 Sept–18 Apr. 8 rooms: half-board only. Reservations essential. Restaurant* 😊😊*. The sounds of wind and waves lull you in this white house set in a flower garden. A few simple rooms. Seafood gathered or bred on the island can be enjoyed in the dining room while admiring the view.*

Arriving by sailboat

S.Targat/MICHELIN

CHERBOURG-OCTEVILLE

MANCHE, POPULATION 25 370 (METROPOLITAN AREA 117 855)
MICHELIN MAP 303: C-2 – LOCAL MAP SEE PRESQU'ÎLE DU COTENTIN

Cherbourg is a seafaring town with the largest artificial harbour in the world. Here, on the northern shore of the Cotentin Peninsula, this city boasts beautiful monuments, and is known for its remarkable breakwater.

- **Information:** 2 quai Alexandre III, 50100 Cherbourg-Octeville. ☎02 33 93 52 02. www.ot.cherbourg-cotentin.fr.
- **Orient Yourself:** The N 13 ends in Cherbourg, after passing through Caen (123km/77mi southeast) and Bayeux (96km/60mi).
- **Don't Miss:** The Cité de la Mer and a boat tour of the port area.
- **Organizing Your Time:** Count on 3hrs to see the Cité de la Mer.
- **Especially for Kids:** See the acquarium and the submarine at Cité de la Mer.
- **Also See:** The marked itineraries Cobra-La Percée (The Breakthrough) and Objectif-Un Port (Objective-A Harbour), described in the Historical Area of the Battle of Normandy, both go by Cherbourg.

A Bit of History

Titanic Undertakings – The great military architect Vauban (1633-1707) saw the possibilities of Cherbourg as an Atlantic port. An attempt in 1776 to create an offshore barrier by submerging 90 huge timber cones filled with rubble failed when the sea washed it all away. Howwever, over time all of the material that had accumulated on the seabed began to form an artificial island. A fortified breakwater was eventually completed in 1853. Today the breakwater remains essential for maintaining a safe haven against often violent storms.

Frogmen at Work – The capture of Cherbourg on 26 and 27 June 1944 marked a decisive stage in the Battle of Normandy, allowing for the landing of heavy equipment on a large scale. When the American 7th Corps took Cherbourg they found the harbour completely devastated and mined. Mines were cleared by Royal Navy frogmen, so that Cherbourg could supply the Allied armies. The undersea pipeline **PLUTO** (**P**ipe **L**ine **U**nder **T**he **O**cean) from the Isle of Wight emerged at Cherbourg, bringing gasoline to the Allies from 12 August 1944.

Sights

Six historic trails wind through the city, with explanatory markers in

Harbour

S. Targat/MICHELIN

Address Book

⚓ For coin ranges see the Legend on the cover flap.

WHERE TO STAY

⚓ **La Croix de Malte** – *5 r. des Halles. ☎02 33 43 19 16. hotel.croix.malte@ wanadoo.fr. Closed 15 days at Christmas. Reservations advised. 24 rooms. ⌷. A* stone's throw from the theatre and the casino. The rooms, furnished in pine, are well soundproofed. Ask for one of the larger rooms when you reserve.

⚓ **Hôtel Angleterre** – *8 r. P.-Talluau. ☎02 33 53 70 06. www.hotelangleterre. fr.com. 23 rooms. ⌷.* Situated in a quiet part of the town centre, a simple hotel with a white façade. Rooms are a bit small, but renovated and perked up with pastel colours. Reasonable prices.

⚓⚓ **Hôtel Ambassadeur** – *22 quai de Caligny. ☎02 33 43 10 00. www.ambassadeurhotel.com. 40 rooms. ⌷.*This hotel overlooks the port, providing a view of constant activity. But have no doubts, the rooms are well soundproofed. Reasonable prices.

⚓⚓ **Hôtel Renaissance** – *4 r. de l'Église. ☎02 33 43 10 00. www.hotel-renaissance-cherbourg. com. 12 rooms. ⌷.*This name is accuate: the hotel has benefitted from a recent make-over. Bright, soundproofed rooms, modern bathrooms. An address that starts of on the right foot.

⚓⚓ **Manoir St-Jean Bed and Breakfast** – *Le hameau St-Jean, 50110 Tourlaville, 1km/0.6mi beyond the château des Ravalet via D 322 and the road marked centre aéré, Rte de Brix. ☎02 33 22 00 86. 3 rooms. ⌷⌷.* Located on the edge of the château des Ravalet park, this converted 18C farmhouse overlooking the green Trotebec Valley has retained its authentic character. You will be well taken care of by the owner, who has a great knowledge of the natural and cultural wealth of her region. Two self-catering cottages.

WHERE TO EAT

⚓ **Au Tire-Bouchon** – *17 r. Notre-Dame. ☎02 33 53 54 69. Closed Sun. Reservations advised.* The owner also owns a wineshop and a grocery, and the bistrot specialities are meant to accom-pany a good bottle. Dishes include confit de canard and the andouillette sausage as we1l as fresh seafood.

⚓⚓ **L'Antidote** – *41 r. au Blé. ☎02 33 78 01 28. Closed Sun and Mon. Reserva-tions advised.* A pleasant terrace and a wood-paneled dining room. The specialties include *rillets de saumon de Cherbourg* (a salmon patty), black pud-ding with pineapple, ginger and apples, and *foie gras*. Warm welcome.

⚓⚓ **Café de Paris** – *40 quai Caligny. ☎02 33 43 12 36. www.manchegastron-omie.com. Closed 16 Jan–7 Feb, 7–22 Nov, Mon lunch and Sun from 29 Sept to 13 Apr.* This bistro-style restaurant is bright and warm with its decor reflected in mirrors. Enjoy a selection of seafood while admiring the view of the harbour in one of the two dining rooms.

⚓⚓ **Le Faitout** – *25 r. Tour-Carrée. ☎02 33 04 25 04 . Closed 2 weeks Dec. Reservations required .* An attractive rétro façade outside, a handsome wood-panelled decor like that of a ship inside. Traditional cuisine and Norman specialities.

⚓⚓ **Sel et Poivre** – *17 r. du Port. ☎02 33 01 24 09. seletpoivre@alicepro.fr .* A pinch of salt, a dusting of pepper and a good dollop of know-how bring out the best in typical local fare served in a charming dining room.

ON THE TOWN

Cherbourg is a sailors' town and, just like their beloved sea, under its peaceful daytime atmosphere runs an unsuspected agitation which surfaces after midnight.

Casino de Cherbourg– *18 quai Alex-andre-III. ☎02 33 43 00 56. cherbourg@ groupecogit.com. Open daily 10.30am-3am.* Built in 1827, this casino is the oldest in France. Gamblers can try their luck with slot machines or boule. Some might prefer the leather armchairs of the elegant bar, or the 1950s style pub "Fifty's Diner". The discotheque plays golden oldies.

SHOPPING

La Cave au Roy – *47 r. Tour-Carrée. ☎02 33 53 01 21. Open Tue–Sat 9am–12.30pm, 2.30-7:30pm, Sun and public holidays 10am–12.30pm. Closed spring school* *holidays.* This well-stocked wine store in the town centre carries a variety of regional specialities.

Les 3 Marches – *13 r. Grande-Rue. ☎02 33 53 24 94. Tue–Sat 9am–12.15pm, 2.30–7.55pm.* One of the oldest shops in Cherbourg, a grocery featuring products from all the regions of France, with an accent on Normandy.

Les Tonnelles du Val – *102 r. Médéric. 50110 Tourlaville. ☎02 33 22 44 40. Tue–Sat 9am–noon, 3-7pm. Closed public holidays.* This huge warehouse, decorated with beams and casks, was once a foundry, then a dairy before becoming the haunt of connoisseurs of fine wine and old Calvados. Charming.

SPORT-LEISURE

Station Voile Nautisme et Tourisme de Cherbourg Hague – *R. du Diablotin. ☎ 02 33 78 19 29. station-voile-cherbourg-hague@wanadoo.fr. Open summer: daily 9am-6pm. Winter Mon–Fri 9am–12.30pm, 1.30–5pm. Closed 1 May.* This water sports club offers many activities: canoing, kayaking, sailing, diving, beach sports, mountain biking, paragliding, hang-gliding, etc. Lessons and rentals.

French and English. They start across from the SNCF train station, across from Saint-Trinité and across from the former Transatlantique station.

Parc Emmanuel-Liais
The park, created by the naturalist and astronomer **Emmanuel Liais** (1826-1900), is famous for its tropical plants.

Place Napoléon
A bronze statue of the emperor dominates the square. Nearby is the **Église de la Trinité** a Flamboyant Gothic church.

Musée Thomas-Henry
Open May–Sept daily 10am–noon, 2–6pm, Sun and Mon 2–6pm. The rest of the year daily except Mon and Tue 2–6pm. No charge. ☎02 33 23 39 30.
The first gallery is devoted to paintings with Cherbourg and the sea as themes. The 15C-19C paintings are on display in the other galleries: Fra Angelico's altarpiece panel, *The Conversion of St Augustine*, Filippo Lippi's *Entombment*. The 17C-19C collection has works by Murillo, Vernet and Chardin as well as canvases by Poussin, Largillère and Rigaud and a Nude by David. The local artist **Jean-François Millet** (1814-75) is well represented.

Muséum d'Ethnographie, d'Histoire naturelle et d'Archéologie
Open May–Sept daily 10am–noon, 2–6pm, Sun and Mon 2–6pm. The rest of the year daily except Mon and Tue 2–6pm. Closed on public holidays. No charge. ☎02 33 53 51 61.
On the ground floor are exhibits of shells, mammals and birds. Upstairs Egypt, Asia, Africa, Oceania and the Americas are represented.

Cité de la Mer★★
Open July– Aug daily 9.30am–7pm. May–June & Sept 9.30am–6pm.The rest of the year 10am–6pm. (Last entry one hour before closing). Closed 3 weeks in Jan, 1 Jan, 25 Dec. 14€ Apr–Sept (children under 6 no charge; ages 7–17 10€). The rest of the year 12.50€ (ages 7–17 9€). ☎02 33 20 26 26. www.citede-lamer.com.
Located at the Transatlantique station, facing the marina, this museum has basins and tanks that present marine fauna and flora. *Le Redoutable★*, the first French nuclear submarine, is here.

Port militaire (Arsenal)
For security reasons, visits are no longer allowed.
The Arsenal is the headquarters for ship-building and naval armament including the building of submarines.

Boat Trip Round the Roadstead
Guided tours Apr–Sept 10am, 11.30am, 2pm, 3.30pm and 5pm. 11.50€ (children 4-12 years 6.50€). ☎02 33 20 09 00. Ticket booth and embarcation point at Cité de la Mer.

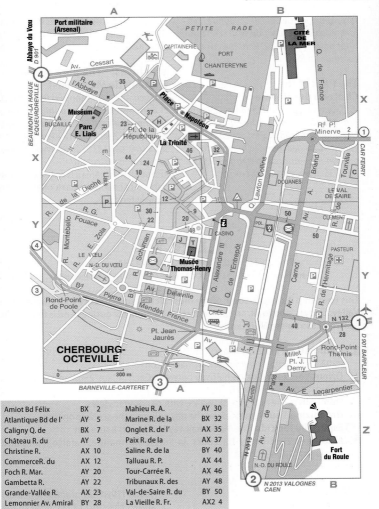

Amiot Bd Félix	BX 2	Mahieu R. A.	AY 30
Atlantique Bd de l'	AY 5	Marine R. de la	BX 32
Caligny Q. de	BX 7	Onglet R. de l'	AX 35
Château R. du	AY 9	Paix R. de la	AX 37
Christine R.	AX 10	Saline R. de la	BY 40
Commerce R. du	AX 12	Talluau R. P.	AX 44
Foch R. Mar.	AY 20	Tour-Carrée R.	AX 46
Gambetta R.	AY 22	Tribunaux R. des	AY 48
Grande-Vallée R.	AX 23	Val-de-Saire R. du	BY 50
Lemonnier Av. Amiral	BY 28	La Vieille R. Fr.	AX2 4

Visitors sail past the central fort of the seawall, which Napoléon called his pyramid, and the military port.

Fort du Roule

A road winds up to the fort on Roule Hill (112m/367ft). In June 1944, the Germans entrenched here offered fierce resistance before surrendering. The ramparts offer a good panorama★(Viewing table).

Musée de la Libération

♿ ⏰ Open May–Sept 10am–noon, 2–6pm, Sun and Mon 2–6pm. The rest of the year Wed–Sun 2–6pm, except by reservation. ⏰Closed public holidays except 8 May, 11 Nov and Jan. ⏰3.20€ (children 1.70€). ☎02 33 20 14 12.

The museum retraces the dark years of French history from 1940 to 1944 as well as hopeful events such as the D-Day landing, the liberation of Cherbourg and the rebuilding of the port.

Excursions

Tourlaville

5km/3mi E. From Cherbourg take avenue de l'Amiral-Lemonnier SE. In Tourlaville, at the crossroads before the Hôtel Terminus, *turn right onto rue des Alliés. 800m/875yd farther on at the junction with D 63 turn right again onto D 32. Park the car and continue on foot.*

The Park of the Château des Ravalet★

&◯*Open June–Aug daily 8am–7.30pm. Apr–May & Sept daily 8am–7pm. Mar & Oct daily 8am–6pm. Rest of year hours vary.* ⟶*Guided tours (1h30min) offered on Mon July –Aug.* ⟶*No charge.* ☏*02 33 22 01 35. www.ville-cherbourg.fr.*

The park of this lovely Renaissance château includes tropical plants, lovely stretches of water and fine beech trees.

Martinvast - The park of the Château de Martinvast

◯*Open Apr–Sept Mon–Fri 9am–noon, 2–6pm, weekends and public holidays 2–6pm. The rest of the year Mon–Fri 9am–noon, 2–6pm, Sun 2–6pm.*◯*Closed Sat.* ⟶*6€.* ☏*02 33 87 20 80. www.ifrance. com/jardins-en-cotentin.*

Although the château is not open to the public, its charming **park** offers seven signposted trails.

CLÉCY★

CALVADOS, POPULATION 1 252
MICHELIN MAP 303: J-6 – LOCAL MAP SEE LA SUISSE NORMANDE

This township is close to some of the most picturesque beauty spots in the Orne Valley. Clécy is, above all, an excellent starting point for outings and is the tourist centre of the Suisse Normande,

- ❂ **Information:** Place du Tripot, 14570 Clécy.
  ☏ 02 31 69 79 95. www.suisse-normande.com
- ▶ **Orient Yourself:** Clécy is halfway between Caen (40km/25mi north) and Flers (23km/14.4mi south) via D 562.
- ⊛ **Don't Miss:** The many scenic walks, with panoramic views.
- ◯ **Organizing Your Time:** Spend the day enjoying the scenery on foot.
- Kids **Especially for Kids:** The Model Railway Museum is a sure bet.
- ⚲ **Also See:** Vire, Thury-Harcourt, la Suisse normande, Falaise, Flers and Aunay-sur-Odon.

Walks

Croix de la Faverie★

45min round-trip on foot. Leave from the car park between the post office and the church and drive towards La Faverie Cross. At the stop sign turn right; then turn left and continue to climb. Follow the signposts to the crossroads where the cross stands.

From the pine trees *(picnic site)* there is a very pretty **view**: the Rochers des Parcs overlook the Lande Viaduct.

- ▶ *From Clécy take the route de La Serverie. Cross the bridge over the Orne and the level crossing; after*

100m/110yd turn right. A sign (left) shows the start of the path to the Sugar Loaf.

Le Pain de Sucre★

▲*Allow 3hr round-trip on foot.* This path *(blazed with red and white markers)* climbs up a valley on the right bank of a stream. Cross the stream. Entering the copse, keep to the right of a trail that rises obliquely to the right and leads to the foot of a hillock; climb up. The **panorama** brings in a vast sweep of the Orne. Going down, on reaching the foot of the hillock, keep to the right along the slope opposite the one you came by, and follow a winding path (blazed with markers) which, passing below the

Address Book

♿For coin ranges, see the Legend on the cover flap.

WHERE TO EAT

🍽 **La Guinguette à tartines** – *1 Le bord de l'Orne.* ☎*02 31 69 89 38. Closed Oct–Mar. Open daily in July–Aug.* Sandwiches and simple dishes served in generous portions in a relaxed atmosphere. On the banks of the Orne, enjoy the wide terrace or the dining room with panoramic views. Miniature golf, rental of kayaks.

LEISURE

Vélorail – ☎*02 31 69 39 30. www.rail-suissenormande.fr. Open July–Aug daily 10.30am–6pm. Apr–June & Sept–Oct Mon–Fri 2–4pm, weekends and public holidays 10.30am–6pm. 13€ for a 4- person railbike (1hr30min trip).* Leave Condé via D 911 towards Pont-d'Ouilly. The train station at Pont-Éram-bourg has reopened. You can take a 6km/3.6mi journey by railbike *(vélorail)* until Berjou. A novel way to discover the area.

Rochers de la Houle, comes out at the rustic church of Vey.

▶ *From Clécy Church take D 133C towards La Serverie. Cross the bridge over the Orne, turn left to St-Rémy; after 1.5km/0.9mi turn right into a hairpin bend and follow the Ridge Road.*

Promenade des Crêtes★

8km/5mi – about 45min.
The road overlooks the valley and offers beautiful views of the Orne. Follow the wooded banks and bear left on the road *(sharp bend)* which returns to St-Omer.

Sight

Musée du Chemin de fer miniature

♿ Kids 📷 Guided tours (45min) June–Aug 10am–noon, 2–6.30pm (6pm in June). Sept daily except Mon 10am–noon, 2–6pm. Oct Sun and public holidays 2–5pm. Mar–Easter Sun and public holidays 2–5.30pm. ⏰Closed Nov–Easter. ☎5.50 € (Children 3.50 €) ☎02 31 69 07 13. Model locomotives and wagons speed round landscapes from the Suisse Normande or Flanders.

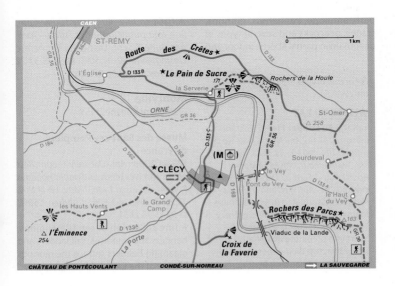

CLÈRES★

SEINE-MARITIME, POPULATION 1 266
MICHELIN MAP 304: G-4

One of Normandy's greatest attractions is the animal park at the château of Clères. The original castle, now in ruins, was built in the 11C. The present château consists of a 19C western wing in the neo-Gothic style, and an eastern wing dating from the 15C, which was remodelled towards 1505. In the market square stands the wooden structure and slate roof of an 18C covered market.

- 🛈 **Information:** 59 av. du Parc, 76690 Clères. ☎02 35 33 38 64. www.ot-cleres.fr
- ▶ **Orient Yourself:** Clères is 30km/19mi north of Rouen, following A 150, A 151 and D 6, or about 50km/31 mi south of Dieppe by N 27 and D 6.
- 👁 **Don't Miss:** The rare birds in the aviary at Clères.
- 🕐 **Organizing Your Time:** Give yourself a good two hours to tour the zoo.
- 👶 **Especially for Kids:** After the Clères zoo, see the amusement park at Bocasse.
- 👣 **Also See:** the Pays de Caux, Dieppe, Neufchâtel-en-Bray, and Rouen.

Sight

Parc Zoologique de Clères-Jean-Delacour★

👶 ♿ 🕐 *Open Apr–Sept 10am–7pm. Mar & Oct 10am–6.30pm. Early Nov 1.30–5.30pm. ⬧4.60€ (children 3 €). ☎02 35 33 23 08.*

In an exceptional natural setting, the park of Clères provides a wonderful opportunity to see the birds and mammals collected by the botanist and ornithologist **Jean Delacour** (1890-1985). The garden is populated by pink flamingos, ducks and exotic geese. In the park, antelope, kangaroos, gibbons, cranes, peacocks and several types of deer roam in partial liberty. Indoor and outdoor aviaries are reserved for lesser-known birds, some on the endangered species list: around 2 000 birds. In the former main room of the château, a gallery houses rare exotic birds.

👁 *To observe the animals under the best possible conditions visit the park before 30 June.*

Excursions

Parc du Bocasse

2km/1 ml W by D 6. 👶 *Park includes a children's amusement park and picnic area.* ♿ 🕐 *Open July–Aug daily 10am–6pm, Sun and public holidays, 10am–7pm. Apr–June & Sept. Last entry 1hr before closing. ⬧10.50–11.50€. ☎02 35 33 22 25. www.parcdubocasse.fr*

Montville

6km/3.7mi S on the D 155.

Musée des Sapeurs-Pompiers de France

👶 ♿ 🕐 *Open Apr–Oct daily 1–6pm. Rest of the year weekends and public holidays 1–6pm.* 🕐 *Closed 1 Jan, 1 May, 1 & 11 Nov, 24,25, 31 Dec. ⬧3.80€ (Children 1.50€) ☎02 35 33 13 51.*

A fine collection of red fire engines, banners and uniforms, tall ladders and gleaming helmets retrace the glorious history of the French fire brigades.

👣 *For coin ranges, see the Legend on the cover flap.*

WHERE TO EAT

🍽🍽🍽 **Au Souper Fin** – *76690 Frichemesnil, 4km/2.4mi NE of Clères via D 6 and D 100.* ☎02 35 33 33 88. *buisset. eric@wanadoo.fr. Closed 24 Mar–1 Apr, 11 Aug–2 Sept, 22 Dec–6 Jan, Sun evening Oct– Apr, Wed and Thu.* This restaurant is situated in a brick house that was once Frichemesnil's grocery shop-café. The owner-chef puts his heart into preparing imaginative cuisine. Attractive dining room, garden terrace. Three charming bedrooms.

CONCHES-EN-OUCHE★

EURE, POPULATION 4 280
MICHELIN MAP 304: F-28

The town of Conches, on the edge of the woodlands that mark the northern limits of the Pays d'Ouche, is remarkably situated on a spur encircled by the River Rouloir. There is a particularly good view of the town if it is approached along the Rouloir Valley (from Évreux). The keep of the ruined castle is illuminated from April to September.

- **Information:** Place Aristide-Briand, 27190 Conches-en-Ouche.
  ☎02 32 30 76 42.
- ▶ **Orient Yourself:** From Aigle (30km/19mi southwest) or Évreux (14km/9mi northeast) take D 830. From Bernay (30km/19mi northwest) take D 140, and from Rouen (50km/31mi north) pass by Neubourg.
- **Don't Miss:** The beautiful windows of the Ste-Foy church.
- **Organizing Your Time:** Visit Conches in the morning, then stroll along the many paths in the area.
- **Also See:** Évreux, le Bec-Hellouin, Brionne, Bernay and Verneuil-sur-Avre.

A Bit of History

From Rouergue to the Pays d'Ouche
– On his return from a campaign against the Spanish Moors (1034), **Roger de Tosny** made a pilgrimage to Conques, in Rouergue (south-west France) and brought back relics of St Foy. This may be the origin of the town's name. Roger dedicated a church to **St Foy**; at the end of the 15C it was replaced by the present building.

Sights

Jardin de l'hôtel de ville
The Gothic doorway of the town hall – entrance to the former castle – leads to a garden in which stands the ruined keep of the lords of Tosny, surrounded by 12C towers.
From the terrace there is a fine view of the Rouloir Valley and the elegant Flamboyant apse of St Foy Church. Below another terrace offers a similar view.

Rue du Val
There are two interesting buildings here. One is the 16C half-timbered **maison Corneille**, home to the family of the famous dramatist (1606-1684). At the end of the street, the **hospital** stands on the site of the abbey; the vaulted cellars are open to visitors.

The Communauté des communes de Conches publishes a ⓩwalking guide to the area, which also shows trails for ⓑ bike and ⓗhorseback riding, on sale at the tourist office. There are four suggested tours though town.

Église Ste-Foy★
The south tower is crowned by a tall spire of wood and lead, a copy of the one blown down in a storm in 1842. The fine carved panels of the façade doors are early 16C. Notice the many gargoyles. Inside there are some beautiful statues including that of St Roch (17C) in the south aisle and near the great organ.
Stained-Glass Windows★– The Renaissance windows, dating from the first half of the 16C, have retained their unity in spite of restoration. Those in the north aisle depict the life of the Virgin.
The seven windows (10.5m/34ft) in the chancel are divided into two, the upper part illustrating the Life of Christ, the lower to that of St Foy and portraits of the donors.
The windows in the south aisle were made in either Île-de-France or at Fontainebleau. The Mystical Wine Press (fifth window) is the best-known.

LEISURE

🐎**Village équestre de Conches** – Horseback riding. ☏02 32 30 22 56.
Lac de la Noë – *1 rte d'Évreux, 27190 La Bonneville-sur-Iton. June–Sept 10am–7pm.* ☏02 32 37 61 87. *www. conches-en-ouche.fr.* Miniature golf, tennis, swimming, fishing, boating, etc., equipment rentals.
Markets – *Thursdays and Sundays.*

The houses facing the church are 15C and 16C. The vaulted cellars (11C-12C) are open to visitors.

Musée du Terroir Normand

🕐*Open June–mid-Sept Wed–Sun 10am–noon, 2–5pm.* 🕐*Closed public holidays.* 🎫*3€ (under 16 years no charge).* ☏02 32 37 92 16.
The Museum presents an exhibition of old tools and farming implements as well as re-creations of various work-shops.

Musée du du Verre

♿🕐*Open June–Sept Wed–Sat 10am–noon, 2–5.30pm, Sun 2.30–6pm. Mar–May and Oct–Nov Wed–Fri 2–5.30pm.*

🎫*3€(Under 16 years no charge)* ☏02 32 30 90 41.
This museum has a collection of objects made of molten glass by the man known as the sorcerer of Conche, François Décorchement (1880-1971).

Excursion

Breteuil-sur-Iton
14km/9mi S by D 840.
The town stands on the eastern edge of Breteuil Forest in a loop of the River Iton which forms a small lake in the public gardens laid out on the site of the old castle. The **church**, where in 1081 William the Conqueror's daughter Adèle the Beautiful married Stephen, Count of Blois, dates from the 11C; the local reddish stone (*grison*) gives it a rustic appearance. The belfry is a large square tower above the transept crossing. The interior is dominated by the great nave arches supported on 12 massive stone pillars. The pillars in the transept cross-ing date back to the days of William the Conqueror. The balustrade of the organ loft is decorated with Italian Renaissance motifs and 12 angelic musicians.

PRESQU'ÎLE DU COTENTIN★★

MICHELIN MAP 303: A-1 TO B-2

The pronounced thrust of the Cotentin peninsula into the Atlantic corresponds with an equally uncharacteristic landscape: the austere surroundings of La Hague is more like Brittany than Normandy. Geographically speaking, the area can be divided into three parts: the Cotentin Pass is the lower plain, the Val de Saire includes the river valley and the whole north-east part of the peninsula, the Cap de la Hague is the granite spine jutting out into the sea. The wooded hinterland was the cradle of Norman adventurers who once controlled the central Mediterranean area.

▶ **Orient Yourself:** Surrounded on three sides by the sea, and separated from the mainland by swamps, the penninsula extends from Portbail to the west (71km/44.5mi north of Granville) to Carentan on the east (44km/27.5mi west of Bayeux), passing through Cherbourg.
☺ **Don't Miss:** The splendid view of the Nez de Jobourg and the bay of Écalgrain.
🕐 **Organizing Your Time:** Spend two days; each tour below takes half a day.
Kids **Especially for Kids:** The Ludiver planetarium at La Hague provides a glimpse of the universe.
♿ **Also See:** Cherbourg-Octeville, Barfleur, Valognes, Ste-Mère-Église, the Parc naturel régional des marais du Cotentin at du Bessin, St-Sauveur-el-Vicomte and Barneville-Carteret.

A Bit of History

Norman Kings of Sicily (11C-12C) – Early in the 11C, the harsh rule of the Duke of Normandy drove many dissatisfied inhabitants of the Cotentin to set out for the Holy Land. En route they wandered into southern Italy where feudal barons were in a perpetual state of war. A lord in Apulia, in revolt against Byzantium, asked the Normans to return home and raise troops for him; they had no difficulty in finding recruits in the poor and overpopulated Cotentin.

The exploits of three sons of **Tancrède de Hauteville**, a minor baron from the Coutances area, aroused great enthusiasm. The eldest, William, known as Iron Arm, drove out those who had employed him and became William of Apulia in 1102. His two brothers, Robert and Roger followed his lead. The reign of Roger II from 1101 to 1154 was particularly brilliant. The last Norman king of Sicily was Manfred, who was killed at Benevento in 1265 by Charles of Anjou, brother of St Louis, and whose tragic fate was celebrated by Dante, Byron and Schumann.

Visit

Marais du Contentin et du Bessin Regional Nature Parc

🏠 *Maison d'Acceuil, 50500 St-Côme-du-Mont. ☎02 33 71 65 30. www.parc-cotentin-bessin.fr. ♿The marked itineraries D-Day-Le Choc (The Impact), Objectif-Un Port (Objective-A Harbour) and Cobra-La Percée (The Breakthrough) described in the Historical Area of the Battle of Normandy, pass through the Parc des Marais.*

This nature park, formerly known as the Marais de Carentan, was inaugurated in June 1991 and embraces 145 communes. With a total area of 120 000ha/465 sq mi these wetlands stretch from the Bay of Veys on the east coast of the Cotentin peninsula to Lessay haven on the west coast. This area of marshland (25 000ha/97sq mi) and *bocage* with its many canals is rich in plant and animal life. The relatively tall vegetation of these treeless wetlands provides good nesting and wintering grounds for migratory species.

Les Ponts d'Ouve★ near Carentan is a visitor centre for the Marais du Cotentin et du Bessin Park. In addition to the exhibits indoors on flora and fauna, there is a **discovery trail** through the park with informative panels. There are observation areas set up for bird watchers.

Driving Tours

East Coast★

①From Carentan to Barfleur
75km/47mi – about 2hr 45min

Carentan
Carentan is an important cattle market town and one of the largest centres of the regional dairy industry. The octagonal spire of the belfry of the **Église Notre-Dame** (12C-15C) dominates the whole region. The fine stone house at the corner of rue de l'Église and place Guillaume-de-Cerisay was described by Balzac under the name Hôtel de Dey in his work *Le Réquisitionnaire*.

The arcades of the old covered market in **place de la République** date from the late 14C. The **hôtel de ville** (town hall) occupies an 17C-19C convent.

▶ *From Carentan take N 13 towards Ste-Mère-Église. Shortly before St-Côme-du-Mont, turn right onto D 913.*

Cotentin vaquelotte (fishing boat)

J. Blonde/Musée Maritime, Tatihou

Ste-Marie-du-Mont

The impressive **church** is identified by its square 14C tower of which the top storey is a Renaissance addition. The nave is early 12C; the transept and chancel date from the 14C. Inside is a late-16C figured pulpit; in the chancel, on the left, is a funerary statue of Henri Robert aux Espaulles carved in the early 17C.

A roadside monument honours 800 Danish sailors who took part in the D-Day landings.

Utah Beach

Musée du Débarquement – ⟨⟩ *June–Sept 9.30am–7pm (last entry 45min before closing). Apr–May & Oct 10am–6pm. Feb–Mar and 1st 2 weeks Nov 10am–5.30pm. Last 2 weeks Nov and school holidays 10am–1.30pm.* ⟨⟩*Closed Jan (except weekends) and 25 Dec.* ⟨⟩*5€ (6–16 years old 2€).* ⟨⟩*02 33 71 53 35. www.utah-beach.com.*

Despite murderous fire from the German coastal batteries, the troops of the American 4th Division (7th Corps) disembarked on 6 June near La Madeleine and Les Dunes-de-Varreville and managed to make contact with the airborne troops of the 82nd and 101st Divisions, who had landed in the region of Ste-Mère-Église. Three weeks later the whole of the Cotentin peninsula had been liberated.

At **La Madeleine** there is a milestone – the first on the Road to Liberty – erected in 1947 to honour soldiers killed during the landings and a memorial to the 4th Division. A German blockhouse (*left*) is now a monument to the dead of the 1st Engineer Special Brigade; a stele and a crypt commemorate the American 90th Division. On an area of dunes, presented by the commune of Ste-Marie-du-Mont as official American territory, there stands a huge stele erected on the 40th anniversary of the landings by the Americans in homage to those who died at Utah Beach. It provides a fine view of the sea; the wrecks of several blockships are still visible at low tide (*north*).

Les Dunes-de-Varreville

In an opening in the dunes, 100m/110yd from the route des Alliés, a rose granite monument in the form of a ship's prow and bearing the cross of Lorraine commemorates the landing of the 2nd French Armoured Division under General Leclerc on 1 August 1944.

Quinéville

This is a family seaside resort. Good view of St-Vaast roadstead from the square near the church.

Mémorial de la Liberté retrouvée

⟨⟩⟨⟩*Open Apr–mid-Nov daily 10am–7pm.* ⟨⟩*6€ (children 4€).* ⟨⟩*02 33 95 95 95.* This museum is re-creates daily life during the dark days of the Occupation. There is a village street, a blockhouse, and miscellaneous documentary material from the period.

Quettehou

The 13C granite church on a height is flanked by a tall 15C belfry. From the cemetery there is a view of Morsalines Bay, the Hougue Fort and the Pointe de Saire.

Val de Saire★

A detour inland from Quettehou runs through a pleasantly green countryside and affords good views of the east coast of the Cotentin peninsula.

▸ *From Quettehou take D 902 N towards Barfleur; turn left onto D 26 which climbs through apple orchards. In Le Vast turn right.*

The countryside offers rolling woodlands and pastures in the valleys.

▸ *In Valcanville turn right onto D 125. At the D 328 crossroads turn left onto the road to La Pernelle; after 300m/300yd turn right at the sign Église, Panorama.*

Beyond the rebuilt church of **La Pernelle** is a former German blockhouse, once an observatory, which commands a **panorama**★★ (*viewing table*) extending from the Gatteville lighthouse (north) to the Grandcamp cliffs (south) by way of the Pointe de Saire, Réville Bay, Tatihou Island, Hougue Fort and the St-Marcouf Islands; in clear weather Percée Point is visible.

Address Book

For coin ranges see the Legend on the cover flap.

WHERE TO STAY

Hôtel - Restaurant L'Escapade – *28 r. du Dr-Caillard, opposite the train station, 50500 Carentan. 02 33 42 02 00. Closed Dec–Feb. 15 rooms.* Restaurant. Under Napoleon III, this stately edifice covered with Virginia creeper was a coaching inn. Today it offers rooms of varying sizes, all recently renovated, and a handsome rustic dining room with an impeccably waxed parquet.

La Dannevillerie Bed and Breakfast – *50630 Le Vast, 6km/3.6mi NW of Quettehou via D 902 and D 26, then 2km/1.2mi further on, take the road on the right before Le Vast. 02 33 44 50 45. www.ladannevillerie.com. 3 rooms.* Nestling in the Val de Saire, near the river, this little farm offers peace and repose. At breakfast time, gourmets will enjoy delicious bread, baked in a wood-fired oven by the village baker, and homemade jam.

Hôtel Le Vauban – *7 r. Sébline, 50500 Carentan. 02 33 71 00 20. 14 rooms.* Small rooms a bit fusty but impeccably kept and a dining room full of green plants. Located in the centre of town.

WHERE TO EAT

L'Estaminet – *Pl. de l'Église, 50480 Ste-Marie-du-Mont-Village. 02 33 71 57 01. Closed Jan, Tue evening and Wed Oct–May.* Stop on the tiny, charming square next to the church, which on 6 June 1944 was stormed by thousands of Allied vehicles on their way from Utah Beach. This lovely Norman inn is the right place to recover from your emotions. Seafood on the menu. A few rooms.

Ferme-auberge La Huberdière – *Le Pommier, 50480 Liesville-sur-Douve,* 8km/5mi NW of Carentan via D 913 to St-Côme-du-Mont then D 270. *02 33 71 01 60. Closed Sun evening and Mon. Reservations required.* You can tour this farm which breeds dairy cows and nanny goats, to learn the secrets of milking and cheese-making. You may also sit down directly for a meal and enjoy the specialities of the house without delay.

Le Moulin à Vent – *50440 St-Germain-des-Vaux, 9km/5.6mi N of Nez de Jobourg via D 202, D 901 then D 45. 02 33 52 75 20. Closed Dec–Jan, Sun evening and Mon, except July–Oct.* This spruce, flower-decked granite house stands on a cliff at the end of the Cotentin peninsula. In the dining room with its exposed beams, you will enjoy fresh seafood and sea views.

LEISURE

École de Surf du Cotentin – *14 bis bd Deveaud, 50340 Siouville-Hague. 06 81 33 57 07. cotentin.surfclub.free.fr. Daily except Sun 9am-6pm. Closed Dec–mid-Mar.* This long beach of fine sand is the ideal spot for surfers. Lessons and rentals.

Club de kayak de mer du Nord-Cotentin – *Rte de Becquet, 50110 Tourlaville. 02 33 22 59 59. http://cotentinkayak.free.fr Daily except Sun and Mon 9am–noon, 2–6pm. Closed Feb and Christmas holidays.* This club offers lessons and kayak trips both on sea and in rivers, as well as rentals.

SHOPPING

Dupont d'isigny – *99 rte Américaine, 50500 Carentan. 02 33 71 66 66. -info@.dupont.isigny.com. Open daily 9am–noon, 2–4.30pm.* This deluxe sweetshop, founded in 1894, offers 8 sorts of caramel and a wide range of candies. The factory can be visited by appointment.

▶ *Take D 909 following signs to Pernelle Bourg.*

▶ *Continue N on D 1 along the port and the coast.*

St-Vaast-la-Hougue
See SAINT-VAAST-LA-HOUGUE.

Beyond Réville the road passes La Crasvillerie, a delightful 16C manor house. As you approach Barfleur, the countryside

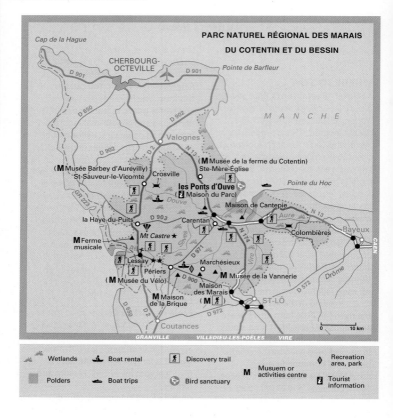

PARC NATUREL RÉGIONAL DES MARAIS
DU COTENTIN ET DU BESSIN

Wetlands	Boat rental	Discovery trail	Museum or activities centre
Polders	Boat trips	Bird sanctuary	Recreation area, park
			Tourist information

begins to look a bit like Brittany, with granite houses, rocky bays and gnarled trees bent by the wind. Gatteville lighthouse stands to the north.

Barfleur and Excursions
See BARFLEUR.

North Coast★★

2 From Barfleur to Cherbourg
38km/23.6mi – about 1hr 30min

Barfleur
See BARFLEUR.

▶ *Between Barfleur and St-Pierre-Église, the road crosses the Saire Valley.*

Tocqueville
This was the family seat of **Alexis de Tocqueville** (1805-59) the author of *Democracy in the United States* and *The Ancien Régime and the Revolution*.

St-Pierre-Église
The fortified 17C church has a 12C Romanesque doorway. The 18C **château** was the family home of the Abbé de St-Pierre, the 17C author of a plan for peace entitled *Projet de Paix Perpétuelle*.
There are several good **viewpoints**★ from the Fermanville-Bretteville corniche, notably those at the Pointe du Brulay and Brick Bay.

▶ *Shortly after Brick Bay turn left at the Auberge Maison Rouge, to climb uphill towards Maupertus-sur-Mer. A track on the right leads to the television relay station.*

Belvedere★
There is a magnificent view of the coast and Cherbourg in the distance.

▶ *Return to D 116; continue W; in Bretteville take D 320 left towards Le Theil.*

War of the Hedgerows

For the American soldiers of 1944, the Cotentin campaign – the advance to Cherbourg and the Battle of St Lô – is summed up in the description "the War of the Hedgerows." Leafy hedges and sunken lanes, such as those that divide the Normandy countryside, are unknown in America and came as an unpleasant surprise for American troops. The hedgerows were ideal for defensive warfare or guerilla tactics. Modern arms were not much help either: 4-inch shells scarcely shook the tree-covered embankments, which doubled as natural anti-tank barriers. Armoured vehicles moved with difficulty along the roads, making foot soldiers key in the fight for victory in this hell of hedges.

It was exhausting fighting an invisible enemy; every field and orchard crossed was a victory in itself. Progress was slow and often estimated by the number of hedges passed. Terrain had to be declared clear before the tanks could move into action. An American sergeant found one solution in his design whereby a sharp steel device, not unlike a ploughshare, was attached to the front of each tank to help them advance through the difficult terrain.

Allée Couverte (Gallery Grave)
This collective burial chamber, which dates back 4 000 years, consists of a double row of upright stones supporting flat slabs laid horizontally.

▶ *Return to Bretteville; take D 116 W.*

On approaching Cherbourg one can see the roadstead and Pelée Island which serves as an anchor for the mole which, with the great breakwater, divides the harbour from the sea. To the left is Roule Fort.

Cherbourg
♿ *See CHERBOURG.*

③ From Cherbourg to Beaumont
47km/29mi – about 2hr.

Cherbourg
♿ *See CHERBOURG.*

▶ *Leave Cherbourg by D 901.*

Ludiver - Observatoire - Planétarium de La Hague
♿ Kids ⏱ *Open Jul–Aug daily 10am–7pm (last entry 1hr before closing). The rest of the year Mon–Fri 9am-12.30pm, 2-5.30pm, Sun 2-6pm.* ⏱ *Closed Jan, 1 May, 1 and 11 Nov, 24-25 & 31 Dec.* ◉7€ *(children 5€).* ☎02 33 78 13 80. www.ludiver.com.

Set up on the Tonneville and Flottemanville-Hague plateau (180m/591ft), this new centre comprises a museum on astronomy and the universe, a planetarium with a seating capacity of 80 and an interior amphitheatre where

Lighthouse on Cap de la Hague, Soury

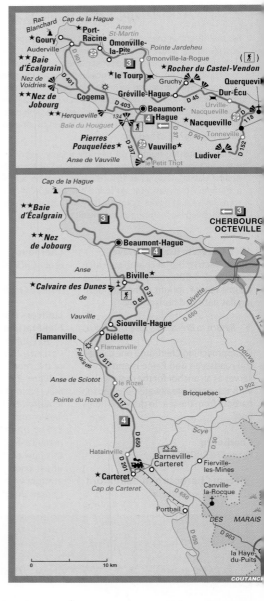

the images of a 600mm telescope are projected live to the public.

▶ *Return to the coast and pass under D 901.*

Querqueville
Beside the parish church stands the 10C **Chapelle St-Germain** (*left*), the oldest religious building of the Cotentin area. From the chevet *(path between the chapel and the church)* there is a view over the Cherbourg roadstead stretching from Cap Lévy (east) to Pointe Jardeheu (west).

▶ *From Querqueville take D 45 W in the direction of Urville-Nacqueville;*

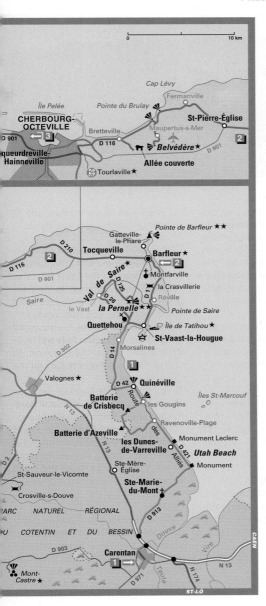

turn left just before the hamlet of La Rivière.

Château de Nacqueville

Guided tours (1hr) Easter–Sept daily except Tue and Fri (except public holidays) at 2pm, 3pm, 4pm and 5pm. ⊕5€ (children 5–15 years old 2€). ☎02 33 03 21 12.

This beautiful 16C edifice, covered with ivy, makes a romantic sight, standing by a pool in its **park**★ of oak trees and rhododendrons. Only the great hall with its beautiful Renaissance fireplace is open to the public.

▶ *Return to D 45; continue W.*

Baie d'Écalgrain

At the entrance to Landemer, on the left, are the towers of the old **Manoir de Dur-Écu** restored in the 16C but resting on 9C foundations. Only the courtyards and dovecot can be visited, but the maze in the field opposite is worth seeing (&.☺*open mid-July–Aug 11am-1pm, 2–7pm; ⊗4.50€; ☎06 10 58 68 41*).

▶ *After Landemer the road rises in the Habilland Ravine, soon a perspective (right) opens up from the Cap Lévy lighthouse to Pointe Jardeheu.*

Gréville-Hague
House – ☚*Guided tours (45min) July–Aug 11am–7pm. June & Sept 11am–6pm. Apr–May and school holidays except Christmas 2-6pm. ⊗4€ (7–15 years 1.60€). ☎02 33 01 81 91.*
The small church was a model for the painter **Jean-François Millet** (1814-75) in his works of Norman landscapes. The artist's bust sits on a rock at the crossroads and the **house** where he was born in **Gruchy** is open to the public.

▶ *From Gréville-Hague, take the D237 to the right for Gruchy.*

Rocher du Castel-Vendon★
Allow 1hr round-trip on foot. Maison Prévert – ☺Open July–Aug 11am–7pm. June & Sept 11am–6pm. Apr–May and school holidays except Christmas 2–6pm. (Last entry 1hr before closing.) ⊗4€ (7–15 years 1.60€). ☎02 33 52 72 38.

▶ *Leave the car at the entrance to the village and continue on foot to the public wash-house by a sunken road*

which then becomes a footpath: ☺ parts of this itinerary are difficult.

🏃 The path follows the right-hand side of the valley. From a rocky promontory, there is a **view** of the coast from Cap Lévy to Pointe Jardeheu. In the foreground stands the granite rock spine called the Rocher du Castel-Vendon.
In **Omonville-la-Petite**, is a graveyard where the poet **Jacques Prévert** (1900-77) is buried (left of the entrance). To visit the **Maison Prévert** park on the church square.
The road towards St-Germain-des-Vaux affords views of the tiny hamlet of **Port-Racine**, one of France's smallest ports. At the entrance to **Auderville** a road down to Goury leads to the north end of the Cap de la Hague. Beyond the shore is the lighthouse of La Hague and, in the distance, the steep cliffs of Alderney.

Goury★
The small harbour is an important coast-guard and lifeboat station. In its octagonal station, the lifeboat swivels around a turntable so it can be launched from two slipways: towards the port at high tide or towards the open sea at low tide.

Baie d'Écalgrain★★
This desolate beach backed by heathland is one of the area's wild beauty spots. To the left of Alderney are Guernsey and Sark and on the horizon the west coast of the Cotentin peninsula.

▶ *From Dannery take D 202 to the headland, Nez de Jobourg.*

Nez de Jobourg★★

🕐 *The information centre at the Avra Centre for storage of nuclear waste is open Mon–Fri 8.30am–noon, 1.30pm–5pm.* ☛*Guided tour (2hrs) Mon–Fri by reservation.* ✆*No charge; identification card required.* 🅿 *Parking inside site.* ☎ *0810 120 172 (same price as local call).*

The long, rocky and barren promontory is now a bird sanctuary (seagulls). Walk along the **Nez de Voidries**. From the Auberge des Grottes there is a view north of Écalgrain Bay, the lighthouse off Cap de la Hague and the Channel Islands: Alderney, the nearest, Sark, Guernsey and Jersey. Farther south the Nez de Jobourg itself comes into view, separated from the Nez de Voidries by Senneval Bay. In the distance Vauville Bay curves south to the cliffs at the Cap de Flamanville.

▷ *Take D 403, a steep downhill road, opposite the* **Usine Areva**.

Leave the car in a lay-by in a bend beyond Herqueville to look at the **vista**★★ across Vauville Bay and over the Flamanville cliffs. The descent continues with Houguet Bay on the right.

Beaumont-Hague

This was the home town of the 17C smuggling family, the Jallot de Beaumont.

West Coast★★

④ From Beaumont-Hague to Carteret

45km/28mi – about 1hr 30min.
Between Beaumont-Hague and Biville, the road goes down towards the shore and then climbs up again to the plateau.

Pierres Pouquelées★

45min round-trip on foot from D 318.
🚶 Leave the car 200m/220yd before the first houses of Vauville and walk inland up a path on the right. When it reaches the plateau turn left to reach the Pierres Pouquelées gallery grave. Continue right to a small rise from which there is a **panorama**★ of the coast from the Nez de Jobourg to the Flamanville cliffs.

Vauville

Botanical Garden – 🚻☛*Guided tours (1hr) May–Aug daily 2–6pm. Sept Tue, Fri, weekends and public holidays 2–6pm. Easter–Apr & Oct weekends and public holidays 2–6pm.* ✆*6€ (6–12 old 5€).* ☎*02 33 10 00 00.*

The 12C church and the 17C manor make an attractive picture. The **Botanical Garden**★ on the grounds of the manor specialises in evergreen plants.

Beyond the village of Petit-Thot the road affords a good **view**★ of the moor land around the bay of Vauville.

Biville★

The village is set on a plateau overlooking the desolate shoreline of Vauville Bay. The Blessed **Thomas Hélye** (1187-1257), a native of Biville, lies the 13C chancel. On the north side is a 19C bronze group showing Thomas Hélye with some of his followers.

The arrival of the Allies and the liberation of the region is commemorated in a stained-glass window by Barillet (1944) *(first on the right in the nave).*

▷ *Walk along the street beside the church; by a fence make some sharp turns and take the path which passes in front of a chapel dedicated to the Virgin and continue to the Calvary.*

Calvaire des Dunes★

🚶 *45min on foot there and back.*

▷ *At the end of the street next to the church, go through the gate and take the path which passes by a little chapel and leads up to the cross.*

From the foot of the cross there is a panoramic view: in the foreground the desolate landscape of Vauville Bay stretches from the Nez de Jobourg to the cliffs at Flamanville.

▷ *At Siouville-Hague the road runs once again beside the dunes, the hills and the sea.*

Diélette

The small port of Diélette, at the foot of the dark cliffs, is the only refuge between Goury and Carteret. As the tide goes out, a beach of fine sand appears between its two breakwaters.

Centre nucléaire de production d'électricité de Flamanville

☞ *For security reasons, the nuclear power station no longer receives visitors.* ☎*02 33 78 70 17.*

This nuclear power station, occupying 120ha/300 acres, stands in part on the granite bedrock, and in part on an artificial platform that juts into the ocean. Two production units have an installed capacity of 1 300 million kW each. Each unit produces 9 000 million kWh.

Between Flamanville and Le Rozel the road overlooks a small bay, the **Anse de Sciotot**; Cap de Flamanville and, to the south, the Pointe du Rozel are visible. The cliffs become lower, giving way to dunes.

Between Hatainville and Carteret the road runs along the dunes, the highest on the Norman coast. The grass covered hollows between the dunes are known locally as *mielles*.

Carteret★
ఢ*See BARNEVILLE-CARTERET.*

COUTANCES★★

MANCHE, POPULATION 9 522
MICHELIN MAP 303: D-5

Coutances is perched on a hillock crowned by the town's magnificent cathedral, miraculously saved from the bombardments that destroyed two-thirds of the town in June 1944. The name of this religious and judicial centre of the Cotentin peninsula recalls the Roman emperor Constantins-Chlorus (293-306). In the 14C Coutances acquired an aqueduct (*ancien aqueduc*) of which only three arches remain standing to the north-west of the town on the Coutainville road.

- ℹ **Information:** Place Georges-Leclerc, 50200 Coutances, ☎02 33 19 08 10.
- ▶ **Orient Yourself:** Coutances is at a crossroads: D 972 links it to St-Lô (29km/18mi east), D 900 heads towards Cherbourg (77km/48mi north) and D 971 leads to Granville (29km/18km south). The seacoast is 10 minutes to the west.
- ☺ **Don't Miss:** The cathedral, a miracle of Gothic architecture, and the display of old Nativity crèches at the manor of Saussey.
- ⏱ **Organizing Your Time:** Take 2hrs to see the town and cathedral, before embarking on one of the excursions in the area.
- 🧒 **Especially for kids:** The cathedral offers guided tours for children in July–August
- ఢ **Also See:** The marked itinerary Cobra-La Percée (The Breakthrough), one of several described in the Historical Area of the Battle of Normandy, goes through Coutances.

Cathédrale★★★

🧒*Guided tours for children (6–12 years) – July–Aug Mon, Wed and Fri 2.30pm. Tour of the cathedral, art project, stone-carving, visit to cathedral tower.* ☜*4.50€.* ☎*02 33 19 08 10.*

☺ One of the best views of the cathedral is when arriving at Coutances from the south; the elegance of the proportions and the purity of the lines are starkly outlined against the sky.

Geoffroy de Montbray, one of those great prelate knights Duke William gathered round him, completed the first nave in 1056. Then, thanks to the generosity of the sons of **Tancrède de Hauteville** whose amazing Mediterranean adventure had just begun, he built the chancel, transept, central tower and the façade with its twin octagonal towers reminiscent of those at Jumièges.

In 1218, after the town had been burnt down, a new Gothic cathedral was literally mounted on the remains of the 11C church, involving prodigious adaptations of style as can be seen from the way the Romanesque towers of the old façade were incorporated into a new rectangular front and surmounted by spires.

Exterior

Above the great window a beautiful gallery crowns the façade whereas on either side rise the towers, quartered at their highest, octagonal level, by graceful elongated pierced turrets. The profusion of ascending lines, so remarkable in their detail, culminates in the flight of the spires which rise to 78m/256ft. The bold turreted lantern tower at the transept crossing is noteworthy for its slender ribbing and fine, narrow windows.

Interior

Pause at the beginning of the nave for a remarkable general view of this singular building with its upswept lines: to right and left wide arcades are lined above by galleries where the lower windows, surmounted by blind rose windows, have been blocked up; above again, along the bottom of the clerestory windows, a second balustrade of a different design, lines the walls.

Dominating the transept crossing is the octagonal **lantern tower★★★**. It is 41m/135ft high at its apex and the best example of its type in Normandy. At the base of the south transept pillar stands the beautiful and deeply venerated 14C statue of Our Lady of Coutances, which miraculously survived the 1944 bombing of St Nicholas' Church. The north transept contains the oldest, 13C stained-glass windows; the south, a 14C window, in sombre tones, of the Last Judgement. The chancel, with the same architectural simplicity as the nave, is later in date and wider. As you walk round the two ambulatories, note the false triforium formed from two arches each covering twin bays. The radiating chapels are shallow and the ribs of their vaulting combine with the corresponding ambulatory bay rib to form a single arch. The central apsidal chapel, known as the Circata, was enlarged during a late-14C rebuilding by Sylvestre de la Cervelle. Above the slender painted columns small figures and animals peer out from the foliage of the capitals.

Upper Storeys★★

Guided tour (1hr30min) Reserve beforehand. July–Aug daily except Sat 10.30am, 2.30pm, 4pm, Sun 2.30pm, 4pm. May–June & 1st 2 weeks Sept Tue, Thur and Sun 2.30pm. 5.50 € (under 10 years not permitted). The walk, which explores the the Romanesque parts of the original building, starts at a west front tower, continues through the attic of the aisle then on to the third-floor galleries to finish at the top of the lantern tower. The **panorama** extends from Granville, over the Chausey Islands to Jersey and on a clear day even Mount Pinçon is visible.

Sights

Jardin des plantes★

Open July–mid-Sept 9am-11:30pm. Apr–June & last half Sept 9am–8pm. Rest of the year 9am–5pm. Sound and light show in July–August. No charge. ☎02 33 19 08 10.

The garden's entrance is flanked by an old cider press on one side and the Quesnel-Morinière Museum on the other. The terraced promenade traverses the sloping gardens with its many flower beds and pine trees.

Musée Quesnel-Morinière

Open July-Aug daily except Tue 11am–6pm, Sun 2–5pm. Rest of the year daily except Tue 10am–noon, 2–5pm, Sun 2–5pm. Closed 1 Jan, Pentecost Mon, 25 Dec. 2.40€, Sun no charge. ☎02 33 07 07 88.

The museum is in the former Hôtel Poupinel, which was bought in 1675 by the king's counsellor of the same name. The collections are mainly local: regional pottery, paintings by local artists. Outstanding, however, are Rubens' *Lions and Dogs Fighting* and the *Last Supper* by Simon Vouet. The popular arts and traditions section includes 18C-20C costumes from the Coutances area, 18C-19C regional pottery, headdresses, furniture and kitchen utensils.

Les Unelles

A new steel frame and glass-walled building adjoins the former seminary buildings which have been transformed to house an arts centre, the tourist office and the local authority offices. The name is derived from the Unelli whose capital was Cosedia, present day Coutances.

Église St-Pierre

This fine 15C-16C church built by Bishop Geoffroy Herbert was given a lantern tower over the transept crossing. In accordance with Renaissance custom, it was decorated ever more richly as the height increased.

Excursion

▶ *Leave Coutances to the N on D 971 heading for St-Sauveur-Landelin, then turn right onto D 53. Just after Moncuit, turn left towards Hauteville (D 435).*

Hauteville-la-Guichard

15km/9.3mi NE. Musée Tancrède de Hauteville – ⊙Open Jul–Aug daily except Mon 2–6pm. Sept–Nov and Feb–June last Sun of month 2–6pm. ⊙Closed Dec–Jan and public holidays. ☞4€ (children 1.5€) ☎02 33 19 19 19.

The **Musée Tancrède de Hauteville** plunges you into the heart of the Norman conquest of Sicily and southern Italy at the beginning of the 11C. Tancrède and his 12 children (the most famous were Robert Guiscard and Roger I of Sicily) were the true founders of Norman power in the Mediterranean. Incredibly well organised and extremely cunning, they created a powerful state remarkable for its military achievements as well as for its cultural influence.

Driving Tour

From Coutances to the Coast

Round-trip of 50km/31mi.

▶ *Leave Coutances by ④, D 44 and then turn right onto D 244.*

On the way out of Coutances the road passes the overgrown remains of the aqueduct.

Château de Gratot★

⊙*Open daily 10am-7pm. ☞3€ (children 1.50€) ☎02 31 57 18 20.*

For five centuries the château belonged to the Argouges family. Abandoned for many years, the château has been converted into an arts centre after extensive restoration starting in 1968.

A small three-arched bridge over the moat leads to the entrance gatehouse and then the inner courtyard. On either side are the bare walls of the service buildings; to the west are the ruins of a square corner tower. Within the courtyard from left to right are the 18C pavilion and the 17C main building, flanked by the Round Tower, and the Fairy's Tower with the North Tower to the rear.

Maison seigneuriale

Two flights of steps lead up to the entrance of the now roofless former living quarters. The ground floor was lit by tall windows, the upper floor by dormers.

Tour ronde

This early-15C round tower is quite medieval in appearance. The narrowing of the staircase as it moved upwards was devised to hinder an attack as only one person could pass at a time.

The entrance to the basement is at the foot of this tower.

Caves

The groined vaulting of these fine cellars is supported by stout piers. The masonry is composed of stones placed edgewise.

The late-15C tower, now called the Fairy's Tower, is reinforced by a powerful buttress. It is octagonal at the base but becomes square at the top and is crowned by a saddleback roof. The wall head is decorated with gargoyles and a balustrade.

Tour d'angle

This corner tower, the only part of the medieval castle which remains, prob-

Address Book

For coin ranges, see the Legend on the cover flap.

WHERE TO STAY

Village Grouchy Bed and Breakfast – *11 r. du Vieux-Lavoir, 50560 Blainville-sur-Mer, 2km/1.2mi N of Agon-Coutainville via D 72. ☎02 33 47 20 31. jr.sebire@free.fr. Closed Jan– Mar. 5 rooms.* This little village used to be comprised exclusively of fishermen's homes. In this house, large bedrooms with wood panelling make for a fine halt right near the sea. A summer kitchen is at guests' disposal in the garden.

Le Quesnot Bed and Breakfast – *3 r. du Mont-César, 50660 Montchaton, 6.5km/4mi SW of Coutances via D 20 then D 72. ☎02 33 45 05 88. Closed 15 Nov– Easter. 3 rooms.* Guests have the use of a small 18C stone-built house with its own terrace and tiny garden and a view of a little church perched on a promontory. Modern bedrooms above the large country-style dining room.

Hôtel Cositel – *Rte Coutainville, Delasse. ☎02 33 19 15 00. hotelcositel@ wanadoo.fr. 55 rooms.* A modern building on a hilltop overlooking the town. The rooms are bright and functionally furnished. Wine bar, restaurant with a terrace on a small lake, bistrot.

WHERE TO EAT

Le Jules Gommes – *34 r. du Vaudredoux, 50590 Regneville-sur-Mer, 10km/6.2mi SW of Coutances via D 20, rte de Montmartin-sur-Mer and then D 49. ☎02 33 45 32 04. Closed Mon–Tue except schoolholidays. Reservations required weekends.* This address, which shares its name with a late-19C three-masted schooner, positively exudes charm. Handsome rustic interior featuring exposed stone, a fireplace and watercolours. Both seafood and inland cuisine, crepes and a pub featuring a healthy choice of ales and whiskeys.

Le Tourne-Bride – *585 r. d'Argouges, 50200 Gratot. ☎02 33 45 11 00 Closed 1–15 July, Feb holidays, Sun evening and Mon.* The proprietors of this former post-coach relay, Martine and Denis Poisson, offer a warm and attentive welcome. In the two rustic-style dining rooms, the menu accents traditional Norman cuisine, with produce straight from the sea and local fields.

La Verte Campagne – *Le Hameau Chevalier, 50660 Trelly, 13km/8.1mi S of Coutances via D 7, D 49, then D 539 and a minor road. ☎02 33 47 65 33. Closed 17–24 Mar and 22 Nov –15 Dec.* This 18C farm, covered with Virginia creeper in summer, has retained its authentic charm: wide ceiling beams, stone walls and old fireplaces. This renowned restaurant serves dishes prepared with care. A few rooms available upstairs.

MARKET

Market – *Pl. du Gén.-de-Gaulle, 50560 Blainville-sur-Mer – Sun morning.* A very animated and colourful market. Country produce of every kind can be found here, including, naturellement, the local cheese: le coutances.

LEISURE

Several beaches are found on this part of the west coast, within 15–15km/7.5– 9mi of Coutances. From north to south: **Anneville-sur-Mer,** a little beach with fine sand set in the dunes; **Gouville-sur-Mer,** a beach 6km/4mi long with several acres of oyster beds (*for a guided tour of the oyster beds, call the tourist office at ☎02 33 47 84 33);* **Blainville-sur-Mer,** another beach with a reputation for oysters, also offers fishing and a wide sand beach much appreciated by families; **Agon-Coutainville** is the furthest south, and you will find here a golf course, a casino and all sorts of sports and nautical activities.

ably dates from the late 13C or the early 14C; the door has been walled up.

Communs

One of the rooms in these 16C outbuildings hosts an exhibition on the château, its construction and restoration.

▶ *In St-Malo-de-la-Lande take D 68 towards Tourville-sur-Sienne then turn right onto D 272 to Agon-Coutainville.*

Agon-Coutainville

Coutainville is one of the more popular resorts on the west coast of the Cotentin peninsula. Its long beach of fine sand is bounded by the Channel to the west and the Sienne estuary to the east. At low tide these great wet sandy stretches are popular for those looking for shrimps, cockles and clams.

▶ *Take the road leading to the Pointe d'Agon.*

Pointe d'Agon

The line of stones on the right-hand side of the road is a memorial to the author **Fernand Lechanteur** (1910-71) who wrote in the Norman dialect. From the headland there is a good view of this part of the Channel coast and especially of the port of Regnéville on the other side of the estuary.

▶ *Return to Agon-Coutainville, then follow the road to the hamlet, rue d'Agon.*

The D 72 road soon overlooks the silted up port of Regnéville.

Tourville-sur-Sienne

The roadside statue is of Admiral de Tourville, who lost the Battle of La Hougue (1692). From the terraced cemetery (*road from the statue*) there is a good view of Regnéville harbour closed off by the sandy headland, Montmarin belfry, the Rocher de Granville, and in clear weather, the Chausey Islands.

▶ *Drive to Pont-de-la-Roque along D 650, then to Regnéville-sur-Mer along D 49.*

COUTANCES

Albert-1er Av.	Z	2
Croûte R. de la	YZ	3
Daniel R.	Y	5
Duhamel R.	Z	6
Écluse-Chette R. de l'	Y	8
Encoignard Bd	Z	9
Foch R. Mar.	Z	10
Gambetta R.	Y	12
Herbert R. G.	Z	13
Leclerc Av. Division	Y	15
Legentil-de-la-Galaisière Bd	Z	16
Lycée R. du	Z	17
Marest R. Thomas-du	Y	18
Milon R.	Y	19
Montbray R. G.-de	Z	20
Normandie R. de	Y	21
Palais-de-Justice R. du	Y	23
Paynel Bd J.	Y	24
Quesnel-Morinière R.	Z	26
République Av. de la	Y	27
St-Dominique R.	Y	29
St-Nicolas R.	Y	30
Tancrède R.	Y	32
Tourville R.	Y	33

Musée Quesnel Morinière	Y	M

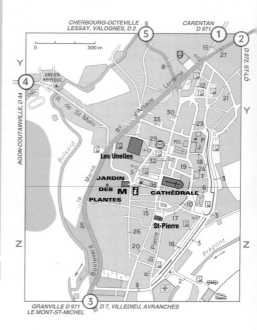

Regnéville-sur-Mer

Musée du Littoral et de la Chaux – ⏰*Open July–Aug daily 11am–7pm. June & Sept 11am–6pm. Apr–May and school holidays, except Christmas 4–6pm.* 👛*4€ (Children 1.60 €)* ☎*02 33 46 82 18.*

This small port located at the mouth of Sienne harbour was prosperous until the site silted up, causing the locality's influence to decline.

From the 13C **church**, follow signposts to the **Musée du Littoral et de la Chaux** set up in the former Rey lime kilns. This splendidly restored example of mid-19C industrial architecture presents traditional activities connected with the Channel coast: sea-sand and kelp picking, rope making, the manufacturing of fishing craft etc. The various uses of lime as well as the techniques involved in its making are illustrated by a number of models and ancient tools.

▶ *Leave Regnéville on D 49 towards Montmartin-sur-Mer, then Hyenville (D 73). Continue on D 73 until you cross D 7 and drive towards Coutances via Saussey.*

Manoir de Saussey★

⏰*Open Easter–Sept daily 2-6.30pm (last entry 1hr before closing).* 👛*6€ (Children 1.50€).* ☎*02 33 45 19 65.*

The 17C buildings are enhanced by a pretty rose garden, an orchard, a vegetable patch and a series of delightful flower beds. Note the collection of **Nativity scenes**, including some made of bread and one lovely 17C Napolitan scene with sumptuous robes. There is also a lovely exhibition of **glassware**.

▶ *Go back to D 7 and follow signs to the Manoir d'Argences.*

Jardins d'Argences

⏰*Open mid-May–mid-Oct daily 2–6pm.* 👛*5.50€ (under 12 years no charge).* ☎*02 33 07 92 04.*

The grounds surrounding this manor house (15C-18C) are enchanting and laid out along a series of pretty itineraries.

▶ *Drive back to Coutances.*

Tour à la Fée

According to legend, one of the lords of Gratot fell hopelessly in love with a beautiful young maiden whom he had met at the fountain. In reply to his proposal of marriage the damsel avowed she was a fairy and that she could marry him only on the condition that he never pronounced the word *death*. The lord promised. One day during a reception at the château, the lord grew impatient waiting for her ladyship; he went up to her room and in an ill-considered reprimand pronounced the fateful word. The fairy gave a heart-rending cry, then clambered onto the window sill and was seen no more.

CRÈVECŒUR-EN-AUGE

CALVADOS, POPULATION 554

MICHELIN MAP 303: M-5 – LOCAL MAP SEE PAYS D'AUGE

Crèvecœur is a pleasant town situated in the Auge Valley. Some 500m/500yd to the north and to the right of N 13 is the Château de Crèvecœur.

- **Information:** Consult tourist offices in Lisieux and the Pays d'Auge
- ▶ **Orient Yourself:** Crèvecoeur is on N 13 between Caen (43km/21mi west) and Lisieux (20km/12.5mi east).
- **Don't Miss:** The wonderful dovecot at the château.
- **Organizing Your Time:** As the château opens only at 11am, use the morning to see the manor of Coupesarte.
- **Also See:** Pays d'Auge, Lisieux, Pont-l'Évêque, Houlgate and Cabourg.

Sights

Château★

1hr ○*Open July–Aug daily 11am–7pm. Apr–June & Sept daily 11am–6pm. Oct Sun 2–6pm.* ○*Closed Nov–Mar.* ∞*5€ (under 10 years no charge).* ☎*02 31 63 02 45. www. chateau-de-crevecoeur.com.*

Encircled by trees and moats, the timber-framed buildings of the **château** – its motte was erected in the 11C – were transformed in the 15C and restored in 1972. They now form a highly picturesque sight: an outer bailey and feudal motte surrounded by a filled-in moat. The 16C gatehouse used to stand beside the former Château de Beuvilliers near Lisieux. The 16C barn and 15C manor are home to the collections of the **Musée Schlumberger,** named after two Alsatian brothers Conrad and Marcel; in 1928 these geophysicists and petroleum engineers invented the continuous electric logging of boreholes, a technique that was to be extended to countries all over the world. The museum displays equipment used in oil drilling and prospecting. The **dovecot**, a remarkable construction, is square-shaped. Note the projecting eaves formed by the shingled roofing, visible on all four sides of the building. On the side facing winds, is a shelf from which the pigeons are released. The interior woodwork is pierced with 1 500 pigeon-holes (*boulins*).

For more information on dovecots, see the Introduction.

The 12C chapel features oak framework in the shape of an upturned hull, as well as fragments of a medieval wall painting. The farm buildings contain the second part of the museum, devoted to **Normandy architecture**, which presents examples of traditional timber-framed architecture from the Pays d'Auge. The History Room (Salle d'Histoire) displays miscellaneous objects retracing the history of Crèvecœur-en-Auge over the centuries.

Excursion

Manoir de Coupesarte★

15km/9 mi southeast. Leave Crèvecoeur-en-Auge by D 16 towards St-Pierre-sur-Dives. At Mesnil-Mauger, turn left onto D 47. Cross Authieux-Papion, then just after St-Julien-le-Faucon, turn right onto D 47. Coupesart is 1.5km/1mi further. Exterior only ○*Open daily 9am-7pm.* ∞*No charge.* ☎*02 31 63 82 12.*

This charming residence (○ *closed to the public)* surrounded by water on three sides is the main house of a farm building. The construction goes back to the end of the 15C or beginning of the 16C. From the field on the left beyond the small lock there is a good view of the half-timbered façade with its two corner turrets reminiscent of watchtowers.

The half-timbered outbuildings contribute to the originality of the whole.

DEAUVILLE ☲ ☲ ☲

CALVADOS, POPULATION 4 364

MICHELIN MAP 303: M-3 – LOCAL MAPS SEE PAYS D'AUGE AND VALLÉE DE LA SEINE - ROUEN

Deauville, a popular resort since the mid -19C, is known for the luxury and refinement of its various establishments and the elegance of its entertainments. Events of the the summer season include racing (including the Grand Prix), the polo world championship, regattas, tennis and golf tournaments, galas, and the international yearling fair. Every year, in early September, the city hosts the prestigious **American Film Festival.**

- **Information:** Place de la Mairie, BP 79, 14800 Deauville. ☎02 31 14 40 00. www.deauville.org.
- ▶ **Orient Yourself:** Located 94km/59mi from Rouen and 43km/27mi from Le Havre, Deauville stretches along a beach between Trouville and Mont Canisy on the Côte Fleurie. The Touques estuary, crossed by the Pont des Belges, near the train station, separates Deauville from the older resort, Trouville.
- **Don't Miss:** The pretty villas as well as the view from Mont Canisy and the coastal road from Honfleur to Cabourg.
- ○ **Organizing Your Time:** Try to see Deauville in the morning; afternoons bring crowds.
- **Also See:** Trouville, Honfleur, Houlgate, Cabourg and the Pays d'Auge.

Visit

The Resort

The season in Deauville opens in July and ends with the Deauville Grand Prix on the fourth Sunday in August and the Golden Cup of the international polo championship. Horse racing takes place alternately at La Touques (flat racing) and Clairefontaine (flat racing and steeplechasing) and the international yearling sales are held in Deauville in August. Out of season the resort accommodates numerous conventions as well as seminars.

The coming and going on the **Planches** – a wooden plank promenade running the whole length of the beach – is the most distinctive feature of beach life in Deauville. It is lined with elegant buildings – the Pompeian Baths and the Soleil Bar, where stars and celebrities like to be seen.

Between the Casino and the Planches, the Centre International de Deauville (C.I.D.) is a remarkable ensemble of suspended gardens, fountains and transparent façades which welcomes all kinds of professional, cultural and festive events.

A walk along the seafront boulevard Eugène-Cornuché will prove that Deauville is not called the "beach of flowers" *(plage fleurie)* for nothing.

The yacht marina on the Touques and the Yacht Club strike an elegant note.

A little **tourist train** will take you on a guided tour of the city (with commentary), and the tourist office has information about walking tours and bicycle trails.

Deauville Port

The port is enclosed on the west side by a breakwater extending from the beach to the mouth of the Touques and on the east by a jetty marking the port entrance to the channel. The deep access channel means that the port is accessible 80% of the time. It consists of three docks, entered though a double lock, which provide deep water moorings and ample capacity: 800 berths along 4 000m/4 360yd of quays. At the centre are the slate-roofed marinas, the Deauville harbour master's office, an annexe of the Marina Deauville Club (quai des Marchands, near the lock) and space for shops and hotel services.

Driving tours

The mileage given is calculated from the Pont des Belges, which links Deauville to Trouville.

In summer, the coast between Honfleur and Cabourg is one of the busiest in France, but is lovely despite the crowds.

Le Mont Canisy★

Round-trip of 15km/9 miles (about 45min).

▶ *Leave Deauville to the SW by the D 513.*

Bénerville Church stands overlooking a crossroads.

▶ *Turn left up the hill before the church; after about 200m/200 yards by the town hall turn left again. At the top bear onto a local road leading to Mont Canisy. Leave the car by a gate.*

A path leads to the blockhouses where the view extends from Cap de la Hève to the Orne estuary.

▶ *Return to the car and go right.*

Once beyond the more recent housing estates of Canisy there are views over the Touques Valley as the road descends to the St-Arnoult crossroads.

▶ *Turn left onto D 278 to Deauville.*

The casino in Deauville

G. Targat/ MICHELIN

The Corniche Normande: From Deauville-Trouville to Honfleur★★

21km/13 miles. Allow about 1hr.

▶ *Leave Deauville-Trouville to the NE by D 513.*

This very pleasant tour passes through magnificent scenery and affords views over the Seine estuary between gaps in the hedges and orchards. Handsome properties are scattered along the road. Just before Villerville there is a fine view of the oil refineries on the estuary. To the left Le Havre can be recognised by its thermal power station and the belfry of St Joseph's Church.

Villerville⌂

This lively seaside resort, with its nearby meadows and woods, has kept its rural character. Notice the Romanesque belfry on the local church. From the terrace overlooking the beach there is a view of Le Havre and Cap de la Hève. The road is thereafter narrow with hidden bends.

Cricquebœuf

The 12C **church**, with its ivy- covered walls, is a familiar feature on travel posters. The countryside around, with its apple orchards, grazing cows and tranquil ponds add to the emblematic beauty.

▶ *In Pennedepie, take D 62; after 2.5km/1.5mi turn right onto D 279.*

Barneville

The church, tucked away in the greenery, is backed by the magnificent park of the 18C château.

▶ *Take D 279 N; after 4km/3 mi turn left by a château to reach Honfleur via the Côte de Grâce.*

Côte de Grâce★★
⌕*See HONFLEUR: Excursions.*

Honfleur★★
⌕*See HONFLEUR.*

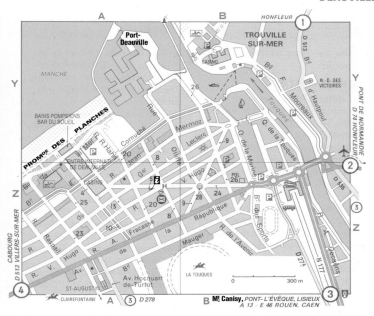

DEAUVILLE			Gambetta R.	BY	9	Le Marois R.	AZ	25
			Gaulle Av. Gén.-de	AZ	10	Mirabeau R.	BY	26
Blanc R. E.	AZ	4	Gontaut-Biron R.	AYZ	13	Morny Pl. de	BZ	28
Colas R. E.	AZ	5	Le-Hoc R. D.	BZ	24	RépubliqueAv. de la	ABZ	
Fossorier R. R.	ABZ	8	Hoche R.	AYZ	20			
Fracasse R. A.	AZ		Laplace R.	AZ	23			

The Côte Fleurie: From Trouville-Deauville to Cabourg★★

To Cabourg: 19km/12 mi.

▸ *Leave Deauville to the SW by D 513.*

Bénerville-sur-Mer and Blonville-sur-Mer

The hillsides are dotted with villas overlooking a long sandy beach.

Blonville-sur-Mer

Its sweeping sandy beach stretches to the slopes of Mont Canisy. At Blonville, there is an amusement park near the sea. The Chapelle Notre-Dame de l'Assomption houses some modern frescoes, the work of the artist **Jean-Denis Maillart**.

Villers-sur-Mer�▨☨

Musée paléontologique – ⟨⟩ ⊙Open July–Aug daily 9am–7pm. Mar–June & *Sept–Oct daily 9.30am–12.30pm, 2–6pm. Rest of the year daily 9.30am–12.30pm, 2–5.30pm. ⊙Closed Sun afternoon Nov– Feb (except school holidays), 1 Jan, 25 Dec. ⊠No charge. ☎02 31 87 01 18.*

This elegant seaside resort with its casino and excellent sports facilities is known for its large beach and its wooded hilly countryside crisscrossed with small paths leading down to the town centre. The **Musée Paléontologique** *(access through the tourist office)* has exhibits of fossils and stuffed birds from the area together with a stone armchair and seashells which belonged to Ferdinand Postel, artist and photographer who lived in Villers from 1880 to 1917.

Just before Houlgate, on a downhill hairpin bend, a viewing table *(right)* offers a **panorama** from the mouth of the River Dives to the mouth of the River Orne.

Falaise des Vaches Noires★

🄰Between Villers-sur-Mer and Houlgate, the Auberville plateau ends in a

195

Address Book

For coin ranges, see the Legend on the cover flap.

WHERE TO STAY

Hôtel Le Patio – *180 av. de la République. ☎02 31 88 25 07. www.hotel-patio.fr - Closed Feb. 13 rooms.* The name tells it all: this century-old edifice with an immaculate façade possesses an enticing, flower-filled patio where breakfasts are served as soon as the weather warms up. The rooms, each one different, are regularly spruced up.

Hôtel Hélios – *10 r. Fossorier. ☎02 31 14 46 46. www. hotelheliosdeau-ville.com. Closed 7–21 Jan. 36 rooms.* A practical address at the centre of the resort. Simple rooms have been freshened up and a small apartment is appreciated by families. Mini-swimming pool.

La Maison Pommerose Bed and Breakfast –*St-Sylvestre-l'Eglise, 27260 St-Sylvestre-de-Cormeilles. ☎02 31 57 13 05. www.pommerose.com. 3 rooms. Meals* . Nestled in a thicket of green, this magnificent Norman residence will charm you with its comfort. The stone fireplace warms rooms decorated with tile floors and carved woodwork. Pretty garden with apple trees. Breakfasts are delicious and generous.

Hôtel Normandy – *38 r. Jean-Mermoz. ☎02 31 98 66 22. www.lucienbarriere.com. 272 rooms.* This elegant timber-framed manor house dating from 1912 is situated in the liveliest part of town: facing the sea, a stone's throw from the casino and the shopping district. A sumptuous hotel that will cater to your each and every desire. The place to be in this town where everything glitters.

WHERE TO EAT

Dupont avec un thé – *20 Pl Morny. ☎02 31 88 20 79. sasnupont.dives@ wanadoo.fr. Closed Mon, Thur and Fri out of season, except school holidays from 1–2.30pm.* This shop offers wonderful desserts such as lemon-scented sugar cookies and coffee-flavoured macaroons. Light meals and a hearty breakfast menu.

Le Nautica – *2 r. Désir.-Le Hoc. ☎02 31 88 03 27. Closed Wed out of season, except during school holidays.* The atmosphere of an English pub prevails, with a little touch of the sea, in this brasserie near the train station. The menu offers only dishes prepared right in the kitchen, smoked salmon and foie gras included. Service from noon to midnight.

La Flambée – *181 r Général-Leclerc. ☎02 31 88 28 46. restaurant. laflambee@wanadoo.fr. Closed 2–15 Jan.* In the the vast open hearth are prepared, under your eyes, grilled steaks and chops. There is also more traditional cuisine and, in a tank for your inspection, lobsters.

Bar de la Mer – *Casino Barrière de Deauville. ☎02 31 88 27 51. Closed Nov –15 Feb except public holidays and Mon–Fri during school holidays.* This restaurant, located right on the famous boardwalk, offers a pleasant dining room, decorated with a fresco depicting the first paid holidays, an enormous terrace on the beach, and a splendid view of the ocean. Completely renovated, it offers shellfish, grilled meat and salads.

La Table d'Auge – *Pl. du Marché. ☎02 31 88 30 58 . www.deau-ville-terroir.com. Reservations advised summer and weekends.* Shellfish served in this restaurant is guaranteed fresh: it goes directly from the tank to the kitchen. If your tastes lie elsewhere, don't fret: delicious, authentic regional recipes are also available. In the evening, weather permitting, why not enjoy your meal on the terrace?

La Galerie de Tourgéville – *14800 Tourgéville, 6km/3.75mi S of Deauville via D 278 and D 27. ☎02 31 87 31 11. www.galeriedetourgeville.com. Closed Tue–Wed.* A restaurant decorated with sundry bric-a-brac and an art gallery. The menu is simple and rather trendy, with scads of atmosphere; the Deauville Parisians simply *adore* it!

ON THE TOWN

Martine Lambert – *76 bis r. Eugène-Colas. ☎02 31 88 94 04. martine.comb-ert@wanadoo.fr. Open daily Apr–Sept and July–Aug 10am–1pm, 3–8pm, week-*

end 10am–midnight. The reputation of Martine Lambert's ice cream reaches far beyond Deauville. Made from Norman cows' milk and fresh eggs, each flavour is subtle and delicious: nuts, chocolate, caramel ice cream, sprinkled with toasted walnuts and almonds, simply irresistible.

Casino – *R. Edmond-Blanc.* ☏*02 31 14 31 14. www.lucienbarriere.com.* 325 slot machines, punto-banco, and more.

Les Planches – *Le Bois Lauret, 14910 Blonville-sur-Mer, 6km/3.7mi SW of Deauville in the countryside; route well-indicated.* ☏*02 31 87 58 09. www. lesplanches.com. Open Fri–Sat and school holidays 11pm–dawn. Closed Jan.* All of preppy Paris haunts this discotheque known for its Cuban bar, loft and heated pool. During the Deauville festival, it's packed (but never before midnight) with people hoping to bump into some stars (which does happen!).

LEISURE

Kid Le Circuit de Deauville – *Rte de Caen, 14800 St-Arnoult, 4km/2.5mi S of Deauville by D 27.* ☏*02 31 81 31 31 www. dupratconcept.com. Open daily 9.30am-12.30pm, 1.30-6.30pm.From 16€.* Sizeable amusement park specialised in motor sports: go-carting (adults

and children), speed boats and jet skis, safety driving courses and more.

HORSEBACK RIDING

Kid Poney Club – *R. Renaldo-Hann.* ☏*02 31 98 56 24. Open daily during school holidays. Rest of the year open weekends and public holidays. Closed Jan. 30€/1hr.* Rides on the beach astride a pony or horse. Go in the morning, it's less crowded and you can watch race horses being trained in the seawater to strengthen their tendons.

TOURING DEAUVILLE

Tourist train: There is a tour of the town (35mn) in a small tourist train from Easter through Sept, from 10.30am to 18.30 pm. The tour leaves from the Place de la Mairie or the restaurant Ciro's. 5.50€ (Children 3.50€). Information at tourist office.

CALENDAR OF EVENTS

June – International Sailing Week and Jumping International. Opening of the horseracing season.

August – Musical August (Août musical) music festival, polo championship, horse races, sale of yearlings.

September – Festival of American Cimema. 10 days from the beginning of Sept.

---

crumbling and much-eroded cliff face. It is best to walk along the beach at low tide (*about 2hr on foot round-trip*) to enjoy the panorama which extends from Trouville to Luc-sur-Mer and over most of the Seine bay.

In places large pieces of limestone have broken away from the cliff top and piled up at the base where they have been colonised by seaweed; these are the Black Cows (Vaches Noires).

Houlgate⌂⌂

Houlgate is set in the verdant Drochon Valley; the shady avenues and the houses and gardens add to the overall charm of this resort.

The promenade overlooks the fine sandy beach, which is popular for bathing. The road runs along the coast and, before Dives-sur-Mer, passes in front of a monument commemorating the departure of **Duke William** for the conquest of England.

Dives-sur-Mer★

See DIVES-SUR-MER.

Cabourg⌂⌂

See CABOURG.

▶ *Head to Cabourg via D 45.*

PLAGES DU DÉBARQUEMENT★★

MICHELIN MAP 303: F-3 TO K-4

This tour includes that part of the Calvados coast between the mouths of the Orne and the Vire, also known as the Côte de Nacre where the D-Day landings took place on 6 June 1944. The marked itineraries, known as Overlord-L'Assaut (Overlord-The Onslaught) and D-Day-le Choc (D-Day-The Impact), are two of several such itineraries in the Historical Area of the Battle of Normandy.

- **Information:** Quai Baron-Gérard, 14520 Port-en-Bessin.
  ☎02 31 22 45 80. www.bayeux-bessin-tourism.com.
- ▶ **Orient Yourself:** This section covers the Calvados coast between the mouths of the Orne and the Vire, also known as the Côte de Nacre (Mother-of-Pearl coast) where the Normandy landings took place on D-Day, 6 June 1944.
- **Don't Miss:** La Pointe du Hoc, the gun emplacements of Longues-sur-Mer and the château of Benouville.
- **Organizing Your Time:** Each of the circuits described below takes a half day.
- **Kids Especially for Kids:** The Maison de la Mer at Courselles-sur-Mer will help them identify the shells they find on the beach.
- **Also See:** Omaha Beach, Arromanches-les-Bains, Ouistreham-Riva-Bella, Bayeux, Fontaine-Henry, Caen, the Cotentin Penninsula, Ste-Mère Église.

The D-Day Landings

Dawn of D-Day – The formidable armada, which consisted of 4 266 barges and landing craft together with hundreds of warships and naval escorts, set sail from the south coast of England on the night of 5 June 1944 (*for further details, see The Battle of Normandy in the Introduction*); it was preceded by flotillas of minesweepers to clear a passage through the mine fields in the English Channel.

As the crossing proceeded, airborne troops were flown out and landed in two detachments at either end of the invasion front. The British 6th Division quickly took possession of the Bénouville-Ranville bridge, since named Pegasus Bridge after the airborne insignia, and harried the enemy positions between the River Orne and the River Dives to prevent reinforcements arriving. West of the River Vire the American 101st and 82nd Divisions mounted an attack on key positions such as Ste-Mère-Église or opened up the exits from Utah Beach.

The name Calvados: A Source of Controversy

According to tradition, the Calvados *département* owes its name to *El Salvador*, a Spanish ship belonging to the Armada that sank off the rocky Norman coast: on several maps dating from the 17C one can find the spelling *Salvador* or Calvador. However, it would seem that this legend is unfounded since no boat bearing that name and belonging to Phillip II's fleet is believed to have been shipwrecked in the area.

The other possible explanation for the origin of the word Calvados was put forward by a lecturer of Caen University, who claims that the name comes from the Latin *calva dorsa*, meaning barren hills. This expression, used as a proper noun and gallicized without ever being translated, was subsequently mentioned on many oceanographic charts. Admittedly, seen from the sea, the heights running along the Côte du Bessin are, in parts, quite bare! The variety of the Calvados coast reflects its hinterland; the open farmlands of the Caen countryside produce a perfectly flat shoreline.

Address Book

For coin ranges, see the Legend on the cover flap.

WHERE TO STAY

La Ferme d'Escures Bed and Breakfast – *At Escures village, 14520 Commes, 2.5km/1.5mi S of Port-en-Bessin via D 6.☎02 31 92 52 23. 4 rooms.* Located a few miles from the beaches and Bayeux, this 17C farm built with local Caen stone, is the ideal starting point for a tour of the area. The decoration of the rooms is simple but pleasant and the self-catering cottage, located in the former bakery, has its own garden.

Le Logis Bed and Breakfast – *Escures village, 14520 Commes, 2.5km/1.5mi SE of Port-en-Bessin via D 6. ☎02 31 21 79 56. http://monsite.wanadoo.fr/le.logis. 4 rooms.* You will be won over by the charm of these old houses inhabited by a family with a great sense of hospitality. Breakfast is served in the former stable, which still has a stone drinking trough. The rooms and the self-catering cottage are comfortable.

Ferme du Mouchel Bed and Breakfast – *At lieu-dit "Le Mouchel", 14710 Formigny. ☎02 31 22 53 79. 4 rooms.* On a little country road, a pleasant dairy farm probably from the 16C. Three pretty rooms, with another in an annex where breakfast is served.

La Faisanderie Bed and Breakfast– *14450 Grandchamp-Maisy. ☎02 31 22 70 06. 3 rooms.* Attractive house covered in Virginia creeper in the midst of a horse farm. Pretty rooms, each different. Breakfast is served in pleasant dining room with fireplace.

Domaine de L'Hostréière– *R. du Cimetière américain. 14170 Colleville-sur-Mer. ☎02 31 51 64 64. www.domainedelhostreiere.com. Open Easter–15 Nov. 20 rooms.* Modern, well-equipped rooms, each with a terrace, now occupy the outbuildings of this old farm, next to the American cemetary of St-Laurent-sur-Mer. Gym and swimming pool.

Le Petit Val Bed and Breakfast – *24 r. du Camp-Romain, 14480 Banville, 3km/1.8mi SW of Courseulles-sur-Mer via D 12. ☎02 31 37 92 18. fermelepetitval@wanadoo.fr. 5 rooms.* Dating probably from the 17C, this typical Bessin farm is the ideal spot for a nature break. Discreet decor in the cosy bedrooms, attractive breakfast room and a garden filled with flowers.

Manoir de l'Hermerel Bed and Breakfast – *14230 Géfosse-Fontenay, 7km/4.2mi N of Isigny via D 514 then D 199. ☎02 31 22 64 12. www.manoir-hermerel.com . Closed 15 Nov– 15 Feb. 4 rooms.* This fortified 17C farm once belonged to the local squire, as the dovecot facing the entrance porch testifies. Visit the small 15C Gothic chapel before retiring to one of the attractive bedrooms. Simple, convivial welcome.

Château de Vouilly Bed and Breakfast – *14230 Vouilly-Église, 8km/5mi SE of Isigny via D 5. ☎02 31 22 08 59. www.chateau-vouilly.com. Closed Dec–Feb.5 rooms.* A moat abounding with fish, handsome gardens, an orangery, imposing drawing rooms and dual-coloured paving in an 18C residence. In 1945, it was the general headquarters of the American press.

WHERE TO EAT

Café Gondrée – *Pegasus Bridge – 12 av. du Cdt-Kieffer, 14970 Bénouville, 9km/5.6mi N of Caen via D 514. ☎02 31 44 62 25. Closed 15 Nov–8 Mar.* This small, authentic pre-war café, the first house on French soil to be liberated in 1944, has strong historic and emotional connotations. Arlette Gondrée, who was four at the time, still prepares the traditional family omelette with salad. **La Flambée** – *2 r. Émile-Demagny, 14230 Isigny-sur-Mer. ☎02 31 51 70 96. la.flambee.isigny@wanadoo.fr. Closed 2 weeks Feb–Mar, 2 weeks June–July, Tue in winter and Wed.* The wood fire gives off a wonderful smell in this typical Norman restaurant. Fish and meat are grilled in the vast fireplace of the dining room with its exposed beams.

Les Alizés – *14 quai Ouest, 14470 Courselles-sur-Mer.* This kitchen which highlights local produce has won a loyal clientèle. In a comfortable dining room with a nautical theme, you can sample oysters and mussels at any hour, against a background of classical music. Some guestrooms.

Le Vauban – *6 r. du Nord, 14520 Port-en-Bessin. ☎02 31 21 74 83. dgance@aol.com. Closed mid-Dec–mid-Jan, Tue evening out of season and Wed.* One of the locals' favourite eating places. The owner-chef relies upon appetizing fresh produce and his expertise to bring out the best qualities of land and sea.

Le Bistrot d'à Côté – *10–12 r. Michel-Lefournier, 14520 Port-en-Bessin. ☎02 31 22 71 34. www.barque-bleue.fr. Closed Jan, Tue–Wed from 15 Sep–15 Jun.* This dining room, a study in contrasting blues and yellows, features old photographs of the harbour. The day's fish and shellfish dishes are listed on the large blackboard menu.

La Pêcherie – *Pl du 6-Juin, 14470 Courselles-sur-Mer. ☎02 31 37 45 84. www.la-pecherie.com.* Storm lanterns, oars and portholes announce a nautical theme. The cuisine follows suit, with oceanic specialties. A few guestrooms decorated like ship's cabins.

La Trinquette – *7 rte du Joncal, 14450 Grandcamp-Maisy. ☎02 31 22 64 90. www.restaurant-la-trinquette.com. Closed Tue–Wed Oct–Easter.* The sea is hidden by the fish-auction market but never mind, the fish ends up on your plate: leeks slowly melted in butter, simmered in an earthenware dish or served as a soup with a Norman rouille sauce. Try the local fishermen's dish, *la marmite grandcopaise.*

Restaurant de l'Hôtel Mercure – *On the golf course, 14520 Port-en-Bessin. ☎02 31 22 44 44. www.accorhotels.com. Closed 22 Dec–12 Jan.* This hotel restaurant, open to the public, has a superb view over the Omaha Beach Golf Club, whose facilities it shares. The Sunday brunch is particularly generous. A brasserie-type restaurant at the club house.

L'As de Trèfle – *420 r. Léopold-Hettier, 14990 Bernières-sur-Mer. ☎02 31 97 22 60. asdetrefle3@wanadoo.fr.* This building, constructed after the war, is unattractive, but the quality of the kitchen is well worth the trip. Delicious seafood and dishes from the interior. Terrace for fine weather.

Manoir d'Hastings et la Pommeraie – *18 av de la Côte-de-Nacre (near the church), 14970 Bénouville, 10km/6.2mi NE of Caen via D 515 - ☎02 31 44 62 43. www.manoirhastings.com. Closed 10 Nov –14 Dec, Feb school holidays, Sun evening and Mon.* This former 17C priory, enclosed within its garden, has retained its old-world aspect with weathered stone walls and exposed beams. Several dining rooms including an attic one. A few bedrooms.

LEISURE

Spa Le Hammam de la Mer – *2 r. Guynemer,14530 Luc-sur-Mer. ☎02 31 97 32 22. www.thalasso-normandie.com. Closed 3–23 Jan.* An authentic oriental steam bath, with Moroccan tiles on the floor, mosaics, screens in sculpted wood, and all the necessary details. The accessories are also thoroughly Moroccan: perfumes, olive-oil soap, clay scrubbing compounds, tough loofah sponges for exfoliations. Tea is served along with delicate pastries.

British Sector – Although preliminary bombing and shelling had not destroyed Hitler's Atlantic Wall, they succeeded in disorganising German defences. Land forces were able to reach their objectives, divided into three beachheads. A German counterattack was crushed under naval bombardment.

Sword Beach – The Franco-British commandos landed at Colleville-Plage, Lion-sur-Mer and St-Aubin. They captured Riva-Bella and the strongpoints at Lion and Langrune and then linked up with the airborne troops at Pegasus Bridge. The main strength of the British 3rd Division then landed. This area, exposed to the Germans' long range guns in Le Havre, became the crucial point in the battle.

Juno Beach – The Canadian 3rd Division landed at Bernières and Courseulles, reaching Creully by 5pm. They were the first troops to enter Caen on 9 July 1944.

S. Sauvignier/MICHELIN

Beach near Arromanches

Gold Beach – The British 50th Division landed at Ver-sur-Mer and Asnelles; by the afternoon they held Arromanches and the artificial Mulberry harbour could be brought into position. The 47th Commandos advanced and captured Port-en-Bessin during the night of 7 June. On 9 June the British sector joined up with the Americans from Omaha Beach. On 12 June, after the capture of Carentan had enabled the troops from Omaha and Utah beaches to join forces, a single beachhead was established.

American Sector – 🚶 The events involved in the landing of American troops at **Omaha Beach** and **Utah Beach** are described under OMAHA Beach and Presqu'île du COTENTIN.

The Beaches★

1 Sword Beach – Juno Beach – Gold Beach

▶ *71km/43mi – about 1hr 15min. From Caen take D 515 NE.*

The road to Riva-Bella runs down the lower Orne Valley west of the ship canal.

Bénouville

Château – 🚶🕐Open during temporary exhibitions, usually late June–mid-Sept daily except Tue 2–6pm. 1.50€ (under 18 years no charge) ☎02 31 95 53 23.

The town hall, which stands alone in a fork in the road near Pegasus Bridge, was occupied by the British 5th Parachute Brigade at 11.45pm on 5 June. The **château**★, one of the major works by the Parisian architect **Claude-Nicolas Ledoux** (1736-1806), is a fine example of French neo-Classical architecture at the end of the 18C.

The interior contains a suite of five rooms and a magnificent **staircase**★★ rising through three landings to the first floor.

Pegasus Bridge

The two Ranville-Bénouville bridges were captured soon after midnight during the night of 5-6 June 1944 by the British 5th Parachute Brigade: **Pegasus** was their emblem. Major Howard had won the Battle of Pegasus – a field where the Horsa and Hamilcar gliders could land, a mobile bridge made of steel, a house at the water's edge... and the Gondrée family, who waited until **Lord Lovat** (1911-95) and his Green Berets arrived, to the strains of Bill Millin's bagpipes (🚶*see sidebar, next page*).

Mémorial Pegasus★

Av. du Major-Howard, 14860 Ranville. 🚶🕐Apr–Sept 9.30am–6.30pm. Feb–Mar & Oct–Nov 10am–1pm, 2–5pm. 🕐Closed Dec–Jan. ☜5.50€ (children 4€). ☎02 31 78 19 44. www.normandy1944.com

Near the commemorative stelae stands a museum devoted to life during the Occupation and the Normandy landings.

Ouistreham-Riva-Bella♨♨

🚶 *See OUISTREHAM-RIVA-BELLA.*

Bill Millin and his Bagpipes

"Down the road came Lord Lovat's commandos, cocky in their green berets. Bill Millin marched at the head of the column, his pipes blaring out *Blue Bonnets over the Border*. On both sides the firing suddenly ceased, as soldiers gazed at the spectacle. But the shock didn't last long. As the commandos headed across the bridges the Germans began firing again. Bill Millin remembers "just trusting to luck that I did not get hit, as I could not hear very much for the drone of the pipes."

The most famous literary work about the Battle of Normandy is undoubtedly *The Longest Day*, written by the late Irish author **Cornelius Ryan** (published by Simon & Schuster in New York).

▶ *From Riva-Bella to Asnelles, the D 514 follows the Mother-of-Pearl coast.*

Colleville-Montgomery

At dawn on 6 June the 4th Anglo-French commandos landed here under the command of Captain Kieffer. In gratitude, the commune of Colleville-sur-Orne added to its name that of General (later Field Marshall) Bernard Montgomery, the Victor of El Alamein and commander of the British forces.

South of the town, going towards Biéville-Beauville, a former coastal defence has been transformed into a **memorial** for the Suffolk Regiment. ◷*Open all year. Museum open 6 June and July–Sept Mon–Sat 3–7pm.* ↝ *Guided tour (1hr30min) Tue at 3pm.* ☎*02 31 97 12 61. www.amis-du-suffolk-rgt.com*

Lion-sur-Mer

This seaside resort has a 16C-17C **château**. The **church** has a 11C Romanesque tower and handsome capitals.

Luc-sur-Mer

Luc is a seaside resort known for its bracing air. The spa (*see Address Book*) offers hydro-sodium-iodate cures. The beautiful **municipal park**★ *(35 rue de la Mer)*, is an oasis of greenery.

Langrune-sur-Mer

The name of this resort on the Mother-of-Pearl coast is Scandinavian in origin and means green land, probably due to the abundant seaweed which fills the air with iodine. The 13C **church** has a very handsome bell-tower similar to the tower of St-Pierre in Caen.

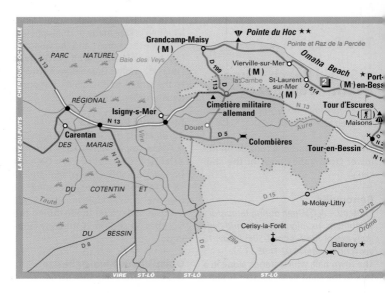

▶ *Take D 7 inland.*

La Délivrande

The tall spires of the basilica in La Délivrande, the oldest Marian sanctuary in Normandy, are visible for miles across the Caen countryside and far out to sea. The present **basilica**, Notre-Dame de la Délivrande, is a neo-Gothic 19C building housing a highly venerated statue of the Virgin (late 16C). At the Convent of **Notre-Dame-de-Fidélité** (Our Lady of Fidelity), the last house on the Cresserons road, the chapel chancel is lit by three stained-glass windows (1931), made of crystal and chrome, by **René Lalique** who was also responsible for the door of the tabernacle.

▶ *Continue on D 7 for 3km/2mi until you reach D 404 leading to Courseulles-sur-Mer. Follow signs for the Musée-Radar up to D 83 on the right.*

Douvres-la-Délivrande

Musée-Radar – ⏰*Open daily July–Aug 10am–6pm (Last entry 30mn before closing). 5.50€ (10–18 years 3€).* ☎*02 31 06 24 24.*

The **Musée-Radar** retraces the history of radar equipment. Blockhouses, situated on the site of the German radar station at Douvres, have been renovated and provide insight into the daily life of Ger-man soldiers stationed along the Atlantic Wall. The role of aerial or maritime search equipment in the last war and their evolution since 1945 is explained with the help of realistic scenery.

St-Aubin-sur-Mere ⌂

Bracing seaside resort with an offshore reef for shrimping and crab catching.

Bernières-sur-Mer

The French-Canadian Chaudière Regiment landed on this beach. Press and radio reporters came ashore here and sent the first reports of the landings. The church has a justly famous 13C **belltower**★; the three storeys and the stone spire together measure 67m/220ft.

Courseulles-sur-Mer ⌂

Centre Juno Beach

♿ ⏰*Apr–Sept 9.30am–7pm. Mar & Oct 10am–8pm. Nov–Dec & Feb 10am–1pm, 2–5pm.* ⏰*Closed Jan, 25 Dec.* ☞*6.50€ (under 8 years no charge, older children 5€).* ☎*02 31 37 32 17. www.junobeach. org.* At Centre Juno Beach, a short film introduces you to the role of Canadian soldiers and sailors, as well as the heroic performance of Canadian industry. Multi-media guideposts and interactive exhibits enliven the displays.

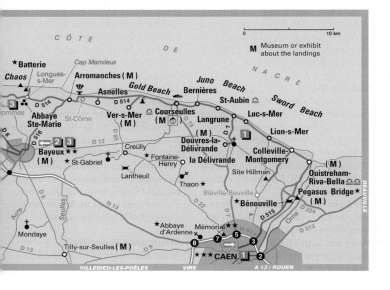

Crabs and AVREs and DD Tanks
Ingenious Fighting Machines to Breach the Atlantic Wall

These bizarre fighting machines, known as Hobart's Funnies, formed the 79th Armoured Division, commanded by their foremost inventor Major-General Sir Percy Hobart. The tanks were designed to swim ashore (Duplex Drive: Sherman amphibious tank); to clear a path through the minefields (Crab: Sherman flail tank): to double as flame-throwers (Crocodile: Churchill VII tank); to lay matting on soft sand (Bobbin); and to double as bridges to carry other tanks over obstacles (Ark: Churchill tank). The tanks were a complete surprise to the enemy and after the Normandy landings the 79th Armoured Division pursued its advance, crossing the Rhine and entering Germany.

Eisenhower paid a vibrant tribute to Hobart's Funnies, pointing out that many lives had been saved thanks to the "successful utilisation of our mechanical inventions". A Duplex Drive can still be seen on Canada Beach (Plage du Canada) at Courseulles-sur-Mer.

In 1944 several important people landed on the west beach at Courseulles, then part of Juno Beach: on 12 June **Winston Churchill**, on 14 June **General de Gaulle** on his way to Bayeux and on 16 June **George VI** on a visit to the British troops.

Courseulles is also a seaside resort well known for its large marina.

The **Maison de la Mer**, at the entrance to the harbour, displays an astonishing collection of sea shells and is equipped with an aquarium (100 000l/2 200gal of sea water) containing local marine fauna, and a diorama on the cultivation of oysters. Kids ⚓ ◷*Open July–Aug 9.30–7pm, May–June 9.30am–12.30pm, 2–7pm. Feb – Apr & Sept 10am–noon, 2–6pm. Oct–Nov & Jan open during school holidays 2–6pm.* ◷*Closed Dec. except school holidays.* ⚓*6.50€ (5-12 years 4.70€).* ☏*02 31 37 92 58.*

Ver-sur-Mer
On 6 June 1944 this tiny resort was the main British bridgehead in the Gold Beach sector. A monument commemorating the landing stands where D 514 meets avenue du Colonel-Harper. The **tower**★ of St Martin's Church is the original robust 11C Romanesque structure of four storeys.

The **lighthouse** works in conjunction with the lights of Portland and St Catherine's Point in England and at Antifer, Le Havre and Gatteville in France to guide the shipping in the Channel. There is an extensive view from the lantern.

America-Gold Beach Museum
◷*Open July–Aug daily 10.30am–1.30pm, 2.30–5.30pm. May–June & Sept–Oct daily except Tue, 10.30am–1.30pm, 2.30–5.30pm.* ⚓*4€ (5–15 years 2.40€.* ☏*02 31 22 58 58. www.versurmer.fr* The first exhibit describes pioneering transatlantic flights, notably that of the triple-engine Fokker *America* which landed at Ver in 1927. Hommage is also paid to the British troops who landed at Gold Beach on 6 June 1944 to liberate Bayeux.

West of Ver-sur-Mer, the cliffs of Arromanches come into view.

Asnelles
This little resort with its sandy beach lies at the eastern end of the artificial harbour established at Arromanches. From the mole there is a good view of the cliffs and the roads of Arromanches (traces of the Mulberry harbour still exist). On the beach stands a monument raised to the memory of the British 231st Infantry Brigade.

West of Asnelles the road climbs to the eastern edge of the Bessin plateau; the Romanesque church in St-Côme comes into view. West of St-Côme, on the right-hand side of the road, a belvedere *(viewing table and parking area)* offers a beautiful view★ down over the harbour of Arromanches and the last remaining elements of the Mulberry harbour.

Arromanches-les-Bains
↪ *See ARROMANCHES-LES-BAINS.*

After Arromanches, the road goes through the fields of Bessin. Further on, you can see the bell-towers of Bayeux.

2 Omaha Beach★

From Bayeux to Carenton 75km/47mi, about 2hr45min.

▶ *Leave Bayeux by the N 13 going W.*

Tour-en-Besson

The church has a 12C doorway. The spire above the transept crossing dates from the early 13C. The Romanesque nave with its pure lines has been renovated. Admire the beauty of the Gothic chancel (early 15C). On the columns of the arcade to the right, notice 12 sculpted scenes representing the months of the year.

Tour d'Escures

🚶 *Park beside D 100; take the private path (left) uphill (15min on foot there and back).* Steps on the outside of the wall lead to the top of the round tower which provides an extensive view of the rolling Bessin countryside and of Bayeux.

Port-en-Bessin★

👣 *See itinerary below. From Port-en-Bessin, as far as Grandcamp-Maisy, the road continues through the Bessin region, which is crisscrossed by hedgerows.*

Omaha Beach

👣 *See OMAHA BEACH.*

Pointe du Hoc★★

▶*From D 514 coming from Bayeux, just after a manor-house, turn right to the* 🅿*car park.* 🕐*1hr on foot.*
The Pointe du Hoc was heavily defended by the Germans; their observation post covered all the area where the American invasion fleet appeared on the morning of 6 June 1944. As the troops landing on **Omaha Beach** would have been particularly vulnerable to attack from this battery, the **Texas** fired 600 salvoes of 14-inch shells. The 2nd Battalion of Rangers captured the position by assault at dawn on 6 June, scaling the cliffs with ropes and extendible ladders but with heavy losses – 135 Rangers out of 225. Commandos of the 116th Regiment of

the US infantry, assisted by tanks, subdued the German defence. The gaping craters and battered blockhouses give some idea of the intensity of the fighting. Fine **views**★ of the sea and the coast westwards to the Cotentin peninsula.

▶ *Continue W on D 514.*

Grandcamp-Maisy

Little fishing port and marina. A small **museum** describes the exploits of the American Rangers. 🕐*Open mid-May–Oct daily except Mon 9.30am–1pm, 2.30-6.30pm. Feb–mid-May & Nov daily except Mon 1–6pm* 🕐*Closed Jan–Dec.* 🎟*4€ (Children 2€).*

▶ *Take D 199 and D 113 inland.*

Cimetière militaire allemand de la Cambe

This impressive German cemetery with its rectangular lawn (2ha/5 acres) is the last resting place of 21 500 German soldiers who fell in the fighting in 1944.

Château de Colombières

The **château** was one of the most important strongholds in the Bayeux region and today it makes a most attractive picture with its massive 14C machicolated round towers reflected in the waters of the moat. The rest of the château was heavily restored in the 17C and 18C.

Isigny-sur-Mer

The town has been famous for production of milk and butter since the 17C.

Carentan

👣 *See Presqu'île du COTENTIN: East Coast.*

3 La Côte du Bessin★

▶ *From Bayeux to Port-en-Bessin – 34km/20mi – about 1hr 45min. Leave Bayeux on D 516.*

Arromanches-les-Bains

👣 *See ARROMANCHES-LES-BAINS.*

▶ *After visiting Arromanches, return to the road you came in on and, about 1km/0.5mi outside of town, turn*

The Norman Ancestors of Walt Disney?

As is well known, in 1066, Duke William of Normandy sailed across the Channel and conquered England. After these historic events, two Norman soldiers who had accompanied his troops, **Hugues d'Isigny** and his son **Robert**, chose to settle on British soil. They were born in Isigny-sur-Mer, a small village near the mouth of the River Vire.

Over the years, their surname d'Isigny underwent a series of changes, becoming Disgny, then Disney, which sounded decidedly more Anglo-Saxon. In the 17C, a branch of the Disney family emigrated to Ireland. In 1834, Arundel Elias Disney and his brother Robert, along with their families, embarked on a voyage to North America. Leaving from Liverpool, they arrived on Ellis Island off New York on 3 October, after travelling for one month. That was the start of their American adventures. On 5 December 1901, Elias Disney's fourth child was born in Chicago: he was to become the famous illustrator **Walt Disney**, whose legendary animated cartoon characters like Mickey Mouse and Donald Duck have delighted many a generation of children. He died on 15 December 1966.

right on the road to Port-en-Bessin. At Longues-sur-Mer, turn right on D 104 towards the sea.

Batterie allemande de Longues-sur-Mer★

Half a mile down this road, a surfaced road *(left)* leads to the site of the powerful German battery. In spite of the release by 124 RAF planes of 600t of bombs during the night preceding 6 June, the four German guns began firing at 5.37am on June 6. The French cruiser *Georges-Leygues* returned fire, followed by the *Montcalm* and the American battleship *Arkansas*. The Germans were silent for a while but resumed firing in the afternoon; the battery was finally silenced at 7pm by two direct hits from the *Georges-Leygues*. Built on a picturesque cliff, it was composed of four 150mm guns with a range of 20km/12.5mi which enabled it to control Omaha and Gold beaches. The observation post and control room, on the cliff-edge, appeared in a famous scene from the film *The Longest Day*.

Le Chaos

The track descends steeply and is liable to rockfalls; there is a view of the coast from Cap Manvieux in the east to the Pointe de la Percée in the west.
This part of the Bessin coast has eroded into a chaotic jumble: entire sections have collapsed into heaps of fallen rocks, perched in the most extraordinary positions.

▶ *Take D 104 S towards Bayeux.*

Abbaye Ste-Marie

🕓*Open 1st 3 weeks of July & Sept Mon–Fri 2–6pm. Easter–Oct Thu 2–6pm. For other days apply to gardian.* ✎*4€ (under 18 years no charge.)* ✆*02 31 21 78 41.*
All that remains of the 12C abbey church is the main door and a few footings of the chancel and transept. The tombstones of the lords of Argouges can be admired in the refectory.

▶ *Return N to D 514; continue W to Port-en-Bessin.*

Port-en-Bessin★

The town, which is known locally as Port, is made more picturesque by its narrow confines.
From the jetties, a favourite haunt of rod fishermen, there is a view of the cliffs of the Bessin coast, from Cap Manvieux to the Pointe de la Percée. A tower erected by Vauban in the 17C dominates the eastern outer harbour. There is a good **view** of the whole harbour from the blockhouse on the clifftop.
Just outside Bayeux on D6, there is a good **view** of the **Château de Maisons** (15C-18C), surrounded by a moat fed by the river.

DIEPPE ★★

SEINE-MARITIME, POPULATION 34 653
MICHELIN MAP 304: G-2 – LOCAL MAP SEE PAYS DE CAUX

Dieppe, the beach closest to Paris, is France's oldest seaside resort. The harbour is modern but many old corners and alleys remain, along with churches, a castle and a museum. In the square du Canada stands a monument commemorating the men of Dieppe who explored Canada in the 16C, 17C and 18C, a reminder of more than 350 years of common history. A plaque recalls the Commando Raid in 1942.

- **Information:** Pont Jehan-Ango – 76204 Dieppe. ☎*02 32 14 40 60. www.dieppe.fr.*
- ▶ **Orient Yourself:** Dieppe is 65km/40.6mi north of Rouen and 108km/67.5mi from Le Havre. The city is cut in two by the River Béthune, with the picturesque old districts on the right bank and the commercial and government buildings on the left bank around the Grande-Rue and the Rue de la Barre.
- **Parking:** Look for free parking along the seafront (Bl de Verdun), along the quai de Bérigny (cultural centre) and behind the train station. The parking lot opposite the town hall (Mairie) on Maréchal-Joffre is paying.
- **Don't Miss:** The 18C buildings along Rue de la Barre and the wonderful view of the city from the château museum, as well as the Forest of Eawy.
- **Organizing Your Time:** You need a day to see Dieppe, and a half-day to tour the Forest of Eawy.
- **Also See:** Varengeville-sur-Mer, Arques-la-Bataille, le Pays de Caux, Le Tréport and Eu.

A Bit of History

Jean Ango and the Privateers' War (16C) – When the Portuguese decided to treat any vessel found off the African coast as a pirate ship, François I riposted by issuing letters of marque.

The seamen of Dieppe took the lead. **Jean Ango**, shipbuilder and naval adviser to François I, produced a fleet of privateers, "which would make a king tremble". Among his captains was **Verrazano** from Florence who discovered the site of New York (1524).

Within a few years Ango's ships had captured over 300 Portuguese vessels. Fearing ruin, the King of Portugal forced Ango to give up his letter of marque. The captain built himself a splendid mansion in Dieppe and a country residence in Varengeville. In 1535 he was appointed Governor of Dieppe. In 1551 he was buried in a chapel of St James' Church.

Dieppe Spa – According to the chronicler Pierre de l'Estoile, in 1578 Henri III, who was suffering from scabies (a skin disease), was advised by his doctors to bathe in the sea at Dieppe.

Later Madame de Sévigné mentioned in her letters that some of the court ladies, who had been bitten by a dog, went to Dieppe. She wrote of one of them, "The sea received her bare naked and thus was made proud; I mean to say the sea was proud, for lady was greatly embarrassed."

Throughout the 19C the baths and casinos of Dieppe attracted extravagant people showing off their fine clothes and celebrities such as King Louis-Philippe, Napoleon III, Eugène Delacroix, Camille Saint-Saëns, Alexandre Dumas and Oscar Wilde.

Canadian Commando Raid in 1942 – On 19 August 1942, Operation Jubilee, the first Allied reconnaissance in force on the coast of Europe, was launched, with Dieppe as the primary objective. Seven thousand men, mostly Canadians, were landed at eight points between Berneval and Ste-Marguerite, but the Churchill tanks floundered hopelessly on the beach under intense fire. Five thou-

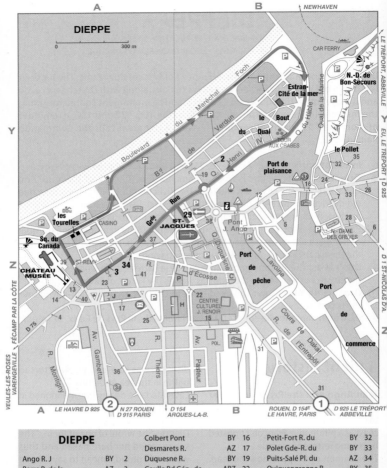

DIEPPE			Colbert Pont	BY	16	Petit-Fort R. du	BY	32
			Desmarets R.	AZ	17	Polet Gde-R. du	BY	33
Ango R. J	BY	2	Duquesne R.	BY	19	Puits-Salé Pl. du	AZ	34
Barre R. de la	AZ	3	Gaulle Bd Gén.-de	ABZ	22	Quiquengrogne R.	BY	35
Barre R. du Fg-de-la	AZ	4	Grande-Rue	ABY		République R. de la	AZ	36
Belleteste R. Jean	BY	5	Groulard R. C.	AZ	23	St-Jacques R.	AYZ	37
Bonne-Nouvelle R.	BY	6	Guerrier R.	BY	24	St-Jean R.	BY	38
Brunel R. J.	BY	7	Joffre Bd Mar.	AZ	25	Sygogne R. de	AZ	39
Carénage Q. du	BY	12	Leclerc Av. Gén.	BY	26	Toustain R.	AZ	40
Chastes R. de	AZ	13	Levasseur R.	BY	28	Victor-Hugo R.	AZ	41
Citadelle Ch. de la	AZ	14	Nationale Pl.	BY	29			
Clemenceau Bd G.	BZ	15	Normandie-Sussex Av.	BZ	31			

sand men were killed or taken prisoner; the Allies learned from this raid that German defences were concentrated round the ports and, as naval losses were small, that amphibious operations on a larger scale might be successful; the Germans, however, concluded that future Allied attacks would be directed particularly at the ports.

Downtown and the Beach

🚶 *About 1hr 30min from the parking at place Nationale, near St-Jacques. Other car parks are on quai Henri-IV and the corner of quai Duquesne and rue d'Écosse.*

Place Nationale

In the centre of the circle stands a statue of Abraham Duquesne (1610-88), famous for defeating the Dutch navy and for hunting down and disarming pirate ships in the Mediterranean. Two of the buildings on place Nationale (nos 18 and 24) date from the early 18C.

Église St-Jacques★

Begin by going round the outside of the church, which has been considerably rebuilt over the centuries. Over the 14C central doorway is a fine rose window; the façade tower is 15C, the east end and radiating chapels are 16C; the unrenovated south transept, on the other hand, is a good example of early Gothic.

Interior

The well-proportioned nave, which is 13C, was ornamented in the 14C with a triforium and given tall windows a century later.

The first chapel in the south aisle, the Chapel of the Holy Sepulchre, is 15C. The transept, the oldest part of the church, supports the dome which was rebuilt in the 18C. A fine 17C wooden statue of St James stands above the high altar. The Sacred Heart Chapel on the right facing the high altar has original Flamboyant vaulting; the centre chapel is known for carved organ consoles (1635). Left, above the sacristy door, is a frieze of Brazilian Indians that recalls the voyages of Dieppe explorers.

Grand-Rue

Many of the houses in white brick date from the reconstruction of Dieppe after the British naval bombardment of 1694. No 21 (now the Globe Café) was once the home of the dreaded pirate Balidar, terror of the English Channel. In the courtyard of no 77, there is a fountain dating from 1631. At no 186, an apothecary's old sign on the first floor illustrates three elements of nature: an obelisk (mineral), a palm (vegetable) and a sun (fire).

Place du Puits-Salé

At the junction of six roads, this is the liveliest quarter of Dieppe. The name recalls an old salt-water well (the current well is purely decorative). The large white façade of the early 18C Café des Tribunaux has a clock from 1709.

Rue de la Barre

The pharmacy at no 4 was founded in 1683. Voltaire lodged here when he returned from exile in England, at the home of his friend the apothecary **Jacques Féret**. The houses here are once again early 18C, with period balconies (nos 40, 42, 44). The Protestant church at no 69 was once the chapel of a Carmelite convent (1645).

▷ *Take rue de la Sygogne, which overlooks the château, to the right.*

A monument in the **square du Canada** recalls the 350 years of history uniting Dieppe and Canada, starting with the 17C colonists who left for Québec and continuing through the raid of 19 August 1942. In the summer, you can enter the château-museum from the square.

Boulevard de Verdun leads to the beach through the monumental gate **Les Tourelles**, the only survivor of five gates (15C) in the old fortifications.

Continue along quai du Hâble in the neighbourhood known as **le Bout du Quai**. The little streets off place du Moulin-à-Vent have traditionally been home to local fishermen. The **Maritime Museum** *(Estran Cité de la Mer Museum, see below)* is on the north side. Just before the corner of rue de la Rade and quai du Hâble, are the vestiges of a 14C tower (Tour aux Crabes. Follow quai Henri-IV along the marina.

▷ *Return to place Nationale on the left, via Grand-Rue.*

The Port, le Pollet and the Cliff

▣ *About 2hrs, starting from the tourist office.*

▷ *Go up the cliff from the fishermen's neighbourhood known as Le Pollet for a great view.*

Avant-Port

Tall, dark stone buildings surround the basin where the Newhaven-Dieppe ships used to moor.

E. Baret

The fishing port in Dieppe

A yachting marina designed to accommodate up to 400 boats was recently built following the 1994 transfer of the car ferry terminal onto the new outer port. To reach the terminal on foot, cross two bridges, Pont d'Ango and Pont Colbert, built in 1889 from designs by Gustave Eiffel. They lead to the Pollet district. Follow along the base of the cliffs, where you can see *gobes*, former cliff dwellings, now walled up.

▶ *Go back to the Colbert Bridge and take ruelle des Grèves (next to a butcher's shop). From rue Guerrier, take rue du Petit-Fort which ends in a stairway to the top of the cliffs.*

Le Pollet and Cliff
There is a very old street leading off rue Guerrier, rue Quiquengrogne; the strange name was a rallying cry of pirates on the Channel in the 15C. Next to no 3 rue du Petit-Fort, a tiny fisherman's cottage, its roof caved in, predates the 1694 bombardment of Dieppe by the English. On top of the cliff stands the **Chapelle Notre-Dame-de-Bon-Secours**, built in 1876. The military light signal is operational 24hr. Step away from the mast for an extensive **view**⋆ of the city and harbour.

Port de pêche (bassin Duquesne)
Dieppe has a large fishing fleet which goes out to sea on shortish expeditions (one to five days), bringing back fish and seafood for auction. The early-morning fish market is a colourful sight. Dieppe is France's leading source of scallops *(coquilles St-Jacques)*, as well as of sole and other fine fish.

Château and Maritime Museum

Château
From the east end of **boulevard de la Mer**, there is a magnificent view⋆ of the city and the beach. Dieppe Castle was built round a massive circular tower which formed part of the earlier, 14C, town fortifications. 17C curtain walls link the castle to the square St-Rémy Tower. Formerly belonging to the governors of the town, it now houses the Municipal Museum.

Museum⋆
🕐*Open June–Sept daily 10am–noon, 2–6pm. Oct–May daily except Tue 10am–noon, 2–5pm (Sun 6pm). Last entry 30mn before closing.* 🕐*Closed 1 Jan, 1 May, 1 Nov, 25 Dec.* ⊜*3€(under 12 years no charge).* ☏*02 35 06 61 99.*
The collections centre on two themes: the navy and ivory. At the entrance is a display of ship models, maps and navigational tools. On the first floor, several rooms are devoted to Dutch painting and furniture – many seascapes and still-life pictures of fish (Pieter Boel,

Address Book

👛*For coin ranges, see the Legend on the cover flap.*

WHERE TO STAY

🛏 **Le Logis d'Eavy Bed and Breakfast** – *1 r. du 31-Aug-1944. ☎06 19 15 52 04. www.logisdeavy.com. 2 rooms and 2 suites. ;▭.* This former post-coach relay has, behind a half-timbered façade, a pretty paved courtyard. The interior, much of it original, is splendid. Delicious breakfasts. Good value for money.

🛏 **Hôtel au Grand Duquesne** – *15 pl St-Jacques. ☎02 32 13 61 10. www. augrandduquesne.fr. 12 rooms. ▭. Restaurant 🍽🍽.* While the guestrooms are somewhat Spartan, the restaurant is remarkable. Everything is made in the kitchen, even the bread. Vegetarian menu, along with traditional dishes. Try the house dessert, a caramel crêpe.

LEISURE

⚓**Armement Legros** – *54 r. du Dauphin-Louis-XI. ☎02 35 84 82 85. Daily from 2pm. Closed Sept–June except public holidays.* Monsieur Legros proposes fishing trips and 40min sea cruises. Equipment may be rented. Invigorating and fun.

⚓**M. Dubois** – *10 r. de la Charpenterie. ☎02 35 84 93 51. Sea-fishing excurions from May–Oct. Daily 8.30am–6pm. Price for 5 people 230€. By reservation.*

WHERE TO EAT

🍽 **Le Sully** – *97 quai Henri IV. ☎02 35 84 23 13. rest.-le-sully@wanadoo.fr. Closed mid-Jan–mid-Feb, Tue evening and Wed. Reservations advised on weekends.*

This family restaurant has three dining rooms, each different: rétro style with a veranda on the port; the second contemporary and the last rustic in theme. Seafood is the house specialty.

🍽🍽 **Le New Haven** – *53 quai Henri IV. ☎02 35 84 89 72 restaurant.newhaven@ wanadoo.fr. Closed Tue and Wed except in July–Aug.* A straight-forward and pleasant restaurant. The interior is nautical in theme, and the view on the marina is charming. The chef produces traditional cuisine, generously served.

🍽🍽 **Au Trou Normand** – *76550 Pourville-sur-Mer, 5km/3mi W of Dieppe via D 75. ☎02 35 84 59 84. Closed 1–19 Aug, 21 Dec–4 Jan, Tue evening, Wed evening and Sun.* This inn overlooks the beach where the Canadians landed in the 1942 Operation Jubilee. On the menu: products of both sea and land.

🍽🍽 **La Marmite Dieppoise** – *8 r. St-Jean. ☎02 35 84 24 26. Closed 28 June–6 July, 22 Nov–10 Dec, Sun except noon during Apr–Oct, Thu evening and Mon.* The yellow-brick façade in the centre of town conceals a small restaurant with a faithful following. Cuisine with a spotlight on seafood; try the house speciality, the delectable *marmite dieppoise.*

🍽🍽 **Le Bistrot du Pollet** – *23 r. de Tête-de-Bœuf. ☎02 35 84 68 57. Closed 10-23 Apr, 14–17 Aug, Sun and Mon. Reservations required.* The sort of small bistro we like. A pretty façade of marine tiles, yellow walls hung with old posters, and flavoursome cuisine blending the best of surf and turf. No wonder the place is often packed!

17C) – as well as to 19C and 20C French painting: Isabey, Noël, Boudin, Renoir, Pissaro, Mebourg, Sisley, Jacques-Émile Blanche and Walter Sickert. There is an important collection of Pre-Colombian (Peruvian) pottery.

On the first floor is an incomparable collection of **Dieppe ivories**★. The craftsmanship is meticulous: model ships and navigational instruments, as well as religious items and secular pieces (toilet articles, sewing requisites, fans, snuff boxes, etc.).

A small workshop has been reconstituted to show the tools of local craftsmen who carved ivory imported from Africa and the Orient. In the 17C there were 350 ivory carvers in the town. One gallery is dedicated to the musician **Camille Saint-Saëns**.

Estran-Cité de la Mer★

♿.🕐*Daily 10am–noon, 2–6pm.* 🕐*Closed 1 Jan, 25 Dec.* 🎫*5€ (children 3€). ☎02 35 06 93 20. www.estrancitedelamer.free.fr*

Situated at the heart of an old fishermen's district, this museum is devoted to local maritime professions and to the ecosystem of the eastern Channel.

Excursions

Varengeville-sur-Mer ⌂
☺ *See VARENGEVILLE-SUR-MER. 8km/5mi SW via D 75.*

Offranville
12km/7mi SW via D 54B/D54. Standing next to a 16C church is a thousand-year-old tree more than 7m/23ft around. The William-Farcy gardens are planted with lovely flowers and trees.

Arques-la-Bataille
☺ *See ARQUES-LA-BATAILLE.*
5km/3mi S via D 154 or D 154E.

Château de Miromesnil★
12km/7mi S via D 915 or D 54B. ☺ *See ARQUES LA BATAILLE: Excursions.*

Forêt d'Eawy
67km/40mi from Dieppe to Neufchâtel-en-Bray.
This beautiful beach wood covers a jagged ridge (6 600ha/16 300 acres) flanked by the Varenne and Béthune valleys. A straight ride, allée des Limousins, bisects it. Leaving from Dieppe (D 915) the road crosses the plateau between the River Varenne and the River Scie. Going downhill (D 107) from Le Bois-Robert there are pretty views of the wooded crest separating the Varenne from one of its tributaries. Brick manor houses are dotted all along the Varenne Valley *(D 149, D 154)*. A pretty detour is offered by the Road of the Long Valleys *(D 97)* between Rosay and the carrefour de l'Épinette junction. The village of **St-Saëns** lies on the road back through the woods *(D 12)*.

DIVES-SUR-MER★

CALVADOS, POPULATION 5 812
MICHELIN MAP 303: L-4 – LOCAL MAP SEE PAYS D'AUGE

If Cabourg is known as a holiday resort, its sister city Dives tends to be associated with history, for it was from here that William the Conqueror, Duc de Normandie, set out to invade England in the 11C.

- **Information:** R. du Général-de-Gaulle 14160 Dives-sur-Mer. ☎02 31 28 12 50
- ▶ **Orient Yourself:** Dives is across the estuary of the River Dives from Cabourg.
- **Don't Miss:** The old marketplace (Halles) and the church.
- **Organizing Your Time:** Give yourself an hour to enjoy the town.
- **Also See:** Cabourg, Houlgate, Deauville, Trouville, Honfleur, Pays d'Auge

Sights

Halles★
The magnificent oak frame of the covered market (15C-16C) is in very good condition. Wrought-iron signs identify the stalls of the merchants.
On the other side of place de la République stands Bois-Hibou Manor (16C).

Église Notre-Dame de Dives
This massive church, a centre of pilgrimage until the Religious Wars, is 14C and 15C, except for the transept crossing, a remnant of an 11C sanctuary. Inside, the elegant 15C nave contrasts sharply with the massive pillars and plain arches of the Romanesque transept crossing. The transepts themselves, the chancel and the Lady Chapel, were built in the Rayonnant Gothic style of the 14C.

Village Guillaume-le-Conquérant
This pleasant enclave of art and craft shops is located within the precincts of the old inn of the same name, dating from the 16C.

Address Book

For coin ranges, see the Legend on the cover flap.

WHERE TO STAY

M. et Mme Roussel Bed and Breakfast – *Lieu-dit «La Roculière», 61700 St-B0omer-les-Forges, 10km/6 mi N of Domfront via D 962.* ☎02 33 37 60 60. *4 rooms.* 🍴🚗. This pretty farm surrounded by fields and orchards is the essence of Normandy. Comfortable rooms and copious breakfasts near the fireplace. In summer, you can barbecue supper in the old bread-oven.

WHERE TO EAT

Relais de la Forêt – *61700 Dompierre, 9km NE of Domfort cia D 21.* ☎02 33 30 44 21. *Closed Mon through Thu evenings.* Despite its rather tired decor, this little village restaurant often has to turn away diners at noon or weekends. The cuisine is traditional and prepared with local products, especially cider.

Auberge Le Grandgousier – *1 pl. de la Liberté.* ☎02 33 38 97 17. *Closed Feb, Oct, Mon evening, Wed evening and Thu.* A family inn at the heart of the old town, two steps from the post office. Chequered tablecloths and exposed beams create inviting dining rooms: one features a 16C hearth. Good value.

SHOPPING

Les Chais du Verger Normand – *R.du Mont-St-Michel.* ☎02 33 38 53.96. *Open Mon–Fri 9am–noon, 2–8pm, Sat 9.30–noon. Closed Sunday.* Calvados produced in Domfront received its official "appellation" in 1997. Here, the Comte L. de Lauriston sells his product and displays distilling equipment.

DOMFRONT★

ORNE, POPULATION 4 262
MICHELIN MAP 310: F-3

Domfront lies spread along a rocky ridge over a gorge carved by the River Varenne, affording a panorama of the Passais bocage country. In addition to its strategic site★ on the old route between Mont-St-Michel and Paris, the town features historic ruins and a well-restored town centre.

- **Information:** 12 place de la Roirie, 61700 Domfront. ☎02 33 38 53 97. www.domfront.com
- ▶ **Orient Yourself:** Domfront is on the D 962 between Mayenne (36km/22.5mi south) and Flers (22km/14mi north).
- **Don't Miss:** The Romanesque church Notre-Dame-sur-l'Eau.
- **Organizing Your Time:** Several bike tours have been mapped by the tourist office.
- **Especially for Kids:** The tourist office has a guidebook for children
- **Also See:** Flers, Bagnoles-de-l'orne, Lassay-les-Châteaux and Mortain.

A Bit of History

Under English Rule – In 1092 the townspeople of Domfront rose up against their overlord Roger de Montgomery and rallied to **Henry Beauclerc**, the son of William the Conqueror. In 1100 Henry became King of England and Domfront an English possession.

In the 12C Henry II Plantagenet and his queen, Eleanor of Aquitaine, often visited with their brilliant court. In August 1170 papal legates met here to attempt to reconcile Henry and his estranged Archbishop of Canterbury, Thomas Becket.

Domfront passed from English to French hands and back again during the Hundred Years War. it became French for good in 1450.

Matignon's Siege – In 1574. Gabriel, Comte de Montgomery (1530-74), who had mortally wounded the French King Henri II in a tournament, defended Domfront against the royal forces under the Comte de Matignon. Montgomery surrendered believing that his life would be saved but was executed on the orders of Henri's widow, Catherine de' Medici.

Old Town Centre★

30min

The old town is enclosed by a wall and 13 of the original 24 towers. The best preserved are those on the south side; one is still crowned with machicolations. For a good view walk along rue des Fossés-Plisson. Several 16C stone houses, formerly inhabited by noble or well-to-do families, have been restored.

Grande-Rue

This sloping street, now a pedestrian zone, has kept its original paving.

Rue du Docteur-Barrabé

There are some lovely timber-framed houses, notably at no 40 and at the corner of ruelle Porte-Cadin.

Église St-Julien

This modern church (1924) in neo-Byzantine style is dominated by a tall cement belfry. Inside, an immense mosaic depicts Christ in Majesty. The area around the church, in particular rue St-Julien and place du Commerce, is a pleasant area for a stroll.

Hôtel de ville

Guided tours (1hr) daily except weekends and public holidays 9am–noon, 1.30–4.45pm. No charge. 02 33 30 60 60. www.domfront.com
In the town hall, the **Salle Charles-Léandre** houses paintings and drawings imagined by the local artist.

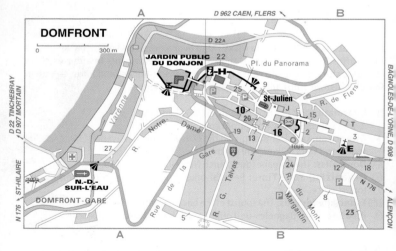

DOMFRONT								
			Commerce Pl. du	B	9	Montgomery R.	B	19
			Dr-Barrabé R. du	B	10	Porte-Cadin R.	B	20
BarbacanesR. des	B	2	Foch R. Mar.	B	12	Porte-de-Normandie R.	B	22
Champ-de-Foire Pl. du	B	3	Fossés-Plisson R. des	B	13	Pressoir R. du	B	23
Champ-Passais R. du	A	5	Godras R. de	B	15	République R. de la	B	24
Clemenceau R. G.	B	7	Grande-Rue	B	16	St-Julien R.	B	25
Colombier R. du	B	8	Joffre R. Mar.	B	18	Tanneries R. des	A	27

Croix du Faubourg	B	E		Hôtel de ville (salle Charles-Léandre)	B	H

Additional Sights

Jardin public du Donjon★

Cross the bridge over the old moat to the public gardens laid out on the site of the fortress razed in 1608. Nothing remains of the early-11C timber fortress built by Guillaume Talvas. Of Henry Beauclerk's 1092 fortress there remain two imposing sections of the keep's walls and two towers from the flattened curtain wall. Inside the curtain walls stand the ruins of the late-11C Chapelle St-Symphorien. Eleanor of Aquitaine's daughter was born in Domfront and christened in this very chapel. Skirt the ruins of the keep to reach the terrace *(viewing table)* which affords a **panorama**★ of the Passais countryside and its three rivers, the Mayenne, Varenne and Égrenne.

Église Notre-Dame-sur-l'Eau★

This charming Romanesque Church of Our Lady on the Water (late 11C) was badly mutilated in the 19C when five of the seven nave bays were destroyed to make way for a road. Following damage in 1944 the church was restored.
According to legend, at Christmas in 1166 Thomas Becket, Archbishop of Canterbury, celebrated Mass in this church while in exile in France.
Several 12C frescoes have been uncovered in the south transept representing the Doctors of the Church (theologians who expounded the Christian doctrine). A Gothic canopy covers a recumbent figure with a lion at its feet.

Croix du Faubourg

From the foot of the Calvary, there is a **panorama**★ similar to the one from the public gardens, but it extends further east towards Andaines Forest.

Driving Tour

Northwest of Domfront
Round tour of 35km/22mi – about 2hr.

▶ *Leave Domfront by D 22.*

The roads recommended, particularly those from Lonlay-l'Abbaye to D 907, are narrow but beautiful.

Lonlay-l'Abbaye

The church, once part of an 11C abbey, enjoys a pleasant country setting. It was damaged in 1944. The 15C porch opens directly into the transept; the south arm is typical of Romanesque construction and decoration. The Gothic chancel and its granite pillars have been restored.

▶ *5km/3mi W of the village turn left onto D 134.*

La Fosse-Arthour

The most interesting part of the drive is between two bridges. From a rock height on the left there is a view of the setting in which La Fosse-Arthour lies with the River Sonce running swiftly between two steep sandstone banks and opening out into a pool before continuing on its way in a series of small cascades. Fishing and canoeing enthusiasts are able to indulge in their favourite sport on the 3ha/7-acre stretch of water.

▶ *Take D 134 S towards St-Georges-de-Rouelley; at the first junction turn left onto the Rouellé road. In Rouellé turn left onto D 907 to Domfront. After 1.5km/1mi turn right onto a narrow road, unsurfaced towards the end, which leads to the Saucerie Manor.*

Manoir de la Saucerie

The entrance pavilion flanked by two round towers with loopholes is all that remains of this 16C manor house. The combination of different building materials (stone, brick and timber) provides a certain charm.

▶ *Return to D 907 for Domfront.*

DREUX★

EURE-ET-LOIRE, POPULATION 31 849
MICHELIN MAP 311: E-3 – LOCAL MAP SEE VALLÉE DE L'EURE

Dreux is set on the boundary between Normandy and Île-de-France; it is a lively regional market town earning its living from diverse industrial activities. The town is the final resting place of members of the Orléans family, one of France's royal lines; they can be viewed in the crypt of the Royal Chapel of St-Louis where their tombs comprise an impressive collection of 19C sculpture. Nearby, the Eure valley contains lovely suprises, notably the château of Anet.

- 🛈 **Information:** 6 r. des Embûches, 28100 Dreux.
  ☎02 37 46 01 73. www.ot-dreux.fr
- ▶ **Orient Yourself:** Dreux is 85 km/53mi west of Paris via N 12, and 48km/30 mi east of l'Aigle. The historic centre is on the left bank, and the Grand-Rue (Rue Maurice-Viollette) is the liveliest street.
- ◉ **Don't Miss:** The Royal Chapel and the Renaissance château of Anet.
- 🕓 **Organizing Your Time:** You'll need 2hrs to see the town, and another 2 hrs for the château of Anet. Make time for a picnic on the site of the château d'Ivry.
- **Kids Especially for Kids:** The musée Marcel-Dessai has a children's itinerary.
- 🖑 **Also See:** Verneuil-sur-Arve, Conches-en-Ouche and Évreux.

A Bit of History

Dreux rose to importance when the Normans settled west of the River Avre and Dreux Castle had to defend the French frontier against a very belligerent neighbour. The castle, which stood on the hill now occupied by St Louis' Chapel, was besieged many times. It was dismantled on the orders of Henri IV, who razed the town in 1593 after a three-year siege.

In 1556 the Paris Parliament decided that the County of Dreux should in the future be the exclusive property of the French royal family. In 1775 Louis XVI ceded Dreux to his cousin, the Duc de Penthièvre, son of the Comte de Toulouse. Eight years later, when at the King's insistence the Duc was forced to give up his magnificent property at Rambouillet, he arranged for the family tombs in the parish church of Rambouillet (subsequently destroyed) to be transferred to the collegiate church adjoining Dreux Castle.

When the Duc's daughter married Louis Philippe d'Orléans, known as Philippe Égalité, her dowry included the County of Dreux. It was thus that Dreux, which until the Revolution had been a simple family burial place, became the mausoleum of the Orléans family.

Sights

Belfry★

⚒ *Closed for renovations.*
At the end of the Grand-Rue (Maurice-Viollette) rises the ornate façade of the Hôtel de Ville (town hall), which was built from 1512 to 1537. The ground and first floors are decorated in the Flamboyant style; the Renaissance second floor shows the skill of a young architect from Dreux, **Clément Métézeau** (1479-1555).

Église St-Pierre

🔎 *Ask at the tourist office for tour info.*
Built in the early 13C and partly damaged during the Hundred Years War, St Peter's Church was heavily remodelled from the 15C to the 17C. The façade dates from the 16C. Of the two towers designed to flank it, only the left one was actually completed. The gate, chancel and left arm of the transept are 13C. The right arm of the transept dates from the 16C to the 17C. The church interior is notable for its fine 15C and 16C **stained-glass windows**, to be found especially in the side chapels *(1st, 2nd and 3rd on the right; 2nd, 3rd and 4th on the left)* and apsidal chapel. The outstanding organ case (1614) is the work of the local cabinetmaker Toussaint Fortier.

Chapelle royale St-Louis

🎧 *Guided tour (1hr) July–Aug daily except Tue 9.30am–12.30pm, 1.30–6.30pm. Apr–June & Sept daily except Tue, 9.30am–noon, 2–6pm.* 🎫*6.50€ (Children 3€).* ☎*02 37 46 07 06.*

Before the Revolution this site was occupied by the Collegiate Church of St Stephen (St-Étienne). In 1783 it received the remains of members of the Toulouse-Penthièvre families.

In 1816 the dowager Duchess of Orléans, widow of Philippe Égalité, erected a chapel in the neo-Classical style. It was enlarged by her son Louis-Philippe (1773-1850) when he became king, and the exterior was embellished with bell turrets and Gothic pinnacles. The building as a whole is a monument to the 19C both for the quality of its architecture and the work of talented artists.

The side windows make it possible to admire the stained glass representations of the patron saints of France and the royal family: (*left*) St Philip, St Amelia, St Ferdinand (the heads are portraits). The stained glass in the apse illustrates the life of St Louis.

The main crypt contains the tombs of the Princes of Orléans; the recumbent figures form a little museum of 19C statuary by Mercié, Pradier, Dubois, Chapu, Millet, Lenoir etc.

On the lower level, five extremely rare **glass panes painted with enamels**★★ catch the visitor's attention. They were made in the Sèvres workshops, as was the other glasswork.

The park contains several remains of old fortifications. A fine **view** can be had of the town.

Musée d'Art et d'Histoire Marcel-Dessal

🕐*Open daily except Sun and Tue 2–6pm.* 🕐*Closed public holidays (except 14 July) and 2nd half Dec.* 🎫*2.17€ (Under 10 years no charge).*☎*02 37 50 18 61. www.musees.regioncentre.fr*

Set up in a neo-Romanesque chapel, the museum displays furnishings taken from the Collégiale Saint-Etienne, a 12C church which stood on the site of the Royal Chapel.

Shown alongside local archaeological exhibits, dating from Prehistoric, Gallo-Roman and Merovingian times, are exhibits evoking the history of the Dreux region. A set of 18C furniture taken from the Château de Crécy-Couve, formerly owned by the Marquise de Pompadour, is also on show. The painting gallery displays both ancient and contemporary works. Impressionist and post-Impressionist movements are well represented with canvases by Vlaminck, Montezin and Le Sidaner, arranged around a painting by Claude Monet (*Wisteria*).

Driving tours

1 From Dreux to Pacy-sur-Eure

42km/25mi – about 3hr (including château visit).

▶ *Leave Dreux via D 928 N and take D 161 to the left.*

Outside Dreux, the aqueduct crosses the valley, carrying water from the Avre to Paris. Off to the right, you can see the church in the little town of Montreuil as you drive by, and Dreux Forest off to the left. In Ézy-sur-Eure, an old humpback bridge (Pont St-Jean) crosses the river to Saussay.

Château d'Anet★

🎧 *Guided tours (45min) Apr–Oct daily except Tue 2–6.30pm. Feb–Mar & Nov weekends 2-5pm.* 🎫*7€ (Children 4€).* ☎*02 37 41 90 07.*

Of all the French Renaissance châteaux, Anet was reputedly the most ornate. Successive owners since 1840 have endeavoured to maintain the original appearance of the buildings.

A Queen without a Crown

Shortly after her arrival at court, **Diane de Poitiers** (1490-1566), widow of Louis de Brézé, Seneschal of Normandy and Lord of Anet, caught the attention of Henri, second son of François I and 20 years her junior. Beautiful, intelligent and a patron of the arts, Diane was 32 when the dauphin met her and he was still fascinated by her when he became King Henri II. When in 1559, Henri was

Address Book

For coin ranges, see the Legend on the cover flap.

WHERE TO STAY

Hôtel Le Beffroi– *12 pl Métézeau.* 02 37 50 02 03. hotel.beffroi@club-internet.fr. *Closed 23 July–16 Aug. 15 rooms.* . *If you intend to visit St-Pierre Church, you couldn't be closer. Although not particularly luxurious, the rooms are suitably functional. We prefer those, more peaceful, on the riverside.*

Château de Berchères – *18 r. du Château, 28560 Berchères-sur-Vesgre, 7km/4.2mi NW of Houdan via D 933.* 02 37 82 28 22. www. chateaudebercheres.com. *Closed Sun. 18 rooms.* . *This handsome 18C château is set in a vast park featuring ancient trees and a pond. The spacious bedrooms are named after fruits and vegetables and are decorated accordingly with brio.*

WHERE TO EAT

Le St-Pierre – *19 r. Sénarmont.* 02 37 46 47 00. www.lesaint.pierre. com. *Closed 7–15 Mar, 12–28 July, Sun evening, Thu evening and Mon. Delectable menus and reasonable prices have brought renown to this small restaurant in the town centre. Bistro-style decor.*

Aux Quatre Vents – *18 pl. Métézeau.* 02 37 50 03 24. *Closed evenings except Fri. Located in the heart of Dreux, this family eatery offes an array of traditional dishes served in a brasserie-style dining room. Terrace by the river the summer.*

SHOPPING

Calvados Morin – *10 rue d'Ézy, 27450 Ivry-la-Bataille.* 02 32 36 40 01. calvadosmorin@tiscali.fr - *Open Mon-Fri 2–4pm. Closed public holidays.* This family firm, founded in 1889, offers a superb array of Calvados from 3 to 30 years old. The caves where the brew is aged in oak casks are certainly worth a visit.

killed by Montgomery during a tournament, Diane had reigned for 12 years over sovereign, court, artists and royal finances. Anet, which she had rebuilt, was the symbol of her power and taste. In 1559 Henri's widow Catherine de' Medici took Chenonceau but left Anet to Diane, who died there in 1566.

Work began c 1548 under the architect **Philibert Delorme**.

The centrepiece of the main building overlooking the courtyard was well ahead of its time; it now stands in the courtyard of the Fine Arts School (École des Beaux-Arts) in Paris.

The greatest artists of the day embellished the château: the sculptors Goujon, Pilon and the silversmith Cellini, the enameller Limosin and the Fontainebleau tapestry makers.

In the 17C alterations were made by the Duke of Vendôme, grandson of Henri IV and his mistress Gabrielle d'Estrées. The duke added a break-front and main stairway to the left wing of the main courtyard, the only one surviving today, and had the court of Diane closed to the west by a hemicycle.

Entrance gate

The work of Philibert Delorme. Above the central arch, the tympanum consists of a casting of Benvenuto Cellini's bronze low relief now in the Louvre (*Diane Recumbent*). Above the door is a clock dominated by a stag held at bay by four dogs. Once the animals told the time, the dogs barking, the stag stamping its foot. The outlying buildings are surmounted by chimneys capped with coffins as evidence of Diane's constant mourning.

Left wing of the main courtyard

The visit begins on the first floor with Diane's bedroom. The main attraction is the Renaissance bed, decorated with the three crescents of Diane. The stained-glass windows include fragments of the original greyish monochrome designs

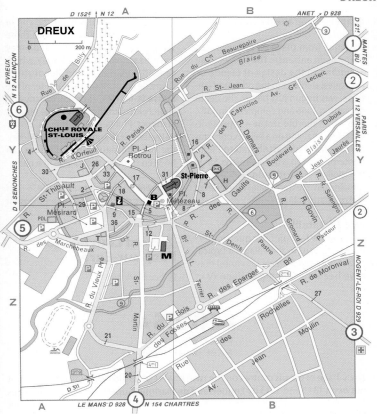

DREUX		Esmery-Caron R.	AZ	12	Parisis R.	AY	
		Fusillés Pl. des	AZ	15	Prés.-Kenned Av. du	BZ	27
Anatole-France Pl.	AY	2	Gaulle R. du Gén.-de	BY	16	Renan R. Ernest	AZ	29
Bois-Sabot R. du	AY	4	Gde-Rue M.-Violette	AY	17	Sainte-Barbe Pl.	AY	30
Chartraine R. Porte	AZ	5	Illiers R.	AY	18	Senarmont R. de	AY	31
Châteaudun R. de	BY	7	Marceau Av. du Gén.	AZ	20	Tanneurs R. aux	AY	33
Doguereau R.	BY	8	Melsungen Av. de	AZ	21	Teinturiers R. des	AZ	36
Embûches R. des	AYZ	9	Palais R. du	AY	26			

Beffroi	AY	B	Musée d'Art et d'Histoire Marcel-Dessal		AZ	M

(*grisailles*), a discreet decoration in keeping with Diane's mourning.

The **main stairway**, added by the Duke of Vendôme in the 17C, affords views of the lake and park. The vestibule, dating back to the same period, leads to the Salon Rouge containing furniture from the French and Italian Renaissance.

The Faïence Room, which has kept part of its original tiling, leads into the dining room where the huge fireplace is supported by two atlantes by Puget. In the centre note the Jean Goujon medallion depicting Diane snaring the royal stag.

Chapel

It was built in 1548 by Philibert Delorme and is in the form of a Greek cross. A dome and lantern cover the circular nave, one of the first to be built in France. The skilfully executed diamond-shaped drawing on the coffers produces a surprising optical illusion, the whole cupola seeming to be drawn upwards. The design of the floor tiling recalls this geometrical subtlety. Diane de Poitiers used to attend Mass from the gallery, which communicated with her rooms in the right wing (*demolished*).

Chapelle funéraire de Diane de Poitiers

Entrance from place du Château, left of the main entrance. The chapel, built according to the design of Claude de Foucques, architect to the princes of Lorraine, was begun just before the death of Diane in 1566 and completed in 1577. The white-marble statue★ representing Diane kneeling on a tall sarcophagus in black marble, is attributed to Pierre Bontemps; so too is the altarpiece. Since the spoiling of the tomb in 1795, Diane's remains have rested against the chevet of Anet parish church.

Ivry-la-Bataille

There are a few picturesque timber-framed houses in the village: a typical local house *(no 5 rue de Garennes)* may have been the lodging of Henri IV in 1590; the 11C doorway *(at the end of rue de l'Abbaye),* decorated with three sculpted key stones (renovated), may have been part of Ivry Abbey which ceased to exist at the Revolution. Diane de Poitiers was the founder of the **Église St-Martin,** a late-15C to early-16C church, attributed in part to the famous architect, Philibert Delorme.

Between Neuilly and the mills of Merey, the 16C **Château de la Folletière** can be seen through the foliage in a park.

▶ *From Chambine to Pacy, D 836 rises above the Eure and there are pleasant views upstream.*

②From Louviers to Pacy-sur-Eure

See LOUVIERS.

ÉCOUIS★

EURE, POPULATION 714
MICHELIN MAP 304: I-6

The village of Écouis centres on the twin towers of its old collegiate church, built between 1310 and 1313 by Enguerrand de Marigny, Superintendant of Finances to Philip the Fair. Opponents accused him of sorcery, and he died on the gibbet in 1315. His artistic patronage may be seen from the remarkable works of art in the church.

- **Information:** 6 place du Cloître, 27440 Écouis.
  ☎02 32 69 43 08. www.collegiale-ecouis.asso.fr.
- ▶ **Orient Yourself:** Écouis is 12km/7.5mi south of Lyons-la-Forêt via D 2.
- **Don't Miss:** The Collégiale Notre-Dame and the Abbaye de Fontaine Guérard.
- **Organizing Your Time:** See the Collégiale, then take a drive to the abbey.
- **Also See:** Lyons-la-Forêt, Forges-les-Eaux, Les Andelys and Rouen.

Visit

Collégiale Notre-Dame★

Open 7am–7pm For a guided tour, make an appointment at the presbytery.
☎02 32 69 43 08.
The sober building of the Collegiate Church – the roof timbers were replaced by the present brick and stone vaulting at the end of the 18C – has an immense chancel terminating in a three-sided apse. The chancel contains some beautiful furnishings and remarkable **statues★** dating from the 14C to the 17C.

1) Chapel of the Immaculate Conception (16C)
2) Christ on the Cross (13C)
3) St Nicaise
4) St Ann and the Virgin (14C)
5) Our Lady of Écouis (14C)
6) Statue of St Margaret (14C)
7) Statue of Jean de Marigny, brother of Enguerrand, who was Archbishop of Rouen when he died in 1351.
8) St John Chapel – The wooden vault enables us to imagine the former vault of the nave. Statue of Alips de Mons, wife of Enguerrand de

Marigny. Stained glass (14C) depicting the Crucifixion with St John and Mary at the foot of the Cross.

9) 14C choir stalls; 16C doors and woodwork
10) Door of former rood screen.
11) Christ and his Shroud (16C)
12) North side chapel: St Martin, St Francis, St Laurent (14C), St Cecilia
13) Madonna of the King (14C)
14) St Agnes (14C)
15) St Veronica (14C)
16) Ecce Homo in wood (15C)
17) Annunciation (15C) — The statue of the Virgin is supported by a charming group of small angels reading prophecies relating to the mystery of the Incarnation. The hands and face of the Virgin, together with the face of Archangel Gabriel, are in marble encrusted in stone.
18) St John the Baptist (14C)
19) Organ case (17C)

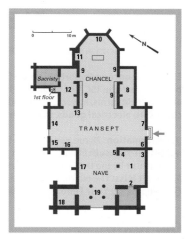

In a **room** on the first floor beautiful works of art are displayed including a cope chest and the chalice of Jean de Marigny (14C).

Excursion

Abbaye de Fontaine-Guérard★
12km/7mi NW via N14. Just before Fleury-sur-Andelle, take D 321 left, then the second road on the right. Count about 30min to visit. ♿ 🕐*Open July–Aug daily except Mon 2–6.30pm. Apr–June and Sept–Oct daily except Mon 2–6pm.* 👁*4.75€ (Children 3.25€)* ☎*02 32 49 03 82. www.cister.net*
The ruins of the 12C abbey, on the north bank of the Andelle, are both evocative and moving, owing to their isolation and the threat of flooding.

Beside the path stands the 15C St Michael's Chapel (left). The abbey church dates from 1218; the square chevet and some apsidal vaulting have survived. The **chapter-house** (right) is a fine example of early-13C Norman architecture.

Abbaye de Fontaine-Guérard

B. Kaufmann/MICHELIN

ELBEUF

SEINE-MARITIME, POPULATION 16 666
MICHELIN MAP 304: G-6 – LOCAL MAP SEE VALLÉE DE LA SEINE

Elbeuf was once an important centre for French cloth-making, an industry that began here in the 15C. The decline of this industry, described by the famous novelist André Maurois, has since been offset by modern manufacturing, including chemicals, electrical goods, machinery, metallurgy and automobiles.

- ▨ **Information:** 28 rue Henry, 76504 Elbeuf Cedex. ☏02 35 77 03 78.
- ▶ **Orient Yourself:** Elbeuf is reached by N 15 and D 7 from Rouen (20km/12.5mi north) or by the D 313 from Louviers (14km/9mi south).
- ⊘ **Don't Miss:** The old cloth-making neighborhoods; a River Oison excursion.
- ⊙ **Organizing Your Time:** Attractions are more likely to be open on afternoons.

Old Town Walking Tour *Allow 45min.*

- ▶ *Leave your car in the parking lot ℗ across from the town hall. Take rue Henry and when you reach St-Jean Church, turn left on rue Guymener.*

Place St-Jean and the Puchot district are at the heart of the old town.

- ▶ *Straight along rue R.-Poulain and take the first right to place de la République.*

On the square the old cloth manufactory (18C, attic and chimneys 19C) is being restored. More than 350 people worked here in 1889; it closed in 1961.

- ▶ *Rue aux Bœufs; cross rue Boucher-de-Perthes. Go through the gardens to St-Étienne Church, then continue up rue de la République on the right.*

The **Jardins de la Source,** opened 1994, enlivened this old manufacturing area.

- ▶ *Continue straight on rue des Martyrs and take the first left to the town hall.*

WHERE TO EAT

⊖⊜**La Pomme** – *44 Rte de l'Eure, 72340 Pont de l'Arche, 11km/6.6mi E of Elbeuf via D 921 and D 321.* ☏02 35 23 00 46. *A pretty thatched Norman cottage on the banks of the Eure with a pleasant dining room serving dishes based on local ingredients.*

Sights

Musée municipal d'Elbeuf

🕭*(Except Sun)* ⊙*Open July–Aug and school holidays daily except Mon 2.30–5.30pm. Rest of the year closed Mon and Tue, except school holidays.* ⊙*Closed public holidays.* ⊜*No charge.* ☏02 32 96 90 15. www.mairie-elbeuf.fr*

This **natural history museum** comprises nine rooms where large collections of zoological, mineral and archaeological (remarkable Gallo-Roman burial places) exhibits are displayed.

Église St-Jean-Baptiste

⊙*Open Mon–Fri 9am-1.30pm.* ⊶*Choir closed for repairs.*

Gothic church with Classical ornamentation and furnishings. Notice the 16C stained-glass windows on the 1st, 3rd, 4th and 5th windows in the north aisle and the first in the south aisle. They are the oldest (1500) and best conserved.

Église St-Étienne

⊙*Open May–Oct Sat 10.30pm–1pm*

This Flamboyant church has retained its 16C stained-glass windows. Note the Crucifixion on the top window to the right in the apse and other windows retracing scenes from the life of the Virgin in the north aisle. Near the Lady Chapel in the north aisle there is a fine stained-glass representation of the Tree of Jesse. St Roch is depicted in the stained glass of a chapel in the south aisle. One of the panels shows the drapers in work-

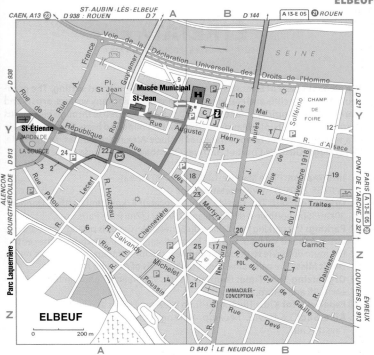

ELBEUF			Fontaine R. Jean-de-la	BY	12	Maurois R. André	BY	19
			Fraenckel R. Paul	BY	13	Mitterrand Pl. F.	BZ	20
Bœufs R. aux	AY	2	Gambetta Av.	AZ	14	Pavée R.	BZ	21
Boucher-de-Perthes R.	AY	3	Gaulle R. Gén.-de	BZ		Poulain R.	AY	22
Briand Pl. A.	BY	5	Guynemer R.	AY		Prés.-Roosevelt R.	BY	23
Céleste R.	AZ	6	Jean-Jaurès R.	BY		République Pl. de la	AY	24
Cousin-Corblin R.	BZ	7	Leclerc R. Général	BY	17	République R.	AY	
Curie R. Pierre	AY	9	Libération Pl. de la	BY	18	St-Jacque R.	BZ	25
Dendeville R.	BY	10	Martyrs R. des	ABY				

ing clothes. Woodcarving is represented by a Louis XV style rood beam, a 13C recumbent figure of Christ (lower north aisle) and, on either side of the chancel, statues of St Stephen and St John.

Excursions

Saint-Ouen-de-Pontcheuil

6km/3.5mi S via D 840. Moulin Amour – ⊙Open July–Aug daily except Mon 2.30-6.30pm. May–June & Sept–mid-Oct Sun and public holidays 2.30–6.30pm.(Last entry 30 min before closing.) ∞4€ (Children no charge). ☏02 32 35 80 27. www.avpn.asso.fr
The **Moulin Amour**, the very last water mill officially registered along the banks

of the River Oison, is still operated during presentations to the public.

Les roches d'Orival ★
  See HONFLEUR.

Château de Robert le Diable★

Musée des Vikings. ⊶*Closed to visitors*
The castle is a popular viewpoint over the Seine Valley. Robert the Devil, its legendary builder, is vaguely based on Robert the Magnificent, the father of William the Conqueror. The fortress was destroyed by John Lackland (King John of England) in 1204; it was rebuilt by Philippe Auguste, King of France, and was probably destroyed again in the 15C by the French to prevent it from falling into the hands of the English.

ÉTRETAT★★

SEINE-MARITIME, POPULATION 1 615
MICHELIN MAP 304: B-3

The elegant resort of Étretat is renowned for its magnificent setting. The grandeur of the high cliffs and crashing waves has inspired many writers, artists and film directors. Maurice Leblanc described the Aiguille Creuse through his famous character, Arsène Lupin. Maupassant spent his childhood here, "leading the life of a wild foal." Other famous habitués include Alexandre Dumas, André Gide, Victor Hugo, Gustave Courbet, Jacques Offenbach and Claude Monet.

- **Information:** Place Maurice-Guillard, 76790 Étretat.
  ☎02 35 27 05 21. www.etretat.net
- ▶ **Orient Yourself:** This seaside resort is located 47km/29mi north of Honfleur, 90km/56mi northwest of Rouen and 219km/137mi from Paris.
- **Parking:** The parking lot on place du Général-de-Gaulle is paying. There are free lots: the Grand Val lot (r. Guy-de-Maupasssant, 300m/275yds from the centre), the route du Havre to the south and near the former train station to the north.
- **Don't Miss:** The panoramic view from the cliffs of Aval and Amont.
- **Organizing Your Time:** From the beach, you need an hour on foot to reach each cliff and return.
- **Especially for Kids:** The Tourist Train between Étretat and Les Loges..
- **Also See:** Le Havre, Fécamp, Varengeville-sur-Mer, Dieppe and the Pays de Caux.

Cliff Walks

Falaise d'Aval★★

Allow 1hr on foot there and back. From the west end of the promenade climb the steps (180 steps, handrail) to the path which scales the cliff face. Walk along the edge of the cliff as far as the ridge of Porte d'Aval.

The view is magnificent: the massive Manneporte arch (left), the Aiguille opposite and the Amont Cliff on the far side of the bay. The variations of colour according t time of day and natural lighting are truly enchanting.

Falaise d'Amont★★

Allow 1hr on foot there and back. From the east end of the promenade take the steps cut into the chalk cliffs and the path to the clifftop.

Access by car: take D 11 Fécamp par la Côte; just before the sign indicating the end of the built-up area, turn sharp left

Falaise d'Aval

G. Targat/MICHELIN

Address Book

For coin ranges, see the Legend on the cover flap.

WHERE TO STAY

M. et Mme Delahais Bed and Breakfast – *54 r. du Prés.-Coty, 76790 Le Tilleul, 3km/1.8mi S of Étretat via D 940. 02 35 27 16 39. Closed 2 weeks in Oct. 4 rooms.* Looking for the keys to your room? Try the village grocery! Basic comfort, a very considerate reception, ambient quietude and, above all, highly attractive prices for a room just 3min from Étretat by car!

Hôtel La Résidence – *4 bd René-Coty, B.P. 24. 02 35 27 02 87. 15 rooms.* This downtown mansion was built in the 14C. Pleasant rooms with amusing, eclectic furniture. Mind the steps: the superb period staircase leading to the reception is uneven owing to its venerable age! Cycle hire.

WHERE TO EAT

Lann Bihoué – *45 r. Notre-Dame. 02 35 27 04 65. Closed Dec, Tue except during school holidays and Wed.* To make a change from Norman cuisine, try this crêperie near the town centre. Besides the classic Breton crêpes, there's a specialty with Guémémé sausages and caramelized apples. Friendly service.

Le Clos Lupin – *37 r. Alphonse-Karr. 02 35 29 67 53. Closed Mon–Tue except school holidays. Reservations required weekends.* Behind its stylish painted façade and lace trimmings, a long dining room, recently redecorated, in the heart of town. The menu features classic fare at decidedly reasonable prices.

Le Galion – *Bd René-Coty. 02 35 29 48 74. Closed 15 Dec–26 Jan, Tue and Wed.* Situated right in the town centre, this house built with materials taken from an old Lisieux residence has a noteworthy ceiling of carved beams dating from the 14C. Good cuisine and competitive prices.

LEISURE

Kids **Étretat Tourist Train - Vélorail** – *At the train station. 6km/3.6mi from Étretat via D 940, 76790 Les Loges. 02 35 29 49 61. www.trains-fr.org/unecto/ttepac. Hours vary; call for information. Reservations required. Closed Nov–Mar.* Across the green countryside between Étretat and Les Loges. You can pedal the vélorail (a sort of bicycle on train tracks) from Loges.

---

onto a steep and narrow uphill road. Park near the monument.

From **Notre-Dame-de-la-Garde** there is a magnificent **view★** of Étretat and its surroundings. Below is the long shingle beach between the Aval arch and the Aiguille. Behind the chapel an immense spire points towards the sky. The memorial was erected to Nungesser and Coli, French aviators who made the first, unsuccessful attempt to fly the Atlantic on 8 May 1927. It was here that their aircraft, the *Oiseau Blanc*, was seen for the last time.

Musée Nungesser-et-Coli

Closed for repairs.

The museum contains mementoes of the two pioneering aviators, "the first to dare."

Sights

Halles

This wooden covered market in place du Maréchal-Foch is a reconstruction.

Église Notre-Dame

It has a Romanesque doorway with a 19C tympanum. The rest of the building is 12C. Go forward to the transept crossing to admire the 13C lantern turret.

Le Clos Lupin★

15 r. Guy-de-Maupassant. Open Apr–Sept 10am–5.45pm. Rest of the year Fri, weekends and school holidays 11am–4.45pm. Audioguided tours (45min) Closed mid-Nov–mid-Dec, 1 Jan and 25Dec. 6.50€ (Children 4 €). 02 35 10 59 53. www.arsene-lupin.com.

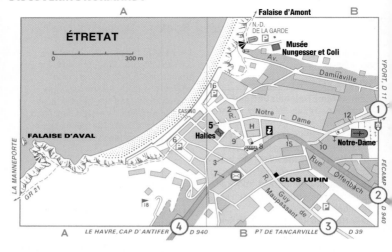

ÉTRETAT			Gaulle Pl. Gén.-de	A	6	Nungesser-et-Coli Av.	B	12
			George-V Av.	B	7	Verdun Av. de	B	15
Abbé-Cochet R. de l'	B	2	Guillard Pl. Maurice	B	8	Victor-Hugo Pl.	B	16
Alphonce-Karr R	B	3	Monge R.	B	9			
Coty Bd R.	B	5	Mottet R. Charles	B	10			

Arsène Lupin is a gentleman burglar created by Maurice Leblanc. The museum, in a vast Norman family home, mingles mementoes of the two.

Excursion

To Le Havre-Antifer Port and Terminal

15km/9mi S

▶ *Leave Étretat by D 940; turn right onto D 111, direction La Poterie, cap d'Antifer.*

⚠ *The cliffs can collapse without warning. Do not walk directly beneath them, and beware of the tides.*

Bruneval

A German radar installation near the beach was the objective of an Allied raid on the night of 27-28 February 1942. Three detachments of British parachutists destroyed the enemy position and re-embarked almost without loss.

▶ *Between Bruneval and St-Jouin, the road passes through picturesque countryside and leads to the oil terminal.*

Le Havre-Antifer Terminal

The Le Havre-Antifer port was created in 1976 to receive oil tankers too big for the facilities at Le Havre. On the way back to St-Jouin, a narrow road on the right (signalled Port du Havre/Antifer/Belvédère), leads to a belvedere with a fine **view**.

"On a sun-drenched beach when the galloping waves toss the fine shingle, a charming sound rings out, dramatic as the tear of a canvas sail and merry as an elfin peal of laughter, a soft rumbling that echoes all along the coastline, racing against the foamy peaks, resting a while, then resuming its lively, intoxicating dance with the ebbing of the ocean waters. The very name Étretat – spirited and lively yet deep and melodious – seems to have sprung from the sound of pebbles being rolled by the receding waves. And its beach, whose beauty has been immortalised by so many painters, is the embodiment of magic, with its two formidable tears in the cliff face known as the doors."   Guy de Maupassant – *Étretat*

EU ★

SEINE-MARITIME, POPULATION 8 081
MICHELIN MAP 304: I-1

Eu is a small town on the River Bresle set between the sea and the forest from which it gets its name. The town centres around its beautiful 11C collegiate church. It was in Eu that the two Anguier brothers, François (1604-69) and Michel (1612-86), were born: these Baroque sculptors contributed to the building of the Louvre and the Val de Grâce in Paris.

- **Information:** 41 rue Paul-Bignon, 76260 Eu. ☎02 35 86 04 68. www.ville-eu.fr
- ▶ **Orient Yourself:** Eu is 4km/2.5mi east of Le Tréport by D 1915 and 34 kim/21mi northeast of Dieppe by D 925.
- **P Parking:** There is parking on the square between the château and the church.
- **Don't Miss:** The château and its museum; the historic centre of town for its lively pedestrian streets.
- **Organizing Your Time:** Spend the morning seeing the city, then head towards the pretty forest of Eu.
- **Kids Especially for Kids:** Take them to the archeological site at Bois-Abbé and the Glass-making Museum.
- **Also See:** Le Tréport, Dieppe, Arques-la-Bataille and Neufchâtel-en-Bray.

Visit

Collégiale Notre-Dame-et-St-Laurent★

Allow 30min

Apr–Oct 9am–noon, 2-6pm (except Sun during mass). Nov–Mar 9am–noon, 2–5pm (except Sun during mass). Closed 1 Jan. No charge. ☎02 35 86 27 11.

The collegiate church, dedicated to Our Lady and St Lawrence O'Toole, Primate of Ireland who died in Eu in 1180, was erected in the 12C and 13C in the Gothic style. In the 15C the apse was remodelled and in the 19C Viollet-le-Duc, the architect and restoration specialist, undertook a general restoration of the building.

The **interior** is striking for its size and harmonious proportions. The second ambulatory chapel on the right, the Chapel of the Holy Sepulchre, has, beneath a Flamboyant canopy, a 15C **Entombment**★; opposite is a magnificent head of Christ in Sorrow, also 15C.

Crypt

The crypt, which is beneath the chancel, was restored in 1828 by the Duke of Orléans who reigned as King Louis-Philippe from 1830 to 1848. The 12C-13C recumbent statue of St Lawrence O'Toole is believed to be one of the oldest in France.

Additional Sights

Château

Nothing remains of the original castle where William the Conqueror married Matilda of Flanders in 1050. It was destroyed in 1475 on the orders of Louis XI. The present château, a huge brick and stone building begun by Henri of Guise and Catherine de Clèves in 1578, has been restored several times since. It passed to the Orléans family and became one of the favourite residences of Louis-Philippe, who received Queen Victoria there twice. Viollet-le-Duc was commissioned to redecorate it between 1874 and 1879 for the Count of Paris, grandson of the king. The château, which now belongs to the town of Eu, is occupied by the town hall and the communal archives, and houses the **Louis-Philippe Museum**.

Musée Louis-Philippe

Open mid-Mar–early Nov daily except Tue 10am–noon, 2-6pm, Fri 2–6pm (last entry 1hr before closing). 4€(Children 2€). ☎02 35 86 44 00.

On the ground floor visitors are shown the grand staircase and the Duchesse d'Orléans' suite, redecorated by Viollet-le-Duc in 1875, as well as the two salons and the bedroom where Queen Victoria and Prince Albert slept in 1843 and 1845, embellished with a superb inlaid parquet floor made under Louis-Philippe. In the newly restored portico overlooking the garden, note the dazzling **wall of light** conceived by Viollet-le-Duc and master-glazier Oudinot.

On the first floor you can visit the 19C bathroom, the gold bedroom with its pretty green and gilt wainscoting bearing the monogram of the Grande Demoiselle, the Louis-Philippe **dining hall** with its lovely 17C coffered ceiling, the Black Salon, with its strange pink and black colour scheme, and the vast **Galerie des Guise** containing 10 000 volumes, including books from the library of Eu's Jesuit College and those belonging to the last Comte d'Eu.

The south wing of the first floor, which once housed the private suites of Louis-Philippe and Marie-Amélie, is currently being restored to its former glory.

The Park
Most of the trees are beeches, one of which, known as the Guisard★, was planted in 1585.

Chapelle du Collège★
The Jesuit college now bears the name of the 17C Anguier brothers, who studied here. The chapel was commissioned in 1624 by Catherine de Clèves, widow of Henri de Guise, to whom she brought the County of Eu as a dowry in 1570. The Louis XIII **façade**★ is quite remarkable. The beautifully restored brick and stone masonry lends both warmth and harmony to the whole ensemble.

Musée des Traditions verrières
Rue Semichon, follow the signs from the Salle Audiard. 🚸 ♿ 🕒 *Open July–mid-Sept Tue, Wed, weekends and public holidays 2.30–6pm. Apr– June and mid-Sept–early Nov Tue, weekends and public holidays 2.30–6pm.* 💶 *3€ (Under 12 years no charge)* ☎ *02 35 86 21 91.*

The former stables of the Bresle cavalry house this museum devoted to glass-making techniques.

The Forêt d'Eu
This beech wood covers three isolated massifs with beautiful beech glades: St Martin's Priory Chapel (pretty doorway); **St Catherine's Viewpoint** (a 45min walk leads up to a view of the Yères Valley); **La Bonne Entente** (an oak and a beech growing intertwined); **St-Martin-le-Gaillard** (13C **church**). The interior has cornices carved with humourous human figures; 18C Virgin and Child. Note that that Baby Jesus is receiving a fig.

EU	
Abbaye R. de l'	2
Bignon R. P.	3
Collège R. du	4
Conquérant Pl. G.-le	5
Duhornay R. J.	6
Hélène Bd	7
Leconte R. O.	8
Morin R. Ch.	9
Normandie R. de	10

Address Book

For coin ranges, see the Legend on the cover flap.

WHERE TO STAY

Manoir de Beaumont Bed and Breakfast – *Rte de Beaumont, 2km/1.2mi E of Eu via D 49 dir. Forêt d'Eu* ☎02 35 50 91 91. www.demarquet.com. *3 rooms.* This former hunting lodge of the Château d'Eu overlooks the valley. From your appealing, comfortable rooms, you'll savour the tranquillity of the park, the charm of the house, and, above all, the first-class welcome. An excellent address from every point of view.

Hôtel restaurant Maine – *20 pl. de la Gare.* ☎02 35 86 16 64 www.hotel-maine.com. *19 rooms.* *Restaurant.* Built in 1897, this bourgeois house has an old-fashioned, discreet appeal. Rooms, generally plainly fitted out, may be embellished with small touches from the past. Belle Epoque dining room brightened up by knick-knacks, paintings and bouquets.

WHERE TO EAT

La Gare aux Gourmets – *2 r. de la Gare, -80520 Woincourt, 8.5km/5.3mi E of Eu via D 925.* ☎03 22 30 92 42. gare-aux-gourmets@cegetel.net. *Closed Aug and Sat lunch.* A stone's throw from the Channel, near the village train station, this friendly rustic inn offers traditional fare in a family atmosphere.

LEISURE

Cycles Joostens – *1 r. Ch.-Morin.* ☎02 35 86 22 24. Joostens@nerim.net. *Daily except Sun and Mon 9am–noon, 2–7pm. Closed 2 weeks in Feb and in Aug.* Bicycle rentals. Tourist offices have maps for some marked trails. If you dislike dirt paths, head for the Bois de Cise (before Ault and N of Mers), where the trails are paved and lead you to a little-frequented beach. The Hyères valley circuit (50km/31.25mi), starting from the beach at Mesnil-Val, passes through lovely countryside but you need to be in shape. There's an alternate, more relaxed circuit of only 25km/15.6mi.

ÉVREUX★★

EURE, POPULATION 60 108
MICHELIN MAP 304: G-7

Évreux, on the River Iton, is the religious and administrative capital of the Eure. The city centre was rebuilt after 1945, providing attractive settings for the town ramparts, the old bishop's palace, the cathedral and the 15C belfry, all of which had escaped damage. Flower gardens along the banks of the Iton offer a pleasant place to stroll.

- **Information:** 3 place du Gén-de-Gaulle, 27000 Évreux. ☎02 32 24 04 43. www.ot-pays-evreux.fr
- **Orient Yourself:** Évreux is 96km/60mi west of Paris, 58km/36mi south of Rouen and 48km/30mi northest of Dreux.
- **Parking:** There is parking (fee) behind the Cathedral, near the tourist office and near the Cloître des Capuchins public garden.
- **Don't Miss:** The Flamboyant beauty of Notre-Dame cathedral and the rich collections of the museum.
- **Organizing Your Time:** Allow yourself two hours to see the museum.
- **Especially for Kids:** The Roman ruins at Gisacum will interest them as will the train through the valley of the Dure.
- **Also See:** Vernon and Giverny, Les Andelys, Louviers, Le Bec-Hellouin, Brionne, Bernay and Conches-en-Ouche.

A Bit of History

A French City throughout the Wars of History – Évreux's story is a lengthy chronicle of fire and destruction:

5C – Vandals sack old Évreux, a prosperous market town dating back to the time of the Gauls.

9C – Vikings destroy the fortified town established by the Romans on the present site beside the Iton.

1119 – Henry I, King of England, sets fire to the town when fighting the Count of Évreux.

1193 – King Philippe Auguste, betrayed here by King John of England, burns the city in reprisal.

1356 – Jean the Good, King of France, lays siege to Évreux in his struggle against the House of Navarre, and sets fire to the town.

1379 – Charles V besieges the town, which suffers cruelly.

June 1940 – Following German air raids the centre of the city burns for nearly a week.

June 1944 – Allied air raids raze the district round the station.

Walking Tour

3km/2mi. Allow about 1hr 30min (not including the cathedral and the museum). Park at place Clemenceau.

▸ *Begin at place du Général-de-Gaulle.*

Place du Général-de-Gaulle

A castle once stood on this square. Today, there is a fountain which represents the River Eure as a woman holding an oar and the city's coat of arms.

Promenade des remparts

The walk runs beside the River Iton.

Tour de l'Horloge

The elegant 15C clock tower stands on the site of a tower which flanked the town's main gateway.

Ancien évêché

The 15C former bishop's palace looks out onto the cathedral and has a fine Flamboyant air with dormer windows, ornamented window pediments and a staircase tower. The Municipal Museum is inside *(see Sights on the following page)*.

Ancien cloître des Capucins

Open mid-Apr–mid-Sept 8am–8pm. Mar–mid-Apr & mid-Sept–Oct 8am–7pm. Rest of the year 8am–5pm. No charge. These old Capuchin cloisters comprise four galleries with timber roofs and monolithic columns. In the cloister close is a flower garden with a central well.

Église St-Taurin

This former abbey church established in 660 and dedicated to the first Bishop of Évreux dates back to the 14C and 15C. The well-proportioned 14C chancel is lit by superb 15C windows. Three windows in the apse trace the life of St Taurinus.

Châsse de St-Taurin★★

This masterpiece of 13C French craftsmanship in the north transept was given to the abbey by St Louis to contain St Taurinus' relics and was probably made in the abbey workshops. The silver gilt reliquary enriched with enamel is in the form of a miniature chapel and even shows St Taurinus with his crosier.

Sights

Cathédrale Notre-Dame★★

The great arches of the nave are the only extant part of the original church, which was rebuilt between 1119 and 1193, before being damaged a second time by fire. The chancel was built in 1260. The chapels are 14C. Following the fire of 1356 the lantern tower and the Lady Chapel were added. The magnificent north transept façade and doorway are early 16C. The upper parts of the cathedral suffered in the 1940 conflagration: the silver belfry melted and the west façade towers lost their crowns.

Exterior
Walk along the north side.
The aisle windows were redesigned in the 16C in the Flamboyant style. The

north door is a perfect example of the Flamboyant style, then at its height.

Interior

To view the **stained glass**★ *(see illustration in the Introduction: Religious architecture)* and the **carved wood screens**★ of the ambulatory chapels stand in the transept, between the pillars supporting the graceful lantern tower.

The light chancel is closed by a superb 18C wrought-iron grill and is very beautiful. The apse windows have been declared the most beautiful and the most limpid of the 14C.

Fine wood screens dating from the Renaissance mark the ambulatory entrance. The 15C **Treasury Chapel** is quite unique: closed off by wrought-iron bars to which an iron frame has been attached. The **screen**★ to the fourth chapel is a masterpiece of imagination and craftsmanship, particularly the lower figures; the chapel glass is early 14C. The central or Lady Chapel, given by Louis XI, has 15C windows of considerable documentary interest. The upper parts depict the peers of France at the king's coronation. Two windows further on is Louis XI himself.

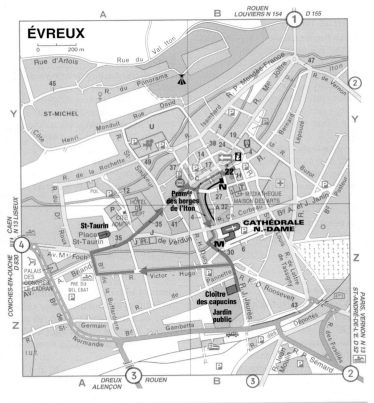

ÉVREUX								
			Feray R. Édouard	BY	19	Lombards R. des	BY	38
			Gaulle Pl. de	BY	22	Meilet R. du	AZ	41
Borville-Dupuis R.	BY	4	Grand-Carrefour Pl. du	BY	24	Résistance R. de la	BZ	4
Chambaudoin Bd	BZ	6	Grenoble R. de	BY	27	St-Michel R. de	AY	45
Chartraine R.	BZ	8	Harpe R. de la	BZ	30	Vigor R.	BY	47
Chauvin Bd G.	AY	12	Horloge R. de l'	BZ	32	7e-Chasseurs R. du	AY	49
Clemenceau Pl.	BY	14	Joséphine R.	AZ	35			
Dr-Oursel R.	BY	17	Leclerc R. Gén.	AY	37			

Ancien évêché (Musée)	BZ	M	Tour de l'Horloge	BY	N

Address Book

For coin ranges, see the Legend on the cover flap

WHERE TO STAY

Manoir de la Boissière Bed and Breakfast – *Hamlet "La Boissaye", 27490 La Croix-St-Leufroy, 16km/10mi NE of Évreux via D 316, towards Gaillon, then D 836.* 02 32 67 70 85. *www.chambres-de-la-boissiere.com. Reservations required. 5 rooms.* This 15C manor is a working farm. The rooms are each different, with family furniture and tile floors. Pretty duck pond and veranda. Meals by reservation.

WHERE TO EAT

La Boulangeraie – *130 av. Aristide-Briand, 27930 Gravigny, 2km/1.25mi N of Évreux.* 02 32 62 22 35. *Daily except Sun 7am–8pm.* The concept is unusual: the bakery on one side and on the other a place where you can sit and enoy a sandwich, a pizza an omelette or a salade. All food is irreproachably fresh.

La Croix d'Or – *3 r. Joséphine.* 02 32 33 06 07. Seafood served in a long, sober dining room or on the veranda is the star of this establishment next door to St-Taurin Church. A favourite with the local population, for being a simple address with mild prices.

Hôtel de France – *29 r. St-Thomas.* 02 32 39 09 25. *www.hoteldefrance-evreux.com. Closed Sat lunch, Sun evening and Mon. Reservations advised.* Relatively quiet despite its downtown location, this eatery, identified by its salmon-coloured façade, offers seasonal menus. Dining room with a veranda. Private parking. Comfortable, quiet rooms.

ON THE TOWN

Le Grand Café – *11 r. de la Harpe.* 02 32 33 14 01. *Mon–Thu 7.30am–9pm, Fri–Sun 7.30am–1am.* Located in a pedestrian street on the banks of the canal, this traditional café has two terraces that offer a view of the cathedral.

SHOPPING

Chocolatier Auzou – *34 r. Chartraine.* 02 32 33 28 05. *jmauzou@aol.com. Open Tue–Thu 9am–12.45pm, 1.45–7.30pm, Fri 9am–7.30pm, Sat 8am–7.30pm, Sun and public holidays 8.30am–1pm. Closed 1 Jan, 1 May, Sun in July-Aug.* This confectioner's produces several house specialities: cakes and sweets based on chocolate, pralines and meringe, all with evocative names.

Museum★★

Open daily except Mon 10am–noon, 2–6pm. Closed 1 Jan, 1 May, 1 and 11 Nov, 25 Dec. 4€ (No charge for children and on 1st Sun of month). 02 32 31 81 90. On the ground floor of the museum, the first two rooms are devoted to the history and geography of the Eure region and of the town itself.

The former chapter-house (Room 3) has a monumental fireplace and contains medieval and Renaissance collections. Notice the series of 17C Aubusson tapestries on the theme of the Prodigal Son. Room 4 contains medieval exhibits: tomb inscriptions in engraved stone, capitals. In the basement the **Archaeological Room**★ uses the former Gallo-Roman rampart enhanced by an appropriate lighting arrangement. The collections include domestic and religious objects, from the Palaeolithic (300 000–9 000 BC) Age to the Gallo-Roman Era (1C-4C AD).

The first floor contains 17C and 18C paintings as well as various decorative items, including apothecary jars in Nevers and Rouen faience from Évreux Hospital. Contemporary art exhibitions and a collection of 19C paintings and objects (Lebourg, Jongkind) take up the second floor; the third floor, with its diagonal vaulting at the top of the stairway, is devoted to 20C art, in particular Abstract painting (Hartung, Soulages).

ÉVRON

POPULATION 7 283

MICHELIN MAP 310: G-6

This small town at the foot of the Coëvrons possesses one of the finest churches in the Mayenne, visible from 10km/6.7mi away. In the 19C the town's linen mills prospered; today it is classified as a "station verte de vacances"– recognised for the beauty and preservation of the natural surroundings.

- **Information:** 4 Place de la Basilique, 53600 Évron. ☎02 43 01 63 75.
- ▶ **Orient Yourself:** Evron, surrounded by forests and lakes, is 26km/16mi southeast of Mayenne via D 7, and 33 km/21mi northwest of Laval via D 20, then N 157.
- **Don't Miss:** The St-Crespin chapel in the Notre-Dame Basilica.
- **Organizing Your Time:** After an hour seeing the town, make an excursion to the surrounding countryside.
- **Also See:** Mayenne, Jublains, Sillé-le-Guillaume, Ste-Suzanne, Saulges and Laval.

Basilique Notre-Dame★

Allow 30min

A massive square 11C tower, embellished with corner buttresses and turrets, links the Romanesque part of the nave to the 18C abbey buildings.

The nave's four original bays are Romanesque, while the remainder of the basilica was rebuilt in the 14C in the Flamboyant Gothic style. Note the very fine 16C organ case and in the trefoil the fragments of a fresco depicting the Nursing Virgin.

The bare Romanesque nave enhances the sense of space, soaring height, luminosity and contrasts with the Gothic decoration elsewhere (restored 1979).

Chancel

Slender columns, pure lines and subtle decoration give the chancel considerable elegance. The overall effect is embellished by five windows with 14C stained glass, restored in 1901. During repair work to the chancel paving, a crypt and several sarcophagi were discovered, one dating to the 10C..

Chapelle St-Créspin★★

The 12C St. Crespin's Chapel opens off the north side of the ambulatory. Christ is shown in a mandorla surrounded by the symbols of the Evangelists. Four lovely Aubusson tapestries represent Abraham's Sacrifice of Isaac, Hagar and Ishmael in the desert, Lot and his daughters leaving Sodom and Jacob's Dream.

Address Book

WHERE TO STAY

▣▣ **Le Chêne Sec Bed and Breakfast** – *14700 Pertheville-Ners - 9km/5.6mi E of Falaise via D 63 towards Trun, then a minor road -* ☎*02 31 90 17 55 - closed in winter -* ▱ *- 2 rooms - meals* ▣▣*.* Quietude and character are the main features of this 15C manor house situated in a hamlet. Reached by an attractive spiral staircase, the two rooms upstairs feature exposed beams, stone walls and country furniture. Remember to visit the small 11C house in the grounds.

WHERE TO EAT

▣▣ **L'Attache** – *Rte de Caen – 1.5Km/0.9mi N of Falaise -* ☎*02 31 90 05 38 - closed 19-31 July, Tue evening and Wed – reserv. advisable*. You'll find this restaurant quite appealing: the owner is very keen on wild herbs and he will impart his enthusiasm to you through recipes prepared with local produce and culinary savoir faire. Discretion is the keynote in the dining room of this former coaching inn.

Chapelle St-Crépin, Fresco

At the altar is a large 13C statue of Our Lady of the Thorn in wood plated with silver. Beneath a remarkable 13C crucifix, a cabinet contains two outstanding pieces of metalwork: a delightful 15C silver Virgin and a 16C reliquary.

Driving Tours

Le Bois de Mirebeau

Allow about 1hr 45min.

▶ *35km/22mi – From Évron take D 20 N*

As the road climbs there are views to the west over woods and lakes.

▶ *Beyond Ste-Gemmes-le-Robert turn right onto the Mont Rochard road which is sometimes in poor repair.*

Le Gros Roc

From this rocky escarpment surrounded by vegetation there is an extensive view over the bocage countryside.

▶ *Turn left onto D 241 just before a bridge.*

The itinerary passes the **Château de Montesson**, encircled by a moat; the entrance pavilion is crowned by an unusual roof. The adjoining round tower has a highly original onion-domed roof.

▶ *In Hambers, opposite the church, turn left onto D 236. After 2.5km/1.3mi turn left again onto the narrow road leading to the Butte de Montaigu.*

Butte de Montaigu★

Allow 15min on foot there and back from the car park.

The mound, crowned by an old chapel, is only 290m/925ft high but, because of its isolation, makes an excellent viewpoint from which to see the Coëvrons rising to the south-east, Évron, Ste-Suzanne on its rock spike, to the south, Mayenne and its forest, to the north-west and the forests of Andaines and Pail to the north and north-east.

▶ *Return to D 236 and continue S through Chellé. At the T-junction turn left onto D 7 at the entrance to Mézangers village; turn right to the Château du Rocher.*

Château du Rocher★

Allow 30min on foot there and back. Exterior of château: mid-June–Sept 10am–noon, 3–6pm. No charge.

A gallery of five low rounded arches runs the length of the Renaissance façade. Delicate sculptures adorn the buildings. The more austere 15C façade faces the lake in the park.

▶ *Return to D 7 and continue S to return to Évron.*

Les Bois des Vallons

36km/22mi – Allow about 1hr From Évron take D 32 W. On the W side of Brée turn right onto D 557. On approaching St-Ouen-des-Vallons turn right to the Château de la Roche-Pichemer.

Château de la Roche-Pichemer

Open July–mid-Aug 2–6pm. No charge. Park near the moat, outside the gate.

The château consists of two main Renaissance wings built at right angles and covered with tall slate roofs. Massive square pavilions project from each corner, adding considerable dignity to the building, fronted by formal gardens.

▶ *From St-Ouen-des-Vallons take D 129 and D 24 S via Montsûrs to La Chapelle-Rainsouin.*

La Chapelle-Rainsouin

A room off the church chancel contains a beautiful 16C polychrome stone **Entombment**★.

▶ *Take D 20 NE. In Châtres-la-Forêt turn right onto D 562. Further on turn right again to the Château de Monteclerc.*

Château de Monteclerc

☞ *Not open to the public. Leave the car at the beginning of the avenue.*

The château, built at the very beginning of the 17C, stands in sober dignity at the far end of a vast courtyard. The drawbridge lodge has a rounded roof crowned by a lantern turret.

▶ *Return to Châtres-la-Forêt; turn right onto D 20 to return to Évron.*

FALAISE★

CALVADOS, POPULATION 8 434
MICHELIN MAP 303: K-6

Falaise suffered cruelly during the fighting in the Falaise-Chambois pocket in August 1944. The town's setting in the Ante Valley is dominated by the enormous fortress, one of Normandy's first stone castles, where William the Conqueror was born. Falaise is a centre for excursions into Suisse Normande.

🛈 **Information:** Blvd de la Libération, 14700 Falaise.
☎02 31 90 17 26. www.otsifalaise.com

▶ **Orient Yourself:** Falaise is is on N 158 between Caen, 41km/26mi to the north and Argentan, 22km/14mi to the southeast.

☺ **Don't Miss:** The château of William the Conqueror.

🕐 **Organizing Your Time:** Visit the château in the morning, lunch in Falaise and finish the day by touring the valley of the River Laizon.

Kids **Especially for Kids:** Children will enjoy the Automates Avenue exhibit.

👁 **Also See:** The marked itinerary Le Dénouement (The Outcome), one of several described in the Historical Area of the Battle of Normandy, goes through this town.

The Town

Église de la Trinité★

The west front of the church features a triangular Gothic porch. On the south side note the gargoyles and small carved figures. At the east end the Renaissance flying buttresses are highly ornate.

Fontaine d'Arlette

From the fountain of the Val d'Ante (Fontaine d'Arlette) there is an impressive view of the castle towering above.

Église St-Gervais

The church was built from the 11C to the 16C; the lantern tower is 12C. Inside, the contrast between the two architectural styles is striking: the south side is Romanesque, the north Gothic.

Porte des Cordeliers

This lovely stone gateway was part of the town wall. It is flanked by a round tower and has a pointed arched 14C-15C porch.

Château Guillaume-Le-Conquérant★

🕐*Open July–Aug 10am–7pm. Sept–Dec & Feb–June 10am–6pm.* 🕐*Closed Jan through Feb school holiday, 25 Dec.* ✎6€ *(Children 3€).* ☎02 31 41 61 44.

This medieval ensemble (12C-13C), characteristic of defensive Anglo-Norman architecture, has been heavily restored: the two keeps have been given roofs, while the stronghold now has a surprising concrete gatehouse. William the Bas-

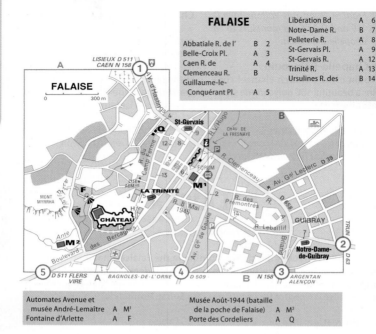

FALAISE

			Libération Bd	A	6
			Notre-Dame R.	B	7
			Pelleterie R.	A	8
Abbatiale R. de l'	B	2	St-Gervais Pl.	A	9
Belle-Croix Pl.	A	3	St-Gervais R.	A	12
Caen R. de	A	4	Trinité R.	A	13
Clemenceau R.	B		Ursulines R. des	B	14
Guillaume-le-Conquérant Pl.	A	5			

Automates Avenue et musée André-Lemaître	A	M¹
Fontaine d'Arlette	A	F
Musée Août-1944 (bataille de la poche de Falaise)	A	M²
Porte des Cordeliers	A	Q

tard, Duke of Normandy, was born here in 1027, to a local girl, Arlette.

Inner courtyard

Visitors walking through the Porte St-Nicolas enter a large area of about 1ha/2.5 acres, defined by 15 towers.

Main keep

This rectangular structure, built as late as the 12C, is surprisingly large; the great flat buttresses, which mark the line of the walls, still convey an impression of impregnability. The huge *aula* on the second floor was the main reception room. Its ambitious restoration involved sophisticated techniques: the flooring is made of alternating squares of glass and lead, whereas the ceiling consists of a Teflon covering stretched over an iron frame. Note the Chapelle St-Prix, a small oratory.

Small keep

This luminous, well-balanced construction commissioned by Henri I Plantagenet in the late 12C was designed to guard the main keep from attack from the rock platform.

Tour Talbot

This impressive round tower, 35m/115ft tall with walls 4m/12ft thick, was allegedly named after John Talbot, governor of the castle in 1449. An incredibly deep well (65m/197ft) carved out of the wall provides water to the entire castle.

The rock platform commands a lovely **view** of the surrounding countryside.

Musée Août-1944 (Battle of the Falaise Pocket)

⏲ *Open Easter–11 Nov 10am–noon, 2–6pm* ⏲ *Closed Tue except June–Aug. Closed 11 Nov– Easter.* ⊜*6€ (Children 2.80€).* ☎ *02 31 90 37 19. www.normandie-museeaout44.com*

This private collection displays heavy English, American and German war equipment. Several realistic scenes, enhanced by uniformed dummies, depict the spots where the fierce fighting of the Falaise Pocket took place.

Automates Avenue

Kids *Blvd de la Libération.* ♿ ⏲*Open Apr–Sept 10am–12.30pm, 1.30–6pm. Oct– Mar open weekends, school and public holidays 10am–12.30pm, 1.30–6pm, Sun 2–6pm.* ⏲*Closed mid-Jan– early Feb,*

1 Jan, 25 Dec. 5€ *(4–11 years 4.50€).* ☏*02 31 90 02 43.*

Until the 1950s, the Decamps company decorated the windows of Parisian department stores with animated scenes during Christmas time. The collection of more than 300 of these automatons includes some of the shop window displays.

Musée André-Lemaître

♿ *Same address, ticket booth and hours as Automates Avenue.* 3€ *(4–11 years 2€).* ☏*02 31 90 02 43.*

This museum is devoted to the local artist **André Lemaître,** renowned for his more than 4,000 still-life paintings.

Église Notre-Dame-de-Guibray

The church dates from the days of William the Conqueror. The apse and the apsidal chapels are still pure Romanesque. The organ is by Parizot (1746).

Driving tours

▶ *2.5km/1mi N of Falaise by rue Victor-Hugo. After crossing the bridge over the Ante turn right onto the path to Versainville.*

Versainville

The 18C château (🔑 not open to the public) features a central wing with a peristyle, linked by a gallery to a huge pavilion forming the left wing.

▶ *4km/2.5mi W of Falaise by V along D 511. Then turn right onto D 243.*

Noron-l'Abbaye

This village has a 13C church with a charming two-storey Romanesque belfry.

▶ *26km/16mi round trip – leave Falaise on D 658, N. Allow about 1hr.*

Vallée du Laizon

Aubigny

At the entrance to the village, on the left, stands a late-16C château and its outbuildings. The parish **church** contains statues of six consecutive lords of Aubigny, kneeling in the chancel, which provide

---

Guibray Fair

For nine centuries the suburb of Guibray to the south-east of Falaise was famous for its fair. Already in the 11C the horse fair was attended by thousands from all over Europe. The streets, lanes and alleys of Falaise, with their many inns and taverns, were alive with minstrels and dancers. Since the 19C increasing mechanisation has reduced the horse to a minor role.

---

interesting details of contemporary dress. As you continue, notice the tall 13C belfry of **Soulangy** to the left.

▶ *Right onto D 261. In Ouilly-le-Tesson turn right. Right at the next junction.*

Assy

A magnificent avenue (left) leads to the Château d'Assy, a handsome 18C mansion with an elegant Corinthian portico; the chapel dates from the 15C.

▶ *Return to the junction and turn right; turn left onto D 91.*

Soumont-St-Quentin

The 12C-14C church belfry is Romanesque below and Gothic above.

▶ *Return to Falaise by N 158.*

Beautiful Arlette

One evening in 1027, on returning from the hunt, Robert (later known as The Magnificent), younger son of King Richard II, Duke of Normandy, was struck by the beauty of a local girl, her skirts drawn high as she worked with her companions washing clothes at the stream. A lad of 17, he watched for her daily and desired her. Arlette's father, a rich tanner, let her decide for herself and she, refusing all secrecy, entered the castle over the drawbridge on horseback, finely apparelled.

Then, as the chroniclers of the time wrote, "When Nature had reached her term, Arlette bore a son who was named William."

FÉCAMP★★

SEINE-MARITIME, POPULATION 21 027
MICHELIN MAP 304: C-3 – LOCAL MAP SEE PAYS DE CAUX

Fécamp is a fishing port as well as a centre for pleasure boats. The town is also the home of Benedictine liqueur – a link with its monastic past. Guy de Maupassant was one frequent visitor to the town, which features in several of his works.

- **Information:** Quai Sadi-Carnot, 76403 Fécamp.
  ☎02 35 28 51 01. www.fecamp-tourisme.com
- ▶ **Orient Yourself:** Fécamp is 43km/27mi northeast of Le Havre and 72km/45mi northwest of Rouen.
- **Don't Miss:** The rich collections of the Bénédictine palace, the abbey of La Trinité and the superb view from Cap Fagnet and Valmont Abbey.
- **Organizing Your Time:** Fécamp and its surroundings will take up a day.
- **Especially for Kids:** The museum of Terre-Neuvas et de la Pêche.
- **Also See:** Pays de Caux, Étretat, Varengeville-sur-Mer and Dieppe.

A Bit of History

As early as the 7C there was a monastery in Fécamp with a relic of the Precious Blood. Richard II, Duke of Normandy from 996-1027, established a Benedictine community here. Before the rise of Mont-St-Michel, this was the foremost place of pilgrimage in Normandy.

Sights

Abbatiale de la Trinité★

The abbey church built by Richard II was struck by lightning and burned down. The subsequent building (12C-13C) was modified several times between the 15C and 18C.

Exterior

The cathedral is one of the longest (127m/416ft) in France. The Classical façade does not accord with the rest of the building and the nave walls are austere. Skirt the south porch: the tympanum above the door is a good example of Norman Gothic decoration.

Above the transept crossing rises the square lantern tower (65m/210ft high), designed in the typical Norman style.

Interior

The south transept contains a beautiful late-15C **Dormition of the Virgin**★. On the right of the altar is the Angel's Footprint. In 943, when the reconstructed church was being consecrated, an angel appeared and left his footprint on the stone.

The chancel's dimensions make it magnificent. The stalls, baldaquin and high altar are all good 18C works by the Rouen artist De France. A Renaissance altar stands behind the high altar. In the centre of the sanctuary is an ancient shrine adorned with low-relief sculptures dating from the 12C. The chapels off the chancel aisles and radiating chapels were embellished with wonderful **carved screens**★ in the 16C. In the fourth chapel, on the right, is the **tomb**★ of Abbot Thomas of St-Benoît, who died in 1307; the tomb is decorated with scenes from the abbey's history on its base.

The 15C **Lady Chapel**★ forms a separate group in the Flamboyant style. The wood medallions are 18C; the windows are 13C, 14C and 16C. Facing the chapel is the white-marble **tabernacle**★ of the Precious Blood.

The 17C tomb in the chapel of the Sacred Heart belongs to **Guglielmo da Volpiano**, first abbot of Fécamp, who died in 1031.

Palais Bénédictine★★

Open July–Aug 10am–7pm. Apr–June & Sept 10am–1pm, 2–6.30pm. Oct–Dec & Feb–Mar 10.30–12.45pm, 2–6pm (last entry

Address Book

📖 *For coin ranges, see the Legend on the cover flap.*

WHERE TO STAY

🛏 **Hôtel de la Plage** – *87 r. de la Plage.* ☎*02 35 29 76 51. 23 rooms.* 🚗.
Situated close to the waterfront, this very simple family hotel is a modest stopover. Rooms are spic-and-span and the breakfast room is picturesque with its marine decor and counter shaped like a ship's hull.

🛏🛏 **Mireille Le Thuillier Bed and Breakfast** –*37 Le Val de la Mer – 76400 Senneville-sur-Fécamp, 5km/3mi E of Fécamp direction Dieppe, then secondary road.* ☎*02 35 28 41 93. www.val-de-la-mer.com. Closed 15 Aug–15 Sept. 3 rooms.* 🍽🚗.
This charming Norman house, which appears quite old, is named for the little road that runs by it, leading to the sea. Guestrooms are decorated with exquisite taste. The biggest, sun-filled room is on the ground floor.

WHERE TO EAT

🍽 **Chez Nounoute** – *3 pl Nicholas-Selle.* ☎*02 35 29 38 08. Closed Wed from Sept–Feb. Reservations advised.* Occasionally one likes to find an unusual place, managed by a rather special but friendly owner. Here you find seafood *choucroute* and fresh fish wonderfully cooked.

🍽🍽 **Le Maritime** – *2 pl. Nicolas-Selle.* ☎ *02 35 28 21 71.Reservations advised.* You get a strong whiff of the sea air when you enter this restaurant situated in the marina: navigational instruments and wood panelling add to the maritime decor. The menu offers seafood, as well as meat for famished buccaneers.

LEISURE

Tourisme et loisirs maritimes – *15 rue Vicomte.* ☎*02 35 28 99 53. tlm76@wana-doo.fr.* A variety of excursions on boats along the Norman coast are proposed, including fishing expeditions, both from Fécamp and from LeHavre.

The tourist office has suggestions for bicycle excursions and hikes in the area.

1hr before closing). 🕐Closed Jan, 25 Dec and 1 May. ➜6€ (under 12 years no charge) ☎02 35 10 26 10. www.benedictine.fr

The building, designed by Camille Albert in the late 19C, is a mixture of neo-Gothic and neo-Renaissance styles.

The **museum** displays a large collection of objets d'art: silver and gold work, ivories, Nottingham alabasters (late 15C), wrought-iron work, statues and many manuscripts.

The Gothic Room is covered by a fine pitched roof made of oak and chestnut, shaped as the upturned hull of a ship; it houses the library: 15C Books of the Hours with fine **illuminations**, numerous **ivories**, a collection of **oil lamps** dating from the early days of Christianity and a Dormition of the Virgin, a painted low-relief wooden carving of the German School. The Alexander Le Grand Room, named after the Fécamp merchant who first marketed the Bénédictine liqueur in 1863, displays objects and documents relating to its history.

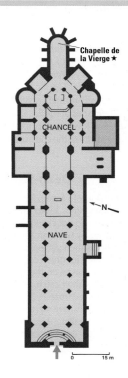

Chapelle de la Vierge ★

CHANCEL

N

NAVE

0   15 m

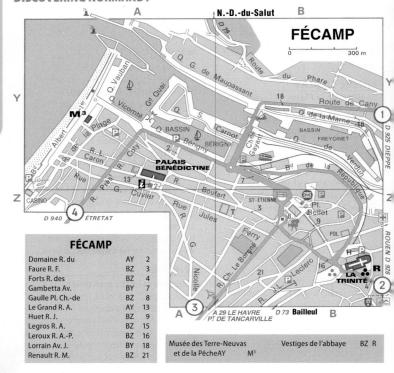

FÉCAMP

FÉCAMP		
Domaine R. du	AY	2
Faure R. F.	BZ	3
Forts R. des	BZ	4
Gambetta Av.	BY	7
Gaulle Pl. Ch.-de	BZ	8
Le Grand R. A.	AY	13
Huet R. J.	BZ	9
Legros R. A.	BZ	15
Leroux R. A.-P.	BZ	16
Lorrain Av. J.	BY	18
Renault R. M.	BZ	21

Musée des Terre-Neuvas et de la Pêche	AY	M³	
Vestiges de l'abbaye	BZ	R	

Musée des Terre-Neuvas et de la Pêche★

&⏱Open July–Aug daily 10am–7pm. Rest of the year daily except Tue 10am–noon, 2–5.30pm. ⏱Closed 1 Jan, 1 May, 25 Dec. ⊜3€ (under 18 years no charge)⊚02 35 28 31 99.

The Newfoundland and Fishing Museum evokes memories of the Fécamp fishing industry. The lower gallery explores the great adventure of the cod fishermen on the Newfoundland banks in the days of the sailing ship and the dory, a flat-bottomed craft rising at bow and stern.

One room is devoted to ship-building, featuring a model of the Belle Poule, the naval training ship built in Fécamp in 1931.

Exhibits trace the development of fishing methods and types of craft.

The outdoor terrace provides a magnificent **view**★ of the sea.

Deep-Sea Fishing, an Old Tradition

The herrings of Fécamp have been renowned since the Middle Ages. During the Renaissance ships sailed from Fécamp to Newfoundland to fish for cod. Fishing techniques did not change much for nearly 400 years: the fish was caught with a ground line by two men aboard a 5m/6yd-long flat-bottomed boat called a *doris*. The fish was then gutted, cleaned, boned, salted and stored in the hold; this was called fishing for green cod. Fishing for dried cod, meant fishermen had to settle during the season on the coast of Newfoundland, where they would build drying racks for their catch. During the 1970s, 15 huge trawlers with a crew of 900 men salted and froze 21 000t of cod in the icy waters of the North Atlantic. Today, pleasure boats have replaced trawlers, but until recently one could still meet old fishermen recalling their memories at the Bout Menteux (Liars' Corner, situated between quai de la Vicomté and quai de Bérigny).

Excursions

Château de Bailleul

10km/6mi SE by D 73.

This elegant 16C château (☞ not open to the public) consists of a central square building flanked by four pavilions. The medieval side façades are almost blind. A chapel stands in the wooded park.

Valmont

11km/7mi E via D 150.

Located in the very heart of the Pays de Caux and dominated by a castle built on a rocky spur, the village of Valmont possesses the ruins of a Benedictine abbey.

Abbey★

Church open daily; Chapelle de la Vierge and mausoleum open daily July–Sept daily except Tue 2.30–5pm. ≈2€ (Children no charge).☎02 35 27 34 92

Founded in the 12C, the Benedictine abbey of Valmont was rebuilt in the 14C following a fire and was radically altered in the 16C. After the Revolution the abbey became a private residence The **Chapelle de la Vierge★**, or Six o'Clock Chapel (the monks celebrated mass at this time every day), which has remained intact among the ruins, has an overall effect of great grace. Above the altar is a tiny room which has exquisite decorations and also a picture of the Annunciation attributed to Germain Pilon.

Château

Open mid-July–Aug Mon–Fri 9am–noon, 2–5pm. Closed public holidays. ≈3€ (under 16 years 1.50€)

Property of the Estoutevilles, lords of Valmont, this former military fortress preserves a Romanesque keep flanked by a Louis XI wing, crowned by a covered watch-path, and a Renaissance wing.

FLERS

ORNE, POPULATION 16 947
MICHELIN MAP 310: F-2

Situated in the heart of a "bocage"—a region of traditional hedgerows—Flers has managed to modernise itself: textiles, originally based on local linen and hemp, have given way to new industries, notably mechanical engineering and electrical appliances.

- **Information:** 2 Place du Dr-Vayssières, 61100 Flers. ☎02 33 65 06 75
- **Orient Yourself:** Flers is at the crossroads of the Paris-Granville and Caen-Laval routes. It is 92km/57.5mi south of Caen via D 562, 58km/36mi north of Mayenne via D 962 and D 23, 30km/19mi southeast of Vire and 44 km/27.5mi west of Argentan via D 924.
- **Don't Miss:** The view from the château at Mont de Cerisy.
- **Organizing Your Time:** You need half-day to see Flers and its surroundings.
- **Also See:** Clécy, the Suisse Normande, Bagnoles-de-l'Orne, Mortain, Domfront and Vire.

The Castle

Musée du Château

Open May–Oct daily except Sat morning 10am–noon, 2–6pm, Sat 2–6pm. Closed 1 May. ≈2€ (Children no charge). ☎02 33 64 66 49.

The present castle, with a moat on three sides, has a 16C main building by the alchemist, **Nicolas Grosparmy**, lord of Flers from 1527 to 1541, with an 18C Classical main front.

The first-floor rooms contain the painting and decorative art sections. In the gallery devoted to the regional schools of the 19C there are works from the Barbizon School by Corot and Daubigny, pre-Impressionists such as Boudin and Lépine and Impressionists (Caillebotte).

Address Book

For coin ranges, see the Legend on the cover flap.

WHERE TO EAT

Au Bout de la Rue – 60 r. de la Gare. 02 33 65 31 53. lebouleux@wanadoo.fr. Closed 1–25 Aug, Wed evening, Sat lunch, Sun and public holidays. This place is a genuine neighbourhood bistro: its red walls decorated with old posters and black-and-white photographs contribute to the charming and convivial atmosphere. You can enjoy more privacy in the separate cubicles. Several menus including one for children.

Auberge de la Mine –Le Gué-Plat, 61450 La Ferrière-aux-Étangs, 12km/7.5mi S of Flers via D 18, then D 21 and D 825. 02 33 66 91 10. aubergedelamine@free.fr. Closed 6–31 Jan, 3–27 Aug, Sun evening, Tue and Wed. This completely renovated restaurant was formerly the cafeteria of an iron mine. Carefully prepared cuisine, based on what's fresh at the market. Good value for money.

WHERE TO STAY

Galion Hotel – 5 r. Victor-Hugo. 02 33 64 47 47. 30 rooms. Situated in a peaceful district close to the town centre, this small hotel is a recent construction. From here you can walk to the foot of the castle for a visit or a stroll in the park. Rooms are traditional. Buffet breakfast.

Around Mont de Cerisy

▶ *Round-trip of 24km/15mi – Take D 924 W. Allow 3hrs*

La Lande-Patry

Two giant yews grow in the old cemetery.

▶ *Continue W on D 924.*

Tinchebray

Prison royale – ⏱*Open July–Aug Tue–Sat 10.30am–noon, 2-5.30pm, Sun 3–6pm.* 3€. 02 33 66 78 00.

On 28 September 1106 a battle took place near this market town between two of William the Conqueror's sons. As a result the elder son, Robert Curthose, was forced to cede the Duchy of Normandy to Henry I of England, known as Henry Beauclerk.

The **Prison royale** (rue de la Prison) houses an Ethnographic Museum. The revolutionary tribunal was set up on the first floor. Two cells have fireplaces, as some prisoners could pay for coal. The thick walls and wooden doors with impressive locks bear many graffiti, the oldest of which dates from 1793.

▶ *From Tinchebray take D 911 NE. In St-Pierre-d'Entremont turn right onto D 18. Before crossing the River Noireau turn right onto a narrow road along the river bank.*

Les Vaux

After passing between Mont de Cerisy (*left*) and St-Pierre Rocks (*right*), the road ends in the old hamlet of St-Pierre where a small Roman bridge spans the river.

▶ *Continue SE on D 18 to Cerisy-Belle-Étoile.*

Mont de Cerisy★

⏱*Open daily 9am–6pm.* 02 33 66 52 62. A road *(fee to enter)*, bordered by rhododendrons (in flower May to June), climbs up the slope to the ruined castle, which commands extensive **views**★ over the countryside (*bocage*) even to the foothills of the Suisse Normande. The plateau is the venue for the **Rhododendron Festival** (*last Sunday in May*).

▶ *Continue on D 18 to return to Flers.*

CHÂTEAU DE FONTAINE-HENRY ★★

CALVADOS, MICHELIN MAP 303: J-4

This beautiful building is a fine example of Renaissance architecture. A member of the Harcourt family built it in the 15C and 16C over the dungeons, cellars and foundations of the original 11–12C fortress.

▶ **Orient Yourself:** Fontaine-Henri is in the Mue valley, near the Côte de Nacre and the D-Day beaches, 18km/11mi north of Caen and 25mi/16mi east of Bayeux.

☺ **Don't Miss:** The stone stalls in the château chapel.

◷ **Organizing Your Time:** You need 1hr 30mins to see the château.

🖒 **See also:** Arromanches-les-Bains, Ouistreham-Riva-Bella, Caen, Bayeux and the Normandy landing beaches.

Visit

🔊 *Guided tours (1hr 30min) mid-June–mid-Sept daily except Tue 2.30–6.30pm. Easter–mid-June & mid-Sept – 2 Nov weekends and public holidays 2.30–6.30pm. ⌨6€ (children 4€). Evening visits Fri in summer.⌨8€ (children 6€). ☎06 89 84 85 57. www.chateau-de-fontaine-henry.com.*
An immense, steeply sloping slate roof, taller than the building itself, covers the 16C pavilion on the left. The main building is a wonder of delicately worked stonework. Inside is similar stonework, including the François I **staircase**. Furnished throughout, the château has some fine paintings. The nave of the 12C chapel was altered in the 16C.

Excursion

🚶*Allow 15min on foot there and back. The lane branches off D 170 on a corner, about 500m/550yd from Thaon parish church. This downhill path will take you to the bottom of the valley.*

Ancienne église de Thaon★

Allow 15min there and back.
◷*Visits possible on Sun. Contact M. Paunet of the AVET association. ☎02 31 80 04 76.* This small 12C Romanesque church is enhanced by its attractive setting in an isolated valley. The belfry, one of the most original in Normandy, is capped by a pyramid roof and deeply recessed twin bays.

The château

FORGES-LES-EAUX

SEINE-MARITIME, POPULATION 3 465
MICHELIN MAP 304: J-4

Located in the green heart of the Pays de Bray, Forges-les-Eaux is a spa resort and source of iron-rich waters reputed to be both refreshing and stimulating.

- **Information:** Rue Albert-Bochet, 76440 Forges-les-Eaux. ☎02 35 90 52 10. www.ville-forges-les-eaux.fr.
- ▶ **Orient Yourself:** Forges-les-Eaux is 60km/37.5mi northeast of Rouen.
- **Don't Miss:** Excursions into the Pays de Bray to see the pretty villages.
- **Organizing Your Time:** After a morning in town, see the Pays de Bray.
- **Also See:** Neufchâtel-en-Bray, Clères and the château of Martainville.

Sights

Collection Faïence de Forges

In the Tourist Office. ◷*Open Tue–Friday on request.* ◷*Closed public holidays.*👁*2€.* ☎*02 35 90 52 10.*
A hundred or so examples of Forges faïence, manufactured until the 19C, are displayed at the town hall.

Musée de la Résistance et de la Déportation

◷*Open daily 2–6pm (Last entry 5.30pm).* ◷*Closed 1 Jan, 14 July, 15 Aug and 25 Dec.* 👁*3€ (Under 10 years no charge).* ☎*02 35 90 64 07*
Insignia, arms and uniforms as well as documents recount the dark days of the Occupation in Haute Normandie.

The Spa

Rue de la République boasts some half-timbered façades (17C-18C), and leads onto avenue des Sources, where it passes under the old railway line (now a footpath).
The resort grounds and casino are to the left, just after the bridge.
The **park** and spa are managed by the Club Méditerranée in an elegant setting.

Parc Montalent and Épinay Forest

On the other side of avenue des Sources, four pleasant and well-marked **nature trails** wind among the ponds and into the woods.

Excursion

La Ferme de Bray

Leave Forges via D 915 NW, after 8km/5mi, turn left before Sommery and follow the signs. &◷*Open July–Sept daily 2-7pm. Apr– June & Oct weekends and public holidays 2–6pm.* 👁*5€ (under 12 years no charge)* ☎*02 35 90 57 27.*
On the banks of the Sorson, this restored site shows what a prosperous 17C-18C farm was like. The bread oven, the cider press and the mill are in use. There are regular exhibits in the main house, a spacious 16C building whose façade was redone in the 17C.

Driving Tours

Southern Pays de Bray

▶ *52km/31mi. Leave via D 921 S.*

The Pays de Bray is a lush strip at the centre of the vast bare stretches of the Caux plateau. It owes its chief characteristic, known as the Bray Buttonhole, to a geological accident, which created a hollow in the surrounding chalk. Running parallel to the valley of the River Seine, the region is a sparsely inhabited patchwork of vales, limestone bluffs, hills, meadows and forests.

La Ferté-Saint-Samson

The village is perched just before the main edge of the Bray "Buttonhole" and from the approach to the church there is an extended view of the depression with its clearly defined rim. In the main square is the 16C house of Henri IV.

▶ *In Fry, before church, turn left onto D 1*

The road runs along the south-west Bray escarpment of massive bare mounds crowned with beech trees (Mont Robert).

Beauvoir-en-Lyons★

🅿️*Park beyond the town hall; walk up the street on the left to the church.*
From the east end there is a **view**★ of the green Bray Valley cutting away in a straight line south-east. In clear weather Beauvais Cathedral is visible.

▶ *Return to the car and continue SE on D 1. At a crossroads, turn left downhill onto D 57. Then follow D 21.*

Gournay-en-Bray★

Gournay and Ferrières are the busiest towns in the Pays de Bray. The local dairy industry supplies most of the fresh cheese consumed in France.

Collégiale St-Hildevert

The church, which is largely 12C, has withstood several wars but the late-12C doors have suffered from excessive restoration. Inside, the massive columns are surmounted by carved capitals. The oldest and most worn, at the end of the south aisle, are among the earliest examples of attempts at human portrayal during the Romanesque period.

▶ *Take D 916 N.*

Beuvreuil

Church – ⊶ *Closed for repairs.*
The wooden porch of the small 11C country **church** is decorated with enamelled bricks. Inside the church are an 11C font stoup, a 15C holy-water stoup, Gothic statues, a 15C altarpiece and a 16C lectern.

▶ *Take D 84 W; turn right onto D 915 to Forges.*

Vallée de l'Andelle

▶ *56km/34mi – From Forges take D 919 and D 13 SW. Allow about 2hr 30min.*

Sigy-en-Bray

The **abbey church** is all that remains of Sigy Abbey, founded in the 11C by Hugh I. It has kept its 12C chancel and seven-sided apse, a 13C portal and the nave vaulting, restored in the 18C. The 15C bell-tower overlooks a cemetery with a late-15C sandstone calvary.

▶ *Take D 41 E towards Argueil, then D 921 S.*

Le Héron

This small village enjoys a pleasant site alongside the park – designed by Le Nôtre – of the château where, it is said, Gustave Flaubert, then 16 years old, discovered the worldly life, an inspiration used in *Madame Bovary*.

▶ *Continue to Vascoeuil by the D 46.*

Vascœuil

At the château (🕐*Open July–Aug 11am–6.30pm. Mid-Mar–June & Sept–mid-Nov daily except Mon 2.40–6pm.* 🕐*Closed public holidays.* ✍7.50€ *(Children 5 €)*) the historian Jules Michelet (1798-1874) wrote his famous *Histoire de France*.
The road continues past a surprising sight, the ruins of a spinning mill built at the turn of the 20C in imitation of the Medieval and Gothic styles.

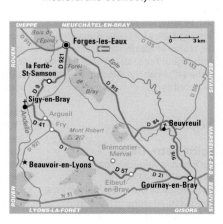

Pont-St-Pierre

The town, which stretches across the Andelle Valley, owes much to its 12C-18C château and surrounding park, glimpsed through a gap in the main street.

The 11C-12C church is decorated with **woodwork**★, complemented by Henri II stalls and a 17C altarpiece from Fontaine-Guérard. A 14C Virgin in the chancel wears a dress inlaid with cabochon stones.

▶ *After Romilly station turn right; follow D 19 which crosses D 20. After the Sabla factory, turn left along the Seine.*

Écluses d'Amfreville★

The locks, together with the Poses Dam, control the water flow in the Lower Seine and divide the stretch below Paris from the tidal section flowing into the Channel. Take the footbridge overlooking the locks to see water pouring over the Poses Dam; go over to the left bank where the 8 000kW power station stands. A spillway specially designed for fish with an observation room shows how different species make their way upstream.

▶ *To return to the coast, continue on D 19 as far as Amfreville-sous-les-Monts and take D 20 up a steep hillside.*

FRESNAY-SUR-SARTHE

SARTHE, POPULATION 2 335
MICHELIN MAP 310: J-5

Fresnay occupies a picturesque site perched high above the River Sarthe. The town is a centre for excursions into the Alpes Mancelles or Sillé Forest, but also has plenty to offer on-site in the form of a preserved network of narrow streets bordered by old houses.

- **Information:** 19 av du Dr-Riant, 72130 Fresnay-sur-Sarthe. ☎02 43 33 28 04.
- ▶ **Orient Yourself:** Fresnay is 21km/13mi south of Alençon.
- **Don't Miss:** The beautiful medieval houses in the town centre.
- **Organizing Your Time:** You'll need 1hr30min to see this pretty town.
- **Also See:** Alençon and Sillé-le-Guillaume.

A Bit of History

In 1063 the town was occupied by the troops of William, Duke of Normandy; he put down revolts in 1068 and 1078 himself. In 1100, following incessant local fighting, Henry I of England abandoned the region of Maine, which allied itself with Anjou. Peace lasted until the end of the 14C, when the Hundred Years War reignited strife.

Sights

Église Notre-Dame

Open July–Aug 3.30–6pm, by appointment ☎02 43 97 24 98.
The Church of Our Lady, built of local rust-coloured stone in the transitional Romanesque style, is dominated by a remarkable octagonal belfry. The round-headed doorway frames the oak door (1528); its carved panels depict *(left)* the Tree of Jesse and *(right)* Christ

Terrace de l'Hôtel de Ville

A public garden has been laid out in the castle's former precincts. From the terrace there is a view★ down over the Sarthe with its attractive bridge and old houses.

Cave du Lion

Open July–Aug daily except Mon 4–7pm, on appointment with Jean-Gilles 8 days in advance. ☎02 43 33 64 42. No charge.
This underground cellar opens off ruelle du Lion, on the far side of the covered market. The chamber has an octagonal central pillar and ribbed vaulting.

GISORS

EURE, POPULATION 9 481

MICHELIN MAP 304: K-6

Gisors is the capital of the Norman Vexin: it was once a frontier town belonging to the dukes of Normandy. The town owes its origins to the castle, which formed part of a line of defence running from Forges-les-Eaux to Vernon and included the castles of Neaufles-St-Martin and Château-sur-Epte.

- **Information:** 4 rue du Gén.-de-Gaulle, 27140 Gisors.
  ☎02 32 27 60 63. www.tourisme-gisors.fr
- **Orient Yourself:** Gisors is 76km/47.5mi northwest of Paris and 64km/40mi northeast of Rouen.
- **Don't Miss:** The château and the Tree of Jesse in St-Gervais-et-St-Protais.
- **Organizing Your Time:** See Gisors in the morning, then tour the Epte valley.
- **Also See:** Giverny, Vernon, Les Andelys and Lyons-la-Forêt.

Visit

Château Fort★★

Guided tours (1hr) Apr–Sept daily except Tue at 10am, 11am, 2.30pm, 3.45pm and 5pm. Oct–Mar weekends and public holidays at 10.30am, 2.30pm, and 4pm. Closed Dec–Jan and 1 May. ☜5€ (Children 3€). ☎02 32 55 59 36. www.ville-gisors.fr.

The castle was built as early as 1097 by William II, King of England and son of the Conqueror. It was fortified in the 12C by Henry II. In 1193 it was taken by Philippe Auguste of France. During the Hundred Years War the castle changed hands several times before returning to the French crown in 1449.

The 11C **keep**, on its 20m/65ft artificial mound in the centre of the fortified perimeter and surrounded now by a public garden, is flanked by a watch-tower. This 12C surrounding wall was added by Philippe Auguste.

A staircase leads to the top from where there is a fine **view** over the surrounding woodland.

Église St-Gervais -et-St-Protais★

The oldest parts of the church date back to the 12C, but construction continued to the end of the 16C, as is evident both outside and inside. The Gothic chancel was completed in 1249; the side chapels adjoining the ambulatory were added in 1498 and 1507. The transept doors are 16C and Gothic, as is the very tall nave. The monumental west front is Renaissance: the doorway is flanked by two towers, that on the north being built in 1536, that on the south left unfinished in 1591.

In spite of the mixture of architectural styles the church as a whole appears perfectly harmonious, particularly inside.

The large monochrome window in the chapel on the right of the choir dates from the 16C. The chapel below the South Tower contains a charming spiral staircase by Jean Grappin and a huge late-16C Tree of Jesse.

WHERE TO STAY

☜☜ **Le Four à Pain Bed and Breakfast** – 8 r. des Gruchets, 27140 St-Denis-le-Ferment, 7km/4.2mi NW of Gisors heading for the château, a side road and D 17. 2 rooms. ☎02 32 55 14 45 - . Can you imagine a room built in an old bread oven amid a charming garden bursting with flowers? Another room, in the farm renovated à l'ancienne, is larger and has a handsome wood frame ceiling.

The History of the Dukedom of Normandy

It was at St-Clair-sur-Epte in the year 911 that Charles the Simple – a nickname, meaning honest and straightforward – met with Rollo, the ruler of the Vikings. Dudon de St-Quentin, Normandy's first historian, recounts that, to ratify the agreement creating the Dukedom of Normandy, the Viking placed his hands between those of the French king. This informal deal, concluded in the manner of tradesmen, carried the same legal weight as a formal exchange of seals and signatures, for a written treaty was never signed. The dukedom is bordered by the River Epte north of the River Seine and by the River Avre to the south. The boundaries of Normandy were often fought over throughout history by the kings of France and the dukes of Normandy, who became the kings of England in the late 11C.

Driving Tour

Epte Valley

41km/25mi – allow 2hr
The road from Gisors to Vernon follows the west bank of the Epte. The riverside is shady, in contrast with the bareness of the slopes hewn out of the chalk bed of the Vexin plateaux.

▶ *From Gisors take D 10 W.*

Neaufles-St-Martin

The village is dominated by a keep standing upon a perfectly preserved artificial mound.

▶ *At the junction turn left onto D 181.*

Dangu

Church – ⏱Can be visited on request at the town hall. ☎02 32 55 22 15.
The main features of the Gothic **church** are the 18C woodwork and painted panelling in the chancel, the 16C Montmorency Chapel in which a *grisaille* window above the altar shows St Denis, St Lawrence and, on his knees, William, fifth son of Anne of Montmorency.

▶ *Take D 146 S into the valley.*

Château-sur-Epte

Standing on an artificial mound surrounded by a moat are the remains of a massive keep built by William Rufus, King of England from 1087 to 1100, to protect the Norman frontier from France.

GIVERNY★

EURE, POPULATION 548
MICHELIN MAP 304: J-7 – 2KM/1MI SE OF VERNON

Claude Monet lived in this village from 1883 until his death in 1926, and attracted many other artists to the area. It was here that he painted the huge canvases of the water lilies which can be seen in Paris at the Orangerie Museum and the Marmottan Museum.

- 🛈 **Information:** An information point is open from April to October, 10am–7pm, in the parking lot opposite the Museum of American Art.
- ▶ **Orient Yourself:** Giverny is 2km/1.25mi southwest of Vernon, which is (69km/43mi) from Rouen via D 313/D 5.
- 🅿 **Parking:** Parking lots are found on both sides of D 5.
- 👁 **Don't Miss:** The home of Claude Monet and the American Art Museum.
- ⏱ **Organizing Your Time:** Give yourself 2 hours for each of the museums.
- 👁 **Also See:** Vernon, Les Andelys, Évreux and Dreux.

Address Book

&*For coin ranges, see the Legend on the cover flap.*

WHERE TO STAY

◎◎ **Le Bon Maréchal Bed and Breakfast** – *1 r. du Colombier.* ☎*02 32 51 39 70. 3 rooms.* 🍽 🍷. This house used to be a small café where Monet and his artist friends would meet. Ideally situated between the gardens and the American Art Museum, it now offers cosy, comfortable rooms with reasonable prices to match.

WHERE TO EAT

◎◎ **Restaurant-Musée Baudy** – *81 r. Claude-Monet.* ☎*02 32 21 10 03. restaurantbaudy@yahoo.fr. Closed Nov– Mar, Sun evening and Mon except public holidays.* The former Hôtel Baudy used to lodge Impressionist painters. Savour the dish of the day and salads. Delectable old rose garden concealing the studio just beyond… A must!

◎◎**Le Moulin de Fourges**– *38 r. du Moulin, 27630 Fourges.* ☎*02 32 52 12 12. www.moulindefourges.com. Closed Nov–Mar, Sun evening and Mon except July–Aug.* A former watermill on the banks of the Epte, a place Monet would have appreciated. No waterlilies, but a country setting. Traditional cuisine.

Visit

Maison de Claude Monet★

🕓*Open Apr–Oct daily except Mon 9.30am–6pm.* ◎*5.50€ (Children 3€) www.fondation-monet.com*

Claude Monet's garden slopes gently to the banks of the River Epte. The house has been converted into an exhibition area with reproductions of his greatest paintings. The tour includes the blue salon, the bedroom with the bed and roll-top desk, the old studio, the yellow dining room with its painted wooden furniture and the tiled kitchen.

The garden comprises the walled garden *(clos normand)*, planted according to Monet's own design, and *(via a tunnel to the other side of the road)* the Japanese-inspired water garden, fed by the River Epte.

Musée d'Art américain Giverny★

&🕓*Open Apr–Oct daily except Mon 10am–6pm (Last entry 30min before closing.)* 🕓*Closed public holidays.* ◎*5.50€ (Children 4€) Free first Sun of month .* ☎*02 32 51 94 65. www.maag.org.*

This museum, which stands within a few hundred yards of the house of Claude Monet, contains about 100 works of art by 40 American artists, largely from the Terra Museum of American Art in Chicago. It is housed in three adjoining galleries.

Claude Monet's pink and green house

GRANVILLE★

MANCHE, POPULATION 12 687
MICHELIN MAP 303: C-6

This lively seaside resort, set on a rocky promontory, is also a busy port with an active fishing fleet and a marina. Granville is also the departure point for ferries to the Chausey and Channel islands.

- **Information:** 4 cours Jonville, 50406 Granville. ☎02 33 91 30 03. www.ville-granville.fr
- ▶ **Orient Yourself:** As the bird flies, Granville is 150km/94mi from Paris;106km/66mi from Cherbourg; 109km/68mi from Caen; 50km/31 mi from Mont St-Michel.
- 🕿 **Don't Miss:** A look at haute couture in the Villa Dior.
- 🕐 **Organizing Your Time:** Try to fit in a day trip to the Iles Chausey.
- **Kids** **Especially for Kids:** There is an aquarium they will enjoy.
- 🖐 **Also See:** Iles Chausey, Villedieu-les-Poêles, the Abbaye de la Lucerne and Carolles.

A Bit of History

In the 15C, the English fortified the rocky promontory as a base from which to attack Mont-St-Michel, then occupied by the Normans. The town was recaptured permanently by the knights of Mont-St-Michel in 1442. Prosperity came with deep-sea fishing for cod in the 18C, and Granville flourished with the rising popularity of sea bathing in the 19C.

Upper Town

Allow 2hr
The Main Gate (Grand'Porte) with its drawbridge remains the principal entrance to the fortified, upper part of town which concentrates all Granville's military and religious past within its ramparts.

Église Notre-Dame

The oldest parts of this austere granite church with a fine tower go back to the 15C. The nave itself and the west front were erected in the 17C and 18C. The 14C statue, in the north chapel, of Our Lady of Cape Lihou is greatly venerated locally.

Pointe du Roc

This is an exceptional **site**★. The point which marks the northern limit of Mont-St-Michel Bay is linked to the mainland only by a narrow rocky isthmus. In the 15C the English dug a trench, known as Tranchée aux Anglais, as part of their fortifications.

🚶 *The walk (the path starts from the harbour) to the lighthouse offers a fine view of the sea and the rocks.*

The Carnival at Granville

This long-standing tradition was originated by local fishermen. Before leaving for long fishing expeditions out in Newfoundland, cod fishermen would go out to spend their money in the streets of the city, dressing up in various costumes for the occasion. Today the carnival takes place during Shrove Tuesday celebrations; it lasts for four days and includes a funfair with a procession of floats, an orchestra and majorettes. On the last day the residents, dressed up and masked, pay a visit to their friends; a Carnival effigy is burned on the beach, marking the end of festivities.

Address Book

&For coin ranges, see the Legend on the cover flap.

WHERE TO STAY

🍽 **Hôtel des Bains** – 19 r. G.-Clemenceau. ☎02 33 50 17 31. www.hoteldesbains-granville.com. 54 rooms. ☐. Waves break just beneath the terrace of this century-old hotel. Ask for a room with a view over the sea, or one equipped with a relaxing jacuzzi.

🍽 **Le Hamel Bed and Breakfast** – Lieu-dit "Le Hamel", 50380 St-Aubin-des-Préaux, 7km/4.4mi from granville via D 973 and D 154. ☎02 33 51 42 65. 4 rooms. 🍴 ☐. An old stone farm building in a peaceful, verdant setting with spacious, comfortable rooms. Lounge and breakfast room with a fireplace that is welcome on cold days. Pretty garden.

WHERE TO EAT

🍽 **Crêperie Grill l'Échauguette** – 22-24 r. St-Jean. ☎02 33 50 51 87. Nestling in one of the narrow streets of old Granville, this unassuming creperie is sought after by the locals. In addition to buckwheat galettes, you will enjoy grills cooked in the fireplace.

🍽 **L'Horizon** – Pl. du Mar.-Foch. ☎02 33 50 00 79. www.casino-granville.com. Closed Mon–Tue from Oct to Mar. This restaurant belongs to the stylish Casino. You'll have a first-rate view of the sea from the dining room, and when the weather is fine you can make out the Channel Islands. Seafood and contemporary cuisine.

🍽🍽 **La Citadelle** – 34 r. du Port. ☎02 33 50 34 10. www.restaurant-la-citadelle.com. Closed Feb and Christmas school holidays, Tue from Oct– Mar and Wed. Before setting off for the islands, stop and have a meal in the dining room with its blue-wood panelling or sit on the small raised terrace. Specialities: seafood, including lobster.

LEISURE

Spa **Institute de Thalassothérapie Préwithal** – 3 r. Jules-Michelet. ☎ 02 33 90 31 10. www.prewithal.com. Open 10am–noon, 2–8.30pm. Closed 11-25 Dec. Granville's invigorating climate has favoured the creation of a physical therapy and re-education centre directly on the sea coast. Spa treatments are offered in the afternoon, while the morning is spent on revivifying hikes studying flora and fauna.

🔦**Old ships** – Granville is famous for its traditional fishing vessels, such as la bisquine, a sailing ship that challenged those of Cancale during fierce regattas as early as the 1850s. Today, cruises are offered aboard some of these, superbly restored by ardent craftsmen:
La Granvillaise (☎02 33 90 07 51),
Le Charles-Marie (☎02 33 46 69 54)
Le Lys Noir (☎02 33 90 48 63),
Le Courrier des Îles (☎02 33 50 49 80)
Le Strang Hugg (☎02 33 90 69 06).
CRNG (Centre régional de nautisme de Granville – Bd des Amiraux. ☎02 33 91 22 60. www.crng.asso.fr. Open 9am–6pm. Closed Christmas holidays. Some 170 boats of all sorts are available for rental, lessons or excursions. Activities for all ages and levels of skill.

Rampart Walk★

P Park on the parvis of Notre-Dame Church.

▶ Go through the Grand'Porte and over the drawbridge. Turn right onto rue Lecarpentier to follow the south rampart to place de l'Isthme.

🔭The **view**★ from the square extends, on a clear day, to the coast of Brittany (viewing table).

▶ Continue along the inside of the ramparts by rue du Nord.

At this point the view is spectacular in stormy weather. The Chausey Islands lie to the north-west.

▶ Turn left onto rue des Plâtriers to reach rue St-Jean, then turn right.

Note, at no 7 rue St-Jean, an old house with a ground-floor shop and then, at no 3, a house dating from 1612.

▶ *The street opposite, montée du Parvis, leads back to the starting point.*

Lower Town

La Plage

The narrow beach at the foot of shale cliffs is overlooked by the Plat-Gousset Breakwater promenade.

Jardin public Christian-Dior et Villa des Rhumbs

🕐*Garden open 9am–8pm. ⦾No charge. Museum open mid-May–mid-Sept 10am–6.30pm. ⦾5€ (Under 12 years no charge). ☎02 33 61 48 21.*

This public garden and museum are located in the childhood home of the famous couturier. From the upper terrace you look down on the Granville promontory, north towards Regnéville and out to the Chausey Islands.

The cliff path passes the cemetery to reach the great expanse of Donville Beach.

Aquarium du Roc

Enter from boulevard Vaufleury. 🄺🄸🄳🅂 🕐*Open Feb holidays–11 Nov daily 10am–12.30pm, 2–7pm (Last entry 1hr before closing.)* 🕐*Closed Mon in Mar. ⦾7€ (Children 3.50€). ☎02 33 50 19 83. www.aquarium-du-roc.com*

The **tanks** contain fish from local waters – note the sea perch with its powerful jaw and conical teeth for eating shellfish – as well as exotic and freshwater species.

Musée du Vieux Granville

In the fortified gatehouse, Grand'Porte. 🕐*Open July–Sept daily except Tue 10am–noon, 2–6.30pm (Last entry 30min before closing.) Apr–June daily except Tue 10am–noon, 2–6pm. Oct–mid-Dec & Feb holidays–Mar open Wed and weekends 2–6pm.* 🕐*Closed last half Dec– Feb holidays, 1 May, 1 Nov. ⦾1.70€. ☎02 33 50 44 10.*

On the first floor, is a collection of Norman costumes and headdresses as well as household furnishings. On the second floor are exhibitions about the sea.

Musée Richard-Anacréon

🕐*Open June–Sept daily except Mon 11am–6pm. Rest of the year daily except Mon and Tue 2–6pm.* 🕐*Closed 1 and 8 May and when exhibits are being changed. 2.60€ (Under 11 years no charge). ☎02 33 51 02 94.*

This museum of modern art presents a collection of works by 20C artists, displayed as temporary exhibitions.

Harbour

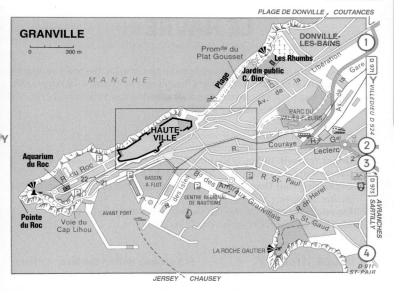

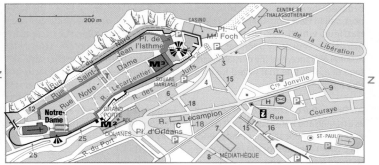

GRANVILLE		Hauteserve Bd d'	Z	9	Ste-Geneviève R.	Z	17
		Juifs R. des	Z		Saintonge R.	Z	18
Clemenceau R. G.	Z 3	Lecampion R.	Z		Terreneuviers Bd	Y	21
Corsaires Pl. aux	Z 4	Leclerc R. Gén.	Y		Vaufleury Bd	Y	22
Corsaires R. aux	Z 6	Parvis-Notre-Dame			2e-et-202e-de-		
Couraye R.	Z	Montée du	Z	12	Ligne Bd des	Z	25
Desmaisons R. C.	Z 7	Poirier R. Paul	Z	15			
Granvillais Bd des Amiraux	Z 8	St-Sauveur R.	Z	16			

Musée Richard-Anacréon	Z M³	Musée du Vieux-Granville	Z M²

Excursion

Îles Chausey
 See Îles CHAUSEY.

St-Pair-sur-Mer ⚓
Kids St-Pair has a breakwater promenade protecting a beach of golden sand which is perfect for children. The

church is said to have been founded in the 6C by two local Evangelists, St Pair and St Scubilien. The building consists of the Romanesque belfry and the bay beneath, the 14C chancel and a 19C neo-Gothic nave and transepts. Inside are several religious artworks from the 15C through the 18C, as well as 6C sarcophagi.

LE HAVRE★

SEINE-MARITIME, POPULATION 184 000 MICHELIN MAP 304: A-5

In 1945 Le Havre was Europe's worst damaged port; today the town, including the residential area of Ste-Adresse and the old port of Harfleur, is a remarkable example of large-scale reconstruction and successful town planning. Le Havre's university is new, it opened here in 1986.

- **Information:** 186 blvd Clemenceau, 76059 Le Havre.
  ☎02 32 74 04 04. www.lehavretourisme.com
- ▶ **Orient Yourself:** 197km/123mi from Paris and 90km/56mi from Rouen.
- **Don't Miss:** Car ferries operate to England and the Republic of Ireland.
- **Organizing Your Time:** The best time to visit is Wednesday or weekends, when all sites are open.
- **Especially for Kids:** The Malraux museum has a tour map for children.
- **Also See:** Honfleur, Étretat, Pays de Caux, Lillebonne.

A Bit of History

A Judicious Choice – In 1517 **François I** ordered the construction of a new port, called Havre-de-Grâce, to replace Harfleur, which had silted up. The marshy site chosen by Bonnivet, Grand Admiral of France, had the crucial advantage of a high tide that lasted for over two hours.

An Ocean Port – The career of Le Havre as a trading and transatlantic port began during the American War of Independence when supplies for the rebels were shipped from Le Havre.
Le Havre bustled in the 19C when great transatlantic passenger liners reduced the journey time New York.

Le Havre during the War – Le Havre suffered 146 raids, in which more than 4 000 were killed. The siege of the town began on 2 September 1944 – the Battle of Normandy was over and Paris liberated, but Le Havre was still occupied. Allied air raids went on ceaselessly for eight days from 5 September; the Germans were determined to blow up any port installations still in existence. On 13 September 1944 Le Havre was liberated. It took two years to clear the destruction and reconstruction began only in 1946.

The Port★★

Traffic

Le Havre is a deep-water port situated in the Seine estuary; it ranks first among French ports for exports and container traffic, and fourth in Europe for total traffic. Le Havre also has frequent car-ferry links with Great Britain (Le Havre-Portsmouth) and Ireland (Le Havre-Rosslare, Le Havre-Cork).
Each year 7 000 merchant ships dock in Le Havre, including 2 250 container ships.

Port Tour

Allow 1hr 15min – ▯ *information from the tourist office.*
For information about the port and shipping movements, see the receptionist at the Centre Administratif, Port Autonome, Terre-plein de la Barre. Audio-

Le Gac/MICHELIN

guides can be hired for unaccompanied visits of the port.

Boat trips from quai de la Marine take their passengers round the port facilities.

The Modern Town★

The old town was virtually wiped out in 1944. A new town was planned by **Auguste Perret** (1875-1954), the pioneer of reinforced concrete construction, who achieved remarkable architectural unity.

Bassin du Commerce and Espace Niemeyer

The commercial dock is the focal point of the new district accessible by an elegant footbridge, designed by the architects Gillet and Du Pasquier.

At the west end, facing the war memorial, is the new **Espace Oscar-Niemeyer** complex on place Gambetta. The main pavilion (Grand Volcan) has a large theatre, a cinema and exhibition rooms.

Place de l'Hôtel-de-Ville★

The square, which was designed by Auguste Perret, is bordered by three-storey buildings, punctuated by taller 10-storey blocks. The open space is laid out with fountains, lawns, arbours and yew hedges. The **hôtel de ville**, an austere building, is distinguished by a great tower (72m/236ft high) in concrete.

Avenue Foch★

The central roadway is bordered by lawns shaded by trees; the Porte Océane marks the west end of the street on the seafront.

North dike and the beach

The north breakwater, supplemented by a jetty, encloses the marina. The Le Havre and Ste-Adresse Beach stretches from the North Breakwater to the Hève Cape.

Église St-Joseph★

This sober **church** typical of Auguste Perret's style was built of concrete between 1951 and 1957. It is surmounted by an octagonal lantern-belfry (109m/358ft high). The **interior**★★ is monumental and impressive.

Sémaphore

The view from the end of the pier embraces the harbour entrance and the long southern breakwater protecting the outer harbour.

Sights

Cathédrale Notre-Dame

Built between 1575 and 1630, the cathedral is a combination of Gothic and Renaissance styles and bristles with buttresses decorated with gargoyles. The organ (1637) was presented by Richelieu and bears his arms.

A. de Valroger/MCIEHLIN

Le Volcan by Oscar Niemeyer, Basin du Commerce

Musée des Beaux-Arts André-Malraux★

&. ©Open daily except Tue 11am–6pm (weekends 11am-7pm). ©Closed 1 Jan, 1 and 8 May, 14 July, 11 Nov, 25 Dec. ≈5€ (Children no charge, and on 1st Sat of month.). ☎02 35 19 62 62. www.ville-lehavre.fr

The glass and metal building looks out to the sea through a monumental concrete sculpture known locally as Le Signal. The roof, designed to provide the best possible light to the galleries inside, consists of six sheets of glass covered by an aluminium sun blind.

The museum presents a fine **collection**★ of works by **Raoul Dufy** (1877-1953), who was born in Le Havre and **Eugène Boudin** (1824-98), a native of Honfleur.

Muséum d'Histoire naturelle

©Open daily except Tue 2.30–5.30pm, Wed, weekends and public holidays 10–11.30am, 2.30–5.30pm. ©Closed 1 Jan, 1 May, 14 July, 11 Nov, 25 Dec. ≈No charge. ☎02 35 41 37 28.

The Natural History Museum is housed in the old 18C law courts. One room displays works by the naturalist painter **Charles-Alexandre Lesueur** (1778-1846).

Ste-Adresse★★ Allow 1hr.

This a pleasant district extends from the edge of Le Havre towards the Hève Cape and consists of a seaside resort and the old town of Ste-Adresse.

Walking Tour★

Boulevard Albert-1er runs alongside the beach to place Clemenceau and the statue of Albert I, King of the Belgians from 1909 to 1934.

▶ Follow the signs for Pain de Sucre and Notre-Dame-des-Flots.

After a few bends in the road you arrive at the **Pain de Sucre**. A little higher up on the right the **Chapelle Notre-Dame-des-Flots** contains sailors' votive offerings.

▶ Turn left onto route du Cap.

The road passes in front of the École Nationale de la Marine Marchande (Merchant Navy College).

Cap de la Hève

Continue to the lighthouse. 🔝Allow 15min on foot there and back.

This rocky site overlooks the mouth of the Seine. Boulevard du Président-Félix-Faure, to the right and facing the ocean, offers an extensive **view**★.

▶ Return to place Clemenceau.

Harfleur

Église St-Martin

Access by rue Aristide-Briand and rue de Verdun following the direction of Rouen.
The 15C bell-tower (83m/272ft) of the Église St-Martin is famous in the Caux region.

Take rue des 104 and rue Gambetta, right, to the **bridge** over the Lézarde from which there is a good view.

Montivilliers

8km/5mi from the centre of town. Leave Le Havre on D 489.

An 11C lantern tower above the transept crossing and a Romanesque belfry surmounted by a spire (restored in the 19C) identify the **Église St-Sauveur**★.

Château de Filières

20km/12mi NE via N15; take D 31 left after St-Romain, then D 80 to the right. ☜Guided tours (30min) July–Aug daily 11am–6pm. May–June & Sept Wed, weekends and public holidays 2-6pm. ≈5€ (Children 3€). ☎02 35 20 53 30.

The château stands in a fine park. The building, built in white Caen stone after designs by Victor Louis, is in two parts: a late-16C wing (left) and a plain 18C central pavilion with a Classical façade. In the park, west of the château, are seven rows of magnificent beech trees, known as the **Cathedral**★ because their branches meet overhead to form a living vault.

Address Book

For coin ranges, see the Legend on the cover flap

WHERE TO STAY

Richelieu – *132 r. de Paris.* ☎*02 35 42 38 71. hotel.lerichelieu@wanadoo.fr 19 rooms.* 🖵*.* Located on a celebrated shopping street with many boutiques. Pleasant lobby in ocean colours. Restful, well-kept rooms.

Hôtel Terminus – *23 cours de la République.* ☎*02 35 41 72 07. www.grand-hotel-terminus.fr. Closed 22 Dec–1 Jan. 44 rooms.* 🖵*.* Just opposite the train station, this hotel has excellent sound-proofing. Ask for one of the renovated rooms, which have bright colours and modern furniture. Buffet breakfast.

Hôtel Marly – *121 r. de Paris.* ☎*02 35 41 72 48. www.hotellemarly.com. 37 rooms.* 🖵*.* Located along the boulevard leading to the harbour, this somewhat austere-looking hotel is quite practical. The rooms are suitably large, well equipped and functional. A good address for both business and tourism.

WHERE TO EAT

Le Wilson – *98 r. Prés-Wilson.* ☎*02 35 41 18 26. Closed 3–20 July, Sunday evening Tue evening and Wed.* A bistrot atmosphere and lively activity characterize this little restaurant on a small square in a commercial district. In fine weather, sit on the terrace. Traditional cuisine.

Le Bistrot du Chef...en gare – *28 cours de la République, SNCF train station.* ☎*02 35 26 54 33. mediarestaurant@wanadoo.fr. Closed Aug, Sat lunch, Mon evening and Sun.* This attractive rétro-style dining room is right at the train station. Daily specials based on fresh produce.

La Petite Auberge – *32 r. Ste-Adresse.* ☎*02 35 46 27 32. Closed 20 Feb–1 Mar, 124 Aug, Sat lunch, Sun evening and Mon.* Not far from Ste-Adresse, this small restaurant with its dapper façade offers a menu based on regional recipes and fresh market produce.

ON THE TOWN

Les Trois Pics – *Sente Alphonse-Karr. 76310 Ste-Adresse.* ☎*02 35 48 20 60. landure.alain@club-internet.fr. Tue–Sat noon 10am–1am.* Whether you sit on the terrace overlooking the sea in summer or behind the large picture windows in winter, you can enjoy fish and seafood or choose something from the café-tearoom while admiring the exceptional panoramic view of the bay.

LEISURE

Sea tour: "Ville du Havre" – On the *Ville du Havre,* a sailboat fitted out for passenger tours, discover the maritime side of the city. The skipper is also a reliable tour guide. Ticket office and information at the tourist office ☎*02 32 74 04 04.*

Rental of kayaks and wind-surfers – *Place du Havre.* ☎*02 35 41 49 76. 1–7pm.*

Aéro-club du Havre - Jean-Maridor – *R. Louis-Blériot, Le Havre-Octeville Airport.* ☎*02 35 48 35 91. aeroclub@ club-internet.fr. Daily except Sun 2–7pm, Sat 10am–noon, 2-6pm.* First flights and beginners' flights lasting 30min! Short, but intense... On board a 2 or 4 seat aircraft, you'll fly along the coast to Étretat, then return via the countryside and the Normandy Bridge before going round Le Havre over the estuary.

SHOPPING

Les Gobelines – *R. du Prés.-Wilson. Mon, Wed, Fri 7.30am–1.30pm.* This market is not very large, but it has the advantage of a central location, on a wide street neara the town hall. Locals come here to buy fresh fruit and vegetables, meat and fish.

Les Halles Centrales – *Daily except Sun and public holidays.* This major market place is spread out, so stalls have plenty of room. Many of the most prestigious of the town's shopkeepers have stalls here, including some 30 that sell food.

Calendar

The Office of Tourism publishes a monthly newspaper, *Agenda*, that gives a schedule of events as well as arrivals of all the big cruise ships.

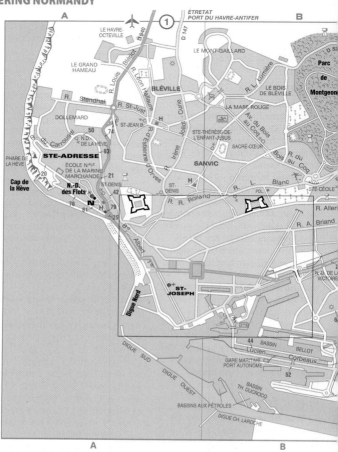

HARFLEUR

104 R. des	D	98
Doumer R. Paul	D	30
Foch Av. Mar.	D	
Verdun Av. de	D	90

LE HAVRE

Abbaye R. de l'	C	2
Albert-1er Bd	EY,A	
Allende R.	B	
Alma R. de l'	EY	3
Amériques Quai des	C	
Anatole-France R.	GY	
Anfray R.	GZ	5
Aplemont Av. d'	C	7
Archinard Av. Gén.	GZ	9
Asie Quai de l'	C	
Atlantique Quai de l'	C	
Aviateur-Guérin R.	HZ	
Bellanger R. F.	EY	
Bellot R.	HZ	
Bernardin-de-St-Pierre R.	FZ	13
Bert Av. Paul	C	
Blanc R. L.	B	
Blériot R. Louis	A	
Bois-du-Coq Av. du	B	
Bois-du-Coq R. du	B	
Bougainville Quai	D	

Bougainville R.	HY	
La Bourdonnais R.	EY	54
Braque R. G.	EFY	
Bretagne R. de	FGZ	14
Briand R. A.	HY,B	
Brindeau R. L.	EFZ	15
Cavée Verte R. de la	FY	
Chevalier-de-la-Barre Cours	HZ	18
Churchill Bd W.	B,HZ	24
Clemenceau Bd	EZ	
Cochet R.	EY	
Colbert Quai	GHZ	
Colomb Av. C.	BC	
Corbeaux Av. L.	FGZ,B	
Coty Av. René	FGY	
Courbet R. Amiral	HZ	
Cronstadt R. de	GY	
Delaroche R. M.	FY	
Delavigne Quai C.	GZ	29
Delavigne R. C.	GHY	
Demidoff R.	HY	
Dr-de-Boissière R.	EFY	
Doumer R. Paul	EFZ	
Drapiers R. des	FZ	32
Durand Bd Jules	CD	
Estienne-d'Orves R. d'	A	
Étretat R. d'	EY	

Europe Quai de l'	C	
Eyriès R. J.-B	GY	
Faidherbe R. Gén.	GZ	36
Faure R. P.	FY	
Félix-Faure R.	EFGY	
Féré Quai Michel	FZ	37
Flaubert R. G.	FGY	
Foch Av.	EFY	
Fort R. du	EY	
Foubert R.	EY	
François-1er Bd	EFZ	
François le Chevalier Passerelle	GZ	39
Frissard Quai	HZ	
Gallieni R. Mar.	GY	
Gaulle Av. Gén.-de	C	
Gaulle Pl. du Gén.-de	FZ	41
Gaulle R. Gén.-de	EY	
Genestal R. H.	FY	43
George-V Quai	FGZ	
Gobelins R. des	EFY	
Guillemard R.	EY	
Hallaure R. Léon	A	
Hélène R.	HY	
Hermann-du-Pasquier Quai	B	44
Honegger R. A.	FZ	46
Hôtel-de-Ville Pl. de l'	FYZ	47
Huet R. A.-A.	FY	49

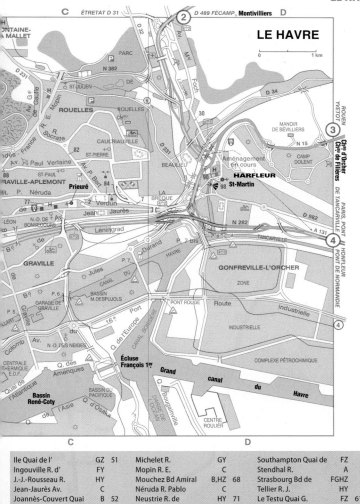

LE HAVRE

Ile Quai de l'	GZ	51	Michelet R.	GY		Southampton Quai de	FZ	
Ingouville R. d'	FY		Mopin R. E.	C		Stendhal R.	A	
J.-J.-Rousseau R.	HY		Mouchez Bd Amiral	B,HZ	68	Strasbourg Bd de	FGHZ	
Jean-Jaurès Av.	C		Néruda R. Pablo	C		Tellier R. J.	HY	
Joannès-Couvert Quai	B	52	Neustrie R. de	HY	71	Le Testu Quai G.	FZ	61
Joffre R. Maréchal	GHY		Notre-Dame Quai	FZ	72	Tourneville R. de	GHY	
Joliot-Curie R. Irène	A		Octeville Rte d'	A	74	Val-aux-Corneilles Av.	C	88
Kennedy Chée J.	EFZ	53	Osaka Quai d'	C		Verdun R. de	C	
Lafaurie R. G.	FGY		Paris R. de.	FZ		Verlaine R. Paul	C	
Laffitte R. Ch.	HZ		Pasteur R.	HY	75	Victor-Hugo R.	FZ	91
Lamblardie Quai	FGZ	57	Péri R. Gabriel	GY		Videcoq Quai	FZ	92
Lang R. Ed	FZ		Perret Pl. Auguste	FZ	76	Voltaire R.	EFZ	94
Lebon R. Ph.	HY		Picasso Av. Pablo	C	77	Wilson R. Président	EY	96
Lecesne R. Jules	FGHZ		Pompidou Chée G.	GZ	78	16e-Port Av. du	C	
Leclerc Av. Gén.	FY	58	Renan R. Ernest	GY		24e-Territorial Chée du	GZ	97
Lemaître R. F.	EZ	60	République Cours de la	HY		329e R. du	GHY	
Leningrad Bd de	C		Richelieu R. de	EFZ				
Lesueur R.	GHY		Risson R. F.	GY	80	**SAINTE-ADRESSE**		
Louer R. J.	FY	63	Rolland R. R.	AB				
Lumière R. L.	B		Rouelles R. de	C	82	Cap Rte du	A	20
Mac-Orlan R.	HY		St-Just R.	A		Carroussel R. du	A	
Mailleraye R. de la	EZ		St-Roch Square	EY		Cavell R. E.	A	21
Marceau R.	HZ		Ste-Adresse R. de	EY		Clemenceau Pl.	A	25
Marical R. Clément	EY		Sakharov R. Andrei	C	84	Gaulle R. Gén.-de	A	42
Marine Quai de la	FGZ		Saône Quai de la	HZ		Ignauval R. d'	A	50
Massillon R.	HY	65	Sarrail R. Gén.	GY		Prés.-F.-Faure Bd	A	78
Maupassant R. G.-de	EY	67	Séry R.	EZ		Reine-Élisabeth R.	A	79
Mendès-France R. P.	BC		Socrate R	.C		Roi-Albert R. du	A	81
						Vitanal R. de	A	93

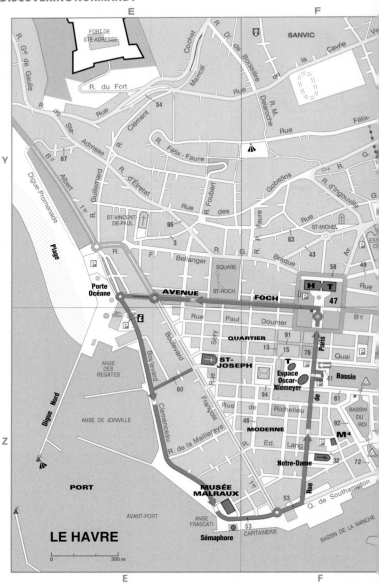

LE HAVRE

LE HAVRE SIGHTS INDEX						
Street Names index is on the preceding page.	Digue Nord	EZ	Pain de Sucre	A	N
	Espace Oscar-Niemeyer	FZ	Plage	EY	
	Foret de Montgeon	B	Prieuré de Graville	C	
	Harfleur	D	Ste-Adresse	A	
	Hôtel de ville	FY H	Sémaphore	EZ	
Bassin du Commerce	FGZ	La " Porte océane"	EY	Église St-Joseph	EZ	
Cap de la Hève	A	Le Quartier Moderne	EFZ	Église St-Martin	D	
Cathédrale Notre-Dame	FZ	Musée Malraux	EZ	Theatre	FY T	
Chapelle N.-D.-des-Flots	A	Muséum d'histoire naturelle	FZ M⁴			

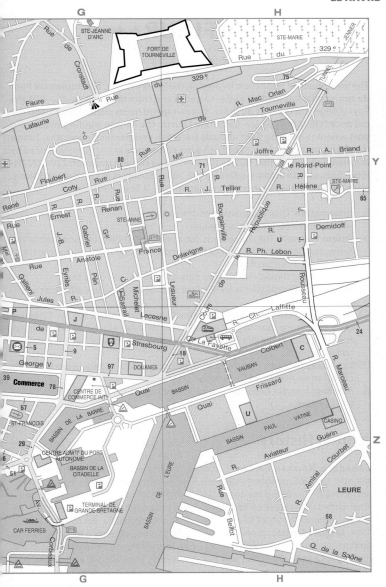

HONFLEUR★★

CALVADOS, POPULATION 8 178
MICHELIN MAP 303: N-3

The lovely town of Honfleur is located on the Seine estuary. The impressive Pont de Normandie has made it easier to get to and from the town, and to visit the Pays d'Auge and the Côte de Grâce. You can spend hours wandering around the old dock (Vieux Bassin), Ste-Catherine Church, the narrow winding streets and port where the fishing fleet unloads fresh fish and shellfish every day. Today, Honfleur can rightly claim to be both a river port and a seaport, as evidenced by the many large liners that choose the welcoming city as a stopover: 220m/722ft-long ships, able to accommodate up to 1 200 passengers in optimal conditions, glide along the quays, where the waters are 7.5-9.5m/24-31ft deep.

- **Information:** Quai Lepaulmier,14602 Honfleur.
  ☎02 31 89 23 30. www.ot-honfleur.fr.
- ▶ **Orient Yourself:** The city spreads out along the left bank of the mouth of the Seine, 3km/2mi from the Pont de Normandie. It is 25km/15.6 mi from Le Havre and 91 km/57mi from Rouen.
- 🅿 When touring the old city, you can park your car on quai de la Tour.
- **Don't Miss:** The old streets on Honfleur and the wooden Ste-Catherine church, built by shipwrights.
- 🕐 **Organizing Your Time:** Photo bugs should station themselves on Ste-Catherine quay early in the morning to capture the remarkable elongated reflections of the old houses in the still water. In the evening, sunset lights up the *greniers à sel* just opposite.
- **Especially for Kids:** Visit the tropical gardens of Naturospace to see hundreds of butterflies floating in an immense greenhouse.
- ⓒ **Also See:** Trouville, Deauville, Houlgate, Cabourg, the Pays d'Auge, Pont-l'Évêque and Le Havre.

A Bit of History

Canada, a Norman Colony – Ever since the early 16C, navigators had been anchoring briefly along the coast of a land named Gallia Nova by Verrazano, the discoverer of the site of New York. in 1534, **Jacques Cartier** stepped ashore and claimed the territory for France, naming it Canada. François I was less than impressed with the explorer on his return as he brought back no spices, gold, or diamonds. Canada was thus left unexplored until the 17C when the experienced navigator **Samuel de Champlain** received orders to colonise this vast territory. He set sail from Honfleur, and in 1608 founded Quebec.

On Colbert's advice Louis XIV took an interest in Canada and the country rapidly became a Norman and Percheron colony settled by over 4 000 peasants who made their living by agriculture, fishing, hunting and fur trading.

The Iroquois Indians bitterly opposed the French colonists who by 1665 had to appeal to France for aid against mounting attacks. A thousand soldiers arrived; simultaneously a decree was issued compelling each man to marry, within a fortnight upon her arrival, one of the women, known as the king's daughters *(filles du roy)*, who were sent out from France to help increase the sparse population. The queen took an interest in the selection of the young women who were to be "not ugly... not repulsive... healthy and strong enough for working on the land."

From Canada, **Cavalier de La Salle** journeyed south to explore and colonise Louisiana in 1682. He established the communication route along the Ohio Valley which was to lead to war with the

Address Book

For coin ranges, see the Legend on the cover flap.

GUIDED TOUR

Honfleur's tourist office offers tours (1hr30) led by highly qualified guides trained by the Ministry of Culture. This is the only way to see certain places, such as the famous *greniers à sel* (salt stores). Contact the tourist office or www.vpah.culture.fr. 5 €. In English 6 € (Under 12 years no charge).

WHERE TO STAY

Chambre d'hôte Le Vieux Pressoir – *Hameau le Clos-Potier, 27210 Conteville, 13.5/8.5mi from Honfleur via D 580, rte de Pont-Audemer then left on D 312.* ☎02 35 57 60 79. www.la-ferme-du-pressoir.com. 7 rooms.; Evening meal. Set in the countryside, this 18C half-timbered farm will delight those who appreciate calm and simplicity. Every room contains 19C and 20C objects and furniture found in second-hand shops. Flower garden, duck pond and 300-year-old cider press add to the charm.

Camping La Briquerie – ☎02 31 89 28 32. www.campinglabriquerie.com. Open Apr–Sept. 430 sites. ;. Reservations advised. Restaurant on site. Set on the edge of a forest, this campground has sites separated by hedges of shrubs or flowers. Some small but well-kept self-catered cottages. Large swimming pool, game-room and miniature golf. Restaurant-bar with meals in season.

Hôtel Otelinn – *62 cours A.-Manuel.* ☎02 31 89 41 77. www.otelinn-honfleur.com. 50 rooms. 🅿🛏. Restaurant. At a distance from the city centre, this hotel has the considerable advantage of proposing rooms at reasonable prices. Small and functional, they make for an agreeable halt. A garden and a terrace give you the opportunity of basking in the gentle Norman sun.

La Cour Ste-Catherine Bed and Breakfast – *74 r. du Puits.* ☎02 31 89 42 40. wwwgiaglis.com. 6 rooms. Closed Jan. 9 rooms. Housed in a 17C convent, this pleasant inn offers 5 elegant guestrooms, opening onto a flower garden. In the lounge, pretty furniture from second-hand shops around the fireplace. Breakfasts served in the old cider-press. Charming welcome from the owners.

Le Clos Deauville Saint-Gatien – *4 chemin des Brioleurs, 14130 St-Gatien-des-Bois, 9km/5.4mi S of Honfleur via D 579.* ☎02 31 65 16 08. www.clos-St-Gatien.fr. 58 rooms. 🅿🛏. The charm of the Norman countryside a few short miles from the shore characterises this half-timbered house nestled in a verdant setting. Comfortable, cosy rooms. Three pools, one covered, a sauna and a fitness room.

WHERE TO EAT

Bacaretto – *44 r. de la Chaussée.* ☎02 31 14 83 11. Closed Wed evening. This little 2-storey wine bar offers more than 120 bottles to sample, accompanied by a plate of delicious snacks and a piece of "organic" bread.

Ex-Voto – *8 pl. Albert-Sorel.* ☎02 31 89 19 69. Closed 1 Nov, 25 Dec and Wed. Reservations advised. One of the few inexpensive yet good value restaurants in town, this place will make you nostalgic for the neighborhood bistro. The proprietress concocts special dishes and short orders from fresh market produce. Very few tables, best reserve.

Le Bistrot des Artistes – *14 pl. Berthelot.* ☎02 31 89 95 90. Closed Jan, Tue from Oct to Apr and Wed except in July–Sept. Antiques, paintings of the sea, photos of Honfleur and leatherette wall seats make up the decor of this restaurant with a Parisian bistro flair. Tables near the window have a lovely view of the Vieux Bassin. On the menu: salads and slices of bread with various toppings.

La Grenouille – *16 Quai Quarantaine.* ☎02 31 89 04 24. www.absinthe.fr. Closed 12 Nov–15 Dec. The main room of this establishment in a 17C house has an especially pleasant décor: red walls, chairs and banquettes in bistro style, a collection of frogs and toads, and old Michelin Guides. Typical bistro cuisine, seafood and, of course, frogs' legs!

ご乃器 **Au Vieux Honfleur** – *13 quai St-Étienne* - ☎*02 31 89 15 31*. This restaurant by the old harbour extends its terrace along the quay when the weather is fine. Al fresco or inside, nice and warm among bibelots, posters and paintings, you'll be able to savour Norman dishes and seafood while gazing upon the splendid port.

SHOPPING

Markets – Pl. Ste-Catherine. Antique market 2nd Sun of each month. Weekly market Sat. Organic produce market Wed. Flower market Sat morning Pl. Arthur-Boudin.

Griboulle – *16 r. de l'Homme-de-Bois.* b*02 31 89 29 54*. Open *9,30am–1pm, 4_6.30pm*. Closed *25 Dec*. M. Griffoul, nick-named Gribouille, is an unforgettable local character. The products in his boutique are special too: Norman shortbread, milk jam, potted rabbit, preserved pork, cider products etc. Sample the pommeau or Calvados.

La Cave Normande – *13 r. de la Ville and 12 quai Ste-Catherine.* ☎*02 31 89 38 27 and 02 31 89 4928*. Open summer season *9am–10pm*. Winter *10am–12.30pm, 4.30–7pm*. Closed *Jan and Tue in winter*. This is where you'll find top-quality Calvados as well as cider, perry and pommeau.

SPORT

Centre équestre du Ramier – *Chemin du Ramier, 14600 Équemauville, S of Honfleur, towards Équemauville, follow signs.* ☎*02 31 89 49 97. Reception: Wed, weekends and public holidays 9am–5pm, other days by appointment.* Located in the heart of the (authentic!) Norman countryside, this pretty riding centre has 15 training horses available. Rides last for 1hr-1hr 30min.

TAKE A BREAK

La Petite Chine – *14–16 r. du Dauphin.* ☎*02 31 89 15 31. Open daily except Mon 11am–7pm, weekends 10am–7pm. Closed 2 weeks in Jan and 2 weeks in June.* This lovely tea shop, decorated in blue and yellow, looks on the port. It has wonderful desserts such as caramelized orange tarte, meringue with whipped cream, gingerbread or caramels. Chocolate and jams as well.

ON THE TOWN

Evenings in Honfleur, the Old Port comes alive. Restaurants, brasseries and bars are clustered on the quais Ste-Catherine, La Quarantaine and St-Etienne. Terraces remain open until 2am in summer.

British and finally the loss by the French of Canada in 1760.

Honfleur, an Artist's Paradise –

The character and atmosphere of Honfleur has inspired painters, writers and musicians.

Musset came to stay in St-Gatien In the period when the Normandy coast was fashionable with the Romantics. Honfleur began to fill with painters – not only those who were Norman-born such as Boudin, Hamelin and Lebourg, but also Paul Huet, Daubigny, Corot and others from Paris and foreigners such as Bonington and Jongkind.

It was in the small St-Siméon Inn- "chez La Mère Toutain" -that the Impressionists first met. Ever since artists have continued to visit Honfleur.

Baudelaire, who stayed in the town with his mother in her old age, declared, "set-tling in Honfleur has always been the dearest of my dreams" and while there wrote his *Invitation au Voyage*.

Other Honfleur citizens include the composer Erik Satie (1866-1925), the poet and novelist Henri de Régnier (1864-1936), the author Lucie Delarue-Mardrus, the economist Frédéric Le Play and the historian Albert Sorel.

Old Town Walking Tour★★

Allow 1hr 30min.

▶ *Leave from place Arthur-Boudin to the east of the old dock.*

Place Arthur-Boudin

Old slate-shingled houses stand around the square; no 6 is a Louis XIII house with

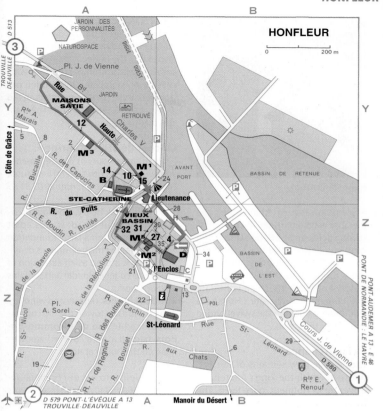

HONFLEUR

0   200 m

HONFLEUR

Albert-1er R.	AY	2
Berthelot Pl. P.	AZ	3
Boudin Pl. A.	BZ	4
Cachin R.	AZ	
Charrière-de-Grâce R.	AY	5
Charrière-St-Léonard R.	BZ	6
Dauphin R. du	AZ	7
Delarue-Mardrus R. L.	AY	8

Fossés Cours des	AZ	9
Hamelin Pl.	AY	10
Homme-de-Bois R.	AY	12
Lingots R. des	AY	14
Logettes R. des	AY	15
Manuel Cours A.	AZ	19
Montpensier R.	AZ	21
Notre-Dame R.	AZ	22
Passagers Quai des	ABY	24
Le-Paulmier Quai	BZ	13

Porte-de-Rouen Pl. de la	AZ	25
Prison R. de la	AZ	27
Quarantaine Quai de la	BZ	28
République R. de la	AZ	
Revel R. J.	BZ	29
St-Antoine R.	BZ	30
St-Étienne Quai	AZ	31
Ste-Catherine Quai	AZ	32
Tour Quai de la	BZ	34
Ville R. de la	BZ	35

Clocher de Ste-Catherine	AY	B	Musée Eugène-Boudin	AY .M³
Greniers à sel	BZ	D	Musée d'Ethnographie	
			et d'Art populaire	AZ M²
			Musée de la Marine	AZ M⁵

stone and flint chequered decoration. The Saturday-morning flower market brings colour and life to the area.

Greniers à sel

Open during temporary exhibits or as part of the city's guided tour. Tourist office ☎02 31 89 23 30.
Rue de la Ville. These tile-covered stone buildings were constructed in the 17C in order to store the salt required by the cod fishing fleet.

Rue de la Prison

Very picturesque with its line of old timber-framed houses. At the end of the street, on the right, is the former church of St-Étienne, its bell-tower rising up above the old port. The building now houses the **Musée de la Marine** (Naval Museum).

Vieux Bassin★★

The quaysides of the old dock – designed by Duquesne on the orders of Colbert

G. Targat/MICHELIN

Église Ste-Catherine

– are picturesque, enhanced by the pleasure boats alongside. The contrast is striking between **St-Étienne Quay,** with its splendid two-storey stone dwellings, and **Ste-Catherine Quay,** where the tall – rising up to seven storeys high – slender houses are faced with slate and timber. The Governor's House (La Lieutenance), next to the swivel bridge completes the scene.

La Lieutenance

Only a relic now remains of the 16C house in which the king's lieutenant, Governor of Honfleur, once lived. The façade facing the square now incorporates, between two bartizans, Caen Gate, one of the two main entrances to the city in the Middle Ages. From the corner of the passenger quay you get a good view of the house, the old dock and, on the other side, the outer harbour.

Rue de Logettes, a reference to the numerous wooden stalls that once lined the street, leads to place **Ste-Catherine,** in the heart of the neighbourhood of the same name. In addition to the pretty street and half-timbered houses, the neighbourhood is famous for its unique church and bell-tower.

Église Ste-Catherine★★

This church is a rare example in Western Europe of a building constructed, apart from the foundations, entirely of wood. After the Hundred Years War all masons and architects were employed on the inevitable post-war reconstruction, but the Honfleur axe masters from

the local shipyards determined to thank God immediately for the departure of the English and built a church with their own skills. The interior has twin naves and side aisles, the timber roof over each nave being supported by wooden pillars. The carved panels ornamenting the gallery are 16C, the organ 18C. There are also many wooden statues.

Clocher de Ste-Catherine★

🕐*Open same hours as Musée Eugène-Boudin.* ✍*2€ (With ticket from Musée Eugène-Boudin, no charge).* ☎*02 31 89 54 00.*

The massive oak belfry, a building covered in chestnut wood, stands apart from the church on a large foundation which contained the bell-ringer's dwelling. Today it is used as an extension of the Musée Eugène-Boudin and contains religious works.

Rue des Lingots, narrow and winding, goes around the tower; the old cobblestones lead to **rue de l'Homme-de-Bois,** named after a covered wooden head on the house at no 23.

▶ *Turn left onto rue de l'Homme-de-Bois; 400m/440yd further on, across from the Hôtel-Dieu Chapel, take rue du Trou-Miard to the right, then turn right again onto rue Haute.*

The hospital's old lighthouse, on place Jean-de-Vienne, is now mostly used by seagulls. **Rue Haute,** formerly a pathway outside the fortifications, was home to many local shipbuilders. The composer Erik Satie was born at no 88, where the timbers are painted red; inside there is an unusual museum. Continue onto **place Hamelin,** birthplace of Alphonse Allais (no 6), a French humorist of the late 19C.

▶ *End your tour of Honfleur by walking straight on (quai de la Lieutenance and quai de la Quarantaine) to return to place Arthur-Boudin on the right. Or turn and go through the public garden, walking as far as the Seine along the digue de l'Ouest, where a pleasant pedestrian path has been created on the jetty.*

Sights

Musée Eugène-Boudin

Place Érik Satie ⓒOpen mid-Mar–Sept daily except Tue 10am–noon, 2–6pm. Rest of the year daily except Tue 2.30–5pm, weekends and public holidays 10am–noon, 2.30–5pm. ⓒClosed Jan to mid-Feb, 1 May, 14 July, 25 Dec. ☜5.20€ (Under 10 years no charge). ☎02 31 89 54 00.

An old Augustinian chapel and a more recent building house this museum, which is chiefly devoted to the painters of Honfleur and of the estuary.

On the first floor is a rich collection of household items from 18C 1n3 19C Normandy. The second and third floors display works by 20C artists who, for the most part, worked in the region: Dufy, Marquet, Friesz, Villon, Lagar, Grau-Sala, Saint-Delis, Gernez, Driès, Herbo, Vallotton, Bigot etc.

Galleries adjoining the chapel feature 19C paintings by Eugène Boudin (the museum possesses 89 of his paintings and drawings) and by Monet, Jongkind, Dubourg, Isabey, Pécrus, Courbet, Cals. A second holds the Hambourg-Rachet bequest of some 300 canvases (19C-20C) by Derain, Foujita, Garbell, Marie Laurencin, Van Dongen and Hambourg. The third is a drawings room in which about 100 works are rotated each year.

Musée du Vieux Honfleur

The museum presents three sections – one on the navy, one on popular art and finally the Manoir du Désert (&see Aditional Sights).

Musée de la Marine

&ⓒ*Open same hours and conditions as for the Musée d'Ethnographie et d'Art populaire.* The museum, which is housed in St Stephen's Church (deconsecrated), traces the history of the port of Honfleur and contains a large number of scale models and topographical information on the town.

Musée d'Ethnographie et d'Art populaire

ⓒ *Open Apr–Sept daily except Mon 10am–noon, 2–6.30pm. Mid-Fev–Mar & Oct–mid-Nov daily except Mon 2.30–5.30pm, weekends 10am–noon, 2.30–5.30pm. ⓒClosed 1 May, 14 July. ☜3.10€ or 4.30€ for a combined ticket with the Musée de la Marine. ☎02 31 89 14 12. www.musees-basse-normandie.fr.*

Ten Normandy interiors have been reconstructed in this museum located in 16C residences. Note particularly the timbered manor house, the bourgeois dining room, the weaver's and printer's workshop, the bedroom and a shop on the ground floor.

Maison Satie★

Entrance at 67 blvd Charles-V (running parallel to the rue Haute). ☛Audioguided tour 1hr. ⓒOpen May–Sept daily except Tue 10am–7pm. Oct–Dec & mid-Feb – Apr daily except Tue 11am–6pm. ⓒ Closed Jan–mid-Feb and 25 Dec. ☜5.20€. ☎02 31 89 11 11.

Wearing headphones, you are guided through a series of stage-like settings recalling the career of Erik Satie (1866-1925) – "born young in an old world". The museum offers the opportunity to hear the music and understand more about the life of the man who came out with such conversational pearls as: "Give me a minute to get my skirt on, and I'll be right with you!"; "Although our information is false, we cannot guarantee it."; "What do you prefer, music or cold-cuts?"; "The piano is like money, it's only agreeable when you've got your hands on it."

Église St-Léonard

S of the Vieux-Bassin, take the rue de la République, then left into the rue Cachin, which leads to the place St-Léonard.

Pont de Normandie

The façade of this church is a bizarre combination of an ornate Flamboyant doorway and a 17C belfry tower.

Inside are two immense shells which have been converted into fonts. At the entrance to the chancel stand statues of Our Lady of Victory and St Leonard with two prisoners kneeling; note in the chancel the wooden statues of St Peter, St Paul and the four Evangelists. The narthex is furnished with an 18C copper lectern from Villedieu-les-Poêles.

Naturospace★

Opposite the hospital lighthouse, Bd Charles V. ⚬ Kids ⏲Open Apr–Sept 10am– 1pm, 2–7pm. Feb–Mar & Oct–10am–1pm, 2–5.30pm (Last entry 1hr before closing). ⏲Closed Dec–Jan. 7.40 € (Children 5.80€). ☎02 31 81 77 00.

Inside an enormous greenhouse, 60 species of butterflies from 6 continents float gracefully in perfect freedom. Surrounded by the whispering of their wings, you stroll among tropical plants and observe cocoons from which, early in the morning, a few caterpillars emerge. Good explanations and special exhibits.

Additional Sights

Pont de Normandie

3km/2mi E via the D 580. There is a 5€ toll for cars, but no charge for pedestrians, cyclists and motorcyclists. ⚬ *But watch out—the wind can be ferocious!*

The bridge was started in 1988 and officially opened in January 1995; it is the third largest bridge to span the Lower Seine after the Pont de Tancarville and the Pont de Brotonne.

Its impact on the economy is three-fold: it brings Le Havre and Honfleur closer together by removing the detour via Tancarville Bridge (24km/15mi instead of 60km/37mi); it is one of the major motorway links between the Channel Tunnel and the west and south-west of France; it represents one of the many connections in the so-called **Estuaries Route**, which ties up the north and south of Europe without going through Paris.

The Pont de Normandie, a truly remarkable work of art and a technological feat, was seen as a milestone in the history of civil engineering, since it established the record of the longest cable-stayed bridge (more elegant and cheaper to build than a suspension bridge). Although Lisbon's Vasco de Gama Bridge (1998) is now the longest in Europe, the Pont de Normandie is higher. This steel and concrete mass, which seems to defy the laws of gravity, is surprisingly light and extremely stable. Careful attention was devoted to the subject of safety: the bridge is designed to withstand winds of up to 440kph/274mph; it can resist shocks caused by the largest cargo boats, which could only collide with the north tower, protected by 9m/30ft of concrete; the road surfacing has in-built sensors triggered off by the presence of black ice; tollbooth operators can monitor traffic continually thanks to surveillance cameras.

Besides the standard lighting for road traffic, the Breton architect **Yann Kersalé** conceived a sophisticated lighting system called *Rhapsody in Blue and White* – a bi-coloured display of static lights outline the two towers (blue on the underside, white on the outside), whereas a row of blue twinkling lights run underneath the deck.

Côte de Grâce★★

The peaceful beauty of this famous hillside, appreciated by all Honfleur enthusiasts, is also appealing to passing tourists.

Calvaire★★

Telescope. From the cross there is a good **panorama** of the Seine estuary, the Le Havre roadstead, to the right, the Pont de Normandie and, in the distance, Tancarville Bridge.

Chapelle Notre-Dame-de-Grâce

In the centre of the esplanade beneath tall trees stands the small chapel of Our Lady of Grace and within it the statue after which it is named. This graceful 17C building has replaced a sanctuary said to have been founded by Richard II, 4th Duke of Normandy. It was here that navigators and explorers came to pray before leaving on journeys of discovery or colonisation to the North American continent; a borough of Montréal bears this name. The north transept chapel is dedicated to all Canadians of Norman origin. There are numerous small, ex-voto vessels.

Mont-Joli viewpoint

The view complements the one from Calvaire: in the foreground are the town, the port and the coast; to the east is the semicircle of hills. Tancarville Bridge can be seen in the distance.

Driving Tour

South Bank of the Seine – Honfleur to Rouen★★

130km/81mi – Allow about 5hr.
This charming drive takes you through forests and along roads overlooking the river below.

▶ *Leave Honfleur via cours Jean-de-Vienne and take D 312 towards Berneville and Pont-Audemer.*

The road follows the lower Risle Valley. Beyond Berville, there are many fine views of the estuary. In the spring, the blooming apple orchards turn the landscape into a wonderland.

Pont-Audemer★
See PONT-AUDEMER.

▶ *Take D 810.*

Ste-Opportune-la-Mare
See QUILLEBEUF.

▶ *Take D 95.*

After a section on a crest road, between Val-Anger and Vieux-Port, the Seine Valley comes into view again.

Vieux-Port★
The thatched cottages are half hidden by their orchards.

Aizier
The stone bell-tower of the 12C church looks very old. Near the church there is a manhole slab – the remains of a covered way dating from around 2000 BC.

▶ *From Aizier to Quesney, D 95 and D 65 follow the edge of Brotonne Forest.*

Vatteville-la-Rue
The nave of the church dates from the Renaissance; it bears a black mourning band which was painted on the wall for the funeral of the lord of the manor. The Flamboyant chancel is lit by 16C stained-glass windows.

▶ *Turn left onto D 65 which leads to La Mailleraye (ferry).*

Running alongside the Seine to the right, the road offers views of typical Norman thatched cottages half hidden by trees. After Notre-Dame-de-Bliquetuit, you can see the two ferries which cross at Yainville and Jumièges. Road D 65 then rises in hairpin bends.

Viewpoint★
Picnic area. Viewing table. To the right can be seen the towers of Jumièges Abbey, particularly impressive at sunset, and to the left the Seine Valley.

▶ *300m/330yd farther on, stop on the right in the La Mailleraye lay-by.*

Chêne à la Cuve
100m/110yd from D 913, opposite the 11km post.
Four oak trunks growing from a single bole form a kind of natural vat, 7m/23ft in circumference.

▶ *Take D 313 towards Bourg-Achard and turn right on D 101.*

Moulin d'Hauville
Open July–Aug 2.30–6.30pm. Apr–June & 1st 2 weeks Sept Sun and public holidays 2.30–6.30pm. 2.50€ (Children 1.50€). 02 32 56 57 32.
This 13C windmill is one of the few surviving stone mills in Upper Normandy and once belonged to the monks of Jumièges Abbey. Its cap can be ori-

ented according to the direction of the wind and is supported by oak beams. The stone tower and large sails are most impressive. If weather allows, you can see the mill in operation.

▶ *Take D 101 in the other direction and turn left on D 712. Going down the hill, turn onto D 45 (nice views on the forest and the river), then take D 265 which crosses Mauny Forest, then D 64 towards La Bouille.*

Between La Ronce and La Bouille, the road goes along the river's edge.

La Bouille

La Bouille, which enjoys a handsome setting at the foot of the wooded slopes of the Roumois plateau, has always attracted artists, and over the years a great many writers, poets and painters have succumbed to the irresistible charm of its landscapes.

In the old days, people from Rouen would come here to sample local gastronomic delights: eels stewed in cider, La Bouille cheese and *douillons aux pommes* (apples hollowed out, filled with butter, wrapped in pastry and baked). Today the village still offers a charming combination of terraces, inns and avenues. The town has remained popular among painters, who set up their easels and draw sketches of the quaint streets and surrounding countryside.

On the quayside, a plaque on one of the houses reminds visitors that the author **Hector Malot** was born in the locality.

Moulineaux

Church – ⊙*Make appointment at the mairie to visit.* ☎*02 35 18 02 45.*
The **church** with its slender spire dates from the 13C. Inside there is an attractive woodwork group formed by the pulpit and rood screen (one side of the latter is Gothic and the other Renaissance). In the apse is the 13C **stained-glass window**★ that was the gift of Blanche de Castille. Note the 16C tableau of the Flemish School depicting the Crucifixion and a monk in prayer. There is a far-reaching view of the Seine Valley from the cemetery.

▶ *Take D 3, a steep hill.*

Monument Qui Vive

At the crossroads of D 64 and D 67A.
There is a remarkable view (viewing table) of the Seine as it curves round to encircle Roumare Forest.
Road D 64 goes down to the Seine so that one gets a view of the river bend commanded by Robert the Devil's castle and the Rouen industrial suburbs.

Château de Robert le Diable★

⤶*See ELBEUF: Excursions.*

▶ *Go back to D 64 up a steep climb. Take D 64 right through Londe Forest. At the crossroads known as Le Nouveau Monde, follow D 938 to Orival, to the S.*

Orival★

From Oissel to Orival the road is overhung by curious rocks which are part of the chalk escarpment. They dominate the peaceful riverine landscape. Orival Church is an unusual semi-troglodytic 15C building.

▶ *Return to Le Nouveau Monde.*

Roches d'Orival★

⚠*Park on D 18 by the sign Sentier des Roches; 1hr on foot there and back* ☺*by a steep path which is slippery when wet. At the top turn right onto a path which passes in front of some caves hollowed out of the rocks.*
The path follows the cliff. By a grassy knoll (300m/330yd) there is a **view** of the Seine and of the rock escarpment, broken by a grassy corniche on which the path continues.

▶ *Follow D 18 along the Seine.*

Oissel

Pleasant public garden.

▶ *To return to Rouen, take D 13, then N 138 to the right.*

The pine forest of Rouvray is an oasis of calm, reminiscent of the Landes of south-west France.

VILLE ROMAINE DE JUBLAINS★

MAYENNE, POPULATION 711, MICHELIN MAP 310: G-5 – 14KM/9MI NW OF EVRON

This archaeological site offers a valuable insight into urban life under the Romans. The baths, the ruins of a Roman fort, the temple and the theatre are the best Gallo-Roman period remains in the region.

- **Information:** ☎02 43 04 3033. www.jublains.fr.
- ▶ **Orient Yourself:** The remains of the Roman city are 10km/6.25mi southeast of Mayenne and 14km/9mi northwest of Évron.
- **Don't Miss:** The remarkably preserved theatre.
- **Organizing Your Time:** If you are near Jublains in late July or early August, try to attend a musical performance organized by Les Nuits de la Mayenne (*www. nuitsdelamayenne.com*).
- **Especially for Kids:** The museum has a booklet to help guide them around.
- **Also See:** Mayenne, Évron, Ste-Suzanne and Laval.

A Bit of History

Following the conquest of Gaul by Julius Caesar (50BC), the Romans divided the country into districts and built towns; the town of Noviodunum (Jublains) was built at an ancient crossroads as an important link in the road network of the Roman Empire. Its main role as a sanctuary is shown by the alignment of the public buildings along the axis of the temple.

Sights

Musée départemental d'Archéologie

Situated at the entry to the fortress. &Open May–Sept 9am–6pm. Oct–Apr daily except Mon 9.30am–12.30pm, 1.30–5.30pm. Closed 1 Jan, 31 Dec. 3.50€ (Children and on 1st Sun of month no charge). ☎02 43 04 30 16.

This museum uses modern techniques to present archaeological themes of the Mayenne region, in particular the palaeolithic site at Saulges with its decorated cave, the Gaulish and Gallo-Roman sanctuaries and the development of the Roman town of Jublains. A large model gives a good idea of what Jublains looked like in ancient times.

Forteresse gallo-romaine

The fortress consists of three concentric parts. The central building, the oldest part of the fortress dating from the early 3C, is a massive rectangular storehouse with four angle towers. During the crisis which shook the Roman Empire at the end of the 3C (invasions, military anarchy, peasant rebellions...), the storehouse was surrounded by a rampart of raised earth and a moat. This moat was later filled in and fortified walls were erected around AD 290, just before the whole site was abandoned.

Public baths

Below the church; entrance through the Syndicat d'Initiative. &Entry permitted during museum opening times.

The building, which dates from the late 1C, was altered in the 3C and transformed into a Christian church at the end of the Gallo-Roman period. The west side, facing the church, was occupied by the furnace which supplied hot air to the hypocausts (a system of

Gallo-Roman stag

Conseil Général de la Mayenne

underfloor heating) in the warm and hot rooms.

The layout of the baths is shown on a plan; one can see the main rooms: the cold bath (*frigidarium*) paved in blue schist, the warm room (*tepidarium*), the sweating room (*laconicum*). The hot bath (*cella soliaris*) is situated beyond the excavated part.

Theatre

The theatre was offered to the town by a rich Gaul, Orgetorix (c 81-83).

Temple

The temple can be visited freely; brochures are distributed at the museum or at the Syndicat d'Initiative. The temple is situated at the other end of the Roman town, 800m/0.5mi from the theatre. Its proportions were vast (each side being about 80m/262ft long) and limestone was brought from the Loire region.

ABBAYE DE JUMIÈGES★★★

MICHELIN MAP 304: E-5

Jumièges is one of the most impressive ruins in France, occupying a splendid site on the Lower Seine. The history, galleries, south aisle, the nave roof, the transept crossing, the chancel apse and the roofless cloisters are described below.

- 🛈 **Information:** 10 Bd des Belges, 14510 Houlgate.
  ☎02 31 24 34 79. www.ville-houlgate.fr
- ▶ **Orient Yourself:** Jumièges is located on a graceful meander of the Seine, between the villages of Duclair and Trait, 28km/17.5mi west of Rouen.
- 🔎 **Don't Miss:** Not far from Jumièges, in Mesnils sous Jumièges *(5km/3mi SE via the D 65),* sits the 13C manor where the lovely and astute Agnès Sorel, mistress of Charles VII, died in 1450.
- 🕐 **Organizing Your Time:** You may wish to spend time admiring the view and strolling near the Seine.
- 👌 **Also See:** Rouen, St-Wandrille, Caudebec-en-Caux, Lillebonne and the Parc naturel des Boucles de Seine normande.

Abbaye de Jumièges

A. De Valroger/MICHELIN

A Bit of History

Jumièges Almshouse – In the 10C Duke William Longsword rebuilt Jumièges on the ruins of the 7C abbey destroyed by the Vikings. The new Benedictine abbey soon became known as the Jumièges Almshouse as well as a centre of learning. The abbey church was consecrated in 1067 in the presence of William the Conqueror.

The last monks dispersed at the Revolution, and in 1793 the abbey was bought by a timber merchant who intended to turn it into a stone quarry and used explosives to bring down the church lantern. A new proprietor in 1852 set about saving the ruins which now belong to the nation.

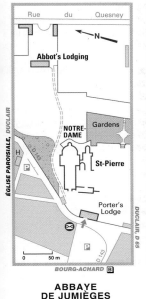

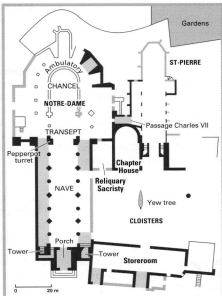

ABBAYE DE JUMIÈGES

👁Jumièges is a ruin and open to the sky in places. Consider this an outdoor venue, and dress accordingly.

The Abbey★★★

Allow 30min ♿ 🕐 *Open July–Aug 9.30am–6.30. mid-Apr–June & 1st half Sept Mon–Fri 9.30am–1pm, 2.30–6.30pm, weekends and public holidays 9.30am–6.30pm. Rest of the year 9.30am–1pm, 2.30–5.30pm. (Last entry 30min before closing).* 🕐*Closed 1 Jan, 1 May, 1 and 11 Nov, 25 Dec.* 💶*5€. (Under 18 years and 1st Sun of the month Oct to Apr no charge).* ☎*02 35 37 24 02. www.monum.fr.*

Église Notre-Dame

The projecting porch is flanked by twin towers (43m/141ft high) whose spires were visible until 1830.

The entire nave (27m/89ft high) still stands, together with part of the transept and the chancel. Only the west side of the lantern has survived, resting on an arch which is impressive for its height and reach.

Passage Charles-VII

The passage leading to St. Peter's Church was named for the visit of King Charles VII (1403-1461) to Jumièges.

Église St-Pierre

The porch and first bays of the nave are Norman Carolingian (oculi and twinned arcades), the remaining ruins date from the 13C and 14C. The arched entrance porch is flanked by two small doors with stairs to the gallery towers behind. The first two bays of the nave are a rare example of 10C Norman architecture.

Chapter-house

Between the abbey and St Peter's is this 12C chapter-house off the cloisters.

WHERE TO STAY

🍽 **Le Relais de l'Abbaye** – *798 r. du Quesney, 76480 Jumièges.* ☎*02 35 37 24 98. 4 rooms.* 🚫🛏 *. In the shadow of the famous abbey, here's a charming rural house. Summertime, breakfast is served in the garden.*

Cloisters
In the middle of the cloisters grows an ancient yew tree. The four galleries once consisted of 26 bays. The refectory was on the south side.

Storeroom
The great cellar dates from the end of the 12C.

Gardens
Beyond a fence, a 17C set of steps leads to a broad terrace and the gardens.

Abbot's Lodging
Beyond the lawn rises the former abbot's lodging, a majestic 17C rectangular building.

Église paroissiale St-Valentin
⏱*Open July–Aug daily except Tue 2–6pm.* ☎*02 35 37 28 97.*
The parish church has an 11C-12C nave and a 16C chancel and ambulatory; inside, altarpieces and 15C-16C stained-glass windows in ambulatory chapels.

LASSAY-LES-CHÂTEAUX★

MAYENNE, POPULATION 2 532
MICHELIN MAP 310: G-4

On the edge of this ancient market town stands an imposing fortress. A few remarkable buildings have been restored, revealing some splendid red-granite façades (Maison du Bailly, a half-timbered inn).

- 🛈 **Information:** 8 rue du Château, 53110 Lassay-les-Châteux. ☎02 43 04 74 33
- ▶ **Orient Yourself:** Lassy is a lovely stop on D 34 between Bagnoles-de-l'Orne (17km/10.6mi northeast) and Mayenne (19km/12mi southwest).
- 👁 **Don't Miss:** For a good overall view of the castle walk down the path that passes under the stone bridge and skirts the foot of the towers and the pool on the right-hand side.
- 🕐 **Organizing Your Time:** Walks have been well marked out In the surrounding countryside among the hedgerows (bocage).
- 👶 **Also See:** Domfront, Bagnoles-de-l'Orne, Jublains and Mayenne.

The Château★

🎧*Guided tours (1hr) June–Sept daily 2.30–6.30pm. In May, weekends and public holidays 2.30–6.30pm.* 💶*5€ (Children 2 €).* ☎*02 43 04 71 22.*

WHERE TO STAY

☕ **La Prémoudière Bed and Breakfast** – *61330 St-Denis-de-Villenette, 11.5km/7.1mi N of Lassay-les-Châteaux via D 117 dir. Domfront, then D 52 at Sept- Forges.* ☎*02 33 37 23 27.* *5 rooms.* 🛏☕ *. Meal* ☕*.* Apple and pear cider is made on this Norman farm where the former cellars have been converted into guestrooms. Peace and quiet is guaranteed and home-made red-berry jam is served for breakfast.

The castle, which dominates the village with its eight pepper-pot towers linked by a strong curtain wall, was built in 1458 in place of an older building dismantled in 1417 during the Hundred Years War. The castle is a prime example of military architecture under the reign of Charles VII. Its history evokes three famous people – King Henri IV, the writer and poet Victor Hugo and the chemist A.L. de Lavoisier who was a prisoner in the castle during the Revolution. The bridge spanning the moat leads to the barbican, a fortified structure defending the entrance to the castle. The two towers guarding the drawbridge are linked by living quarters, in which 16C and 17C weapons and furniture are displayed. The casemates can be seen at the foot of the barbican. The tour ends with a stroll in the park.

LAVAL★

MAYENNE, POPULATION 50 800
MICHELIN MAP 310: E-6

The first thing that strikes any visitor to Laval is the River Mayenne, which flows gently through the centre of town, as it has since the year 1000. The town has a picturesque château and old half-timbered houses, and has produced many distinguished citizens *(see below)*.

- **Information:** *1 allée du Vieux-St-Louis, 53000 Laval.*
  ☎*02 43 49 46 46 www.laval-tourisme.com.*
- ▶ **Orient Yourself:** Laval is is 32km/20mi south of Mayenne by D 162. Le Mans is 86km/54mi to the east on N 157.
- **Don't Miss:** A walk along the docks to see the old *bateau-lavoir* St-Julien.
- **Organizing Your Time:** You can tour the old city by yourself: it should take about one hour, not counting visits to the château, museums and churches.
- **Also See:** Mayenne, Jublains, Évron and Saulges.

Famous Citizens

Laval is the birthplace of many exceptional men. **Ambroise Paré** (1517-90) was the first to practise the ligature of arteries during amputations and is deserving of his reputation as the father of surgery: yet he was modest about his success, "I dress their wounds, God cures them."

Henri Rousseau (1844-1910), whose nickname was Le Douanier (the Customs Officer), was a tax collector in Paris. He was the archetype of the modern naïve artist, and was known for the meticulous approach which he brought to his paintings of lush jungles, wild beasts and exotic figures.

Alfred Jarry (1873-1907) was the inventor of pataphysics, the science of imaginary solutions, and the forerunner of the Surrealists. He created the grotesque satirical character of *Père Ubu, King of Poland*, when he was still in his teens. Jarry died destitute and largely unappreciated. Today, however, he is honoured as one of the creators of the Theatre of the Absurd.

Alain Gerbault (1893-1941) was a renowned tennis player, as well as sailor. In 1923 he made the transatlantic crossing single-handed; he died in the Polynesian islands. His second boat, the *Fire-Crest II*, is exhibited in the Jardin de la Perrine.

Jean Cottereau, called Jean Chouans, led royalist troops during the French Revolution. In 1793 the Royalists *(Les Blancs)* occupied Laval and beneath its walls defeated the Republican army of General Lechelle. The name **Chouans** was adopted from their rallying cry, the hoot of the tawny owl *(chat-huant)*.

Old Town Walking Tour★

Allow 1hr

Place de la Trémoille

The square is named after the last of the local lords. On the east side stands the Renaissance façade of the 16C **Nouveau Château** built for the Count of Laval; it was enlarged in the 19C and now houses the law courts.

Rue des Orfèvres

The narrow street which runs south into Grande-Rue is lined with beautiful 16C overhanging houses and 18C mansions. At the T-junction stands the Renaissance house (1550) of the Master of the Royal Hunt (Grand Veneur).

Grande-Rue

This was the main street of the medieval city; it descends to the River Mayenne between rows of old houses, some half-timbered with projecting upper storeys, others in stone with Renaissance decoration.

▶ *Turn right onto rue de Chapelle.*

The street climbs between medieval and Renaissance houses to a charming statue of St René in a niche *(right)* at the top.

▶ *Go straight ahead onto rue des Serruriers.*

South of the Beucheresse Gate are two slightly askew half-timbered houses.

Porte Beucheresse
In former days this 14C gate, then called Porte des Bûcherons, opened directly into the forest. its two round towers, topped with machicolations were once part of the town walls. Henri Rousseau was born in the south tower, where his father worked as a tinsmith.

Cathédrale
The building has been altered many times but the nave and the transept crossing are covered with Angevin vaulting, characterised by curved rib vaulting in which the keystones are at different heights.

The walls are hung with Aubusson tapestries (early 17C) depicting the story of Judith and Holophernes in six panels. On the left pillar near the chancel is a very beautiful triptych painted by the Antwerp Mannerist School in the 16C; it presents the Martyrdom of St John the Apostle when closed and three scenes from the life of John the Baptist when open. In the north transept there is an imposing revolving door carved in the 18C.

On leaving the cathedral, walk round the east end to admire the north-east door (facing the law courts), which is decorated with 17C terracotta statues.

Rue de la Trinité
One of of the old houses dates from the 16C and is adorned with statues of the Virgin and the Saints.

▶ *Turn left onto rue du Pin-Doré which ends in place de la Trémoille.*

Quays★
🕐*The bateau-lavoir St-Julien: July–Aug daily except Mon 2–6pm.* ⊜*No charge.*
The quays on the east bank provide the best overall **views**★ of Laval across the River Mayenne. From the **Pont Vieux**, a 13C humpback bridge, there is a more detailed view of the old town.
The **bateaux-lavoirs**, the last public wash houses in Laval, are moored along quai Paul-Boudet. One of these, the **St-Julien**, has been restored.

Jardin de la Perrine★
The terraces of these public gardens command attractive views. As well as a rose garden there are many tall trees,ponds, waterfalls, lawns and flower beds.

The Château★ *Allow 1hr*

🕐*Open May–mid-Sept daily except Mon 10am–6pm. 14 July and 15 Aug 2–6pm. Rest of the year daily except Mon and public holidays 2–5pm.* ⊜*Unaccompanied visit 1€.* 📷*Guided tour (1hr, last departure 5pm) 2€ (Children and 1st Sun of month no charge.* ☎*02 43 53 39 89. www.mairie-laval.fr.*
To the right of the railings in front of the law courts stands a noble 17C porch, next to an early-16C half-timbered house. Through the porch is the courtyard of the old castle enclosed by ramparts (from the top of the walls there is a picturesque **view**★ of the old town). In its present state the bulk of the castle dates from the 13C and 15C; the windows and dormers in white tufa, carved with scrolls in the Italian style, were added in the 16C. The crypt and the keep are the oldest parts (12C-13C).

Donjon
Originally separated from the courtyard by a moat, the keep was later incorporated between the two wings of the castle. Within the keep, the most interesting feature is the extraordinary **timber roof**★★ which was built c 1100

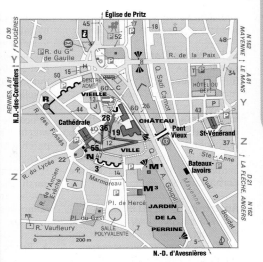

LAVAL

Alègre Prom. Anne d'	Z	3
Avesnières Q. d'	Z	5
Avesnières R. d'	Z	7
Briand Pont A.	Y	8
Britais R. du	Y	9
Chapelle R. de	Z	12
Déportés R. des	Y	13
Douanier-Rousseau R.	Z	14
Droits de l'homme Parvis des	Y	15
Gambetta Quai	Y	17
Gaulle R. Gén.-de	Y	
Gavre Q. B.-de	Y	18
Grande-Rue	Z	19
Hardy-de-Lévaré Pl.	Z	22
Jean-Fouquet Q.	Y	26
Moulin Pl. J.	Y	34
Orfèvres R. des	Z	36
Paix R. de la	Y	
Paradis R. de	Z	37
Pin-Doré R. du	Z	40
Pont-de-Mayenne R. du	Y	43
Renaise R.	Y	44
Résistance Crs de la	Y	45
Serruriers R. des	Z	47
Solférino R.	Y	48
Souchu-Servinière R.	Y	50
Strasbourg R. de	Y	52
La Trémoille Pl. de	Z	28

Espace Alain-Gerbault et Fire-Crest II	Z	M¹
Musée des Sciences	Z	M³
Nouveau château	YZ	J
Porte Beucheresse	Z	N
Tour Renaise	Z	R

to an ingenious circular design. Great beams, radiating from the centre like the spokes of a wheel, project beyond the walls (which are over 2m/6ft thick) to support the wooden defensive gallery that projects out to permit defense of the gate and the base of the walls.

Sights

Musée d'Art naïf★
○*Same hours as for the old château.*
The Museum of Naïve Painting, which can be visited separately from the castle and the keep, displays a number of canvases by painters from France, Croatia, Germany, Brazil etc. A reconstruction of Rousseau's (Le Douanier) studio contains mementoes of the artist.

Musée des Sciences
○ *Open daily except public holidays 10am–noon, 2–6pm.* ○*Closed between exhibits.* ⊘*2€ Children 1€ (1st Sun of month no charge).* ☎*02 43 49 47 81.*
The Science Museum is housed in an imposing building. The archaeological

exhibits are the result of excavations carried out in the Laval region. The 19C astronomical clock in its carved wooden case is a fine exhibit.

Notre-Dame-d'Avesnières Basilica
1.5km/1mi S.
This ancient sanctuary dedicated to the Virgin Mary was made into a basilica in 1898. The Romanesque **east end**★ is best seen from Avesnières Bridge: the chancel, the ambulatory and the five radiating chapels. The attractive Gothic-Renaissance spire is an identical copy, made in 1871, of the original which was erected in 1538.
The fine Romanesque chancel consists of three storeys of arches and bays. The modern stained glass is by Max Ingrand.

Église St-Vénérand
The nave of the church is flanked by double aisles. The north front, facing the street, has a Flamboyant door★ decorated with an attractive 17C terracotta figure of the Virgin.

Tour Renaise – This 15C round machicolated tower belongs to the old walls.

Église Notre-Dame-des-Cordeliers★

Built between 1397 and 1407, this former chapel of a Franciscan monastery contains a remarkable set of seven **altarpieces★★** from the 17C. Six of them can be seen in the north aisle *(lighting is essential; token available from the Tourist Office)*; they were carved out of tufa and marble by the local architect **Pierre Corbineau** (1600-78).

Ancienne église du Pritz

2km/1mi N. Leave Laval by allée de la Résistance, rue du Vieux-St-Louis and D 104. ⚬➤*Private: No visits permitted.* This simple church stands on the right of the road in the hamlet called Pritz and is surrounded by a garden. It dates from about the year 1000 and was altered and enlarged in the Romanesque period.

Driving Tour

▸ *15km/9mi W by rue du Général-de-Gaulle and N 157.*

Abbaye de Clermont

♿🕐*Open Apr–Oct 9am–6.30pm. Rest of the year 9am–4pm.* ✎4€ *(Children 2€).* ☎*02 43 02 11 96.*

The ruins stand in open country watered by many streams. The abbey was founded in 1152, as a daughter house of Clairvaux, by St Bernard with the support of Guy V, Count of Laval; it was a thriving monastic community until the Revolution.

The square east end of the **church** comes into view before the dilapidated west front and the austere Romanesque porch with its three round-headed openings.

South of the church is the **cloister garth**. The wooden cloister galleries have not survived, but the **lay brothers' range** (west) contains the cellar and the refectory.

▸ *Return to Laval and then take quai d'Avesnières and D 1 S out of town.*

The road goes down to the banks of the Mayenne, providing a nice view over the former Porte de l'Huisserie.

▸ *Bear left onto D 112 towards Entrammes; after 1km/0.6mi fork left onto a narrow road to L'Enclos et Bonne (Lock).*

The road descends to the bank of the River Mayenne, offering a very attractive **view★** of the river, the lock, a mill and a castle.

View on the town and castle

G. Guegan/MICHELIN

Address Book

For coin ranges, see the Legend on the cover flap.

WHERE TO STAY

Camping Village Vacances Pêche – *53170 Villiers-Charlemagne, 20km/12.4mi S of Laval via N 162.* ☎*02 43 07 71 68. ccpmg@wanadoo.fr. Open Apr–Oct. 20 sites. Reservations advised.* Keen anglers will be able to indulge in their hobby at leisure. The lake abounds in pike, pikeperch and carp. Campers have their own bathroom installations and room to store fishing tackle. It is possible to rent small chalets with individual terraces raised on piles.

Marin'Hotel – *102 av R-Buron.* ☎*02 43 53 09 63. www.marin-hotel. fr. 25 rooms.* On a streetcorner near the train station, the building is decorated with grotesque masks that testify to its age. The rooms, however, are up-to-date, functional and well soundproofed from the street noise. The breakfast room has a nautical theme.

Grand Hôtel de Paris – *22 r. de la Paix.* ☎*02 43 53 76 20. www. hotel-de-paris-laval.fr. Closed 24–26 Jan and 21 Dec–2 Jan. 50 rooms.* Hotel situated right in the town centre, close to the shopping area. The simple rooms with their white roughcast walls and coloured wood furniture are well soundproofed.

Le Bas du Gast Bed and Breakfast – *6 r. de la Halle-aux-Toiles, across from the Salle Polyvalente.* ☎*02 43 49 22 79. www. chateaulebasdugast. fr. C losed Dec–15 Mar. 4 rooms.* Built in the centre of Laval's old quarter, this 17C-18C castle is surrounded by a beautiful garden featuring trimmed box trees. As you go in, note the lovely smell of wax on the oak parquet flooring and period furniture. The spacious guestrooms have been thoughtfully decorated.

WHERE TO EAT

La Braise – *4-6 r. de la Trinité.* ☎*02 43 53 21 87. Closed 1 week at Easter, 1 week in Aug, Sun and Mon. Reservations advised.* Located in old Laval, this establishment has a faithful clientele that appreciates the pleasant decor of knick-knacks, a bread oven, old grocer's fixtures, a jug collection… not to mention the fine welcome. Meat brochettes and fish cooked in the fireplace.

L'Antiquaire – *5 r. Béliers.* ☎*02 43 53 66 76. Closed 13 July–5 Aug,16–24 Feb, Sat lunch, Sun evening and Wed.* This restaurant occupies the ground floor of an old Laval house. In the well-furnished dining room, turn of the 20th century British decor in tones of red. Generous portions of traditional cuisine, with a few modern touches.

À La Bonne Auberge – *170 r. de Bretagne.* ☎*02 43 69 07 81. labonneauberge@free.fr. Closed 19–26 Feb, 1–22 Aug, 24 Dec–8 Jan, Fri evening, Sun evening and Sat.* The pastel-coloured decoration of the dining room gives this inn an intimate, muted atmosphere. The veranda adds light and an impression of spaciousness. Well-prepared cuisine at reasonable prices.

Gerbe de Blé – *83 r. Victor-Boissel.* ☎*02 43 53 14 10. www.gerbedeble. com. Closed 2–13 Jan, 26 July–19 Aug, Mon lunch and Sun except public holidays.* This renowned family-run establishment is worth a detour. The warm decor of wood panelling in shades of golden wheat is conducive to relaxation. The traditional cuisine is well prepared and appetizing. A few guestrooms as well.

La Table Ronde – *Pl. de la Mairie, 53810 Changé, 4km/2.5mi N of Laval via D 104.* ☎*02 43 53 43 33. Closed 3 weeks in Aug, 1 week in Feb, Sun evening, Wed evening and Mon.* Opposite the château. Upstairs, the gastronomical restaurant: Louis XVI-style chairs and handsome tables laid with care; downstairs, the bistro.

SHOPPING

Abbaye de la Coudre – *R. St-Benoît.* ☎*02 43 02 85 85. www.abbaye-coudre.com. Open Tue–Sat 10am–noon, 2–5pm, Sun and Mon 2–5pm.* Under beautiful rafters and lit by lightwells in the roof, this boutique offers products made by monastic communities:

fruit pastes, jams, preserves of beer and wine, Chimay beer, coffee from Cameroon, spirits, cookies, Bonneval chocolate, honey, nougat, caramels... and the specialty of the house, Trappist cheese aged two months in the abbey cellars.

LEISURE

Kids Golf de Laval-Changé – *La Chabossière, 53810 Changé.* ☎*02 43 53 16 03 - golf53.laval@wanadoo.fr. Open daily 9am–7pm. Winter until 5.30pm. Closed 25 Dec–5 Jan.* Laid out on undulating ground covering 82ha/203 acres, this splendid golf course offers two rounds of 9 and 18 holes by the River Mayenne, suitable for beginners as well as for players with a handicap. From the bar/restaurant, there is a superb view of the course. Beginners' courses and equipment rental. Covered practice area and putting green.

SPECIAL EVENTS CALENDAR

The Nights of the Mayenne– *From mid-July to mid-August.* Shows and performances at three major sites: Ste-Suzanne, Jublains and Laval. Creativity is unleashed as the Mayenne region celebrates its rich heritage with musical and theatrical programs. *Information and reservations at* ☎*02 43 53 34 84. www.nuitsdelamayenne.com.*

Les Uburlesques – *1st weekend of Sept.* A street festival in the spirit of Ubu roi, the play -- or rather, theatrical gesture, by Alfred Jarry.

Night-time musical tours – *Mid-July–mid-August, every Tue.* A pleasant way to visit the sights of Laval, guided by actors in period costumes.

Guided tours –Laval, which is classified as a City of Art and History, offers tours conducted by highly qualified guides trained by the Ministry of Culture. For both night-time musical tours and guided tours contact the Tourist Office. *www.laval-tourisme. com, or www.vpah.culture.fr*

▶ *Return to D 112 and continue S; bear left onto D 103.*

Trappe du Port-du-Salut

No charge.
Until 1959 the famous Port-Salut cheese was made here by the Trappist monks. They still make cheese today but under a different name.
The **large and small chapels** are open to the public.

▶ *Continue E on D 103.*

Entrammes

Ancient baths – Guided tour *(1h15min) mid-July–mid-Aug 10.30am–12.30pm,3–7pm. 1st2 weeks July & last 2 weeks Aug 3–7pm. Apr–June & Sept–mid-Oct Sun and public holidays 2–6pm.* 2.80€ *(Children 1.40€)* ☎*02 43 49 46 46.*

During recent restoration work inside the church, remains of the town's **ancient baths** were discovered. (see *Ville romaine de JUBLAINS).* An audio-visual presentation explains the site.

Parné-sur-Roc

The church belonging to the village on the rock was built in the 11C and contains some interesting **mural paintings** (late 15C to early 16C). On the left one sees the silhouette of the resurrected Christ against a background of red stars and a Madonna Dolorosa; on the right, Cosmas and Damian, two brothers who practised medicine and were popular in the Middle Ages.

▶ *Take D 21 to return to Laval.*

LESSAY

MANCHE, POPULATION 1 763
MICHELIN MAP 303: C-4

Lessay grew up round a Benedictine abbey founded in 1056 by a Norman lord. The first monks came from Le Bec-Hellouin. The town is particularly lively in September during the Holy Cross Fair, which originated in the 13C.

- **Information:** 11 place Saint-Cloud, 50430 Lessay. ☎02 33 45 14 34
- ▶ **Orient Yourself:** Lessay lies between Coutances, 21km/13 mi to the south on D2, and Valognes, 36km/22.5mi north on D 900.
- **Don't Miss:** The impressive view of the abbey nave.
- **Organizing Your Time:** In July and August, concerts are held at the abbey.
- **Especially for Kids:** There are several nature trails; ask at the tourist office.
- **Also See:** Barneville-Carteret, St-Sauveur-le-Vicomte, the Parc naturel régional des marais du Cotentin et du Bessin, the Cotentin penninsula, and Coutances.

Abbey Church★★

Allow 30min

The magnificent Romanesque abbey church was reconstructed between 1945 and 1957, using original building materials wherever possible; the result is one of the most perfect examples of Romanesque architecture in Normandy. Building of the original church started in 1098 with construction of the apse, chancel transept and two bays of the nave with their vaulting; the remaining bays of the nave were completed several years later.

Exterior

The full beauty of the lines of the apse, abutting on a flat gable, can best be seen from the War Memorial Square. The rather squat square belfry with its Hague schist slates is also worth noting.

Interior

The seven broad bays of the nave and the transepts are roofed with pointed vaulting; there is rib-vaulting in the

Vaulted ceiling, Abbey Church

S. Sauvignier/MICHELIN

La Foire de Sainte-Croix

Lessay is extraordinarily lively during the days of the Holy Cross Fair (second weekend in September). The origins of the fair are lost in the 11C – it is supposed that the Benedictines were the first sponsors.

Friday is fair day for horses, donkeys, dogs, ferrets and fowl; Saturday welcomes cattle, sheep and goats. For three days, more than 1 500 exhibitors spread out over 7km/4mi of alleyways and dozens of carnival rides are set up alongside.

To feed the 400 000 visitors, about 2 800 local lambs are grilled up in the traditional manner along an alleyway reserved for this purpose.

aisles. The gallery in front of the clerestory windows passes round the entire building in the thickness of the walls. The chancel terminates in an oven-vaulted apse lit by two rose windows.

A 15C chapel with a cobbled floor *(right of the chancel)* contains the baptistery and the font. The new glass windows are subtly coloured and the design is inspired by Irish manuscripts.

LILLEBONNE

SEINE-MARITIME, POPULATION 9 738
MICHELIN MAP 304: D-4

The small industrial town of Lillebonne was once a Roman military camp named Juliobona, after Julius Caesar. With the arrival of several textile factories towards the end of the 19C, the Lillebonne-Bolbec valley came to be known as the Golden Valley.

- **Information:** Rue Victor-Hugo, 76170 Lillebonne. ☎02 35 38 08 45.
- **Orient Yourself:** Lillebone is 67km/42mi west of Rouen and 37km/23mi east of Le Havre via D 982.
- **Don't Miss:** The Roman theatre and artefacts at the museum.
- **Organizing Your Time:** Although some sights are closed for renovation, you can admire them from the outside while enjoying their surroundings.
- **Also See:** Le Havre, the Pays de Caux, St-Wandrille, Caudebec-en-Caux, Jumièges, the Parc naturel des Boucles de la Seine and Honfleur.

Sights

Théâtre-Amphithéâtre romain

Under renovation for an undetermined length of time. Closed for individual visits.
From place de l'Hôtel-de-Ville it is possible to see the general layout of this Roman amphitheatre, built in the 1C and 2C.
The central arena follows the usual plan of amphitheatres in north-west Gaul, where all kinds of spectacles were held (mythological scenes, gladiator fights, performing animals, hunts with small game). The crowd watched on from the **cave**★, a series of stands probably made of wood.

Château

Access by 46 rue Césarine.
Little remains of the fortress (rebuilt in the 12C and 13C), where William the Conqueror assembled his barons before invading England: one wall of an octagonal tower and, on the left, a round three-storey keep.

Église Notre-Dame

This 16C church has a sweeping spire (55m/181ft) rising above a square tower. Inside, a stained-glass window tells the story of John the Baptist. The stalls were originally from the Abbaye du Valasse.

Musée municipal

Place Félix-Faure, across from Roman theatre. ⏱*Open May–Sept 10am–noon, 2–6pm. Rest of the year daily except Tue 2–6pm.* ⏱*Closed 1 Jan, 25 Dec.* ∞*1.55€ (Children no charge).* ☎*02 32 84 02 07.*
The museum is devoted to popular art and traditions. The basement houses archaeological finds from local excavations (cremation tombs, pottery and ironwork from the 1C to the 3C).

Excursions

Le Mesnil-sous-Lillebonne

2km/1mi S. Church – ⏱*Open June–Sept 2–6pm* ∞*1.55€.* ☎*02 32 84 02 07.*
The extremely ancient parish **church** has recently been restored. It presents a display of religious art and a collection of fossils and minerals.

Abbaye du Valasse

6km/4mi NW by D 173. ☞ Closed for repairs.

The foundation of the abbey resulted from two vows, one made by Waleran de Meulan for escaping a shipwreck, and one made by Empress Matilda, William the Conqueror's granddaughter, for surviving the struggle for the throne of England against her cousin Stephen of Blois. The abbey, consecrated in 1181, prospered until the 14C, when the Hundred Years War and the Wars of Religion brought ruin. The building was sold at the Revolution, converted into a château, then sold to a dairy; in 1984 it was bought by the municipality of Gruchet-le-Valasse.

The main façade is an elegant 18C pedimented composition with two return wings.

The central pediment bears the arms of Empress Matilda: three Normandy leopards (from William the Conqueror) and an eagle (from her husband, the German emperor Henry V).

LISIEUX★★

CALVADOS, POPULATION 23 166
MICHELIN MAP 303: N-5 – LOCAL MAP SEE PAYS D'AUGE

Sitting on the east bank of the Touques, Lisieux has become the most important commercial and industrial town in the prosperous Pays d'Auge. The town is renowned for St Teresa of Lisieux.

- **Information:** 11 rue d'Alençon, 14100 Lisieux.
  ☎02 31 48 18 10. www.lisieux-tourisme.com.
- **Orient Yourself:** Coming from Évreux (73km/45.6mi easst via N13), you immediately see the imposing 20C neo-Byzantine baslica of St Teresa.
- **Parking:** The basilica is equipped for pilgrimages with ample parking nearby.
- **Don't Miss:** The cathedral of St-Pierre and the CERZA zoo.
- **Organizing Your Time:** Visit Lisieux in the morning, then tour the countryside.
- **Especially for Kids:** A short distance outside Lisieux, near Hermival-les-Vaux, is the popular game reserve CERZA.
- **Also See:** Pays d'Auge, Crèvecoeur-en-Auge, Honfleur, Pont-l'Évêque and Vimoutiers.

A Bit of History

Thérèse Martin was born on 2 January 1873 to a well-to-do and very religious family in Alençon; she was an eager and sensitive child who soon showed intelligence and will-power. On the death of his wife, M. Martin brought the family to Lisieux where they lived at Les Buissonnets. At nine years, Thérèse felt the call of the Church. The authorities considered her too young and it was only in April 1888, after a pilgrimage to Rome and a request to the Holy Father, that she entered the Carmelite Order at the age of 15 years and three months. As Sister Teresa of the Child Jesus, she resolved "to save souls and, above all, to pray for the priests". Her gaiety and simplicity cloaked a consuming energy. She wrote the story of her life, *History of a Soul*, finishing the last pages only a few days before entering the Carmelite hospital in which, after an agonising illness, she died in 1897. She was canonised in 1925. On 19 October 1997 Pope Jean-Paul II proclaimed her a Doctor of the Church, an exceptional honour bestowed on saints of great spiritual influence.

The Pilgrimage

Les Buissonnets

🕐Open Palm Sunday–Sept. Audio tours (30min) 9am–noon, 2–6pm. Feb–Mar & Oct 10am–noon,2–5pm. Rest of the year 10am–noon, 2–4pm. 🕐Closed mid-Dec –mid-Jan. ☜No charge. ☎02 31 48 55 08. http://therese-de-lisieux.com.

This house is where Thérèse Martin lived from the age of 4 to 15. The tour includes the dining room, Thérèse's bedroom, her father's bedroom and a display of mementoes from her childhood days.

Chapelle du Carmel

⚟Closed for repairs.

The saint's shrine, a recumbent figure in marble and precious wood, is in the chapel on the right and contains her relics.

Salle des Souvenirs

⚟Closed for repairs.

A series of display windows with recorded commentary shows mementoes relating to the saint's convent life.

Basilique Ste-Thérèse

This impressive basilica was consecrated on 11 July 1954 and is one of the biggest 20C churches. The **dome** is open to visitors.

The construction of the bell-tower was interrupted in 1975; it ends in a flat roof and contains the great bell, three other bells and a carillon of 44 bells. Notice on the tympanum of the door the carvings by Robert Coin depicting Jesus teaching the Apostles and the Virgin of Mount Carmel. The immense nave is decorated with marble, stained glass and mosaics by Pierre Gaudin, a pupil of Maurice Denis. In the south transept stands a reliquary offered by Pope Pius XI containing the bones of the saint's right arm. The **crypt** (entrance outside, beneath the galleries) is decorated with mosaics (scenes in the life of St Teresa).

Muséé-Diorama: Histoire de Sainte-Thérèse

Beneath the north cloister of the basilica. ♿🕐Easter–Oct daily 11am–1pm, 2–6pm. Rest of the year weekends, school and public holidays 2–5pm. 🕐Closed Jan.

☜3€ (Children 1€). ☎02 31 48 55 08. http://therese-de-lisieux.com

This diorama depicts a dozen episodes in the life of St Teresa .

Cathédrale St-Pierre★

Allow 15min

The cathedral was begun in 1170 and completed only in the mid-13C.

Exterior

The façade, raised above the ground on stone steps, is pierced by three doors and flanked by towers.

Walk round the church by the right to the south transept's Paradise Door. The massive buttresses linked by an arch surmounted by a gallery were added in the 15C.

Interior

The transept is extremely simple with the lantern rising in a single sweep at the crossing. Walk round the 13C chancel, to the huge central chapel which was remodelled in the pure Flamboyant style on the orders of Pierre Cauchon, Bishop of Lisieux, after the trial of Joan of Arc. It was in this chapel that Thérèse Martin attended mass. Note the series of 15C carved low-relief sculptures.

Musée d'Art et d'Histoire

🕐Open daily except Tue 2–6pm. 🕐Closed 1 Jan, 1 May, 25 Dec. ☜2.60€ (Children no charge). ☎02 31 62 07 70.

Set up in a handsome 16C half-timbered house, a collection of documents and images explains the history, arts and crafts of Lisieux and the Pays d'Auge.

Additional Sight

Cerza★

12km/7.5mi NE. Leave Lisieux by D 510, S on the plan; 3km/2mi after Hermival-les-Vaux turn right onto D 143. 🧒🕐Open July–Aug 9.30am–7pm. Apr–June & Sept 9.30am–6.30pm. Rest of the year 10am–5pm. ☜13.50€ (Children 7€). ☎02 31 62 17 22. www.cerza.com.

The **Centre d'Élevage et de Reproduction Zoologique Augeron (CERZA)**

Address Book

🪙 *For coin ranges, see the Legend on the cover flap.*

WHERE TO STAY

🛏 **Hôtel St-Louis** – *4 r. St-Jacques.* ☎*02 31 62 06 50. Closed 8–14Mar and 22–28 Nov. 17 rooms.* ⛩. New, bright wallpaper, new furniture, improved bathrooms: the rooms of this family hotel have benefitted from a youth cure. There is a little garden as well.

🛏 **Camping Le Colombier** – *14590 Moyaux, 16km/9.6mi NE of Lisieux via D 510 and D 143.* ☎*02 31 63 63 08. mail@ camping-lecolombier.com. Open 30 Apr–12 Sept. Reservations advised. 180 sites. Food service.* This camp site has character, with its manor, timeworn buildings and garden à la française. The interior decoration has been conceived with authenticity and warmth in mind. Swimming pool.

🛏🛏 **Hôtel de la Place** – *67 r. Henry-Chéron.* ☎*02 31 48 27 27. www.hoteldelaplace.com. Closed 16 Dec–7 Jan. 34 rooms.* ⛩. The rooms are of varying sizes, but all have been renovated and are bright and modern. Well-stocked breakfast buffet.

WHERE TO EAT

🍴 **Le Jardin de Taormina** – *2-4 place du Parvis, 14290 Orbec, 18km/11mi SW of Bernay via D 131.* ☎*02 31 32 01 15. jardin.de.taormina@wanadoo.fr. Closed Sun evening and Mon.* This restaurant just below the church Notre-Dame d'Orbec has 3 dining rooms with a relaxed, southern atmosphere. Summer evenings, enjoy the view of the illuminated bell tower from the terrace. Italian cuisine.

🍴🍴 **La Coupe d'Or** – *49 r. Pont-Mortain.* ☎*02 31 31 16 84. www.la-coupe-d-or.com. Closed Sun evening.* Although this hotel restaurant is on a busy street, all is calm as soon as you enter the door. Dining room recently renovated. 14 guestrooms also renovated. Reasonable prices.

🍴🍴 **Aux Acacias** – *13 r. de la Résistance.* ☎*02 31 62 10 95. Closed 25–31 Dec, Thu evening from Nov to Mar, Sun evening and Mon except public holidays.* An enjoyable restaurant on a small square downtown. The well-prepared regional dishes are interpreted with flair, based on fresh produce. The decor is pastel and the prices are affordable.

TAKE A BREAK

Pâtisserie Chez Billoudet – *44 r. Henry-Chéron.* ☎*02 31 62 17 91. Open daily except Mon 7.30am–7.30pm. Closed 2 weeks during Feb-Mar school holidays and 2 weeks in July.* This confectioner/chocolatier offers delicious specialities such as the caluador (chocolate with calvados creme and caramel), le pom-reine (chocolate filled with apple ganache) and the traditional apples in calvados. Tearoom.

SHOPPING

Le Père Jules – *Rte de Dives-sur-Mer, 14100 St-Désir-de-Lisieux.* ☎*02 31 61 14 57. Open daily 8am–12.30pm, 1.30–8pm.* Located in a gorgeous 19C Norman house, this family concern established in 1919 is named after the founding grandfather. You'll be invited to visit the calvados cellars and, naturally, sample a drop or two.

provides a pleasant, natural setting for a great many endangered animal species. The 52ha/129 acres of the domain offer interesting topographical contrasts – valleys and plains, meadows and forests, barren stretches and lush pockets of vegetation, charmingly dotted with small ponds and burbling streams. Signposted routes will take you through the **African Reserve** (a vast area set aside for rhinoceroses, zebras, watussi, ostriches and giraffes) or on a tour of the valley. A great many primates (gelada baboons, macaques, capuchins, gibbons) as well as lemurs live in semi-liberty, in a biotope specially designed to meet their needs.

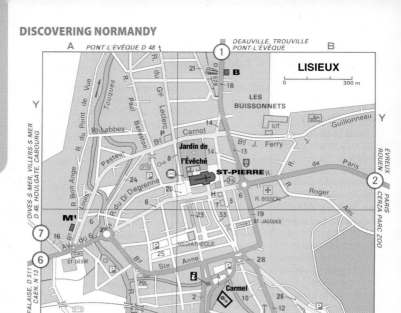

LISIEUX								
			Dr-Lesigne R.		BZ 10	Mitterrand Pl. F.	ABY	20
			Dr-Ouvry R.		BZ 12	Oresme Bd N.	BY	21
Alençon R. d'	BZ	2	Duchesne-Fournet Bd	BY	13	Pont-Mortain R.	BZ	23
Carmel R. du	BZ	4	Foch R. Mar.	BY	14	Remparts Quai des	AY	24
Char R. au	BY	5	Fournet R.		BZ 15	République Pl. de la	ABZ	25
Chéron R. Henry	ABY	6	Guizot R.		AZ 16	Ste-Thérèse Av.	BZ	28
Condorcet R.	AY	8	Herbet-Fournet Bd	BY	18	Verdun R. de	BZ	31
Creton R.	ABZ	9	Jeanne-d'Arc Bd		BZ 19	Victor-Hugo Av.	BZ	33

Les Buissonnets	BY	B	Musée d'Art et d'Histoire	AZ	M¹

Driving Tour

Haute Vallée de la Touques - 75km/47mi. Allow about 3hr from Lisieux and back.

▶ *From Lisieux take D 579 S. After 4km:2mi turn left onto D 64.*

Fervaques

Château – Only the exterior can be visited. Telephone for times. ⊚5€ for a brochure. ☏02 31 32 33 96.

The 16C and 17C **château** overlooking the Touques is a vast building of brick and stone. Fervaques was the retreat of Delphine de Custine, a friend of the author F.R. de Chateaubriand (1768-1848) who also stayed there.

▶ *In Notre-Dame-de-Courson turn right onto D 4; after 3km/2mi turn left.*

Bellou

In the village centre stands Manoir de Bellou, a pleasant 16C timber-framed manor house. The road (D 110) runs south-east through the Moutiers-Hubert Forest and passes the Manoir de Cheffreteau.

▶ *In Les Moutiers-Hubert turn right onto D 64 towards Gacé. At the crossroads turn left onto D 16 and immediately right. Cross the river in Canapville; turn right onto D 33 and continue S. S of Ticheville station cross the railway line. At the next junction turn right onto D 242; after 1km/0.5mi turn right to Vimoutiers.*

Vimoutiers
See VIMOUTIERS.

▶ *Take D 579 N; turn right onto D 268 which climbs steeply. Continue N and W through St-Ouen-le-Houx. From D 110 turn right onto D 579.*

Livarot
Home of the cheese of the same name, this village has some beautiful houses.

▶ *Continue N on D 579; bear right onto D 268.*

St-Germain-de-Livet★
Château – Guided tours (1hr) daily except Tue 11am–6pm (Last entry 5pm). Closed first 2 weeks of Oct, Dec–Jan, 1 May. 6.20€ (Under 18 years no charge). ☎02 31 31 00 03.

This delightful **château** consists of a 16C wing, decorated in a highly original stone and brick check pattern, adjoining a 15C half-timbered structure. The 15C wing contains the guard-room, decorated with 16C **frescoes** (battle scene; Judith bearing the head of Holofernes), and a dining room with Empire-style furniture. On the first floor of the 16C wing are two rooms beautifully tiled in terracotta from the Pays d'Auge, the so-called bedroom of the painter Eugène Delacroix (1798–1863), the gallery with paintings by the Riesener family (19C) and a small round Louis XVI salon.

LOUVIERS★
EURE, POPULATION 18 328
MICHELIN MAP 304: H-6

Badly damaged in 1940, Louviers has been carefully reconstructed, sparing the remaining old houses and delightful avenues along the River Eure. The old town north of Notre-Dame Church has pretty half-timbered houses, such as in rue Tatin, rue du Quai and rue Pierre Mendès-France. Louviers remains an industrial centre, especially in the north of the town.

- **Information:** *10 rue du Maréchal-Foch, 27400 Louviers.* ☎02 32 40 04 41. www.tourisme-seine-eure.com
- ▶ **Orient Yourself:** Louviers is 32km/20mi south of Rouen and 103 km/64mi northwest of Paris via A 13.
- **Don't Miss:** The Flamboyant Notre-Dame church and Acquigny park.
- **Organizing Your Time:** You will need 1hr30min to see the town.
- **Also See:** Les Andelys, Évreux, Elbeuf and Rouen.

Walking Tour

▶ *From the Notre-Dame Church in the town centre, take the Rue de la Poste, which crosses both branches of the Eure River.*

Ancien couvent des Pénitents
Allow 30min
All that remains of this Franciscan convent, built in 1646 on a tributary of the Eure, is the inhabited main building together with three small arcaded galleries belonging to the cloister. The western gallery is in a ruinous state and overlooks a square with lawn and trees.

Rue de la Trinité *(on the left)* leads into the former manufacturing district and to **rue Terneaux,** where the buildings have large attics once used for drying out dyed fabrics.

▶ *Take the short rue Polhomet to the right, then turn right again on rue du Quai. Pretty half-timbered houses*

Normandy's Literary Ghosts

Many of Normandy's towns, villages, manor houses, coastal and rural scenes were described often under a fictional name by one of the region's celebrated writers.
Cabourg – the Balbec in Marcel Proust's *À la recherche du temps perdu*.
Ry – the Yonville-l'Abbaye of Gustave Flaubert's *Madame Bovary* (1857).
Le Havre – Guy de Maupassant's *Pierre et Jean* (1888).
Inland from Yport – Maupassant's *Une Vie* (1883).
The Cotentin – Barbey d'Aurevilly's (the Walter Scott of the region) *Le Chevalier des Touches*, *Une vieille maîtresse* and *L'Ensorcelée*.

line the street. Rue au Coq, on the left, leads to the museum; rue Pierre-Mendès-France takes you back to the east end of Notre Dame Church.

Église Notre-Dame★

The plain 13C church was redecorated in the late 15C in the Flamboyant style and it is for this that it has become famous. The **south front**★ is outstanding for its profusion of Flamboyant features. Pointed gables rival with openwork balustrades, pinnacles, festoons and gargoyles. The **south porch**★, with all its delicately carved detail, looks more like silverwork than masonry. Note the Renaissance door panels and the hanging keystones of the Gothic arcades.

Interior

The 13C nave with double side aisles is an elegant interior which shelters several fine **works of art**★.
1) Entombment (late 15C).
2) Salome and her sons, James and John (16C).
3) Throne.

4) Above the altar are three statues: Christ, the Virgin and St John (15C). On each side are carved panels depicting the Virgin Mary and the Centurion at Calvary (14C).
5) Altar decorated with carved panels depicting the life of the Virgin (16C).
6) and **7)** Early-17C tableaux by local artist Jean Nicolle: the Nativity and Adoration of the Magi.
8) Mausoleum by Robert d'Acquigny (late 15C).
9) Restored Renaissance stained glass.

Musée municipal

 ♿ ⏱*Open daily except Tue 2–6pm.* ⏱*Closed 1 Jan, 1 May, 25 Dec. No charge.* ☎*02 32 09 58 55. www.ville-louviers.fr*
The museum hosts temporary exhibitions of faience, furniture and painting. One room is devoted to the clothing industry.

Maison du Fou du Roy

The half-timbered house in the main street is also the tourist office. It once belonged to Guillaume Marchand, an

Address Book

ⓘ*For coin ranges, see the Legend on the cover flap.*

WHERE TO STAY

⊝⊝ **Manoir de La Haye le Comte** – 4 rte de La-Haye-le-Comte, 700m/0.2mi S of Louviers on D 113. ☎02 32 40 00 40. www.manoir-louviers.com. Closed 23 Dec –15 Jan. 14 rooms. 🅿 ⌇. Restaurant ⊝⊝. A 16C family residence. Snug, personalised rooms. Cosy lounge and dining rooms. The park offers romantic strolls, tennis, pétanque, croquet, a golfing range and mountain biking.

WHERE TO EAT

⊝ **Le Jardin de Bigard** – 39/41 r. du Quai. ☎02 32 40 02 45. Closed Feb holidays, 2 weeks in Aug and Sun. Reservations advised. A traditional restaurant behind a brick façade, located in a neighbourhood that survived World War II unscathed. View of Notre-Dame Church, a park and a manor; terrace in the summer.

apothecary, who became Henri IV's jester (Fou du Roy) after the previous incumbent was killed in battle.

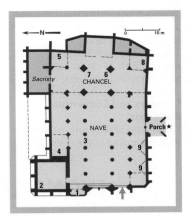

Excursions

Vironvay

5km/3mi E by N 155, then the minor road on the left which crosses A 13 and N 15. The isolated church overlooks the Seine Valley. The **view**★ on approaching extends over the river spanned by the bridge at St-Pierre-du-Vauvray and, farther east, the ruins of Château-Gaillard.

Pont-de-l'Arche

11km/7mi E by D 321 along the south bank of the Seine.

The small town, named after the first bridge to be built over the lower Seine, is pleasantly set in a valley. On the south side is Bord Forest.

The **Église Notre-Dame-des-Arts** exhibits the Flamboyant Gothic style in the doorway and the ornate south side. The interior is lit by 16C and 17C windows The Louis XIII altarpiece shows the Resurrection by CLF Le Tourneur (1751-1817).

Acquigny French gardens

6km/4mi S of Louviers via D 71. ⚷🕓*Open July–Aug daily 2–7pm. Mid-Apr–June &Sept–Oct weekends and public holidays 2–6pm.* ⊙*6.50€ (Children 4€).* ☎*02 32 50 23 31.*

The formal **French gardens** lying at the confluence of the River Eure and River Iton have retained their long avenues and orangery. Waterfalls, artificial streams and a series of fords are reminiscent of the Romantic period.

ABBAYE DE LUCERNE

MANCHE, MICHELIN MAP 303: D-7 – 12KM/8MI SE OF GRANVILLE

The sizeable ruins of Lucerne Abbey stand in a fine parkland setting in the pleasantly green Thar Valley. The abbey was founded in 1143, but it was not before 1164 that construction started.

▶ **Orient Yourself:** The abbey is 12km/7.5 mi southeast of Granville via D 973, then D 580 until just before St-Pierre-Langers. It is on the road between Sartilly and St-Léger-en-Avranchin.

⚷ **Don't Miss:** The remarkable 12C bell tower.

🕓 **Organizing Your Time:** Give yourself 1hr 30min to see the site.

⚶ **Also See:** Granville, Carolles, Villedieu-les-Poêles and Avranches.

Visit

Abbey Church

⚷🕓*Open Apr–Sept daily 10am–noon, 2–6.30pm. Oct daily 10am–noon, 2–5pm; Rest of the year daily except Tue 10–noon, 2–5pm.* 🕓*Closed Jan–mid-Feb, Sun* mornings and during religious holidays. ☞*Guided tours available July–Aug.* ⊙*4€ (Children 2 €).* ☎*02 33 48 83 56. www.abbaye-lucerne.fr*

The doorway in the 12C façade is Romanesque. The Cistercian-style nave consists of seven bays. The transept crossing (restored) supports a late-12C Gothic square **bell-tower**★, pierced on each side with narrow lancets.

The south transept houses a fine 18C **organ**★ with 33 stops. Concerts are given throughout the year.

Cloisters and Conventual Buildings

The arcades of the north-west corner and the entrance to the chapter-house are still standing. In the south-west corner, near the door to the old refectory (entirely rebuilt), is a 12C *lavatorium* with four beautiful little Romanesque arcades.

The way back to the porter's lodge passes the old tithe barn and the dovecot, a huge round tower with 1 500 pigeon-holes.

LYONS-LA-FORÊT★

EURE, POPULATION 795, MICHELIN MAP 304: I-5

The half-timbered houses, old brick buildings and sylvan setting in the heart of the Forêt de Lyons create a picture-book vision of Normandy. Unusually in the French language, the final "s" of Lyons is pronounced, indicating the town's Scandinavian origins.

- **Information:** 20 rue de l'Hôtel de Ville, 27480 Lyons-la-Forêt. ☎02 32 49 31 65.
- **Orient Yourself:** Lyons-la-Forêt is 43km/27mi east of Rouen via N 31 and D 921, and 20km/12.5mi north of Andelys via D 2, on the River Lieurre.
- **Don't Miss:** The château of Vascoeuil and the beautiful Forêt de Lyons.
- **Organizing Your Time:** Spend your afternoon exploring forest paths on your way to Écouis.
- **Also See:** The château of Martainville, Écouis, Forges-les-Eaux, Les Andelys and Rouen

The Village

Halles

The old covered market in the centre of place Benserade was used for scenes in Jean Renoir's film *Madame Bovary*. The fountain appeared in Claude Chabrol's 1990 version of the same novel.

Pretty half-timbered houses surround the square. In the steep street west of the square, **Maurice Ravel** composed *Le Tombeau de Couperin* and completed the orchestration for Mousorgski's *Pictures at an Exhibition*.

Église St-Denis

Rue Bout-de-Bas leads to St-Denis Church, at the edge of the village, on the riverside. Open only to groups. The 12C church was completely renovated in the 15C.

The stonework and the timber belfry are admirable. In the chancel, the statue of St Christopher carrying the infant Jesus dates from the 16C.

Forêt De Lyons★★

70km/42mi – Allow one day.

The forest covers 10 700ha/26 440 acres and is known for its glorious beech trees, some with trunks 20m/60ft tall. You can also admire an old abbey and two interesting châteaux.

- *Leave Lyons via D 6E.*

Notre-Dame-de-la-Paix

From this statue there is a fine view of the town of Lyons.

- *Take D 169 left.*

Chapelle St-Jean

Behind the 17C chapel a path leads to the Chêne St-Jean (St John's Oak) which has a circumference of 5m/16ft at a height of 1.30m/4ft from the ground.

▷ *Take the second road on the left (D 11) towards Rosay.*

Rosay-sur-Lieure

The **church** and churchyard are in a pleasant setting.

▷ *D 11 goes on to Ménesqueville.*

Ménesqueville

The small 12C country **church,** skilfully restored, contains some very old statues. The stained-glass windows by contemporary artist F-E Décorchemont portray the Song of Songs.

▷ *From here, D 12 goes along the pretty Fouillebroc Valley as far as Lisors.*

Lisors

The church contains a 14C crowned Virgin which was found buried in 1936.

▷ *Take D 175; on the right, you will see the ruins of the abbey.*

Abbaye de Mortemer

🌄 *Guided tours (45min) of the museum (45min) May–Aug 1–6pm. Rest of the year Sun and public holidays 2–6pm. Unaccompanied access to park year-round 1–6pm.* ☞ *Park and museum: 7€. Park alone 5€ (Children museum and park 6€, park alone 3€).* ☎ *02 32 49 54 34.www. mortemer.free.fr.*

In the forest stand the ruins of the 12C-13C Cistercian abbey which had a huge church (90m/295ft long; 42m/138ft wide). A **museum** below the conventual building, reconstructed in the 17C, explains monastic life and evokes legends connected with the abbey. A small train will take you on a tour of the very lovely grounds.

▷ *Across from the abbey, on the left-hand side of D 175, a short path leads to the Croix-Vaubois crossroads.*

Les Halles, Lyons-la-Forêt

G. Targat/MICHELIN

Carrefour de la Croix-Vaubois

The monument erected here recalls the foresters who died in the Resistance.

▷ *As you continue along D 175, look for two springs (sources) off to the left.*

Source de Ste-Catherine-de-Lisors

A footbridge spanning the Fouillebroc leads to an oratory, traditionally visited by young girls in search of a husband.

Source du Fouillebroc

This spring is set in pleasant forest surroundings.

▷ *After crossing D 6, the road leads into Beaufcel via the hamlet of La Bouvetière.*

Beaufcel-en-Lyons

Church – 🕐 *Guided tours by appointment with Mme Dufour, 1 rte de Fleury, 27480 Beaufcel-en-Lyons.* ☎ *02 32 49 62 51.* The **church** is preceded by a 17C porch and contains beautiful statues, including a 14C virgin in polychrome stone.

WHERE TO STAY

😊😊 **Les Lyons de Beauclerc**– *7 r. de l'Hôtel-de-Ville.* ☎ *02 32 49 18 90. www.lionsdebeauclerc.com. Closed Mar. 6 rooms.* ⛲. *Restaurant* 😊😊. This old house unites modern comfort with second-hand furniture collected by the owners, who also run an adjacent antique shop. Restaurant and tea shop on the premises.

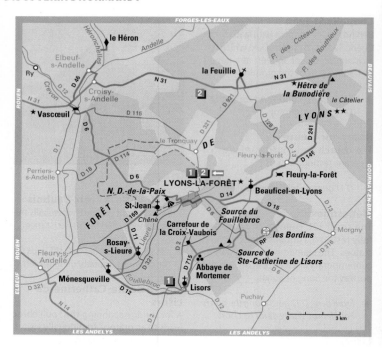

> D 14 goes alongside Fleury-la-Forêt Castle (to the right) and into the village of Bosquentin.

Château de Fleury-la-Forêt

Guided tours (45min) mid-June–mid-Sept 2–6pm. Rest of the year weekends and public holidays 2–6pm. Closed Dec–Feb. 6.50€ (Children 5.50€). 02 32 49 63 91. www.chateau-fleury-la-foret.com
Beyond a magnificent wrought-iron gate, a majestic avenue of ancient lime trees leads to the early-17C château built of red brick, flint and sandstone.
The interior contains interesting displays of dolls, toys and furniture. There is also a huge kitchen abundantly decorated.

> Turn left after Bosquentin and follow D 241.

Hêtre de la Bunodière★

Indicated by a signpost on the right as you leave N 31 to enter the forest, this magnificent beech, which is 40m/131ft tall, stands near the Câtelier Reserve. Its circumference measures 3.3m/11ft.

> N 31-E 46 leads back to La Feuillie.

La Feuillie

The slender church **spire**★ is a bold piece of carpentry.

Vascœuil

This little village (pronounced Va-coy) on the edge of the forest is famous for its **château**★ (14C-16C; 7.50€ (Over 10 years 5€); 02 35 23 62 35; www.chateau-vascoeuil.com).

Musée Michelet

A collection of mementoes of the historian Jules Michelet (1798-1874) .

Église St-Martial

Guided tours on weekdays and certain Sundays by appointment with M. Jean-Joseph Le Brozec, rue des Canadiens. 02 35 02 11 69.
Inside this church is the tomb of Hugues de Saint-Jovinien, a holy man who died in the 12C. The painted stone statues represent the Virgin Mary and St Martial.

> You can return to Lyons-la-Forêt via D6/D6E.

MAYENNE

MAYENNE, POPULATION 13 724
MICHELIN MAP 310: F-5

Mayenne is a bridgehead town whose strategic importance in the past was compounded by the existence of a powerful fortress.

- **Information:** Quai de Waiblingen, 53100 Mayenne. ☎02 43 04 19 37. www.mairie-mayenne.net.
- ▶ **Orient Yourself:** Mayenne is on the route from Le Mans (104km/65mi southeast) to Mont-St-Michel. It is also between Caen (12km/79mi north) and Laval (32km/20mi south).
- **Don't Miss:** The pretty villages in the forest of Mayenne.
- **Organizing Your Time:** Take a day to see the town, and to enjoy the many nautical activities on the Mayenne river.
- **Also See:** Domfront, Lassay-les-Châteaux, Jublains and Laval.

A Bit of History

Cardinal Mazarin originally undertook to make the River Mayenne navigable from Lavalle to Mayenne in the 17C. The town's key role was proved during the Second World War. By 8 June 1944, Mayenne had been nearly levelled, but the bridge remained intact. Thanks to the heroism of an American sergeant, Mack Racken, the only bridge still spanning the River Mayenne was saved to serve the Allies.

Sights

Château Carolingien

⌖Closed for repairs. Scheduled to reopen in 2008.

Abutting on rock escarpments, the 11C castle stands on the hill on the west bank of the river. It suffered frequent siege, and William the Conqueror took it by cunning.

The perimeter wall remains, giving the castle a truly feudal appearance. The promenade between the curtain walls and the town gardens commands an attractive **view**★ of the town.

Basilique Notre-Dame

This church has been remodelled several times. The west front along with the pillars and arches in the nave, are 12C; the transept walls and windows are 16C. The church was rebuilt at the end of the 19C in the Gothic style.

Église St-Martin

Located opposite the château, on the hillside on the other side of the river.
🕐*Open Easter–Oct 9.30am–5pm.* In the 11C the church belonged to Marmoutiers Abbey in Tours, and both the apse and transept date from this period.

The modern stained glass, like that in the Basilique Notre-Dame, is by the master glazier Maurice Rocher.

Excursions

Forêt de Mayenne (oak, elm and coppice): **Fontaine-Daniel** (a pool overlooked by an attractive chapel and an **exhibition centre**), flower-decked houses and an old Cistercian abbey; **Chailland** (statue of a Virgin on top of a rocky escarpment). *Exhibition centre displaying fabrics including Mayenne cloth (toile de Mayenne) –* 🕐*Open daily except Sun and public holidays 9am–noon, 2–6pm* 🚫*No charge.* ☎*02 43 00 34 80.*

MONT-ST-MICHEL★★★

MANCHE, POPULATION 46
MICHELIN MAP 303: C-8

Why is the world fascinated by Mont-St-Michel? No doubt it is not just the beauty of the architecture and the length of the mount's history. Perhaps it is the sense of mystery in the movement of the tides that separate this rocky outcrop from the mainland, or the play of twilight on the water and walls, or the cry of gulls gliding above the salty grass marsh. It is impossible to take the measure of Mont-St-Michel without including its unique natural setting: the rock and the bay of this UNESCO World Heritage Site are truly one.

🛈 **Information:** Corps de garde des Bourgeois, 50116 Le Mont-St-Michel.
☎02 33 60 14 30. www.ot-montsaintmichel.com, www.abbaye-saintmichel.com

▶ **Orient Yourself:** Mont St-Michel is at the northern limit of D 976, which connects with D 175 at Pontorson, 10km/6mi south, which in turn leads to Avranches (21km/13mi northeast) via N 175 and major national arteries.

🅿 **Parking:** Parking lots (4€ per day per vehicle) stretch over 2km/1.25mi of dikes. Arrive early to get a space closer to the Mount.
During very high tides (every other week, twice a day), parking lots are inundated and you must park along the access road. Attendants will inform you if you cannot read the signs.

🚫 **Don't Miss:** Try to catch the miraculous spectacle of sunset over the bay from the steps of the church.

🕐 **Organizing Your Time:** In the summer, night visits are organized, to musical accompaniment, daily except Sunday from 7–11.30pm, last entry at 10.30pm. Information at the Visitors' Service ☎02 33 89 80 00.

Kids **Especially for Kids:** The Maison de la Baie offers guided tours of the bay; just bear in mind that walks cover several kilometres. The nature centre at Relais de Vains-St-Léonard explains the fauna and flora of the Bay. (*see Relais de Genêts*) Alligator Bay, in Beauvoir (*see Beauvoir*), displays alligators, crocodiles, turtles, etc.

👍 **Also See:** Pontorson, Avranches, Carolles and Granville.

A Bit of History

An amazing achievement– The abbey dates back to the early 8C when the Archangel Michael appeared to Aubert, Bishop of Avranches. He founded an oratory on the island, then known as Mount Tombe. In the Carolingian era (8-10C) the oratory was replaced by an abbey. From then until the 16C a series of increasingly splendid buildings, in the Romanesque and then the Gothic style, succeeded one another, on this mount dedicated to the Archangel Michael.

The abbey was remarkably well fortified and never fell to the enemy. The construction is an amazing achievement. The blocks of granite were transported from the Chausey Islands and Brittany, then hoisted up to the foot of the building. The crest of the hill was very narrow, so the foundations had to be built up from the lower slopes.

Pilgrimages – Pilgrims flocked to the mount, even during periods of attrition like the Hundred Years War. The English, who had possession of the area, granted safe conduct to the faithful in return for payment. People of all sorts made the journey: nobles, rich citizens and beggars who lived on alms and were granted free accommodation by the monks.

Hotels and souvenir shops flourished. The pilgrims bought medals bearing the effigy of St Michael and lead amulets which they filled with sand from the beach.

In periods of widespread disaster the pilgrimage incited such excess of fervour that the church authorities were obliged to intervene.

Of the many thousands of people crossing the bay, some drowned, others perished in the quicksands. The deaths lead to the lengthening of the prayer to St Michael in Peril from the Sea.

Decline – The abbey came to be held in commendam (by lay abbots who received the revenue without exercising the duties) and discipline among the monks grew lax. In the 17C the Maurists, monks from St Maur, were made responsible for reforming the monastery, but they only made some disappointing architectural changes, and tinkering with the stonework. Further dilapidation ensued when the abbey became a prison. In 1811, after the Revolution, it was converted into a national prison for political prisoners. In 1874 the abbey and the ramparts passed into the care of the Historic Monuments Department (Service des Monuments Historiques). Since 1966 a few monks have again been in residence conducting the services in the abbey church.

Stages in the Abbey's Construction

The buildings date from the 11C to the 16C.

Romanesque Abbey

11C-12C: Between 1017 and 1144 a church was built on the top of the mount. The previous Carolingian building was incorporated as a crypt – Notre-Dame-sous-Terre (Our Lady Underground) – to support the platform on which the last three bays of the Romanesque nave were built. Other crypts were constructed to support the transepts and the chancel, which projected beyond the natural rock.

The convent buildings were constructed on the west face and on either side of the nave. The entrance to the abbey faced west.

Gothic Abbey

13C-16C: This period saw the construction of:

♦ The magnificent Merveille buildings (1211-28) on the north side of the church, used by the monks and pilgrims and for the reception of important guests.

♦ The abbatial buildings (13C-15C) on the south side comprising the administrative offices, the abbot's lodging and the garrison's quarters.

♦ The main gatehouse and the outer defences (14C) on the east side, which protected the entrance which was moved to this side of the mount.

♦ The chancel of the Romanesque church had collapsed and was rebuilt more magnificently in the

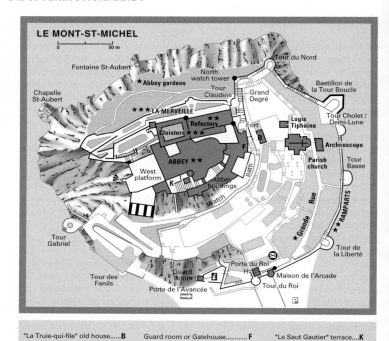

LE MONT-ST-MICHEL

Tour du Nord
Fontaine St-Aubert
★ Abbey gardens
North watch tower
Tour Claudine
Grand Degré
Bastillon de la Tour Boucle
Chapelle St-Aubert
★★★ LA·MERVEILLE
Refectory ★★
Cloisters ★★★
Fort
Logis Tiphaine
Tour Cholet / Demi-Lune
Archéoscope
ABBEY ★★
Parish church
Tour Basse
West platform
Abbey buildings
Watch
Tour Gabriel
Tour de la Liberté
Tour des Fanils
Guard Room
Porte de l'Avancée
Porte du Roi
Maison de l'Arcade
Tour du Roi
RAMPARTS
Grande Rue

"La Truie-qui-file" old house......**B**   Guard room or Gatehouse............**F**   "Le Saut Gautier" terrace....**K**

Flamboyant Gothic style (1446-1521) above a new crypt.

Alterations

18C-19C. In 1780 the last three bays of the nave and the Romanesque façade were demolished.

The present bell-tower (1897) is surmounted by a beautiful spire that rises to 157m/515ft and terminates in a statue of St Michael (1879) by Emmanuel Frémiet. The 4.5m/15ft-tall archangel, in position for over 100 years, was recently restored after lightening has struck off St Michael's sword.

Major project to restore the Bay

After years of planning, the project to dredge the Bay of St-Michel is finally underway. This extremely complex project will reverse the silting-up that has gone on for years, particularly since construction of the 1877 causeway. In the first stage, begun in 2006, a dam is being constructed on the River Couesnon to restrain the influx of sand. Starting in 2008, the parking lots will be moved further inland; as of 2010, shuttles will ferry tourists to and from the Mount. Finally,

the causeway will be partially replaced by a bridge planned for 2012 which will allow tidal water to swirl freely around the bay. Tourist access to the Mont will not be interrupted during these major works. For more information, you can consult the website www.projetmont-saintmichel.fr.

The Village

⊜*The cobbled streets are uneven and steep here, and the abbey is a labyrinth of corridors and cloisters. Wear the most comfortable shoes you own.*

Outer Defences

The outer gate opens into the first fortified courtyard. On the left stands the Citizens' Guard-room (16C) occupied by the Tourist Office; on the right are the Michelettes, English mortars captured in a sortie during the Hundred Years War. A second gate leads into a second courtyard. The third gate (15C), complete with machicolations and portcullis, is called the King's Gate because it was the lodging of the token contingent maintained by the king to assert his rights; this gate opens onto the Grande-Rue where the abbot's soldiers lodged in the fine arcaded house (right).

Grande-Rue★

This picturesque narrow street climbs steeply between old (15C-16C) houses and ends in a flight of steps. In summer it is crowded with stalls of souvenir merchants just as in the Middle Ages.

Ramparts★★

These are 13C-15C. The sentry walk offers fine views of the bay; from the North Tower the Tombelaine Rock, which Philippe Auguste had fortified, is clearly visible.

Musée de la Mer et de l'Écologie

Kids ©Open July–Aug 9am–7pm. Feb – June, Sept–mid-Nov and Christmas school holidays 9am-5.30pm. ∞7€ (children 4.50€). ☎02 33 60 85 12.
Films and an audioguided tour explain the environment of the Mount, including the tides, the dangers in the Bay and the silting-up process. There are also 150 models of old boats.

Musée historique

Kids ©Same hours and conditions as for the Musée de la Mer. ☎02 33 60 07 01.
This historical museum retraces the history of the Mount back 1000 years, using a sound and light show and glass cases of old objects and weapons. The tour ends in the dungeons.

Église paroissiale St-Pierre

The 11C parish church has been much altered. The apse spans a narrow street. The church contains a Crucifix and other furnishings from the abbey; the chapel in the south aisle houses a statue of St Michael covered in silver; in the chapel to the right of the altar there is a 15C statue of the Virgin and Child and another of St Anne and the Virgin as a child.

Logis Tiphaine

©Same hours and conditions as for the Musée de la Mer. ☎02 33 60 23 34.
When the celebrated 14C warrior Bertrand du Guesclin was captain of the Mount, he had this house built (1365) for his wife Tiphaine Raguenel, an attractive and educated woman from Dinan, while he went off to the wars in Spain. The house was heavily restored in the 19C.

The Abbey★★★

©Open May–Aug 9am–7pm (last admission 1hr before closing). Rest of the year 9.30am–6pm. ☜ Guided tour (1hr) offered. ©Closed 1 Jan, 1 May, 25 Dec. ∞8€ (Under 18 years no charge). No charge to attend mass, during which visits are not allowed: daily except Mon noon–12.15pm. ☎02 33 89 80 00.
The tour passes through a maze of corridors and stairs floor by floor, not from building to building or period by period.

Mont-St-Michel

B. Kaufmann/MICHELIN

Address Book

For coin ranges, see the Legend on the cover flap.

WHERE TO STAY

⌐ **Hôtel La Tour Brette** – 8 r. Couesnon, 50170 Pontorson, 9km/5.6mi S of Mont-St-Michel. ☎02 33 60 10 69. www.latourbrette.com. Closed 14–22 Mar, 1–20 Dec and Wed except July–Aug. 10 rooms. ⌐ . Restaurant⌐. This well-situated little hotel owes its name to an old tower that protected Normandy from the dukes of Brittany. Rooms are small but recently renovated. At the restaurant, extensive traditional menu.

⌐ **Hôtel Bretagne** – R. Couesnon, 50170 Pontorson, 4km/2.4mi S of Mont-St-Michel via D 976. ☎02 33 60 10 55. www.lebretagnepontorson.com. Closed 15–30 Jan. 13 rooms. ⌐. Restaurant ⌐. This regional-style house has lovely 18C wood panels, a grey-marble fireplace and a plate-warming radiator (very unusual!) in a little dining room. Cosy, typically British bar and spacious, pleasantly furnished rooms.

⌐ **Mme Gillet Hélène Bed and Breakfast** – Le Val-St-Revert, 35610 Roz-sur-Couesnon, 15km/9.3mi SW of Mont-St-Michel via D 797, the coast road to St-Malo. ☎02 99 80 27 85. 4 rooms. ⌐ ⌐. This 17C family house overlooks the bay and offers a beautiful view of Mont-St-Michel and the surrounding countryside. Four rooms where an old world charm lingers on: three on the sea side and a more recent and brighter one with a terrace facing the garden.

⌐ **Amaryllis Bed and Breakfast** – Le Bas-Pays, 50170 Beauvoir, 2.5km/1.5mi S of Mont-St-Michel dir. Pontorson. ☎02 33 60 09 42. aamaryllis.lume@wanadoo.fr. 5 rooms. ⌐ ⌐. This stone house was renovated specifically as a B&B. The impeccably clean rooms feature well-equipped bathrooms and a furnished terrace. An extra treat: you can visit the farm next door.

⌐⌐⌐ **Âuberge St-Pierre** – Grande-Rue. ☎02 33 60 14 03. www.auberge-saint-pierre.fr. 21 rooms. ⌐. Restaurant ⌐⌐. This inn offers rooms spread across 3 houses. The restaurant, in a 15C house, offers a brasserie on the ground floor, a rustic dining room upstairs or a terrace overlooking the ramparts of Mont-St-Michel.

WHERE TO EAT

⌐ **La Gourmandise** – 21 rte du Mont-St-Michel, 50170 Beauvoir, 4km/2.4mi S of Mont-St-Michel. ☎02 33 58 42 83. Closed Nov–Mar and Tue except July–Aug This Breton house transformed into a crêperie enlivens the tiny village. Simple decor, lit up by large bay windows. The extensive menu offers a choice of crepes and galettes. A few guestrooms.

⌐ **Auberge de la Baie** – La Rive, 50170 Ardevon, 3km/1.8mi SE of Mont-St-Michel dir. Avranches via D 275. ☎02 33 68 26 70. www.aubergedelabaie.fr. Closed Nov and Tue–Wed except during July–Aug. This restaurant on a departmental road is a welcome break from the bustling tourism of Mont-St-Michel, at least for an hour or two. On the menu: traditional and regional dishes, plus a short list of galettes. 12 guestrooms.

⌐⌐ **La Sirène** – Grande-Rue. ☎02 33 60 08 60. Closed 10 Jan–2 Feb, 15 Nov –20 Dec. Take the spiral staircase to enter the crêperie in this 14C house that was an inn for many years. The frosted-glass windows, their panes separated by metal mullions, confirm the genuine flavour of the place.

⌐⌐ **Pré Salé** – Rest. belonging to the Hôtel Mercure, 2km/1.2mi S of Mont-St-Michel via D 976. ☎02 33 60 14 18. contact@hotelmercure-montsaintmichel.com. Closed 12 Nov–6 Feb. Located along the River Couesnon at the start of the dike, the Hôtel Mercure welcomes you into its bright dining room, recently renovated with tables set comfortably apart from each other. Try the delicious salt-meadow (pré salé) meat from Mont-St-Michel Bay.

⌐⌐ **La Promenade** – Pl. du Casino, 50610 Jullouville, ☎02 33 90 80 20. www.la-promenade.fr. Closed Mon and Tue. Reservations advised. It would be difficult to find a better view of Mont-St-Michel Bay than at this elegant restaurant-tearoom on the ground floor of the former casino hotel (1881). Handsome antique furniture and tableware. Menu with an accent on seafood.

Outer Defences of the Abbey

A flight of steps, the Grand Degré, once cut off by a swing door, leads up to the abbey. At the top on the right is the entrance to the gardens; more steps lead up to the ramparts.

Through the arch of an old door is a fortified courtyard overlooked by the fort, which consists of two tall towers linked by machicolations. Even this military structure shows the builder's artistic sense: the wall is attractively constructed of alternate courses of pink and grey granite. Beneath a flattened barrel vault a steep and ill-lit staircase, the Escalier du Gouffre (Abyss Steps), leads down to the beautiful door which opens into the guard-room, also called the Porterie.

Salle des Gardes or Porterie

This gatehouse was the focal point of the abbey. Poor pilgrims passed through on their way from the Merveille Court to the Almonry.

Abbey Steps

An impressive flight of 90 steps rises between the abbatial buildings *(left)* and the abbey church *(right)*; it is spanned by a fortified bridge (15C).

The stairs stop outside the south door of the church on a terrace called the Saut Gautier (**Gautier Leap**), after a prisoner who is supposed to have hurled himself over the edge. The tour starts here.

West Platform

This spacious terrace, which was created by the demolition of the last three bays of the church, provides an extensive view★ of the bay of Mont-St-Michel.

Church★★

The exterior of the church, particularly the east end with its buttresses, flying buttresses, bell turrets and balustrades, is a masterpiece of light and graceful architecture. The interior reveals the marked contrast between the severe, sombre Romanesque nave and the elegant, luminous Gothic chancel.

La Merveille★★★

The name, which means the Marvel, applies to the superb Gothic buildings on the north face of the Mount. The eastern block, the first to be built between 1211 and 1218, comprises, from top to bottom, the refectory, the Guests' Hall and the Almonry; the western block, built between 1218 and 1228, consists of the cloisters, the Knights' Hall and the cellar.

From the outside the buildings look like a fortress although their religious connections are indicated by the simple nobility of the design. The interior is a perfect example of the evolution of the Gothic style, from an almost Romanesque simplicity in the lower halls, through the elegance of the Guests' Hall, the majesty of the Knights' Hall and the mysterious luminosity of the Refectory, to the cloisters which are a masterpiece of delicacy and line.

Cloisters★★★

The cloisters seem to be suspended between the sea and the sky. The gallery arcades display heavily undercut sculpture of foliage ornamented with the occasional animal or human figure (particularly human heads); there are also a few religious symbols. The double row of arches rests on delightfully slim single columns arranged in quincunx to enhance the impression of lightness. The different colours of the various materials add to the overall charm. The *lavatorium* (lavabo) on the right of the entrance recalls the ceremonial washing of the feet every Thursday.

Refectory★★

The effect is mysterious; the chamber is full of light although it appears to have only two windows in the end wall. To admit so much light without weakening the solid side walls which support the wooden roof and are lined with a row of slim niches, the architect introduced a very narrow aperture high up in each recess. The vaulted ceiling is panelled with wood and the acoustics are excellent.

Old Romanesque Abbey

The rib vaulting marks the transition from Romanesque to Gothic. The tour includes the Monks' Walk and part of the dormitory.

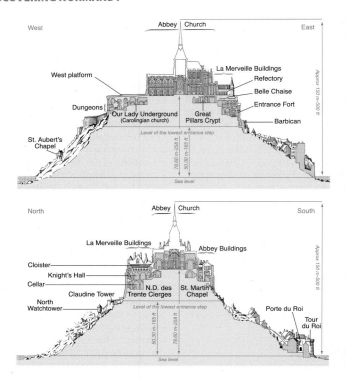

Great Wheel

The wheel belongs to the period when the abbey was used as a prison. It was used to haul provisions and was operated by five or six men turning the wheel from within as if on a treadmill.

Crypts

The transepts and chancel of the church are supported by three undercrofts or crypts; the most moving is **Notre-Dame-sous-Terre** *(accessible only during guided tours)*: the Carolingian structure which stands where St Aubert officiated, is a simple rectangle (8x9m/26x30ft), divided into two small naves by a couple of arches resting on a central pillar. The place is awe-inspiring because of the complete silence which prevails and because of the memory of events which took place here more than 1 000 years ago! The most impressive is the **Crypte des Gros Piliers**★ (Great Pillared Crypt) which has 10 pillars (5m/16ft in circumference) made of granite from the Chausey Islands.

Guests' Hall★

Here the abbot received royalty (Louis IX, Louis XI, François I) and other important visitors. The hall (35m/115ft long) has a Gothic ceiling supported on a central row of slim columns; the effect is graceful and elegant.

At one time it was divided down the middle by a huge curtain of tapestries; on one side was the kitchen quarters (two chimneys) and on the other the great dining hall (one chimney).

Knights' Hall★

The name of this hall may refer to the military order of St Michael which was founded in 1469 by Louis XI with the abbey as its seat.

The hall is vast and majestic (26x18m/85x58ft) and divided into four sections by three rows of stout columns.

It was the monks' workroom or scriptorium where they illuminated manuscripts, read and studied religious or secular texts and, for this reason, it was heated by two great fireplaces. The

Omelette de la Mère Poulard

Annette Boutiaut was born in Nevers in 1851. She was employed as a lady's maid by the architect Édouard Corroyer, a disciple of Viollet-le-Duc, who was commissioned by the Monuments Historiques (a State-run organisation) to restore Mont-St-Michel Abbey. Annette followed her employers there and met the son of a local baker. They married and took over the running of the St-Michel Tête d'Or Hotel. At that time (around 1875), the causeway had not been built yet so that tourists and pilgrims reached Mont-St-Michel on foot, on horseback or aboard a *maringotte* (a small two-wheeled horse-drawn cart), tide permitting. They were usually very hungry and could not bear to wait for food to be prepared. Annette knew that a good innkeeper should not be taken unawares. She therefore always had eggs in store and quickly beat up an omelette for her guests while they waited for more substantial dishes. Her welcome and the quality of the food she served gradually brought her fame. When Annette Poulard died in 1931, food critics speculated on the secret recipe of the omelette. Some talked about fresh cream, specially selected eggs and butter, others argued it was all due to fast cooking; Annette herself explained in a letter dated 1922: "I break the eggs in a bowl, I beat them up well, I put a nice knob of butter in the frying pan, I throw the eggs in and stir continuously."

Curnonsky (1872-1956), the prince of gourmets, said that the secret lay in the recipe of Dr Rouget, the hero of Balzac's *La Rabouilleuse*, who beat up the yolks and whites separately before mixing them in the frying pan!

almonry and cellar occupy the rooms on the lower floor.

Cellar
This was the storeroom; it was divided into three by two rows of square pillars supporting the groined vaulting.

Almonry
This is a Gothic room with a Romanesque vault supported on a row of columns.

Abbey Gardens★
🕐*Closed in winter and in bad weather.* A pleasant place for a stroll with a view of the west side of the mount and St Aubert's Chapel.

Mont-St-Michel Bay★★

▸ *About 100km/60mi of coast line border the bay.*

The islands, cliffs, beaches and dunes form a series of ecosystems which are home to many species of flora and fauna.

Travelling along the coast, you will be rewarded by stunning views of Mont-St-Michel, and you can enjoy walks along pleasant paths rambling between the polders and grassy fields.

Tall tales and natural phenomena
Pilgrims liked to tell frightening tales of the perils of Mont-St-Michel, but the natural phenomena of the site are now well understood. What used to be called quick sand is really the effect of swathes of firm sand sitting on top of pockets of more liquid sand. The fearsome fog which occasionally envelops the whole bay with such speed can now be predicted by weather forecasters, and there is no longer a need to ring the church bell to warn of its imminence. And the tide racing in faster than a galloping horse? Although there are specific points where the action of the spring tide combines with geological features to create a movement of water at a speed of up to 25-30kph/15-18mph, the average rate of speed of the incoming tide is 3.75kph/2.25mph – about the speed of a person walking.

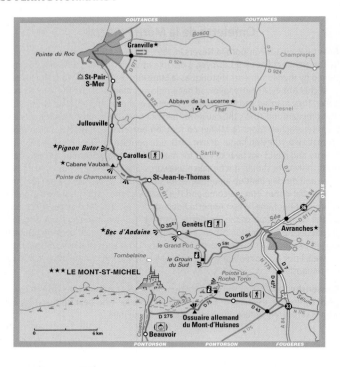

From Granville to Mont-St-Michel

40km/25mi – Allow about 2hr 30min
Between Granville and Carolles, there is a wide open view of the bay.

St-Pair-sur-Mer
⏂*See GRANVILLE Excursions.*

Jullouville
The town is renowned for its fine sand beach. A pleasant walk leads along the seafront, passing 19C houses scattered among pine trees. The view extends from Pignon Butor to the Point du Roc.

Carolles
The village is set on the last headland before the sandy expanse of Mont-St-Michel Bay. As you drive between Carolles and St-Jean-le-Thomas, there is a splendid view ★★ of the bay. Don't hesitate to stop the car!
🚶In the vicinity there are also several attractive walks with fine views.
The **Vallée des Peintres** (Artists' Valley) is an attractive spot, green and rock-strewn (🅿 *car park at Carolles-Plage, N of Carolles*).
The **view**★ from **Le Pignon Butor** *(viewing table)* on the clifftop extends north to Granville Rock and west to the Pointe du Grouin and Cancale in Brittany *(1km/0.6mi – 1hr on foot there and back, NW of the village).*
🚶The path through the **Vallée du Lude** crosses an area of gorse and broom to

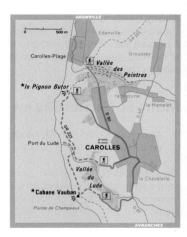

reach the lonely cove, Port du Lude, on the coast.(🅿*Follow the signs to the car park.1hr on foot there and back).*

▸ *S of Carolles on D 911 beyond the small bridge turn right; park at the end of the road; take the downhill path (left) which then climbs (right) towards the cliff.*

The **view**★ from the Vauban Hut, a stone building standing on a rocky mound, includes Mont-St-Michel in the middle of the bay

St-Jean-le-Thomas

This seaside resort is very busy in the summer months.

▸*On entering Genêts turn right.*

Bec d'Andaine★

There is a good **view** of Mont-St-Michel here from this beach backed by dunes.

Genêts

The solid granite 12C-14C **church** is preceded by an attractive porch with a wooden roof. Inside, the transept crossing leaves an impression of considerable strength, as it rises from four square granite piers with animal- and foliage-decorated capitals. The high altar is crowned by a canopy resting on gently swelling columns. Note the 13C stained-glass window at the east end and some lovely statues.

Relais des Genêts

Guides offer visitors an opportunity to join walking tours through the bay area, some with special themes, and all centred around enjoying the natural beauty, learning about the flora and the fauna. *Place de la Mairie, 50530 Genêts, ☎02 33 89 64 00.* Reservations are required, and you are asked to wear boots and warm clothing in winter, and carry a windbreaker, a snack and water at all times.

▸ *On leaving Genêts turn right before the calvary.*

The coastal road goes through Le Grand Port and offers good views, at very close quarters, of Mont-St-Michel, especially from the **Pointe du Grouin du Sud** (Grouin du Sud Point). The famous salt-marshes can also be seen.

Maison de la baie-Relais de Vains-St-Léonard

🎯⏺◐*Open July–Aug 10am–7pm. June & Sept 10am–6pm. Apr–May and school holidays 2–6pm.*◐*Closed Christmas holidays.* ⌨*4€ (7–15 years 1.60 €).*
Before undertaking a walking tour of the Bay, lead your children through this multimedia exhibition to introduce them to the flora and fauna they will encounter.

▸ *Take D 591 and D 911 to Avranches.*

Avranches★

◐*See AVRANCHES.*

▸ *At Bas-Courtils, turn left onto D 75; after 2km/1mi turn right onto D 107.*

Ossuaire Allemand du Mont-d'Huisnes

This circular construction with its 68 compartments, built in 1963, contains the remains of 11 887 German soldiers fallen in France. From the belvedere there is a good view of Mont-St-Michel.

▸ *Continue along D 275.*

The coastal road skirts the salt-marshes where flocks of sheep are put out to graze on the special grass there. The lambs are prized for their succulent tender meat. Again there are fine views of Mont-St-Michel.

Alligator Bay

Located at the entrance to Beauvoir, on the edge of D 976. 🎯⏺◐*Open Apr–Sept 10am–7pm. Feb–Mar & Oct–Dec 2–6pm. Jan weekends and school holidays 2–6pm.* ⌨*11€ (Children 4–12 years 7€, 13–18 years 9€). ☎02 33 68 11 18. www.alligator-bay.com*
Thrills are guaranteed at this reptile breeding centre where you can see a wide variety of tortoises, snakes and crocodiles.

MORTAGNE-AU-PERCHE

ORNE, POPULATION 4 513
MICHELIN MAP 310: M-3

This pretty village retains a medieval design with the houses clustered together, presenting a jumble of brown-tile roofs contrasting with the lighter-coloured façades. The village was once a stronghold of the Perche region.

- **Information:** Halle-aux-Grains, 61400 Mortagne-au-Perche.
  ☎02 33 85 11 18.
- ▶ **Orient Yourself:** Mortagne is 35km/22mi south of L'Aigle by D 930 and 74km/46mi southwest of Dreux by N 12.
- **Don't Miss:** If you approach from the north, on D 930, you will enjoy an excellent view of the town.
- **Organizing Your Time:** After an hour or two in town, spend the day walking in the forests of Perche, la Trappe or Réno-Valdieu.
- **Also See:** Bellême, Nogent-le-Rotrou and L'Aigle.

Visit

Jardin public

These gardens "à la française," offer good views of the Perche countryside. An outstanding equestrian statue by E Frémiet, (1824-1910) depicts Neptune as a horse, setting out to conquer Ceres.

Hôpital

Delightful 16C cloisters with panelled vaulting and an 18C chapel are all that remain of the former convent of St Clare.

Porte St-Denis

Musée Percheron – Open mid-June–mid-Sept daily except Mon 3–6pm.

Closed 14 July. No charge.☎02 33 25 25 87.
The St-Denis Gate is the sole remnant of the town's fortifications. In the 16C two storeys were added to the original 13C Gothic arch and they now house the **Musée Percheron**.

Maison des Comtes du Perche

This 17C house stands on the site of a former manor house. The ground floor houses the public library, and the first floor contains the Musée Alain.

Église Notre-Dame

The church was built between 1495 and 1535 and combines both Flamboyant

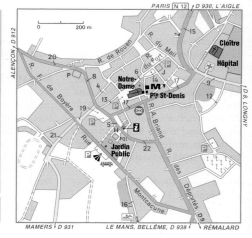

MORTAGNE-AU-PERCHE	
Comédie R. de la	4
Gaulle Pl. Gén.-de	5
Guérin R. du Col.	6
Leclerc R. Gén.	8
Longny R. de	9
Monanteuil R.	12
Notre-Dame R.	13
Palais Pl. du	14
Paris R. de	15
Poudrière R. de la	16
Quinze-Fusillés R. des	17
République Pl. de la	19
St-Éloy R. du Faubourg	20
St-Langis R. du Faubourg	21
Ste-Croix R.	22

Maison des comtes du Perche : Musée Alain	M¹

Gothic and Early Renaissance styles on the exterior decoration.

There is a magnificent 18C **altarpiece**★ in the apse. The stained-glass window in the third chapel, off the north aisle, recalls the role of local people in the colonisation of Canada in the 17C.

Musée Alain

⊙ *Open Tue, Thu, Fri 2–6pm, Wed 10am–noon, 1.30–6pm, Sat 10am–noon, 2–5pm.* ⊙ *Closed Sun, Mon and public holidays and 25 Dec –1 Jan and public holidays.* ◈ *No charge.* ☎ *02 33 25 25 87.*

The French philosopher **Alain** (1868-1951), whose real name was **Émile Chartier**, was born in Mortagne. The museum displays personal belongings.

Driving Tours

The Perche and Trappe Forests

Round-trip of 51km/32mi – Allow about 1hr 30min.

▷ *From Mortagne take N 12 N and after 12km/7mi turn right onto D 290.*

Parc naturel régional du Perche,

created in 1998, covers 182 000ha/449 722 acres of gentle hills, deep forests, hidden ponds, hedgerows, green valleys and interesting architecture.

Autheuil

The Romanesque church (restored) has a fine chancel arch at the entrance to the transept, handsome capitals on the transept's square piers and a 16C statue of St Leonard.

▷ *Make a U-turn and take D 290 W in the direction of Tourouvre.*

Tourouvre

Two stained-glass windows in the **church** tell about local families associated with the founding of Quebec.

▷ *Beyond the church turn right onto a road which climbs steeply towards Perche Forest.*

⊙ *For coin ranges, see the Legend on the cover flap.*

WHERE TO STAY AND EAT

⊖⊖ **Hostellerie Genty-Home** – *4 r. Notre-Dame.* ☎ *02 33 25 11 53. www.genty-home.com. Closed Sun evening except public holidays. 8 rooms.* ⊑. This traditional hostelry gives onto a nice little square in the city centre. The hotel rooms have a modern flair, whereas the elegant dining room is Louis XV. Regional specialties.

After a steep climb the road enters Perche Forest and, after 2km/1mi, reaches the beautiful Étoile du Perche crossroads. Continue straight ahead and on reaching the Avre Valley turn left to admire the various pools. West of Bresolettes the road enters Trappe Forest.

▷ *At the road junction turn right onto D 930 and then left onto the minor road.*

Abbaye de la Trappe

♿ ⊙ *Video shows and exhibition room daily 10.30am–noon, 3–5.45pm, Sun noon–1pm, 3–6pm.* ◈ *No charge.* ☎ *02 33 84 17 00.* The 12C abbey was named after an area where hunters caught game using a *trappe*. The name was adopted by monasteries which, like La Trappe, form the Order of Reformed Cistercians of the Strict Observance.

▷ *Make a U-turn and take D 930 S to Mortagne.*

From Mortagne-au-Perche to Longny

25km/16mi – Allow about 30min – ♿ *for map, see BELLÊME.*

Loisé

The 16C church is flanked by a monumental square tower.

Forêt de Réno-Valdieu

This 1 600ha/4 000-acre forest has beautiful stands of very old trees. A farm has replaced the former Abbaye de Valdieu, joined in 1789 with the forest of the Comte de Réno.

West of the forest the road (D 8) traverses a remarkable landscape of hills, passing Château de la Goyère.

▶ *On leaving the forest, take D 291 right.*

Monceaux-au-Perche

Manoir du Pontgirard – ⬥ ⏱Open May –Sept weekends and public holidays 2.30–6.30pm (Last entry at 6pm). ⏴5€ (Under 16 years no charge). ☏02 33 73 61 49. www.pontgirard.free.fr

This village standing at the confluence of two small valleys is one of the prettiest in the area. Nestling along the banks of the River **Jambée**, the **Manoir du Pontgirard** (16C) features some fine terraced **gardens** tucked away behind its walls.

▶ *Longny is reached by taking D 11, which runs through the shady Jambée Valley.*

Longny-au-Perche

A pleasant location beside the River Jambée. There is a good view of Logny from the charming 16C **Chapelle de Notre-Dame-de-Pitié** (▶*access by rue Gaston-Gibory on the right of the town hall*). The carved wooden doors are by a local 19C-20C artist, Abbé Vingtier. The west door shows the Visitation and the Annunciation; the north door the Virgin of Sorrow and the south door the face of Christ from Veronica's veil.

The **Église St-Martin** dates from the late 15C and the early 16C. The square belfry is supported by carved buttresses and the stair tower.

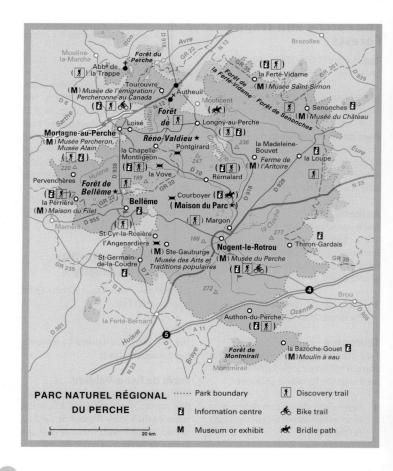

PARC NATUREL RÉGIONAL DU PERCHE

······ Park boundary
🚶 Discovery trail
🅱 Information centre
🚲 Bike trail
M Museum or exhibit
🐎 Bridle path

0 ———— 20 km

MORTAIN ★

MANCHE, POPULATION 2 191

MICHELIN MAP 303: G-8

This small, pleasantly well-kept town is built half way up a hillside in an attractive setting★ where the River Cance, cutting through the last of Basse-Normandie's southern hills, emerges on to the vast wooded Sélune basin, leaving in its wake a rock-strewn countryside. The name of the town is derived from the word Maurus and could refer to the Moors who served in the Roman army.

During the Middle Ages Mortain was the capital of the county held by Robert, the stepbrother of William the Conqueror. The town has been rebuilt over the ruins left after the Battle of Normandy.

- **Information:** Rue du Bourglopin. ☎02 33 59 19 74.
- ▶ **Orient Yourself:** Mortain is 25km/15.6mi south of Vire via D 577 and D 977. Avranches is 42km/26mi west via D 5.
- **Don't Miss:** The picturesque Grande and Petite Cascades and the "Chrismal" treasury at St-Évroult church.
- **Organizing Your Time:** You will need a half day to tour the Cascades, which involve considerable walking and the Abbaye Blanche.
- **Also See:** The marked itinerary La Contre-attaque (The Counter-Attack), one of several described in the Historical Area of the Battle of Normandy, goes through Mortain.

Sights

Grande Cascade★

Either park in avenue de l'Abbaye-Blanche in the lot at a bend in the road and take the path downhill or park in rue du Bassin (signposted) and take the path that follows the river bank.

The waterfall (25m/82ft) is created by the River Cance flowing through a wooded gorge; the foaming waters recall the mountain streams of the Pyrenees or the Alps.

Petite Cascade★

45min on foot there and back. From place du Château take the downhill path S (left) along the wall of the Caisse d'Épargne (signpost).

The path crosses the River Cance and follows the bank upstream past the Aiguille Rock. It then crosses the Cançon stream on stepping stones before reaching the waterfall (35m/121ft) in a rock amphitheatre.

Petite Chapelle★

From Mortain take the road S towards Rancoudray; in front of the Gendarmerie turn left. Park in the car park at the top of the hill; walk up the avenue of fir trees.

To the left and beyond the chapel there is a belvedere (viewing table) providing a **view**★ of the wooded heights of Mortain and Lande-Pourrie. On a clear day Mont-St-Michel and the Breton coast are visible on the horizon (right).

Abbaye Blanche

Open Apr–Dec daily except Tue 10am–noon, 2.30–7pm No charge. ☎02 33 79 47 47.

This 12C former monastery in a landscape of rocky outcrops was founded in

Gyssels/Photononstop

Grande Cascade

Address Book

For coin ranges, see the Legend on the cover flap.

WHERE TO EAT

Auberge Paysanne – *In the Village enchanté de Bellefontaine, 50520 Bellefontaine, 7km/4.3mi N of Mortain via D 33.* ☎02 33 59 01 93. www.village-enchanté.fr. *Closed 15 Jan–15 Mar.* Situated at the entrance of the village, this old barn converted into a restaurant is truly bewitching with its old beams, granite fireplace and original hard-packed earth floor still partly showing to complete the rustic atmosphere. If you wish to stay, there are several possibilities: guestrooms and self-catering cottages.

Auberge du Moulin – *Moulin de la Sée, 50150 Brouains.* ☎02 33 59 50 60. www.aubergedumoulin.fr. *Closed 30 June–10 July, 26 Dec–17 Jan, Sun evening, Mon and Tue.* This inn on the banks of the Sée is part of the Ecomusée de la Vallée de Brouains. The simplicity of the rooms is matched by the low prices. Dining room verandah giving onto the countryside.

---

the 12C by Adeline and her brother Vital, chaplain to Count Robert, stepbrother of William the Conqueror.

The **chapter-house** is composed of two bays with pointed vaulting. The sisters usually sit by order of seniority on the white-stone benches which run round the walls.

The **gallery**, contrary to other Romanesque cloisters in the region, which have twinned columns or clusters as at Mont-St-Michel. consists of a simple row of single columns. The vaulting is of timberwork.

The **church** displays the usual features of the Cistercian plan: flat east end with its oculus and transept chapels. The diagonal ribs are a precursor of the Gothic style.

The groined vaulting of the **Lay Sisters Refectory** is supported by two central columns.

Collégiale St-Évroult

Unaccompanied visit 9am–7pm. To see the Treasury, ask at the tourist office. No charge. ☎02 33 59 19 74.

This old collegiate church reconstructed in the 13C is built of sandstone in a somewhat severe Gothic style. The 13C belfry is attractively plain and simple. The fine door in the second bay shows all the decorative elements known to Norman Romanesque. The **treasury** contains the Chrismal, an exceptional 7C casket of Anglo-Irish origin. The casket or portable reliquary is made of beechwood, lined with copper and engraved with runic inscriptions and images of sacred personages.

Bassin R. du	3
Bourg-Lopin R. du	4
Château Pl. du	6
Grande-Rue	7
Jumelage Pl. du	8
Rocher R. du	10

From Pewterers to Guy Degrenne

In the early 19C men would leave their native village and take to the roads to try their luck throughout France. They would buy used cutlery made of pewter from farms and would melt it to make new kitchen utensils. These men, who were born in Sourdeval, Gathemo or Fresne-Porêt, were known as *grillous*: they were the ancestors of the industrialists who gradually converted their old paper mills into small metalworking factories. Over the years the manufacture of cutlery was to become a speciality of the canton. It was originally made in pewter, then in steel-coated metal and eventually in stainless steel, as is the custom today. The firm Guy Degrenne, named after its original founder, is one of France's most prestigious manufacturers of cutlery today.

Excursions

Ger
On the road to Flers. 15km/9.3mi from Mortain on D 157. Then take D 60 on the left, heading towards Le Placître.

Musée régional de la Poterie ★
&. Ⓒ *Open July–Aug 11am–7pm. June & Sept 11am–6pm. Apr–May 2–6pm. 4.20€ (Children 1.75€). ☎02 33 79 35 36.*
The museum comprises 12 buildings: a potter's house, three long tunnel-kilns from the 17C and 18C, a drying device for pots, various workshops, a bakery etc. There is an interesting **demonstration-★** of manufacturing techniques. Pottery is still made on the premises and is available for sale.

Vallée de la Sée Driving Tour

Round-trip of 58km/36mi – Allow about 3hr. From Mortain take D 977 N towards Vire.
North of La Tournerie, where the road winds downhill, there is a view of the vast Sourdeval basin, through which runs the River Sée.

▶ *In Sourdeval turn left onto D 911.*

The road follows the curves of the narrow **Sée Valley★**, offering a new view at each bend.

Moulin de la Sée
&. Ⓒ *Open July–Aug Mon–Fri 9am–7pm, weekends and public holidays 11am–7pm; Mar–June & Sept–Oct Mon–Fri 9am–12.30pm, 2-6pm, weekends and public holidays 2-6pm. Ⓒ Closed Nov–Feb. 5€ (Children 3.50€). ☎02 33 59 20 50. www.moulin-de-la-see.com*
This mill is also known as the Écomusée de la Vallée de Brouains, a museum devoted to rivers and related activities.

▶ *After passing the church in Chérencé-le-Roussel, turn right onto D 33.*

St-Pois
Fine views south of the Sée Valley.

▶ *In St-Pois turn right and right again onto D 39 which climbs uphill.*

St-Michel-de-Montjoie
Musée du Granit – &. Ⓒ Open mid-June – Aug daily 2–6pm. May–mid-June Sun 2–6pm. 4€ (Children 1.60€). ☎02 33 59 02 22.
The village is known for its granite quarry (▶ *NW off D 282 towards Gast)* and for its mineral water, Eau de Montjoie.
The **Musée du Granit** describes quarrying and displays granite objects – capitals, pediments, sarcophagi, balusters, millstones – in a wooded park.

▶ *Return to Chérencé-le-Roussel. Turn left onto D 33 towards Mortain.*

NEUFCHÂTEL-EN-BRAY

SEUINE-MARITIME, POPULATION 5 103

MICHELIN MAP 304: I-3

The former capital of the Pays de Bray is today the capital of "bondon," a cylinder-shaped cheese. The other local stars are the "petit-suisse," invented near Gournay-en-Bray, and the fromage de Neufchâtel, a farm cheese produced in several shapes.

- **Information:** 6 place Notre-Dame, 76270 Neufchâtel-en-Bray. ☎02 35 93 22 96. www.neufchatel-en-bray.com.
- ▶ **Orient Yourself:** This small villate is 45km/28mi southwest of Dieppe via D 915 and 50km/31mi northeast of Rouen via A 28.
- **Don't Miss:** The church of St-Pierre-et-St-Paul in Aumale.
- **Organizing Your Time:** Count on a good half day to see Neufchâtel and its pretty countryside.
- **Also See:** Eu, Le Tréport, Dieppe, Forges-les-Eaux and the château of Martainville.

Visit

Église Notre-Dame

The doorway dates from the end of the 15C; the early-16C nave contains Renaissance capitals. The eight windows in the aisles depict local saints: St Radegonde, St Vincent, St Anthony. In the 13C chancel round columns support the pointed vaulting; against a pillar is a gilt wood Virgin crowned.

Northern Pays de Bray Driving Tour

46km/28mi – 1hr30min

▶ *Leave Neufchâtel on D1314 to the N.*

From the road, which runs north through the so-called Bray Buttonhole formation, there are extensive views of the Béthune Valley (left) and Hellet Forest (north).

▶ *Turn left on D 56.*

The road crosses through Hellet Forest. From Croixdalle, D 77 *(turn left)* goes down the Béthune Valley as far as Osmoy-St-Valery, where it climbs the south-west slope, and passes through a gap. The view is of Nappes Forest. As you leave the Mesnil-Follemprise Valley the bell-tower of Bures-en-Bray appears.

Bures-en-Bray

Church – ⏱Tour on request from M. Daniel Longin. ☎02 35 93 09 48.

The Bray Buttonhole

The movement of the earth's crust which brought about the raising of the Alps in the Tertiary Era had repercussions as far as the Paris basin. The shocks which disturbed the ancient shelf formed ridges in the upper layers deposited in the Secondary Era. Wide and deep undulations were formed in a south-east/north-west direction and subsequently one of these swelled into a large dome with a steep north-east face.

Erosion relentlessly ate into the dome, exposing subjacent Jurassic soil in its considerable geological complexity. This narrow cut, with its clearly defined rim, is known as a buttonhole and explains the variations in landscape resulting from the differences in the nature of the soil.

The 12C **church** has a modern brick façade. Inside are a 16C stone altarpiece and a 14C Virgin and Child.

▶ *Uphill after the church take the first road, D 114, left near the café-tobacconist.*

The road follows a terrace at the foot of the south-west face on which the villages have been built.

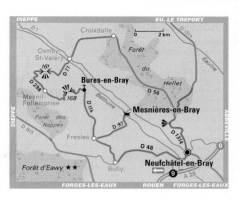

▶ *At Fresle turn left onto D 97.*

Aumale

The **Église de St-Pierre-et-St-Paul** displays both the Flamboyant and the Renaissance styles. The south portal, attributed to Jean Goujon (1510-1566), has been damaged.

▶ *Take N 29 towards Neufchâtel, turn immediately right onto D 920.*

Foucarmont

The squat impression given by the concrete **church** (rebuilt 1959-64) is somewhat alleviated by the wonderful irregular stained-glass windows and by the precious stones inlaid in the walls.

▶ *N 28 leads back to Neufchâtel.*

NOGENT-LE-ROTROU

EURE-ET-LOIRE, POPULATION 11 524
MICHELIN MAP 311: A-6

The capital of the Perche region lies on the banks of the River Huisne, dominated by its castle. The old town borders the main road (N 23) at the foot of St John's Hill; the new town covers the flat land beside the River Huisne.

🛈 **Information:** 44 rue Villette-Gate, 28400 Nogent-le-Rotrou. ☎02 37 29 68 86. www.ville-nogent-le-rotrou.fr

▶ **Orient Yourself:** Nogent-le-Rotrou is 91km/57mi southwest of Dreux via D 928 and 77km/48mi south of L'Aigle via D 918 and D 11.

🅿 **Parking:** Park in the Place de la République and explore the old streets of the town on foot.

☺ **Don't Miss:** The château St-Jean and the tomb of Sully.

🕐 **Organizing Your Time:** Time your visit in the afternoon, when most sites are open.

☋ **Also See:** Bellême, Mortagne-au-Perche and the Parc naturel regional du Perche.

A Bit of History

Between 925 and 1226 the Gallo-Roman town became a powerful fief of the Rotrou family, counts of Perche, who gave the town its name (Nogent derives from the Gallic word *novio-mago* meaning new market). Nogent was burned down in 1449 at Charles VII's command to prevent the English from capturing it. The town was rebuilt soon afterwards, in the Flamboyant or Renaissance style.

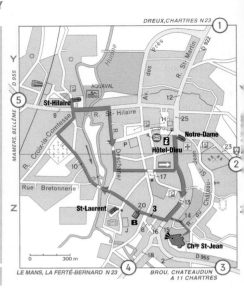

NOGENT-LE-ROTROU

Bouchers R. des	Z 2
Bourg-le-Comte R.	Z 3
Bretonnerie R.	Z
Château-St-Jean R.	Z
Croix-la-Comtesse R.	Y
Deschanel R.	YZ
Dr-Desplantes R.	Z 8
Foch Av. Mar.	Y 9
Fuye R. de la	YZ 10
Giroust R.	Y 12
Gouverneur R.	YZ 13
Marches-St-Jean R. des	Z 14
Paty R. du	Z 15
Poupardières R. des	Z 16
Prés Av. des	Y
République Pl. de la	Z 17
Rhône R. de	Z 18
St-Hilaire R.	Y
St-Laurent R.	Z 20
St-Martin R.	Y
Sully R. de	YZ 23
Villette-Gaté R.	Y 25

Maison du Bailli	Z B

Famous Native Son

Rémi Belleau (1528-77), one of the founders of the Pléiad group, was a graceful and subtle poet who glorified the art of living by depicting banquets and other festive occasions; he was also a great nature lover and would enjoy describing rural landscapes and the beauty of natural shapes. His art was epitomized in the pastoral *La Bergerie*, published in 1565. As a sign of friendship and literary respect at his funeral in Notre-Dame in Paris, his coffin was carried by Ronsard, Baïf, Philippe Desportes and Amadis Jamyn, most of whom came from the region between Chartres and Angers.

Nogent-le-Rotrou is closely associated with **Maximilien de Béthune**, Duc de Sully (1560-1641), renowned financier of Henri IV. The duke owned Rosny, Sully, La Chapelle-d'Angillon, Henrichemont and Villebon. In 1624 he purchased the château and manor of Nogent from Henri II de Condé.

Address Book

WHERE TO STAY

◑ **Le Jardin François Bed and Breakfast** – *Le Clos, 61340 Préaux-du-Perche, 10km/6mi W of Nogent-le-Rotrou via D 935, towards Bellême, then D 11, Rte St-Agnan-sur-Erre.* ☎*02 37 49 64 19. www.jardin-francois. 5 rooms.* 🚬🛁. Pretty rooms with kitchenettes in an old house located near a magnificent garden created by the owner, a keen plantsman. Concerts and exhibitions are held in the orangerie or the outdoor theatre.

◑◑ **Hôtel Au Lion d'Or** – *28 Pl St-Pol* ☎*02 37 52 01 60. hotelauliondor@wanadoo.fr. 18 rooms.* 🛁🚬. Totally renovated guestrooms with white-stained furniture unholstered in bright fabric and modern bathrooms await you in this little hotel, centrally located and practical.

SHOPPING

Virginie Berthier – *41 r. du Paty.* ☎*02 37 52 12 81. Visits by appointment, 10-person maximum.* ✂*30€ per hour.* Creation and restoration of stained-glass windows, painting on glass. Lessons.

Sights

Église Notre-Dame

The building was formerly the chapel of the Hôtel-Dieu (workhouse) and dates from the 13C and 14C. At the end of the north aisle there is a 16C-17C crib; the figures are of painted terracotta.

Tombeau de Sully

Access is through rue de Sully: you will come to a small courtyard containing the oratory and the tomb. The doorway to the Hôtel-Dieu (17C) displays Sully's coat of arms and emblems on the pediment. As Sully was a Protestant, his tomb is next to the church but not part of it. His empty tomb was sculpted by Barthélemy Boudin from Chartres.

Château St-Jean

Access on foot by rue des Marches-St-Jean, or by car along rue de Sully, then rue du Château-St-Jean which provides glimpses of Nogent and the Huisne Valley.

◷*Open daily except Tue 10am–noon, 2–6pm (Last entry 5.30pm).* ◷*Closed 1 Jan, 1 May, 1 Nov, 25 Dec.* ⌖*2.50€ (Children 1.50€)* ☎*02 37 52 18 02.*

This impressive castle stands on a rocky spur. The Rotrous, counts of Perche, lived in the huge rectangular keep (35m/115ft high), which is supported by unusual buttresses. The enclosing wall with its semicircular towers, was built from the 12C to the 13C. The remarkable gatehouse is flanked by round towers with arrow slits and machicolations of tufa stone. The courtyard provides a pleasant view of the town.

▶ *A path runs round outside the walls.*

Rue Bourg-le-Comte

Several of the houses are of interest: a 13C turreted house (no 2), which is better seen from rue des Poupardières; a 16C house (no 4); a Renaissance house with mullioned windows (no 3).

Maison du Bailli

47 rue St-Laurent. Two turrets flank the entrance to the 16C mansion built by Pierre Durant, bailiff of St Denis' Abbey, and his wife Blanche Dévrier. The dormer windows are particularly fine.

Église St-Hilaire

The church (13C-16C) stands beside the River Huisne. Its square tower dates from the 16C. The unusual polygonal chancel (13C) was modelled on the Holy Sepulchre in Jerusalem.

Église St-Laurent

▶ *Visits by appointment with the town hall of Nogent-le-Rotrou.*

The building is in the Flamboyant style, surmounted by a tower with a Renaissance top.

OMAHA BEACH

CALVADOS, MICHELIN MAP 303: G-3
LOCAL MAPS SEE BELOW AND PLAGES DU DÉBARQUEMENT

The name Omaha Beach, which until 6 June 1944 existed only as an operational code name, has continued to designate the beaches of St-Laurent-sur-Mer, Colleville-sur-Mer and Vierville-sur-Mer, in the memories of the American soldiers of the 1st (5th Corps of the 1st Army) Division, who suffered heavy casualties in the most costly of the D-Day battles.

▶ **Orient Yourself:** Omaha Beach is some 20km/12.5mi northwest of Bayeux.

⊜ **Don't Miss:** The American Cemetary at Colleville-sur-Mer holds some 9 400 crosses and Stars of David, perfectly aligned. Note the extreme youth of the fallen soldiers.

◷ **Organizing Your Time:** You will need three hours to see the sights.

⌖ **Also See:** See also the Plages du Débarquement, Arromanches-les-Bains and Bayeux.

A Bit of History

Normandy Landings - When the American forces landed at Omaha Beach on June 6 1944, they met an extremely well-organised German defence that was aided by a strong coastal current that swept landing craft off course, and beach shingle that proved at first insurmountable to heavy armour. Companies at first baulked, later rallied and by evening the 116th Regiment had taken the Port-en-Bessin-Grandcamp road enabling the motorised units to gain the plateau.

The austere and desolate appearance, especially of the eastern part, a narrow beach backing on barren cliffs, makes the invasion scene easy to imagine.

Tour

Colleville-sur-mer to Vierville

9km/6mi – Allow about 1hr – ⏱ see map below.

Colleville-sur-Mer

The last Germans did not leave the area around the village church until 10am on 7 June. The church has been entirely rebuilt.

▷ *Just before the church, turn right towards the coast.*

Monument to the 5th Engineer Special Brigade

The monument, built on the remains of a blockhouse, commemorates those who died protecting movements between the landing craft and the beach. This is the best belvedere on Omaha Beach.

American Military Cemetery (St-Laurent-sur-Mer)

The 9 385 Carrara marble crosses and Stars of David stand aligned in an impressive site. A memorial stands in the central alley and is surrounded by trees. The commemorative list includes 1 557 names.

A belvedere *(viewing table showing the landing operation)* overlooks the sea. The path down to the beach *(30min there and back)* passes a second viewing table.

A monument to the US 1st Infantry Division stands just outside the cemetery.

▷ *Continue W on D 514 to St-Laurent-sur-Mer.*

St-Laurent-sur-Mer

Musée Omaha 6 juin 1944

♿ 🕐 *Open July–Aug daily 9.30am–7.30pm (Last entry 1hr before closing. Mid-May –June & Sept 9.30am–7pm. Mid-Mar –mid-May and mid-Sept–mid-Nov 9.30am–6.30pm. Mid-Feb–mid-Mar 10am–12.30pm, 2.30–6pm. 🕐 Closed mid-Nov to mid-Feb. 💶5.40€ (Children*

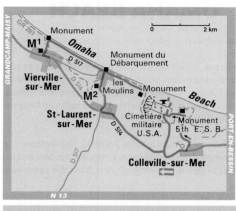

| Musée D.-Day-Omaha | M1 | Musée Omaha-6 juin 1944 | M2 |

Address Book

&For coin ranges, see the Legend on the cover flap. See also the address books for Bayeux and Places du Débarquement.

WHERE TO STAY

⌂ **Ferme du Clos Tassin Bed and Breakfast** – 14710 Colleville-sur-Mer, in the village, on D 514. ☎02 31 22 41 51. www.clostassin.fr.st Closed Jan. 5 rooms. ⌂⌂. Meal ⌂⌂. The owners of this farm make their own cider, calvados and pommeau (a mixture of calvados and apple juice). Tasting in the shop itself, because that's where meals are taken! The bedrooms are simple but very comfortable..

⌂⌂ **Hôtel du Casino** – Bd de Chauvigny, 14710 Vierville-sur-Mer. ☎02 31 22 41 02. Closed 15 Nov–15 Mar. 12 rooms. Ⓟ⌂. Restaurant ⌂⌂. Sea breezes and fine sand await you when you stay in this seaside hotel dating from the 1950s. Ask for a room with a view, then enjoy seafood in the dining room.

WHERE TO EAT

⌂⌂ **L'Omaha** – Pl. du Monument, 14710 St-Laurent-sur-Mer. ☎02 31 22 41 46. Closed 15 Nov–15 Feb. This restaurant's strongest point is its situation facing the sea, a stone's throw from Omaha Beach. Plain interior and two summer terraces. Cuisine with an accent on seafood. A small souvenir shop.

LEISURE

Eolia Normandie – Le Carey Omaha Beach, 14710 Colleville-sur-Mer. ☎02 31 22 26 21. www.eolia-normandie.com. Guided outings on sand-yachts, wakeboards, catamarans and kayaks.

3€). ☎02 31 21 97 44. www.musee-memorial-omaha.com. This village was not liberated until 7 June after heavy combat. The **museum** describes life under occupation.

▷ Take D 517 down to the beach: the road runs through a valley to another memorial.

Les Moulins

This site is marked by the **Monument to the D-Day Landing**. Turn right onto the road that runs along the beach and follow it to the end; there, at the foot of the American cemetery, you can look out onto the Ruquet Valley and the road opened by the Engineers unit after the blockhouse was destroyed around 11.30am. Heavy equipment, motorised units and the infantry were able to reach the plateau and then advance to the town of St-Laurent.

▷ Return to the Monument to the D-Day Landing.

The first units found shelter here at dawn on 6 June 1944. From a platform erected for the Omaha Beach Monument there is a view of the cliffs the infantry had to scale in order to reach the plateau.

Vierville-sur-Mer

▷ Follow boulevard Maritime west several hundred yards towards Vierville.

Here a stele marks the spot where the first to fall in the Battle of the Beaches were temporarily buried.

▷ The road leaves the coast by another beach exit.

A monument to the American National Guard stands on one of the most redoubtable of the German blockhouses.

Operation Overlord

This was the name given to the Allied invasion of Europe on 6 June 1944. Following an initial postponement due to bad weather, the largest invasion fleet in history set out for the Normandy coast and the landing beaches, code-named Utah, Omaha, Gold, Juno and Sword.

ORBEC

CALVADOS, POPULATION 2 564
MICHELIN MAP 303: O-5

Orbec is a small and lively town with a long history, as witnessed by the many old half-timbered houses in the busy shopping street, rue Grande. The town stands quite close to the source of the River Orbiquet in one of the most pleasant valleys in the Auge region. At the entrance to the town stands the famous Pierre Lanquetot factory, which has been producing its delicious Camembert cheeses for the past century.

- ⓘ **Information:** 6 Rue Grande, 14290 Orbec ☎02 31 32 56 68. www.mairie-orbec.fr
- ▶ **Orient Yourself:** Orbec is 18 km/11mi southwest of Bernay via D 131.
- ⊛ **Don't Miss:** The excursion on foot, following the GR 26 itinerary.
- ⓒ **Also See:** Bernay, Lisieux, Vimoutiers

Visit

Musée municipal
For hours and conditions, contact the Tourist Office.
The museum is located in a beautiful 16C timber-framed house, the **Vieux Manoir**★, built for a rich tanner. Carved figures and geometric patterns decorate the exterior.

GR 26 Walk

4.5km/3mi S of Orbec
A small road (Chemin de la Folletière-Abenon), follows along the Orbiquet River. Leave the car by the bridge and take a path on the left. The GR 26 itinerary (signposted in red and white) leads you on a tour of one of the prettiest valleys in the Pays d'Auge.

WHERE TO STAY

⌓⌓ **Le Manoir de l'Engagiste** – *15 r. St-Rémi, 14290 Orbec. ☎02 31 32 57 22. engagiste@wanadoo.fr. 4 rooms.* ⌓. Take the time to fully enjoy this marvellously restored 16C manor. The rooms are veritable cocoons. Wintertime, you'll have a warm breakfast in the exquisite salon by the crackling fireplace.

OUISTREHAM-RIVE-BELLA ⌂ ⌂

CALVADOS, POPULATION 8 679
MICHELIN MAP 303: K-4 – LOCAL MAP SEE PLAGES DU DÉBARQUEMENT

Located at the mouth of the Orne and astride the canal from Caen, the combined facilities of the town of Ouistreham and the beach of Riva-Bella make an excellent seaside resort. As the seaport for Caen, the harbour bustles with trawlers, pleasure craft and the cross-Channel ferries plying between Ouistreham and Portsmouth.

- ⓘ **Information:** Jardins du Casino, 14150 Ouistreham-Riva-Bella. ☎02 31 97 18 63. www.ot-ouistreham.fr.
- ▶ **Orient Yourself:** Ouistreham is 15km/9.4mi from Caen.
- ⊛ **Don't Miss:** Stroll out to admire the yachts anchored in the marina.
- ⓠ **Organizing Your Time:** You might consider taking a sea-water cure.
- ⓒ **Also See:** The marked itinerary Overlord-L'Assaut (The Onslaught), one of several described in the Historical Area of the Battle of Normandy, goes through this town.

Landing beach

The Town

Église St-Samson★

This ancient 12C fortress church was built on the site of a 9C wooden church destroyed by Norsemen. The gabled west front with its three superimposed tiers of blind arcades above the recessed doorway is particularly remarkable. Step back to get a good view of the late-12C belfry supported by buttresses.

In the nave note the round piers with gadrooned capitals and the lovely clerestory windows.

Port de Plaisance

Leave the car in place du Général-de-Gaulle. A large basin on the opposite bank of the canal (Canal de Caen à la Mer) provides berths for many yachts. In season it is a lively and colourful spot.

Lighthouse

Open July–Aug Fri, weekends and public holidays 3–6pm. Rest of the year depending on the weather and the guardian's availability. No charge.
From the top of the lighthouse there is a good view of the harbour and marina.

Address Book

For coin ranges, see the Legend on the cover flap.

WHERE TO STAY

Hôtel de la Plage – *39 av Pasteur, 14150 Riva-Bella. 02 31 9685 16. www. hotel-ouistreham.com. Open Mar–11 Nov. 16 rooms.* Early 20C Anglo-Norman villa, on a quiet street near the beach. Renovated guestrooms; a few large enough for families. Pretty garden.

WHERE TO EAT

Le Normandie – *71 av. Michel-Cabieu. 02 31 97 19 57. www. lenormandie.com. Closed 18 Dec–1 Jan, Sun evening and Mon except Apr–Oct.* This restaurant occupies an old Norman house on the port. The dining room is brightly coloured and well-lit, and the veranda is elegant.

Le St-Georges – *51 av. Andry. 02 31 97 18 79. saint-georges.hotel@ wanadoo.fr. Closed 8–29 Jan, Sun evening and Mon lunch.* The first sea-bathers came here towards the end of the 19C. Try the seaside specialities served in both dining rooms: the modern one with its large picture windows offering a panoramic view of the coast, and the traditional one with its wooden ceiling and fireplace. A few guest rooms.

LEISURE

Thalazur Ouistreham – *Av. du Cdt-Kieffer. 02 31 96 40 40. www.thalazur.fr daily, Sun 9am–5pm. Closed 17–26 Dec.* Salt water treatments, massage, beauty care, and fitness programs. The centre includes a hotel.

The Resort

Big Bunker

Avenue du 6-Juin near the tourist office. ⏱*Open Apr–Sept 9am–7pm. Rest of the year 10am–6pm.* ⏱*Closed 25 Dec and Jan.* ⊛*6.50€.* ☏*02 31 97 28 69.*
This former German range-finding station overlooks the mouth of the River Orne from a height of 17m/56ft.; it sent firing instructions to the artillery units in Ouistreham. Rooms are arranged as they were in 1944. In the range-finding room, you can study the horizon with the range-finder over a 180° angle and a distance of 45km/28mi.

Musée du Débarquement "no 4 Commando"

Avenue Pasteur, near the tourist office. ♿ ⏱*Open Mar–Oct 10.30am–6pm.* ⊛*4.50€ (Children 2.50€)* ☏*02 31 96 63 10.*
The 4th Anglo-French Commando under Commander Kieffer reduced the enemy strong points on the morning of 6 June.

HARAS NATIONAL DU PIN★

ORNE, MICHELIN MAP 310: J-2

Le Pin Stud Farm, one of the most famous horse-breeding establishments in France, is attractively set amid woods and meadows. Its activities include racing and training for the staff of other national and private stud farms (smithery, artificial insemination, etc.).

- 🛈 **Information:** Guided tours (1hr) Apr–7 Oct 10am–6pm. Closed 1 Jan and 25 Dec. ⊛4 €(Children 1.50 €). Tour of the stables 8€(Children 5.50€) Guided tour and stable tour 10€ (Children 5.50€).
- ▶ **Orient Yourself:** The Haras is some 15km/9mi east of Argentan via N 26.
- 😊 **Don't Miss:** The Cour d'Honneur on Thursdays with stallions and carriage teams.

A Bit of History

The stud farm dates from 1665, when Jean-Baptiste Colbert, chief minister of Louis XIV, founded the national stables. The buildings, designed by Pierre Le Mousseux, a disciple of the great architect François Mansart, date from 1715 to 1730; the grounds were designed under the king's landscape architect, André Le Nôtre.

Visit *Allow 45min*

Three magnificent woodland rides converge on the horseshoe-shaped courtyard known as Colbert's Court. The brick and stone stable wings accommodate the 40 or more stallions grouped according to their breed. Other outbuildings house the collection of 19C carriages used for official events in France and abroad.

Excursion

St-Germain-de-Clairefeuille

10km/6mi SE (via Nonant-le-Pin).
The church is distinguished by its magnificent woodwork including 13 **painted panels**★ of the Life of Our Lord by the early-16C Flemish School.

Haras national du Pin

A. de Valroger/MICHELIN

CHÂTEAU DE PIROU★

MANCHE, MICHELIN MAP 303: C-4 – 10KM/6MI S OF LESSAY

The 12C fortress, which once stood on the coast beside an anchorage, served as an outpost for the defence of Coutances under the lords of Pirou. The castle passed to other noble families until the late 18C, when it was used as a hideout for smugglers dealing in tobacco from Jersey.

🗓 **Information:** Open Apr–Sept 10am–noon, 2pm–6.30pm. Rest of the year 10am–noon, 2–5pm. Closed Dec–Jan. ⊚4€ (Children 2P) ☎02 33 46 34 71. www.chateau-pirou.org.

▶ **Orient Yourself:** 10km/6mi from Lessay and 2km/1.25mi from the sea.

⊛ **Don't Miss:** The tapestry describing the conquest of Sicily by the Normans.

🕐 **Organizing Your Time:** For a relaxed visit, take 1hr 30min.

🖐 **Also See:** Lessay, Coutances and the national parks; du Cotentin et du Bessin.

Visit *Allow 30min*

Three fortified gatehouses – there were originally five – lead to the old sheepfold, the outer bailey and then to the castle itself, a massive structure encircled by a moat. The room where justice was dis pensed displays a **tapestry** similar in style to the Bayeux tapestry, recounting the conquest of southern Italy and Sicily by the Cotentin Normans. The original tapestry can be seen only in July and August; otherwise a copy is on display.

WHERE TO EAT

⊜⊜ **La Mer** – *2 r. Fernand-Desplanques, 50770 Pirou-Plage, 2.5km/1.5mi W of Château de Pirou via D 94. ☎02 33 46 43 36. Closed Jan,10 days in Oct, Sun evening, Mon evening, Tue evening and Wed off-season.* From your table you see the coastline and the Channel Islands appear offshore in good weather. The cuisine has a definite sea flavour.

Château de Pirou

S. Sauvignier/MICHELIN

The Legendary Geese of Pirou

When the Norse invaders failed to take the fortress they decided to lay siege to it. After several days of waiting they realised that there was no longer any sign of activity within the castle but, being suspicious, they decided to delay a little longer before making the final assault. Imagine their surprise when they found that the only remaining occupant was a bedridden old man, who informed them that the lord, his wife and other occupants of the castle had transformed themselves into geese, to escape from the hands of their attackers. Indeed the Norsemen recollected having seen a skein of wild geese flying over the castle walls the previous evening. According to Norse traditions, the human form could only be reassumed once certain magic words had been recited backwards. The geese came back to look for their book of magic spells but alas, the Norsemen had set fire to the castle. Legend has it that the geese come back every year in the hope of finding their book of spells, which explains why there are so many skeins of geese in the vicinity of the castle.

PONT-AUDEMER★

EURE, POPULATION 8 981
MICHELIN MAP 304: D-5

Visitors to Pont-Audemer will enjoy this quaint town of 16C houses. it is some-times called the Venice of Normandy in reference to its canals, which once served a prosperous tanning trade.

- **Information:** Place Maubert, 27500 Pont-Audemer. ☎02 32 41 08 21. www.ville-pont-audemer.fr
- ▶ **Orient Yourself:** Pont-Audemer is 24km/15mi east of Honfleur via D 180 and N 175, and 58km/36mi west of Rouen via A 13.
- **Don't Miss:** The itinerary Pont-Audemer au Fil de l'Eau, marked out by compass cards painted on the ground, lets you explore the town at your own pace..
- **Parking:** Leave your car in the lot on the Place Général-de-Gaulle.

Old Town

▶ *Allow 45min. Start from place du Général-de-Gaulle. Take rue des Carmes and turn left on rue de la République; 100m/109yd farther on, turn left again onto impasse de l'Épée. Farther down the street, also on the left, is impasse St-Ouen.*

Walk down these lanes to view the half-timbered houses, and to see the north-ern side of the church.

▶ *Take rue Thiers to the left.*

From the **bridge over the Risle**, there is a nice view of slate-roofed river houses.

▶ *From place Victor-Hugo, continue to place Louis-Gillain, to the right, and enter rue des Cordeliers.*

At the corner of rue des Cordeliers and rue Notre-Dame-du-Pré stands a build-ing with a small tower, the timber beams resting on a ground floor of stone.

▶ *Return to place Louis-Gillain, cross the branch of the Risle and take rue Sadi-Carnot.*

Several residences have sculpted door-ways (nos 8, 16, 18, 20, 27bis). To the right, **rue Place-de-la-Ville**, leads over a little bridge and onto rue de la Répub-lique, in front of St-Ouen Church.

Address Book

⏱*For coin ranges, see the Legend on the cover flap.*

WHERE TO STAY

◎◎ **Les Cloches de Corneville** – *Rte de Rouen, 27500 Corneville-sur-Risle, 6km/3.6mi E of Pont-Audemer via N 175. ☎02 32 56 7 21. www.cloches-de-corneville.fr.* 🅿 ⌣. The Corneville bells peal from the top floor of this hotel, designated a historic monument: you can climb up and see them. The pleasant restaurant and charming, well-soundproofed rooms, combine to make an agreeable halt.

WHERE TO EAT

◎◎ **Auberge du Cochon d'Or** – *27210 Beuzeville, 14km/8.5mi W of Pont-Audemer via N 175. ☎02 32 57 70 46. www.le-cochon-dor.fr.* Comfortably decorated with wide tables and uphol-stered armchairs, this inn is popular with locals who appreciate the varied menus.
◎◎◎ **Le Petit Coq aux Champs** – *La Pommeraie Sud, 27500 Campigny, 6km/3.6mi S of Pont-Audemer via D 810 and D 29. ☎02 32 41 04 19. www.lep-etitcoqauxchamps.fr. Closed 2–29 Jan. Reservations required.* This beautiful thatched cottage houses a restaurant of solid renown.

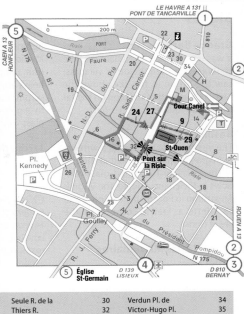

PONT-AUDEMER

Canel R. Alfred	2
Carmélites R. des	3
Clemencin R. Paul	5
Cordeliers R. des	6
Delaquaize R. S.	7
Déportés R. des	8
Épée R. de l'	9
Félix-Faure Quai	
Ferry R. Jules	
Gambetta R.	13
Gaulle Pl. Général-de	14
Gillain Pl. Louis	16
Goulley Pl. J.	
Jean-Jaurès R.	18
Joffre R. Mar.	19
Kennedy Pl.	
Leblanc Quai R.	20
Maquis-Surcouf R.	21
Maubert Pl.	22
Mitterrand Quai François	23
N.-D.-du-Pré R.	
Pasteur Bd	
Place-de-la-Ville R.	24
Pot-d'Étain Pl. du	25
Président-Coty R. du	26
Président-Pompidou Av. du	
République R. de la	
Sadi-Carnot R.	
St-Ouen Impasse	29

Seule R. de la	30	Verdun Pl. de	34
Thiers R.	32	Victor-Hugo Pl.	35

> Go up rue de la République and take the first passage to the right, just after rue des Carmes.

Cour Canal also has some lovely half-timbered buildings to admire.

Churches

Église St-Ouen

The church was begun in the 11C and enlarged in the 16C but the west front was never completed. The nave was given a Flamboyant veneer at the end of the 15C. There are magnificent Renaissance **stained-glass windows**★.

Église St-Germain

Access by rue Jules-Ferry to the S. ⊙*Open Mon 2–6.30pm, Wed and Fri 4.30–6pm, Thu 10am–noon.* Parts of this church date back to the 11C, 14C and 19C. The arches of its squat Romanesque tower have been rebuilt in the Gothic style.

PONTMAIN

MAYENNE, POPULATION 893

MICHELIN MAP 310: C-4 – 6KM/4MI SW OF LANDIVY

In this village on the border of Brittany on 17 January, 1871, during the Franco-Prussian War, the Virgin appeared to several of the village children, including Eugène and Joseph Barbedette, with a message of prayer and hope; 11 days later an Armistice was declared.

🛈 **Information:** 5 rue de la Grange, 53220 Pontmain. ☎02 43 05 07 74.
▶ **Orient Yourself:** Pontmain is 16km/10mi northeast of Fougères, 45km/28mi northwest of Mayenne and 35km/22mi southwest of Mortain.
⊙ **Don't Miss:** The lovely garden of La Pellerine, with its water-lilies.

Sights

Grange Barbedette

It was from this thatched barn that the children, and then the other villagers, saw the Virgin in the sky above the house of Augustin Guidecoq on the far side of the square.

Basilique

The vast neo-Gothic basilica with its twin granite spires was built at the end of the 19C. The 10 stained-glass windows in the chancel depict the Virgin's Apparition in Pontmain in Lourdes and La Salette, as well as scenes from the life of Christ.

Chapelle des Missionaires Oblats

Musée des Missions – &⊙*Open Wed, Sun and public holidays 2.30–6pm. Other days on request.* ⊜*No charge.* ☎*02 43 30 26 46.*

Behind the basilica are the park and Mission of the Oblate Fathers of Mary Immaculate. The 1953 chapel has a heavy appearance from outside – but is surprisingly pleasing within, illuminated by a golden light diffused by stained-glass windows.

Jardin de la Pellerin★

21km/13mi S of Pontmain, on N 12 between Fougères to the W and Ernée to the E. La Larderie, 53220 La Pellerine. ⊙*Open May–15 Oct Thu and Fri 10am–6.30pm, weekends 2–6.30pm. 6€ (Under 14 years no charge).* ☎*02 43 05 93 31.*

Lovely gardens surround a 17C house: roses, shrubs, arbours and ponds with acquatic plants, including water lilies, on a 2ha/5 acre site.

PONTORSON

MANCHE, POPULATION 4 107
MICHELIN MAP 303: C-8

Pontorson is a favourite stopping place for visitors on their way to Mont-St-Michel. The town is named after a local baron, Orson, who in 1031 built a bridge (pont in French) over the Couesnon.

🛈 **Information:** Place de l'Hôtel-de-Ville, 50170 Pontorson. ☎02 33 60 20 65.

▶ **Orient Yourself:** Pontorson is 9km/5.6mi south of Mont-St-Michel on D 976.

⊛ **Don't Miss:** The chapel of the St-James American Military Cemetery.

Visit

Église Notre-Dame

The 11C church is said to have been founded by **William the Conqueror** to thank the Virgin for saving his army from the Couesnon quicksands. The episode is portrayed in a stained-glass window and also in scene 17 in the Bayeux tapestry. The church was given pointed vaulting at a later date and has been remodelled several times. The rough granite west front has kept its Romanesque appearance. in the chapel of St Saviour is a fine 15C altarpiece known as the Broken Saints. Despite being mutilated during the Wars of Religion and the Revolution, it is a work of great richness.

Excursion

St-James

15km/9mi E by D 30. &⊙*Open Mon–Fri 8am–5pm, weekends and holidays 9am–5pm.* ⊙*Closed 25 Dec, 1 Jan.*

This is one of western Normandy's oldest cities, founded by William the Conqueror in 1067. The **Cimetière américain et Mémorial de Bretagne** is on the outskirts of St-James (▶*Take D 230 in the direction of Louvigné*). This cemetery holds the graves of over 4 400 Americans. In the chapel regimental colours, stained-glass windows, coats of arms and maps commemorate the events of 1944.

QUILLEBEUF

EURE, POPULATION 1 044, MICHELIN MAP 304: D-5

Until the 19C captains waited here for high tide, to pass through the dangerous channel known as the cemetery of ships. Today, the old port is overwhelmed by oil refineries and petrochemical installations in Port Jérôme on the north bank. Nonetheless, the town has managed to retain its traditional character. The town has an excellent view of Port Jérôme from the lighthouse. Église Notre-Dame-de-Bon-Port has a fine but incomplete Romanesque tower.

Driving Tour

Quillebeuf to Roque Point
23km/14mi – Allow 1hr

The Vernier Marsh cuts a vast bay of 5 000ha/20sq mi out of the Roumois plateau between Quillebeuf and the Pointe de la Roque. It forms part of the **Parc naturel régional des Boucles de la Seine**.

Ste-Opportune-la-Mare
Follow the signs *Panorama de la Grande Mare* to a viewpoint over the Great Marsh and beyond to the reclaimed Marshland.

Réserve naturelle des Mannevilles
Guided tours (3hrs) July–Aug Sun 2–5pm. 3€ (Under 16 years no charge). Information and reservations. 02 32 20 27 10. Wear boots.
The visitor can observe the flora and fauna of the Marais area and approach Camargue horses and highland cattle.

▶ *West of Bouquelon, take D 39 N to St Samson-de-la-Roque. A narrow winding road leads to the headland.*

Pointe de la Roque★
Picnic area. From the lighthouse on the cliff the **panorama** extends over the Seine estuary to Cap de la Hève and the Côte de Grâce. Tancarville cliffs and bridge can be seen to the right.

ROUEN ★★★

SEINE-MARITIME, POPULATION 109 000 (METROPOLITAN AREA 389 862)

MICHELIN MAP 304: G-5

Rouen, capital of Upper Normandy, has undergone a remarkable campaign of restoration that has given new life to the old city's network of narrow, winding streets lined with magnificent half-timbered houses. In addition, Rouen is a city of first-rate museums – the Musée de Beaux-Arts alone is worth the trip – and possesses one of the most sumptuous Gothic cathedrals in France. Rouen sits in a lovely valley surrounded by high hills, from which there are extensive views over the city and the Seine.

- **Information:** 25 place de la Cathédrale, 76000 Rouen.
  ☏02 32 08 32 40. www.rouentourisme.com.
- ▶ **Orient Yourself:** Some 130km/81mi from Paris, Rouen spreads out along both banks of the Seine. On the right (north) bank, a series of arching boulevards define the city centre, its old residential districts and historic centre. On the left (south) bank are administrative offices, the Préfecture, modern residential and business districts, and the industrial zone.
- **Parking:** Paying lots are found on: Place du Général-de-Gaulle (Hôtel de Ville), Square Verdrel, Palais, Vieux-Marché, La Pucelle, Charettes, la Bourse (rue du Général-Leclerc), la Haute-Vielle-Tour, Saint-Marc, 39e RI and St-Vivien. There are free lots on the lower quays of the left bank and at Boulingrin, near the train station.
- **Don't Miss:** The Gothic splendour of the cathedral and of the churches of St-Maclou and St-Ouen; the lovely half-timbered houses of Old Rouen; the Musée des Beaux-Arts.
- **Organizing Your Time:** One day here is barely adequate. Spend the morning exploring the old streets, reserving the afternoon for museums.
- **Especially for Kids:** Certain museums have special guidebooks for children: the Musée Flaubert, the Musée d'Histoire de la Médecine, and the Musée Maritime, Fluvial and Portuaire.
- **Also See:** Elbeuf, the château de Martainville, Clères, St-Wandrille and Jumièges.

A Bit of History

Rollo the Forerunner – After the **Treaty of St-Clair-sur-Epte** in the year 911, Rollo, the Viking chief and first Duke of Normandy, was baptised at Rouen, the capital of the new duchy, and took the name Robert. He proved to be a far-sighted planner: he narrowed and deepened the river bed, built up unused marshlands, linked the downstream islands to the mainland and reinforced the banks with quays. His works lasted until the 19C, unrivalled for their efficiency.

Goddons – Rouen was hard hit during the Hundred Years War: in 1418 Henry V of England besieged the town, which was starved into capitulation after six months.

Revolts and plots followed against the Goddons – the nickname for the English derived from their common swear word, "God damn." Hope was reborn by the exploits of Joan of Arc and the coronation of Charles VII, then Joan was taken prisoner at Compiègne by the Burgundians. The English threatened the Duke of Burgundy with economic sanctions and through the mediation of Pierre Cauchon, Bishop of Beauvais, Joan was handed over to the English. On Christmas Day 1430 she was imprisoned in the Tower of the Fields in the castle built in the 13C by Philippe Auguste. A strong military presence under Lord Warwick deterred any uprisings.

Trial of Joan of Arc – Bishop Cauchon promised a fair trial and opened the first session on 21 February 1431. An amazing dialogue began between Joan and her judges: the Maid replied to all the tricks and subtleties of the churchmen and lawyers.

On 24 May, in the cemetery of the abbey of St Ouen, tied to a scaffold, Joan was pressed to recant; she finally gave in, was granted her life but condemned to life imprisonment.

The English were furious and threatened the judges; Cauchon replied, "We will get her yet." On Trinity Sunday the guards took away Joan's women's clothes which she had promised to wear, and gave her men's clothing instead. At noon "for the necessities of the body, she was constrained to go out and indulge in the said habit." She was thus said to have broken her promise and was condemned to the stake. On 30 May she was burned alive in place du Vieux-Marché.

In 1449 Charles VII entered Rouen; in 1456 Joan was rehabilitated and in 1920 she was canonised and made Patron Saint of France.

Golden Century – The period between the French reconquest (1449) and the Wars of Religion (1562-1598) was a golden century for all Normandy and particularly for the city of Rouen. Local dignitaries built sumptuous stone mansions and carved woodwork adorned the façade of burgesses' houses.

Rouen merchants in cooperation with Dieppe navigators traded along all the main maritime routes.

Industrial Upsurge – Industrialisation, launched by textile manufacturing, called for changes in the port: in the 19C docks were constructed, the railway was built; the old city on the right bank spread to the tributary valleys and hillsides.

Modern City – Industrial expansion accelerated at the beginning of the 20C. During the Second World War, the old districts close to the Seine and the industrial zone on the south bank were destroyed. During reconstruction, facto-

Joan of Arc was beatified in 1909

S. Sauvignier/MICHELIN

ries were moved to industrial zones and the left (south) bank became a residential area and administrative centre. Lacroix Island, formerly industrial, has become residential with parks and open spaces.

The Port

▶ *Bd Émile-Duchemin, Hangar 13 (on the road to Le Havre from the Pont Guillaume-le-Conquérant*

Rouen is France's fifth busiest port after Marseilles, Le Havre, Dunkerque and Nantes-St-Nazaire, and the third biggest river port. Its location between Paris and the sea is a great advantage.

Owing to improved maritime access, modernisation of port equipment and facilities, and the building of silos and new terminals, the growth of the port has been constant. It now stretches from Rouen to Tancarville on the right bank of the Seine and from Rouen to Honfleur on the left bank.

For displays recounting a great many riverside and maritime adventures, visit the **Musée maritime, fluvial et portuaire** on Quai Émile-Duchemin, Hangar 13 (follow the directions for LeHavre from the Guillaume-le-Conquérant bridge) &. ⦿*Open daily except*

Address Book

⚓For coin ranges, see the Legend on the cover flap.

WHERE TO STAY

⊖ **Hôtel des Carmes** – 33 pl. des Carmes. ☎02 35 71 92 31. www.hoteldescarmes.com. 12 rooms. ⊒. Situated in the town centre, not far from the cathedral, this hotel is an appealing halt. The delightfully decorated reception area hints of artistic tendencies, and the clutter-free bedrooms are charming and well fitted out. A very good address for budget-conscious travellers.

⊖ **La ferme du Coquetot Bed and Breakfast** – 46 r. du Coq, 27380 Bourg-Beaudouin, 18 km/11.25mi NE of Rouen via N 14. ☎02 32 49 09 91. www.fermeducoquetot.free.fr. 3 rooms and one cottage. ⊒. Meal ⊖. This red brick house sits on the grounds of an abandoned château, now a working farm. The rooms are simple and pretty. The cottage is in an old dovecote, with lots of charm. Friendly reception.

⊖⊖ **Brithotel Versan** – 3 r. Jean-Lecanuet. ☎02 35 07 77 07. www.rouen-hotel-versan.com. 34 rooms. ⊒. A practical address on a busy boulevard not far from the town hall. The rooms are all similar, functional and well equipped. Efficient soundproofing.

⊖⊖ **Hôtel Le Cardinal** – 1 Pl de la Cathédrale. ☎02 35 70 24 42. www.cardinal-hotel.fr. Closed 18 Dec–14 Jan. 18 rooms. ⊒. Near the Notre Dame Cathedral, this family hotel offers small guestrooms that are being gradually renovated. Summer, breakfast on the terrace.

WHERE TO EAT

⊖ **Pascaline** – 5 r. de la Poterne. ☎02 35 89 67 44. pascaline.rouen@numericable.fr. Reservations advised. Located next to the courthouse, this restaurant with a bistro façade is very pleasant. Brasserie decor with handsome wood counters, long seats and yellow walls. Choice of attractive fixed-price menus. Book ahead – it's often full.

⊖ **La Toque d'Or** – 11 Pl. du Vieux-Marché. ☎02 35 71 46 29. Closed Wed out of season. Well-placed opposite the Place du Vieux-Marché, this pretty half-timbered house holds two different restaurants: on the ground floor, a large elegant room offers refined fare (the *tête de veau* is remarkable), while upstairs, more relaxed menu features grilled meat served at a faster pace.

⊖ **Les Maraîchers** – 37 pl. du Vieux-Marché. ☎02 35 71 57 73. www.les-maraichers.fr. A restaurant with Parisian bistro airs in a half-timbered house. Banquettes, a bar, close-set tables, old advertising plaques, hat and jug collections – nothing's missing! Improvised cuisine. Norman-style second dining room on the ground floor.

⊖⊖ **Le Gourmand du Sud-Ouest** – 24 r. Rollon. ☎02 35 07 36 08. Closed 15 July–15 Aug, Sun and Mon. Reservations advised. Here, the entire Tessal family bustles about to ensure you're well-fed according to the culinary precepts of southwestern France. The cassoulet of course is highly placed on a menu featuring solid, nourishing dishes. Friendly atmosphere.

⊖⊖ **Guinguette Chez Dédé** – Les Écluses, 27380 Amfreville-sous-les-Monts. ☎02 32 49 80 06. Closed Mon. Afternoons and evenings, the accordion plays for dances featuring walzes and tangos. A vast terrace overlooks the Seine. Traditional cuisine: mussels with French-fries, fried fish, etc.

⊖⊖ **La Marmite** – 3 r.de Florence. ☎02 35 71 75 55. www.lamarmiterouen.com. Delicious odours waft from the cooking pot (*marmite*) situated near the Place du Vieux-Marché. Push open the door to enjoy a delicately flavoured cuisine, prepared with fresh products and presented with care. Dining room freshly renovated.

TEA-TIME

Dame Cakes– 70 r. St-Romain, Cathedral district. ☎02 35 07 49 31. Daily except Sun 10am–6.30, Sat 10am–7pm.
This tearoom occupies the former workshop of the famed ironsmith Ferdinand Marrou. Magnificent old ornamental iron work, including a balcony. The owner has a taste for cakes that grannie used to make: chocolate cake, vegetable crumble, a variety of cakes both sweet and salty. The menu changes every month.

ON THE TOWN

⊙Famed as the spot where Joan of Arc met her end, the Place du Vieux-Marché is today a lively centre of evening activity, with lots of bars and restaurants, many with terraces. Check the *Viking*, a free brochure distributed locally, for more information.

Bar de la Crosse – *53 r. de l'Hôpital.* ☎*02 35 70 16 68. Daily except Sun 9am–9pm (Fri and Sat 11.30pm). Closed 1st 2 weeks Aug and public holidays*. This small bar has gained its popularity from the relaxed and friendly atmosphere you find here. Concerts and exhibitions.

Le Bateau Ivre – *17 r. des Sapins.* ☎*02 35 70 09 05. Wed–Sat 10pm–4am. Closed Aug*. Ever on the lookout for new talents, this bar has been livening up Rouen night life for the past 20 years. Concerts Fridays and Saturdays, ballads and poetry Thursdays, café-theatre or French songs Tuesday evenings. A few programmes are available at the tourist office.

Taverne St-Amant – *11 r. St-Armand.* ☎*02 35 88 51 34. Daily except Sun 11am–4pm, 7–2am, Mon and Sat 7pm–2am. Closed 3 weeks in Aug*. Set up as a restaurant-bar for 32 years, this 17C house welcomes painters, writers, actors and other artistic habitués. On the last Thursday of the month, an evening of popular song.

SHOWTIME

Théâtre de l'Écharde – *16 r. Flahaut.* ☎*02 35 15 33 05. theatreecharde@hotmail.com. Tickets purchased at the theatre before performance.*⊙*6/9€.* Theatre with 100 seats where the troupe's performances and shows for young theatre-goers are performed.

Théâtre des Deux Rives – *48 r. Louis Ricard.* ☎*02 35 70 22 82. devaux.jeanmarc@wanadoo.fr. Opening hours follow schedule of performances. Ticket office Mon–Fri 2–6pm. Closed July–Aug and public holidays.*⊙*8/18€.* Classical and modern theatre, with an emphasis on living playwrights.

SHOPPING

Faïencerie Augy-Carpentier – *26 r. St-Romain.* ☎*02 35 88 77 47. www.fayencerie-augy.com. Open daily except Sun 9am–7pm, Mon 10am–8pm.* *Tour of the workshop by appointment.* The last handmade and hand-decorated earthenware workshop in Rouen! They offer copies of many traditional motifs on white and pink backgrounds, from blue monochrome to multi-coloured, and from lambrequin to cornucopia.

Chocolatier Auzou – *163 r. du Gros-Horloge.* ☎*02 35 70 59 31. Tue–Sat 9.30am–7.15pm, Sun 9.30am–1pm, Mon 2–7.15pm. July–Aug closed Sun. Closed 1 Jan and 1 May.* Located in a half-timbered house, this renowned chocolatier will tempt you with his specialities, such as Les Larmes de Jeanne d'Arc (Joan of Arc's Tears: lightly roasted almonds covered with nougatine and chocolate) or L'Agneau Rouennais (a sort of sponge cake) and candied apples.

Hardi –*22 pl. du Vieux-Marché.* ☎*02 35 71 81 55. Daily except Sun 8.30am–7.30pm. Restaurant open noon–2.30pm.* This delicatessen occupies a suberb half-timbered house on one of the livliest squares in Rouen. Specialities such as sheep's foot *à la rouennaise*, andouilles with hot peppers and Caen tripe cooked in calvados and cider, are among the dishes to discover.

MARKETS

Antiques– **Place St-Marc** Sun 8am–1.30pm

Traditional markets –

Place St-Marc– Tue, Fri, Sat and Sun.
Place des Emmurés – Tue and Sat.
Place du Vieux-Marché – Daily except Mon.

LEISURE

⊙The town hall distributes two useful brochures giving information about the city and its surroundings. *L'Agenda rouennais* appears every 3 weeks and lists cultural events, while the *Rouen magazine*, twice-monthly, is more general and complete. Pick them up at the tourist office.

Cultural events

Evening light shows – ☎*02 32 08 32 40. June–July at 11pm. 1st 2 weeks Sept at 10pm.* A dozen pictures inspired by Monet are projected onto the façade of the Cathedral, using its sculptures to create strange forms and colours.

Tue 10am–12.30pm, 2–6pm (5pm from Nov–Feb), weekends 2–6pm (5pm from Nov–Feb). ⏰*Closed 1 Jan, 1 May and 24,25 and 31 Dec.* ⏺*4€ (Children 2.50€).* ☎*02 32 10 15 51. www.musee-maritime-rouen.asso.fr*

Cathédrale Notre-Dame★★★

Allow 1hr 30min
♿*Tactile map and brochures in braille available.* ⏰*Open daily except Mon morning.* 👥*Guided tour (1hr 30min) including the baptistry, the Chapel of the Virgin and the crypt, usually closed to the public, daily during school vacations, otherwise weekends at 2.30pm.* ⏰*Closed 1 Jan, 1 May, 8 May 11 Nov.* ⏺*No charge.* ☎*02 35 71 71 60.*

The cathedral of Rouen is one of the most beautiful examples of French Gothic architecture. Construction began in the 12C but after a devastating fire in 1200 the building was reconstructed in the 13C. The cathedral took on its final appearance in the 15C under the master builder Guillaume Pontifs and in the 16C under Roulland le Roux. In the 19C it was crowned with the present cast-iron spire. Badly damaged during the Second World War, the cathedral is open but the enormous restoration work started over 50 years ago continues.

Exterior

The attraction of Rouen Cathedral lies in its infinite variety, including an immense façade bristling with openwork pinnacles and framed by two totally different towers: the Tour St-Romain on the left and the Tour de Beurre on the right.

West front

This imposing façade was used in a series of paintings by Monet to study the effects of lighting at different times of the day on the same subject. Dating from the 12C, the **Portail St-Jean** *(left)* and the **Portail St-Étienne** *(right)* doorways each have a delicately carved semicircular arch crowned by a small colonnade. The two tympana are 13C. The lattice-work window gallery (1370-1420) above the two portals is in the Flamboyant style; the niches decorated with statues and topped by openwork gables are 14C and 15C.

The **central doorway** (early 16C) is flanked by two powerful pyramid buttresses decorated with statues of the Prophets and Apostles. The tympanum is decorated with a Tree of Jesse, destroyed by the Huguenots and restored in 1626.

The **Tour St-Romain**, to the left, is the oldest tower (12C), and in the Early Gothic style. The sumptuous **Tour de Beurre** (Butter Tower) was thus named in the 17C when it was believed that it had been paid for by dispensations granted to those didn't fast during Lent. It never received a spire but was surmounted by an octagonal crown. Inside is a carillon of 56 bells.

South side

The **central lantern tower** with its spire is the tallest in France (151m/495ft) and the glory of Rouen. It was started in the 13C and was raised in the 16C. The present spire, in cast iron, replaced in 1876 the wooden spire covered in gilded lead which dated from 1544. The **Portail de la Calende** (Calende doorway), which opens between two 13C square towers, is a 14C masterpiece.

North side

On skirting the **Cour d'Albane** (Albane Court), closed to the east by the cloister gallery, one can see the north side, the lantern tower and spire and the upper section of the Booksellers' transept.

A little further on the **Cour des Libraires** (Booksellers' Court) is closed by a magnificent stone gateway in the Flamboyant style. At the end of the court is the **Portail des Libraires** (Booksellers' Doorway) (🕮*see Introduction: Religious architecture)* which opens on to the north side aisle.

The tympanum (late 13C) is decorated by a Last Judgement depicted in terrifying detail.

▶ *Return to the parvis to enter the cathedral by the main door.*

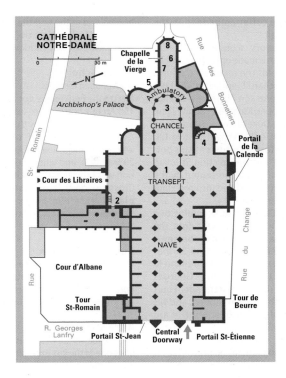

CATHÉDRALE NOTRE-DAME

Chapelle de la Vierge
8
6
7
5
Ambulatory
3
CHANCEL
Archbishop's Palace
4
Portail de la Calende
Rue des Bonnetiers
1
TRANSEPT
Cour des Libraires
2
Rue St-Romain
NAVE
Cour d'Albane
Rue du Change
Rue Georges Lanfry
Tour St-Romain
Tour de Beurre
Portail St-Jean
Central Doorway
Portail St-Étienne

Nave

In the Early Gothic style, the nave is made up of 11 bays four storeys high. Dominating the transept crossing is the **lantern tower** rising with incredible boldness 51m/167ft on enormous piles which sweep upward.

Transept

In the north arm is the famous Escalier de la Librairie (Booksellers' Stairway); from a charming little balcony rise the two flights of the staircase (the first is 15C, the second 18C).

Chancel

The choir of finest 13C style is the most noble part of the cathedral on account of its simple lines and the lightness of its construction.

The high altar is made of a marble slab from the Valle d'Aosta, and dominated by a Christ in gilded lead (18C). Opening off the south arm is the apsidal chapel dedicated to Joan of Arc and embellished with modern stained-glass windows by Max Ingrand.

Crypt, Ambulatory, Lady Chapel

&⟶*Guided tours (1hr30min) For conditions, see above.*

The 11C ring-shaped **crypt** preserves its altar and its curb stone well (5m/16ft deep). The heart of Charles V is pre-

The south doorway of Rouen Cathedral

S. Sauvignier/MICHELIN

served in a coffer embedded in the east end wall.

The **ambulatory** (access south arm – exit north), which is made up of three apsidal chapels, holds the recumbent figures of Rollo, Richard Lionheart (late 13C), Henry (second son of Henry II of England) the Young King (13C), and William Longsword, Duke of Normandy and son of Rollo (14C). Also shown are five 13C **stained-glass windows**★, the bottom one of which, depicting St Julian the Hospitaller, was presented by the Fishmongers' Guild and inspired Flaubert to write a tale.

The **Lady Chapel** (14C) contains two admirable 16C tombs. To the right, the **tomb of the Cardinals of Amboise**★★ of the Early Renaissance (1515-25) was carved after drawings by Roulland le Roux. The two cardinals – Georges d'Amboise (left), Minister under Louis XII and Archbishop of Rouen, and his nephew, also Georges (right) – are shown kneeling.

On the left, stuck on the recess of the Gothic tomb of Pierre de Brézé (15C) is the **tomb of Louis de Brézé**★, Seneschal of Normandy and husband of Diane de Poitiers, who became the mistress of Henri II after her husband's death. It was built between 1535 and 1544.

In addition, the chapel possesses 14C stained-glass windows representing the Archbishop of Rouen and a fine picture by Philippe de Champaigne, *The Adoration of the Shepherds*, framed in a rich altarpiece of 1643.

Old Rouen★★★

Allow about 30min

▶ *Depart from place de la Cathédrale.*

Place de la Cathédrale

Opposite the cathedral on the corner of rue du Petit-Salut stands the former **Bureau des Finances** (House of the Exchequer – Tourist Office), an elegant Renaissance building (1510).

Rue St-Romain★★

One of Rouen's most fascinating streets with its beautiful 15C-18C half-timbered

houses and at the end the spire of the Église St-Maclou. Note no 74, a Gothic house with 15C bay windows.

Archevêché

o━ Not open for tours.

Next to the Booksellers' Court stands the 15C Archbishop's Palace (altered in the 18C). A gable pierced by the remains of a window is all that is left of the chapel where the trial of Joan of Arc ended on 29 May 1431, and where her rehabilitation was proclaimed in 1456.

Cross rue de la République to reach **place Barthélemy** bordered with picturesque half-timbered houses where St Maclou's Church stands.

Rue Martainville★

The street has kept some marvellous 15C-18C half-timbered houses. On the north-west corner of St Maclou's Church is a lovely Renaissance fountain.

Aître St-Maclou★★

184-186 rue Martainville. This 16C ensemble is one of the last examples of a medieval plague cemetery. The half-timbered buildings which surround the yard were built from 1526 to 1533; the south side was built in 1640 and never served as a charnel house.

The ground floor of these buildings is made up of galleries which were once open – as in a cloister. On the column shafts (formerly door frames) are carved figures (damaged) portraying the Dance of Death.

Above the ground floor, the attic was used as a charnel house until the 18C. These buildings now house the School of Fine Arts (École des Beaux-Arts).

▶ *Return to the west end of St-Maclou and turn right.*

Rue Damiette★

The street is lined by half-timbered houses and offers a nice vista of the central tower of St Ouen's Church. Note on the right the picturesque blind alley of the Hauts-Mariages.

In place du Lieutenant-Aubert bear left onto rue d'Amiens to the 17C **Hôtel d'Étancourt** and admire its façade embellished with large statues.

▶ *Return to place du Lieutenant-Aubert; turn left onto rue des Boucheries-St-Ouen; turn right onto rue Eau-de-Robec.*

Rue Eau-de-Robec

In this street, lined with old houses boasting recently restored timber framing, flows a little stream, spanned by a series of footbridges. Several of these tall buildings have workshop-attics, where drapers would leave their skeins of cotton and sheets of fabric out to dry.

Musée national de l'Éducation★

Kids ⬥ ⏱ *Open daily except Tue 10am–12.30pm, 1.30–6pm, weekends 2–6pm. School holidays daily except Tue 2–8pm.* ⏱ *Closed public holidays.* ⬤3€ *(Under 18 years no charge).* ☎ 02 35 07 66 61.

The National Museum of Education is housed in a handsome 15C residence known as the **Maison des Quatre Fils Aymon**★. It was once a notorious trysting spot referred to as the House of Marriages on account of the many casual encounters that took place there.

The museum evokes school life from the 16C up to the present day. A 19C classroom has been reconstituted.

On the corner of rue du Ruissel, note the **Pavillon des Vertus**, a fine 16C mansion decorated with statues of women symbolising the cardinal virtues.

▶ *Return to rue des Boucheries-St-Ouen, take rue de l'Hôpital left in front of* **St-Ouen Church**★★ *(described below).*

At the corner of rue des Carmes stands the attractive Gothic Crosse fountain (restored), and further on at the corner of rue Beauvoisine and rue Ganterie is a handsome half-timbered house.

▶ *Turn right onto rue Beauvoisine which crosses rue Jean-Lecanuet, one of Rouen's most commercial streets.*

In rue Beauvoisine note no 55, a carved half-timbered house with courtyard: no 57 is a Renaissance house. Turn left onto rue Belfroy, bordered at the beginning by 15C-16C half-timbered houses, to

Palais de Justice

reach place St-Godard *(the* **church**★ *is described below).*

Across rue Thiers and square Verdrel, allée Eugène-Delacroix leads to the charming **rue Ganterie**★, lined with old half-timbered houses. In the other direction, towards place Cauchois, this street is **rue des Bons-Enfants**, where several 15C houses still stand; on no 22, notice the sculpted figures.

▶ *Take rue des Carmes to the right, then turn right again on rue des Juifs, which runs alongside the Palais de Justice.*

Palais de Justice★★

This splendid 15C and early-16C Renaissance building was built to house the Exchequer of Normandy (law courts). Renovated in the 19C, it was badly damaged in August 1944.

The **main court** – excavations have revealed a 12C Jewish place of worship – is flanked by two wings, the **façade**★★ (1508-26) of which is exquisite. ⊶ *Closed for restoration.*

The decoration of the façade, is typical of the Renaissance: the base is quite plain but the ornamentation increases on each floor so that the roof line is a forest of chiselled stone with pinnacles, turrets, gables and flying buttresses.

The left-wing stone staircase leads to the **Salle des Procureurs** (Prosecutors'

S. Sauvignier/MICHELIN

Room). This large room has a splendid modern panelled ceiling.

Place du Vieux-Marché★

In the Middle Ages the square was the scene of public mockery and executions. On the North, the foundations of the pillory have been excavated, and on the South, an outline marks the tribune from where the judges of **Joan of Arc** watched her execution. A cross has been erected at the spot where she was burned at the stake on 30 May, 1431.

Rue du Gros-Horloge★★

Connecting place du Vieux-Marché to the cathedral is the abbreviated rue du Gros, a busy commercial street during the Middle Ages and the seat of local government from the 13C to the 18C. With its large cobblestones and attractive 15C-17C half-timbered houses, rue du Gros-Horloge is nowadays one of the city centre's major tourist attractions.

Gros-Horloge

This is the most popular monument in Rouen. The clock, formerly placed in the belfry (🚹 see below), was moved to its present location in 1527 when the arch was specially constructed to receive it. In addition to the single hand which gives the hours, there is the central section telling the phases of the moon and the lower inset indicating the weeks.

Belfry

🔒 Acess limited. Ask at tourist office.

This small tower is topped by a dome added in the 18C to replace the one removed by Charles VI in 1382 to punish the citizens of Rouen, who had organised a tax revolt, known as La Harelle. Within there is a spiral staircase (1457). Inside are the two bells (13C) which gave the signal for the Harelle uprising: on the right the Rouvel (not operated since 1903); on the left, the Cache-Ribaud which sounds the curfew every night at 9pm. From the top of the belfry there is a majestic **vista**★★ of the city, its port and the surrounding countryside.

Next to the belfry is the Renaissance loggia, where the Great Clock keeper used to stand, as well as a beautiful 18C fountain.

On the corner of rue du Gros-Horloge and rue Thouret stands the old town hall (1607).

▷ *Rue du Gros-Horloge leads back to place de la Cathédrale.*

After this long walk around town, you will want to relax in one of the outdoor cafés set up around the square.

▷ *From place de la Calende, rue de l'Épicerie leads to the Fierté St-Romain and the Halle aux Toiles.*

Fierté St-Romain

This charming Renaissance building is crowned by a stone lantern that used to contain the relics of St Romanus. The building adjoins the **Halle aux Toiles** (Linen Hall), a partly modern construction with exhibition, conference and banquet rooms.

St Romain and the Gargoyle

In the 7C, St Romain was the bishop of Rouen, and at the time, a terrible monster known as the Gargoyle was terrorising the city. To rid Rouen of this horrible beast, St Romain needed help. A man who had been condemned to death was the only person brave enough to come forward. Together they set out to confront the dragon. The bishop managed to wrap his stole around the dragon's neck and they led the beast back into town, where it was killed. The courageous prisoner was freed. From the 12C and until the Revolution, one prisoner was chosen by the canons of the church every year to present the reliquary holding the holy remains of St Romain to the crowd from the top of the Haute-Vieille Tower. In return, he would be freed. Nowadays, the legendary event is recalled in the annual fun fair held in the month of October.

Churches

Église St-Maclou★★

🕐For opening hours, contact the tourist office. This beautiful church of Gothic-Flamboyant style, built between 1437 and 1517, is remarkable for its homogeneity, despite being finished during the heyday of the Renaissance. Only the spire of the belfry is modern.

The west façade, the finest part of this building, is preceded by a large five-panelled porch set like a fan. Two of the three doorways, the central one and that on the left, are celebrated for their Renaissance **panels**★★.

These panels are divided into two parts: the leaf of the door has charming little bronze heads of lions and other animals and designs in semi-relief of pagan inspiration, whereas the upper panel, which is a little heavy, has a carved medallion. The medallions on the central door represent the Circumcision on the left and the Baptism of Christ on the right; the upper part of the door represents on the left God the Father before the Creation; on the right, God the Father after the Creation.

The Font Door on the left has only one panel. The medallion represents the Good Shepherd entering the pasture from which he has expelled the thieves.

Inside, the **organ case**★ (1521) is remarkable for its Renaissance woodwork. The **spiral stairs**★ (1517), magnificently carved, are from the choir screen.

Église St-Ouen★★

🕐Open mid-Mar–Oct daily except Mon 10am–12.15pm, 2–6pm (Sun opens at 9am). Rest of the year Tue and weekends 10am–noon, 2–5pm. 🕐Closed mid-Dec –mid-Jan.

Remarkable for its proportions and the purity of its lines, this former abbey church is one of the jewels of High Gothic architecture. The construction, which began in 1318 and slackened during the Hundred Years War, was completed in the 16C.

Exterior

On the south side is the beautiful door named after the wax candle merchants (ciriers) who held their market here. The **east end**★★ is beautiful, with flying buttresses and pinnacles and individually roofed radiating chapels. At the transept crossing, the square **central tower**★, flanked by small towers, rises two tiers before ending in a ducal coronet.

The **Porche des Marmousets** which occupies the lower level is unusual: its arching leans to one side and appears to end in mid-air, resting not on colonnades but on two false keystones.

Interior

The **nave** (🕐see illustration in Introduction: Religious architecture), of a light construction, demonstrates elegance and harmonious proportions. Such perfection could be explained by the golden mean, which in this particular case would be a ratio of 1 to 3: the piers are each separated by 11m/36ft and the vaults reach a height of 33m/109ft.

This slender structure is further enhanced by the warm, radiant light that filters through the large **stained-glass windows**★★. The oldest ones date from before 1339 and are still embedded in the chapels surrounding the chancel. The 16C clerestory windows in the nave are devoted to the Patriarch (north) and to the Apostles (south). The two 15C rose windows in the transept arms illustrate the Celestial Court (north) and a Tree of Jesse (south). The modern Crucifixion adorning the axial bay is by Max Ingrand (1960). The big rosette to the west is the work of Guy le Chevalier (1992).

The chancel is closed off by gilded **grilles**★★ (1747) executed by Nicolas Flambart.

Église St-Godard★

🕐Open Sat 3–5pm.

This late-15C church contains wonderful **stained-glass windows**★, in particular a 16C one on the right side showing the Tree of Jesse.

Close to it is the window of the Virgin, which is made up of six 16C panels.

Église Ste-Jeanne-d'Arc

Completed in 1979, the church is shaped like an upturned ship. Inside are 13 panels of superb **Renaissance stained glass**★★ (16C) from St Vincent's

Abbé Lemire R.	AZ	
Albane Cour d'	BZ	3
Alsace-Lorraine R. d'	CZ	6
Amiens R. d'	CZ	
Anquetil Quai J.	BZ	
Arago R. F.	AZ	
Aubert Pl. du		
Lieutenant	CZ	9
Avalasse R. de l'	BCY	
Barbey-d'Aurevilly R.	AZ	10
Barthélemy Pl.	BZ	12
Beauvoisine R.	BCY	
Beauvoisine Rampe	CY	
Belfroy R.	BY	13
Belges Bd des	AZ	
Bihorel R. de	CY	
Boieldieu Pont	BZ	16
Bons-Enfants R. des	ABY	19
Boucheries-Saint-		
Ouen R. des	CZ	22
Boudin R. E.	BY	24
Boulet Quai G.	AY	25
Bouquet R.	BY	
Bourg-l'Abbé R.	CY	27
Bourse Quai de la	BZ	28
Bouvreuil R. St-André	BY	30
Bouvreuil Rampe	ABY	
Bretagne Av. de	AZ	
Briand Av. A.	CZ	
Cage R. de la	CY	
Calende Pl. de la	BZ	35
Carmes Pl. des	BY	
Carmes R. des	BYZ	
Carnot Pl.	BZ	
Carrel R. A.	CZ	42
Cartier Av. Jacques	AZ	43
Cathédrale Pl. de la	BZ	45
Cauchoise Pl.	AZ	
Cauchoise R.	AY	46
Cavelier-de-la-		
Salle Quai	AZ	
Cécille R. Amiral	AZ	
Champ-des-		
Oiseaux R. du	BY	48
Champlain Av.	BZ	49
Charrettes R. des	AZ	
Chasselièvre R.	AY	52
Chastellain Av. Jacques	BCZ	
Chirol R. P.	AZ	
Clemenceau Cours	AZ	
Cordier R. du	BY	56
Corette R. M.	AZ	
Corneille Pont	BZ	
Corneille Quai Pierre	BZ	57
Crevier R.	AZ	
Croix-de-Fer R.	BYZ	59
Crosne R. de	AY	61
Damiette R.	CZ	63
Delacroix Allée Eugène	BY	66
Donjon R. du	BY	67
Duchamp Espl. M.	BY	68
Eau-de-Robec R.	CZ	70
Écosse R. d'	BY	
Écureuil R. de l'	BY	72
Emmurées R. des	AZ	
Ernemont R. d'	CY	76
Faulx R. des	CZ	81
La-Fayette R.	ABZ	
Flamand R. E.	CZ	
Flaubert Av. du Contrat	AY	
Foch Pl.	BY	84
Fontenelle R. de	AYZ	

Gambetta Bd	CZ		Hauts-Mariages		
Ganterie R.	BY		Impasse des	CZ	94
Gaulle Pl. Général-de	CY	89	Henri-IV Pl.	AZ	
Giraud R. Général	AZ		Herbouville R. d'	ABY	
Grand-Pont R.	BZ		Hôpital R. de l'	BY	96
Gros-Horloge R. du	ABYZ		Industrie R. de l'	BZ	
Guillaume-le-			Jeanne-d'Arc Pont	AZ	100
Conquérant Pont	AZ	93	Jeanne-d'Arc R.	BYZ	

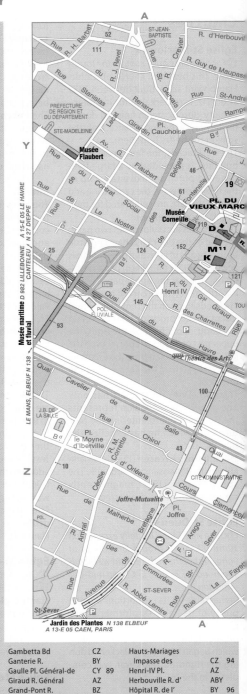

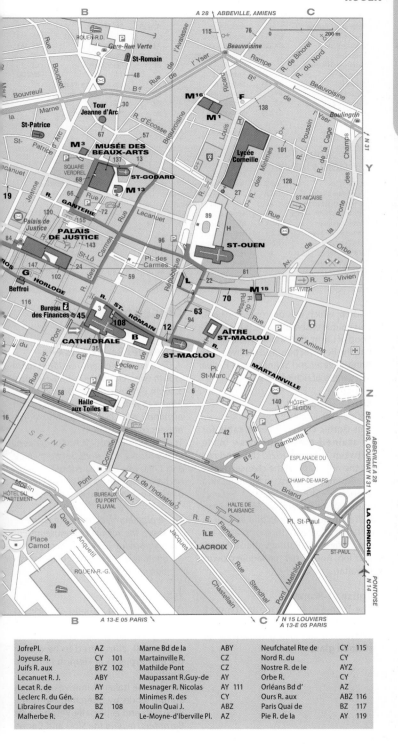

Jofre Pl.	AZ	Marne Bd de la	ABY	Neufchatel Rte de	CY	115
Joyeuse R.	CY 101	Martainville R.	CZ	Nord R. du	CY	
Juifs R. aux	BYZ 102	Mathilde Pont	CZ	Nostre R. de le	AYZ	
Lecanuet R. J.	ABY	Maupassant R.Guy-de	AY	Orbe R.	CY	
Lecat R. de	AY	Mesnager R. Nicolas	AY 111	Orléans Bd d'	AZ	
Leclerc R. du Gén.	BZ	Minimes R. des	CY	Ours R. aux	ABZ 116	
Libraires Cour des	BZ 108	Moulin Quai J.	ABZ	Paris Quai de	BZ	117
Malherbe R.	AZ	Le-Moyne-d'Iberville Pl.	AZ	Pie R. de la	AY	119

Porte-des-Champs		Rollon R.	AY 129	Ste-Marie R.	CY 138
Av. de la	CY	Ruissel R. du	CZ	SchumanR. Robert	CS 140
Poterne R. de la	BY 120	St-Gervais R.	AZ	Socrate R.	BY 143
Poussin R.	CY	Saint-Godard Pl.	BY 137	Stanislas-GirardinR.	AY
Pucelle-d'Orléans		St-Lô R.	BY	Stendhal R.	CZ
Pl. de la	AZ 121	St-Marc Pl.	CZ	Thouret R.	BYZ147
Racine R.	AY 124	St-Maur R.	BY	Vieux-Marché Pl. du	AY
Renard R. du	AY	St-Patrice R.	BY	Vieux-Palais R. du	AY 152
République R. de la	BZ	St-Paul Pl.	CZ	Yser Bd de l'	BCY
Requis R. des	CY 128	St-Romain R.	BZ	19-Avril-1944 Pl. du	BY 155
Revel R. E. J.	AY	St-Sever R.	AZ		
Ricard R. Louis	CY	St-Vivien R.	CZ		

ROUEN SIGHTS INDEX					
		La Corniche	CZ	Musée national	
		Lycée Corneille	CY	de l'Éducation	CZ M¹⁵
		Musée Corneille	AY	Muséum d'Histoire	
Archevêché	BZ B	Musée Flaubert		naturelle d'Ethnographie	
Aître Saint-Maclou	CZ	(Histoire de la médecine)	AY	et Préhistoire	CY M¹⁶
Bureau des Finances	BZ	Musée Jeanne-d'Arc	AY M¹	Palais de Justice	BY
Cathédrale Notre-Dame	BZ	Musée de la Céramique	BY M³	Tour Jeanne-d'Arc	BY
Fierté St-Romain	BZ E	Musée des Beaux-Arts	BY	Église St-Godard	BY
Fontaine-Ste-Marie	CY F	Musée départemental		Église St-Maclou	CZ
Gros-Horloge	BZ G	des Antiquités		Église St-Ouen	CY
Halle aux Toiles	BZ	de la Seine-Maritime	CY M¹	Église St-Patrice	BY
Hôtel d'Étancourt	CZ L	Musée le Secq		Église St-Romain	BY
Hôtel de Bourgtheroulde	AY K	des Tournelles	BY M¹³	Église Ste-Jeanne-d'Arc	AY D
Jardin des Plantes	AZ	Musée maritime et fluvial	AZ		

Church, which was destroyed in 1944. This unique ensemble depicts the Childhood of Christ, the Passion, the Crucifixion, the Resurrection, and the lives of St Anne, St Peter and St Anthony of Padua in a variety of rich colours.

Église St-Patrice
○*Open Sat 3–5pm.*
This Gothic church is remarkable for its **stained-glass windows**★ made between 1538 and 1625. The windows on the north side of the chancel depict the Triumph of Christ; in the adjoining chapels are St Faron, St Fiacre, St Louis and St Eustache, and an Annunciation in Italian Renaissance style as well as a Nativity scene. In the north aisle are the stories of St Barbara and St Patrick and Job. An 18C gilt baldaquin crowns the altar.

Église St-Romain
The former 17C Carmelite chapel, restored in the 19C and again in 1969, contains interesting Renaissance **stained glass**.

Museums and Monuments

Musée des Beaux-Arts★★★
♿○*Open daily except Tue 10am–6pm (South wing closed 1–2pm). Last entry 5.30pm.* ○*Closed public holidays.* ◉*3€, (Under 18 years no charge and on 1st Sun of month).* ☎*02 35 71 28 40. www.rouen-musees.com*
The 19C Museum of Fine Arts underwent heavy renovation work between 1989 and 1994, which both restored its original harmonious proportions and created modern exhibition areas.

⊕ *A plan handed out at the entrance shows the layout of the museum. For a chronological visit, start with the south wing, to the right of the reception area.*

15C-17C Painting
One of the most striking canvases is an oil painting on wood, *The Virgin Among the Virgins*, by Gérard David (c 1460-1523), considered to be one of the masterpieces of Flemish Primitive painting.

Besides the Italian Primitives, you can admire works by Guerchin, Giordano, Bronzino and especially Veronese (*St Barnabus Healing the Sick*) and Caravaggio (The Flagellation of Christ). Spanish masters include Velásquez and Ribera; Dutch art is represented by Martin de Vos, Van de Velde, N Berchem and Rubens (The Adoration of the Shepherds). France, too, is acknowledged with paintings by François Clouet (Diane Bathing), Louis de Boullogne (Ceres or Summer), Poussin (Venus Arming Aeneas and The Storm), Simon Vouet and Jouvenet.

18C Painting

Second floor of the south wing. The most noteworthy painters are Lancret (The Bathers), Fragonard (The Washerwomen), Van Loo (Virgin with Child) and Traversi (The Music Lesson).

19C Painting

This section is unquestionably the highlight of the museum, in terms of both its size and the high standard of its collection. Europe's main artistic movements are represented –**neo-Classicism, Impressionism** or **Symbolism** – and the great masters are all here: Ingres, Monet, David, Géricault, Degas, Caillebotte, Corot, Chassériau, Millet, Moreau, Sisley, Renoir and many others.

In the Salle du Jubé (Rood Screen Room), **Romanticism** is present with a set of five sculptures by David d'Angers which stand opposite *Justice of Trajan* by Delacroix and, on the side, *Les Énervés de Jumièges*, a hyper-realist painting by Vital-Luminais.

20C Painting

Contemporary painting is represented by Modigliani, Dufy (The Seine River), the Duchamps brothers, Dubuffet, Nemours and others..

Musée de la Céramique★★

🕐*Open daily except Tue 10am–1pm, 2–6pm (Last entry 5.30pm).* 🕐*Closed public holidays.* ∞*2.30€. Price changes for temporary exhibits. (Under 18 years and 1st Sun of month no charge).* ☎*02 35 07 31 74. www.rouen-musees.com*

The 17C Hôtel d'Hocqueville houses the Ceramics Museum, which presents an outstanding collection of 16C to 18C Rouen faiance.

The work of Masséot Abaquesne, Rouen's first faience maker, who plied his trade around 1550, is represented by paving flags and portrait vases. After a lull, production resumed with Louis Poterat (1644-1725), whose workshop produced dishes and tiles enhanced with a blue and white decor. The colour red made its first appearance around 1670.

Faience was to enjoy a surge of popularity in the early 18C. Decors featuring five colours (starch or yellow ochre ground) appeared. In the room devoted to polychrome decoration, note the **celestial globe** by Pierre Chapelle, a masterpiece of faience making. After 1721, motifs became more varied. Subsequently, around the mid-18C, the Rococo style came into fashion, embellished with all manner of floral motifs.

Musée Le Secq des Tournelles★★

🕐*Open daily except Tue 10am–1pm, 2–6pm (Last entry 5.30pm).* 🕐*Closed public holidays. 2.30€. Price changes for temporary exhibits. (Under 18 years and 1st Sun of month no charge).* ☎*02 35 88 42 92. www.rouen-musees.com.*

The Wrought Ironwork Museum is housed in old St Lawrence Church, a fine Flamboyant building, and is exceptionally rich (3C–20C).

The nave and transept contain large items, such as balconies, signs, railings etc, and in the display cabinets, locks, door knockers and keys. Their evolution can be studied from Gallo-Roman times.

The north aisle includes displays of locks, belts and buckles from the 15C to 19C. The south aisle exhibits a large variety of domestic utensils and tools.

The north gallery on the first floor is devoted to accessories such as jewels, clasps, combs, and smoking requisites. A rare 16C-19C collection of professional tools is housed in the south gallery.

Musée Jeanne-d'Arc

Place du Vieux-Marché. 🕐*Open mid-Apr–Sept 9.30–7pm. Rest of the year 10am–noon, 2–6.30pm.* 🕐*Closed 1 Jan, 25 Dec.* ∞*4€ (Children 2.50 €).* ☎*02 35 88 02 70. .*

The Musem displays models, a wax museum, documents etc. A vaulted cellar houses a model of the castle where Joan of Arc was imprisoned.

Hôtel de Bourgtheroulde

No 15 place de la Pucelle, behind the Place du Vieux-Marché. ⏱*Open Mon–Fri 8.30am–5.30pm, weekends 10am–6pm.* ✏*No charge.*

This famous mansion (pronounced Boortrood) inspired simultaneously by Gothic and the first precepts of the Renaissance, was built in the first half of the 16C by Guillaume le Roux, Counsellor to the Exchequer and Lord Bourgtheroulde.

Stand back a little to look at the façade and then enter the justifiably well-known inner court.

The end building is pure Flamboyant, with a hexagonal staircase tower. The left gallery is entirely Renaissance with six wide basket-handle arches. It is surrounded by friezes: the upper one, disfigured, shows the Triumphs of Petrarch, the lower, the famous meeting of Henry VIII and François II on the Field of the Cloth of Gold (1520).

Musée Pierre-Corneille

Rue de la Pie. 🗨*Guided tours (30min) July–Aug daily except Mon and Tue 2–6pm, Rest of the year weekends and public holidays 4–8pm (Last entry 5.30pm).* ⏱*Closed 1 Jan and 25 Dec.* ✏*No charge.* ☎*02 35 71 28 82.*

The French playwright **Pierre Corneille** (1606-84) was born and lived here for 56 years. Considered the father of French Classical tragedy he wrote, among others, *Mélite* (1629; first performed in Rouen), *Le Cid, Horace* and *Cinna.*

Musée Flaubert et d'Histoire de la médecine

51 rue de Le Cat. ⏱*Open Tue 10am–6pm, Wed–Sat 10am–noon, 2–6pm.* ⏱*Closed Sun, Mon and public holidays.* ✏*2.20€ (Children no charge).* ☎*02 35 15 59 95. www.chu-rouen.fr*

The Hôtel-Dieu (17C-18C) has a Classical façade. This museum devoted to the history of medicine is set in the home (one of the pavilions) where **Gustave Flaubert** (1821-80) was born. His father worked as a surgeon. Souvenirs of Flaubert are on display.

Tour Jeanne-d'Arc

⏱ *Open Apr–Sept Mon–Sat 10am–12.30pm, 2–6pm, Sun and public holidays 2–6.30pm. Rest of the year Mon–Sat 10am–12.30pm, 2–5pm, Sun 2–6pm.* ⏱*Closed 1 Jan, 1 May, 1 and 11 Nov, 25 Dec. 1.50€ (Children no charge).* ☎*02 35 88 02 70. www.jeanne-darc.com.*

This is the former keep in Philippe Auguste's 13C castle, where Joan was subjected to torture on 9 May 1431. The second floor is devoted to the life of Joan of Arc.

Musée des Antiquités de la Seine-Maritime★★

♿ ⏱ *Open daily except Tue 10am–12.15pm, 1.30–5.30pm, Sun 2–6pm.* ⏱*Closed 1 Jan, 1 May, 1 and 11 Nov, 25 Dec.* ✏*3€ (Under 18 years no charge).* ☎*02 35 98 55 10.* 🗨*Guided tours available on request at* ☎*02 35 98 55 10.*

A 17C convent houses this museum which displays objects from prehistory to the 19C. From the Middle Ages and the Renaissance are items including

---

Rouen Faience

The word *ceramics* covers all aspects of terracotta (baked clay), whereas faience is a type of ceramic made of compound clay covered with a tin-based enamel. White in colour, faience can be decorated. Two types of earth went into the making of Rouen faience: St-Aubin (from the Boos Plateau), clayey and bright red, and earth from Quatre-Mares (between Sotteville and St-Étienne-du-Rouvray), a light, sandy alluvial soil. Mixed in the right proportions, the result was ground, washed, dried, powdered, sifted and placed in decantation containers. When sufficiently consistent, the mixture was placed near an oven to finish the evaporation process, and then trodden to extract fermentation gases. Sand was then added to form a ceramic compound. Finally there were the different processes of shaping, casting, glazing, painting and curing.

stunning religious gold and silver plate (12C Valasse Cross), 12C-13C **enamels★**, 5C-16C **ivories★** (a 14C seated Virgin) as well as a collection of arms and Moorish and Italian majolica. In a long gallery are Gothic and Renaissance **carved façades★** from half-timbered houses in old Rouen. A separate gallery contains the 15C **Winged Deer tapestry★★** and Renaissance furnishings.

There is also an important **Gallo-Roman collection★** noteworthy for its bronzes and glassware. In the centre of the lapidary gallery is the famous **Lillebonne mosaic★★** (4C, restored 19C), the largest signed and illuminated mosaic to be found in France.

Near the museum gardens stands the large **Fontaine Ste-Marie** by Falguière.

Lycée Corneille

The school is in the former 17C-18C Jesuit college and was attended not only by Corneille but later also by Corot, Flaubert, Maupassant and Maurois.

Excursions

Jardin des plantes★

2.5km/1.5mi. Leave Rouen by avenue de Bretagne, or take bus route no 12 and get off at Dufay or Jardin des Plantes. &♿ &🕐*Open daily 8am until dark in winter, 8.30am–8pm in summer.* &💰*No charge.* &☎*02 32 18 21 30.*

In a beautiful 10ha/25-acre park planted with shrubs, flowers and tree species of all kinds, the **tropical hothouses** present an outstanding collection of rare varieties. The park, originally designed in the 17C, contains around 3 000 plant species inside the greenhouses and a further 5 000 out in the open air. One of the star attractions is the legendary **Victoria Regia**, a giant water lily from the Amazon, whose large, flat leaves can reach a diameter of 1m/3.3ft in summer. Its flowers bloom, change colour, and die the same day.

Centre Universitaire

5km/3mi. Leave Rouen by rue Chasselièvre NW on the map.

From the road, which ends on the Mont-aux-Malades plateau on which the university campus has been built, there is a good **panorama★★** of the city, the port and the curve in the river.

Manoir Pierre-Corneille

In Petit-Couronne, 8km/5mi. From Rouen take avenue de Bretagne, on the map; turn right by the first houses of Petit-Couronne onto rue Pierre-Corneille. 🅿*Leave the car before no 502.* 🕐*Open Apr–Sept daily except Tue 10am–12.30pm, 2–6pm, Sun 2–6pm. Rest of the year daily except Tue 10am–12.30pm, 2–5.30pm, Sun 2–5.30pm.* 🕐*Closed 1 Jan, 1 May, 1 and 11 Nov, 25 Dec.* 💰*3€ (Under 18 years no charge).*☎*02 35 68 13 89.*

The Norman "house in the fields" was bought in 1608 by the poet's father. When his father died in 1639, Corneille inherited the house and continued to stay there. The museum evokes the writer's family life with 17C furniture.

Musée industriel de la Corderie Vallois

8km/5mi. Leave Rouen by quai Gaston-Boulet and proceed towards Dieppe; follow N 27 until you reach Notre-Dame-de-Bondeville. ♿💰*Guided tour (1hr30min) daily 1.30–6pm. Machines are run every hour, with commentary by a mechanic.* 🕐*Closed 1 Jan, 1 May, 1 and 11 Nov, 25 Dec.* 💰*3€ (Under 18 years no charge).* ☎*02 35 74 35 35.*

Recently restored, this old factory has retained 19C rope-making machinery in working order. A huge paddle wheel drives the whole complex mechanism.

Forêt Verte

23km/14mi – Allow about 1hr. Leave Rouen by rue Bouquet.

The road passes through the forest, a favourite spot with the people of Rouen.

Barentin

17km/11mi NW. Leave Rouen by A 15 or N 15. Visitors entering Barentin from Mesnil-Roux are greeted by a 13.5/44ft polystyrene Statue of Liberty, made for the French film *Le Cerveau* (The Brain). The town boasts works by contemporary sculptors such as Rodin, Janniot, Bourdelle and Gromaire. On the place de la Libération is a pretty 17C fountain by Nicolas Coustou.

The brick railway viaduct, 505m/1 657ft long, which carries the Paris-Le Havre railway line across the Austreberthe Valley stands in Barentin.

The 19C **church** (○*Open daily except Wed and Sun 9am–5pm. ☎02 35 91 21 35)* has modern windows depicting the lives of St Martin, St Helier and St Austreberthe.

Driving Tours

The Corniche★★★

10km/6mi – plus 15min sightseeing, preferably at sunset.

▶ *Starting from place St-Paul, drive along rue Henri-Rivière and its continuation, rue du Mont-Gargan. Branch right onto rue Annie-de-Pène.*

The road climbs by a hairpin bend to the top of Ste-Catherine Hill, a chalk spur separating the Robec and Seine valleys.

Côte Ste-Catherine★★★
Leave the car on a terrace in a sharp bend to the left. There is a strikingly beautiful **panorama** *(viewing table)* over the river bend and the town with all its belfries.

▶ *Continue along D 95 which meets N 14bis by a school. Turn left; after 200m/220yd turn right before the Café de la Mairie.*

Bonsecours★★
The neo-Gothic basilica of Bonsecours (1840) which crowns the Mount Thuringe spur is an excellent belvedere from which to see the shipping on the river and industrial Rouen. From the monument to Joan of Arc there is a **view** that includes Rouen and the Seine Valley. From the foot of the Calvary *(viewing table)* there is a **panorama** downstream to the river bend: the port and the bridges *(left bank)* and the cathedral *(right bank)*.

▶ *Continue on N 14 towards Paris; turn right onto N 14 to return to Rouen.*

Croisset; Canteleu★

9km/6mi – plus 15min sightseeing.

▶ *Leave Rouen by quai Gaston-Boulet, towards Duclair. Turn left onto D 51 towards Croisset.*

Croisset
Pavillon Flaubert – 🔭*Guided tours (15min) July–Aug daily except Mon and Tue 2–6pm. Rest of the year weekends 2–6pm (last entry 5.45pm).* ○*Closed 1 Jan and 25 Dec.* ✎*No charge.*☎*02 35 71 28 82.*

The **Pavillon Flaubert**, now a museum, is where Gustave Flaubert wrote *Madame Bovary* and *Salammbô*.

▶ *Return to D 982 and continue W to Canteleu.*

Canteleu★
There is an interesting but limited view of the port and part of the town from the church terrace.

Lower Seine Valley Driving Tour★★★

From Rouen to Le Havre

109km/68mi – Allow about 4hr 30min
The route provides a variety of views of the meanderings of the Lower Seine.

▶ *From Rouen take D 982.*

A **view**★ of Rouen can be glimpsed to the east through a small valley.

Canteleu★
See above.
The road *(D 982)* crosses the Forêt de Roumare before emerging near St-Martin-de-Boscherville with a view of the Seine Valley and the old abbey church in the foreground.

St-Martin-de-Boscherville★
See ST-MARTIN-DE-BOSCHERVILLE.

The road between La Fontaine and Mes-nil-sous-Jumièges follows the outer side of the bend for several miles between the river bank and the cliff.

Duclair

From Place de la Libération, you can watch the passage of large cargo vessels, incongruous in such a rural setting.
Eglise St-Denis (o– closed to visitors), which was restored in the 19C, has retained tis 12C belfry surmounted by a 16C spire.

▶ *W of Duclair bear left onto D 65.*

This road across the end of the Jumièges Promontory is part of the picturesque **Route des Fruits**, where blackcurrants, redcurrants, cherries etc are sold directly to the public.

Le Mesnil-sous-Jumièges

It was in the 13C manor house at Mesnil that Agnès Sorel, the favourite of Charles VII, died in 1450.
The road runs past the **country park** and **open-air leisure centre**, part of the Brotonne Regional Nature Park.

Abbaye de Jumièges★★★

See Abbaye de JUMIÈGES.

Yainville

The square church tower and nave are 11C. The goldsmiths Christofle set up a factory in the town in 1971.

Le Trait

The 16C **parish church** of this industrial district includes some delightful alabasters (*Adoration of the Magi* and *Coronation of the Virgin*) beneath the statues surrounding the altar.

▶ *In Caudebecquet turn right to St-Wandrille.*

St-Wandrille★

See ST-WANDRILLE.

▶ *Continue W on D 982.*

Caudebec-en-Caux

See CAUDEBEC-EN-CAUX.

▶ *From Caudebec-en-Caux take D 81 and D 281 S and W.*

West of Caudebec-en-Caux, the wood-land gives way to the alluvial lowland along the estuary and industrial sites.

Villequier★

See CAUDEBEC-EN-CAUX.

Château d'Ételan★

Open mid-June –Sept weekends, Mon, Tue and public holidays 11am–1pm (park and chapel only) 3–7pm (park, chapel and château). Last entry 1hr before closing. 2€ morning only, 4€ afternoon (Under 10 years no charge). ☎ 02 35 39 91 27.
This remarkable Flamboyant Gothic building dating from 1494, which occupies the site of an old fortress, dominates the valley. An elegant, nine-bay staircase turret heralds the Early Normandy Renaissance. The terrace provides a superb **view** (foreground) of the St-Maurice-d'Ételan and Norville marshes and (background) of Brotonne Forest. The boats on the Seine appear to be gliding through the field.

Notre-Dame-de-Gravenchon

Interesting modern church with a lead and copper composition on the façade of St George slaying the dragon.

Lillebonne

See LILLEBONNE.

The whitish cliffs around Tancarville emerge in the distance; the road bridge comes clearly into view.

Tancarville

The last chalk cliff on the north bank of the Seine provides a fine view of the river estuary.
The **Pont de Tancarville**★ (1954-59) is one of the largest suspension bridges in Europe (length 1 400m/4 943ft). Previously all cross-river traffic on the Lower Seine had been carried by ferries so as to allow passage for sea-going vessels.
From the bridge (*leave your car at one end*) there is a lovely **view**★ of the Seine estuary and Tancarville Canal in the foreground; in the far distance you can glimpse the Pont de Normandie, which

channels the traffic above the Seine estuary slightly more downstream. The only part of the feudal 10C château to survive intact is the Tour de l'Aigle (Eagle Tower) built in the 15C.

▶ *West of Tancarville the road (D 982) passes under the north end of the bridge (view of the bridge) and skirts the cliff as far as Le Hode.*

There is a good view of the south bank of the estuary and of the industrial zone south of the Tancarville Canal.

St-Jean-d'Abbetot

The **church**, which dates from the first half of the 11C, is decorated with frescoes (12C, 13C, 16C); the **finest frescoes**★ are in the crypt.

▶ *Continue W to Le Havre.*

ST-ÉVROULT-NOTRE-DAME-DU-BOIS

ORNE, MICHELIN MAP 310: L-2

The ruins of this abbey, a great centre of intellectual life in the 11C and 12C, are set in a lovely valley, through which the River Charentonne flows.

🛈 **Information:** Place Fulbert-de-Beina, 61300 L'Aigle.
☎02 33 24 12 40. www.paysdelaigle.com

▶ **Orient Yourself:** The abbey is 27km/17mi northwest of L'Aigle on D 13.

😊 **Don't Miss:** Enjoy the driving tour through the lovely countryside.

🕐 **Organizing Your Time:** Take time for a stroll in the woods near the abbey.

Kids Especially for Kids: Nearby, at Saints-Pères lake, is a recreation area.

🕭 **Also See:** L'Aigle, Verneuil-sur-Arve, Conches-en-Ouche, Bernay and Vimoutiers.

Visit

Abbey Ruins

Destroyed in the 10C by wars, the Romanesque abbey of Ouche revived in the 11C. It was rebuilt in the 13C in the Gothic style, but little remains.

In front of the main entrance there stands a monument to Orderic Vital (1075-1142), whose work described the abbey in its heyday. Behind the monu-ment, beyond the porch (late 13C), the abbey church is being restored.

Driving Tour

The Charentonne Valley

From St-Évroult to Serquigny, 65km/41mi – about 2hr 30min.

▶ *Leave St-Évroult by D 31 travelling NE. After 5km/3mi, take D 14 left. At La Ferté-Frênel, take D 252 and D 33 N.*

This tour takes you between Anceins and Notre-Dame-du-Hamel.

▶ *In Mélicourt, take D 819 left.*

St-Denis-d'Augerons

From the war memorial there is an attractive view of the two churches of St-Denis-d'Augerons and St-Aquilin.

▶ *Return to Mélicourt; take D 33 N.*

🕭 *For coin ranges, see the Legend on the cover flap.*

WHERE TO STAY

🍽 **Le Manoir de Villers** – *61550 Villers-en-Ouche, 9km/5.5mi N by D 230, direction Bocquencé.* ☎*02 33 34 98 00. http://perso.wanadoo.fr/lemanoir/. Closed Jan, Tue–Thu except hotel. 6 rooms.* 🛏 🐎. *On this 17C farm are a riding school, an Italian restaurant and 6 small bedrooms. Rustic dining room.*

Broglie

This small town was the fief of the famous Broglie (pronounced Broy) family. The 18C **château** (⚿ *private*) is built around a medieval fortress. The pillars and the chancel of the **church** are Romanesque; the rest is 15C and 16C.

Jardin aquatique

♿⏱*Open daily.* 🚫*No charge.* ☎*02 32 44 60 58.* This charming little water garden, irrigated by the River Charentonne, is planted with a variety of floral species.

Ferrières-St-Hilaire

This remains of the forge and the forge master's manor still stand.

St-Quentin-de-Isles

Below the 19C château, there is a textile plant. A dovecot stands on an island.

Bernay

⚭*See BERNAY.*

▶ *Take D 144 E along the opposite side of the river.*

Menneval

The country church with its renovated façade is delightful. The local Brotherhood of Charity dates from 1060.

▶ *5km/3mi farther along, cross the bridge over the Charentonne.*

Fontaine-l'Abbé

Church –A pretty Norman village with a Louis XIII château and a **church** (⚿ *Not open.*) which houses banners of the local Brotherhood of Charity.

▶ *Return to D 133 and continue onto Serquigny.*

Serquigny

The church façade is pierced by a Romanesque doorway. Inside, are a Renaissance chapel *(left)* and stained-glass.

ST-LÔ

MANCHE, POPULATION 20 090
MICHELIN MAP 303: L-5

In 1944 St-Lô acquired the sad title of Capital of Ruins. On 19 July, the day the town was liberated, only the battered towers of the collegiate church and a few houses in the suburbs remained standing. Since then St-Lô has been rebuilt and it is now the site of one of the largest stud farms in France.

🛈 **Information:** Place du Général-de-Gaulle, 5000 St-Lô. ☎02 33 77 60 35

▶ **Orient Yourself:** St-Lô lies between Coutances (29km/18mi west) and Bayeux (37km/23mi northeast).

👁 **Don't Miss:** The outdoor pulpit at the Église Notre-Dame.

🕐 **Organizing Your Time:** In late summer, attend the Thursday exhibition at the stud farm.

🧒 **Especially for Kids:** The Ferme de Boisjugan, on the road to Vire, gives an interactive look at farm life.

👣 **Also See:** The marked itinerary D-Day-Le Choc (The Impact), one of several described in the Historical Area of the Battle of Normandy, goes through this town.

A Bit of History

Key Town – St-Lô, a vital communications centre, was destined to play a strategic role in the Battle of Normandy. Owing to its position at a crossroads, the town underwent heavy bombing from 6 June aimed at dispersing enemy forces.

The battle for St-Lô began early in July in the middle of the War of the Hedgerows to capture the Lessay-St-Lô road, the base for Operation Cobra.

Address Book

⚭For coin ranges, see the Legend on the cover flap.

WHERE TO STAY

⊖ **Hôtel Armoric** – *15 r. de la Marne* ☎*02 33 05 61 32. 20 rooms.* 🅿 ⌂. This 1950s building is out of the town centre yet close to the ramparts and the old town. Simple rooms, with veneer or wicker furniture, are well kept.

⊖⊖ **Château de Dampierre Bed and Breakfast**– *14350 Dampierre, 9km/5.6mi from Torigny-sur-Vire via D 13, then right on D 53.* ☎*02 31 67 31 81. www.chateau-de-dampierre. com. 5 rooms.* ⊟ ⌂. A magnificent tree-lined approach leads to this 16C manor. Well-kept rooms overlooking the moat, the gatehouse and a superb dovecot, in the midst of the *bocage* countryside.

⊖⊖ **Auberge de Campagne** – *Château de la Roque, 50180 Hébécrevon, 7.5km/4.7mi W of St-Lô towards Coutances, then towards Périers via D 900.* ☎*02 33 57 33 20. www.chateau-de-la-roque.fr. 15 rooms. Meals* ⊖⊖. This beautiful 16-17C residence appears at the end of a poplar-lined approach. Tastefully decorated rooms, lovely park for strolls, friendly welcome.

WHERE TO EAT

⊖ **Bistrot de Paul et Roger** – *42 r. du Neufbourg.* ☎*02 33 57 19 00 .* In the middle of this crazy bric-a-brac of glazed tiles, Louis XVI chairs, old posters and black-and-white photographs, don't miss the priceless collection of old radio sets. Copious cuisine.

⊖⊖ **La Petite Auberge** – *1216 Rte de Candol.* ☎*02 33 05 34 11. petite-auberge-candol@wanadoo.fr. Closed Mon.* After long years of travel, the chef has settled here to create delicious seafood dishes served on the terrace or near the fireplace.

⊖⊖ **Le Péché Mignon** – *84 r. du Mar.-Juin.* ☎*02 33 72 23 77. restaurant-le-peche-mignon@wanadoo.fr. Closed 25 Feb–6 Mar, 20 July –10 Aug, Sat lunch, Sun evening and Mon.* Near the Haras national, the owner/chef prepares regional dishes adapted to today's tastes. Two dining rooms, including a more modern one with brightly coloured tablecloths.

The town, which was the centre of German resistance, fell on 19 July. A monument, erected in memory of Major Howie of the American army, recalls a moving episode in the town's liberation. Howie had wanted to be one of the first to enter St-Lô, but he was killed on the 18 July. To fulfil his wish, the first Allied troops to enter St-Lô carried his coffin in with them, setting it down in the ruins of the belfry of Holy Cross Church.

A week later, after an unprecedented aerial bombardment – when 5 000 tonnes of bombs fell on an area of 11km2/4.3sq mi – the German front broke in the west and the Avranches breakthrough was launched.

Reconstruction – A new town has arisen from the ruins, planned so that one can now clearly see the outline of the rocky spur, ringed by ramparts and

St-Lô and the Unicorn

Strolling through the streets of St-Lô, the attentive visitor will glimpse many versions of the unicorn, a handsome white horse with a goat's beard, cloven hooves and a narwhal's spiralled horn growing from his forehead.

Considered as shy, wary creatures embodying purity, chastity and loyalty, unicorns in the Middle Ages came to symbolise the Virgin Mary. The devotion of the inhabitants of St-Lô for the Virgin may account for for the presence of a unicorn on the city's coat of arms, in rue de la Porte-au-Lait, and even leaping from a stone fountain on the corner of rue Leturc and rue du Neufbourg.

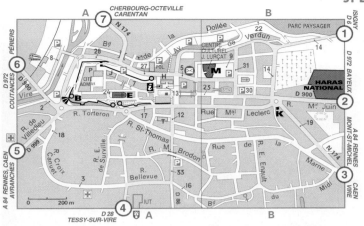

ST-LÔ			Champ-de-Mars Pl.	B	9	Mesnilcroc R. du	B	22
			Feuillet R. Octave	A	12	Neufbourg R. du	B	23
80e-et-136e-			Gaulle Pl. Gén.-de	A	13	Notre-Dame Parvis	A	24
Territorial R. des	A	33	Gerhardt R. Gén.	B	14	Noyers R. des	A	27
Alsace-Lorraine R.	A	2	Grimouville R. de	A	16	Poterne R. de la	A	28
Baltimore R. de	A	3	Havin R.	A	17	St-Thomas R.	A	
Beaucoudray R. de	A	5	Houssin-Dumanoir R.	A	18	Ste-Croix Pl.	B	30
Belle R. du	A	7	Lattre-de-T. R. Mar.-de	B	19	Torteron R.	A	
Briovère Av. de	A	8	Leclerc R. Mar.	B		Vieillard-de-Boismartin R.	B	31

Belvédère	A B	Monument du major Howie	B K	Église Notre-Dame	A E
		Musée des Beaux-Arts	B M		

towers, which have become the land-mark. The oldest district, the Enclos, in the upper part of the town includes the Préfecture and administrative buildings, which make an interesting post-war architectural group. The extremely modern tower in place du Général-de-Gaulle is an amazing contrast to the former prison porch nearby, now a memorial to Resistance fighters and the victims of Nazism.

Sights

Église Notre-Dame
The west front of the church (13C-17C) and the two towers have been shored up but otherwise left as they were in 1944 as a witness to the ferocity of the bombardment. There is an outside pul-pit against the north wall, level with the chancel.

Belvedere
From the tower overlooking the spur on which the town stands there is a view of the Vire Valley and the *bocage*.

Hôpital-Mémorial France-États-Unis
By rue de Villedieu to the SW.
The hospital was built jointly by the two nations and has a Fernand Léger mosaic on one of its façades.

Musée des Beaux-Arts
In the Centre Culturel Jean-Lurçat. ⟨Open daily except Mon and Tue 2–6pm. ⟨Closed 1 jan, Easter Sun and Mon, 1 May, Ascension, 1 Nov, 25 Dec. ⟨2.55€ (Under 12 years no charge). ⟨02 33 72 52 55.
The museum has a good collection of tapestries as well as 19C French painting: Boudin, Miller and Corot.

Haras national★
Rue du Maréchal-Juin in the Bayeux direction. ⟨Kids⟩ ⟨⟩ ⟨Guided tours (1hr) July–Aug daily except Thu afternoon, Sun morning and public holidays 11am, 2.30pm, 3.30pm and 4.30pm. June & Sept 4.30pm (verify with office). ⟨4.50€ (12-16 years 2.50€). Presentation of stallions at 3pm every Thu from the last Thu of July through 1st Thu of Sept. ⟨4€. ⟨02 33 55 29 09.

Vire river valley

The St-Lô stud, the biggest of the 23 national studs, specialises in breeds such as Norman cobs, trotters and French saddle-horses. Every Thursday in season, the stables hold a **presentation**★ of the stallions.

Vallée de la Vire

20km/12mi SE of St-Lô by N 174.

Torigni-sur-Vire
Château des Matignon – ⚫⚫Guided tours (1hr) July–Aug daily 2.30–6pm. (Last entry 5pm). Last 2 weeks of June & 1st 2 weeks of Sept Sun and public holidays 2.30–6pm. ⚫3€. (Children 1€) ☎02 33 56 71 44. Since the 19C the **Château des Matignon** has consisted of only the west wing (restored). The main staircase (17C) leads to the reception rooms which contain a very fine collection of tapestries, Louis XIII, Louis XV and Louis XVI furniture and works by the wildlife artist Arthur Le Duc. The park includes three ponds encircled by shaded paths.

▶ *From Torini take N 174 N; after 5km/2mi turn left onto D 286.*

Roches de Ham★★

Alt 80m/260ft.

From the magnificent escarpment (above the river) there is a **view** of a beautiful bend in the River Vire.

▶ *Return downhill; turn right onto D 551 and right again; pass through Troisgots and descend towards La Chapelle-sur-Vire.*

La Chapelle-sur-Vire

This small village has been a centre of pilgrimage since the 12C. In the church stand a statue of Our Lady of Vire (15C) and a low relief of St Anne, the Virgin and Child.

▶ *Continue along D 159.*

The shaded road crosses the River Vire, then follows its course.

▶ *At the crossroads with D 511, turn right.*

There is a view of the **Château de l'Angotière** (⚫⚫ *not open to the public*).

ST-MARTIN-
DE BOSCHERVILLE★

SEINE-MARITIME, POPULATION 1 551
MICHELIN MAP 304: F-5

The Benedictine abbey was founded in 1144 by William of Tancarville on the site of a collegiate church built around 1050 by his father, Raoul, Grand Chamberlain to William the Conqueror. The monks were driven out during the Revolution.

🛈 **Information:** 227 av du Prés-Coty, 76480 Duclair.
☎ 02 35 37 38 29. www.duclair.fr.

▶ **Orient Yourself:** St-Martin, on the western edge of the Forêt de Roumare, is west of Rouen via D 982, then the D 67

👁 **Don't Miss:** Local tourist offices offer maps of circuits you can take in the Forêt de Roumare.

🕐 **Organizing Your Time:** The abbey can be visited in an hour.

👣 **Also See:** Jumièges, Forêt de Brotonne, Rouen.

Abbaye St-Georges★★

Allow 1hr 15min to tour the area.

Abbey Church

The building, which was constructed from 1080 to 1125, apart from the vaulting in the nave and transept which is 13C, possesses a striking unity of style and harmony of proportion.

The façade is plain: the ornaments on the main door archivolts are geometric, in typical Norman Romanesque style. The nave of eight bays has Gothic vaulting. The monumental confessional in the south transept is 18C.

Abbey Buildings

🕐 *Open April–Oct 9am–6.30pm. Rest of the year 2–5pm.* ✎ *Guided tours Sun Apr–Sept 4pm. Oct–Mar 3.30pm.* 🕐 *Closed 1 Jan, 25 Dec.* ✎ *Apr–Oct 5€, Nov–Mar 4.50€ (Under 12 years no charge).* ☎ *02 35 32 10 82. www.abbaye-sainr-georges.com.*

Chapter-house

The 12C chapter-house is surmounted by a 17C building. Inside, a fine frieze of Hispano-Moorish inspiration runs above the place where the monks' stalls once stood. Excavations have uncovered vestiges of Gaulish and Gallo-Roman temples and a Merovingian funerary church.

Conventual outbuilding

Erected by the Maurists in 1690 and partly demolished during the French Revolution, it was restored in 1994.

Chapelle des Chambellans

It was built in the late 13C to serve the Chambellans of Tancarville.

Park

This formal French garden designed in the tradition of the great landscape architect André Le Nôtre (1680) has recently been restored.

Abbey church of St-Georges

H. Dewynter/MICHELIN

Address Book

&For coin ranges, see the Legend on the cover flap.

WHERE TO STAY

⊜ **Les Hauts du Catel Bed and Breakfast** – 282 chemin du Panorama Le Catel, 76480 Duclair. ☎02 35 37 68 84. Closed Nov to Feb school holidays. 4 rooms. The views from this 1930s villa are simply breathtaking: the meanders of the Seine stretch out below you. The colourful rooms are pleasant; two are located under the roof. Panoramic breakfast room.

WHERE TO EAT

⊜ **Le Bistrot du Siècle** – 75 r. Jules-Ferry, 76480 Duclair. ☎02 35 37 62 36 Closed 25 Dec–1 Jan, Sun and Mon. This little bistro has a fine local reputation. Conviviality reigns in its two dining rooms: one is decorated with old posters; the other is on the veranda. Cuisine with an accent on meat flame-grilled on a wood fire. A few dishes from Reunion Island.

ST-PIERRE-SUR-DIVES★

CALVADOS, POPULATION 3 977
MICHELIN MAP 303: L-5

St-Pierre-sur-Dives, which developed round a rich Benedictine abbey founded in the 11C, still possesses the remarkable old abbey church.

🖪 **Information:** Rue St-Benoît, 14170 St-Pierre-sur-Dives.
☎02 31 20 97 90. www.mairie-saint-pierre-sur-dives.fr.

▶ **Orient Yourself:** St-Pierre-sur-Dives is 43km/21mi southwest of Caen and 15km/9.5mi southwest of Crèvecoeur-en-Auges.

⊘ **Don't Miss:** The restored marketplace of Saint-Pierre-sur-Dives, totally destroyed in 1944.

🕓 **Organizing Your Time:** The Monday morning market is one of the largest in Normandy.

& **Also See:** The Château de Vendeuvre, Falaise and Caen.

Sights

Église★

Church – 🕓Open daily. ☎02 31 20 97 90 The original church was burnt down during the wars between William the Conqueror's sons. The Romanesque south tower dates from the 12C; the west front and the north tower were rebuilt in the 14C.

A copper strip crosses the floor of the nave. Known as the Meridian, it shows the rays of the noontide sun as they pass through a small bronze plaque in one of the windows.

Salle capitulaire

Entrance at 23 rue St-Benoît. 🕓Open all year; ask at the tourist office. ⊜No charge. ☎02 31 20 97 90. www.mairie-saint-pierre-sur-dives.fr.

The early-13C chapter-house has a 13C glazed brick pavement, which was previously in the sanctuary.

Halles★

&🕓May–Sept 8am–8pm. ⊜No charge. ☎02 31 20 97 90. Food market Monday mornings. Antiques market 1st Sun of the month.

The 11C-12C market, which was burnt down in 1944, has been faithfully rebuilt, even to the use of 290 000 chestnut pegs in its **timber-work**.

Excursions

Château de Vendeuvre★★
6km/3.7mi SW by D 271. &*See Château de VENDEUVRE*

Château de Canon
12km/8mi SW of St-Pierre, in Mézidon-Canon, on D 47. ©*Open June–Sept daily except Tue 2–7pm. Mid-Apr–May weekends and public holidays 2–6pm.* ☞*5 €.* ☎*02 31 20 71 50. www.chataudecanon.com.*

This Classical château, built between 1720 and 1768, was the birthplace of Léonce Élie de Beaumont, celebrated 19C geologist.

Parks and gardens★
The gardens and grounds are a delightful mix of the formal French style and picturesque English fashion, embellished with statues and foiies. The **chartreuses**★ are walled gardens where fruits and vegetables are sheltered from the wind.

ST-SAUVEUR-LE-VICOMTE
MANCHE, POPULATION 2 204
MICHELIN MAP 303: C-3

St-Sauveur-le-Vicomte, standing on the banks of the Douve in the heart of Cotentin, is closely associated with the 19C writer **Jules Barbey d'Aurevilly** and St Mary Magdalen Postel who founded the Sisters of the Christian Schools of Mercy in the 19C.

- **Information:** Le Vieux Château, 50390 St-Sauveur-le-Vicomte. ☎*02 33 21 50 44. www.saintsauveurlevicomte.fr.st.*
- **Orient Yourself:** St-Sauveur-le-Vicomte is 15km/9.5mi south of Valognes on D 2.
- **Don't Miss:** The keep of the Vieux Château.
- **Organizing Your Time:** You will need 3hrs to see the château and the abbey.
- **Also See:** The Presqu'île du Cotentin, the Parc naturel régional du Cotentin et du Bessin, Valognes, Ste-Mère-l'Église and Barneville-Carteret.

Sights

Château
Guided tour (45min) July–Aug daily except Sun and public holidays 3pm, 4.30pm. Gardens open all year. ☞*2 €.* ☎*02 33 21 50 44.*

This 12C castle was the ancestral home of two Norman families, the Néels and the Harcourts. The castle has suffered

Address Book

&*For coin ranges, see the Legend on the cover flap.*

WHERE TO EAT AND STAY
☞ **Auberge de la Dives** – *27 bd Collas, St-Pierre-sur-Dives.* ☎*02 31 20 50 50. auberge-de-la-dives@wanadoo.fr. 5 rooms.* Restaurant ☞. This pretty inn is worth the trip: bright, tidy rooms, pleasant country dining room, little terraced on the riverbank and good traditional cuisine.

SHOPPING
Plaisirs des Mets – *2 rue de Lisieux, St-Pierre-sur-Dives.* ☎*02 31 90 33 05. Closed Tue evening, Wed, Sun evening off-season.* The pretty façade of this small grocery shop, which has been made to appear old, draws the eye. Inside, the nostalgic theme is pursued: old crates with advertising still evident, elderly furniture and period bric-à-brac support displays of tea, noodles, oils, sweets, sweet liqueurs, preserved flowers and jams.

Château de Crosville-sur-Douve

many a siege notably by the English in 1356 and the French in 1375. Louis XIV had the castle converted into a hospice in 1691.

Église

Only the transept dates from the 13C, the rest of the church was rebuilt in the 15C. At the entrance to the chancel are a 16C *Ecce Homo* (*left*) and a 15C statue of St James of Compostela (*right*).

Musée Barbey-d'Aurevilly

Enter the castle precinct (which now contains an old people's home), climb the stairs (left) beyond the vault. ⏱*Open 26 May–16 Sept & 7 Apr–6 May 10am–noon, 5–6pm. Rest of the year weekends 3–5pm.* ☞*Guided tours available.* ⏱*Closed Mar & Dec.* ⌖*2.30€ (Under 12 years no charge).* ☎*02 33 41 65 18.*

The museum contains mementoes of Jules Barbey d'Aurevilly (1809-89), a critic and writer of popular fantastical novels who was born in the town and is buried in the castle cemetery *(round the castle, along the curtain walls in the moat, and across the large courtyard).*

Abbaye

♿⏱*Open daily 10am–noon, 2–6pm.* ⌖*No charge.* ☞*Guided tours available on request.* ☎*02 33 21 63 29.*

The abbey was founded in the 10C by Néel de Néhon, Vicomte de St-Sauveur. The Hundred Years War brought ruin on the abbey and forced the monks into exile. At the Revolution the building was further dismantled. In 1832 it was bought by Mother Mary Magdalen Postel to serve as the mother house of the Sisters of St Mary Magdalen which she had founded in Cherbourg in 1807.

Abbatiale

The plain round-headed windows in the south aisle of the abbey church date from the Romanesque period. The tomb of St Mary Magdalen Postel lies in the north transept.

Parc

The well-tended park with its fine trees and colourful flower beds is a pleasant place for a stroll.

Excursion

Château de Crosville-sur-Douve

Proceed towards Valognes for 5km/3mi and in Rauville-la-Place take D 15 towards Pont-l'Abbé, then follow the signposts. ⏱*Open mid-Apr–mid-Oct and during school holidays daily 2–6pm.* ⌖*4€ (Under 12 years no charge) 1€ for the garden.* ☎*02 33 41 67 25.*

The oldest part of this imposing 17C château is the round, machicolated tower with its staircase turret. The granite staircase and the remnants of painted decoration in the great hall are two interesting features of the interior.

ST-VAAST-LA-HOUGUE

MANCHE, POPULATION 2 097
MICHELIN MAP 303: E-2

Among the good reasons to visit this popular seaside resort with a marina and a mild climate are the delicious oysters. The fortifications protecting the harbour date back to Vauban (17C). Offshore lies the "warrior island," Tatihou.

- **Information:** 1 Place du Général-de-Gaulle, 50550 St-Vaast-la-Hogue. ☎02 33 23 19 32. www.saint-vaast-reville.com
- ▶ **Orient Yourself:** St-Vaast is 12km/7.5mi south of Barfleur via D 902 and 17km/10.6mi northeast of Valognes.
- **Don't Miss:** The Île de Tatihou and the view at the Pointe de Saire.
- **Also See:** The Cotentin Penninsula, the Parc naturel régional du Cotentin et du Bessin, Barfleur and Valognes.

Sights

Île de Tatihou★
Crossing (10min) every 30min (high tide) and every hour (low tide). Crossing from mid-Apr–Sept 10am–6pm. Rest of the year weekends 2–4.30pm. Number of visitors limited to 500 per day; book in advance. 7.80€ return fare (ticket includes visit of the museum and the Tour Vauban). ☎02 33 23 19 92.

An amphibious vehicle takes visitors over to Tatihou. The **Musée maritime départemental** (Maritime Museum) has sections on naval architecture and history as well as objects recovered underwater at the site of the Battle of La Hougue (1692). A nature reserve (20ha/50 acres) offers opportunities for birdwatching. In the old fort, there is a bookshop, a cafeteria and a restaurant.

▶ *From St-Vaast-la-Hougue take D 1 N towards Réville; after crossing the bridge over the Saire turn right to the Pointe de Saire.*

Pointe de Saire
Beyond the hamlet of Jonville, by the sea, is an old blockhouse that offers a good **view**★ of the attractive rock-strewn beaches of Pointe de Saire and of Tatihou Island.

▶ *Continue N on D 1.*

Beyond Réville the road passes La Crasvillerie, a delightful 16C manor house. As you approach Barfleur, the landscape changes to granite houses, rocky bays and gnarled trees bent by the wind. Gatteville lighthouse stands to the north.

Port de St-Vaast-la-Hougue

B. Kaufmann/MICHELIN

Address Book

For coin ranges, see the Legend on the cover flap.

WHERE TO STAY

La Ferme de Cabourg Bed and Breakfast *–10 rte du Martinet, 50760 Réville, 3.5km/2.2mi N of St-Vaast via D 1, then D 328 dir. Jonville.* ☎*02 33 54 48 42. 3 rooms.* A poplar-lined alley leads to this fortified 15C farm with its elegant double porch. The guestrooms have retained loophole openings which add to the light from mullioned windows reflected on white walls.

Hôtel de France et Fuchsias *–20 r. du Mar.-Foch.* ☎*02 33 54 42 26. www.france-fuchsias.com. Closed 3 Jan –1 Mar, Mon, Tue in Mar, Nov, Dec and Tue lunch from Apr–Oct. 34 rooms.* Restaurant. When the fuchsias are in bloom, they cover the walls of this hotel set back from the harbour. Some rooms overlook the garden. Meals in the dining room, on the veranda or the terrace.

WHERE TO EAT

Crêperie Léoncie *– 27 Quai Vauban.* ☎*02 33 44 42 50.* You'd best book ahead for this little place with a growing reputation. Try the delicious crêpes with scallops, or with 3 kinds of apples.

Le Chasse Marée *– 8 pl. du Gén.-de-Gaulle.* ☎*02 33 23 14 08. Closed 5–27 Jan, 15–30 Nov, Mon lunch in July–Aug, Sun evening and Mon from Sept–June.* The dishes, mostly seafood, are served in the delightful blue-and-white dining room. On the walls, the flags of prestigious yacht clubs (mainly British) and old marine photos form an appropriate setting for the refined cuisine.

SHOPPING

Market *– r. de Verrüe, pl Belle-île and pl de la République. Sat 7am–2pm.* Some 80 merchants sell fruit, vegetables, charcuterie, cheese, seafood and more.

ABBAYE DE ST-WANDRILLE★

SEINE-MARITIME, POPULATION 1 184
MICHELIN MAP 304: E-4

St-Wandrille Abbey and the renascent abbey of Le Bec-Hellouin are a moving testimony to the continuity of the Benedictine Order in Normandy. Today, the monks earn their living mainly from the manufacture of furniture polish and household products.

- **Information:** *Consult the green Address Boxes for Jumièges, Caudebec-en-Caux and the Pays de Caux for restaurants and hotels.* ☎*02 35 96 23 11. www.st-wandrille.com*
- ▶ **Orient Yourself:** The abbey lies on D 982, 4km/2.5mi east of Caudebec and 51km/32mi west of Rouen.
- **Don't Miss:** The cloister, the only part of the abbey still intact.
- **Organizing Your Time:** Visit the abbey on Sunday morning or, on other days, in the afternoon.
- **Also See:** Rouen, Jumièges, Caudebec-en-Caux, Lillebonne and the Parc naturel des Boucles de Seine.

A Bit of History

God's Athlete (7C) – King Dagobert's court was celebrating the marriage of Count Wandrille, who seemed destined to a brilliant career, when, by common accord, the bride entered a convent and Wandrille joined a group of hermits. The King ordered Wandrille to return to court but in time, Dagobert was enlightened by a miracle and accepted the choice. Wandrille's saintliness and magnificent physique earned him the nickname of God's Athlete.

Valley of the Saints (7C-9C) – In 649 Wandrille founded Fontanelle monastery, a centre of learning "where saints flourish like rose trees in a greenhouse."

Benedictine Continuity – In the 10C monks began to rebuild the abbey, destroyed by Vikings. The abbey survived the Wars of Religion, but the Revolution scattered the monks and a series of owners let the buildings fall into ruin. In 1931, the Benedictines returned permanently.

Abbaye★ *Allow 45min*
The entrance to the abbey is through a 15C door surmounted by a symbolic pelican. The porter's lodge and its twin are 18C. The imposing 18C **Porte de Jarente** leads to the main courtyard, accessible on guided tours only. The only parts of the abbey church still standing are the tall columns in two groups of pillars.

Cloisters★
Guided tours (1hr) Easter–Nov. 1 daily at 3.30pm, Sun and public holidays 11.30am and 3.30pm. Rest of the year Sat 11.30pm, Sun and public holidays 11.30am and 3.30pm. Unaccompanied
visits allowed of abbey buildings and of the exterior. *Closed Easter, 25 Dec. 3.50€(Under 15 years no charge). 02 35 96 23 11. www.st-wandrille.com.*
The 14C south gallery *(only one open to the public)*, parallel with the nave, was linked to it by a door surmounted by a now mutilated tympanum illustrating the Coronation of the Virgin. A niche in the 13C church wall contains the graceful 14C statue of Our Lady of Fontenelle.

Église
Mass conducted in Gregorian chant daily at 9.45am, Sun and public holidays at 10am. Vespers daily at 5.30pm (Thu at 6.45pm), Sun and public holidays at 5pm. No visits during services.
The church is an old 13C tithe barn, the Canteloup Barn, which was transported in 1969 from La Neuville-du-Bosc in the Eure and re-erected at St-Wandrille.

Chapelle St-Saturnin
Not open to the public. By car, follow the signs; on foot about 45min there and back. On leaving the abbey take the path downhill (right) and note the 16C Entombment in a niche. Skirt the wall for 150m/164yd; go around a field and take the path beside the abbey wall.

The chapel stands on the edge of the abbey park; it is a small 10C oratory, probably built on Merovingian foundations. The façade was remodelled in the 16C.

STE-MÈRE-ÉGLISE

MANCHE, POPULATION 1 585
MICHELIN MAP 303: E-3

This town entered modern history brutally on the night of 5-6 June 1944 when troops from the American 82nd Airborne Division landed to assist the 101st Division in clearing the exits from Utah Beach. Ste-Mère-Église was liberated on 6 June but fighting continued until tanks advanced into the town from Utah Beach the following day.

Information: 6 r. Eisenhower, 50480 Ste-Mère-Église. 02 33 21 53 91.
Orient Yourself: The N 13 between Bayeux (59km/37mi east) and Valognes (16km/10mi northwest) passes by Ste-Mère-Église.
Don't Miss: Look up to the church steeple at the paratrooper dangling there.

○ **Organizing Your Time:** Take 2hrs to see the village and the Airborne Museum.

Kids **Especially for Kids:** Children will enjoy the Cotentin Farm Museum

♿ **Also See:** The marked itinerary Objectif-Un Port (Objective-A Harbour), one of several described in the Historical Area of the Battle of Normandy, goes through this town.

Sights

Church

The solid 11C-13C church was damaged particularly during the dislodging of German snipers from the belfry. A dummy at the end of a parachute hangs from the steeple as a reminder of Private John Steele: dropped over the area during the night of 6 June 1944, he dangled from the steeple, playing dead for 2hr, while the church bell rang continuously; The Germans eventually unhooked him.

Borne 0 de la Voie de la Liberté

In front of the town hall. This is the first of the 12 000 symbolic milestones (*bornes*) along the Road of Liberty followed by General Patton's troops to Metz and Bastogne.

Musée Airborne

♿○*Open daily Apr–Sept 9am–6.45pm. Rest of the year daily 9.30am–noon, 2–6pm. ○Closed Dec–Jan. ⊛6€ (Children 3 €). ☎02 33 41 41 35. www.airborne-museum.org.*
A parachute-shaped building houses the Airborne Museum which contains mementoes of the fighting on D-Day.

Ferme-Musée du Cotentin

♿○*Open July–Aug 11am–7pm. (Last entry 1hr before closing). June & Sept 11am–6pm. Apr–May and school holidays (except at Christmas) 2–6pm. ⊛4€ (Children 1.60€). ☎02 33 95 40 20.*
Housed in the Beauvais farm (16C), this Cotentin Farm Museum recreates rural life of the early years of the 20C.

Commemoration of Steel's adventures

B. Kaufmann/MICHELIN

Address Book

♿*For coin ranges, see the Legend on the cover flap.*

WHERE TO STAY

⊜⊜ **Le Sainte-Mère** – *8 r. Rich-edoux. ☎02 33 21 00 30. hotel-le-ste-mere@wanadoo.fr. 41 rooms.* ⓟ⌂. Restaurant ⊜⊜. Imposing modern architecture near milestone 0 on the Voie de la Liberté. Rooms all alike, well soundproofed. Lounge with large-screen TV and billiards. A copious buffet and grilled steaks and chops will assuage your appetite.

WHERE TO EAT

⊜⊜ **Le John Steele** – *4 r. du Cap-de-Laine, 50480 Ste-Marie-du-Mont-Village. ☎02 33 41 41 16. www.aubergejohnsteele.com. Closed Sun evening and Mon Oct–June.*
Situated near the regrettably famous church, this inn pays homage to the soldier John Steele. Typically Norman dining room with exposed beams and stone walls. Regional cuisine enhanced by the chef's personal touch. A few simple rooms.

STE-SUZANNE

MAYENNE, POPULATION 935
MICHELIN MAP 310: G-6

This peaceful village occupies a **picturesque setting**★ on a rocky promontory commanding the north bank of the Erve. In the 11C, the viscounts of Beaumont built on the site one of the most important Maine strong points, the only one to successfully resist William the Conqueror.

- **Information:** *1 rue du Chenil, 53270 Ste-Suzanne.* ☎02 43 01 43 60.
- ▶ **Orient Yourself:** Ste-Suzanne is located on A 81 between Le Mans (50km/31mi east) and Laval (32km/20mi west).
- **Don't Miss:** The view of the town and countryside from the castle keep.
- ○ **Organizing Your Time:** You need a half day to see the local sights.
- **Especially for Kids:** Look into the Théatrales Pitchoun, a summer program for children.
- **Also See:** Évron, Sillé-le-Guillaume, Saulges and Laval.

Sights

Viewing Table

Via rue du Grenier-à-Sel.
From the tower you see the town nestled around its 11C keep, the new town beyond the ramparts and the surrounding countryside.

Promenade de la Poterne

The walk along the ramparts encircling the town starts from the Tour du Guet (watchtower), and passes alongside the castle and the old Porte de Fer (Iron Gate). The second half of the walk, which ends at the Porte du Guichet (Wicket Gate), provides distant views (northeast) of the Coëvrons Hills and (north) of Mont Rochard and the Butte de Montaigu topped by St Michael's Chapel.

Church

Interesting statues include a gracious St Suzanne, a 16C polychrome wood statue and a 14C stone Virgin and Child.

Dolmen des Erves

3km/2mi by D 143 or the Assé-le-Béranger road. This megalithic monument was built during the 4th millennium BC.

Musée de l'Auditoire

○*Open July–Aug daily 2–6pm.* ∞4€ *(Children 2.50€).* ☎02 43 01 42 65.

The former court building now houses an exhibition on the medieval town of Ste-Suzanne.

Château

○*Open May–Sept daily 9am–6pm. Rest of the year daily except Mon 9.30am–12.30pm, 1.30–5.30pm.* ○*Closed 1 Jan, 25 Dec.* ∞*No charge.* ☎02 43 01 40 77.
The second floor of this early 17C château has an astonishing **timberwork roof** in the form of an upturned keel.

Driving Tour

Saulges

19km/12mi S by D 125 and D 235.
The road follows the Erve Valley. In Saulges, in the square opposite the parish church stands **Église St-Pierre**. Steps in the 16C **Chapelle St-Sérénède** lead down into a rare Merovingian building, the 7C **Chapelle St-Pierre**.

Grottes de Saulges

⌁ *Guided tour (45 min) July–Aug 10–11.30am, 2–6pm. Rest of the year 2–4.30pm.* ○*Closed mid-Nov–mid-March* ∞8€ *(2 caves), 5.50€ (1 cave). Children 5.50€ (2 caves), 3.50€ (1 cave).* ☎02 43 90 51 30.
The caves–**Grotte à Margot** and **Grotte de Rochefort**–present some interesting geological formations and traces of human habitation.

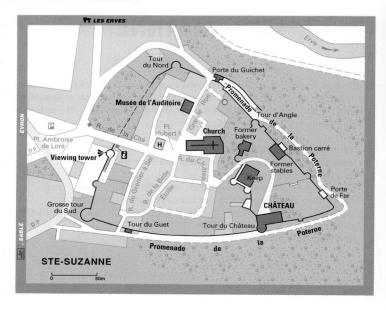

STE-SUZANNE

▶ *Take D 554 NW towards Vaiges; after 1km/0.6mi turn left onto a downhill road to a car park; walk over the footbridge.*

Oratoire St-Cénéré

The hermitage is secluded at the foot of a rocky slope, near where the Erve forms a small lake known for its good fishing.

SÉES★

ORNE, POPULATION 4 504
MICHELIN MAP 310: K-3

Sées has been the seat of an episcopal see since St Latuin converted the district to Christianity in the year 400. The quiet old cathedral town, with its several religious communities, has been sensitively restored.

- 🛈 **Information:** Place du Général-de-Gaulle, 61500 Sées. ☎02 33 28 74 79.
- ▶ **Orient Yourself:** Sées is 22km/14mi southeast of Argentan, or 19km/12mi north of Alençon, near the Forêt d'Écouves.
- ☺ **Don't Miss:** The chancel of the cathedral, and the Forêt d'Écouves.
- ⏱ **Organizing Your Time:** Take a day to see the town and enjoy the forest.
- ✦ **Also See:** Argentan, the Haras du Pin, Alençon and the château de Carrouges.

Visit

Cathédrale★★ *Allow 15min*
⏱*Open daily.*
Despite its difficult history, the cathedral is one of the finest examples of 13C and 14C Norman Gothic.
Exterior - The porch on the west front is disfigured by heavy buttresses added

in the 16C when it began to lean alarmingly.
Interior - In the **chancel**★★ and the **transepts**★★ the triforium is an interesting example of Gothic art, lit by magnificent 13C **stained glass**★★ and rose windows in the transept.

Address Book

For coin ranges, see the Legend on the cover flap.

WHERE TO EAT

Le Cheval Blanc – *1 pl. St-Pierre. ☎02 33 27 80 48. Closed Feb, Nov, and Fri.* A charming "Old France" atmosphere prevails in this century-old half-timbered inn. Traditional dishes in a rustic setting. Guestrooms are clean and simple.

Le Gourmand Candide – *14 pl du Gén.-de-Gaulle. ☎02 33 27 91 28. Closed Feb school holidays, Sun evening, Tue evening and Mon.* The pretty green façade of the restaurant draws the eye. Inside, a contemporary dining room, and a more elegant room with a veranda. Traditional dishes such as the *tête de veau du gourmand Candide*.

WHERE TO STAY

Ferme Équestre des Tertres Bed and Breakfast – *61500 La Chapelle-près-Sées, 4km/2.4mi S of Sées dir. La Ferté-Macé via D 908 then Bouillon via C 14. ☎02 33 27 74 67. www.fedestertres.com. 5 rooms.* This farm is the starting point for fine rides through the Écouves Forest. Hikers can follow blazed paths whereas other guests could try a barouche ride. Three stylish bedrooms with robust furniture.

Hôtel Ile de Sées – *61500 Macé, 5.5km/3.4mi NW of Sées dir. Argentat, via D 303 and D 747. ☎02 33 27 98 65. www.ile-sees.fr. Closed Nov–Feb, Sun evening and Mon. 16 rooms.* Enjoy the peace and quiet of the countryside at this former dairy, set in a park. Dark woodwork adds warmth to the interior decoration. Nice rooms in pastel shades with sedate stained furniture.

SOUND AND LIGHT

Les Musilumières – *July–mid Sept, Fri–Sat evening. 45min. Reserve at tourist office.* Sound and light show in the cathedral, retracing its history.

Additional Sights

Église Notre-Dame-de-la-Place

Guided tour available from the tourist office . ☎02 33 27 81 76.
The organ loft is Renaissance and the 12 low-relief sculptures illustrating scenes from the New Testament, are 16C.

Musée départemental d'Art religieux

Open July–Sept daily except Tue 10am–6pm. 2€ (Under 12 years no charge). ☎02 33 81 23 00.
The Museum, in the former canons' residence, presents a varied collection (12C-19C) of religious art and objects.

Cathédrale de Sées

B. Kaufmann/MICHELIN

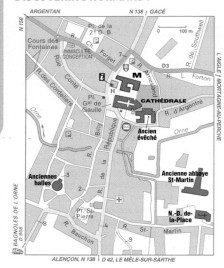

SÉES	
Dr-Hommey R. du	2
Gaulle Pl. Gén.-de	
Halles Pl. des	3t
Leclerc R. Gén.	4
Loutreuil R. A.	7
Paysant R. É.	8
République R. de la	
Verdun R. de	9

Musée départemental d'Art religieux	M

Ancienne abbaye St-Martin

⌐ *Closed to the public.*
The old abbey is now a children's home. Through the great main door one can see the gracious 18C abbot's lodging.

Ancien évêché

This palace was built for Bishop Argentré in 1778. The beautiful wrought-iron gate has an escutcheon and foliated scrolls.

Anciennes halles

This unusual covered market, a rotunda with a peristyle, dates from the 19C.

Excursions

Château d'O★

8km/5mi NW by N 158 and a right turn. ●⌐Guided tour of gardens (30min) mid-July–mid-Aug daily except Sun 1.30–7.30pm. ⌐No charge. ☎02 33 39 55 79 (M. Gascoin).*
This late 15C château combines the Flamboyant Gothic and Renaissance styles. For many generations the château belonged to the O family, who were royal courtiers. The name "O", pronounced the same as *eau* ("water" in French) is appropriate, for the many sloping roofs, slim turrets, delicate ornamentation and façade of brick and stone are beautifully reflected in the moat.

From Sées to Alençon

29km17mi – 2hr 15min

Écouves Forest

🐎🚶⌐Guided tours on foot or on horse-back through the forest massifs (Écouves, Andaines, Bellême and Perche-Trappe, Réno-Valdieu, Moulins-Bonsmoulins) are available from the Office National des Forêts (National Forestry Commission), 36 r. St-Blaise, 61000 Alençon. ☎02 33 82 55 00.* This **forest** (14 000 ha/37 000 acres) covers the eastern promontory of the hills of Basse-Normandie.
The **Signal d'Écouves** is with the Mont des Avaloirs the joint highest point (417m/1 368ft) in western France.

▷ *Take D 204 S. At the Rochers du Vignage crossroads bear right onto D 26 and again right onto a forest road; park the car.*

Rochers du Vignage★

1hr 45min round-trip on foot.
🚶The path *(marked with yellow blazes)* leaves the forest road to a low rock crest from which there are outstanding views over the forest. The path reaches the Chêne-au-Verdier, then parallels the Aubert forest road for 300m/330yd, forks right, then returns downhill to the forest road and the car.

▷ *Take D 26 S to Alençon.*

SILLÉ-LE-GUILLAUME

SARTHE, POPULATION 2 585
MICHELIN MAP 310: I-5

The small town of Sillé-le-Guillaume had a rich and eventful past as one of the strong points, like Ste-Suzanne and Mayenne, which protected northern Maine from Norman invasion.

- **Information:** Place de la Résistance, 72140 Sillé-le-Guillaume. ☎02 43 20 10 32. www.sille-plage.com
- **Orient Yourself:** Sillé-le-Guillaume is on D 304, 35km/22mi northwest of LeMans and 41km/25.6mi southeast of Mayenne.

Visit

Château

Guided tour available July–Aug daily except Mon 2.30 and 4.30pm. 2.50€. ☎02 43 20 10 32 (tourist office).
At the end of the Hundred Years War, the English sacked the 11C fortress. The 15C castle was built on the ruins.

Église Notre-Dame

The church stands upon the site of a former Romanesque church of which the **crypt** and the south transept gable remain. A beautiful 13C door restored in the 15C is decorated with a statue of the Virgin and Child.

Forêt de Sillé

Maps available at tourist offices.
The classic excursion in the Forest of Sillé takes in the **Étang du Defais**, also known as the Lac de Sillé; the 16C **Château de Foulletorte**, and view from **La Croix de la Mare**.

Excursions

Forêt de Sillé

1hr. From Sillé-le-Guillaume take D 310 NE. 42km/26mi
The road rises before entering Sillé Forest which covers the eastern crest of the Coëvrons chain of hills and is well organised for walkers (shelters, signposted footpaths and special riding lanes). The forest was over-exploited at the turn of the 20C and today it is composed trees under tall stands or plantations of conifers on the poorer soils.

- *After 4km/2.5mi turn left onto the forest road; after 800m/875yd turn left again onto a forest road which skirts the north end of Defais Pool.*

Étang du Defais

This stretch of water, also known as the Lac de Sillé, with its attractive surroundings, is a favourite spot with the local townspeople. There is a good bathing area with facilities for yachting, canoeing, swimming, camping etc.

- *From the west side of the pool take the road W; at the crossroads turn right onto D 16.*

From the northern edge of the forest there is a good view of the Norman *bocage*.

- *In La Boissière turn left; in St-Pierre-sur-Orthe take D 143 SW via Vimarcé.*

Château de Foulletorte

Park beside D 143; walk up the avenue which leads to the castle.
The attractive moated château (the water is supplied by the River Erve) was built by Antoine de Vassé at the end of the 16C. The staircase loggia on the entrance front, the projecting cornice on the two wings at right angles, the round-headed or mullioned windows and the tall chimneys are the only decorative notes on this sobre granite building.

- *Return to St Pierre-sur-Orthe; turn right onto D 35.*

LA SUISSE NORMANDE★★

MICHELIN MAP 303: J-6 TO K-7

This extraordinary name denotes an area in Normandy which has neither mountains nor lakes in the Swiss sense and does not even include Normandy's highest points but is nevertheless an attractive tourist area. The River Orne, as it cuts its way through the ancient rocks of the Armorican Massif, produces a kind of hollow relief of which the most typical elements are a pleasantly winding river course bordered by steep banks surmounted by rock escarpments.

▸ **Information:** Place du Tripot, 14570 Clécy.
☏02 31 69 79 95. www.suisse-normande.com.

▸ **Orient Yourself:** The Suisse Normande takes in the Orne river valley and other rivers including the Noireau, the Vère, the Roure and the Baize.

▸ **Don't Miss:** The remarkable view of the Rouvre gorges from the belvedere of the Roche d'Oëtre.

▸ **Organizing Your Time:** Tour the area in your car before deciding on which of the many hikes to try.

▸ **Also See:** Thury-Harcourt, Falaise, Argentan, Flers and Clécy.

Driving Tour

Vallée de l'Orne★★

From Thury-Harcourt to Putanges
99km/61mi – Allow about 3hr. 🐾 *Nearly all sights require a short walk. Be sure to wear suitable shoes.*

Thury-Harcourt
🚶*See THURY-HARCOURT.*

▸ *From Thury-Harcourt take D 562 S.*

The road drops down into the valley. Ahead is the small Chapelle de la Bonne-Nouvelle, perched on a hillock, followed immediately by Caumont with its abandoned sandstone quarry (left) and St-Rémy and its mining installations.

St-Rémy – Fosses d'Enfer
The St-Rémy iron mines were worked from 1875 to 1967.

Maison des Ressources Géologiques de Normandie – Kids ⊙*Open July–Aug daily 10am–12.30pm (Last entry at noon), 2.30–6pm (Last entry 5pm). May–June & Oct daily except Tue 2–6pm. Apr & Oct daily except Tue 2–5.30pm. ⊙Closed*

Nov–Apr. ♿*4.60€ (Children 2.30€). ☏02 31 69 67 77. www.musee-fosses-denfer. com.* An educational program describes all sorts of mineral extraction, especially of energy resources.

Clécy★
🚶*See CLÉCY.*

▸ *Leave Clécy along D 562 S. In Le Fresne turn left onto D 1.*

The road follows the crest of the ridge separating the valleys of the Orne and Noireau and then joins up with the Béron crest. East of the Rendez-Vous des Chasseurs (500m/550yd) there is a view north of the Orne Valle and of the rocks of the Parcs. The downhill stretch offers a view (right) of the Oëtre Rock before reaching **Chapelle St-Roch,** a 16C pilgrimage chapel where a *pardon* is held on the Sunday after 15 August. Continue on to **Pont-d'Ouilly**, a busy tourist centre at the confluence of the River Orne and River Noireau.

▸ *Take D 167 SE along the Orne to Pont-des-Vers. Turn right onto D 43. In Rouvrou, take the road signposted Site de Saint-Jean, then turn right after the cemetery.*

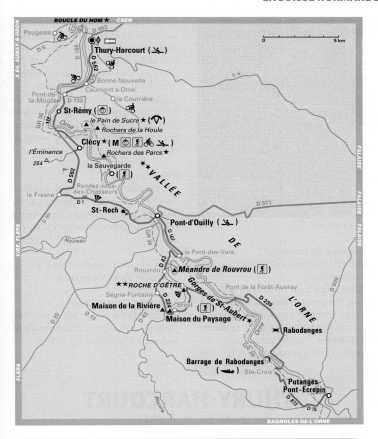

Address Book

🪙 *For coin ranges, see the Legend on the cover flap.*

EATING OUT

🍴🍴 **Au Poisson Vivant** – *61790 Pont-Érambourg, 9km/5.6mi W of Pont-d'Ouilly via D 511 dir. Caen and Pont-Érambourg.* ☎*02 31 69 01 58. Closed 2–6 Jan, Mon and Tue. Reservations advised weekends.* This former dance hall has a small dining room lengthened by a veranda and decorated in 1930s style.

🍴🍴 **Auberge Saint-Christophe** – *61790 St-Christophe, 12km/7.5mi SE of Clécy via D 562 then D 1.* ☎*02 31 69 81 23. aubergesaintchristophe@wanadoo.fr. Closed Feb holidays, 19 Aug–3 Sept, Nov holidays, Sun evening and Mon.* This old house, covered in Virginia creeper, sits on a quiet country road. Rustic dining room, regional cuisine. Some small rooms available.

WHERE TO STAY

🛏 **La Ferme du Vey Bed and Breakfast** – *14570 Le Vey.* ☎*02 31 69 71 02. www.la-ferme-du-vey.com. 3 rooms.* 🍽. This working farm with 80 head of cattle offers 3 comfortable and tidy rooms in an outbuilding. The sociable proprietor is delighted to talk about his farm.

LEISURE

With so many rivers, the Suisse-Normand will thrill water sports enthusiasts. Many sites offer rental of equipment for water sports. At Clécy, look for Au fil de l'eau, le Beau Rivage and Lionel Terray; at Thury-Harcourt, La Roc qui Beu and the Kayak Club; at Pont-d'Ouilly, the Base de Plein Air.

Roche d'Oëtre

S. Sauvignier/MICHELIN

Méandre de Rouvrou

Allow 15min round-trip on foot from the war memorial.

This is the best point from which to view the bend in the river at the narrowest part of the rock ridge. Return to the car and follow the signs to **Roche d'Oëtre**★★ *(The belvedere belongs to a café but there is no obligation to buy any-*

thing). The rock is in a grandiose **setting** dominating the wild and winding Rouvre Gorges with its steep escarpment. East of the Roche d'Oëtre the road runs along the valley; the last viewpoint is the bridge in La Forêt-Auvray.

At this point on its course, north of the Argentan region, the Orne flows through a succession of narrow defiles, known as the **Gorges de St-Aubert**★, which are accessible only on foot.

Rabodanges

The 17C castle is set in a park overlooking the Orne Valley. Further on, at the **Barrage de Rabodanges**, there are fine views of Rabodanges Lake from the road and also from the bridge in Ste-Croix.

▶ *In Ste-Croix turn left onto D 872 just before the war memorial.*

Putanges-Pont-Écrepin

This little town on the Orne is a starting point for visiting the **Gorges de St-Aubert** – accessible only on foot.

THURY-HARCOURT

CALVADOS, POPULATION 1 825
MICHELIN MAP 303: J-6

The town, rebuilt, stands on the banks of the Orne and is now a tourist centre for the Suisse Normande to the south. Thury adopted the name Harcourt from the Harcourt family which came from the town of Harcourt in the county of Évreux; in 1700 Thury became the Harcourt ancestral seat.

- **Information:** 2 place St-Sauveur, 14220 Thury-Harcourt. ☎02 31 79 70 45. www.suisse-normande.com.
- ▶ **Orient Yourself:** Thury-Harcourt lies 23km/14.4mi south of Caen.
- **Don't Miss:** A drive to the Boucle du Hom, where the River Orne describes meanders.
- **Organizing Your Time:** Give yourself a half day to see the château, followed by a walk in the country.

Visit

Park and Gardens of the Château★

Open May–Sept daily 2.30–6.30pm. Apr Sun and public holidays 2.30–6.30pm. Ask about prices. ☎02 31 79 72 05.

Near the ruins of the Harcourt family château, the park has 4km/2mi of walkways bordered with trees and shrubs, as well as flower beds and grassy paths.

Driving Tour

Boucle du Hom★

▶ *5km/3mi. Leave Thury-Harcourt on D 6 to the NW. After 1.5km/1mi take D 212 to the right.*

The road follows the west bank of the Orne and offers good viewpoints overlooking the Orne and its green banks. Turn right at Le Hom where the road leaves the Orne to enter a deep cutting through the rock at the end of the curve's promontory.

▶ *Return towards Thury-Harcourt by D 6.*

Mont Pinçon★
The **Pré-Bocage** is a picturesque rural countryside which borders the Caen plain, the Bessin and the *bocage*.

▶ *At the top of the climb of 365m/1 201ft, near a television transmitter, turn left and continue for another 600m/656yd.*

Leave the car to walk over the heathland (⚠ *The rough stony path can be difficult in winter, take care*); there is a wide-ranging **panorama** of the *bocage*.

Chapelle St-Joseph
The road goes up the Orne Valley. Turn right at Mesnil-Roger to St-Martin-de-Sallen and turn right again here onto a narrow uphill road from which a one-lane road leads off to the right to St Joseph's. From behind the chapel, there is a beautiful **panorama**★ *of the Orne Valley and the heights of the Suisse Normande.*

▶ *Return to St-Martin-de-Sallen and take the next road on the right to rejoin D 6 to Thury.*

LE TRÉPORT

SEINE-MARITIME, POPULATION 5 900
MICHELIN MAP 304: I-1

Le Tréport, a small fishing port at the mouth of the Bresle near the border with Picardy, is a seaside resort which is all the more popular for its close proximity to Paris. During the summer lively crowds round the harbour turn the town into a fair. The long shingle beach, backed by tall cliffs, is packed with visitors on weekends. Mers-les-Bains, on the right bank of the Bresle, is less commercial than Le Tréport and has many devotees, as has Ault, a beach farther north.

🛈 **Information:** *Quai Sadi-Carnot, 76470 Le Tréport. ☎02 35 86 05 69. www.ville-le-treport.fr*

▶ **Orient Yourself:** Le Tréport is 93km/58mi from Rouen and 30km/19mi northeast of Dieppe by D 925, on the border of Picardy.

👁 **Don't Miss:** The view from the Calvaire des Terrasses.

🕐 **Organizing Your Time:** Spend the morning in Le Tréport, then see the pretty resort of Mers-les-Bains.

Sights

Calvaire des Terrasses★
🚶*Allow 30min round-trip on foot. Access by car via rue de Paris, rue St-Michel and boulevard du Calvaire.*
A flight of stairs *(378 steps)* leads up from the town hall to the Calvary on the clifftop. From the terrace, there is a **view** over the town, extending north beyond the Caux cliffs to Hourdel Point, the Somme estuary and inland, along the Lower Bresle Valley to Eu.

Église St-Jacques
The 16C church, which stands half way up the hill, has been extensively restored. The modern porch shelters a Renaissance doorway.

TROUVILLE-SUR-MER★★

CALVADOS, POPULATION 5 411
MICHELIN MAP 303: M-3

Trouville is situated on the coast where the cliffs of the Normandy Corniche slope away at the mouth of the River Touques, to be replaced by a wonderful beach of fine golden sand. The town has all the latest amenities and so maintains its reputation; it was the seaside resort which, as long ago as the start of the Second Empire (1852), launched the Fleurie Coast. As in Deauville, the wooden plank promenade (*planches*) running the full length of the beach is the main gathering place for all holidaymakers. Owing to the coming and goings of the fishermen and the small resident population, Trouville is still worth visiting out of season.

🔢 **Information:** 32 quai Fernand-Moureaux, 14360 Trouville-sur-Mer. ☎02 31 14 60 70, www.trouvillesurmer.org.

▸ **Orient Yourself:** Trouville extends along the north side of the estuary, opposite Deauville, 94km/59mi from Rouen and 43km/27mi south of Le Havre.

Visit

Corniche

Make for the corniche road to the north by way of boulevard Aristide-Briand and a left turn. On the way down there is a magnificent **view** of the Trouville and Deauville beaches and the Côte Fleurie. From the Calvaire de Bon-Secours (*viewing table*) the view is breathtaking.

Aquarium

🧒 ♿ 🕐 *Open July–Aug daily 10am–7.30pm. Easter–June & Sept–Oct 10am–noon, 2–6.30pm. Rest of the year 2–6.30pm. 🕐Closed 25 Dec. ⊜7€ (children 3–14 years 5€). ☎02 31 88 46 04. www.natur-acquarium.com*
Seafront promenade. Fresh and salt water fish together with equatorial forest reptiles provide a colourful spectacle.

Musée Villa Montebello

🕐*Open Apr–Sept daily during exhibitions except Tue 2–6.30pm. ⊜2€ (Wed no charge). ☎02 31 88 16 26.*
This villa is a fine example of seaside architecture during the Second Empire

Address Book

⏷*For coin ranges, see the Legend on the cover flap.*

EATING OUT

⬤ **Crêperie Le Vieux Normand** – *124 quai Fernand-Moureaux, Trouville.* ☎*02 31 88 38 79. Closed 10–31 Jan and Thu. Reservations advised.* This first-rate address for diners of all ages owes its success to its ideal location facing the wharf, the agreeable rustic setting and the menu offering a choice of fondues, raclettes, salads and crepes.

⬤ **Le Cap Horn** – *20 r. des Bains.* ☎*02 31 98 45 06. Closed Mon off-season and Tue.* Behind the pretty stone façade are two dining rooms. The upper floor has a seaside decor and a terrace. Seafood menu based on the daily catch.

⬤⬤ **Tivoli Bistro** – *27 r. Charles-Mozin.* ☎*02 31 98 43 44. Closed 3 weeks in June, 2 weeks in Nov, early Dec, Wed and Thu. Reservations advised.* The decor of the small pastel dining room is a bit minimalist, but the cuisine is ample and delicious, made with products straight from the market. Friendly welcome.

⬤⬤⬤ **La Régence** – *132 blvd F.-Moureaux.* ☎*02 31 88 10 71. www.la-regence.com. Closed 8–18 Mar, 1–27 Dec, Mon and Thu except in Aug.* Opposite the sea, an elegant dining room decorated with 19C painted wood panels. Very fresh fish and traditional cuisine.

WHERE TO STAY

⬤⬤ **Hôtel Le Trouville** – *r. Thiers.* ☎*02 31 98 45 48. www.hotelletrouville. com. 15 rooms.* ⛉. If the façade is a bit tired, the interior is bright and clean.

The rooms, 2 of them for family, are on 3 floors, with complete bathrooms and new beds. Good value for money.

⬤⬤ **Hôtel les Sablettes** – *15 r. Paul-Besson.* ☎*02 31 88 10 66. www.trouville-hotel.com. 18 rooms.* ⛉. In a little street away from traffic, this hotel offers simple, practical accomodation. Most rooms have been redecorated. A family hotel, close to the casino and beach.

⬤⬤ **Hôtel Le Fer à Cheval** – *11 r. Victor-Hugo.* ☎*02 31 98 30 20. www.hotelleferacheval.com. 34 rooms.* ⛉. These two old villas at the centre of the resort, near the beaches, offer functional rooms. The proprietor, a former baker, offers delicious croissants and pastries at breakfast and afternoon tea.

ON THE TOWN

La Maison – *66 r. des Bains.* ☎*02 31 81 94 78. Daily except Tue and Wed mornings 9am–7pm. Sat and July–Aug 9am–10pm. Closed Jan.* Brunch, lunch, tea or ice-cream brea, wine-tastings, all to the best music in the world. Interior redecorated.

LEISURE

Centre équestre de Trouville-Villerville – *Chemin des Terrois, 14113 Villerville.* ☎*02 31 14 99 69. ecurie_villerville@ wanadoo.fr. Open July–Aug and school holidays daily 9am–6pm. Rest of year closed Tue.* Horseback riding is permitted on Trouville Beach during the day. This club, with its 15-horse stable, also proposes rides in the forest and along the cliffs, offering a superb view of Deauville, Trouville and Le Havre.

(1852-1870). The museum shows work by artists who brought fame to the town.

Galerie d'exposition

♿ 🕒*Open all year during temporary exhibits. Check schedules.* 🕒*Closed Tue.* ✎*No charge.* ☎*02 31 14 92 06.* Enter through the tourist office. This gallery hosts temporary art exhibitions.

Excursions

Corniche Normande from Trouville to Honfleur
21km/13mi. ⏷*See DEAUVILLE.*

Côte Fleurie from Trouville to Cabourg
19km/11mi. ⏷*See DEAUVILLE.*

VALOGNES★

MANCHE, POPULATION 7 537

MICHELIN MAP 303: D-2 – LOCAL MAP SEE PRESQU'ÎLE DU COTENTIN

Valognes is an important road junction at the heart of the Cotentin peninsula and is the market town for the surrounding agricultural area. The aristocratic town described by Barbey d'Aurevilly was partially destroyed in June 1944; it has been rebuilt in the modern style and expanded. Several traces of the past have survived including Gallo-Roman ruins, 11C-18C churches, and private mansions built in the 18C when local high society made Valognes the Versailles of Normandy.

- **Information:** Place du Château. ☎02 33 40 11 55.
- **Orient Yourself:** Valonges is at a major crossroads. Cherbourg is 20km/12.5mi north and Carenton 30km/19mi south on A 13; Barfleur is 15km/9.4mi northeast and Barnville-Carteret 29km/18mi southwest on D 902; St-Sauveur-le-Vicomte is 16km/10mi outhwest on D 2.
- **Don't Miss:** The spectacular staircase at the Hôtel de Beaumont.
- **Also See:** The marked itinerary Objectif - Un Port (Objective - A Harbour), one of several described in the Historical Area of the Battle of Normandy, goes through town.

Sights

Hôtel de Beaumont★

☛Guided tours (1hr) mid-July–mid-Aug 10.30am–noon, 2.30–6.30pm (Last entry 5.30pm). First 2 weeks July and mid-

Aug–mid-Sept 2.30–6.30pm. ☛4.80€ (Children 2.80 €). ☎02 33 40 12 30.

This noble 18C residence, miraculously spared by the bombings, has a splendid front in dressed stone. Inside, the sweeping flight of steps with its dou-

---

Address Book

☛For coin ranges, see the Legend on the cover flap.

EATING OUT

☛ **L'Agriculture** –16-18 r. Léopold-Delisle. Valognes. ☎02 33 95 02 02. www.hotel-agriculture.com. In the centre of Valognes, this vine-covered building sits on a quiet little square. The interior is charming and rustic. Delicious house specialties. Guestrooms are modern and comfortable.

WHERE TO STAY

☛ **Le Haut Pitois Bed and Breakfast** – 50700 ùlieusaint, 2km/1.25mi S of Valognes via D2, small road to left on leaving the village. ☎02 33 40 19 92. 5 rooms. ☛ ☛. A superb woodland road leads to this former farm in a calm setting. The rooms, located upstairs in an outbuilding (2 can sleep 4 or 5

people) are spare but functional with complete bathrooms. Ideal for a tight budget and for families.

☛☛ **Grand Hôtel du Louvre** – 28, r. des Réligieuses, Valognes. ☎02 33 40 00 07. www.grndhoteldulouvre.com. Closed 15 Dec–15 Jan. 20 rooms. ☛ ☛. Restaurant ☛☛ . Near the centre of town, this hotel has character: Barbey d'Aurevilly, a 19C Gothic novelist, stayed in Room no. 4. Rooms, reached by a spiral staircase, have been renovated but retain their 19C character, as does the dining room.

GUIDED TOURS

In July–Aug, Valognes offers several tours led by expert guides trained by the Ministry of Culture. Contact Le Clos de Cotentin. ☎02 33 95 01 26. pah.clos. cotentin@wanadoo.fr

Hôtel de Beaumont, interior

ble winding stairwell gives access to the upper floor by a stone arch ending in mid-air. The terraces are laid out as formal gardens.

Hôtel de Grandval-Caligny

32 rue des Religieuses. Guided tours (45min) on request 1 day before to Mme Fauvel. May–Sept daily except Sun and public holidays 10am–noon, 2.30–6pm. 4€ (12–18 years 2.50€). 06 98 89 31 64. The 19C novelist **Jules Barbey d'Aurevilly** once lived in this handsome 17C-18C mansion.

Musée régional du Cidre et du Calvados

The Regional Museum is divided between two locations not too far apart.
Open July–Aug 10am–noon, 2–6pm, Sun 2–6pm. Apr–June & Sept and Nov. holidays daily except Tue 10am–noon, 2–6pm, Sun 2–6pm. 4€ (Children 2 €). 02 33 95 82 00.

Musée du Cidre

The Cider Museum is set up in the **Maison du Grand Quartier**, one of a group which housed a 15C–18C linen factory.

Musée de l'Eau-de-Vie et des Vieux Métiers

Housed in the **Hôtel de Thieuville** (16C-19C), this museum displays equipment for distillation, stonemasonry, iron and copper work from the 11C to the 20C.

Excursions

Bricquebec

From Valognes, go W on the D 902, about 13km/8mi. Castle – Guided tours (1hr 30min) July–Aug daily except last weekend of July 2–6.30pm. 1.80€ (Under 12 years no charge). 02 33 87 22 50.
The town is known for its old **castle** and its Trappist monastery. The 14C **keep** is a handsome polygonal tower (23m/75ft high). The sentry walk between the keep and the clock tower offers a view of the town. The **Tour de l'Horloge** houses a small regional museum.

▶ *From Bricquebec take D 50 and D 121 N; just before the Calvary turn left onto a path.*

Abbaye Notre-Dame-de-Grâce

The abbey is not open for tours but it is possible to attend services, watch an audio-visual presentation at 3pm and purchase items. 02 33 87 56 10.
The Trappist monastery, which is occupied by a community of Cistercian monks, was founded in 1824.

VARENGEVILLE-SUR-MER★

SEINE-MARITIME, POPULATION 1 170
MICHELIN MAP 304: F-2

The resort consists of a series of hamlets in a charming landscape of hedges and half-timbered houses. The church stands on an attractive site★ overlooking the sea. The stained-glass window in the south aisle depicting the Tree of Jesse is by 20C abstract artist Georges Braque, who is buried in the graveyard.

▶ **Orient Yourself:** The pretty coastal road D 75 leads to Varengeville, which is 4km/2.5mi west of Dieppe, between Pourville-sur-Mer and Vasterival.

⊛ **Don't Miss:** The beautiful view from the church; the garden at the Bois des Moustiers, designed by Gertrude Jekyll.

🕐 **Organizing Your Time:** Take 1hr to see the garden.

ॐ **Also See:** Dieppe, Arques-la-Bataille, Fécamp and the Pays de Caux.

Sights

Parc floral du Bois des Moustiers★

🕐Open May–Aug 10am–7pm. Mid-Mar–mid-Apr & Sept–mid-Nov 10am–noon, 2–6pm. ⊛7€ (7–18 years 2.50€). ☎02 35 85 10 02.

In a valley facing the sea, this English-style garden (9ha/22 acres) has a profusion of flowering plants and giant rhododendrons. The **house** (1898) was designed by the renowned Sir Edwin Luytens and the **garden** by his frequent collaborator, Gertrude Jekyll.

Chapelle St-Dominique

On the outskirts of Varengeville, on the left side of the road to Dieppe. 🕐Open June–mid-Sept 9am–5.30pm. ☎02 35 85 12 14. There is more **stained glass** by Braque as well as a painting by 20C artist Maurice Denis.

ॐFor coin ranges, see the Legend on the cover flap.

EATING OUT

⊜⊜⊜**La Buissonnière** – Rte du Phare d'Ailly, 76119 Ste-Marguerite-sur-Mer, 2km/1.2mi NW of Varengeville via D 75. ☎02 35 83 17 13. Closed Jan–Feb, Sun evening and Mon. Reserv. required weekends. Early-20C house set in an exquisite garden. Inventive cuisine, three small dining areas and a charming terrace.

Excursions

Phare d'Ailly★

1km/0.5mi on D 75A off D 75. ☜Guided tour (15min) on request beforehand mid-Apr–mid-Sept daily except weekends and public holidays 10am–noon, 2–4.30pm. ☎02 35 85 11 19.

A modern lighthouse has replaced the two older ones, (18C-19C) which were destroyed in 1944.

Manoir d'Ango

Follow the signs from D 75 onto a little road, and turn right a bit farther on; a drive bordered with a double row of beech trees leads to the parking area. ☜Closed for renovations.

This lovely Renaissance home was built between 1535 and 1545 by Italian artists, and was the home of **Jean Ango**, the great 16C navigator, fleet-owner, governor of Dieppe and naval advisor to François I. He received the king here, and much later the house also enchanted the 20C French poets Louis Aragon, André Breton and Jacques Prévert.

The building is designed around a large inner courtyard. The southern part of the building opens on the ground floor into an Italian-style **loggia**, which was originally embellished by frescoes from the Leonardo da Vinci School. The mullion windows are set in walls of sandstone and flint. The decor is typically Renaissance, with many sculpted ornaments forming the shapes of foliage, seashells and medallions.

CHÂTEAU DU VENDEUVRE★★

CALVADOS, MICHELIN MAP 303: L-6 – 5KM/3MI SW OF ST-PIERRE-SUR-DIVES

In 1750 Alexandre le Forestier d'Osseville, Count of Vendeuvre, commissioned the architect Jacques-François Blondel to build him a summer residence on the banks of the Dives. The château and its beautiful gardens, with their delightful surprise fountains, continue to charm.

- **Information:** ☎02 31 40 93 83. www.vendeuvre.com
- **Orient Yourself:** The château is 5km/3mi southwest from St-Pierre-sur-Dives.
- **Don't Miss:** The Musée du Mobilier Miniature is a collection of tiny masterpieces; the park has remarkable waterworks, including surprise spurts.
- **Organizing Your Time:** You will need 3hrs to see the miniature museum and enjoy the garden. You may spend the day here.
- **Especially for Kids:** There is an amusing collection of shelters for pets.
- **Also See:** Château de Canon, St-Pierre-sur-Dives, and Falaise.

Visit

♿🕐*Open May–Sept 11am–6.30pm. Apr (during Tulip Festival) & Oct–2 Nov Sun and public holidays 2–6pm.* ◉6.50€– 8.50€ (Children 4.90€–6.50€). ☎02 31 40 93 83. www.vendeuvre.com.
The château offers five sights: the Miniature Furniture Museum, the château interior, the collection of shelters for pets, the garden, and the 18C kitchens. Ticket prices depend on how many of these venues you want to visit.

Musée du Mobilier miniature★★

The lovely vaulted rooms of the orangery are the setting for an exceptional collection of miniature furniture, models and masterpieces of skilled craftsmen. About 100 pieces from all over the world, dating from the 16C to the present, are exhibited. Tiny pieces of cutlery and porcelain complete this miniature world.

Château★

Same hours as museum.
The rooms are attractively furnished. In the dining room, looking out on the evening sunset as was the custom, the table is laid with a linen cloth bearing the family arms and with the rear façade of the château woven into the cloth. The reception room has some lovely carved panelling. Two of the more popular 18C games are on display: tric-trac table and loto. Note the special chair for a woman wearing panniers and in the main bedroom the toiletry set, the pastels in the salon, the study (collection of goose feathers), the smoking room (paraphernalia of an 18C smoker) and the kitchens. Behind the château there is a water garden.

Garden of surprises

Among the trees and the fanciful delights of the garden, the spray of fountains may catch you by surprise. True to the playful spirit that motivated 18C landscape artists, there are many wonders, including a not-to-be-missed grotto made of 200 000 seashells. High kitsch!

Château de Veudeuvre

Musée de Mobilier: bed for a cat

VERNEUIL-SUR-AVRE★

EURE, POPULATION 6 619
MICHELIN MAP 304: F-9

Verneuil is composed of three districts, the main streets of which are rue de la Madeleine, rue Gambetta and rue Notre-Dame. In the past each district was like a mini-town protected by a fortified wall and a moat, just as the whole town was surrounded by an outer wall and moat; the water for the moats was supplied by the River Iton. Some very fine half-timbered houses and old mansions (restored) have been preserved in the town, which centres on place de la Madeleine. The jovial and congenial Jean-Marie Proslier (1928-97), a popular figure in French cabaret and theatre as well as a prolific television actor, bought a house in this town and set up a restaurant-cum-grocery which also served as a venue for performers.

- **Information:** 129 Place de la Madeleine, 27130 Verneuil-sur-Avre.
  ☎ *02 32 32 17 17*
- ▶ **Orient Yourself:** *36km/22.5mi west of Dreux on N 12.*

A Bit of History

Verneuil was formerly a fortified city created in the 12C by Henry Beauclerk, Duke of Normandy, third son of William the Conqueror. Together with Tillières and Nonancourt it formed the Avre defence line on the Franco-Norman frontier. In 1204, the town became French under Philippe Auguste, who built the Grise Tower and its defence system. After many battles with the English, the French victory of 1449 was achieved through the guile of miller Jean Bertin.

Sights

Tour Grise

The sentry walk at the top of this 13C tower commands the town and surrounding countryside. It is built of red

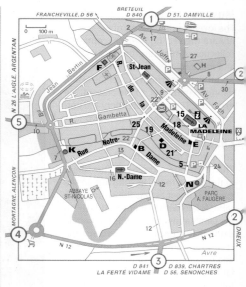

VERNEUIL-SUR-AVRE	
Breteuil Rue Porte de	2
Briand R. A.	4
Canon R. du	5
Casati Bd	7
Chasles Av. A.	8
Clemenceau R.	9
Demolins Av. E.	10
Ferté-Vidame	
Rte de la	12
Lait R. au	13
Madeleine Pl. de la	15
Notre-Dame Pl.	16
Paul-Doumer R.	17
Poissonnerie R. de la	18
Pont-aux-Chèvres R. du	19
Tanneries R. des	21
Thiers R.	22
Tour-Grise R. de la	24
Verdun Pl. de	25
Victor-Hugo Av.	27
Vlaminck R. M.-de	30

Hôtel du 16e s.	B
Maison Renaissance	D
Maison du 15e s.	E
Moulin de Jean-Bertin	F
Tour Gelée	K
Tour Grise	N

agglomerate (*grison*), from which it takes its name.

To the south of the tower, cross the small bridge over an arm of the Iton to view the tower together with a charming little house at its base. The pleasant and relaxing Fougère Park lies near the bridge.

The partly ruined **Église St-jean** has retained its 15C tower and its Gothic doorway.

The term **Promenades** refers to boulevard Casati and its prolongation. Remains of several of the old outer fortifications are visible. From avenue du Maréchal-Joffre and avenue du Maréchal-Foch are interesting views of the town.

The many **old houses** are extremely well restored and undeniably add to Verneuil's charm, notably the 15C residence at the **corner of rue de la Madeleine and rue du Canon**, with its chequered walls and turret. It now houses the public library. Between rue Canon and rue Thiers, on **rue de la Madeleine,** stand a number of attractive stone or timbered houses. The 18C Hôtel Bournonville has wrought-iron balconies. Note also the houses at nos 532, 466 and 401. No 532 stands behind a courtyard.

A Renaissance house stands at no 136, **rue des Tanneries**, with a carved wooden door surmounted by wooden statues. At the corner of rue Notre-Dame and rue du Pont-aux-Chèvres stands a 16C town house with chequered wall and decorated turret. On **place de Verdun, place de la Madeleine, rue de la Poissonerie** are more picturesque old wooden houses.

Église de la Madeleine★

Ascent of the tower Apr–Sept first Sun in the month 3.30pm. Ask at tourist office. Enter by the south doorway.

The **tower**★ abutting the church dates from the late 15C to early 16C. The third of the four tiers is surmounted by a richly decorated belfry.

The Renaissance style porch is flanked by mutilated but still beautiful 16C statues of the Virgin and of St Anne.

The interior is lit by 15C and 16C stained-glass windows and has several 15C and 16C artworks. The nave ceiling is vaulted in wood.

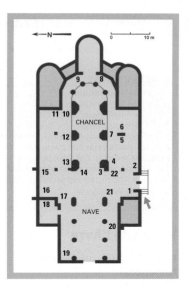

Église Notre-Dame

The church, which was built of the red stone known as *grison* in the 12C and has been remodelled, possesses a number of 16C **statues**★ carved by local sculptors. The illustration shows: **1)**St Denis (14C). **2)**St James the Great. **3)**St Christopher. **4)**St Christine. **5)**St Fiacre. **6)**St Susanna. **7)**St Barbara. **8)**St Francis of Assisi. **9)**St Benedict. **10)**Joan of Arc, as a Lorraine country girl. **11)**Renaissance Pietà. **12)**St Lawrence. **13)**St Augustine. **14)**St Denis with open skull. **15)**St Louis (17C). **16)**Two Prophets (Renaissance woodwork). **17)**St Sebastian (17C woodwork). **18)**15C chest and altar base. **19)**11C font. **20)**14C Trinity (early Norman Renaissance). **21)**Virgin at Calvary (13C). **22)**St John

Excursion

Francheville

9km/5mi NW on D 56. Musée de la Ferronnerie – ♿⏰Easter to 1 Nov Sun and public holidays 3–7pm. ∞No charge. ☎02 32 60 18 89.

The village, attractively set beside the River Iton, has a pretty church, restored. On the square stands a small **Musée de la Ferronnerie** (Ironwork Museum).

Address Book

For coin ranges, see the Legend on the cover flap.

WHERE TO STAY

Hôtel du Saumon – *89 pl de la Madeleine, Verneuil. ☎02 32 32 02 36. www.hoteldusaumon.fr. Closed 22 Dec–12 Jan and Sun evening Nov–Mar. 29 rooms. Restaurant.*
This 18C postal relay surrounds a courtyard. The rooms in the main building, the biggest, are decorated with antique furniture. The restaurant serves salmon in virtually every guise.

Hostellerie Le Clos – *98 r. Ferté-Vidame. ☎02 32 32 21 81. www. hostellerieduclos.fr. Closed 11 Dec–20 Jan. 4 rooms.*
Restaurant. You'll enter another world when you cross the threshold of this elegant mansion. A superb façade of mosaic and brick, refined rooms with sloping ceilings and spacious, almost luxurious suites. Everything here is steeped in elegance for your sole pleasure.

Vallée de l'Avre

From Verneuil-sur-Avre to Nonancourt
20km/12mi – Allow 45min.

▶ *From Verneuil take D 839 S; turn left onto D 316 which continues as D 102 via Montigny-sur-Avre and Bérou-la-Mulotière, to Tillières*

Tillières-sur-Avre
Tillières was the first Norman fortified town built (1013) to guard the Avre defence line. The church, with its Romanesque nave and panelled vault was rebuilt in the 16C. From the garden called the Grand Parterre there is a fine view of the Avre Valley.

▶ *From Tillières-sur-Avre take N 12 E to Nonancourt.*

The **Église St-Lubin** (*south of the river in St-Lubin-des-Joncherets*) was rebuilt in the 16C, also in the Flamboyant style; the façade is Renaissance in style.

Nonancourt
Église St-Martin – Guided tour by request at the tourist office. ☎02 32 58 28 74. Or contact M. Guingnier ☎06 21 10 19 98.
Like Verneuil and Tillières, Nonancourt, built in 1112 by Henry Beauclerk, was a Norman frontier fortress.
The Flamboyant-style **Église St-Martin** dates from 1511. The belfry dates from 1204, the organ from the Renaissance.

▶ *Take N 12 W to Verneuil-sur-Avre.*

VERNON ★

EURE, POPULATION 24 056
MICHELIN MAP 304: I-7

Vernon, which is close to the forest of the same name, was created by Rollo, first Duke of Normandy, in the 9C. It became French early in the 13C and is now an extremely pleasant residential town.

- **Information:** 36 rue Sadi-Carnot, 27200 Vernon. ☎02 32 51 39 60. www.cape-tourismef.fr.
- **Orient Yourself:** Vernon is 65km/40.6mi southeast of Rouen on A 13.
- **Parking:** Two lots are located at each end of the Clemenceau bridge.
- **Don't Miss:** The Église Notre-Dame and the park of the château of Bizy.
- **Organizing Your Time:** The château of Bizy is open only to guided tours. The park can be seen in 30min.
- **Also See:** Giverny, Les Andelys, Évreux and Dreux.

Walking Tour

Park near the Clemenceau Bridge (access from boulevard du Maréchal-Leclerc or rue de la Ravine).

Bridge Viewpoint

From the bridge there is a view of Vernon, the wooded islands in the Seine and the ruined piles on which the 12C bridge stood. On the right bank are the towers of Tourelles Castle, which formed part of the defences of the old bridge.

▸ *Turn left and walk along the Seine.*

The walk takes you by the 18C Bourbon-Penthièvre house, named for the last Duke of Vernon. The street of the same name leads into the **old town**. Notre-Dame Church stands at the end of the pretty street with some half-timbered houses. Notice the 16C façade embellished with Gothic sculptures at no 15.

Église Notre-Dame★

This 12C collegiate church was remodelled several times before the Renaissance. The 15C west front has a beautiful rose window flanked by galleries. In rue du Chapitre, on the right side of the church, is a 17C house (nos 3-5). There are other interesting old houses in rue Carnot and rue Potard, in particular.

Côte St-Michel★

Allow 1hr round-trip on foot.

▸ *From Vernonnet (north); rue J.-Soret to the church, turn right; follow signs.*

From the top of the hill there is a good view of Vernon and the Seine Valley.

Sights

Musée A.-G.-Poulain

Entrance on rue Dupont. &. ○*Apr–Sept daily except Mon 10.30am–12.30pm, 2–6pm. Oct–Mar 2–5.30pm.* ○*Closed public holidays.* ∞*2.60€. (Children and Wed no charge).* ☎*02 32 21 28 09. www. ville-vernon27.fr/musee.*

The museum occupies several buildings dating from the 15C to the 19C. The collection includes works by Monet, Rosa Bonheur, Maurice Denis, Pierre Bonnard, Vuillard and Steinlen (1859-1923).

Excursions

Giverny★
&*See GIVERNY.*

Château de Bizy★

2km/1.25mi W of Vernon by D 181. &. ☛*Guided tours of the interior (45min) Apr–Oct daily except Mon 10am–noon, 2–6pm. Mar weekends 2–5pm.* ∞*7.50€ (5–18 years 5€).* ☎*02 32 51 00 82.*

The château was begun in 1740 for the Maréchal de Belle-Isle, and was remodelled by subsequent occupants. The Classical front faces the park. The rooms are decorated with beautiful Regency woodwork, 18C tapestries and Empire style furniture. The **park** was laid out in the 18C and redesigned in the English style by King Louis-Philippe. Thanks

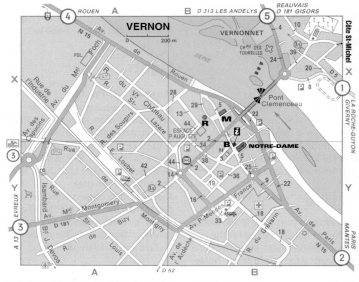

VERNON			Écuries-des-Gardes R.	BX	13	Potard R.	BX	29
			Évreux Pl. d'	BY	14	République Pl. de la	BY	33
Albuféra R. d'	BXY	2	Gambetta Av.	BY	16	Riquier R. Ch.-J.	BXY	34
Barette Pl.	BY	3	Gamilly R. de	BY	18	St-Jacques R.	BY	36
Bonnard R. P.	BX	4	Gaulle Pl. Charles-de	BY	19	Ste-Geneviève R.	BY	38
Carnot R.	BXY	5	Giverny R. de	BX	20	Soret R. Jules	BX	39
Combattants-			Leclerc Bd du Mar.	BXY	22	Steiner R. E.	AY	42
d'Indochine R. des	BX	8	Ogereau R. F.	BX	24	Victor-Hugo Av.	BX	44
Dr-Burnet R.	BY	9	Paris Pl. de	BY	25			
Dr-Chanoine R. du	BX	10	Point-du-Jour R. du	ABX	28			

Maison du temps jadis	BY	B	Musée A.-G.-Poulain	BX	M	Tour des Archives	BX	R

to recent renovation work, the *chemin d'eau* (waterway) has been restored to its former glory.

Signal des Coutumes
8km/5mi from Vernon. Take N 15 out of town and after 5km/3mi, just before Port-Villez, turn right on D 89.

Notre-Dame-de-la-Mer
The **look-out point**★ gives a view of the river between Bonnières and Villez.

▶ *Carry on along D 89; left at the town hall of Jeufosse and leave the paved road on the right. Outside the hamlet of Les Coutumes, take a paved road to the right, which leads to the edge of the woods.*

Signal des Coutumes
There is a lovely, broad **view**★ over the Bonnières meander.

The Vexin Normand★★

From Vernon to Rouen
100km/63mi – Allow 5hr.
The road runs parallel to the right bank of the Seine through farmlands and between the river bank and the escarpment found at each hollow bend.

▶ *From Vernon take D 313.*

Near the D 10 junction, in a field, stands a dolmen (*right*), known as the Gravier de Gargantua (Gargantua's Pebble).

▶ *Courcelles-sur-Seine; cross to south bank.*

Gaillon
⌒ *Closed for renovation.*
The vast **château** (*the access roads branch N off N 15 going W to Rouen*) was made famous in the late 15C

by **Georges d'Amboise**, the first of France's great Cardinal-Ministers. After an expedition to Italy, the prelate rebuilt the château, launching the Renaissance style in Normandy.

▶ *From Gaillon take D 65 N. In Villers-sur-le-Roule turn right onto D 176.*

There is a fine **view**★ south of Tosny. A suspension bridge carries the road over the Seine to Les Andelys.

Les Andelys★★
See Les ANDELYS.

From Les Andelys to Muids, the road (D 313) runs at the foot of chalk escarpments bordering the river. Beyond Muids (D 65) the escarpment is visible across the river.

▶ *In Amfreville-sous-les-Monts turn right onto D 20 which climbs rapidly to the top of the hill; park 50m/55yd beyond the TCF viewing table.*

Côte des Deux-Amants★★
From a bend in the road there is a magnificent view of the Seine Valley: Amfreville locks and dam and the bend in the Seine.

In the 12C, Marie de France, the first French woman writer, told the touching story of Caliste and Raoul. The King of Pitres did not want to give away his daughter so he decreed that her future husband would have to be strong enough to run non-stop to the top of the nearby hill with Caliste in his arms. Raoul, the son of a count, made an attempt but collapsed and died from exhaustion at the top of the hill and Caliste fell dead beside him; the two young people were buried on the spot and so the hill acquired their name.

Écluses d'Amfreville★
The locks and the Poses Dam control water flow in the Lower Seine. Take the footbridge overlooking the locks to see the dam. Follow the towpath over a distance of 1.7km/1mi to reach the river boat Musée de la Batellerie sur la Seine (River Transport Museum). Take the footbridge overlooking the locks to see the water pouring over the Poses Dam.

Fonderie de Cloches

Le Manoir
The new church is a plain, modern building. A vast composition in glass gives a warm light to the interior.

▶ *In Igoville turn right onto N 15, which cuts across a promontory that points towards Elbeuf on the south bank.*

Les Authieux-sur-le-Port-St-Ouen
The church has a fine series of Renaissance stained-glass. Opposite Le Port-St-Ouen, the outskirts of Rouen appear.

▶ *N of St-Adrien turn right onto D 7; continue to the plateau at Belbeuf.*

Chapelle St-Adrien
Situated 20m/65ft below the road, the 13C chapel is partly built inside the cliff and partly thatched.

▶ *S of Belbeuf turn sharp right onto rue de Verdun; bear left, then right, cross a forest crossroads and take the first right; park near the housing development; take the path (45min on foot there and back) to the rocks.*

Roches St-Adrien★
A very attractive view of the river and of the city of Rouen to the north.

Belbeuf
The small church is guarded by its old yew tree. The park of the 18C château has been restored.

▶ *Turn left onto N 14. As the road descends below the basilica in Bonsecours, there is a grand* **panorama**★★.

VILLEDIEU-LES-POÊLES

MANCHE, POPULATION 4 102
MICHELIN MAP 303: E-6

The town occupies a bend in the River Sienne and is an important road junction. It takes part of its name (*poêle* means pot or frying pan) from the making of pots and pans which was a local activity as early as the 12C. At the height of this activity in 1740, there were as many as 139 workshops in the town. From making the great round-bellied copper milk churns (*cannes*) the local factories have converted to the manufacture of copper and aluminium boilers for domestic and industrial use and of souvenirs. Other industries, such as the bell foundry and leather tanning, contribute to Villedieu's reputation. The town has retained its medieval appearance with many attractive inner courtyards (cour des Trois Rois, cour aux Lys, cour aux Moines), stepped streets and alleys and old houses.

- 🛈 **Information:** Place des Costils, 50800 Villedieu-les-Poêles. ☎02 33 61 05 69. www.ot-villedieu.fr.
- ▶ **Orient Yourself:** From Granville, Villedieu is 26km/16mi to the east.
- 🧒 **Especially for Kids:** The zoo in Champrepus.

Sights

Églis e Notre-Dame
This 15C church in the Flamboyant Gothic style was built on the site of a 12C church. The square transept tower over the crossing is emblazoned with various heraldic emblems.

Atelier du Cuivre
♿🐟Guided tours (45min) July–Aug daily 10am–noon, 2–5.30pm. Rest of the year daily except Sun 9am–noon, 1.30- –5.30pm, Sat 9–noon, 2-5.30. 🕐Closed 1 Jan, Easter, Pentecost, 1 Nov, 25 Dec. 👛4.50€ (Children 3.50€). ☎02 33 51 31 85. The story of copper working in Villedieu is explained: the copper deposits, techniques of copper working and a tour.

Musée du Poelserie and Maison de la Dentellière
🕐Open May–Sept daily 10am–12.30pm, 2–6.30pm, Tue and Sun 2–6.30pm. Rest of the year until 6pm. 🕐Closed 1 Sun out of 2 and from mid-Nov–4 Apr. 👛4€ (10–17

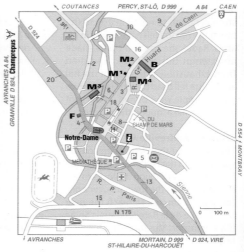

VILLEDIEU-LES-POÊLES	
Bourg-l'Abbesse R. duy	2
Carnot R	.3
Chignon R. du Pont	4
Costils Pl. des	5
Dr-Havard R. du	6
Ferry R. Jules	8
Flandres-Dunkerque R.	9
Gasté R. Jean	10
Gaulle R. Gén.-de	13
Leclerc Av. Mar.	15
Perrière Pl. de la	16
République Pl. de la	18
Tetrel R. Jules	20

Atelier du cuivre	B
Fonderie de cloches	F
Maison de l'étain	M¹
Musée du Cuivre et	
Maison de la dentellière	M²
Musée du	
Meuble normand	M³
Royaume de l'horloge	M⁴

Address Book

⚲For coin ranges, see the Legend on the cover flap.

WHERE TO STAY

🛏 **La Gaieté Bed and Breakfast** – 2 r. St-Georges, 50320 Beauchamps, 10km/6.2mi W of Villedieu-les-Poêles dir. Granville from Beauchamps. ☎02 33 61 30 42 . 5 rooms. 🍽 🛏. This impressive stone house with adjacent garden has recently decorated rooms accessible up a staircase with a lovely old boxwood banister.

WHERE TO EAT

🍽🍽 **Manoir de l'Acherie** – In l'Acherie - 3.5km/2mi E of Villedieu via N 175 bypass and D 554. ☎02 33 51 13 87. www.manoir-archerie.fr. If you wish to admire at leisure the Norman bocage landscape, spend a moment in this 17C manor house with colourful garden, dark patined wood and old stonework. The fare is plentiful, with grills sizzling on a wood fire.

---

years 2€, under 10 years no charge) Combined ticket with the Musée du Meuble normand 5€ (10–17 years 2.50€). ☎06 80 45 51 08.

A reconstruction of an old workshop shows the copperware-making process. The lacemaker's house displays Villedieu lace, popular in the 18C.

Fonderie de Cloches★

♿🔊Guided tour (1hr) 13 July–Aug 9am– 6pm. Rest of the year 10am–12.30pm, 2–5.30pm, Sun and public holidays times differ. ⒸClosed Mon from mid-Nov–mid Feb. ☞4.60€ (Children 3.80€). ☎02 33 61 00 56. www.cornille-havard.com.

The foundry still produces bells for belfries, ships and other public buildings, exported worldwide.

Maison de l'Étain

ⒸOpen daily 10am–noon, 2.30–5.30pm. ☞3.50€ (Children 3€). ⒸClosed Mon, Sun and public holidays. ☎02 33 51 05 08.

In a house dating to the middle ages, an exhibit illustrates the art of pewterworking in the past.

Musée du Meuble normand

ⒸSame times and conditions as for the Musée de la Poeslerie. ☎02 33 61 11 78. The collection of Norman furniture dates from 1680 to 1930.

Excursions

Abbaye de Hambye★★

12km/8mi N of Villedieu by D 9 and D 51. ⒸGuided tour (45min, last tour 30min

before closing) Apr–Oct daily except Tue 10am–noon, 2–6pm. ☞4€ (7–15 years 1.60 €) ☎02 33 61 76 92.

Beside the River Sienne are the majestic ruins of Hambye Abbey, which was founded around 1145. The **church**★ is imposing, although it lacks a roof, a west front and the first bay of the nave. The narrow 13C nave was extended in the 14C by three bays. The exceptionally large Gothic chancel has pointed arches, an ambulatory and radiating chapels. The lay brothers' refectory is furnished with 17C Rouen tapestries and a collection of old furniture.

Mont Robin

13km/8mi N by D 999. About 2km/1mi beyond Percy turn right towards Tessy-sur-Vire and right again almost immediately to Mount Robin.

From this point (276m/905ft) there is an expansive **view** east in the direction of the Suisse Normande.

Parc zoologique de Champrepus

8km/5mi W by D 924 toward Granville. Picnic area and adventure playground. 𝙆𝙞𝙙𝙨 ♿ⒸOpen Apr–Sept 10am–6pm. Feb & Oct 1.30–6pm. Mar weekends 1.30–6pm. ☞12€ (3–12 years 7€). ☎02 33 61 30 74. www.zoo-champrepus.com

Over 80 species are presented in a pleasantly shaded setting of parkland covering 6ha/15 acres. There is also an amusement park and snack shops.

VIMOUTIERS

ORNE, POPULATION 4 418
MICHELIN MAP 310: K-1

The small town of Vimoutiers is tucked away in the valley of the River Vie between hills covered with apple trees which supply the local cider factories. Vimoutiers has close ties with Marie Harel, who gave us the famous Camembert cheese. A statue to her memory, offered by an American cheesemaker, stands on the town hall square.

- **Information:** 21 place Mackau, 61120 Vimoutiers. ☎02 33 67 49 42.
- ▶ **Orient Yourself:** Vimoutiers is 28km/17.5mi south of Lisieux via D 579, and 45km/28mi southwest of Bernay.

Visit

Musée du Camembert
In the tourist office. ♿☞ *Audio-guided tours (30min) Apr–Oct daily 9am–noon, 2–6pm, Mon 2–6pm, Sun and public holidays 10am–noon, 2.30–6pm.* ☞3€ *(Children 2€).* ☎02 33 39 30 29.
The exhibition describes the history and manufacturing process of Camembert. Note the collection of Camembert labels.

Excursions

Camembert
5km/2mi S by D 246.

Maison du Camembert
♿☼*Open May–Aug daily 10am–6pm. Mar–Apr & Sept–Oct daily except Mon and Tue 10am–6pm.* ☞*No charge.* ☎02 33 12 10 37.
Enter through the tourist office. Here is information on this famous cheese and where it is made. A few farms where cheese is still made in the traditional way can also be visited.

Prieuré St-Michel de Crouttes★
5 km/3.1mi W via the D 916, then take the third road to the right. ♿☼*Open May–Sept daily except Mon and Tue 2–6pm. (Last admission 30 min before closing).* ☞6€ *(Children 3€).* ☎02 33 39 15 15.
The origin of this monastic house dates from the 10C. The noble rustic architecture of the buildings is admirably set off by an orchard, gardens and water. Beyond the 18C dairy is the 13C **tithe barn**. One can also see the 18C prior's lodging, the chapel (13C) and the bakery, an 18C timber-framed building.

VIRE

CALVADOS, POPULATION 12 815
MICHELIN MAP 303: G-6

Vire stands on a hillock overlooking the rolling Normandy *bocage*. The town grew up around its castle in the 8C. In the 12C Henry Beauclerc, King of England, strengthened the castle's fortifications and built the keep. In the 13C the population increased, trade flourished and Vire developed apace. The Wars of Religion were detrimental to the town and it lost its military significance in 1630 when Richelieu dismantled the castle. The 17C and 18C were once again a period of prosperity for Vire when both agriculture and trade flourished. Vire is an important road junction and as such it was almost annihilated in 1944.

- **Information:** Square de la Résistance, 14500 Vire. ☎02 31 66 28 50.
- ▶ **Orient Yourself:** On the route between Caen and Fougères.

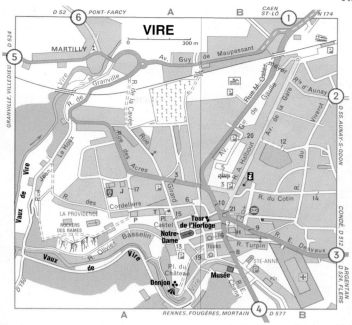

VIRE			Gasté R. A.	B	8	Notre-Dame R.	A	15
			Haut-Chemin R. du	B	9	Remparts R. des	B	16
Aignaux R. d'	AB	3	Leclerc R. Gén.	B	10	Sous-Péfecture R. de la	A	17
Champ-de-Foire Pl. du	B	5	Morgan R. A.	B	12	Valhérel R. du	AB	19
Chénedollé R.	A	6	Nationale Pl.	A	13	Vieux-Collège R. du	B	20
Deslongrais R.	B	7	Noes-Davy R. des	B	14	6-Juin-1944 Pl. du	B	21

Sights

Êglise Notre-Dame

This 13C-15C Église Notre-Dame was erected on the site of a Romanesque chapel built by Henry Beauclerk, Henry I of England.

Access via rue du Valhérel. The **Vaux de Vire** refers to where the steep-sided Vire and Virenne valleys meet, as well as to the 15C songs from which the word *vaudeville* was derived.

Tour de l'Horloge

🕐*Open 18 June–17 Sept Mon–Thu 2–6pm, Fri and Sat 10am–12.30pm, 2–6pm.* 🕐*Closed Sun and public holidays.* ✍*No charge.*

The old main gate (13C) to the fortified town is flanked by twin towers and surmounted by a 15C belfry.

Excursion

Plan d'Eau de la Dathée

7km/4.3mi S on D 577, then turn right onto D 76.

There are good views and a walk (7km/4mi) round the shore, as well as a water sports centre, a bird reserve and picnic area.

Vire Chitterlings

This well-known local speciality (*andouille*) is prepared to a traditional recipe. The stomach and the smaller intestines of the pig are cleaned, chopped, salted and marinated and then stuffed into the larger intestine which is smoked over a beechwood fire for several weeks. The black colour produced by the process is proof of authenticity. The sausage-like chitterlings are then cooked in water and tied off.

South Coast Cliffs, Guernsey

©Chris George/VisitGuernsey

THE BAILIWICKS

The Channel Islands are divided into the **Bailiwick of Jersey**, which includes two rocky islets – the Minquiers and the Ecréhou – and the **Bailiwick of Guernsey**, which includes Alderney, Sark and Brecqhou, Herm and Jethou. All the islands encourage tourism, constructing marinas to attract sailors, ensuring clean beaches for surfers and swimmers, and conserving the countryside to the delight of birdwatchers, walkers and cyclists.

A Bit of History

Although the Channel Islands have been associated with the English crown since the Norman conquest, they lie much nearer to the French coast and were largely French-speaking until the 20C. English is now the universal language of the islands; the native tongue, a dialect of Norman French, the language of William the Conqueror, is rarely spoken. Beneath their apparent Englishness lie 1 000 years of Norman tradition and sturdy independence. The original Norman laws and systems were enshrined in the first charters granted by King John in

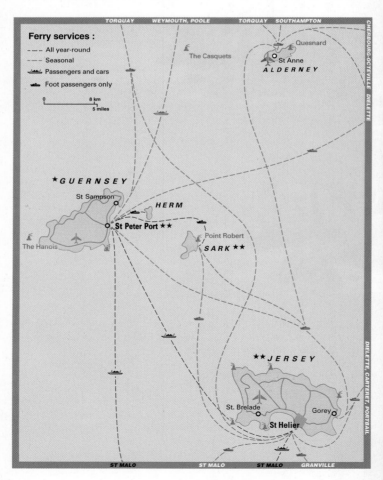

the 13C; modifications were introduced in 1949 to separate the judiciary from the legislature.

Geological Notes

Owing to their situation and the Gulf Stream, the islands enjoy a mild climate that nurtures spring flowers and semi-tropical plants. Long sandy beaches contrast with rugged cliffs; quiet country lanes meander between traditional granite houses. Tidal currents in the islands are among the strongest in the world; at low tide, when the sea may retreat as much as 12m/40ft, huge areas of rocky reefs are exposed, greatly increasing the land mass and making it possible to walk seaward (up to 3km/2mi).

Wrecks and Lighthouses

The Channel Islands are surrounded by extensive offshore reefs and rocky islets which, together with strong tides, treacherous currents and fog, make these seas some of the most hazardous in Britain. Among documented shipwrecks are a Roman galley that sank off St Peter Port; the *White Ship* carrying the heir to the English throne which foundered on the Casquets in 1119; *HMS Victory*, which went down on the Casquets in 1774 with the loss of 1 000 men; the *Liverpool*, which ran aground off Corblets Bay due to fog in 1902; the *Briseis*, which

Clameur de Haro

The ancient legal remedy that is still in force is thought to invoke Rollo, a 10C Norse chieftain. A victim of wrongdoing must kneel down in the presence of two witnesses and say "Haro, haro, haro, à l'aide, mon Prince, on me fait tort" (Help, my Prince, someone is doing me wrong). This must be followed by the recital of the Lord's Prayer in French. The wrongdoer must then desist until a court ruling has been obtained.

struck a reef off Vazon Bay in 1937 with 7 000 casks of wine on board; the *Orion*, an oil rig mounted on an ocean-going barge, which ran aground off Grand Rocques in Guernsey in 1978. There are now four lighthouses owned by Trinity House in the Channel Islands.

The earliest to be built was the one marking the **Casquets** (1723); then followed the three towers, known as St Peter, St Thomas and Donjon (30ft high), which were lit by coal fires. In 1770 oil lamps were introduced, and in 1818 revolving lights. The main light (37m/120ft above sea level) now has a range of 27km/17mi in clear weather.

The **Hanois Lighthouse** was built in 1862 on the treacherous Hanois Reef. **Quesnard Light** (1912) on Alderney and **Point Robert** (1913) on Sark are sited on land and can be visited.

ALDERNEY

POPULATION 2 400
MICHELIN MAP 503

The island (5.6km/3.5mi long by 2.4km/1.5mi wide) slopes gently from a plateau in the south-west, to a tongue of low-lying land in the north-east. There is one main settlement, St Anne, also known as The Town.

Alderney is a haven for nature lovers. The flora includes wild broom, thrift, sea campion, ox-eye daisies, wild orchids and the bastard toadflax (*thesium humifusum*); among the fauna are black rabbits and blonde hedgehogs. Birdwatchers have much to choose from – hoopoes and golden orioles, birds of prey and the occasional white stork or purple heron, and the seabirds, fulmars, guillemots and kittiwakes, especially the colonies of gannets and puffins.

Information: Victoria Street, Alderney, Channel Islands GY9 3TA. ☎01481 823 737. www.visitalderney.com.

▶ **Orient Yourself:** Alderney is the most northerly of the Channel Islands and lies west (12km/8mi) of the Cherbourg Peninsula, separated from the Cap de la Hague headland by the treacherous tidal current known as the Alderney Race.

Don't Miss: The best beaches are in the bays of Bray, Clonque and Telegraph.

Also See: The Cotentin Penninsula and Cherbourg.

A Bit of History

Owing to its key position, nearest to England, France and the Channel shipping lanes, Alderney has frequently been fortified. The Romans seem to have used it as a naval base; there are traces of a late-Roman fort at the Nunnery. The first English fortifications were initiated by Henry VIII (1491-1547), on the hill south of Longis Bay. In the Napoleonic period, the British strengthened existing defences and sent a garrison of 300.

Between 1847 and 1858, alarmed by the development of a French naval base at Cherbourg, the British Government created a safe harbour at Braye by constructing a huge breakwater and built a chain of 10 forts along the north coast. In June 1940 almost all the population left the island and the livestock was evacuated to Guernsey. During their five-year occupation, the Germans re-fortified most of the Victorian forts and built masses of ugly concrete fortifications. When the islanders began to return late in 1945 they found their possessions gone and their houses derelict or destroyed. It took 10 years and substantial government aid to make good the damage.

Constitution

Alderney is part of the Bailiwick of Guernsey. Since the introduction of the new constitution on 1 January 1949, the budget and other financial matters have to be approved by the States of Guernsey. Otherwise all island business is decided by the Committees of the States of Alderney, which consists of 10 elected members and an elected President, who serve for four years. The court consists of six Jurats under a chairman, all of whom are appointed by the Home Office.

St Anne

St Anne, with its cobbled streets and smart whitewashed granite houses, lies about half a mile from the north coast on the edge of the best agricultural land, known as La Blaye.

The original medieval settlement was centred on **Marais Square**. As in ancient times, narrow lanes or *venelles* lead out to the un-enclosed fields divided into *riages*, each consisting of a number of strips: Alderney is one of the few places in Britain still to use this archaic system of managing open agricultural land.

Another settlement grew up at **Le Huret**, where the people assembled to decide when to gather the seaweed (*vraic*) used to fertilise the land. In the 15C more houses were built to the east of the square and the Blaye was extended to support a population of 700. In the 18C the huge profits made from privateering led to a building boom; thatch was replaced by tiles, the first Court House was built and the Governor improved the communal buildings as well as his own residence. The northern part of the town – **Queen Elizabeth II Street, Victoria Street and Ollivier Street** – developed in the early Victorian era. Workmen's cottages were built at Newtown and elsewhere. Many attractive houses and gardens line the green lanes, such as La Vallée, which run from St Anne down to the north coast.

St Anne's Church

Consecrated in 1850, this church was designed by Sir Gilbert Scott in the transitional style from Norman to Early English cruciform.

English was then replacing Norman French as the local language; the lectern holds two Bibles, and the texts in the apse and near the door appear in both languages.

During the war the church was used as a store and the bells were removed; two were recovered on the island and the other four were found in Cherbourg. The churchyard gates in Victoria Street, erected as a memorial to Prince Albert, were removed by the Germans but replaced by a local resident.

Museum

&♿🕐*Open Apr– Oct daily 10am–noon, 2–4pm, weekends 10am–noon.* 🎟️*£2.* ☎*01481 823 222. www.alderneysociety. org/museum.*

The Alderney Society's museum, installed in a former school founded in 1790, presents island geology; flora and fauna; archaeology, particularly finds from the Iron Age Settlement at Les Hughettes; domestic and military history, including the Victorian fortifications and the German Occupation.

The **Clock Tower** (1767) standing nearby is all that remains of the old church which was pulled down when the present one was built.

The elegant **Royal Connaught Square**, renamed in 1905 after a visit by the Duke of Connaught, third son of Queen Victoria, was the town centre in the 18C.

Island Hall (*north side*), a handsome granite building which is now a community centre and library, was enlarged in 1763 by John LeMesurier to become Government House. Mouriaux House was completed in 1779 by the governor as his private residence.

Courthouse

🕐*Open all year Mon–Fri except Thu afternoon 9.30am–12.30pm, 2–4pm.* ☎*01481 822 817.*

The present building in Queen Elizabeth II Street dates from 1850. Both the court and the States of Alderney hold their sessions in the first-floor courtroom.

The name of **Victoria Street**, the main shopping street, was changed from rue du Grosnez to celebrate Queen Victoria's visit in 1854.

The **Butes** recreation ground provides fine views of Braye Bay (*north-east*), across Crabby Bay and the Swinge to the Casquets (*north-west*) and the English Channel.

WHERE TO STAY

🪙🪙🪙 **Farm Court** – *Les Mouriaux, GY9 3UX Alderney.* ☎*01481 822 075. relax@farmcourt-alterney.co.uk Closed 1 week at Christmas. 9 rooms.* 🍽️. In a tranquil corner of St. Anne, old stone farm buildings, nicely renovated, around a paved courtyard and garden. Spacious rooms, breakfast with delicious home-made jam.

Excursions

Tour of the Island

14km/9mi. Allow one day.

It is possible to 🥾walk round the island following the clifftop footpath or to drive around.

Braye

The harbour is protected by Fort Grosnez (1853) which was built at the same time as the massive **breakwater** (1 000yd long plus another 600yd submerged). The first quay, the Old Jetty, was built in 1736 by the governor to provide a safe landing-stage for the privateers and smugglers he protected. The modern concrete jetty dates from the turn of the 20C.

Braye Bay★

The largest bay on the island offers a sandy beach with good bathing and a fine view of the harbour. Skirting the beach is a strip of grass, Le Banquage, where the seaweed (*vraic*) was left to dry.

Fort Albert

Mount Touraille, at the east end of Braye Bay, is crowned by **Fort Albert** (1853). There is a fine view inland to St Anne, westwards across Braye Bay to Fort Grosnez and the breakwater with Fort Tourgis in the background, and eastwards over the northern end of the island.

Hammond Memorial

At the fork in the road E of Fort Albert.
Labourers of the Todt Organisation – paid volunteers from Vichy France, political refugees from Franco's Spain, Ukraine, Russia and North Africa who worked under duress during the Nazi Occupation – are recalled by plaques inscribed in their languages. Three camps on Alderney each held 1,500 men.

North Coast

Three excellent sandy bathing bays cluster round the most northerly headland beneath the walls of Fort Château à l'Étoc (1854), now converted into private flats: **Saye Bay**, nearly symmetrical in shape; **Arch Bay**, named after the tunnel through which the carts collecting seaweed reached the shore; **Corblets Bay**, overlooked by Fort Corblets (1855), now a private house with a splendid view.

Mannez Garenne

The low-lying northern end of the island, known as **Mannez Garenne** (Warren), is dominated by the remains of a German observation tower.

Quesnard Lighthouse

Guided tour (weather permitting) Easter–Sept weekends and bank holidays. £2. Steep steps; children under 1m in height are not permitted to ascend. 01481 823 077 (Lighthouse attendant) or 01481 823 737 (Tourist Information Centre).
Built in 1912, it stands 121ft high and casts its beam nearly 17mi. From the lantern platform there is a magnificent **view**★ of the coast and the Race and, on a clear day, of the nuclear power station on the French coast.

Three forts command the coastline: Les Homeaux Florains (1858), now in ruins, was approached by a causeway; Fort Quesnard, on the east side of Cats Bay, and Fort Houmet Herbe, another offshore fort reached by a causeway, were built in 1853.

Longis Bay

The retreating tide reveals a broad stretch of sand backed by a German tank trap which provides excellent shelter for sunbathing. The shallow bay was the island's natural harbour from prehistoric times until it silted up early in the 18C. Traces of an Iron Age settlement were discovered at **Les Huguettes** in 1968. Various relics indicate the existence of a Roman naval base protected by a fort (c 2C-4C AD).

Raz Island

A causeway, which is covered at high tide, runs out to **Raz Island** in the centre of Longis Bay. The fort (1853) has been

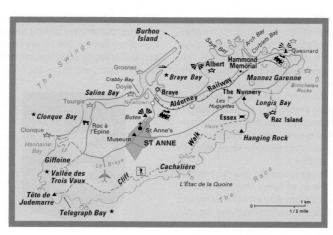

partially restored and there is a fine **view** of Essex Castle and Hanging Rock *(to the south-west).*

The Nunnery
This building, parts of which date to the 4C and which is thought to be the oldest on the island, stands on a rectangular site enclosed within a wall. John Chamberlain converted it to his use when he became Governor in 1584. It was named by British soldiers garrisoned there in the late 18C. It is now private dwellings owned by the States of Alderney.

Essex Castle
The first fort on Essex Hill overlooking Longis Bay was begun in 1546 by Henry VIII but abandoned in 1553. It was razed in 1840 when the present structure was built, to be used first as a barracks and then as a military hospital; it is now private property. Governor John Le Mesurier started a farm to feed the garrison at the Nunnery and called it Essex Farm; the name ascended the hill to the castle.

Hanging Rock
The tilt of the 50ft column of projecting from the cliff face is said to have been caused by the people of Guernsey trying to tow Alderney away.

Cliff Walk
From Haize around to Giffoine there is a magnificent walk served by frequent paths running inland back to St Anne. The view of the steep cliffs plunging into the rock-strewn sea is spectacular.

Cachalière
A path leads down past the old quarry to an abandoned pier. From here the rocks of **L'Étac de la Quoire** can be reached at low water.

Telegraph Bay★
Access to the tower by a path and steps, which are not recommended as they are steep and difficult. Beware of being cut off from the base of the steps by the rising tide. The Telegraph Tower (1811), which provided communication with Jersey and Guernsey, has given its name to the bay below. Except at high tide there is excellent bathing, sheltered from all but a south wind, and a fine view of La Nache and Fourquie rocks.

Tête de Judemarre
The headland provides a fine **view** of the rock-bound coast and of the islands of Guernsey, Herm and Sark.

Vallée des Trois Vaux★
This deep cleft is in fact three valleys meeting on a shingle beach.

Giffoine
From the cliff it is possible to see the birds on their nests in the gannet colony on Les Étacs. At Hannaine Bay, sandy spits between the rocks provide reasonable bathing. Fine **view** of Burhou, Ortac and the Casquets (north).

Clonque Bay★
A zigzag path descends the gorse and heather-clad slope above the attractive sweep of the bay. A causeway runs out to Fort Clonque (1855) now converted into flats. The *vraicing* carts to descend two causeways to the beds of seaweed.
Just south of Fort Tourgis (1855), at the northern end of the bay, is the best-preserved burial chamber on the island, **Roc à l'Épine**.

Saline Bay
The shore, exposed to heavy seas so that bathing can be hazardous, is commanded by Fort Doyle, now a youth centre; beyond lies **Crabby Bay** in the lee of Fort Grosnez.

Burhou Island
For permission to spend the night, contact the Harbour Office. ☎*01481 822 620.* *£10 per night;* *take drinking water.* The island, which lies north-west across The Swinge (about 2km/1.2mi), supports large colonies of puffins, razorbills, gannets and storm petrels as well as other seabirds. A hut provides simple accommodation for an overnight stay for birdwatching.

GUERNSEY★

POPULATION 59 807, MICHELIN MAP 503

Less sophisticated than its larger neighbour, Guernsey has its own particular charm: a slower tempo, the Regency elegance of the capital St Peter Port, the proximity of other islands – Sark, Herm and Jethou. Since the Second World War its main sources of income have been tourism, offshore finance, insurance, and tomatoes.

- **Information:** North Esplanade, St Peter Port, GY1 2LQ, Guernsey. ☎01481 723 552. www.visitguernsey.com
- ▶ **Orient Yourself:** Guernsey is the second largest of the Channel Islands (63km²/ 24sq mi). The south coast, higher, rocky and ragged, contrasts with the sandy bays of the rest of the coast.
- **Don't Miss:** A stroll down the streets of St Peter Port, a swim in Côbo Bay, and the panoramic view from Icart Point in the south.
- **Organizing Your Time:** You'll need a half-day at St Peter Port, plus a day or two to tour the island by car or bicycle, with time for swimming, of course.
- **Kids Especially for Kids:** The Folklore Museum offers a look at the life of sailors and farmers in olden times, and the Aquarium has tortoises and tropical fish.
- **Also See:** Herm, Sark, Jersey, Barneville-Carteret and the Cotentin Penninsula.

Victor Hugo's Exile

Hauteville House★

38 Hauteville. ➤◄ *Guided tour (1hr) May–Sept Mon–Sat 10am–4pm. April noon–4pm.* ◯ *Closed Sun.* ◐*£4.* ☎*01481 721 911.*
Victor Hugo was exiled from his native France for political reasons in 1851. After time in Brussels and Jersey, he bought this great white house in 1856.
During his 14 years' residence Hugo redecorated the interior, doing much of the work himself. The result is certainly eccentric: mirrors are placed so as to enhance the effect of various features. Hugo used to work on his poems and novels standing at a small table in the **Glass Room** on the third floor overlooking the sea. From the **Look-out** where

he sometimes slept, he could see the house up the road (*La Fallue at 1 Beauregard Lane*) into which his faithful mistress, Juliette Drouot, settled in November 1856. In April 1864 she moved down the road (*No 20 Hauteville*).

Candie Gardens

Splendid gardens laid out in 1898 extend below the museum and the Priaulx Library.

St Peter Port★★

The island capital is built on the east coast overlooking an anchorage protected from high seas by Herm and Sark. The medieval town by the shore was rebuilt after bombardment during the Civil War (1642-1646). Profits from privateering in the late 18C produced a delightful Regency town. Guernsey's popularity as a tourist destination was assured when Queen Victoria visited in 1846.
As you walk up Market St, to the right is the **covered market**, comprising Les Halles with the Assembly Rooms above, completed in 1782. Opposite is the Doric-style meat market (1822). Les Arcades, 1830 (*on the left*), is very hand-

some despite the loss of the final bay. The Fish Market was finished in 1877. Finally, the Vegetable Market was constructed in 1879.

The large modern **harbour** bustles with car and passenger ferries, fishing boats and private yachts. Stroll out to White Rock or visit the castle for a fine **view** of the town, the harbour and the neighbouring islands.

The Town Church, as **St Peter's**★ is known, was begun by William the Conqueror in 1048, and completed around 1475. The nave and west door are part of the original Norman structure, which doubled as a fort.

Elizabeth College was founded in 1563 by Elizabeth I. The pseudo-Tudor style building dates from 1826-29.

Sights

Castle Cornet★

Allow 2hr. ◷*Open Apr–Oct daily 10am–5pm. Living history exhibit (20min) Fri and weekend afternoons.* ✆*£6.50; joint ticket with Guernsey Museum and Fort Grey: £9.* P *nearby.* ☎*01481 721 657 (Castle);* ☎*01481 726 518 (Guernsey Museum).*

The castle suffered its greatest misfortune in 1672 when a lightning strike ignited the gunpowder store in the old tower keep.

The original castle (c 1206) was reinforced under Elizabeth I and again under Victoria. An exhibition in the Main Guard relates the **Story of Castle Cornet** from prehistoric to present times.

On the Saluting Platform in the outer bailey the ceremony of the **noonday gun** takes place daily.

From the Citadel there is a fine **view**★ of the harbour and town *(west)*, St Sampson, Vale Castle and Alderney *(35km22mi north)*, Herm, Sark and the French coast *(east)* and Jersey *(south)*.

The **Maritime Museum** relates the island's maritime history from the Gallo-Roman period to the present day.

A **Militia Museum**, housed in the hospital building (1746), contains artefacts of the Royal Guernsey Militia which was disbanded in 1939. Collections of weapons are housed in the **Armoury**.

Guernsey Museum

♿ ◷*Open Apr–Oct 10am–5pm. Rest of the year 10am–4pm. Living history show 11.15am Thu.* ◷*Closed 25-26 Dec and Jan.* ✆*£4; joint ticket with Castle Cornet and Fort Grey £9.* ☎*01481 726 518. www.museum.guernsey.net.*

A cluster of modern octagonal structures arranged alongside a former Victorian bandstand (now a tearoom), houses the Lukis archaeological collection of artefacts retrieved from La Varde chambered tomb in 1811 and the Wilfred Carey Collection of paintings, prints and ceramics.

St James' Concert and Assembly Hall

College Street. Consult website for programs. Box office: ☎*01481 711 361. www.stjames.gg.*

Royal Court House

◷*Daily except weekends 9.30am–5.30pm. Parliament: debates last Wed of month (except Dec, when 2nd Wed of month). Details of debates available from the Greffe.* ◷*Closed Aug.* ✆*No charge.* ☎*01481 725 277.*

The elegant neo-Classical church of **St James'** is now a concert hall. The law courts and the States of Deliberation hold their sittings in the elegant **Royal Court House** (1792); its archives go back 400 years.

Excursions

Saumarez Park★

From St Peter Port take the main road (St Julian's Avenue) uphill opposite the harbour; continue straight past the St Pierre Park Hotel on the left, and straight over at the crossroads with Rectory Hill (left) and rue du Friquet (right). Follow the one-way system by bearing left, turning right and immediately left (sign) on route de Côbo. From the car park walk back parallel with the main road to reach the museum.

The trees and shrubs of this beautiful park are matched by the formal rose gardens; the pond is alive with wildfowl. The house **(St John's Residential Home)** dates from 1721.

DISCOVERING THE CHANNEL ISLANDS

Address Book

Coin ranges for the Channel Islands are derived from approximate conversions of the euro coin ranges on the cover flap into Great Britain Pounds (£).

WHERE TO STAY

Hôtel La Michèle – *GY4 6NB, St Martin. ☎01481 238 065. info@lamichelehotel.com. 16 rooms. ☐. Restaurant (evening only)*. Near Fermain Bay, behind a pleasant façade in painted wood, comfortable, well equipped rooms. Relaxing lounge, garden, terrace and swimming pool.

Maison Bel Air Bed and Breakfast – *Le Chêne, GY8 0AL Forest, 9.6km/6mi W of St Peter Port. ☎01481 238 503. juliette@maisonbelair.com. Closed Dec–Feb. 6 rooms. ☐.* This smart Victorian guesthouse overlooks Petit Bot Bay, accessible on foot. Restful large south-facing garden. Spacious rooms. No smokers.

Sunnydene Hôtel – *R des Marettes. GY1 1ZN St Martin. ☎01481 23870. info@sunnydenecountryhotel.com. Closed mid-Oct–Easter. 20 rooms. ☐☐.* Miniature golf at the end of the garden, comfortable family lounge, tablecloths spread for breakfast, pretty swimming pool and green space. Rooms in the main house or in an outbuilding set in the park.

Hôtel La Frégate – *Les Cotils, GY1 1ZN St Martin. ☎01481 724 624. enquiries@lafregatehotel.com. 12 rooms. ☐. Restaurant.* A panoramic view over the port and St Peter, through large windows that beam light into the rooms of this charming hotel on the hillside. Peaceful site and friendly welcome.

WHERE TO EAT

Fleur du Jardin – *GY5 7JT Kings Mills Castel, 5km/3mi from St Peter Port towards Vazon Bay. ☎01481 257 996. www.fleurdujardin.com.* This 15C house has a lovely garden. Dinner is served in the rustic dining room, lunch at the bar. Contemporary cuisine. Spacious bedrooms.

Zest – *Lefebvre St, GY1 1ZN St Martin. ☎01481 723 052. Closed 2 weekends in Jan and Sat.* Set in the town centre, simply decorated and with comfortable booths. The menu offers a large choice of contemporary dishes, frequently updated.

The Absolute End – *Longstore, GY1 2BG St Peter Port, North of St Peter Port, via St George's Esplanade. ☎01481 723 822. Closed Jan and Sun.* This restaurant is a favourite with locals for its excellent seafood and friendly atmosphere. Interesting lunch menu. Comfortable bar upstairs.

The Pavilion – *Le gron, GY1 9RN. St Saviour. ☎01481 264 165. lecnleck@cwgsy.net. Closed Jan, Mon in winter and Christmas.* This restaurant is found beneath the jewelry store Bruce and Son. Pleasant decoration with displays of jewelry. Delicious food based on products of the sea.

The Auberge – *Jerbourg Rd, GY4 6BH St. Saviour. ☎01481 238 485. theauberge@cwgsy.net. Closed 25, 26 and 31 Dec.* From the garden and the terrace, you will enjoy a splendid view over the sea and the neighboring islands. The rather austere contemporary dining room offering an up-to-date cuisine, served brasserie-style.

TRANSPORTATION

Watch out! The roads of Guernsey are often extremely narrow and if you're not accustomed to driving on the left, you'll want to pay close attention. A parking disk will help you get space in town. Just behind the tourist office, **Economy Cars** rents tiny cars well-suited to Guernsey's roads for £30 a day.

Guernsey Folk Museum★

Kids ☐ ☐ *Open Mar–mid-Oct daily 10am–5pm. ☐£3.50 (Children no charge). ☐. ☎ 01481 255 384. www.national trust-gsy.org.gg.*

Inside the farmstead buildings of Saumarez House a series of Victorian interiors is re-created. Outbuildings display items from the **Langlois Collection of Agricultural Implements**.

Castel

From St Peter Port take the main road (St Julian's Avenue) uphill opposite the harbour; continue straight past the St Pierre Park Hotel on the left, and turn left down Castle Hill/Les Rohais de Haut. The church is on the right before the crossroads.

Parish Church

Early documents list the castle's 12C church of St Mary (**Ste-Marie-du-Castel** or Our Lady of Deliverance) as belonging to the abbey of Mont-St-Michel in 1155; before then, the site may have had a pre-Christian sanctuary and Roman fort.
Fine **views** extend to the coast and across to Vale Church.

St Andrew

From St Peter Port take the main road (St Julian's Avenue) uphill opposite the harbour; bear left onto Queen's Road and continue straight onto Mount Row/Le Vauquiedor/Mauxmarquis Road, after passing the church (left) turn left to the German Underground Hospital (sign).

German Underground Hospital and Ammunition Store

La Vassalerie Rd. Allow 20min. For hours contact the Information Centre. Closed in winter. £3.50 (Children £1) 01481 239 100.
The hospital took nearly three and a half years to build and consists of a series of tunnels excavated down into the granite bedrock. Today the miles of hollow corridors and interlocking wards are eerily vacant, with some departments (operating room, store etc.) open.

▷ *Return to the main road, turn left and drive W; as the road descends, turn right (sign) to the Little Chapel and Guernsey Clockmakers.*

Little Chapel★

Les Vauxbelets, 1km/.6mi from Underground Hospital. Allow 20min.
The Unknown Little Jewel is a model of the grotto and shrine at Lourdes built in 1925 by Brother Deodat, a Salesian monk from Les Vauxbelets College.

Tour of the Island

1 Clos du Valle: St Peter Port to Vale Church

8km/5mi – Allow half a day.
Until 1806 the northern part of Guernsey, known as Clos du Valle, was cut off by the Braye du Valle – a tidal channel of mudflats and salt-marsh. The channel was filled in and the reclaimed land (300 acres) is now covered with glasshouses.

▷ *Leave St Peter Port by the coast road (Glategny Esplanade) N towards St Sampson. Turn left in Belle Greve Bay onto Le Grand Bouet and then take the second right.*

The ruined medieval **Château des Marais** crowns a low knoll: it was first used in the Bronze Age, protected by the surrounding marshy ground. The castle was refortified in the 18C.
Guernsey's second port, **St Sampson**, lies at the eastern end of the Braye du Valle.
St Sampson, the oldest church in Guernsey, was allegedly built where the saint came ashore (c 550), either from Llantwit Major in South Wales or from Dol in Brittany. Its churchyard overlooks the disused Longue Hougue Quarry.

▷ *From the bridge take Vale Avenue N and bear left onto the main road (Route du Braye). Oatlands Craft Centre is located opposite a garden centre on Gigandis Road.*

Oatlands Craft Centre

Braye Road, St Sampson. Open daily year-round 9.30am–5pm. 01481 244 282.
An old brick farmstead and its thatched outbuildings arranged around a courtyard house a craft centre.

Vale Castle★

The medieval castle, now in ruins, was built on the site of an Iron Age hillfort (c 600 BC) on the only high point in Clos du Valle. There is a fine **view** inland, along the east coast and out to sea to the reef,

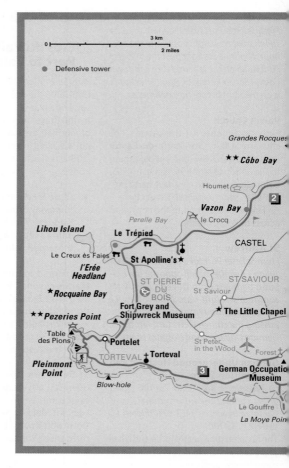

```
0 |————————————| 3 km
       |——————————| 2 miles
```

● Defensive tower

Grandes Rocques

★★ *Côbo Bay*

Houmet

Vazon Bay
le Crocq   **2**

Perelle Bay

Lihou Island   Le Trépied   CASTEL

Le Creux ès Faies
St Apolline's ★

l'Erée
Headland   ST PIERRE
DU BOIS   ST SAVIOUR
St Saviour

★ *Rocquaine Bay*

★★ *Pezeries Point*   Fort Grey and
Shipwreck Museum   ★ The Little Chapel

Table
des Pions   ○ Portelet
St Peter
in the Wood   Forest

TORTEVAL + Torteval

*Pleinmont
Point*   **3**   German Occupation
Museum

Blow-hole

Le Gouffre
La Moye Point

Alderney (*north*), Herm and Sark (*west*), and Jersey (*south*).

Bordeaux Harbour provides mooring for fishing boats and the only safe swimming in the area.

▶ *Follow the main road N; as it curves gently left, turn right onto the minor road; bear left; park by the dilapidated glasshouses (right) opposite the passage tomb.*

Dehus Dolmen

🕐*Open daily sunrise to sunset year-round. Light switch on the left as you enter.*
This passage grave has four side chambers covered by seven capstones: crouch down to see Le Gardien du Tombeau, the figure of an archer (*switch for spotlight*).

▶ *Several minor roads meander N to the coast.*

The **Beaucette Quarry Marina** was created by a well-placed blast in an old diorite quarry, which opened a breach to the sea.

From **Fort Doyle** there is a **view**★ of the Casquets reef and Alderney (*north*), the French coast, Herm and Sark (*west*).

Fort Le Marchant is the most northerly point in Guernsey. It offers a fine view, particularly of **L'Ancresse Common,** the only extensive open space on the island, much used for recreation, and of **L'Ancresse Bay**, a popular spot for bathing and surfing.

La Varde Dolmen is the largest passage grave in Guernsey. **Les Fouaillages** burial ground is 7 000 years old.

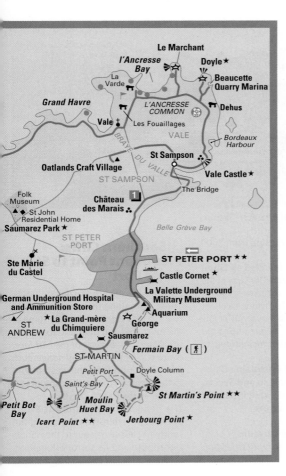

St-Michel-du-Valle Church was consecrated in 1117 on the site of an earlier chapel dedicated to St Magloire, who with St Sampson brought Christianity to Guernsey in the 6C.

② West Coast: Le Grand Havre to Pezeries Point

5km/10mi – Allow about half a day.
The **Grand Havre**, an ample inlet at the west end of the Braye du Valle, is best admired from the Rousse headland with its tower and jetty. A more extensive horizon is visible from the German gun battery on the granite headland, the **Grandes Rocques**.
Côbo Bay★★ is a charming combination of sand and rocks. Swimming is safe.

The huge beach between Fort Houmet (*north*) and Fort le Crocq (*south*) at **Vazon Bay** is excellent for swimming and other recreation.
St Apolline's Chapel★ in the Grande-Rue at Perelle received its charter in 1394. It is decorated with a **fresco** *(light switch)* of *The Last Supper*. The original dedication to Ste Marie de la Perelle was changed in 1452 to St Apolline, a popular saint at the time.
Le Trépied Dolmen burial chamber at Le Cationoc was excavated in 1840 by Frederic Lukis, whose finds are in the Guernsey Museum. In past centuries the site was used for witches' Sabbaths.
The tall defensive tower on the **L'Erée Headland** is called Fort Saumarez. To the south stands **Le Creux ès Faies Dolmen**, a passage grave. Excavation

The Albert Marina in St Peter Port, Guernsey

has produced items dating from 2000 BC to 1800 BC.

In 1114 a priory was founded on **Lihou Island** and dedicated to Our Lady of the Rock (now in ruins). On the west coast a 30m/100ft rock pool provides excellent bathing. (*Accessible by causeway at low tide; check tide tables before setting out and take note of the time for returning to the main island.*)

The grand sweep of **Rocquaine Bay**★ is interrupted by the Cup and Saucer, originally a medieval fort. It is painted white as a navigation mark.

Fort Grey Maritime Museum

⊙ *Open Apr–Oct daily 10am–5pm.* £2.50. 🅿. ☎01481 265 036. *www.museums.guernsey.net.*
The tower accommodates a small museum on two floors dedicated to the many shipwrecks in Guernsey waters.

The picturesque harbour of **Portelet**, full of fishing boats, is backed by the houses of the Hanois Lighthouse keepers. Nearby is the **Table des Pions**, where the *pions* or footmen of the Chevauchée de St Michel ate their lunch sitting at the grass table with their feet in a trench. **Pezeries Point** ★★ is the most westerly point in all the Channel Islands, a remote and unfrequented place. The fort was built in the Napoleonic era.

③ Southern Cliffs: Pleinmont Point to St Peter Port

26km/16mi – Allow half a day.
These cliffs along the south coast and round to St Peter Port provide some of the most wild and dramatic scenery in the island (⊙ *beware of the cliff face, which can be unstable and dangerous*); a footpath runs from the western end to the town, following the contours up and down the valleys and bays.

The headland at **Pleinmont Point** provides an extensive **view**: along the southern cliffs (*east*), out to the Hanois Lighthouse and its surrounding reefs (*west*), across Rocquaine Bay to Lihou Island (*north*).

A footpath stretches all along the clifftops, past all the watch houses before coming out by the Aquarium in St Peter Port. **La Moye Point**, the smallest of the three promontories on the south coast, is wild and beautiful.

German Occupation Museum

In the forest south of the church. Allow 1hr. ♿⊙*Open daily 10am–5pm (winter: 10am–1pm).* ⊙*Closed in Jan.* £3.50. 🅿. ☎01481 238 205.
The museum has grown out of a private collection of artefacts from the Nazi occupation of the Channel Islands: weaponry, uniforms, vehicles, personal effects, etc. **Petit Bot Bay**, which has good bathing and sand at low water, lies at the foot of a green valley guarded by a defensive tower (1780).

Image Courtesy VisitGuernsey

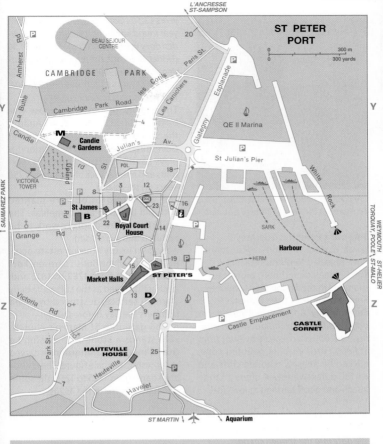

ST PETER PORT						
		Cornet Street	Z	9	Quay (The)	Z 19
		Forest Lane	Y	12	St-George's Esplanade	Y 20
Ann's Place	Y	3	Fountain Street	Z	13	St-James Street	Z 22
Beauregard Lane	Y	4	High Street	Z	14	Smith Street	Z 23
Bordage	Z	5	Market Street	Z	15	South Esplanade	Z 25
Charroterie	Z	7	North Esplanade	YZ	16		
College Street	YZ	8	Pollet	Y	18		

26 Cornet Street	Z	D	Elizabeth College	Z	B	Guernsey Museum and Gallery	Y M

▶ *Return uphill to the main road; turn right down rue de la Villette, which turns inland to rejoin the valley leading down to Moulin Huet Bay.*

Icart Point★★ is the highest and most southerly headland with very fine **views** of the coast. On the east side is **Saint's Bay**, a favourite mooring for fishermen. A water lane runs down the valley, one of the most beautiful in Guernsey, to **Moulin Huet Bay**, where the stream plunges down the cliff face to the sea. Both this bay and its eastern neighbour are good for bathing but **Petit Port** is superior. **St Martin** parish occupies the southeast section of Guernsey and is principally residential. Near the parking lot at **St Martin's Point**★★ there is a magnificent view down to the lighthouse on the point, north up the coast to St Peter Port and seaward to the other islands.

▶ *Follow the path along the cliff*

Image Courtesy VisitGuernsey

L'Ancresse common with Loop Holed Towers; home to the Royal Guernsey Golf club

Jerbourg Point★ is Guernsey's south-eastern extremity: excavations have revealed Neolithic remains.
The Château de Jerbourg protected islanders in the Middle Ages when the French occupied Castle Cornet.
Fermain Bay (*Access on foot from the car park or cliff path from Jerbourg; in summer, the bay is accessible by boat from St Peter Port.*) with its pebbled cove, backed by densely wooded cliffs and an 18C defensive tower, offers a sandy beach and good bathing at low tide.

▶ *Continue E on the main road; on a left-hand curve, turn left beyond main gate into the shaded car park.*

Sausmarez Manor

♿⚓House: guided tour daily Apr–Oct 10.30am and 11.30am; June–Sept additional tour at 2pm. ✆£5.90 (Under 12 years £3.50.) Garden: 🕐Daily 10am–5pm year round. ✆No charge. Subtropical Garden daily year-round 10am–5pm. ✆£4.50 (Under 12 £3.50). Art park sculpture garden daily 10am–5pm year round.✆£4.50 (Under 12 years £3.50). ☎01481 235 904. www.sausmarezmanor.co.uk..

The elegant Queen Anne house was built in 1714-18 by Sir Edmund Andros, the Seigneur of Sausmarez and former Governor of New York. The interior displays handsome family furniture, portraits and mementoes of the family's 750 years on the island.

The wooded **grounds** are planted with tall bamboo and camellias. The **sculpture park** displays work to be admired and purchased.

A modern luxury housing estate occupies the site of the British garrison, **Fort George**, built from 1782 to 1812 and, because it served as the Luftwaffe early warning service, destroyed by Allied bombers the day before D-Day.

At the gate into St Martin's churchyard stands a Stone Age menhir, **La Grand'mère du Chimquière**★ carved to represent a female figure. The church itself dates from 1225 to 1250; the south porch was added in the 1520s.

▶ *Return to the main road; turn right to Jerbourg.*

La Valette Underground Military Museum

🕐Open Mar–mid-Nov daily 10am_5pm. ✆£3.50 ☎01481 722 300.

Defensive Towers

In 1778-79 the shoreline of Guernsey was reinforced by a chain of 15 loopholed granite towers. The 12 that survive, numbered in an anticlockwise sequence, illustrate how advanced they were for their period – an adapted design was later used when similar towers were built in Jersey. The ground level was used for storage; entrance to the first floor was by a retractable wooden ladder and gave access to two levels of accommodation loopholed for musketry defence; the open roof was subsequently altered to make room for a 12-pounder gun. The shortcomings of the design, however, were soon realised by Royal Engineers who advocated a different format for the Martello Towers built at Fort Saumarez, Fort Grey and Fort Hommet (1804), in keeping with those being constructed on the south coast of England. Detached magazines were built alongside in which kegs or barrels of black powder would be stored protected from the damp sea winds and where muskets could be serviced.

The museum occupies five tunnels that were excavated to hold fuel tanks (*Höhlgang*) for refuelling U-boats. The museum displays uniforms and apparel belonging to the Guernsey Militia, German artefacts and mementoes of the Occupation.

Guernsey Aquarium

Kids ♿ 🕐*Open daily year-round 10am–6pm (Sun and public holidays 5.30pm).* 🕐*Closed 1 Jan, 25-26 Dec.* ⚭*£3.75 (Children £2.75).* ☎*01481 723 301.*

Installed in a disused tunnel is a series of water tanks housing a variety of aquatic creatures.

HERM

POPULATION 50

MICHELIN MAP 503

Herm (2.4km/1.5mi long by 0.8km/0.5mi wide) lies half way between Guernsey and Sark. The broad sandy beaches on its north coast contrast with the steep cliffs at the southern end of the island. Herm is a haven of tranquillity having neither roads nor cars; walking is the only way to enjoy the profusion of wild flowers, the dunes, the trees and cliffs. The deep fringe of rocks which lies offshore is most impressive at low tide. South-west of Herm, across a narrow channel, the islet of Jethou (private property leased from the British Crown) rises like a hillock in the sea, the home of many seabirds.

🛈 **Information:** www.herm-island.com. ☎*01481 722 377. admin@herm-island.com.*

▶ **Orient Yourself:** Herm (2.4km/1.5mi long by 8km/0.5mi wide) lies half way between Guernsey and Sark.

👁 **Don't Miss:** The countryside from the Grand Monceau.

🕐 **Organizing Your Time:** You need one day for the island.

👣 **Also See:** Guernsey, Sark, Jersey, Barneville-Carteret and the Cotentin.

A Bit of History

Prehistoric tombs made of granite slabs found in the north of the island are evidence of human settlement in 2000 BC. In the 6C Christianity was introduced by St Magloire who founded monasteries in Sark and Jersey. In the 17C pirates used the island as a base; it was later deserted until the 19C when, for a brief period, granite was quarried for export. In 1947 Herm was sold by the Crown to the States of Guernsey and in 1949 Major Peter Wood and his wife became tenant. In 1987 the lease was transferred to their family company. During the 50

Coin ranges for the Channel Islands are derived from approximate conversions of the euro coin ranges on the cover flap into Great Britain Pounds (£).

WHERE TO STAY

⬭⬭ **White House** – *GY1 3HR Herm - ☎01481 722 159 - Closed Oct-Mar - 39 rooms.* This hotel will seduce you with its splendid view of the island's scenery, its small harbour and the beach. Choice of rooms in the main house or in the cottages. Traditional or more relaxed meals depending on which dining room you choose. Garden with summer swimming pool.

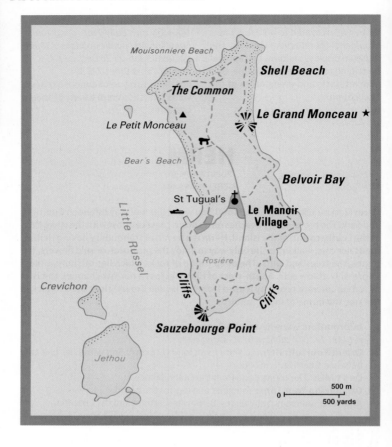

years of family tenancy the island has been carefully developed for tourism while the outstanding natural beauty has been maintained.

Visit

Le Manoir Village

A surfaced road climbs up to the farm and the handful of cottages which make up the hamlet next to the 18C manor house with its square tower.

St Tugual's Chapel was built of island granite in the 11C when Robert the Magnificent was Duke of Normandy.

The northern end of the island is composed of sand dunes, known as **The Common**, covered by prickly vegetation and fringed by sandy beaches which are very popular in summer (Bear's Beach, Mousonnière Beach, **Shell Beach** so called because it is composed of millions of shells deposited by the tides and currents from the Gulf Stream). From this hillock of **Le Grand Monceau**★ there is a splendid panoramic view of the sands, the rocks and the islands. North on the horizon lies Alderney; to the east the French coast. **Le Petit Monceau** beyond is a smaller hillock, overlooking the Bear's Beach.

In contrast with the low land in the north, the southern end of the island is composed of steep granite cliffs dropping sheer into the sea. In **Belvoir Bay** nestles a small sheltered beach, good for bathing. The southern headland, Sauzebourge Point, provides a view of Jethou (south-west) with Guernsey in the background (west) and Sark (south-east).

JERSEY ★★

POPULATION 88 200
MICHELIN MAP 503

In addition to the delights of the beaches and the countryside, visitors to Jersey can enjoy a wide range of more sophisticated pleasures – theatre and cinema, cabaret and floor shows, discotheques and disco-bars.

Victor Hugo, who spent three years in Jersey (1852-55) before moving to Guernsey, was enchanted: "It possesses a unique and exquisite beauty. It is a garden of flowers cradled by the sea. Woods, meadows and gardens seem to mingle with the rocks and reefs in the sea."

- **ℹ Information:** Liberation Square, St Helier, Jersey JE1 1BB. ☎ 01534 44880. www.jersey.com.
- **▶ Orient Yourself:** Jersey is the largest of the Channel Islands (116km2/45sq mi; 9x5mi); it lies close to the coast of France (19km/12mi).
- **😊 Don't Miss:** The walking paths along the north and east coasts.
- **🕐 Organizing Your Time:** Spend a half-day seeing St Helier on foot, then take a day to drive around the island.
- **Kids Especially for Kids:** The Jersey Zoo is a world-renowned refuge for endangered species. The Living Legend recreation park offers rides and shows.
- **👟 Also See:** Sark, Herm, Guernsey, Barneville-Carteret, the Cotentin Penninsula.

A Bit of History

The tombs and prehistoric monuments found on the island indicate human habitation between 7500 and 2500 BC. The Roman presence was brief, and in the 6C St Helier arrived and established Christianity. The dominant influence is that of the Normans who invaded in the 10C and left a rich heritage of customs and traditions.

After 1204, when King John was forced to cede mainland Normandy to France, the French made repeated attempts to recover the Channel Islands: the last attempt occurred in 1781 when Baron de Rullecourt, a soldier of fortune, landed by night in St Clement's Bay. Under Major Peirson, a young man of 24, the militia and British forces defeated the enemy in the main square in what came to be known as the **Battle of Jersey**; both leaders were mortally wounded.

Constitution

Jersey is divided into 12 parishes, which together with two groups of islets, the Minquiers to the south and the Ecréhous to the north-east, make up the Bailiwick of Jersey. The Parliament, known as the States of Jersey, is headed by four officers appointed by the Crown and a fifth officer, the Dean of Jersey, an Anglican clergyman. Together, they preside over 12 Senators, 12 Constables and 29 Deputies, elected to serve for a period of three to six years.

Economy

Agriculture has long sustained the islanders: wheat and rye, turnips and parsnips, four-horned sheep supplying wool for the famous Jersey stockings and knitwear (17C), apples for cider (18C), table grapes grown under glass and famous Doyenne de Comice pears. The mild climate continues to favour the cultivation of flowers (daffodils, freesias,

Address Book

Coin ranges for the Channel Islands are derived from approximate conversions of the euro coin ranges on the cover flap into Great Britain Pounds (£).

WHERE TO EAT

⊖⊖ **Old Court House Inn** – *St Aubin's Harbour, JE3 8AB St Aubin.* ☎01534 746 433. ochstaubins@jerseymail.co.uk. *Closed 25 Dec.* This 15C inn specializes in seafood dishes. One room is a former tribunal, another the reconstructed stern of a galleon. Terrace overlooking the harbour. Spacious guestrooms.

⊖⊖ **Suma's** – *Gorey, JE3 6ET Gorey Hill.* ☎01534 853 291. *Closed 23 Dec–Jan. Reservations required.* This elegant restaurant is a favourite of locals and tourists alike. The bright interior displays works by local artists. From the terrace, views of Mont-Orgueil Castle and the harbour.

⊖⊖ **Bistro Soleil** – *Route de la Haule, JE3 7BA Beaumont.* ☎01534 720 249. *Closed Sat evening and Mon.* A series of rooms opening into each other, with views over St Aubin Bay. Minimalist style, just a few modern paintings. Audacious menus with a Mediterranean touch.

⊖⊖ **Village Bistro** – *JE3 9EP Gorey Village.* ☎01534 853 429. thevillagebistro@ yahoo.co.uk. *Closed 2 weeks in Nov, Sun evening and Mon. Reservations required.* A family cottage with a relaxed atmosphere. Specialities include prawn-and-mushroom risotto and orange-flavoured crème brûlée. Lunch menu at an attractive price.

⊖⊖⊖ **Le Frère** – *Le Mont de Rozel, JG3 6AN Rozel Bay.* ☎01534 861 000. www.lefrerejersey.com. *Closed Sun evening and Mon .* This *frère* (brother) is very much in demand! His secret? A menu to satisfy every taste, reasonable prices and a splendid terrace with a view of the sea and the French coast, the latter in fine weather only.

⊖⊖⊖ **Green Island** – *JE2 GLS St Clement.* ☎01534 857 787. greenisland@ jerseymail.com. *Closed Sun evening and Mon.* This place is very popular with both locals and tourists attracted by its menu based on the local catch and provisions fresh from the market. Relaxed atmosphere in a nautically-themed dining room.

WHERE TO STAY

⊖⊖ **La Bonne Vie Bed and Breakfast** – *Roseville St., JE2 4PL St Helier.* ☎01534 735 955. www.labonnevie-guesthouse-jersey.com. 10 rooms. ⌂. Situated close to the beach and the town centre, this flower-decked Victorian house is meticulously looked after. Warm welcome and rather sweet guestrooms with their flowery cushions, curtains, and eiderdowns.

⊖⊖ **Au Caprice Bed and Breakfast** – *Route de la Houle, JE3 8BA La Houle.* ☎01534 722 083. aucaprice@jerseymail. co.uk. *Closed Nov–Mar.* 12 rooms. ⌂. Meal ⊖. White, luminous and airy, with large doors and windows, this house offers comfortable rooms at a reasonable price. Near a long sandy beach.

⊖⊖⊖ **Hôtel Beau Couperon** – *JE3 6AN Rozel Bay.* ☎01534 865 522. beaucouperon@southernhotels.com. 33 rooms. Restaurant ⊖. This fortress from the Napoleonic era, near the Jersey Zoo, offers a splendid view of Rozel Bay. Most of the spacious rooms have balconies. The dining room windows open onto the sea.

⊖⊖⊖ **Hôtel Moorings** – *JE3 6EW Gorey Pier.* ☎01534 853 633. www. themooringshotel.com. 15 rooms. The location of this small unpretentious hotel, just below Mont-Orgueil Castle and facing the harbour, will certainly appeal to you. The rooms are well fitted, and you will receive a cordial welcome.

LEISURE

Beaches and Swimming – Jersey has some 30 beaches and bays suitable for swimming; they are among the cleanest in Europe. During summer months, this is generally the hottest place in Great Britain and precautions such as sun screen are recommended.

Biking and Walking – Jersey has networks of footpaths, bike trails and green lanes for non-motorized traffic.

Nightlife – Jersey has 11 discotheques and discobars, and many hotels offer dancing and cabarets. In addition, the island abounds in pubs, many of which also offer meals. Check to be sure children are allowed in.

carnations and lavender) and vegetables for export. Some crops are grown in the open fields, others under glass. Unique to Jersey is the giant cabbage *(Brassica oleracea longata)* which grows up to 3m/10ft tall.

In recent years, lucrative businesses have developed in tourism and financial services, industries driven by competitive young residents who have benefited from excellent local education.

St Helier

St Helier is a lively town, the main commercial centre on the island and the seat of government, situated in a sheltered position on the south side of the island. The shops in the pedestrian precinct formed by **King and Queen Streets** are a popular attraction for visitors to the island. The town is named after St Helier, one of the first Christian missionaries to land in Jersey, who was murdered by pirates after living as a hermit there for 15 years (c 555). The scant local population was swelled by refugees fleeing the St Bartholomew Day Massacre (1572) and the Revolution (1789) in France.

Royal Square

Royal Court House – ⊙*For hours, contact the Visitor Service Centre on Liberation Square.* ☎ *01534 44880 www. gov.je.* ⊙*Closed Aug.* The gilded-lead statue of George II, dressed as a Roman emperor, looks down on this charming small square with its spreading chestnut trees; from this point are measured the distances to all the milestones on the island. It was here where the Battle of Jersey erupted. Bordering the south side are the granite buildings of the **Royal Court House**. At the east end of the range of buildings are the **States Chambers** *(entrance round the corner)* where the Jersey Parliament sits in session.

Central Market

The granite building (1882) is furnished with cast-iron grilles at the windows and entrances, and covered with a glass (perspex) roof supported by iron columns. Beneath it open-stall holders proffer local produce to the sound of the

fountain. The fish market is around the corner in Beresford Street.

St Helier Parish Church

The foundation of the present pink-granite church with its square tower pre-dates the Conquest. It continues to be the seat of the Dean of Jersey – hence the epithet "Cathedral of Jersey." The altar cross and candlesticks were a gift from Queen Elizabeth, the Queen Mother.

Sights

Elizabeth Castle

Access on foot by a causeway at low tide (30min); otherwise by amphibious vehicle from West Park Slipway. ⊙*Open Apr– Oct daily 10am–6pm (last admission 5pm).* ⊗*£5.10. (Children £4.60).* ☛*Guided tour (1hr).* ☎*01534 723 971 (Castle). www.jerseyheritagetrust.org.*

☛In the 12C William Fitz-Hamon, one of Henry II's courtiers, founded an abbey on St Helier's Isle in St Aubin's Bay. The castle buildings were completed shortly before Sir Walter Raleigh was appointed Governor (1600) and called Fort Isabella Bellissima in honour of Queen Elizabeth I. It was considerably reinforced during the Civil War (1642-

ST HELIER			Elizabeth Place	Y	9	Royal Square	Z	20
			Gloucester Street	Y	10	St-Saviours Hill	Y	23
Beresford Street	Z	2	Halkett Place	Z	13	Simon Place	Y	24
Broad Street	Z	3	King Street	Z		Union Street	Z	26
Burrard Street	Z	4	La Colomberie	Z	16	Victoria Street	Y	27
Cannon Street	Y	5	La Motte Street	Z	17	Windsor Road	Y	28
Charing Cross	Z	6	Minden Place	Z	18	York Street	Y	30
Cheapside	Y	7	Queen's Road	Y	19			
Conway Street	Z	8	Queen Street	Z				

Central Market	Z	E	Jersey Museum	Z	M²	Royal Court House	Z	J
Fish Market	Z	F	Occupation Tapestry Gallery	Z	M³	Steam Clock	Z	S
Island Fortress			St Helier Parish Church	Z	R			
Occupation Museum	Z	M¹	States chambers and					

1646) while occupied by Royalists who, after resisting the repeated assaults from Parliamentary forces on the island, surrendered after a 50-day siege. The young Prince of Wales stayed here when fleeing from England in 1646, and again three years later when returning to be proclaimed King Charles II. During the Second World War the Germans added to the fortifications by installing a roving searchlight, bunkers and gun batteries. In 1996 Queen Elizabeth II handed the castle, together with Mont Orgueil, to the islanders.

The guard-room displays the various stages in the construction of the castle. The **Militia Museum** contains mementoes of the Royal Jersey Regiment.

From the keep, known as the Mount, There is a fine **view**★ of the castle itself and also of St Aubin's Fort across the bay.

South of the castle a breakwater extends past the chapel on the rock where, according to legend, St Helier lived as a hermit *(procession on or about 16 July, St Helier's Day)*.

Jersey Museum★

⏱️Open Apr–Oct 10am–5pm. Nov–Mar 10am–4pm. ⏱️Closed 1 Jan, 24–16 Dec. 🎟️£5.40 (Children £4.60). ☎01534 633 300. www.jerseyheritagetrust.org.

Housed in a former merchant's house and adjoining warehouse belonging to Philippe Nicolle (1769-1835) is the local museum.

The **ground-floor** area is shared by temporary exhibitions and films about Jersey. The treadmill, which was turned by 12 men and operated a pepper mill, was used in St Helier prison during the 19C. By the stairs is displayed a number of silver toilet articles from the set which accompanied Lillie Langtry on her travels.

On the **first floor**, the history of the island from the Stone Age to the present is unfurled as a series of tableaux.

The **second floor** displays the Barreau-Le Maistre collection of fine art with paintings, drawings and watercolours by local artists or of topographical interest: Sir John Everett Millais PRA (1829-96), PJ Ouless (1817-85), "the Jersey Turner" J Le Capelain (1812-48) and the illustrator Edmund Blampied (1886-1966). Works by **Sir Francis Cook** (1907-78) bequeathed to the Jersey Heritage Trust are on permanent display in their own gallery, a converted Methodist Chapel, in Augrès *(A 8, Route de Trinité)*.

The **third-floor** rooms re-create domestic interiors (1861) typical of a middle-class Jersey family.

Lilly Langtry

New North Quay

The most prominent landmark is the world's largest **steam clock** (36ft tall), modelled on a traditional paddle steamer of a type that once shuttled between the islands and Southampton. It was inaugurated in August 1997 as part of the development of the St Helier waterfront.

Maritime Museum and Jersey Occupation Tapestry

⏱️Open daily 10am–5pm (Out of season 10am-4pm). ⏱️Closed 1 Jan, 24-26 Dec. 🎟️£6 (Children £5.20). ☎01534 811 043. www.jerseyheritagetrust.org.

Installed in converted 19C warehouses, the Jersey **Maritime Museum** is has changing displays relating to the fishing, ship-building and trading industries and to piracy.

The **Jersey Occupation Tapestry** comprises 12 panels (6x3ft) illustrating the story of the Occupation of Jersey from the outbreak of war to the Liberation: each scene, based on archive photographs and contemporary film footage, has been embroidered by a separate Parish.

Fort Regent

Access by escalators in Pier Road. 🧒⏱️Open year round. Summer Mon–Fri 7am–9pm (Last entry 8pm), weekends 8.15am–5pm, public holidays 10am–5pm.

Asking the Way

Jersey has a number of **cycling routes**, marked by blue signs with white writing, and a network of tree-lined lanes, known as **green lanes**, where walkers, cyclists and horse riders have priority over the car (maximum speed 15mph/24kmph). There are also long stretches of **coastal footpath**. Most of the principal tourist sites are flagged by brown signs with white writing.

When local Jersey people give directions, they tend to refer to the roads by name rather than number; it is therefore well worth obtaining a Perry's Pathfinder map, which marks footpaths, car parks and refreshment facilities, or the Town and Island Map, which contains information on green lanes, coastal footpaths, sites of special interest, heritage sights and Second World War sites; it is produced by Jersey Tourism which also publishes a cycling and walking guide.

For other times contact Visitor Services Centre. ☐. ☞*Prices depend on activity.* ⏰*Closed 1 Jan, 25–26 Dec.* ☎*01534 499 609. www.gov.je.*
The massive fortifications of Fort Regent were built to protect Jersey from invasion by Napoleon. Within, topped by a shallow white dome, is a modern leisure centre providing a variety of sports facilities and entertainment: swimming pool, badminton, squash, table tennis, snooker, play area for children, puppet theatre, exhibitions, aquarium, and audio-visual shows on the history and culture of the island. It is also home to the Jersey Signal Station. The rampart walk provides splendid **views**★ of the town and St Aubin's Bay (west).

Island Fortress Occupation Museum

♿ ⏰*Open Apr–Oct daily 9.30am–6.30pm. Nov–Mar 10am-4pm.* ☞*£3.75.* ☎*01534 734 306.*
A limited collection of military uniforms, flak sheds, weaponry and equipment evoke the five-year German occupation (1940-45). A video tells of the anguish endured and of the relief of the eventual liberation.

Excursions

Jersey Zoo★★

From St Helier take A 8 N to Mont de la Trinité; at rue Aslet turn right onto B 31 towards Trinity Church; this road soon becomes rue des Picots passing in front of the zoo (right). Kids ♿ ⏰*Open all year daily 9.30am–6pm (9.30am–5pm in winter) Last entry 1hr before closing.* ⏰*Closed 25 Dec.* ☞*£9.95.* ☞*Guided tour (1hr, until 3pm) by arrangement.* ☐. ☎*01534 860 000; www.durrellwildlife.org.*

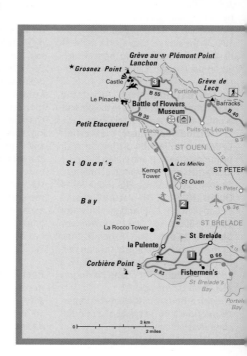

The Durrell Wildlife Conservation Trust, with its headquarters at Jersey Zoo (Les Augrès Manor), was founded by the naturalist **Gerald Durrell** in 1963 as a unique centre for research and breeding of rare and endangered species. The undulating park (10ha/20.5acres) provides compatible environments for some 1 000 animals. Exotic species of plants provide the animals with both food and natural cover.

Residents include babirusas from Indonesia; spectacled bears from the forest uplands of Bolivia and Peru (the only bear indigenous to South America); snow leopards and cheetahs; and a long list of birds.

The most popular animals, however, are probably the primates: a dynasty of lowland gorillas descended from the silverback Jambo (1961-92); orangutans from Sumatra and lemurs from Madagascar, marmosets and tamarins from Brazil, some of which roam freely in the thick shrubbery.

Tortoises, terrapins, snakes, frogs, toads and lizards, happy to lounge in their warmed enclosures among sprigs of flowering orchids, thrive in the **Gaherty Reptile Breeding Centre**.

Ring-tailed Lemur

J. Morgan/DWCT Photo library

Eric Young Orchid Foundation★

Victoria Village, Trinity. Even with signs in Victoria village, the Orchid Foundation is difficult to find. Wed–Sat 10am–4pm. Closed 1 Jan, 25-26 Dec. £3 (Children £1). ☎ 01534 861 963. *www.ericyoungorchidfoundation.co.uk.* A fabulous show of prize orchids is presented here in a display house. Dis-

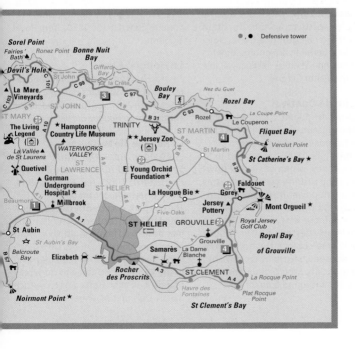

plays are regularly reorganised to ensure constant shows of species, the groups arranged to allow close study of their distinctive blooms.

Jersey War Tunnels★

5km/3mi W. Leave St Helier on the St Aubin road, at Bel Royal, turn right. ♿○*Open mid-Feb–mid-Dec daily 10am–6pm (last entrance 4.30pm).* ✆£9. ☎01534 860 808. *www.jerseywartunnels.com.*

This large complex of tunnels is kept as a compelling memorial to the forced labourers (Spaniards, Moroccans, Alsatian Jews, Poles, Frenchmen, Russians) who worked on its construction for three and a half years under the severest conditions. Note that some visitors may find the visit rather harrowing, others may suffer from claustrophobia.

Hohlgangsanlagen 8 was intended as a secure, bomb-proof artillery barracks. In January 1944, still incomplete, it was converted into a hospital equipped with an operating theatre, five 100-bed wards, X-ray room, mortuary, stores, kitchen, staff quarters etc. Wartime films, archive photographs, newspaper cuttings, letters and memorabilia document the personal suffering and trauma of those caught up in the events.

The **Occupation Walk** opposite the complex leads to an area fortified by anti-aircraft gun positions, crawl trenches, barbed wire entanglements and personnel shelters (leaflet available from the Visitor Centre).

Moulin de Quétivel

○*Open June–Aug Sat 10am–4pm.* ✆£2 *(Children no charge).* 🅿. ☎01534 483 193. *www.nationaltrustjersey.org.je*

The **mill** (pre-1309), on a bend in St Peter's Valley, is one of several powered by the rushing water of streams until steam power made them obsolete. During the German Occupation the machinery was restored before being largely destroyed by fire (1969). Since 1979, re-equipped with parts from other disused Jersey mills, Quétivel has ground locally grown grain and produced stone-ground flour for sale.

Living Legend

Take the A 11, St Peter's Valley Road, to the C112, then follow posted signs. Kids ♿○*Open summer daily 9.30am–5pm. Rest of the year daily except Thu and Fri 10am–5pm.* ○*Closed Dec-Feb.* ✆£7.10 *(Children £5.80)* ☎01534 485 496. *www. jerseyslivinglegend.co.je.*

Inside the granite buildings unfurls the entertaining multi-sensory experience that relates the history and myths of Jersey. The time travellers explore a labyrinth of mysterious chambers, make their way through castle towers and across the decks of a Victorian paddle steamer to discover the lives of past islanders and stories told of heroes and villains.

St Peter's Village

On the square is an underground bunker built by the German Organization Todt in 1942, strategically placed so as to keep surveillance over the airport and access roads to the west of the island.

St Peter's Church

The parish church has a remarkable steeple (124ft high); at its apex is a red navigation light used by aircraft coming in to land at the airport nearby. Behind the altar is a reredos by George Tinworth, commissioned in the 1880s from Royal Doulton.

La Hougue Bie★

From St Helier take either A 6 (Route Bagatelle) or A 7 (St Saviour's Hill) NW; at Five Oaks take A 7 (Princes Tower Road) to the entrance to La Hougue Bie (left).

La Hougue Bie Museums

♿○ *Open Apr– Oct daily 10am–5pm.* ✆£5.40 *(Children £4.60).* 🅿. ☎ 01534 853 823 *(La Hougue Bie). www.jerseyheritagetrust.org.*

The tiny park, encircled by trees, is dominated by a high circular mound. Its name may be derived from the old Norse word *haugr* (meaning barrow) and *bie*, a shorthand for Hambye, a Norman lord who in the Middle Ages came to rid Jersey of a dragon that stalked St Lawrence marsh. During the German occupation, the site was heavily fortified, as it provides an excellent **view** over outlying countryside.

Archaeology and Geology Museum

 ♿ 🕐 *Open mid-Mar–Oct daily 10am–5pm.* 💷*£5.25.* ☎*01534 853 823.*
Artefacts displayed were brought to light by local excavations – notably from La Cotte de St Brelade, a sea cave in the Ouaisné headland and the Belle Hougue caves on the north coast: remains of mammoths, objects belonging to Neolithic farmers and hunters; Bronze Age metal objects found in St Lawrence etc. The geology section presents samples of the various rocks and minerals found on the island.

Neolithic Tomb★

The cruciform passage burial chamber, excavated in 1924, dates from 3500 BC. Similar tombs have been discovered in England and Brittany. The grave was originally built above ground with upright stones and roofed with granite slabs before being covered by a mound of earth and rubble (12m/40ft). A passage (10m/33ft long) leads to the funeral chamber (3x9m/10x30ft), which is covered with huge capstones (the heaviest weighing 25t). The central granite pillar is a modern addition to support the large capstones which were found to be cracked.

Chapels

The mound is surmounted by two medieval chapels: the **Chapel of Our Lady of the Dawn** (Notre-Dame-de-la-Clarté) dates from the 12C; the altar (Late Medieval) came from Mont-Orgueil Castle. The abutting **Jerusalem Chapel** was built in 1520 by Dean Richard Mabon after a pilgrimage to Jerusalem. The interior bears traces of frescoes of two archangels.

German Occupation Museum

A German bunker, built in 1942 as a communications centre, houses radio equipment, weapons, medals, original documents (orders and propaganda) and photographs of the period.

Driving Tours

①From St Helier to Corbière

18km/10mi. Allow about 2hr.

▶ *From St Helier take A 1 (Route de St Aubin) W.*

Millbrook

The Villa Millbrook was once home to Sir Jesse Boot, first Baron Trent of Nottingham, founder of Boots the Chemists, who is buried at St Brelade.

St Matthew's Church

🕐 *Open year round daily except Sat 9am–6pm.* 🅿. ☎*01534 502 864.*
The **Glass Church**, as it is also known, was unexceptional until 1934 when **René Lalique** (1860-1945), the French specialist in moulded glass, was invited by Lord Trent's widow to redecorate the interior with distinctive **glasswork★**: the entrance doors are made of panels presenting a row of four angels. The flowering lily appears in the windows, screens and in the Lady Chapel. The luminescent, ethereal quality is most apparent at dusk when the lights are switched on.

▶ *Follow the main road (Route de La Haule) and then A 1 (Route de La Neuve).*

R. Besse/MICHELIN

Lalique angel, Millbrook

St Aubin

The little town, which faces east across St Aubin's Bay, is particularly picturesque with its long sandy beach, fishermen's cottages and tall granite merchants' houses lining steep, narrow streets or clinging to the cliffs along the shore. St Aubin was invoked as protector against pirates.

The local church (1892) has a fine stained-glass window made by William Morris & Co. **St Aubin's Fort** on the island *(access at low tide)* was built in the reign of Henry VIII, 1509-1547.

The Corbière Walk from St Helier to Corbière follows the line of the old **Jersey Railway** which opened in 1870.

▷ *Turn left off the main road onto B 57 (Route de Noirmont) for access to the promontory and Portelet Bay.*

Noirmont Point★

Command Bunker – ○*Open Apr–Sept. Hours vary. Consult Channel Island Occupation Society www.ciosjersey.org.uk.* ⊜*£2 (Children no charge).* ℗.

The local saying warns of the onset of gales from the south-west:

> *Quand Nièrmont met san bonnet, Ch'est signe de plyie*
> *("When Noirmont (Black Hill) dons his cap, / It is a sign of rain").*

Beyond the pebble beach nestling in **Belcroute** stretches the headland, still scarred by the remains of substantial German fortifications (1941 and 1943-44) including the **Command Bunker**. The most advanced bastion gives fine views of the rocks immediately below and round westwards to the Île au Guerdain.

▷ *Return to the main road A 13 (Route des Genets) and then fork left down B 66 (Mont Sohier).*

St Brelade

This favourite seaside resort is situated in a sheltered bay; its sandy beaches and usually safe waters (☝*certain areas can be tricky*) are ideal for swimming and water-skiing. **Winston Churchill Memorial Park** backs the bay.

At the western end of the beach, behind a screen of trees, the parish church and detached medieval chapel are surrounded by a graveyard.

Parish Church

☝*Light switch inside on the left of the entrance.*

The cherished church of St Brelade is built of granite from the cliffs of La Moye. The chancel, nave and belfry date from the 11C. In the 12C the church became cruciform with the addition of a transept; the aisles were added later.

The altar is a solid slab of stone, marked with five crosses representing the five wounds of the Crucifixion. The 15C font is made of granite from the Chausey Islands, which lie south of Jersey and belong to France.

Fishermen's Chapel

Light switch inside on the left of the entrance.

The family chapel, which is built of the same granite as the church, is decorated in the interior with delicate medieval **frescoes**★. At the east end is an Annunciation dated as c 1375; the other paintings are from a second phase of work c 1425: the south wall (right of the altar) shows *Adam and Eve* followed by *The Annunciation* and *The Adoration of the Magi*; the west wall bears *The Last Judgement*; on the north wall fragments have been deciphered as scenes from *The Passion*. The paintings survived because from c 1550 to the mid-19C the chapel was used as an armoury and as a carpenter's shop.

Behind the chapel a short flight of steps leads to a path through the churchyard to the beach; this is the only surviving example of a *perquage*: once commonplace in medieval Europe, these paths were escape routes from a church, traditionally a place of sanctuary, to the shore and away out to sea.

▷ *Continue along the road back into town; turn left onto A 13 (Route Orange); bear left down B 83 (Route du Sud) to Corbière.*

Corbière

All that remains of the terminus of the Jersey Railway is the concrete platform. As the road descends, a magnificent view is steadily revealed of the rock-strewn point and the white lighthouse rising from its islet: a good place to watch the sun set over the Atlantic. Before the lighthouse (*access on foot at low tide but closed to the public*) was built in 1874, this was a perilous stretch of water where a number of ships foundered; in clear weather the electric beam carries 28km/17mi.

2 From Corbière to Petit Étacquerel

13km/8mi. Allow 1hr.

▷ *Follow the road round to the junction with B 35 (rue de Sergente); turn left towards the coast.*

St Ouen's Bay

The deep surf which rolls into the bay makes it a favourite spot for experienced surfboard and windsurf enthusiasts. The firm sand attracts car and motorcycle racing fans.

In the middle of the bay sits **La Rocco Tower**, the last round tower to be built in Jersey (1800).

Beyond the beach, the landscape is wild and uncultivated, the vegetation sparse. **La Pulente** used to be the main centre for gathering seaweed (*vraic*) which was traditionally used as fertiliser. La Sergenté, also known as the Beehive Hut, is another important Neolithic tomb near to which a large hoard of coins from Brittany was found. The **St Ouen Pond** on the right of the road is a haven for birds and wild flowers, notably the Jersey or lax-flowered orchid. The three upright stones, Les Trois Rocques, are presumed to be part of a dolmen.

Kempt Tower

🕐*Open May–Sept daily 2–5pm.* ⊗*£2 (Children £1).* 🅿. ☎*01534 483 651.*
This defensive tower has been converted into an interpretation centre for a nature reserve called **Les Mielles** (the Jersey dialect word for sand dunes), set up to monitor and protect indigenous plants, birds and butterflies.

▷ *Follow B 35 (Route des Laveurs); turn left onto C 114 (Mont des Corvées).*

Battle of Flowers Museum

Kids 🚶♿🕐*Open Easter– Oct daily 10am–5pm (Last entry 4.30pm).* ⊗*£4 (Children £2).* 🅿. ☎*01534 482 408.*
The **Battle of Flowers**, held on the second Thursday in August along Victoria Avenue in St Helier, was started in 1902 to celebrate the coronation of Edward VII. Traditionally, the floats were broken up after the parade and the crowd pelted one another with the flowers, then mostly hydrangeas. Today, a collection of floats is presented. The tableaux are made up of different grasses and concentrate on animal subjects.

▷ *Return to the coastal road; bear right onto B 35 (Route de l'Étacq).*

Petit Étacquerel

A defensive tower guards the point which marks the northern end of St Ouen's Bay. It is here that in 1651 Admiral Blake landed with the Parliamentary forces which defeated the Royalists.

3 From Grosnez Point to Rozel Bay

27km/17mi. Allow 2hr 30min.
The northern coast of the island is less densely populated. Cliff paths, which stretch from Plémont Bay to Sorel Point and beyond, provide spectacular views of the uneven coastline and the open sea to France, Guernsey and Alderney.

▷ *Continue N by bearing left onto B 55 (Route de l'Ouest): bear left again to reach the car park and look-out point at Grosnez.*

Grosnez Point★

An area of desolate heathland, covered with gorse and heather and known as Les Landes, extends from Étacquerel to Grosnez Point. South-west of the racecourse sits **Le Pinacle**, an impressive rock associated with pagan rituals since Neolithic, Bronze Age, Iron Age, even Roman times. Little remains of **Grosnez Castle** (c 1373-1540); it enjoys magnificent views out to sea, of Sark and the other islands (north-west).

▶ *Return to B 55; in Portinfer turn left onto C 105 (Route de Plémont); fork left to Grève au Lançon; eventually the road skirts the holiday village to end in a car park from where a footpath runs along the coast to Grève de Lecq.*

Steep cliffs containing caves shelter this attractive small bay, **Grève au Lanchon**, which has a sandy beach at low tide. The rocky promontory **Plémont Point** projects into the sea giving a fine view of the cliffs.

▶ *Return along C 105 (Route de Plémont); turn left onto B 55 (Route de Vinchelez) from Grosnez, which leads to Leoville in the parish of St Mary. Turn left onto B 65 (Mont de la Grève de Lecq).*

Grève de Lecq

Barracks (North Coast Visitor Centre) – ⏱Open May–Sept Wed–Sun 10am–5pm. ∞Donations welcome. 🅿. ☎01534 482 238. www.nationaltrustjersey.org.je
The defensive tower on a charming sandy bay with its stream and mill was built in 1780; the conical hill behind is from an Iron Age fortification.
The **barracks** were built between 1810 and 1815 to accommodate the 150 British soldiers who manned the gun batteries on the slopes around the bay. In spring and early summer the area is abloom with wild flowers: gorse, daffodils, bluebells, foxgloves.
The water's edge is broken by jagged rocks locally known as **Paternoster Rocks** after the many prayers uttered by passing fishermen, remembering colleagues who perished there. Far out to sea is the French coast.

▶ *From Grève de Lecq continue along B 40 (Mont de Ste-Marie); turn left onto B 33 (La Verte Rue) and left again before the West View Hotel onto C 103.*

La Mare Vineyards

♿⏱*Open Easter–Oct daiy except Sun 10am–5pm. ∞£5.50 (Children £1.50). 🅿. ☎01534 481 178. www.lamarevineyards.com.*
The estate of an 18C farmhouse has been planted with the only vineyards and cider orchard in Jersey. You can tour the winery and learn about the process. German-style white wines are produced and may be tasted: Clos de la Mare, Clos de Seyval and Blayney Special Reserve.

▶ *Continue along C 103 to the Priory Inn.*

Devil's Hole★

🚶*Park by the inn and take the concrete path down to the cliff.* The blow hole is an impressive sight dramatised by the amplified thunder of the sea entering the cave below. The name is thought to derive from the old French term *creux de vis* meaning screwhole.

▶ *Minor roads run E to St John's Parish and N to the coast.*

Sorel Point

The section of road named **Route du Nord** is dedicated to the islanders who suffered during the German Occupation (stone marker in the car park). It runs from Sorel Point where a mysterious pool (7.3m/24ft wide by 4.6m/15ft deep) known as the Fairies' Bath (Lavoir des Dames) is revealed in the rocks at low tide. To the east is Ronez Point, a headland scarred by granite quarries.

▶ *Drive through St John; turn left onto A 9 (Route des Issues); after the Jersey Pearl Centre fork left again onto B 67 (Route de Mont Mado). Turn left onto C 99, a minor road to Bonne Nuit Bay and Giffard Bay.*

Bonne Nuit Bay

This bay, haunted by smugglers and pirates in the past, is a favourite place for swimming and sailing. Charles II is supposed to have returned from exile to England from this attractive bay. The fort, La Crête, at the east end was built in 1835.

▶ *From here a footpath follows the coast to Bouley Bay; to reach Bouley Bay by car, take C 98, B 63, C 97 (rue des Platons).*

Bouley Bay

This deep sandy bay protected by a jetty and backed by high granite cliffs is a safe, popular place for swimming.

▶ *Return towards Trinity; turn left onto B 31 (rue ès Picots) past Jersey Zoo before turning sharp left onto C 93 (rue du Rocquier) to Rozel Bay.*

Rozel Bay

Part of the bay is taken up with a fishing port where the boats go aground at low tide. Above the bay, at the northern end, traces of a great earth rampart survive from the Castel de Rozel, an Iron Age settlement. At the opposite end, sits Le Couperon, a Neolithic passage grave (2500 BC).

Hamptonne Country Life Museum★

  ⟁ ◷*Open daily Apr–Oct 10am–5pm. ⊗£5.40 (Children £4.60).* ▣ *. ☏01534 863 955.*
Jersey's rural heritage is brought alive in farm buildings with the help of talkative, costumed characters.

④ From Rozel Bay to St Helier

8km/13mi – 1hr 30min
The road turns inland before returning to the coast above Fliquet Bay and finally meandering down to the water line.
Fliquet Bay is a rocky bay between La Coupe and Verclut points: an ideal place for deciphering the volcanic evolution of the island.

▶ *Either follow the road to St Martin or make a detour to explore the country roads – B 38 (Grande Route de Rozel), B 91 (rue des Pelles), B 91 (Route du Villot), B 29 (Mont des Ormes) to Verclut Point (left) and to Gorey Harbour (right).*

St Catherine's Bay★

From the lighthouse at the end there is a magnificent **view**★★ of sandy bays alternating with rocky promontories along the coast southwards. Out to sea lie the Ecréhou islets, once a favoured trading bank for smugglers and now a popular spot for a Sunday picnic.

▶ *Bear right off the coast road (Route d'Anne Port).*

Faldouet Dolmen

A tree-lined path leads to this dolmen, which is 15m/49ft long and dates from 2500 BC. Excavation has revealed a number of vases, stone pendants and polished stone axes.

Gorey

This little port at the northern end of Grouville Bay is dominated by the proud walls of Mont Orgueil Castle on its rocky spur. Attractive old houses line the quay where yachts add colour to the scene in summer.

Mont-Orgueil Castle★

◷ *Apr–Nov daily 10am–6pm (Last entry 5pm) Rest of the year Fri and weekends from 10am to dusk. ⊗£6 (Children £5.20).* ☏ *01534 853 292. www.jerseyheritagetrust.org.*
Gorey Castle received its present name in 1468 from Henry V's brother, Thomas, Duke of Clarence, who was so impressed

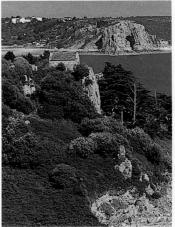

The Parish of Baie de St-Brelade

by the castle's position and its defensive strength that he called it Mount Pride (Mont Orgueil in French). Over the centuries the castle has served as a residence to the lords and governors of the island, including **Sir Walter Raleigh** (1600-03), a prison for English political prisoners, and a refuge for a spy network during the French Revolution.

The earliest buildings date back to the early 13C when King John lost control of Normandy and built a castle to defend the island from invasion. In 1996 Queen Elizabeth II handed the castle over to the islanders.

The **view**★★ from the top is extensive: down into Port Gorey, south over the broad sweep of Grouville Bay, north to the rocks of Petit Portelet and west to the French coast.

A series of waxwork tableaux in the rooms of the castle illustrates significant events in the history of Mont Orgueil.

▶ *Take A 3 (Gorey Coast Road) along the waterfront.*

Royal Bay of Grouville

Grouville is graced with Jersey's finest bay, a magnificent crescent of sand stretching from Gorey harbour to La Rocque Point. The Seymour and Icho Martello towers (1811) may be reached on foot at low tide.

Jersey Pottery★

&⌚◷*Open year-round daily 9am–5.30pm Sun 10am-5.30pm.* ◷*Closed 1 Jan, 25 Dec.* ⊜*No charge.* 🅿. ☎*01534 850 850. www.jerseypottery.com.*

A paved garden, hung with baskets of flowers and refreshed by fountains, surrounds the workshops where the distinctive pottery is produced. You can watch the craftsmen at work, and the show room displays the full range of products for sale.

Royal Jersey Golf Club

The local golf course enjoys a particularly picturesque position; founded in 1878, it was granted its Royal Charter by Queen Victoria.

Grouville Church

Originally dedicated to St Martin of Tours, the church has an unusual 15C granite font.

St Clement's

St Clement is Jersey's smallest parish, named after the church dedicated to Clement I, the third Pope (AD 68-78); it was here that Victor Hugo wrote two volumes of poetry, *Les Châtiments and Les Contemplations*, before departing to Guernsey in 1855.

The dolmen at Mont Ubé, the 3.4m/11ft menhir known as **La Dame Blanche**, and a tall granite outcrop called Rocqueberg suggest that this section of the island was inhabited by Neolithic man. The oldest extant parts of the present church date from the 12C; the wall paintings from the 15C *(St Michael Slaying the Dragon; The Legend of the Three Living and Three Dead Kings).*

St Clement's Bay

This sandy bay stretches from Plat Rocque Point, past Le Hocq Point, marked by a defensive tower, to Le Nez Point (3.2km/2mi). Out to sea strong tides sweep through, continually churning the water.

▶ *From A 4 (Grande Route de St Clement) turn onto B 48 (rue du Pontille), which leads onto A 5 (St Clement's Road), to reach Samarès Manor (right).*

Samarès Manor

&⌚◷*Open June–mid-Oct daily 9.30am– mid-Oct. Garden open daily 10am–5pm. House* ☛⟿*guided tour (40min) morning and afternoon. Gardens and manor* ⊜*£5.85 (Children £1.95).* 🅿. ☎ *01534 870 551. www.samaresmanor.com.*

The name Samarès is probably derived from the Norman *salse marais*, the salt pans which provided the lord of the manor with a significant part of his revenue. In the 11C William Rufus, son of William the Conqueror and King of England, granted the Samarès fief to Rodolph of St Hilaire. In the 17C Philippe Dumaresq drained the marsh by building a canal to St Helier and imported trees and vines from France. The gardens were landscaped and replanted by Sir James Knott who acquired the property in 1924. On the grounds is a rare 11C dovecot; in the house there is the Norman undercroft or manor chapel crypt and the walnut-panelled dining room.

▶ *Continue W on A 4 (the coast road) to Dicq Corner; ⌖ see map of St Helier.*

Le Rocher des Proscrits
Small plaque facing the road.
On the east side of the White Horse Inn, a slipway descends to the beach and a group of rocks, Le Rocher des Proscrits (The Rock of the Exiles), where **Victor Hugo** used to meet regularly with fellow exiles.

SARK ★★

POPULATION 600
MICHELIN MAP 503

Sark, the last feudal fief in Europe and also the smallest independent state in the Commonwealth, offers peace and tranquillity and a traditional way of life without cars. It is located at the very heart of the Channel Islands (12km/7.5mi E of Guernsey, 30.4km/19mi S of Alderney, 19.2km/12mi NW of Jersey). Its two parts – Great Sark and Little Sark – are linked by La Coupée, a high narrow neck of land which inspired Turner, Swinburne and Mervyn Peake, who set the closing scenes of his novel *Mr Pye* here. The island (5.6km/3.5mi long by 2.4km/1.5mi wide) consists of a green plateau bounded by high granite cliffs dropping sheer into the sea or flanking sheltered bays and sandy beaches. Many walks give access to the spectacular coastal scenery. Sark is a haven for wildlife – marine creatures in the rock pools and caves; a wide range of bird species; wild flowers in spring and summer.

▶ **Orient Yourself:** Sark is located at the very heart of the Channel Islands, 12km/7.5mi E of Guernsey, 30.4km/19mi S of Alderney, 19.2km/12mi NW of Jersey. The island is 5.6km/3.5mi long by 2.4km/1.5mi wide.

☺ **Don't Miss:** The magnificent view from the heights of La Coupée.

A Bit of History

In the middle of the 6C St Magloire, the nephew of St Sampson, landed in Sark from Brittany with 62 companions and founded a monastery. Little is known of the island's history before it became part of the Duchy of Normandy. In 1042 Sark was given to the abbey of Mont-St-Michel by William the Conqueror, Duke of Normandy. After centuries of intermittent invasions and lawlessness, during which the monks fled, Sark finally returned to English control in the 16C. In 1565 Elizabeth I granted Sark to Helier de Carteret, Lord of the Manor of St Ouen in Jersey, on condition that he establish a colony of 40 settlers prepared to defend the island. He divided the land into 40 holdings, attributing one to each of the 40 families who had accompanied him

from Jersey. Half of the island population traces decent to these colonists.

The island of Brecqhou (just off the west coast across the Gouliot Passage), a dependent of the fiefdom of Sark since 1565, was acquired in 1993 by the reclusive multi-millionaire British twins David and Frederick Barclay, who have built a massive neo-Gothic mansion, which they rarely visit.

Constitution

At its head is the hereditary Lord (seigneur) who holds the fief of Sark; the present holder is Michael Beaumont, grandson of Sybil Hathaway, the Dame of Sark, who reigned from 1927 to 1974. Sark has its own Parliament, the Chief Pleas. Formerly, it was composed of the 40 tenants and 12 deputies elected for three years. In 2006, however, under the influence of the Barclay twins, the Chief Pleas voted to install a democratically elected legislature.

Excursion *Allow one day.*

Great Sark

Maseline Harbour

The lighthouse (1912) looks down over the harbour, where visitors arrive, from the cliffs on Point Robert.

Creux Harbour★ – Opposite the tunnel to Maseline Harbour is a second tunnel to Creux Harbour, which is picturesque as well as dry at low tide.

La Collinette

A short tunnel leads to Harbour Hill (0.8km/0.5mi); at the top is the crossroads called La Collinette.

Straight ahead stretches **The Avenue**, the main street lined with shops. The small barrel-roofed building on the left at the far end is the two-cell island prison built in 1856. Beyond is **Le Manoir**, built by the first Seigneur and bearing the De Carteret arms. **St Peter's Church** dates from the 19C. The embroidered hassocks are the work of the island women.

La Seigneurie★

La Seigneurie Gardens – ♿ ⏰ *Open Easter –Sept daily except Sun 10am–5pm. £1.80 (Children £.90 . ☎01481 832 345 (Sark Tourism). www.sark-tourism.com).*

The residence of the Seigneur of Sark, stands on the site of St Magloire's 6C monastery. Begun in 1565, it was considerably enlarged in 1730. The square tower, built in 1860, provides a splendid view of the island.

The house is sheltered from the wind by a screen of trees and high walls. The gardens, on which the Dame of Sark lavished so much attention, are luxuriant with flowers and shrubs.

Port du Moulin★★

A road along the north side of the Seigneurie grounds soon turns onto a path following the windings of the clifftop. The sign Window and Bay marks the way to the **Window in the Rock**, which the Rev William Collings, then Lord of Sark, had made in the 1850s to provide an impressive **view** of Port du Moulin.

▶ *Return to the fork in the path and take the other branch to Port du Moulin.*

The bay, popular with bathers, is flanked by stark rocks in strange shapes. On the right stand **Les Autelets**, three granite columns accessible as the sea retreats.

Address Book

Coin ranges for the Channel Islands are derived from approximate conversions of the euro coin ranges on the cover flap into Great Britain Pounds (£).

WHERE TO EAT

⊜⊜🖩 **La Sablonnerie** – *Little Sark, GY9 0SD Sark. ☎01481 832 061. Closed mid-Oct–Easter.* A country lane leads to this restaurant located in a beautifully renovated 16C farm. The wood furniture and the fireplace contribute to the genuine rural atmosphere. Spacious, comfortable but expensive guestrooms.

WHERE TO STAY

⊜⊜ **Dixcart** – *GY9 0SD Sark. ☎01481 832 015. Dixcarthotelsark@wgsy.net. Closed Oct–Easter. 15 rooms. Restaurant* ⊜⊜. This is the oldest hotel on the island, housed in a 16C farm. Exposed beams, antique furniture, fireplaces and stone walls add to the warmth of the place, ideal for a restful stay in the bay area. Restaurant with terrace overlooking the gardens.

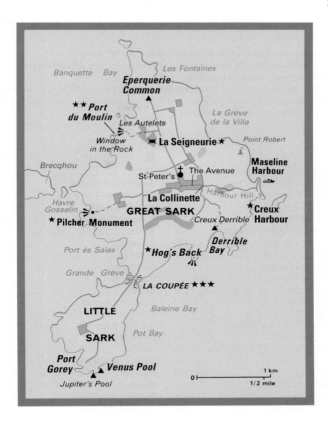

Derrible Bay

At Petit Dixcart turn left onto a stony path, then right onto a path beside a field; a left fork leads down through the trees to Derrible Bay which at low tide has a large sandy beach.

Part way down, a turning to the right leads to the **Creux Derrible**, an enormous hole in the granite cliffs (🖙 take care in poor light).

Return to the first fork and bear left; at the seaward end of this high ridge known as the **Hog's Back**★ stands an ancient cannon, from which there is a magnificent **view**: to the left Derrible Bay and Derrible Point; to the right Dixcart Bay with La Coupée and Little Sark in the background.

La Coupée★★★

The narrow isthmus joining Great Sark and Little Sark is impressive, as on either side steep cliffs drop into the sea. The view is magnificent: to the right lie Brecqhou, Jethou, Herm and Guernsey; to the left is the coast of Jersey before the more distant shadow of the French coast. At the foot of the cliff is Grande Grève Bay, a good place for bathing.

Little Sark

On the southern headland are the chimneys of the abandoned 19C silver mines. A footpath to the left of the old mine chimney runs down to Venus Pool, formed by the sea and visible at low tide. At low tide (🖙 to avoid being stranded, check the time of high tide) visitors can walk from the Venus Pool westward round the headland via Jupiter's Pool, several caves and the rocks in Plat Rue Bay, to Port Gorey which served the silver mines.

The clifftop path is always open and provides a fine view down into Port Gorey.

The following abbreviations appear below: **NP** National Park; **FP** Forest Park.
Sights are listed alphabetically by name and are followed by the name of the district *(amphoe)* or province *(changwat)* where the sight is located.
At the end of the Index are listings of **Where to Eat** and **Where to Stay**. Each entry is listed alphabetically according to its location. *For listings by region, see the Address Books throughout the Discovering Normandy sections of the guide.*

A

Abbaye-aux-Dames, Caen 147
Abbaye-aux-Hommes, Caen 145
Abbaye d'Ardenne, Caen 152
Abbaye de Bec-Hellouin 125
Abbaye de Clermont 278
Abbaye de Fontaine-Guérard 221
Abbaye de Hambye 377
Abbaye de Jumièges 272
Abbaye de Lucerne 289
Abbaye de Mondaye 122
Abbaye Notre-Dame-de-Grâce 367
Abbey of Mont-St-Michel, The 297
Accessibility 21
Acquigny French gardens 289
Agon-Coutainville 190
L'Aigle 86
Air 22
Aizier 269
Alençon 88
Alligator Bay 303
Allouville-Bellefosse 159
Almenêches 99
Alpes Mancelles 12, 92
Ancienne Abbaye de Cerisy-
    La-Forêt 165
Ancienne Abbaye St-Georges 347
Les Andelys 93
Ango, Jean 207
Architecture 64
Argentan 95
Argentan-Sées-Alençon 51
Arlette 237
Arques, Forêt d' .101
Arques-la-Bataille 100
Arromanches-Les-Bains 101
Art and Culture 64
Asnelles 204
Assy 237
Aube 87
Auberge Le Grandgousier 213
Aubigny 237
Auge 12
Aumale 311
Autheuil 305
Avranches 107

B

B&B's 28
Bagnoles-de-l'Orne 110
Bagnoles-de-l'Orne 31
Baie d'Écalgrain 184
Balleroy, Château de 113
Banks 45
Barentin 339
Barfleur 114, 180
Barnevilles 115
Barre-y-Va 158
Barville 164
Basic Information 44
Battle of Caen 141
Battle of Normandy 17, 60
Battle of Odon 153
Bayeux 117
Bayeux Tapestry 117
Beauclerc, Henry 213
Beaumesnil, Château de 131
Beaumont-en-Auge 104
Beauvoir-en-Lyons 245
Le Bec-Hellouin .125
Bec d'Andaine 303
Belbeuf 375
Belle Échappée, La 91
Bellême 127
Bellême, Forêt de 127
Bellou 286
Belvedere 180
Benedictines 64
Bénerville-sur-Mer 195
Bénouville 201
Bernay 129
Bernières-sur-Mer 203
Bessin 52
Beuvreuil 245
Beuvron-en-Auge 103
Biéville-sur-Orne 151
Bishop Aubert 107
Biville 185
Blainville-Crevon 132
Blonville-sur-Mer 195
Bocage normand .52
Boieldieu, François-Adrien 81
Bois de Mirebeau, Le 234
Bois des Vallons, Les 234
Bonington, Richard 79
Bonneville-sur-Touques 105

INDEX

Bonsecours 340
Books............................. 41
Boucle du Hom.................... 363
Boudin, Eugène 79
Bouille, La. 270
Boutiaut, Annette 301
Bradley, General Omar............. 63
Bray Buttonhole, The 310
Breteuil-sur-Iton 176
Bricquebec........................ 367
Brionne........................... 133
Broglie............................ 343
Bruneval.......................... 226
Bures-en-Bray..................... 310
Bus Travel......................... 23

C

Cabourg 103, 136, 195
Caen............................. 138
Caen-Falaise 51
Caen Stone 74
Calendar of Events 35
Calvados..................... 83, 198
Calvados Market 16
Calvaire des Dunes 185
Camembert................... 82, 378
Camping........................... 28
Canapville 105
Canoeing 32
Canteleu 340
Cany-Barville...................... 164
Cap de Carteret 115
Carentan.......................... 177
Carnival at Granville, The 250
Carolles........................... 302
Car Rental......................... 24
Carrouges, Château de 154
Carteret........................... 115
Cartier, Jacques 262
Cathédrale Notre-Dame, Bayeux 118
Cathédrale St-Pierre 284
Caudebec-en-Caux............ 134, 156
Caux Farmsteads 160
Cellular phones 46
Ceramics........................... 77
Cerza 284
Chambois.......................... 98
Champ de Bataille, Château du...... 165
Champlain, Samuel de............. 262
Channel Islands, The........ 21, 381
    Alderney......................... 383
    Bailiwicks, The 382
    Battle of Flowers Museum 409
    Braye............................ 385
    Burhou Island..................... 387
    Castle Cornet 389
    Corbière 409
    Coupée, La........................ 415

Cycling routes....................... 404
Dehus Dolmen 392
Derrible Bay 415
Elizabeth Castle..................... 401
Eric Young Orchid Foundation 405
Essex Castle........................ 387
Fort Albert......................... 386
Fort Regent........................ 403
German Occupation Museum........... 394
Grand Havre, Le 393
Great Sark 414
Grève de Lecq...................... 410
Grosnez Point...................... 409
Guernsey 388
Guernsey Aquarium 397
Guernsey Folk Museum................ 390
Guernsey Museum 389
Hamptonne Country Life Museum 411
Hauteville House..................... 388
Herm 397
Hougue Bie, La...................... 406
Jersey 399
Jersey Museum 403
Jersey War Tunnels 406
Jersey Zoo......................... 404
La Collinette 414
La Mare Vineyards................... 410
La Valette Underground
    Military Museum.................... 396
Le Manoir Village.................... 398
Little Sark......................... 415
Millbrook 407
Mont-Orgueil Castle.................. 411
Moulin de Quétivel................... 406
Pleinmont Point..................... 394
Port du Moulin 414
Pottery 412
Quesnard Lighthouse 386
Raz Island......................... 386
Rozel Bay 411
Sark 413
Saumarez Park 389
Sausmarez Manor 396
Seigneurie, La...................... 414
St Andrew 391
St Anne........................... 384
St Aubin 408
St Brelade......................... 408
St Clement's 412
St Helier 401
St Ouen's Bay 409
St Peter's Village 406
St Peter Port 388
Telegraph Bay....................... 387
Vale Castle......................... 391
Chapelle de Janville 164
Charentonne Valley 342
Châsse de St-Taurin................ 230

Château-Gaillard 93
Château-sur-Epte. 248
Château d'O. 358
Château d'Ételan 341
Château d'Harcourt 166
Château de Bailleul 241
Château de Balleroy 123
Château de Bizy 373
Château de Brécy. 124
Château de Cany 164
Château de Couterne 111
Château de Crosville-sur-Douve. 350
Château de Filières 256
Château de Fontaine-Étoupefour 153
Château de Fontaine Henry 243
Château de Gratot. 188
Château de Lantheuil 124
Château de Launay 134
Château de Martinvast. 172
Château de Miromesnil 101
Château de Monteclerc 235
Château de Nacqueville. 183
Château de Pirou 319
Château de Robert le Diable 223
Château des Feugerets 128
Château des Ravalet 172
Château de Vaussieux 124
Château du Bec 164
Château du Champ De Bataille 165
Château du Mesnil-Geoffroy 162
Château du Vendeuvre 369
Château Guillaume-Le-Conquérant . 235
Cheese 82
Chêne à la Cuve 269
Chêne de l'École. 127
Cherbourg 181
Cherbourg-Octeville 168
Chitterlings (Vire) 379
Cider 83
Cinema 41
Cintheaux. 151
Clameur de Haro 383
Classical Period, The. 73
Clécy 172
Clères. 174
Clermont-en-Auge 103
Climbing. 34
Collégiale Notre-Dame-et-St-Laurent 227
Collégiale St-Hildevert. 245
Colleville-Montgomery 202
Colleville-sur-Mer 314
Conches-en-Ouche. 175
Coquainvilliers 104
Corneille, Pierre 80, 338
Corniche. 364
Corniche du Pail. 92
Corniche Normande 194
Côte d'Albâtre. 52, 160

Côte d'Auge. 103
Côte de Grâce 268
Côte de Nacre 12, 52
Côte des Deux-Amants 375
La Côte du Bessin. 205
Côte Fleurie 12, 52, 195
Cotentin 52
Côte St-Michel 373
Côte Ste-Catherine 340
Cottereau, Jean 275
Courseulles-sur-Mer. 203
Coutances 186
Crépon 124
Crèvecœur-en-Auge. 192
Creully. 124
Criqueville-en-Auge. 103
Croisset. 340
Croix de la Faverie 172
Cruises on the river Seine 29
Curnonsky 301
Currency. 21, 45
Cycling 34

D
d'Aurevilly, Barbey 80
D-Day 313
D-Day Landings 198
Dangu 248
Deauville 31, 193
Débarquement, Plages du 198
Délivrande, La. 203
Delorme, Philibert. 218
Diélette. 185
Dieppe 207
Disney, Walt. 206
Dives-sur-Mer. .212
Documents 20
Domfront. 213
Donjon, Brionne. 133
Dreux. 216
Driving in France 23
Driving tours. 12
Duclair. 341
Dufy, Raoul 79
Dukedom of Normandy. 248
Duty-Free. 20

E
Écluses d'Amfreville 246, 375
Écouché 97
Écouis 220
Écouves Forest 358
Église de Blosseville 162
Église de la Madeleine 371
Église Notre-Dame 156
Église Notre-Dame-des-Cordeliers . . 278
Église Notre-Dame-sur-l'Eau 215
Église Ste-Catherine, Honfleur 266

INDEX

Eisenhower, General Dwight 63
Elbeuf 222
Electricity. 44
Entrammes 280
Épinay Forest 244
Épron. 151
Epte Valley 248
Étang et Fontaine de la Herse 127
Étretat. 224
Eu 227
Eure, The. 13
Eure Market. 16
Évreux 229
Évreux-St-André. 51
Évron 233

F
Faience 338
Falaise 235
Falaise d'Amont 163, 224
Falaise d'Aval. 162, 224
Falaise des Vaches Noires 195
Fécamp. 238
Ferme de Bray, La 244
Fervaques 286
Fierville-les-Mines. 116
Fishing 31
Flamboyant Style, The 72
Flaubert, Gustave 80
Flers 241
Flights 22
Fonderie de Cloches. 377
Food and Drink. .81
Forêt d'Eawy. 212
Forêt De Lyons 290
Forêt de Mayenne 294
Forêt des Andaines 112
Forges-les-Eaux 244
Fort du Roule 171
Foucarmont. 311
Francheville. 371
Franks 54
Fresnay-sur-Sarthe 246
Fresnel, Augustin. 52
Furniture 77

G
Gaillon. 374
Gardens of Normandy 16, 30
Geese of Pirou .319
Genêts. 303
Ger 309
Gerbault, Alain 275
Getting There 22
Gisors. 247
Giverny 248
Glyn, Elinor 401
Gold Beach 201

Gothic Period, The. 71
Gouffern forest. .98
Gournay-en-Bray. 245
Goury. 184
Grand Siècle, The. 73
Grange aux Dîmes. 124
Granville. 30, 250, 302
Gréville-Hague. 184
Grillous 309
Grosparmy, Nicolas. 241
Guibray Fair 237
Guy Degrenne 309

H
Halle au Blé 91
Haras National 345
Haras National du Pin. 99, 318
Harcourt. 166
Harfleur. 256
Hauteclocque, General Philippe de 63
Haute Vallée de la Touques 106
Hauteville-la-Guichard 188
Health 21
Heritage Trails. 14
Herluin 125
Héron, Le 245
Hiking 33
Hobart's Funnies 204
Hoc Point 205
Holidays 44
Honegger, Arthur 81
Honfleur. 262
Horseback Riding 34
Horses. 52
Hostels 28
Hôtel d'Escoville 141
Hôtel de Beaumont. 366
Hôtel de Grandval-Caligny. 367
Hôtel de Thieuville 367
Hôtel du Doyen 121
Hotels (See Where to Stay at the
    back of index). 25
Houlgate. 197
Hugo, Victor 388, 413
Hunting. 35

I
Igoville 375
Île de Tatihou 351
Îles Chausey. 167
Impressionism 79
International Visitors 19
Ivory and Spice Road 14

J
Jardin de la Pellerin. 322
Jardin des plantes 187, 339
Jardin public du Donjon 215

Jarry, Alfred....................... 275
Jullouville.......................... 302
Juno Beach 201

K

Kayaking............................32
Kersalé, Yann...................... 268
Know Before You Go.................18

L

La Belle Échappée 91
La Bouille 270
La Délivrande 203
La Ferme de Bray.................. 244
La Ferté-Macé.......................111
La Ferté-Saint-Samson............. 244
La Foire de Sainte-Croix 281
La Fosse-Arthour...................215
La Haye-de-Routot 134
La Lande-Patry.....................242
Land sailing........................31
Langrune-sur-Mer.................. 202
Langtry, Lillie 401
La Perrière........................128
La Pierre Procureuse...............129
Lassay-les-Châteaux................274
La Suisse Normande............... 360
Latham-47 Monument 158
Laval 275
Laval Château......................276
Le Bec-Hellouin 125
Le Bois de Mirebeau 234
Le Bourg-Dun......................162
Le Bourg-St-Léonard 99
Le Clos Lupin...................... 225
Le Havre 254
Le Havre-Antifer Port and Terminal.. 226
Le Héron.......................... 245
Le Mémorial, Caen 149
Le Mesnil-Durden 162
Le Mesnil-sous-Lillebonne 282
Le Molay-Littry....................123
Le Mont Canisy.................... 194
Le Pain de Sucre...................172
Le Roc au Chien 110
Les Authieux-sur-le-Port-St-Ouen 375
Les Bois des Vallons 234
Les Dunes-de-Varreville 178
Les Moulins 315
Lessay 281
Les Unelles....................... 188
Les Vaux 242
Le Tréport........................ 363
Le Trou Normand...................82
Le Vaudobin 98
Lieuvin 51
Lighthouses...................... 383
Lillebonne 282

Lion-sur-Mer....................... 202
Lionheart, Richard...................93
Lisieux............................ 283
Literature 79
Livarot.......................82, 287
Livet-sur-Authon...................134
Logny-au-Perche...................128
Loisé 305
Longny-au-Perche 306
Lonlay-l'Abbaye....................215
Louviers 287
Luc-sur-Mer.................. 31, 202
Ludiver 181
Lyons-la-Forêt 290

M

Mail 45
Maison d'Henri IV 163
Maison de Claude Monet 249
Maison de Julie Postel 114
Maison des Templiers...............157
Maison du Camembert 378
Manche Market 16
Manéglise 164
Manoir d'Ango 368
Manoir de Coupesarte 192
Manoir de l'Angenardière...........129
Manoir de la Saucerie...............215
Manoir de Saussey 191
Manoir Pierre-Corneille............. 339
Marais du Contentin et du
    Bessin Regional Nature Parc.......177
Markets.............................16
Martainville, Château de.............132
Martell, Jean 401
Martinvast 172
Maupassant, Guy de............80, 226
Maurois, André......................80
Mayenne 293
Mayenne, The.......................12
Mayenne River, The................ 278
Médavy............................99
Mémorial de Montormel..............99
Ménil-Glaise 97
Menneval 343
Menus 29
Merville-Franceville-Plage...........137
Millais, Sir John Everett 401
Millin, Bill 202
Minitel.............................46
Mirbeau, Octave 80
Monasticism........................58
Monceaux-au-Perche.............. 306
Monet, Claude 79, 249
Mont-Joli 269
Mont-St-Michel 12, 15, 294
Mont Canisy, Le 194
Mont Castre........................116

INDEX

Mont de Cerisy 242
Mont des Avaloirs 92
Montfarville 115
Montgomery, General Bernard 63
Montivilliers 164, 256
Mont Pinçon 363
Mont Robin 377
Mortagne-au-Perche 304
Mortain 307
Motorhome Rental 24
Moulin d'Hauville 269
Moulineaux 270
Musée-Mémorial de la
    Bataille de Normandie 122
Musée Août-1944
    (Battle of the Falaise Pocket) 236
Musée d'Art naïf, Laval 277
Musée d'Ethnographie et
    d'Art populaire, Honfleur 267
Musée d'Art et d'Histoire
    Marcel-Dessal 217
Musée de la Mer et de l'Écologie 297
Musée des Beaux-Arts
    André-Malraux 256
Musée du Camembert 378
Musée du Cidre 367
Musée du Débarquement 102
Musée du Débarquement
    "no 4 Commando" 318
Musée du Mobilier miniature 369
Musée du Poelserie and Maison
    de la Dentellière 376
Musée Eugène-Boudin 267
Musée industriel de la
    Corderie Vallois 339
Musée Louis-Philippe 227
Musée régional du Cidre et
    du Calvados 367
Music 81

N

Nature 50
Naturospace, Honfleur 268
Neubourg 126
Neufchâtel 82
Neufchâtel-en-Bray 310
Nez de Jobourg 185
Nogent-le-Rotrou 311
Nonancourt 372
Normandie-Maine Regional
    Nature Park .155
Norman Dovecotes 75
Normandy Sauce .82
Noron-l'Abbaye 237
Noron-la-Poterie 123
Norrey-en-Bessin 152

O

Oath of Bayeux 117
Odon 153
Offranville 212
Oissel 270
Omaha Beach 205, 313
Operation Overlord 315
Orbec 316
Orival 270
Orne Market 16
Ossuaire Allemand du
    Mont-d'Huisnes 303
Ouilly-le-Vicomte 104
Ouistreham 31
Ouistreham-Rive-Bella 201, 316

P

Painting 77
Palais Bénédictine, Fécamp 238
Parc du Bocasse .174
Parc floral du Bois des Moustiers 368
Parc Montalent 244
Parc zoologique de Champrepus 377
Parc Zoologique de
    Clères-Jean-Delacour 174
Paré, Ambroise 275
Parks 30
Parné-sur-Roc 280
Passport 20
Patton, General George 63
Pays d'Argentan 97
Pays d'Auge 52
Pays d'Ouche 51
Pays de Bray 51, 244
Pays de Caux 50
Pegasus Bridge 201
Perche normand .51
Perret, Auguste 73, 255
Perrière, Madame de la 89
Perry 83
Perseigne, Forêt de 91
Petit-Suisse 82
Phare 114
Phare d'Ailly 368
Pierrefitte-en-Auge 104
Pierres Pouquelées 185
Pigeons 75
Pirou, Geese of 319
Plages du Débarquement 198
Plaine du Neubourg 51
Plan d'Eau de la Dathée 379
Plateau de Caux 164
Pointe de Barfleur 114
Pointe de la Roque 323
Pointe du Hoc 205
Pommeau 83
Pont-Audemer 320
Pont-de-l'Arche 289

Pont-l'Évêque 82, 104
Pont-St-Pierre 246
Pont de Brotonne 135
Pont de Normandie, Honfleur 268
Pontmain 321
Pontorson 322
Port-en-Bessin 205, 206
Portbail 116
Post 45
Pottery 77
Pourville-sur-Mer 161
Presqu'île du Cotentin 176
Prices 45
Prieuré St-Michel de Crouttes 378
Promenade des Crêtes 173
Proust, Marcel 136

Q
Queneau, Raymond 81
Querqueville 182
Quettehou 178
Quillebeuf 323
Quinéville 178

R
Rail Travel 22
Rânes 112
Ranville 137
Regnéville-sur-Mer 191
Relais des Genêts 303
Renaissance, The 72
Réserve naturelle des Mannevilles . . 323
Restaurants 28
Richard II, King 237
Richard Lionheart 93
River Orne 97
River Seine 13, 29
Rocher du Castel-Vendon 184
Rochers du Vignage 358
Roches d'Orival 270
Roches de Ham 346
Roches St-Adrien 375
Rocques 104
Rollo 117
Romanesque Period, The 64
Romans 54
Rommel, Field Marshal Erwin 63
Roque Point 323
Rots 152
Rouen **324**
   Aître St-Maclou 330
   Archevêché 330
   Cathédrale Notre-Dame 328
   Église St-Maclou 333
   Église St-Ouen 333
   Gros-Horloge 332
   Hôtel de Bourgtheroulde 338
   Musée de la Céramique 337
   Musée des Antiquités de
     la Seine-Maritime 338
   Musée des Beaux-Arts 336
   Musée Flaubert et d'Histoire
     de la médecine 338
   Musée Jeanne-d'Arc 337
   Musée Le Secq des Tournelles 337
   Musée national de l'Éducation 331
   Musée Pierre-Corneille 338
   Old Rouen 330
   Palais de Justice 331
   Place du Vieux-Marché 332
Roumois 51, 126
Rousseau, Henri 275
Route de la Pomme et du Cidre 16
Route des Colombiers Cauchois 16
Route Historique des
   Abbayes Normandes 15
Route Historique du Patrimoine
   Cultural Québécois 15
Routot 134
Ry 132

S
Sailing 30
St-Aubin-sur-Mere 203
St-Denis-d'Augerons 342
St-Évroult-Notre-Dame-du-Bois 342
St-James 322
St-Laurent-sur-Mer 314
St-Lô 343
St-Martin-de-Boscherville 340
Saint-Ouen-de-Pontcheuil 223
St-Pair-sur-Mer 253
St-Pierre-sur-Dives 348
St-Pois 309
St-Rémy 360
Saint-Saëns, Camille 81
St-Sauveur-le-Vicomte 349
St-Vaast-la-Hougue 351
Sainte-Croix, La Foire de 281
Ste-Suzanne 355
Ste-Adresse 256
St Romain 332
Salacrou, Armand 81
Satie, Erik 81
Saulges 355
Seasons 14
Sea Travel 22
Secqueville-en-Bessin 152
Sées 356
Seine-Maritime Market 16
Seine Valley (Lower) 340
Serquigny 343
Shopping 40
Sieux 103

INDEX

Sightseeing 40
Sigy-en-Bray 245
Sillé-le-Guillaume 359
Skin Diving. 31
Spas 30
St-Céneri-le-Gérei. 92
St-Cyr-la-Rosière .129
St-Germain-de-la-Coudre. 129
St-Germain-de-Livet 287
St-Hymer 104
St-Jean-le-Thomas 302
St-Léonard-des-Bois. 92
St-Loup-Hors 123
St-Pierre, Bernardin de. 80
St-Sulpice-sur-Risle. 87
St-Valery-en-Caux. 162
St-Wandrille. 158
Ste-Foy, Église. 175
Ste-Marguerite-sur-Mer 161
Ste-Marie-du-Mont 178
Suisse Normande, La 360
Sword Beach 201

T

Tancarville 341
Telephones 46
Themed Tours. 14
Thermes de Bagnoles-de-l'Orne 31
Thury-Harcourt 362
Tillières-sur-Avre 372
Time Line 54
Tinchebray. 242
Tipping 45
Tocqueville 180
Tocqueville, Charles Alexis de 80
Tosny, Roger de 175
Touques 105
Tourist Offices. 18
Tourlaville 171
Tourouvre. 305
Tourville-sur-Sienne 190
Trappe du Port-du-Salut 280
Tréport, Le 363
Troarn 151
Trou Normand, Le 82
Trouville-Deauville 195
Trouville-sur-Mer. 364

U

Useful Web Sites .18
Utah Beach 178

V

Val de Saire 178
Vallée d'Enfer 91
Vallée de l'Avre. 372
Vallée de l'Eure. 217

Vallée de l'Orne 360
Vallée de la Cour 112
Vallée de la Durdent. 164
Vallée de la Lézarde 164
Vallée de la Sée 309
Vallée de la Touques. 104
Vallée de la Vire 346
Vallée de Misère. 92
Vallée du Laizon. 237
Valmont 241
Valognes. 366
Varende, Jean de la. 80
Varengeville-sur-Mer 161, 368
Vascœuil. 245
VAT. 40
Vatteville-la-Rue 269
Vauban, architect 168
Vaudeville 379
Vaudobin, Le. 98
Vauville. 185
Vaux, Les. 242
Ver-sur-Mer 204
Verneuil-sur-Avre 370
Vernon 372
Versainville 237
Veules-les-Roses 162
Veulettes-sur-Mer 163
Vexin Normand, The. 51, 374
Vierville-sur-Mer 315
Vieux Bassin, Honfleur. 265
Vikings 54
Village Guillaume-le-Conquérant 212
Villedieu-les-Poêles 376
Villequier 159
Ville Romaine de Jublains. 271
Villers-sur-Mer 104, 195
Villerville 194
Vimoutiers. 378
Vire. 378
Vironvay 289
Visa. 20

W

Wace, Robert. 79
War of the Hedgerows. 181
When and Where to Go. 14
William the Conqueror 57
Windsurfing 31
Words & Phrases 42
Wrecks 383

Y

Yport 164
Yvetot 159

WHERE TO EAT

Aleçon
Au Petit Vatel 90

Alençon
Auberge Normande 90
Le Chapeau Rouge 90
Le Saint-Léo 90

Amfreville-sous-les-Monts
Guinguette Chez Dédé 326

Ardevon
Auberge de la Baie 298

Argentan
Restaurant de Fleuré 97

Avranches
Le Littré 108

Bagnoles-de-Lorne
Auberge de Clouet 111
Chez Marraine 111
La Terrasse. 111
Maison Chatel EURL Le Goff. 111

Barneville-Carteret
Le Berlingot. 116

Bayeux
Hostellerie St-Martin 119
L'Amaryllis 119
La Ferme des Châtaigniers Bed
and Breakfast 119
Le Bistrot de Paris 119
Le Pommier. 119

Beaumont
Bistro Soleil 400

Bellefontaine
Auberge Paysanne 308

Bénouville
Café Gondrée - Pegasus Bridge 199
Manoir d'Hastings et la Pommeraie . . . 200

Bernay
Auberge de la Truite. 130
Le Bistrot de Bernais. 130

Bernières-sur-Mer
L'As de Trèfle 200

Beuzeville
Auberge du Cochon d'Or 320

Brouains
Auberge du Moulin 308

Cabourg
Dupont avec un Thé. 137
Le Champagne. 137

Caen
L'Embroche 139
L'Insolite. 139
Le Bouchon du Vaugueux 139
Maître Corbeau 139
Saint-Andrew's. 139

Campigny
Le Petit Coq aux Champs 320

Caudebec-en-Caux
Auberge du Val au Cesne 158

Changé
La Table Ronde. 279

Château de Carrouges
Le Jean-Anne 155

Cherbourg-Octeville
Au Tire-Bouchon. 169
Café de Paris 169
L'Antidote. 169
Le Faitout. 169
Sel et Poivre 169

Clécy
La Guinguette à tartines. 173

Clement
Green Island 400

Clères
Au Souper Fin. 174

Courselles-sur-Mer
La Pêcherie 200
Les Alizés 199

Coutances
La Verte Campagne 189
Le Jules Gommes. 189
Le Tourne-Bride. 189

Deauville
Bar de la Mer. 196
Dupont avec un thé 196
La Flambée 196
La Galerie de Tourgéville 196
La Table d'Auge 196
Le Nautica 196

Dieppe
La Marmite Dieppoise 211
Le Bistrot du Pollet 211
Le New Haven. 211
Le Sully 211

Domfront
Auberge Le Grandgousier 215

Dompierre
Relais de la Forêt 213

Dreux
Aux Quatre Vents 218
Le St-Pierre 218

Duclair
Le Bistrot du Siècle 348

Étretat
Lann Bihoué 225
Le Clos Lupin. 225
Le Galion 225

Évreux
Hôtel de France 232

Évron
L' Attache. 233

Fécamp
Le Maritime. 239

Flers
Au Bout de la Rue 242

INDEX

Giverny
Le Moulin de Fourges 249
Restaurant-Musée Baudy.............249
Gorey
Suma's.............................. 400
Gorey Village
Village Bistro........................ 400
Grandcamp-Maisy
La Trinquette 200
Granville
Crêperie Grill l'Échauguette 251
L'Horizon 251
La Citadelle.........................251
Guernsey
Fleur du Jardin 390
The Absolute End 390
The Auberge........................ 390
The Pavilion........................ 390
Zest 390
Honfleur
Au Vieux Honfleur................... 264
Bacaretto..........................263
Ex-Voto............................263
La Grenouille 263
Le Bistrot des Artistes 263
Isigny-sur-Mer
La Flambée 199
L'Aigle
Le Manoir de Villers 86
La Ferrière-aux-Étangs
Auberge de la Mine 242
Laval
À La Bonne Auberge 279
Gerbe de Blé 279
L'Antiquaire.........................279
La Braise............................279
Le Bec-Hellouin
Le Canterbury........................125
Le Havre
La Petite Auberge 257
Le Bistrot du Chef...en gare 257
Le Wilson 257
Les Andelys
De Paris..............................94
La Chaîne d'Or 94
Lisieux
Aux Acacias......................... 285
La Coupe d'Or........................ 285
Little Sark
La Sablonnerie.......................414
Louviers
Le Jardin de Bigard.................. 288
Mont-St-Michel
La Gourmandise 298
La Promenade 298
La Sirène........................... 298
Pré Salé............................ 298

Moulay
Beau Rivage 293
La Marjolaine 293
Orbec
Le Jardin de Taormina 285
Ouistreham-Riva-Bella
Le Normandie........................317
Le St-Georges........................317
Pays d'Auge
Auberge de la Boule d'Or..............105
Pays de Caux
La Boussole.........................161
Le Belvédère.........................161
Pirou-Plage
La Mer...............................319
Pont de l'Arche
La Pomme 222
Port-en-Bessin
Le Bistrot d'à Côté................... 200
Le Vauban 200
Restaurant de l'Hôtel Mercure 200
Pourville-sur-Mer
Au Trou Normand 211
Presqu'île du Cotentin
Ferme-auberge La Huberdière.........179
L'Estaminet 179
Le Moulin à Vent 179
Rouen
La Marmite 326
La Toque d'Or........................326
Le Gourmand du Sud-Ouest 326
Les Maraîchers.......................326
Pascaline 326
Rozel Bay
Le Frère............................ 400
St Aubin
Old Court House Inn................. 400
Ste-Marie-du-Mont-Village
Le John Steele 354
St-Laurent-sur-Mer
L'Omaha.............................315
St-Lô
Bistrot de Paul et Roger 344
La Petite Auberge 344
Le Péché Mignon.................... 344
St-Vaast-La-Hougue
Crêperie Léoncie 352
Le Chasse Marée 352
Sées
Le Cheval Blanc 357
Le Gourmand Candide 357
Woincourt
La Gare aux Gourmets............... 229

WHERE TO STAY

Alderney
Farm Court. 385
Alençon
Château de Sarceaux 90
Hôtel Marmotte. 90
La Garencière Bed and Breakfast. 90
Le Moulin de Linthe Bed and Breakfast. 90
Argentan
Le Refuge du P'tit Fischer. 97
Pavillon de Gouffern 97
Avranches
Hôtel La Croix d'Or 108
La Maraîcherie Bed and Breakfast. 108
Bagnoles-de-Lorne
Auberge de la Source. 111
Hôtel Ermitage. 111
Banville
Le Petit Val Bed and Breakfast 199
Barneville-Carteret
La Tourelle Bed and Breakfast 116
Bayeux
Hôtel Reine Mathilde. 119
Le Grand Fumichon Bed and Breakfast. 119
Le Manoir de Crépon
Bed and Breakfast. 119
Berchères-sur-Vesgre
Château de Berchères 218
Bourg-Beaudouin
La ferne du Coquetot
Bed and Breakfast. 326
Cabourg
Ferme de l'Oraille Bed and Breakfast . . 137
Le Moulin du Pré 137
Caen
Hôtel Bernières 139
Hôtel du Château 139
Hôtel du Havre. 139
Hôtel St-Étienne 139
Le Bristol 139
Caudebec-en-Caux
La Normandie. 158
Les Poules Vertes Bed and Breakfast . . 158
Cherbourg-Octeville
Hôtel Ambassadeur 169
Hôtel Angleterre 169
Hôtel Renaissance. 169
La Croix de Malte. 169
Manoir St-Jean Bed and Breakfast. 169
Colleville-sur-Mer
Domaine de L'Hostréière 199
Ferme du Clos Tassin
Bed and Breakfast. 315
Conteville
Chambre d'hôte Le Vieux Pressoir. 263
Corneville-sur-Risle
Les Cloches de Corneville. 320

Coutances
Hôtel Cositel 189
Le Quesnot Bed and Breakfast 189
Village Grouchy Bed and Breakfast. . . . 189
Dampierre
Château de Dampierre
Bed and Breakfast. 344
Deauville
Hôtel Hélios. 196
Hôtel Le Patio 196
Hôtel Normandy 196
La Maison Pommerose
Bed and Breakfast. 196
Dieppe
Hôtel au Grand Duquesne 211
Le Logis d'Eavy Bed and Breakfast 211
Dives-Sur-Mer
M. et Mme Roussel Bed and Breakfast. 213
Dreux
Hôtel Le Beffroi 218
Duclair
Les Hauts du Catel Bed and Breakfast . 348
Escures
La Ferme d'Escures Bed and Breakfast. 199
Le Logis Bed and Breakfast 199
Étretat
Hôtel La Résidence 225
Eu
Hôtel restaurant Maine. 229
Évreux
La Croix d'Or 232
Fécamp
Chez Nounoute 239
Hôtel de la Plage 239
Flers
Galion Hotel 242
Forêt d'Eu
Manoir de Beaumont
Bed and Breakfast. 229
Formigny
Ferme du Mouchel Bed and Breakfast. 199
Géfosse-Fontenay
Manoir de l'Hermerel
Bed and Breakfast. 199
Giverny
Le Bon Maréchal Bed and Breakfast . . . 249
Gorey Pier
Hôtel Moorings 400
Grandchamp-Maisy
La Faisanderie Bed and Breakfast 199
Granville
Hôtel des Bains 251
Gravigny
La Boulangeraie. 232
Guernsey
Hôtel La Frégate 390
Hôtel La Michèle 390
Maison Bel Air Bed and Breakfast 390
Sunnydene Hôtel. 390

INDEX

Hébécrevon
Auberge de Campagne 344
Herm
White House 397
Honfleur
Camping La Briquerie 263
Hôtel Otelinn 263
La Cour Ste-Catherine
Bed and Breakfast. 263
Îles Chausey
Hôtel Fort et des Îles 167
Jumièges
Le Relais de l'Abbaye 273
L'Aigle
Hôtel du Dauphin 86
La Boissaye
Manoir de la Boissière
Bed and Breakfast. 232
La Chapelle-près-Sées
Ferme Équestre des Tertres
Bed and Breakfast. 357
La Houle
Au Caprice Bed and Breakfast. 400
Laval
Grand Hôtel de Paris 279
Le Bas du Gast Bed and Breakfast 279
Marin'Hotel 279
Le Bas-Pays
Amaryllis Bed and Breakfast 298
Le Bec-Hellouin
Château de Boscherville
Bed and Breakfast. 125
Le Chêne Sec Bed and Breakfast
Pertheville-Ners 233
Le Havre
Hôtel Marly 257
Hôtel Terminus. 257
Richelieu 257
Les Andelys
Mme Vard Bed and Breakfast 94
Le Tilleul
M. et Mme Delahais Bed and Breakfast. 225
Lisieux
Hôtel de la Place 285
Hôtel St-Louis. 285
Louviers
Manoir de La Haye le Comte 288
Lyons-La-Forêt
Les Lyons de Beauclerc 291
Mont-St-Michel
Âuberge St-Pierre 298
Mortagne-au-Perche
Hostellerie Genty-Home. 305
Moyaux
Camping Le Colombier 285
Nogent-Le-Rotrou
Hôtel Au Lion d'Or 312
Orbec
Le Manoir de l'Engagiste 316

Ouistreham-Riva-Bella
Hôtel de la Plage 317
Pays d'Auge
Les Marronniers Bed and Breakfast 105
Pays de Caux
Château de Mesnil Geoffroy
Bed and Breakfast. 161
Le Château de Grosfy
Bed and Breakfast. 161
Mme Genty Bed and Breakfast. 161
Pontorson
Hôtel Bretagne. 298
Hôtel La Tour Brette 298
Préaux-du-Perche
Le Jardin François Bed and Breakfast. . .312
Presqu'île du Cotentin
Hôtel - Restaurant L'Escapade 179
Hôtel Le Vauban 179
La Dannevillerie Bed and Breakfast 179
Réville
La Ferme de Cabourg
Bed and Breakfast. 352
Rouen
Brithotel Versan. 326
Hôtel des Carmes .326
Hôtel Le Cardinal. .326
Roz-sur-Couesnon
Mme Gillet Hélène Bed and Breakfast . 298
Rozel Bay
Hôtel Beau Couperon 400
St-Denis-le-Ferment
Le Four à Pain Bed and Breakfast. 247
St-Lô
Hôtel Armoric. 344
St-Pierre-sur-Dives
Auberge de la Dives 349
St-Vaast-La-Hougue
Hôtel de France et Fuchsias. 352
Ste-Mère-Église
Le Sainte-Mère. 354
Sark
Dixcart 414
Senneville-sur-Fécamp
Mireille Le Thuillier Bed and Breakfast . 239
St-Aubin-des-Préaux
Le Hamel Bed and Breakfast 251
St-Gatien-des-Bois
Le Clos Deauville Saint-Gatien 263
St Helier
La Bonne Vie Bed and Breakfast 400
Vierville-sur-Mer
Hôtel du Casino 315
Villers-en-Ouche
Le Manoir de Villers 342
Villiers-Charlemagne
Camping Village Vacances Pêche 279
Vouilly-Église
Château de Vouilly Bed and Breakfast. .199

LIST OF MAPS

THEMATIC MAPS

Principal Sights . . . . inside back cover
Regional Driving Tours . . . . inside front cover
Geography of the region. 51
D-Day in Normandy 61
Boucles de la Seine
    Regional Nature Park 135
Perche Regional Nature Park 306
Normandie-Maine
    Regional Nature Park 155
Marais du Cotentin et du Bessin
    Regional Nature Park 180
Places to stay. .26-27

MONUMENTS

Château Gaillard 94
Artificial port, Arromanches. 102
Le Bec-Hel
louin Abbey 126
Notre-Dame d'Écouis. 221
Trinity Abbey, Fécamp. 239
Jumièges Abbey 273
Notre-Dame de Louviers. 289
Mont-St-Michel Abbey. 300
Rouen Cathedral 329
Notre-Dame Church,
    Verneuil-sur-Avre. 372

LOCAL MAPS FOR TOURING

Perseigne Forest and the Alpes Man-
    celles (from Alençon) 92
Pays d'Argentan. 99
Pays d'Auge. 106
Around Bayeux. 123
Le Perche 306
Around Caen. 152
Pays de Caux 162-163
Îles Chaussey. .167
Around Clécy 173
Cotentin Peninsula 182-183
D-Day beaches. 202-203
Pays de Bray 245
Lyons Forest 292
Mont-St-Michel Bay 302
Carolles. 302
Omaha Beach 314
Marais Vernier (from Quillebeuf) 323
Swiss Normandy: Orne Valley 361
Channel Islands 382
Alderney. 386
Guernsey 392-393
Herm 398
Jersey 404-405
Sark 415

TOWN PLANS

Alençon 88
Argentan 96
Avranches 109
Bagnoles de l'Orne 112
Barneville-Carteret. 115
Bayeux 118
Bellême. 128
Bernay. 132
Brionne 133
Cabourg 136
Caen. 142-143
Caudebec-en-Caux. 157
Cherbourg 171
Coutances 190
Deauville 195
Dieppe 208
Domfront. 214
Dreux. 219
Elbeuf 223
Étretat 226
Eu 228
Évreux 231
Falaise 236
Fécamp. 240
Granville. 253
Le Havre 258, 260
Honfleur. 265
Laval 272
Lisieux. 286
Mont-St-Michel 296
Mortagne-au-Perche 304
Mortain. 308
Nogent-le-Rotrou 312
Pont-Audemer 321
Rouen 334-335
Saint-Lô 345
Sainte-Suzanne 356
Sées 358
Verneuil-sur-Avre 370
Vernon 374
Villedieu-les-Poêles 376
Vire. 379
Saint Peter Port (Guernsey) 395
Saint Helier (Jersey) 402
Regional and Local Maps 429

MAPS AND PLANS

COMPANION PUBLICATIONS

Regional and Local Maps

To make the most of your journey, travel with Michelin maps at a scale of 1:200 000: Regional maps nos 512 and 518 and the new local maps, which are illustrated on the map of France below.

And remember to travel with the latest edition of the map of France no 721 (1:1 000 000), also available in atlas format: spiral bound, hard back, and the new mini-atlas – perfect for your glove compartment.

Michelin is pleased to offer a route-planning service on the Internet: www. ViaMichelin. com. Choose the shortest route, a route without tolls, or the Michelin recommended route to your destination; you can also access information about hotels and restaurants from The Red Guide, and tourist sites from The Green Guide.

Bon voyage!

LEGEND

	Sight	Seaside resort	Winter sports resort	Spa
Highly recommended	★★★	凸凸凸	❋❋❋	‡‡‡
Recommended	★★	凸凸	❋❋	‡‡
Interesting	★	凸	❋	‡

Selected monuments and sights

◉ ━	Tour - Departure point
🏠 ♦	Catholic church
🏠 ♦	Protestant church, other temple
▦ ▣ ▥	Synagogue - Mosque
▬	Building
■	Statue, small building
‡	Calvary, wayside cross
◎	Fountain
━●━	Rampart - Tower - Gate
⤫	Château, castle, historic house
∴	Ruins
◡	Dam
✿	Factory, power plant
☆	Fort
∩	Cave
▣	Troglodyte dwelling
⚑	Prehistoric site
▼	Viewing table
Ⅶ	Viewpoint
▲	Other place of interest

Sports and recreation

🏇	Racecourse
⛸	Skating rink
≋ ▱	Outdoor, indoor swimming pool
🎬	Multiplex Cinema
⚓	Marina, sailing centre
⛺	Trail refuge hut
▱▬▱▬▱	Cable cars, gondolas
▱┼┼┼┼▱	Funicular, rack railway
🚂	Tourist train
◆	Recreation area, park
🎢	Theme, amusement park
Ⅴ	Wildlife park, zoo
⊕	Gardens, park, arboretum
◐	Bird sanctuary, aviary
🚶	Walking tour, footpath
😊	Of special interest to children

Abbreviations

A	Agricultural office (Chambre d'agriculture)	**P**	Local authority offices (Préfecture, sous-préfecture)
C	Chamber of Commerce (Chambre de commerce)	**POL.**	Police station (Police)
H	Town hall (Hôtel de ville)	🛡	Police station (Gendarmerie)
J	Law courts (Palais de justice)	**T**	Theatre (Théâtre)
M	Museum (Musée)	**U**	University (Université)

Additional symbols

🅸	Tourist information	✉	Post office
═ ═	Motorway or other primary route	☎	Telephone
❶ ❶	Junction: complete, limited	▭	Covered market
⇥ ═	Pedestrian street	⨯	Barracks
ⲭ═══ⲭ	Unsuitable for traffic, street subject to restrictions	△	Drawbridge
▥ ┄	Steps – Footpath	∪	Quarry
🚆 🚉	Train station – Auto-train station	✗	Mine
🚌 🚏	Coach (bus) station	Ⓑ Ⓕ	Car ferry (river or lake)
—	Tram	⛴	Ferry service: cars and passengers
Ⓜ	Metro, underground	⇀	Foot passengers only
🅿	Park-and-Ride	③	Access route number common to Michelin maps and town plans
♿	Access for the disabled	Bert (R.)...	Main shopping street
		AZ B	Map co-ordinates

430

Michelin Apa Publications Ltd

A joint venture between Michelin and Langenscheidt

Suite 6, Tulip House, 70 Borough High Street, London SE1 1XF, United Kingdom

No part of this publication may be reproduced in any form
without the prior permission of the publisher.

© 2007 Michelin Apa Publications Ltd
ISBN 978-1-906261-06-1
Printed: August 2007
Printed and bound in Germany

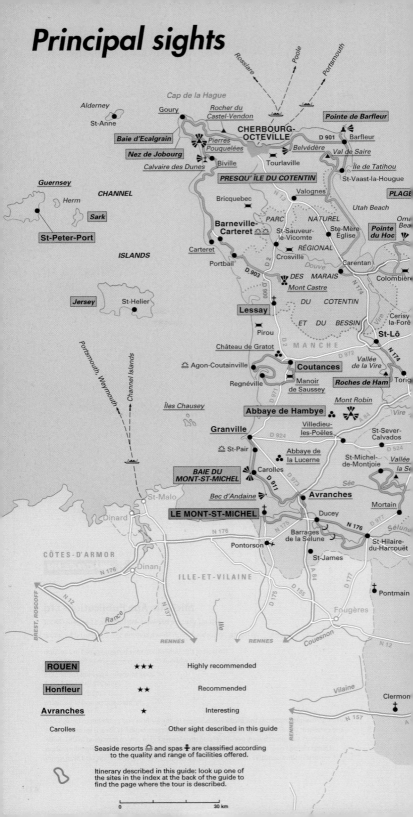

Principal sights

Rosslare → Poole → Portsmouth →

Cap de la Hague

Alderney
St-Anne

Goury
Rocher du Castel-Vendon
Pointe de Barfleur

CHERBOURG-OCTEVILLE
D 901
Barfleur

Pierres Pouquelées
Baie d'Ecalgrain
Belvédère
Val de Saire

Nez de Jobourg
Biville
Calvaire des Dunes
Tourlaville
Île de Tatihou
St-Vaast-la-Hougue

PRESQU'ÎLE DU COTENTIN

PLAGE

Guernsey
Herm

CHANNEL

Bricquebec
Valognes
N 13

Utah Beach

Sark
PARC
NATUREL
Pointe du Hoc
Oma Bea

St-Peter-Port
Barneville-Carteret
St-Sauveur-le-Vicomte
Ste-Mère-Église

ISLANDS
Carteret
D 2
Crosville
RÉGIONAL
Carentan

Portbail
D 903
Douve
Colombière
N 174

DES MARAIS

Jersey
St-Helier
D 900
Mont Castre
DU COTENTIN
Cerisy la-Forê

Vire

Lessay
ET DU BESSIN
St-Lô

Pirou
MANCHE

Château de Gratot
D 2
N 174

Agon-Coutainville
D 972
Vallée de la Vire

Coutances
Torig
Roches de Ham

Regnéville
Manoir de Saussey
D 971

Mont Robin

Portsmouth, Weymouth

Îles Chausey
Abbaye de Hambye
Vire

Channel Islands
Villedieu-les-Poëles
St-Sever-Calvados
D 524

Granville
D 924

St-Pair
Abbaye de la Lucerne
St-Michel-de-Montjoie
Vallée la Se

BAIE DU MONT-ST-MICHEL
Carolles
D 911
Sée

Bec d'Andaine
Avranches
Mortain

St-Malo
LE MONT-ST-MICHEL
Ducey
N 176
D 977

Dinard
N 176
Barrages de la Sélune
St-Hilaire-du-Harcouët

Pontorson
St-James
Séluné

CÔTES-D'ARMOR
N 176
Dinan
ILLE-ET-VILAINE
D 155
D 177
Pontmain

BREST, ROSCOFF
N 12
Rance
N 137
Ille
Couesnon
N 12

RENNES
RENNES
Fougères

Vilaine

Clermon

RENNES
A
N 157

ROUEN	★★★	Highly recommended
Honfleur	★★	Recommended
Avranches	★	Interesting
Carolles		Other sight described in this guide

Seaside resorts ☖ and spas ⴲ are classified according to the quality and range of facilities offered.

Itinerary described in this guide: look up one of the sites in the index at the back of the guide to find the page where the tour is described.

0 ——————— 30 km